Fifth Edition

SOCIAL PSYCHOLOGY

DAVID O. SEARS

University of California, Los Angeles

JONATHAN L. FREEDMAN

University of Toronto

LETITIA ANNE PEPLAU

University of California, Los Angeles

PRENTICE-HALL, INC., Englewood Cliffs, N.J. 07632

Library of Congress Cataloging in Publication Data

FREEDMAN, JONATHAN L.
  Social psychology.

  Includes bibliographies and indexes.
  1. Social psychology.   I. Sears, David O.
II. Peplau, L. Anne.   III. Title.
HM251.F68 1985   302   84-18360
ISBN 0-13-817858-5

Editorial/production supervision: *Edith Riker*
Manufacturing buyer: *Barbara Kittle*
Photo research: *Anita Duncan*
Cover design: *Lundgren Graphics, Inc.*
Cover photograph: *Stan Wakefield*

Printed in the United States of America

10 9 8 7 6 5 4 3 2 1

ISBN 0-13-817858-5 01

Prentice-Hall International, Inc., *London*
Prentice-Hall of Australia Pty. Limited, *Sydney*
Editora Prentice-Hall do Brasil, Ltda., *Rio de Janeiro*
Prentice-Hall Canada Inc., *Toronto*
Prentice-Hall Hispanoamericana, S.A., *Mexico*
Prentice-Hall of India Private Limited, *New Delhi*
Prentice-Hall of Japan, Inc., *Tokyo*
Prentice-Hall of Southeast Asia Pte. Ltd., *Singapore*
Whitehall Books Limited, *Wellington, New Zealand*

CONTENTS

PREFACE

When we wrote the first edition of this book nearly twenty years ago, our task was a much simpler one. The field of social psychology then was relatively new and relatively small. In the intervening decades, it has changed dramatically.

There has been an explosion of research and theory, and a corresponding proliferation of journals meeting the specialized needs of social psychologists. There has been a renewed interest in the practical applications of social psychology for understanding urgent social issues. Women and ethnic minorities have been attracted to social psychology and have enriched the field with new perspectives and new research questions. The students who take social psychology courses today are also a more diverse group: Minority students are better represented than ever before; women are now over half the students in American colleges; and more and more older students are taking our courses.

Our book has grown and changed with the times as well. This edition incorporates the major new topics of research, the best new studies, the most contemporary examples. But all is not focused on newness: Certain basic principles and goals have guided us in the development of this edition.

We believe that social psychology, like any science, is cumulative. As researchers push toward exciting new frontiers, they build on the accumulated knowledge of the field. Our primary goal is to present the "basics" of the field—the core theories and findings that form the shared heritage of our discipline. We believe the new findings of today are best understood as adding to a body of knowledge.

We have also been sensitive to the many changes taking place in social psychology. Over time, the core of the field has gradually shifted. There is less emphasis today on group dynamics, and more on intimate relationships; less interest in attitude change and more in social cognition, and so on. This changing core is reflected in this new edition.

A third goal has been to offer an integrated presentation of the field. As we discuss different topics, we have tried to keep the main theoretical ideas and traditions of social psychology firmly in mind, so that students can see the underlying conceptual continuities in the field. For example, we initially introduce attribution theory in our discussion of social perception, and then show how the theory has been used to understand such topics as attitude change, aggression, and bias against women.

The application of research methods and theories to understanding social issues has been a major theme in social psychology. Throughout the text, we highlight ways in which social psychology sheds light on everyday experiences and social problems. We conclude with a section on applied social psychology that explores areas in which we have special expertise—prejudice and politics, environmental psychology, and gender roles.

The success of any text depends ultimately on its ability to communicate clearly to student readers and to spark student interest in the field. Our goal has been to present materials simply, without oversimplifying. The text is comprehensive, but not encyclopedic. We have paid special attention to selecting examples that illustrate basic principles in a lively way and to sharing our own enthusiasm for the field.

Special Features of the Fifth Edition

This book has been successful throughout its life. And although our basic philosophy about this text remains the same, much has changed in the fifth edition. We think the old book was good, but we have not left well enough alone. Here are some of the changes you'll find.

ORGANIZATION We've reorganized the book to provide a more systematic presentation of the material. Two beginning chapters on theory and methods are followed by five major sections that progress from individual-level topics to dyads and groups, and then to specific applications of social psychology. The first section on social perception includes expanded coverage of new work on social cognition and attribution. The section on attitudes provides a somewhat shorter presentation of work on attitude formation and change than previous editions. The interpersonal relationships section discusses interpersonal attraction, close relationships, aggression, and prosocial behavior. The fourth section on groups incorporates work on conformity and compliance as well as group behavior. The final section on applied social psychology has chapters on prejudice and politics, gender, and environmental psychology. We think that this sequence will fit well with the teaching preferences of many instructors. However, each chapter is self-contained and can be used in any order.

STYLE A major effort has been made to improve the clarity and interest level of the text. We scrutinized every line of text, every table and figure, and every photograph. We enlisted the aid of undergraduates in our classes to help make the book more readable. We have streamlined our language and avoided unnecessary technical terms. Many concrete examples have been added. For instance, the book now begins with several vignettes about social behavior for students to try to understand. These illustrations raise questions about such topics as conformity, bystander intervention, TV violence, and the arms race. In Chapter 2, we use specific studies that address the topics in these vignettes to illustrate different research methods.

LEARNING AIDS   Various teaching aids further increase the effectiveness of the text. Each chapter begins with an outline. At the end of each chapter is a comprehensive summary of major concepts and findings. Key terms are shown in boldface in the text and defined in the Glossary. The Bibliography at the end of the book is extensive and current.

CONTENT   The topics covered in this edition have been revised to reflect significant shifts of emphasis in social psychology. In every chapter, we have added the best of recent work. Some of the highlights of the revision include:

- an enlarged section on the ethics of research including consideration of informed consent, minimal risk, and confidentiality
- more extensive coverage of nonlaboratory research methods, including surveys, correlational studies, and the use of data archives
- a more detailed discussion of nonverbal communication, especially work on the accuracy of detecting deception, the leakage hypothesis, and multiple channels of communication
- a new chapter on social cognition that presents some of the most active research areas in social psychology, including categorization, vividness, salience, prototypes, schemas, and person memory
- expanded coverage of attribution processes that includes new material on when people make attributions, self-serving biases, and overjustification, plus applications of attribution theory to ghetto riots, the sports page, and responses to physical illness
- an updated discussion of attitudes that gives greater attention to expectancy-value theory, the theory of reasoned action, and cognitive response theory
- new sections on loneliness and the impact of divorce on children in the chapter on interpersonal attraction
- a new chapter on close relationships that applies principles of social exchange to understanding dyadic interactions, examines the dynamics of social power, and presents the latest research findings on romantic love
- an aggression chapter that includes new work on deindividuation, contagious violence, and instrumental aggression, as well as practical implications for problems of family violence, pornography, and violence in the media

- in the chapter on prosocial behavior, the addition of a decision-making analysis of helping, a discussion of whether TV can teach kids to be helpful, and profiles of "good samaritans" who have risked their lives to aid others in distress
- the groups chapter includes basic work on group dynamics and leadership, plus applications to social loafing, and mass hysteria
- a new chapter on prejudice and politics that presents the latest work on relative deprivation, self-fulfilling prophecies, and the effects of stereotypes, and discusses the impact of the media on political campaigns
- a chapter on gender in social life supplements the extensive coverage of gender throughout the book and provides in-depth coverage of stereotypes, androgyny, and gender differences in social behavior
- an environmental psychology chapter that presents new findings on personal space and the homefield advantage in sports, discusses research on designing better college classrooms, and considers the impact of city life on social networks and mental health

INSTRUCTOR'S MANUAL   The text is accompanied by a comprehensive *Instructor's Manual* prepared by Karen G. Duffy of State University of New York—Geneseo. The manual outlines learning objectives for each chapter and provides detailed suggestions for lectures. Also included are numerous ideas for classroom discussions, student projects, paper topics, and other activities. There is a complete listing of films, references, and other materials to enrich the course. An extensive testbank of multiple-choice questions test students' recall of material as well as their ability to comprehend and apply the concepts presented in the text. Essay questions are also provided.

Acknowledgments

Special thanks go to Carolyn Drago for her heroic efforts, to Deborah J. Stipek and Steven L. Gordon for their excellent critiques, to Edie Riker for production, to Jeannine Ciliotta for copy editing, and to Gail Boucher and Gloria Piceno for their research assistance. We are very grateful to all the students who gave us such useful feedback on the earlier edition. This book has benefited greatly from thoughtful reviews of the manuscript by:

- Joan F. DiGiovanni, Western New England College
- Gary Long, University of North Carolina at Charlotte
- Elaine Nocks, Furman University
- Barry Ruback, Georgia State University
- Philip E. Tetlock, University of California at Berkeley
- Timothy Wilson, University of Virginia
- Janice Yoder, Webster College

Finally, on a sadder note, this edition goes to press with the loss of our friend and collaborator, J. Merrill Carlsmith of Stanford University, too fresh in our minds. Freedman, Carlsmith, and Sears planned the first edition of this book together in the mid 1960s in a shared spirit of youthful exuberance, in the youth of an exciting and rapidly growing field, and in the early years of our own careers. Merrill was a major force in the original plan of the book. He was a perceptive, brilliant, and exciting human being. His year-long struggle against lung cancer was remarkable for his courage, generosity to others, and good cheer. He was taken from us too early and we feel his loss very deeply. The remaining two original authors feel fortunate indeed to have Anne Peplau bring her impressive background and skills to our venture.

We dedicate the book to Merrill, as a small token of the meaning he had for us.

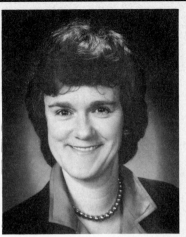

DAVID O. SEARS   JONATHAN L. FREEDMAN   LETITIA ANNE PEPLAU

ABOUT THE AUTHORS

DAVID O. SEARS is Professor of Psychology and Political Science, and Dean of Social Sciences, at the University of California, Los Angeles. Dave received his B.A. in History from Stanford University, and his Ph.D. from Yale University in Psychology. He has taught at UCLA since then, chairing the social psychology program from 1977 to 1982. He has been a visiting professor at Harvard University and the University of California, Berkeley, and a Guest Scholar at the Brookings Institution. He has served on the review panel on social psychology for the National Science Foundation, on the Council of Representatives for the American Psychological Association, on the Board of Overseers of the National Election Studies, and as Chair of the Human Subject Protection Committee at UCLA. His other books include *Public Opinion* (with Robert E. Lane), *The Politics of Violence: The New Urban Blacks and the Watts Riot* (with John B. McConahay), and *Tax Revolt: Something for Nothing in California* (with Jack Citrin). He has published articles and book chapters on a wide variety of topics in social and political psychology, including attitude change, mass communications, ghetto riots, political socialization, voting behavior, and racism.

JONATHAN L. FREEDMAN is Professor of Psychology and chair of the psychology department at the University of Toronto. He received his B.A. from Harvard University and his M.A. and Ph.D. from Yale University. Jonathan taught at Stanford University where he was assistant and associate professor, and at Columbia University as full professor. He was associate editor of the *Journal of Experimental Social Psychology* and has served on the boards of many other journals. His early work was on various topics in social influence, compliance, and deviancy resulting in his book, *Deviancy* (with Anthony Doob). He has studied the effects of crowding and his book, *Crowding and Behavior,* won the American Psychological Association Gold Medal Award. The effects of time pressure is his current research topic. He is the author of many books and articles in social psychology.

LETITIA ANNE PEPLAU is Professor of Psychology and chair of the graduate program in social psychology at the University of California, Los Angeles. Anne received her B.A. in Psychology from Brown University and her Ph.D. in Social Psychology from Harvard University. Since 1973, she has taught at UCLA, where she helped to found the campus Women's Studies Program and has developed popular undergraduate courses in the psychology of gender and close relationships. Her other books include *Loneliness: A Sourcebook of Current Theory, Research and Therapy* (with Daniel Perlman) and *Close Relationships* (with Harold H. Kelley et al.) She has published numerous articles and book chapters in social psychology on such topics as loneliness and social support, friendship, heterosexual dating, homosexual relationships, and social power.

1

INTRODUCTION

OVERVIEW: WHAT DO SOCIAL PSYCHOLOGISTS STUDY?

Social psychology is the systematic study of social behavior. It deals with how we perceive other people and social situations, how we respond to others and they to us, and in general how we are affected by social situations. To start with, let us take a look at the kinds of things social psychologists are interested in understanding. Here are five vignettes, each illustrating a somewhat different area of interest in social psychology.

First Impressions and Lasting Relationships

While you are driving to class at a moderate rate of speed and listening to some music on the radio, you are suddenly jolted out of your dreamlike state by a young woman who cuts in front of you. She is driving a bright red sports car considerably faster than the speed limit. She speeds on, finally squealing around a corner and disappears into the distance. You are a little startled, but then you reflect on the experience. You are surprised to find how quickly you came to have a strongly negative feeling toward her, even though you had only the briefest encounter. You quickly categorized her as a spoiled rich kid, probably from the wealthy neighborhood up in the hills near the campus. You also find that you came to a quick judgment about the causes of her behavior—you concluded that

she cut in front of you because she is a generally reckless driver, not because she was avoiding a pothole or another driver or because she was getting ready to turn. When you think about it, you are a little surprised to realize that you have such a clear impression of a person with whom you have had only the briefest and most fleeting contact.

Then your mind drifts to the mixer you went to last Friday afternoon. You start to think about Mark, the student you met and talked to for about three-quarters of an hour. He seemed quite attractive and had a good sense of humor. Your roommate's brother went to high school with him and said he was a good student and people liked him. But you wonder. You noticed that he was wearing a religious medallion, and it is not your religion. He talked about going to religious services earlier in the week, so he seems to be fairly religious himself, and you are not. You had been telling him about the beautiful house your mother had just put on the market with her real estate firm, and Mark had asked how your father felt about that because he wasn't sure *he* wanted his wife to have a full-time job. You were certainly interested in Mark, but you have begun to wonder. How important is attractiveness over the long haul? Is it always important to feel that your partner is attractive? What about differences in values? Are those issues that can iron themselves out over time, or be negotiated to mutually satisfactory agree-

What are these people attending to as they try to form an impression of each other?

ments? Or do they just get more important over time, causing increasing amounts of conflict? What kinds of problems might they create? How could those problems be dealt with?

Social relationships always involve elements such as these. They raise many questions about how we form impressions, what is important in a relationship, how relationships change over time, and so on. The study of interpersonal relationships is central to social psychology.

Conformity and Attitude Change

In your modern history class, you see a documentary on student protest on your campus in the 1960s. All the students have long hair, and wear jeans and various kinds of old clothes. The males all seem to have beards or mustaches. They are passing marijuana cigarettes around, and they are constantly coming together in crowds, carrying signs and posters, and listening to speakers argue politics. There is an atmosphere of rebelliousness, of great activity in large crowds, and certainly a feeling of general carelessness, sloppiness, untidiness, and even dirtiness about personal appearance.

After the film, you walk out onto your mid-1980s campus. The students all are quite nicely dressed, and some of the clothes look quite expensive. Everyone is neat, clean, and tidy. The men all have fairly short hair. The students occasionally see someone they know and call out a greeting to them. No one seems to be angry or rebellious; on the contrary, almost everyone is smiling and friendly. There are no crowds, just groups of two or three or four friends walking along or talking. There are no signs or posters in evidence, or anything political at all. War and protest seem a million light years away.

Why have things changed so much? Can this be the same campus that was shown in the documentary? How can everything be so different? Why are the students of today so uninterested in protest? Why were students in the 1960s so upset and angry about everything? Where did their attitudes come from? Have their attitudes changed? Are they now driving imported cars and living in the suburbs and wearing coats and ties or dresses to work every day? What about the overt behavior the students were exhibiting? Is everyone just an incredible conformist, so that whatever clothing or hair style is in fashion is adopted by everyone?

You do not feel much like a blind conformist yourself, yet you notice that you are dressed much like everyone else. What makes people behave so similarly? And what about those large groups and crowds the 1960s students got into? What makes people join such groups? How are people different when they are in groups? Does a group make people do extreme things? Hostile things? Out of the corner of your eye, just as you are lost in these thoughts, you see two students walking along in punk rock outfits, and you see that one of them was your straight roommate's best friend in junior high school. What *is* going on?

Violence on Television and In the Streets

Violent crime is a major problem in America. All over the country, people have become afraid to leave their houses at night because of the danger of being assaulted. For example, 47 percent of those surveyed in 1982 (National Opinion Research Center) said there were areas within a mile of their homes where they would be afraid to walk alone at night. Many observers have noted that the rate of violent crime has increased during the same period that television has become the dominant entertainment medium in America. Almost all Americans seem to watch huge amounts of television—virtually every household has a set, and the average set is on about seven hours a day. Young people are exposed to enormous amounts of television: by the age of 18, the average American child has spent 20,000 hours watching television, more time than that spent in classrooms, churches, and all other educational and cultural activities put together.

Much television programming depicts violent physical force. By the early 1980s, prime-time television exposed viewers to almost five acts of violence involving physical force per hour, involving more than half of all the leading characters in prime-time shows. And almost three-fourths of all the shows contained violence (Comstock, 1982).

Many have linked the two developments and concluded that such widespread crime must

stem at least in part from violent television. Sometimes they offer vivid anecdotes to support this view. For example, in San Francisco, an 11-year-old girl was raped with a soda bottle shortly after a television movie had depicted an assault with a similar weapon. In Miami, the lawyer for a boy who had killed someone pleaded that the boy was not responsible for the death because he was just imitating what he had seen on television. The belief that television violence causes crime is widely held. In the mid-1970s, the national PTA began a campaign to monitor television content. The American Medical Association adopted a resolution calling on broadcasters to reduce television violence as a menace to the nation's health. An advisory committee to the U.S. Surgeon General said there was reasonable evidence of a link between television violence and aggressive behavior.

The origins of violent crime, or of aggressive behavior in general, is a central topic for social psychology. That violent television breeds violent crime is a popular theory. But is it true? And if so, under what conditions does media violence have such an effect? Does it occur for all kinds of people? Of all ages? What about the effects of going to a boxing match, or watching a football game? In asking whether or not viewing television violence increases aggression, we may really be raising a more general question: Namely, what are the effects of watching *any* kind of violence, be it on television or anywhere else? These are among the many questions social psychologists have raised about violence.

Woman in Distress: No One Came to Help

At about 9 P.M. on Sunday, March 6, 1983, a 21-year-old woman walked into a bar in a blue-collar neighborhood of New Bedford, Massachusetts, and stopped to have a drink. She later stated that when she tried to leave, a man blocked the door, tackled her, stripped off her clothes except for a sweater, and attacked her. Two other men held her down and tried to force her to perform oral sex acts. As she struggled, screaming and pleading for help from the other customers at the bar, she was lifted onto the pool table and raped. In the words of the police, "She cried for help, she asked for help, she begged for help—but no one helped her." The bartender told police he gave a customer a dime to call the police, but that the customer dialed a wrong number. No one went to the woman's aid, the bartender said, because one of the attackers brandished a butter knife.

The woman finally broke free and ran out of the tavern, naked from the waist down. She flagged down a car, and the driver took her to a telephone. She was treated at a hospital and released. Police later arrested six men between the ages of 23 and 26, though the men who witnessed the incident did not come forward. Under public pressure, the bar owner handed in his liquor license two days later, and the bar was closed for good. Ultimately, four men were convicted of aggravated rape, and sentenced to long prison sentences.

There have been other highly publicized cases of refusal to help, notably that of another young woman, Kitty Genovese. In 1964, as she was coming home from work late at night, she was attacked and repeatedly stabbed in front of her apartment building in Kew Gardens, New York. During her half-hour struggle with the attacker, she repeatedly screamed that she was being stabbed and begged for help. Thirty-eight people living in adjacent houses and apartments later said they had heard her screams. But no one came to her aid or even called the police. They said they did not want to get involved. The police were not called until twenty minutes after she died; then they arrived in two minutes. Even then, none of her neighbors would come out onto the street until an ambulance arrived to take her body away.

Why did no one help? How did the bystanders perceive these two victims? How did they perceive their own responsibility, and the morality of what others were doing? Under what conditions do people step forward to help others, and when do they just passively permit suffering to continue? Social psychologists are concerned with discovering when people will help one another, just as they are with learning when they will be violent.

Why does this woman get help, unlike those in the text? Why are only policemen seeming to help?

The Eichmann Defense: Just Obeying Orders

Before World War II, nearly 9 million Jews lived in Europe. The European Jewish community had had a long and brilliant tradition of culture, artistic and intellectual achievement, and religious devotion. Adolf Hitler and the Nazi party came to power in Germany in 1933, contending that the Aryan race was superior to such "mongrel races" as the Jews and gypsies, and that Europe needed to be racially purified. Within a few years, the Nazi regime had begun to arrest and imprison Jews in Germany. By 1939, when Germany invaded Poland, hundreds of thousands were already in concentration camps.

Soon thereafter, Nazi officials began secretly exchanging memos on "a final solution to the Jewish problem." Under the effective management of Adolph Eichmann, a dedicated career bureaucrat, Jews from throughout Europe were systematically rounded up and shipped to concentration camps such as Dachau and Auschwitz, mostly by train, where they were starved, gassed, shot, cremated, and buried in mass graves. By 1945, when World War II ended, about 6 million European Jews had died. Of those Jews who had lived before the war in the 21 countries fully occupied by the Germans, three out of every four were dead. Atomic bombs would have had to have been dropped on 100 cities to have killed as many Japanese.

Eichmann fled to Argentina after the end of the war, where he was ultimately captured by Israeli investigators in 1961. He was taken to Israel and tried for murder. His defense was that he was not personally responsible for the deaths of the Jews, because he had simply been following orders. The argument was rejected, and he was held accountable for his crimes and put to death. The "Eichmann defense" has come to stand for the claim that a person is justified in committing terrible actions because he or she is "just following orders."

There can be no question that the virtual annihilation of the European Jewish community could have been carried out only with the conscious cooperation of thousands of ordinary Germans—bureaucrats, soldiers, janitors, doctors, railroad workers, carpenters. Did these behaviors emerge from pathological characteristics of the German people? More frighteningly, did they arise out of the normal operation of everyday social processes, such as simple obedience to authority? Under what conditions will people commit terrible acts when ordered to? For social psychologists, such events raise fundamental questions about obedience to authority, and the conditions under which people will comply with or resist directives that violate their own standards of morality.

The Arms Race

As the 1980s began, the nations of the world were spending $500 billion each year on their military forces. There had been about 50 wars or armed conflicts in the previous 10 years, almost all in Third World countries—those most oppressed by poverty, disease, and overpopulation. Most of these wars used weapons exported by the United States and the Soviet Union. But the greatest threat to humankind comes from the threat of nuclear war. The nuclear firepower of the great powers has increased consistently since an atomic bomb was first dropped on Hiroshima. For example, the United States in the early 1980s had 1052 ICBMs (intercontinental ballistic missiles). The nuclear warhead on each Titan II missile has the explosive power of 9 million tons of TNT—the equivalent of 700 Hiroshima bombs. And these single warheads were gradually being replaced with triple warheads.

If the United States or the Soviet Union were to launch an ICBM, it would take about 30 minutes to reach the other nation. Experts estimate that of those 30 minutes, about 10 would be required to communicate word of the attack throughout the entire command structure of the targeted nation, including getting word to the chief of state. There is much uncertainty about whether or not each nation's ICBM launching pads would survive a nuclear attack by the other nation. Hence the American president or the Soviet premier would have about 20 minutes to decide whether or not to push his own nuclear buttons, guaranteeing a quick end to life for most citizens of the opposing nation, as well as the devastation of his own nation.

Each nation now possesses much more firepower than would be required to kill most of the other's citizens, flatten all its major cities, and incinerate virtually all its military forces. Even the chances of war by miscalculation have grown steadily. Strategists concede that such large collections of nuclear weapons are excessive for any military purpose they can imagine.

But they argue that vast quantities of nuclear arms are necessary as "bargaining chips"; that they can only bargain with their opponent for arms reduction "from a position of strength." Each nation interprets any momentary advantage for the opposition as threatening, and immediately takes steps to equal or overcome it.

How did we ever get to this point, where civilization can be destroyed within a matter of minutes? How is it that two such powerful nations have allowed themselves to get into such an apparently self-defeating situation? Many observers believe the answers lie in the nature of the relationship between the two nations—in the structure of their interdependence, and in the interpretations each makes of the other's behavior. They argue that the USA and USSR behave toward each other much as two ordinary people do when they are partially dependent on each other and able to threaten each other.

THE SOCIAL PSYCHOLOGICAL APPROACH

These are the kinds of events social psychologists try to understand: problems of impression formation, interpersonal relationships, conformity, attitude change, aggression, obedience, and helping behavior.

More generally, social psychology begins with the study of perceptions and attitudes: how people perceive each other, how they interpret other people's behavior, and how their attitudes form and change. It includes all forms of interaction between people—attachment and affiliation, liking and close relationships, aggression, altruism, and conformity and influence. It is concerned with how people act in groups, and how groups affect their members. Applications of these ideas focus on, among other things, how people behave politically, prejudice, sex roles, and how the environment affects us. The discipline of social psychology tries to answer any and all questions about how people affect one another and how they behave in social situations. Not all of these questions have been answered fully. The job of social psychologists is to ask the important questions and then to look for answers.

Of course, many other fields also deal with these matters. Sociologists, urban geographers, anthropologists, economists, political scientists, and other types of psychologists are all concerned with social behavior. What is distinctive about the social psychologist's approach? At the simplest level, scholars from the other social sciences tend to use the *societal* level of analysis—they use broad societal factors to explain social behavior. People behave as they do because of economic, historical, or social forces, such as class conflicts, clashes between competing ethnic groups, the crops a particular area can produce, the governmental institutions of the nation, or technological changes in the economy. At the other extreme, clinical and personality psychologists use an *individual* level of analysis—they use the person's unique individual characteristics to explain behavior. In particular they use each person's unique personality traits and conflicts to explain why we all behave somewhat differently in any given situation.

Social psychologists adopt a level of analysis somewhere in between—what we might call the *interpersonal* level. They mainly explain behavior in terms of a person's current social or interpersonal situation. That social situation would include the other people in the environment, their attributes and their behaviors, the context within which they are acting, and so on. For example, what aspects of other people determine whether we will like them or not? Is physical attractiveness or religious feelings more important? What aspects of another person, and the situation, will make us more likely to obey? Must the person have an official role? Act in an authoritative way? Issue commands from an official place, like an office or a laboratory? Threaten us with punishment if we disobey? In all these cases, social psychologists seek to identify those aspects of the immediate social situation that determine human behavior.

Let us compare these three levels of explanation in terms of a specific example. Suppose we are interested in analyzing the origins of violent crime. The societal level approach, typical of economists, political scientists, and sociologists, looks for broad social explanations. These social scientists might point out that high rates of violent crime tend to be associated with poverty, rapid urbanization, and the industrialization of a society. To provide evidence for such a conclusion, they might point to certain facts: poor people commit many more violent crimes than wealthy people do; violent crime is much more common in slum areas than it is in wealthy neighborhoods; crime rates go up in economic

recessions and drop when the economy recovers. Such explanations simply relate the large social forces on the extreme left of Figure 1–1 with the outcomes shown at the extreme right. They do not concern themselves with individual persons at all, or with their immediate situations.

The individual approach of other disciplines within psychology would tend to look for explanations for crime in the unique histories and characteristics of the criminal individual. Developmental, personality, and clinical psychologists would ask what individual differences lead some people to commit crime when others in seemingly identical situations (city dwellers with the same income, age, race, and so on) do not. To understand the individual differences that lead to crime, they focus on the person's background. How was the person raised? What kind of discipline did the parents employ? Were they abusive or alcoholic or not affectionate to the child? Perhaps abusive parents tend to produce children who do not learn to behave properly,

At the societal level, we might ask why protest marches are especially common in the United States, or why this one occurred when it did. At the interpersonal level, we might ask what situations caused these people to protest. At the individual level, we might ask why some individuals in those situations participated and others did not.

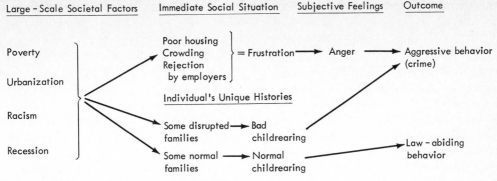

FIGURE 1–1 Contrasting approaches

who become angry at the world, or who do not learn the usual cultural values and morals. One line of research might compare the incidence of criminal behavior among children who were abused by their parents with that of children whose parents did not use physical punishment. Or it might compare the family backgrounds of delinquent and nondelinquent children, or follow a large group of children over many years and relate their criminal or noncriminal behavior to their family backgrounds. The bottom of Figure 1–1 shows how such analyses focus on how people in the same situation may behave differently because of unique past experiences.

In contrast, the special focus of social psychology is to understand how people respond to immediate social situations. It considers what subjective feelings are generally produced in a particular kind of social situation, and how those in turn affect overt behavior. What kinds of interpersonal situations lead to feelings of anger, and increase or decrease aggressive behavior?

For example, one basic principle of social psychology is that frustrating situations make people angry, and they become more likely to engage in aggressive behavior. This effect of frustrating situations is one explanation for crime. It has been tested in laboratories and in the outside world. This particular relationship

can explain not only why aggression occurs in a certain situation, but also why certain economic and societal factors lead to crime. For instance, people who are poor and crowded into urban slums are frustrated: They cannot buy what they want, cannot get good jobs, cannot live in the way they would like. This frustration may in turn be the direct cause of much criminal behavior. The social psychological approach also usually involves some subjective feelings produced by the interpersonal situation, which in turn influence the individual's overt behavior. In this example, the frustrating situation produces anger, which in turn produces aggressive behavior. Thus the frustration-aggression hypothesis explains criminal behavior at quite a different level from either the societal or individual explanations. It focuses on the immediate social situation, and on the subjective feelings such situations produce in people of many different backgrounds.

Each of these approaches is worthwhile and indeed essential if we are to understand complex social problems. And there is, of course, considerable overlap among disciplines in the kinds of studies that are done. The point is that a single question—Why does crime occur?—can be asked and answered in many different ways. The focus can shift from general to specific explanations, and from sociological to psychological processes.

THEORIES IN SOCIAL PSYCHOLOGY

Just as a problem can be studied from different viewpoints by several disciplines, it can be approached within a single discipline from different theoretical orientations. Within psychology, students are often introduced to the major comprehensive theories of human behavior popular in the earlier part of the century. Almost all psychology students have heard of **psychoanalytic** theory and Sigmund Freud; of **behaviorism** and John B. Watson and B. F. Skinner; of **Gestalt** theory and the European psychologists Wolfgang Kohler, Kurt Koffka, and Kurt Lewin. Each of these theories arose from the work of a few charismatic individuals who inspired a fierce sense of loyalty to their own ideas and equally fierce attacks on the supposedly grievous errors of other schools of thought. These pioneers modeled their theories on those of the physical sciences. Their goal was to explain and predict all human behavior, and they wanted theories as detailed, universal, and complete as, for example, atomic theory in physics.

Many of these theories were applied to the problems of social psychology and began to structure its research. The idea of developing general theories is useful and important—but in the long run the problems studied by social psychologists have turned out to be too complex to fit one general, simple theory. So these grand theories have been replaced by more specific **middle-range theories.** These theories attempt to account for a certain limited range of phenomena, such as attitude change, aggression, or interpersonal attraction. Even so, social psychologists' approaches to a wide variety of different problems have been guided by a few general (and often rather simple) basic ideas easily traced back to the general theories of yesteryear. Present-day controversies are often modern versions of old feuds. We think today's research in social psychology can be understood better if we understand its roots in the large, general theories, developed nearly a century ago.

Today, social psychologists who have been influenced by these different traditions emphasize somewhat different factors when they analyze human behavior. But they do not radically disagree—indeed, most would generally agree on the facts. So the most useful way to think about these theories may be to view them as perspectives or approaches to analyzing behavior, rather than as distinctive and contrasting formal theories. Each of these basic approaches applies, in one form or another, to most areas of social psychology.

Here we present a few of these core ideas. We do not intend to be comprehensive or detailed; rather, we want to convey their essence and particularly the contrasts between them, so that we can refer to them in explaining controversies in later chapters. To emphasize the contrasts, we will apply each approach to the specific problem of understanding crime that we mentioned earlier. Here is the situation: Let us suppose a police officer catches a high school dropout, Claude, coming out of the rear door of a liquor store at 3 A.M. with a bag full of money. The store, like everything else in the neighborhood, has long since closed. The officer shouts at Claude to stop and put his hands up. Claude turns, pulls a pistol from his pocket, and shoots the officer, wounding him in the leg. Claude is apprehended and ultimately sent to jail. The statistics predict that his stay in jail will not be productive or happy; it will be costly for society, and the chances of his committing further crimes are fairly high.

Let us consider how researchers using four major theoretical approaches would view this event and explain it. The learning, incentive, and cognitive approaches are most common in social psychology. A fourth, the biological approach, has had relatively little impact, but outside our field it is a common theory for many social phenomena, so we begin by saying a little about it as well.

BIOLOGICAL APPROACHES

The influence of biological factors on human behavior has been stressed by McDougall, Freud, Lorenz, and others. Human beings are born with many biological characteristics that distinguish them from other animals and from each other. There is no question that to some extent such characteristics play a role in determining behavior. At the simplest level, they limit the behavior humans are capable of and the stimuli they respond to. Humans cannot fly, they can eat meat, they are quite strong and physically adept relative to many other animals, and so on. Humans are also intelligent, have language (or the capacity to develop it), have good memories, and live long lives. They have excellent hearing and vision, but respond to only a limited range of sounds and light. Humans also mature slowly, being quite helpless as babies; and until they have lived at least six years or so, they are unable to fend for themselves. Goats, in contrast, can walk almost at birth and can manage by themselves soon after. The list of important innate characteristics could be much longer, but clearly all these qualities affect the kind of animal we are and our social behavior.

Instinct

The question is not whether any of these innate characteristics affect our social behavior, but how big a role they play and just what difference they make. It has been suggested that humans have an *instinct* to be aggressive. Konrad Lorenz and others have argued that built into the human organism, present at birth and unalterable, is an aggressive impulse. In slightly different terms, Freud's psychoanalytic theory also proposes an innate drive toward destructiveness (though Freud thought it could be channeled into nondestructive behavior). The notion that aggression is instinctive does not help us much

in understanding why Claude robbed the store or shot the police officer, except to say that the potential for aggressiveness is part of human nature. It does not tell us why Claude fired the gun whereas others might not have; or why Claude is a criminal and the police officer is not. But this view does provide one way of looking at human behavior.

Genetic Differences

A second version of the biological approach focuses on how genetic differences between people produce differences in behavior. Some people grow up to be much bigger and stronger than others; some are smarter than others; some have better vision and finer coordination than others. Some of us are female (and can give birth to young), others are male and cannot. Similarly, some people may be, for genetic reasons, more aggressive than others. It has been argued that people who have a particular type of genetic structure (specifically XYY chromosomes instead of the more usual XY or XX) are likely to become criminals. Although there is as yet little evidence to support this idea, it would obviously be a partial explanation of criminal behavior. Perhaps Claude has an extra Y chromosome (all XYY people are males), and that is why he is so violent. A related version of the biological approach invokes other physiological factors such as hormonal imbalance or brain defects to explain aggressiveness. It is known that damage to certain parts of the brain, especially the hypothalamus, can produce uncontrolled aggressiveness in animals.

The general idea is that the causes of all behavior, including social behavior, can be found in the biological nature of the person—in the genetic structure, in innate characteristics, in physical characteristics that develop after birth, or in temporary physiological states of arousal, such as those caused by hormone production or brain stimulation. This approach has so far had relatively little impact on social psychology. Social psychologists generally assume that few instinctive or innate behavioral mechanisms exist in humans. Those that do exist seem to have minor effects compared to social factors. We can explain why some adolescent boys engage in gang violence and others spend their time in computer clubs much better by understanding the norms of their cultural groups than by understanding their chromosome structures. However, biological factors are now under intense investigation, and they may become more influential in social psychology in the near future.

LEARNING APPROACHES

For many years, the dominant approach in social psychology in the United States and Canada emphasized the role of learning. The central idea was that prior learning determines behavior. In any given situation, a person learns certain behaviors as habits, and when presented again with that situation, the person tends to behave in the same habitual way. When a hand is extended to us we shake it, because that is how we have learned to respond to an extended hand. When someone says something nasty to us, we may be nasty back or we may try to make the other person like us, depending on what we have learned to do in the past. So perhaps Claude shot the police officer because he had learned to behave violently in situations in which he was challenged by authority. The learning approach became popular in the 1920s and was the basis for **behaviorism.** Pavlov and John B. Watson were its most famous early proponents, a role filled later by Clark Hull and B. F. Skinner. Neal Miller and John Dollard applied the principles of learning to social behavior, and more recently Albert Bandura has extended this application in an approach called **social learning theory.**

Learning Mechanisms

There are three general mechanisms by which learning occurs. One is **association,** or classical conditioning. Pavlov's dogs learned to salivate at the sound of a bell because they were presented with meat every time the bell was rung. After a while they would salivate to the sound of the bell even in the absence of the meat because they associated the bell with meat. We learn attitudes by association. For example, the word "Nazi" is generally associated with horrible crimes. We learn that Nazis are bad because we have learned to associate them with terrible things.

A second learning mechanism is **reinforcement.** People learn to perform a particular behavior because it is followed by something pleasurable and need-satisfying (or they learn to avoid behavior that is followed by unpleasant consequences). A boy may learn to retaliate against insults in school by fighting with a tormentor because his father praises him for sticking up for his rights when he does it. Or a student may learn not to contradict the professor in class because each time he does, she frowns and looks angry, and snaps back at him.

The third major learning mechanism is **imitation.** People often learn social attitudes and behaviors simply by observing the attitudes and behaviors of models. A little boy may learn how to light fires in the fireplace by watching his mother do it. Children and adolescents may acquire their political attitudes simply by listening to their parents' conversations during election compaigns. Imitation may occur without any external reinforcement at all, through simple observation of the model.

Special Features

The learning approach has three distinctive features that set it off from the other core ideas in social psychology. First, the causes of behavior are supposed to lie mainly in the past learning history of the individual. Perhaps in Claude's previous encounters with the police, they had been rough, rude, antagonistic, suspicious, and unsympathetic. Perhaps he had been reinforced in the past for responding violently to situations involving conflict with authority, and nonviolent responses had not brought him satisfaction as often. Or perhaps his father often acted in a violent way himself, so Claude had learned to imitate a violent model. The learning theorist is especially concerned with past experience and somewhat less with the details of the current situation.

Second, the learning approach tends to locate the causes of behavior mainly in the external environment and not in the individual's subjective interpretation of what is happening. It emphasizes the external events previously associated with a stimulus, or the past reinforcement contingencies operating on a response, or the role models to which a person has been exposed. All these are external to the individual. Learning approaches would not emphasize, as causes of behavior, such subjective states as perceptions of the situation (for example, whether or not Claude expected the police officer to attack or shoot him), or emotions (for example, whether Claude was fearful, angry, or calculating).

Third, the learning approach usually aims to explain overt behavior instead of psychological or subjective states. It would try to explain Claude's overt act—shooting the police officer

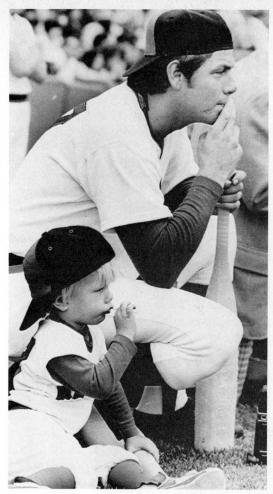

One of the most powerful mechanisms of learning is imitation. In particular children tend to imitate adults, especially their parents and others with whom they are close.

—not his perceptions or thoughts or such emotional states as fear, anger, or guilt. The learning approach would try to explain why Claude's behavior in this situation was violent: He could have argued, run away, frozen in place, or obeyed the officer. Instead, he shot him.

INCENTIVE APPROACHES

A third general approach views behavior as determined by incentives available for various acts. People act on the basis of what they have to gain or lose by any given behavior. Go back to Claude. Let us say he has the choices of fleeing, surrendering, or shooting. He expects that if he flees, he will be chased and probably shot, which adds up to a considerable negative incentive. If he surrenders, he is sure to go to jail, which is also a negative incentive. He may think that by shooting the police officer, he will be able to get away—and with the money too—which is both an absence of negative incentives and a strong positive incentive. Incentive analysis simply considers the pros and cons of any given behavior, and from that predicts how a person will behave.

Conflict Analysis

Often an incentive analysis is expanded to deal with conflicts between two possible behaviors. It considers whether the incentives attached to each behavior are positive or negative, and how positive or negative they are. *Approach-approach* conflicts involve two behaviors, each of which has only positive incentives—for example, two people ask you out for dinner on the same evening, and you like them both and would enjoy spending the evening with either. *Avoidance-avoidance* conflicts involve two negative alternatives—for example, going to the dentist and spending hundreds of dollars for new fillings, or letting your teeth gradually rot away. An *approach-avoidance* conflict concerns behavior that has both positive and negative incentives. Going to visit a senile relative in an old-age home is a kind and affectionate act, but it may also prove embarrassing and boring.

Major Incentive Theories

There are, broadly speaking, three different versions of incentive theories in social psychology. One is rational choice, or *rational decision-making theory*. This assumes that people calculate the costs and benefits of various actions, and pick the best alternative in a fairly rational way. They choose the one that gives them the greatest benefit at the least cost. Numerous such theories have been developed, of which **expectancy-value** theory is perhaps most typical (Edwards, 1954). This holds that decisions are made on the basis of the product of the (1) values of various possible outcomes of the decision, and (2) degree of expectation that each outcome will actually result from the decision.

Suppose you are trying to decide between two new cars, a racy sports car and a solid family-type car. In comparing the two cars, you feel almost certain (high expectation) that the sports car will give you more fun (high positive value). There is also some possibility (low expectation) that the sports car will cost you more in repair bills, but since your brother-in-law owns a repair shop, you feel those bills will not be very expensive (low negative value). A definite high positive value outstrips an uncertain low negative value, so you buy the sports car. Such rational models generate clear predictions about how decisions *ought* to be made, so they are useful normative models. They are also widely used by economists as descriptive models to predict the economic choices made by individuals, firms, and governments. Social psychologists, however, are more likely to emphasize departures from rationality than adherence to rationality, as we will see.

An important extension of rational choice theories to the case of interaction between two people is **exchange theory.** This theory analyzes interpersonal interaction as a series of rational decisions each person makes. That is, each person's behavior toward the other is treated as determined by the costs and benefits to each party of various possible outcomes of the interaction. The interaction between Claude and the police officer would be analyzed as turning hostile because of their conflicting interests: Claude would benefit by escaping, while the police officer would benefit by arresting him. In contrast, an exchange theory analysis of the interaction between a nurse and a patient would focus on the benefits to the patient from cooperating with the nurse (the patient gets the right medication and is helped toward recovery) and the benefits to the nurse from being friendly (the patient cooperates, and the nurse gets a reputation for doing a good job). In this case the two parties' interests converge on sharing a cooperative and friendly interaction. An exchange theory analysis of interpersonal interactions therefore shares the assumption of rationality inherent in other incentive theories, but focuses on the relative costs and benefits to both parties of various possible joint actions. It is particularly

useful for analyzing bargaining situations in which two parties must come to a common agreement despite their separate interests.

A third version of incentive theory places more emphasis on *need satisfaction*. It views the individual as having certain specific needs or motives and as behaving in such a way as to satisfy those needs. Consider, for example, how we might explain which of two women a particular man falls in love with. He might be a person with a great need to have his self-esteem built up, and another need to have a lot of peace and quiet in his life. One woman might constantly boost his ego by telling him how smart and handsome he is. The other might want to give parties all the time. The incentive approach would lead us to look at what needs he has (for esteem and for quiet), and at what need satisfaction is offered by the two women (an esteem booster, and a destroyer of peace and quiet, respectively) in order to predict which woman he would choose. Similarly, we might explain Claude's actions in terms of the tremendous amounts of frustration and anger stored up in him. His shooting of the police offi-

How did you group the objects in this photo when you first looked at it? How would you label those categories?

cer could be understood as a way of satisfying his need to express his anger, whereas giving up quietly would not satisfy that need.

These versions of incentive theory differ somewhat in the image of human nature they convey. The rational choice and exchange theory versions depict a rather calculating, almost scientific chooser, while the need-satisfaction version describes a more impulsive person driven primarily by internal forces. But all three versions focus on the same situation: a person confronted with a choice between alternative behaviors and having to decide on the basis of how much he or she stands to gain or lose from each.

All these versions of the incentive analysis, however, differ from the learning approach in one important way. They deal with the relative advantages and disadvantages of possible responses in the *current* situation, not the habits learned long ago. The causes of behavior, then, lie in the immediate situation surrounding a person. Moreover, an incentive analysis is very much concerned with internal states and not just the external environment. Our perceptions of the situation, our positive or negative feelings about it, our expectations about the consequences of alternative acts, our hopes and fears, all are central to an incentive analysis.

COGNITIVE APPROACHES

The main idea in the cognitive approach to social psychology is that a person's behavior depends on the way he or she perceives the social situation. And the laws of social perception are very similar to the laws of object perception. People spontaneously and automatically organize their perceptions, thoughts, and beliefs about a social situation into simple, meaningful form, just as they do with objects. No matter how chaotic or arbitrary the situation, people will impose some order on it. And this organization, this perception and interpretation of the world, affects how we behave in social situations.

Basic Principles

This is easy to see in terms of our perceptions of the world around us. Put this book down and look around. You will notice that you tend first spontaneously to *group* and *categorize* objects. Instead of seeing objects individually, you see them as parts of a group. You see a row of books as a group, not as so many individual books. You probably perceive other people in the library in groups—perhaps students and librarians, or females and males. You experience that pile of dirty dishes by the kitchen sink as an oppressive heap, not as individual dishes. We tend to group objects according to some very simple principles, such as *similarity* (dishes look more like each other than the stove and refrigerator do, so we group the dishes together), *proximity* (books stacked in a pile go together; the isolated books strewn all over the library table do not), or *past experience* (tables and chairs go together; so do David and Goliath or Dick and Jane; but a stove and chair do not, nor do Woody Allen and a B-52 bomber).

Second, you will notice that you immediately perceive some things as standing out (**figure**) and some as just being in the background (**ground**). Usually colorful, moving, noisy, unique, nearby stimuli are figure, whereas bland, drab, stationary, quiet, common, faraway stimuli are ground. Our attention is drawn to cheerleaders at a football game not because they are so numerous—there may be only a dozen in a crowd of nearly 100,000 people

—but because they move a lot, yell, wave their arms, and wear colorful uniforms. In contrast, we experience the crowd as just that—a crowd—not as a collection of thousands of unrelated fascinating individuals.

These two principles—that we spontaneously group or categorize the things we perceive, and that we focus attention particularly on the most prominent (figural) stimuli—are central not only to our perceptions of physical objects, but of the social world as well. You can see how strong these organizing tendencies are if you try to resist them. Try to see the social world around you as composed of ungrouped, individual persons. Look at a pair of students walking across the campus and see how difficult it is to focus on each one as an individual; it is much easier to see them as a couple. Look at a group of students walking across the campus, and try

to pay exactly equal amounts of attention to each one; it is much easier to focus attention on the one or two who are talking loudly, gesturing animatedly, or dressed unusually or colorfully. The principles of grouping, and of focusing attention on the most figural stimuli, are such routine and automatic features of our perception that it is almost impossible to avoid using them.

Interpreting the Intangible

The cognitive approach is also important for our interpretations of the intangible aspects of people, the things we cannot see, hear, touch, or smell, such as intentions, motives, attitudes, and personality traits. Just as we try to arrive at meaningful interpretations of those aspects of people we can see and hear, so we try to devel-

Expectations and attitudes determine our reaction to a situation. Are the police here being kind and understanding or are they causing trouble for an innocent person?

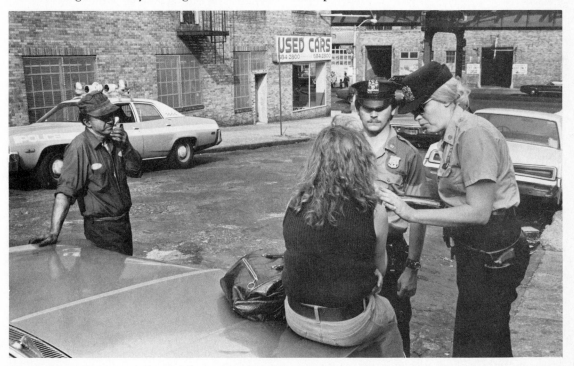

op coherent understandings of how they feel, what they want, what kind of people they are, and so forth. How do we know whether or not someone is ambitious, a chauvinist, or likes us? The cognitive approach to social psychology is crucial for understanding how we arrive at such judgments about people's underlying qualities. We tend to see a pattern in a series of nasty comments or a person's unwillingness to look at us in the eye; we conclude that she doesn't like us. If your boyfriend says "I love you" in the midst of a long conversation and he has never said that to you before, his statement is just as figural against the ground of the conversation as the cheerleaders are against the ground of a huge crowd in the football stadium.

The processes of cognitive organization and interpretation are particularly important for social psychology because of their implications about how people perceive other people and social situations. Claude does not perceive merely the individual parts of the police officer —his eyes, hair, clothes, and so on. Instead, he perceives the whole person—a police officer whose job is to arrest criminals, or perhaps who is prejudiced against people like Claude. Claude will also go beyond what he can actually see and impute meaning to what is going on. He categorizes the man as a police officer, not just another human being. He may see the police officer as threatening, as biased, as cruel. He may stereotype the police officer as being like other police officers (as Claude knows them). And Claude will respond to the police officer and the situation in general according to his own view of them.

Some Important Cognitive Theories

Such simple cognitive principles form the basis for a number of important theories in social psychology. **Attribution theory,** as developed by Harold Kelley and others, deals primarily with how we arrive at interpretations of causality. For example, how do we decide that the salesperson's ingratiating behavior is caused by a genuine liking for us as opposed to the desire to butter us up for a big sale? What do we think is causing someone's cries for help? Our interpretations of the causes may strongly influence whether we come to their aid or not. They are also central to the theory of **cognitive dissonance,** developed by Leon Festinger, which concerns how we change and rearrange our views of the world to make it seem consistent. And they are the basis of much of the research we will discuss on social perception, which attempts to describe the kinds of organization we impose on our judgments of other people.

Cognitive theories differ in emphasis from learning theory in two important ways. They focus on the perceptual organization and interpretation of the moment, not on the past. They are concerned with how Claude perceives the situation, not with his childhood or past experience with the police. Second, they look for the causes of behavior in the individual's perception or interpretation of the situation, and not in the realities of the situation itself. How Claude interprets the situation is more crucial than what the situation actually is.

SUMMARY

1. Social psychology has a unique vantage point on social behavior. It emphasizes factors in immediate social situations that induce the same general response from all people. It is less concerned with large social forces than are the other social

sciences, and less concerned with unique individual responses and individual differences than are personality or clinical psychology.
2. There are several general theoretical approaches to social psychology, but they are not necessarily

contradictory. Rather, each emphasizes one aspect of the causes of behavior without necessarily claiming that the others are unimportant or irrelevant. They differ in emphasis in some important ways and therefore can give us very different insights into social behavior. Each is particularly helpful in trying to understand some phenomena, and perhaps less valuable for others.

3. The biological approach looks for causes in innate characteristics or physiological mechanisms. Although the other approaches pay little attention to such factors, they would certainly include them if it were necessary. Learning theorists or cognitive psychologists would accept that the behavior of people who are hungry or tired differs greatly from that of those who are not, or that the social responses of a person with specific brain damage are far different from those of a person with normal brain function.

4. Learning theories stress a person's life history; they analyze current behavior in terms of what a person has learned in the past. Since they emphasize the connection between the external environment and overt behavior, they typically have understated the role of intellect, of thought, and of complex perceptual processes. Traditionally learning theorists have ignored people's expectations or beliefs, treating them as responding automatically to any current stimulus. In recent years, most learning theorists have begun to incorporate more cognitive processes in their models, so that we now have what might be called learning-cognitive theories, not just learning theories.

5. Incentive theorists believe that, all else being equal, people act to maximize gains and minimize losses. How they make such decisions and how often they actually have to make them are complex questions. Incentive theories tend to be ahistorical, but acknowledge that people's preferences are rooted in their past experiences. They have tended increasingly to build cognitive mechanisms into their analyses of decision-making.

6. The cognitive approach considers behavior as determined mainly by people's perceptions of the social situation. They group and categorize objects, focus attention on the most prominent aspects of the situation, and in general attempt to form a coherent understanding of it. The cognitive approach is probably now the most influential in social psychology. Some cognitive theorists have absorbed a great deal of learning theory, while others stick mainly to cognitive and perceptual processes. But no one denies that both present cognitive processes and past learning history determine social behavior. All these approaches help us understand social behavior. Each approach seems to be especially useful in explaining certain social phenomena. Throughout the text, we will focus on the theory that seems most relevant and useful to a particular issue. But they are all necessary for a full understanding of social behavior.

SUGGESTIONS FOR ADDITIONAL READING

ARONSON, E. 1980. *The social animal* (3rd ed.). San Francisco: W. H. Freeman. A brief, well-written introduction to some of the most interesting aspects of the field. Not complete, but entertaining.

BANDURA, A. 1977. *Social Learning Theory.* Englewood Cliffs, N.J.: Prentice-Hall. The best recent treatment of social learning theory, illustrating some of its adjustment to a more cognitive approach.

DEUTSCH, M., & Krauss, R. M. 1965. *Theories in social psychology.* New York: Basic Books. Still the best coverage of the classic theories.

FEATHER, N. T. (Ed.) 1982. *Expectations and actions: Expectancy-value models in Psychology.* Hillsdale, N.J.: Erlbaum. An up-to-date collection of papers that develops the many applications and implications of expectancy-value models.

WILSON, E. O. 1980. *Sociobiology, the abridged edition.* Cambridge, Mass.: Harvard University Press. The most influential recent effort to apply a biological approach to social behavior.

2

RESEARCH METHODS

One of the most fascinating aspects of social psychology is that we all know a lot about social behavior without having studied it systematically. We live our lives surrounded by other people and we are constantly observing them. We have some idea of what people do in many social contexts. Most other scientific disciplines are very different. We know little about nuclear physics, high-pressure chemistry, or laser technology before studying them. We come to physics or chemistry in almost total ignorance; but we come to social psychology with a great deal of relevant experience.

Much of what is taught in social psychology will fit in with what you already know from your own experience and should be relatively easy to relate to and to learn. One of the exciting aspects of social psychology, therefore, is that you can become familiar with and discuss the very latest findings almost from the beginning. The disadvantage is that you may often believe that you already know much of the material, that research is not needed because the facts are obvious, or that a particular finding is wrong because it is not consistent with your own experience.

But personal experience is not always a very good indicator of how people generally behave. Our observations are usually quite casual. We are not systematic; we do not write down each incident and describe it in an objective, unbiased way. We form *impressions* of how people behave that are sometimes correct and sometimes incorrect. For example, consider the following statements:

- When we are anxious, we like to be with other people.
- Advertisements that try to make people afraid backfire and are less effective than ads that do not arouse fear.
- People in groups will cooperate rather than compete if it is in their own self-interest, and raising the stakes increases the amount of cooperation.
- The more you pay people to make speeches against their own beliefs, the more they will change their minds to agree with the speech they make.
- In choosing friends and lovers, the most important principle is that opposites attract.
- People who live in cities have higher rates of mental illness than people in small towns.

You may not agree with some of these statements, but it is fair to say that they all sound plausible. Yet research has demonstrated that all of them are either false or oversimplifications.

Why do our casual observations lead us to wrong conclusions? Sometimes we are biased and misinterpret what happens. Sometimes we see correctly but remember wrong. Sometimes what we see is a very unusual group of people or situations. Systematic research collects data in such a way as to rule out any sources of bias, to make sure the people observed are representative, and to keep track of the "numbers" so we do not rely on memory or general impressions. Casual observations, even by very careful people, cannot replace systematic research in any field.

The main task of social psychology is to conduct scientific research on social behavior. Our research has several goals. One is to provide careful and systematic descriptions of social behavior that permit us to make reliable generalizations about how people act in various social settings. Another goal is to develop theories about social behavior that help us to understand why people behave the way they do. As we learn more about general principles and the specifics of particular types of behavior, we become better able to control behavior. The application of social psychology may help people learn to control their own aggressive impulses or to develop more satisfying personal relationships. It may also help social planners to design interventions that can help many people—by reducing smoking, by creating more cooperation in the workplace, and so on. The possibilities are exciting—but they must be based on a firm research foundation.

AT THE BEGINNING: THE QUESTION

In this chapter we will describe the research process from start to finish, from generating an idea to the completed empirical test of that idea. All research begins with a question. We then design a study to answer the question as directly as possible. Of course, this is not always easy. In fact, the main difficulty is taking a problem that may be extremely complex and finding a way to get an answer. As we will see, this often involves ingenuity and patience—and even then any one study or series of studies may not give us a firm conclusion. That is why psychologists do many studies on the same problem. Each is designed to answer one part of the question or to narrow down the possible answers.

Theoretical vs. Nontheoretical Questions

Before discussing how we go about designing a study, we need to know what kind of question we have. There are two basic kinds of questions: those that are directly related to a theory and those that are not.

A **theoretical question** starts with a theory we want to test. A theory can be any abstract generalization that tells us what to expect in more specific, concrete cases. A good example is Darley and Latané's theory of the diffusion of responsibility in helping situations. In Chapter 1 we described two cases in which women were attacked in front of a number of witnesses, yet no one helped stop the attack or even called the police. One woman was repeatedly raped, and the other was ultimately killed. What makes people help or not help others in such situations? Darley and Latané (1968) hypothesized that people are least likely to help when they think there are other witnesses to the emergency, so that they do not feel directly and personally responsible. This hypothesis follows from their more general theory of diffusion of responsibility: Anything that diminishes an individual's sense of responsibility for solving a problem makes that person less likely to help others with it. This general theory leads to many more specific, concrete, and detailed *hypotheses,* such as that people will help out less in an emergency when there are other witnesses (as in their experiment; see Box 2–1), that they will work less hard to solve a common problem when in a large group, or that they will pay less attention to instructions when co-workers are also listening. From that one theoretical statement, we can deduce what to expect in numerous more specific situations. Put another way, a general theory generates hypotheses or predictions about how people will behave in a number of more specific situations.

As we saw in Chapter 1, social psychology has moved slowly toward middle-range theories and away from the all-encompassing general theories popular earlier in the century. Diffusion

BOX 2–1
Diffusing Responsibility in an Emergency

To test this "diffusion of responsibility" idea, Darley and Latané conducted a laboratory experiment in which every subject overheard an apparent emergency. Some subjects thought they were the only witnesses. Others were told that other people were waiting with them, and therefore thought that others overheard the emergency as well. The hypothesis was that the subjects would be more likely to try to help when they thought they were the only witnesses to the emergency because they would feel more personal responsibility for the victim's fate. In the study itself, all subjects were placed in separate rooms, and communicated only over intercoms. Some were told there were just two subjects; others, that there were six subjects. A confederate of the experimenters, who acted as if he were one of the real subjects, said initially that he was prone to seizures. Later he said, "I think I need a little help . . . I've got one of these things coming on and I could really use some help . . . (choking sounds) . . . I'm gonna die . . . (chokes, then he was quiet)."

Consistent with the hypothesis, helping was reduced with more witnesses. When the subjects thought no one else had heard the cries for help, 85 percent reported the incident to the experimenters before the confederate fell silent. Of the subjects who thought they were in six-person groups, only 31 percent reported the incident. Bystanders were indeed less likely to intervene to help a stranger in distress when they thought other bystanders were present.

Source: Darley & Latané (1968).

of responsibility is a good example of a middle-range theory because it deals with a moderate range of phenomena—situations in which individuals are trying to solve problems, and their responsibility for the solution varies. It does not attempt to deal with all social behavior. But whether the theory is a grand general theory or a middle-range theory, theoretical research is based on the specific hypotheses derived from theory.

Theoretical research begins with a specific prediction or hypothesis from a theory. The major goal of the research is to evaluate the theory. If the hypothesis is confirmed, the theory is supported. If the hypothesis is disconfirmed, it might suggest that the theory is at least partially wrong. We could then go back and discard the

theory or alter it to make it consistent with the new finding. On the other hand, no matter how the research came out, we would want to evaluate the accuracy of the study very carefully. The study might support the hypothesis, but we might conclude that the study was so flawed it should not be taken as support at all. Or it might disconfirm the hypothesis, but we might reject the study as so poorly done it should not count.

Often, however, research is not concerned with a theory at all. Researchers may simply be interested in discovering more about a particular behavior. We might be interested in what differentiates divorced couples from those who have been married for many years. We might find out how similar the members of the couple are in political and religious values, whether or not they both come from similar ethnic groups and social classes, whether or not they have children, and how many; whether they differ in age a great deal; how overtly they argue and fight when they have conflicts; whether or not they are financially well off; whether both members of the couple work; and so on. There might be a great many variables we would take into consideration not to test any particular theory, but just to describe the differences between successful and unsuccessful marriages. Research motivated by nontheoretical questions is not designed to test predictions from a more general theory and provide a test of the general theory. It is simply designed to gather information about the specific phenomenon in question.

The ultimate goal of psychology, indeed of any science, is to have simplifying theories that explain known facts in a particular realm. Theories help us understand, appreciate, and cope with the world. Data without a theory are difficult to understand and to fit into the rest of our knowledge. On the other hand, sometimes we just need to begin collecting exploratory data because we do not yet have a good theory. So there is great value in both kinds of research—research that focuses on testing particular hypotheses that have been generated from clear theories, and research that simply collects interesting facts about an important phenomenon.

Basic vs. Applied Questions

Another major distinction is whether the researcher is interested in building up knowledge for knowledge's sake, and is therefore doing **basic research,** or is trying to gain knowledge in order to solve some practical problem, which is called **applied research.** Research on the effects of televised violence, for example, can be motivated by either goal. Its aim might be to understand how people respond to any kind of observed violence just because it is an interesting scientific problem. For example, what is the ef-

fect of watching a cowboy movie or a football game? What about a performance of *Romeo and Juliet*, in which the main characters are killed or commit suicide? The answers may tell us a little about the effects of any given program now being shown on prime-time television, and in that sense may have application, but that is not the main goal.

In contrast, the research may start with a specific, real world problem. One practical question is whether watching the crime shows currently being shown on prime-time television actually causes people to commit violent acts themselves. If the research shows that it does, there could be a practical consequence: Reduce the violence on television in order to reduce crime. Unlike basic research, here the emphasis is on a particular problem. It may be that the effects of television are quite different from the effects of any other form of communication, and that the research has no general value except for what it tells us about TV and crime. But someone doing applied research is relatively unconcerned about the broader issues. At least for

How is watching this program likely to affect this viewer's aggressive behavior? How would you isolate the effects of this program from other factors?

Charles Gatewood

the moment, the emphasis is on the immediate problem and how to solve it.

Clearly, both basic and applied research are important. In fact, the distinction is really a continuum: Much research is really a blend of basic and applied research. If we conducted a study on the effects of a popular crime show, it might tell us about prime-time television, but it also tells us something more general about the effects of observed violence. Moreover, basic research almost always grows out of a concern with real problems and must necessarily be related to them, even if indirectly; and applied research has to start somewhere and relies on principles derived from basic research. The ideal arrangement is for each type of work to take ideas from the other.

Basic research is most often also theoretical research, and applied work is usually nontheoretical. However, the other two combinations also exist. For example, the learning theory idea that watching violence produces imitative behavior might be conveniently tested in an applied research project designed to discover the effects of prime-time television viewing. The applied situation may simply be a convenient place to test a general theory. Similarly, nontheoretical but basic research is common in the early stages of studying a particular area; research may be quite exploratory, and guided by little more than hunch. Research on helping, for example, began with some hunches developed from cases like the Kitty Genovese killing, and then tried to test the effects of some of those factors, such as the presence of other people. Theory came later.

CORRELATIONAL VS. EXPERIMENTAL DESIGNS

After an investigator has decided what research question to ask, the most difficult decision still remains: how to do the study. Although variations in study design are virtually unlimited, there are two basic structures: correlational and experimental. Each has advantages and disadvantages. As we will see, the type chosen depends largely on the problem being studied and the goals of the research.

A **correlational** research design consists of passively observing the relationship between two or more variables. It asks this question: When variable A is high, is variable B also high (a positive correlation), low (a negative correlation), or is B's value unrelated (no correlation)? Height and weight are positively correlated, because tall people tend to weigh more than short people; the temperature on a given day and the amount of clothing worn tend to be negatively correlated—that is, people usually wear less clothing on hot days. However, height and amount of clothing worn are probably uncorrelated; tall people and short people probably wear about the same amount of clothing, in general.

A good example of correlational research comes from studies of whether or not watching violence on television is a cause of increased aggressive behavior. Correlational studies have simply measured how much a child watches violent programs on television and the amount of aggressive behavior he or she engages in, and tested for the level of correlation between the two. Are the children who watch the most violence on television also the most aggressive in their daily behavior? Huesmann (1982) found that those elementary school children who watched violent programs the most were also described by their peers as the most aggressive, suggesting just such a link between television viewing and aggression. So we would say that viewing violent programs on television was positively correlated with aggressive behavior among those children.

In an **experimental** design, we arrange two (or more) conditions that differ in exactly specified ways, randomly assign people to experience these different conditions, and then measure the behavior we are interested in. In experiments on media violence, one group of children might be shown a violent film, while another group is shown a nonviolent film. All the children might then be placed in a test situation in which their aggressive behavior can be measured. If those shown the violent film behave more aggressively, filmed violence is concluded to be a cause of aggressive behavior. Hartmann (1969) had one group of teenage boys view a two-minute film showing two boys shooting baskets and then getting into an argument and finally a fistfight. A second group was shown another two-minute film depicting an active but cooperative basketball game.

After watching the film, each boy was asked to help out in what was described as a study of the effects of performance feedback on learning. The subject was supposed to be a "teacher," and to administer shock to a "learner" every time that "learner" made a mistake in the learning task. The "teacher" could deliver as strong a shock as he wanted, within certain limits. It turned out that the subjects who had seen the violent film delivered more shock than those who had seen the nonviolent one. In this situation, at least, observed violence increased aggressive behavior.

Correlation and Causal Ambiguity

Most correlational studies, and all experimental studies, aim first to establish a cause-and-effect relationship between the **independent variable** (the cause) and the **dependent variable** (the effect). In the Huesmann and Hartmann studies, the intent was to assess the causal role of observed violence in producing later aggressive behavior. The point of correlating elementary school children's viewing preferences with their aggressive behavior is to understand the causal role of viewing television violence (the independent variable) in producing aggressive behavior

(the dependent variable). The point of experimentally comparing the effects of a violent with a nonviolent film is to determine whether or not observed violence affects aggressive behavior.

The major weakness of correlational studies is that they leave the cause and effect relationship ambiguous in two ways. One is that the direction of causality is ambiguous. If viewing violent television is correlated with high levels of aggressive behavior, maybe the viewing does indeed cause more aggression. But the correlation could also reflect causality in the reverse direction: Maybe children who are very aggressive in their daily lives, getting into fights and yelling and screaming all the time, especially like to watch other people fighting. Maybe engaging in the aggressive behavior causes the viewing of violence. In other words, a correlation between two variables does not, by itself, tell you which variable is the cause and which is the effect. This **reverse-causality** *problem* occurs whenever two variables are correlated with each other, and each one can just as plausibly be the cause as the effect of the other.

The other serious ambiguity in correlational research is the possibility that neither variable is directly affecting the other. Some other unspecified factor may influence both of them. This is called the **third-variable problem.** For example, aggression is much more common in the homes of lower-class disadvantaged people, where there are typically high levels of unemployment and marital instability, not much money, and a great deal of frustration and anger. In such households, family members may prefer violent television because it seems more realistic and familiar to them. And children in those households may grow up being unusually aggressive themselves because of the high levels of anger and frustration surrounding them. In contrast, children who grow up in more comfortable middle-class homes may enjoy family comedies more and may be much less aggressive themselves. If all this were true, viewing television violence would be correlated with aggressive behavior—but the correlation would be due to a third variable that caused both of them: the level of frustration and anger in the child's family. The correlation between viewing televised violence and aggressive behavior would be called "spurious" because it was artificially created by a third variable that was not considered.

These two ambiguities are often a problem in correlational studies. But sometimes we can be sure that reverse causality could not be operating. Many studies have found a correlation between gender and aggressive behavior—boys are more aggressive than girls. But we can be confident that it is their "boyness" that causes their aggressiveness and not the other way around. Children do not begin sexually neutral and then become physiologically male or female depending on whether or not they fight on the playground.

Nor is the "third-variable" problem always a fatal difficulty, since we can check to see whether or not the most plausible third variable is really responsible for the correlation we have observed. For example, we could add measures of frustration and anger in the child's family to Huesmann's (1982) correlational study of elementary school children. Then we could check to see whether the correlation of television viewing with aggressive behavior was in fact due to home life. The strategy would be to see if the original correlation between television viewing and aggression holds with the third variable held constant; that is, for people at all levels of that third variable. Does it hold both in angry, aggressive families and in happy, peaceful families? If so, we can conclude that the third variable (home life) was not responsible for the original correlation.

Of course, this procedure does not eliminate the third-variable problem. There still could be some other "third-variable" (now actually a fourth, of course) that we still had not measured, such as intelligence. Perhaps the less intelligent children like to watch crude, brute force rather than the subtleties of more verbal drama, and maybe they are more aggressive in school because of the frustration from constantly doing poorly. Again the solution would be to measure this new "third variable," intelligence,

and then see if the original correlation held up for both highly intelligent children and those below average in intelligence.

This sounds as if it could go on and on. But at some point the process ends, because we can no longer think of any more plausible "third variables." That does not mean there are none, but it at least means that for the moment, we will accept the correlation as reflecting a cause-and-effect relationship until someone else thinks of some further possible variable and it is examined.

Causality In Experiments

The great strength of the experimental method is that it avoids ambiguities about causality. In social psychology, experiments consist of randomly assigning people to different conditions and seeing if there is any difference in their responses. If the experiment has been done properly, any difference in responses between the two conditions must be due to the difference in the conditions. To put it in more formal terms, the causal variable, which is called the *independent variable,* must have caused the difference in the *dependent variable.* In the example of media violence, the independent variable is the amount of violence in the film, and the dependent variable is the amount of aggressive behavior.

There are two crucial elements in an experiment. First, the causal or independent variable is deliberately controlled by the experimenter. This is called "varying" or "manipulating" that particular factor. For example, the experimenter might vary or manipulate the amount of violence shown in a particular film by randomly assigning some subjects to view a violent film, and others to view a nonviolent film. If the experimenter is attempting to manipulate only the amount of violence in a film, the violent and nonviolent films should not differ in other ways, such as being cartoon vs. realistic, or black and white vs. color, or old-fashioned vs. modern. The experimenter's control over the independent variable is crucial because it later allows us to pinpoint the exact cause of any differences that emerge between the two groups of subjects. Hartmann (1969) treated the two groups of adolescent boys identically in every respect with just one exception: One group watched a filmed fistfight; the other group watched a friendly basketball game. Any differences between the two groups in their later behavior (the dependent variable) must be attributed to this one difference in how they were treated.

The second crucial element is that subjects must be randomly assigned to conditions. **Random assignment** is crucial because we must assume that the two groups of subjects did not differ before they were placed into the two different conditions. If they differed in some way before we introduced the experimental conditions, we cannot interpret any later differences in behavior as being solely due to those conditions. The differences in behavior could be due to those prior factors and not to the independent variable.

We could try to rule out such previous differences by measuring all the boys' aggressiveness before the experiment began, and then deliberately ensuring that the boys in the two groups did not differ to begin with. This procedure risks not catching some real differences on dimensions we did not think to measure. As a result, more often, we ensure the initial equality of the two groups by leaving it up to chance. We make the assignments by deciding by chance which condition to put each subject in. This can be done by flipping a coin, cutting a deck of cards, or more commonly and more precisely by using a set of random numbers.

Perhaps the most dangerous departure from random assignment lies in allowing the subjects themselves to select their experimental condition, directly or indirectly. Suppose you asked subjects whether they preferred to watch violent or nonviolent television programs and assigned them according to their choices. Then, after having subjects watch either violent or nonviolent TV for some period of time, you

might find that those who watched violent programs were more aggressive. But you could not conclude that the programs made them more violent, because they might have been more aggressive in the first place. It would be no surprise to find that more aggressive people liked more violent programs. The "experiment" would be meaningless.

Advantages of the Correlational Method

Correlational techniques sometimes let us study problems to which experimental methods may not be applicable. Many real world problems do not allow us to control the situation. For example, the experimental method generally cannot be used to study the effects of natural disasters or many of the most important events in people's lives. We cannot assign people to air raids, floods, and surgery entirely at random. It is not chance alone that leads some people to be poor, to live in cities, or to get divorced. It is difficult for both practical and ethical reasons to expose people to such extreme conditions in an experiment. We could not actually conduct an experiment in which a person was given an order to kill another person, and given the opportunity to do so. So any research on such variables must be correlational rather than experimental. We must settle for doing experiments that operate within a range of rather mild and inoffensive human experiences.

A second advantage of a correlational study is that it allows us to collect more information and test more relationships than we can in most experiments. If we wanted to explore what caused some children to be more aggressive than others, we could collect information on a great many potential causal factors, including television viewing, family lives, intelligence and personality, relationships with other children, and so on. Moreover, we could measure aggressive behavior in a number of different ways —in terms of teachers' impressions, observing

Table 2–1 Characteristics of Correlational and Experimental Research	CORRELATIONAL	EXPERIMENTAL
Advantages of Experiments		
Independent variable	Varies naturally	Controlled by researcher
Random assignment	No	Yes
Unambiguous causality	No	Yes
Theory testing	Often	Usually
Advantages of Correlational Studies		
Exploratory	Often	Usually not
Real world problems	Often	Usually not
Tests many relationships	Usually	Usually not

children in school, their reputations for aggressiveness among other children, parents' reports, and so on. The experimental method is inefficient for collecting large amounts of data on many variables. Since experimenters must produce each independent variable, they are usually limited to studying one or two at a time. They could not test 20 variables at once, as is often done in correlational studies. It would take a tremendous number of experimental studies to investigate the effect of each of these factors on each behavior. So correlational studies are often used in nontheoretical or exploratory research because they make possible the efficient collection of large amounts of data.

Correlational and experimental work complement each other. There are many cases in which both methods are useful. In general, correlational studies are particularly effective in the collection of large amounts of data; they provide us with ideas and hypotheses that can then be studied in more detail experimentally. They do have the disadvantage of causal ambiguity, which can never be completely overcome, so it is always helpful when experimental research supplements correlational studies.

FIELD VS. LABORATORY SETTINGS

The next step is to decide where research should be done, in a field setting or in a laboratory. Research done in a field setting means that we study the kind of behavior the person normally engages in as it occurs in its natural habitat. We might study a factory worker's productivity or morale right in the factory itself, a person's television viewing in his own living room, a commuter's response to an emergency on the subway train she normally rides home from work, a third-grader's aggressive behavior toward schoolmates on the school playground, or a college student's relationship with her roommate in a college dormitory. Laboratory research, in contrast, is done in an artificial situation, one the person normally does not inhabit. Usually laboratory research is conducted in some specially outfitted room in a psychology building at a university or research institute. It may have all kinds of special equipment, such as video equipment to show stimuli to subjects, audio equipment to record interaction between subjects, one-way mirrors to permit observation of group interactions, physiological recording equipment, or intercoms to limit interaction between people to audio channels only. Or it may simply have tables and chairs at which people fill out questionnaires. The point is that the researcher brings the subject to an artificial environment.

Although most research in social psychology during the last 25 years has been conducted in the laboratory, some has always been conducted in the field. Both experimental and correlational research can be done in either the laboratory or the field, and each setting has advantages and disadvantages.

Advantage of the Laboratory

The major advantage of work in the laboratory is the control it permits over the situation. Researchers can be quite certain about what is happening to each subject. If they are doing experimental work, they can randomly assign the subjects, expose them to the exact experiences necessary to study the problem, minimize extraneous factors, and go a long way toward eliminating unwanted variations in the procedure. Laboratory researchers have great control over the dependent variable and can measure it in

considerably more detail and in a more uniform manner than in the field. Therefore, the laboratory is the ideal place in which to study the exact effects of one variable on another.

In contrast, in field settings, it is generally extremely difficult to assign subjects to conditions randomly, to be certain they are all experiencing the same thing, to get accurate measures on the dependent variable, and so on. A great many extraneous events and conditions enter into a field study and often obscure the effects of the variables in which the researcher is interested.

In particular, it is difficult to find pure manipulations of the independent variable and pure measures of the dependent variable. The experimenter must find or arrange circumstances that produce specific differences—and no others—between conditions. For example, Feshbach and Singer (1971; see Box 2–2) were able to assign some boys to a constant diet of violent television in their boarding schools, and other boys to a diet of nonviolent television. But most of the boys preferred the more violent programs, so those assigned to nonviolent television may have been more frustrated than the other group because they were not allowed to watch their favorite programs. As a result, it is not clear whether the observed lack of effect of the violent diet is due to its real lack of effect, or due to the frustrations brought on by the assignment itself. This would not be such a problem in a laboratory study, because the researchers would not have had to interfere with the subjects' normal television viewing practices, and therefore would not have induced frustration in one group and not in the other.

Another advantage of the laboratory is convenience and cost. It is usually much easier and cheaper to set up research in a room down the hall from your office than it is to set it up at a site where people are living their daily lives. With sufficient ingenuity and hard work, it is sometimes possible to arrange easy field situations. For example, one team of researchers was interested in whether people tended to choose dating or marital partners of the same level of physical attractiveness as themselves. They observed couples in the lobbies of movie theaters, and indeed found the couples matched each other very closely (Silverman, 1971). However these tailor-made situations for research tend to be few and far between in the field. The world is generally not set up to facilitate the study of a specific problem that psychologists want to study.

Advantage of the Field

The most obvious advantage of field settings is that they are more realistic, and therefore allow the results to be generalized more readily to real life situations. This is called **external validity** to reflect the fact that the results are more likely to be valid in situations outside (external to) the research situation itself (Campbell & Stanley, 1961). This can be seen if we compare the Hartmann (1969) laboratory experiment on observed violence described earlier in this chapter with the Feshbach and Singer **field experiment** on the same topic (see Box 2–2).

In Hartmann's laboratory study, the independent variable, observed violence, was artificial—a brief film on a fistfight especially prepared for the study itself. In Feshbach's and Singer's field study, it was the violence shown on prime-time television shows all over the country. The dependent variable, aggressive behavior, was artificial in the laboratory study—the amount of shock delivered in the "teacher-learner" situation constructed especially for the study. In the field study, the dependent variable consisted of observers' ratings of how much physical and verbal aggression the boys engaged in in their normal interactions with peers and teachers. Suppose we want to generalize from these studies to the effects of prime-time television on teenage boys' aggression in their everyday lives. In the field study we are already dealing with exactly the kinds of observed violence, aggressive behavior, and situation to which we want to generalize. So it would be more appropriate to generalize from the field study.

Another advantage of work in the field is that we are sometimes able to deal with extremely powerful variables and situations that could not be studied in the laboratory. This is particularly true of correlational work. We can observe people in extreme situations—when they are waiting for open-heart surgery in a hospital or huddled together under artillery bombardment. This advantage sometimes applies to field experiments when the manipulation is done not by the experimenter, but by some natural event that just happens to affect people randomly and therefore fits the criteria for an experiment. Researchers wanting to investigate the effects of heat on violence could take advantage of the fact that the hottest days occur at random through the summer. If ghetto riots occurred on the hottest days of the summer, then heat must be one causal factor (Carlsmith & Anderson, 1979).

Because research in the field deals with everyday life, it tends to minimize suspicion by the subjects. Their responses are more spontaneous and less susceptible to the kinds of bias suspicion produces. Whenever a college student knows she is a subject in an experiment, there is

Table 2–2
Characteristics of Field and Laboratory Research

	FIELD	LABORATORY
Advantages of Laboratory		
Control over variables	Low	High
Random assignment	Rarely	Almost always
Convenience and economy	Low	High
Advantages of Field		
Realism	High	Low
Impact of independent variables	Tends to be higher	Tends to be lower
Minimizes suspicion and bias	Yes	No
External validity	High	Low

always the possibility that she is not behaving naturally or spontaneously. She may be trying to please or displease the experimenter, may be behaving in the way she thinks she should, may not accept the experimental manipulation because she is distrustful, and so on. Any of these effects could produce bias in the results or obscure actual relationships and effects.

Nevertheless, although field and laboratory research do differ in the ways we have described, these differences are easily exaggerated. It is possible to obtain considerable control of variables outside the laboratory, and it is possible to make laboratory situations extremely realistic. Research in both types of settings is necessary to avoid the pitfalls of either.

DATA COLLECTION

The next step is to decide on a technique of data collection. Basically, we have three options. (1) We can observe behavior directly. (2) We can get the subjects to report on their own behaviors, perceptions, or attitudes. (3) We can go to an archive and use data originally collected for other purposes.

Observational Research

Direct observation is a widely used research technique. In studying group behavior, you can observe the interactions and note what everyone says, how often they talk, and how often they look at or touch one another. With children, you might observe the number of fights,

sharing, talking, and playing with toys. This is the same technique ethologists (people who study animals in their natural habitat) use to study the behavior of animals. We obviously cannot ask a lion how often he fights or a chimp whether she uses tools. Of necessity, ethologists have had to observe what the animals *do*.

Observational research in natural situations is usually quite difficult and time-consuming. The first task is to decide what actions to record. In doing this, the researcher must face the fact that one cannot observe and record everyting. For example, even a brief conversation is enormously complex. It is easy to record how often each person talks and what he has said; but each act of speaking also involves the pitch, amplitude, and speed of the utterance, the tone used, the number of pauses between words,

Our coding categories depend on what we want to know. How would you code this behavior? Piling up boxes? Cooperation? Interaction with opposite sex?

Teri Leigh Stratford

and so on. As a result, people who study speech can spend hours analyzing a two-minute conversation. Moreover, people use complicated facial and body gestures when they are talking. To make the project manageable, we would need to decide what aspects of the conversation we were most interested in.

Next, a simple method of recording the observed behaviors must be devised. It is essential that observers agree on what happened. For example, a category called "acted friendly" might not be useful because it is often difficult to decide whether or not an act is friendly. Instead, observers use more specific categories, such as "smiled at other person," "offered to share toy," or "helped up from ground," which they can agree on. It can be decided later whether or not all these are indications of friendliness. Much of the difficulty with observation in research and in the real world is that we disagree on what a particular behavior means.

Observational research can be conducted in natural field situations. As indicated earlier, Feshbach and Singer (1971) had supervisors in boarding homes rate teenage boys' levels of aggressiveness in normal interactions with friends and teachers after the boys had seen either violent or nonviolent television. Observational research can also be done in artificial, controlled

situations such as in the Darley-Latané (1968) study of bystander intervention. They created an artificial emergency, and the subject's response was observed.

The advantage of observing behavior in a field situation is its external validity. If the independent variable influences people's behavior in their everyday worlds, it must be important. Also, the meaning of behavior in natural settings is often easier to interpret. When children fight in a schoolyard, we can conclude with some certainty that aggression is being expressed. When someone in the laboratory is told to give electric shock to another subject and does it, it is not so clear that only aggression is involved. Giving the shock may also indicate obedience to authority.

On the other hand, one disadvantage of naturalistic observation is that the behavior of interest may not occur frequently enough to make the study useful—children in fact do not come to blows in a schoolyard very often. So we could wait a long time before such a spontaneous aggressive act occurred. The advantage of the controlled situation is that it is constructed to induce the behavior being studied. The Hartmann and Darley-Latané studies were set up so that agressive and helping behavior were sure to occur in at least some conditions.

Self-Report

Perhaps the most common technique of data collection in social psychology uses people's self-reports of their own perceptions, attitudes, or behaviors. A person can be asked for her preference between two presidential candidates, as in Gallup polls done before each election. Children can be asked to report on their perceptions of their classmates' aggressiveness, or on their own actual television viewing behavior, as in Huesmann's study. In all these cases, the basic data are the individuals' own reports about their thoughts, feelings, and actions.

Self-reports are obtained in a wide number of different settings. The Huesmann study collected information from children in a classroom, and questionnaire studies are often done in a laboratory, especially as part of a controlled experiment. Survey research is another common method of collecting self-report data. In most surveys, people are interviewed by a professional interviewer. Surveys are done about almost every conceivable topic, ranging from product preferences to politics to sexual relations. Until recently, surveys were most often done face-to-face in the home. Now this is increasingly expensive and difficult. People have become more suspicious of strangers coming to the door; rising gasoline prices have made driving to homes more expensive for interviewers; and the increasing number of working women has made it harder to find people at home. So survey researchers have turned to telephone or mail surveys.

Telephone surveys yield data that are similar to those from home interviews, except that they usually must be somewhat shorter and are much less expensive to do. Almost everyone now has a telephone, so telephone surveys do not yield biased samples of respondents. Mail surveys are not usually very reliable, because relatively few people will return mail questionnaires, and the ones who do are not usually representative of the general population.

The big advantage of self-report question-

Ken Karp

How might their answers to this marketing survey be affected by their answering together?

naire or interview techniques is that they allow the investigator to measure subjective states such as perceptions, attitudes, or emotions. These can only be inferred indirectly from observational studies, and as we will see in Chapter 3, observers' inferences of such internal states from overt behavior are not very reliable. Any study that requires us to have information about internal states must almost always use self-report techniques. For example, it would be very difficult for observers to tell how lonely another person feels without getting that person's self-report.

The principal disadvantage of self-report techniques is that we must rely on the people to give honest reports of their own internal feelings. But people sometimes disguise socially unacceptable feelings (such as racial prejudices), and sometimes they are not fully aware of their own feelings. These are precisely the reasons that led behaviorists like Watson and Skinner to reject introspectionist techniques years ago. However, social psychology has come a long way toward learning the conditions under which such self-reports can be trusted, and they have become the dominant data-gathering technique.

Archival Research

A final kind of research is the **archive study,** in which the investigator uses data that had previously been collected in earlier research projects. An example of the use of archives is the study described in Chapter 10 on the relationship between cotton prices and lynchings of blacks in the South. The investigators (Hovland & Sears, 1940) used the general hypothesis that frustration leads to aggression. They argued that drops in cotton prices produced frustration that would in turn produce an increase in aggression in the form of lynchings. The data on

cotton prices and on the number of lynchings were readily available in statistics collected by the United States government and others. The investigators simply looked up these data and ran correlations between the two variables. The years with low cotton prices had the most lynchings, supporting the hypothesis.

Almost all major universities now have their own data archives. They usually include data on a wide variety of topics. Perhaps the best-known archival data are the census reports that have been collected every 10 years for two centuries. The government collects and stores vast quantities of economic statistics. Another important source is the Interuniversity Consortium for Political and Social Research (ICPSR). This is an organization headquartered at the University of Michigan which has stored and distributed the data from most of the major studies done in the social sciences in the past 30 years. It has the major studies of presidential elections done by the National Election Studies, the General Social Survey done at the University of Chicago, and the New York Times/CBS News polls, all of which provide survey data on

The U.S. Census is a major source of archival data. Such massive data collection efforts must be carried out by large research teams with large funding resources.

Fred Gatlin, U.S. Census Bureau

the American people over many years. Many colleges and universities subscribe to the Consortium, which means that all these data are available to any researcher at those institutions.

There are many advantages of using archival data. Most obvious is that it is very cheap to use data that may have been enormously expensive to collect. The U.S. Census costs millions of dollars to collect, but the data can be used for next to nothing. Archival data also allow us to test hypotheses over time, rather than at just one point. We might want to know how many people say they would vote for a woman for president, and the availability of archival data on that question over many years can give us a rich historical context for our findings. On the other hand, archival data almost always were collected with some research question in mind other than the one we wish now to use them for. As a result, the questions are usually not exactly the ones we would ask, or they may be worded the wrong way for our purposes, or the persons in the study may not be exactly the group we would prefer. As a result, the uses of data archives are limited in some ways. Nevertheless, as they continue to expand in the years ahead, they will prove of increasing importance to social psychology.

DEVELOPING AND CONDUCTING THE STUDY

Once the questions and the method have been chosen, the investigator must design and conduct a study. Let's take as an example the design and execution of a laboratory experiment. An investigator has gotten interested in the effects of fear on attitude change. Sometimes advertisers or politicians claim dire consequences will follow if people do not use a product or vote for them. People will be stranded with a flat tire at midnight in a rainstorm on a deserted highway, or their taxes will go up. Does making people fearful make them more susceptible to a propaganda message? Or does it just frighten them so much they don't want to think about anything at all?

Suppose the researcher hypothesizes that fear arousal produces attitude change, and she has decided to do an experimental study. She must set up a situation in which the independent variable (fear) is experimentally manipulated, and in which subjects are randomly assigned to high and low fear groups in such a way that the groups differ only in terms of fear arousal, the independent variable. Then the experimenter must measure attitude change, the dependent variable, in order to see what effect the independent variable has had.

The Independent Variable

The first step in the process generally is to decide on the specific way to manipulate the independent variable. The psychologist starts with a *conceptual definition.* Let us say she defined *fear* as the internal feeling produced by the anticipation of pain or harm from a known source. This conceptual definition may sound impressive, but it is very general. The experimenter's big problem is deciding on the particular way in which she is going to arouse fear; that is, to decide on an *operational definition* of fear. An operational definition is the specific procedure, or operation, that is used to implement the much more general conceptual variable we are interested in. According to the conceptual definition, she must set up a situation in which the person anticipates harm from a known source. The operational definition provides the specific procedure by which this is done.

There are several criteria for a good manipulation. One is that it should work in a similar manner on all subjects. If a manipulation uniformly creates the same experience for all individuals, its effects are more likely to be significant. Therefore, the psychologist wants to use something everyone or almost everyone is afraid of.

A second point is that social psychologists typically deal with several levels of a particular variable rather than simply its presence or absence. It might be that without any fear at all, people simply won't pay attention to the propagandist. With too much fear, they may get too frightened and tune out. With moderate fear, they may be maximally responsive. So we want to think of the independent variable as a continuum, ranging from low to high levels of fear, and the experimental conditions as falling at various points on that continuum.

How can we be certain that the manipulation really created differences in the independent variable we have conceptually defined? There are two main ways of pinning down the meaning of the experimental manipulation. One is to use many different kinds of fear manipulations, all derived from our conceptual definition. If all these different manipulations produce the same effect on the dependent measure (for example, if in all cases the high-fear group was more persuaded than the low-fear group), we can be quite confident that fear is producing the effect. The other way is to provide a direct check on the manipulation by the use of self-reports or by some other variable that we know from previous research to be highly correlated with fear. For example, we could ask people how fearful or nervous they felt. Or we could take measures of blood pressure and pulse rate. Although physiological measures are generally poor indicators of the presence of fear, they do tend to be correlated with it. The greater the fear, the higher should be the blood pressure and pulse

rate. Unfortunately, neither approach is particularly easy in most instances. A great deal of care is required to be certain of our interpretation of the manipulation, and much controversy often revolves around different interpretations of the same experimental manipulation.

The Dependent Variable

We must now decide how to measure the dependent variable, attitude change. Again we must go from a conceptual to an operational definition with a minimum of ambiguity because we would like to be absolutely sure it is attitude change we are measuring. In this case, the researcher might operationally define attitude change as a change in the subject's desire to buy a particular brand of flashlight battery from before to after viewing a fear-arousing commercial or magazine advertisement about it.

Often experimenters cannot find a perfect measure of the variable they are interested in. One solution to this problem is to use many different measures of the same variable. If the measures all produce the same results and are all designed to tap the same variable, we can have increased confidence in the meaning of the findings. Any one measure might be interpreted in a variety of ways, but if 10 different measures produce the same result, it is more likely that the intended variable has been measured.

This, then, is the basic procedure for conducting an experiment in social psychology. A hypothesis is formed, an independent variable is chosen, the manipulation is constructed, the experimental situation is designed, and a dependent measure is selected. Generally, a considerable amount of pretesting is necessary to work out the exact method of manipulating the independent variable, smooth out the procedure, and make as certain as possible that the dependent measure is appropriate. When the pretesting has been completed and the type of subject selected, the experiment is ready to be run.

BIASES

Before actually running the experiment, however, the researcher must anticipate the various kinds of biases that might arise and take steps to minimize their effects. All scientists are concerned about bias, and social psychologists are no exceptions. Three kinds of bias are particularly troublesome in social psychology: the selection of a subject population, the experimenter's behavior, and bias associated with a subject's feelings about being in an experiment.

Subject Population

How do we decide what people to study? One obvious starting point might be that we want to study the people about whom we later want to generalize. If we want to generalize about women who work full time, we should study working women. But clearly we will never be able to afford to study all the people we want to generalize to. So instead we study some smaller number of them, but chosen in such a way that they are representative of the larger group. We cannot study the television habits of all fourth-grade boys in the United States, but we can study some smaller group of them, and if they are representative of fourth-grade boys in general, we will have some confidence that our conclusions will hold for the population as a whole. This is known as a *representative sample.*

The best way to ensure this general representativeness is to study a random sample of the larger population to which we want to generalize. In formal terms, a **random sample** means that each person in the larger population has an equal chance of being included in the study. If we selected a sample of telephone numbers from the phone directory at random (using a table of random numbers, for example), we could be assured that ours was a random sample of all listed phone numbers in the area covered by that telephone book. The laws of probability assure us that a large and truly random sample will almost always be representative of the population within a certain margin of error. It will include approximately the same proportion of women, minorities, unemployed, elderly, and so forth as the population from which we have sampled.

Most of the time social psychologists want to generalize to people in general, not just some subgroup like elementary school children in Austin, Texas, or people who use laundromats in Nashville, Tennessee. Yet it is extremely expensive to study random samples of people in general, as you can readily imagine. It would be especially unrealistic to try to get a random sample of people in general into an experiment in your laboratory at your university. Even Supersaver airfares are not that cheap. So social psychologists try to make realistic compromises between the goal of collecting valid data that can be generalized beyond the few people they test, on the one hand, and practicality on the other.

One very common compromise is to use college students as subjects. It has often been said that American social psychology is based on college sophomores, because they are the ones who are most available for experiments in laboratories. About 75 percent of all published articles in social psychology use undergraduate subjects, and about two-thirds use undergraduates in the laboratory. College students clearly are not random or representative samples of the general population, and social psychologists usually do not make any pretense that they are. How dissatisfied should we be with such unrepresentative samples?

Our need for a representative sample depends on the question we are asking. If we are trying to describe the characteristics of a given population, plainly we need a representative sample. If, for example, we are trying to determine how many hours a day fourth-grade boys normally watch television, we need a representative sample. It would not do to interview boys on the local playground or our friends' sons; soccer players and college professors' sons may not watch as much television as other boys. Suppose we are commissioned to do a study to find out how to introduce automated office equipment into offices where the workers have worked together for decades, are almost all women, and never went past high school. We would not be confident of understanding what techniques would work with them if we did our study on college students who had never met each other before the study and who had no experience with any kind of office machinery or work.

On the other hand, in basic research the representativeness of the sample is not so crucial. The basic researcher is not interested in specific groups but in laws that apply to all people. For example, either Ivy League college students or passersby on Fifth Avenue should help less in the presence of other people than when alone, according to Darley and Latané's diffusion of responsibility theory. The assumption is that all people work in about the same way. So, just as chemicals form the same compounds in about the same way no matter what laboratory you are working in or what company produced the chemicals, almost any subject population is regarded as appropriate for basic research in social psychology.

Moreover, college students may be especially appropriate for studying some phenomena. Suppose we were studying loneliness. National samples indicate that loneliness is greatest among young adults, and that the transition to college induces even more loneliness. So it may be that freshmen college students would be an optimal subject population for that purpose. However, there are probably some areas in which college students may actually be somewhat misleading as a source of data. College students are much younger, in a higher social class, and superior in cognitive skills, especially in test situations, than the general population. For problems in which these are central factors,

college students may be misleading. For example, studies of friendship and social influence would need to take into account the fact that college students' relationships with their friends have generally been rather brief compared to the most important friendships of older people.

Experimenter Bias

One problem that is particularly troublesome in social psychology is experimenter bias. Subjects in an experiment are extremely susceptible to influence by the experimenter. They will do virtually anything the experimenter asks. The social psychologist Martin Orne tells of asking several students to sit in a room and add 2,000 pages of random numbers. He told them: "Continue to work, I will return eventually." Five and one-half hours later, he returned; the students were still adding. Finally, the *experimenter* gave up! Subjects tend to be compliant even when the experimenter does not make any direct request. If the experimenter implies, consciously or otherwise, that he or she would like subjects to respond in a certain way, there is a tendency for them to respond in that way. Subtle cues tend to be picked up by subjects and to influence their behavior. For example, consider the studies of media violence that have subjects shock another person after the subject has viewed a violent or a nonviolent movie. A well-intentioned but perhaps overly eager experimenter, knowing that the subjects who had seen the violent movie were supposed to be the most aggressive, might subtly encourage these subjects to give more shock. She might smile, giggle, make eye contact, or act encouraging in a wide variety of subtle ways. For the subjects who had seen the nonviolent movie, she might frown or act cold when they give the shock, because they are violating the hypothesis.

There are two solutions to this problem. One is to keep the experimenter ignorant as to the experimental condition of the subject. This is usually referred to as keeping the experimenter *blind*. If she does not know which experimental condition she is dealing with, there is no way for her to affect the conditions. In this case, we could have one experimenter show the movies and a second one administer the shock task, and arrange it so that the second experimenter did not know which movie the subject had seen.

A second solution is to standardize the situation in every way possible. If everything is standardized and there are no differences between conditions other than those that are deliberate, there can be no bias. In the extreme case, a subject might appear for an experiment, find a written instruction on the door telling her to enter, have all instructions presented on tape, and complete the experiment before she meets a live experimenter. In this way, every factor in the situation would be absolutely standardized, and experimenter bias would be eliminated.

In actual practice, the solution to the problem of bias is usually a combination of the two procedures we have described. As much as possible, the experimenter is kept blind as to the subjects' experimental conditions; also as much as possible, instructions are standardized by the use of tapes or written materials.

Subject Bias

An even subtler source of bias in a social psychology experiment is the subject's desire to give the "correct" response in the situation. Most subjects want to give the socially acceptable response, in part because they want to impress the experimenter. The *subject bias* occurs when a person's desire to give the "right" answer leads the person to give biased responses.

For example, an experimenter might be interested in the effects of frustration on whites' aggression toward blacks. She might frustrate white subjects and then give them the choice of aggressing against either a white or a black. If this were done in a straightforward manner, many subjects might suspect that the experimenter was interested in whether whites or blacks were the targets of aggression. Most

white college students think it is wrong to be prejudiced against blacks. So the "correct" response would be to aggress equally against whites and blacks, or even to bend over backward and aggress more against whites. However, in a real-life situation many whites do feel considerable prejudice against blacks and may have a tendency to aggress more against them than against other whites. In this example, then, subject bias may interfere with the subjects' natural behavior and bias their responses.

Subject bias is almost impossible to eliminate entirely, but it can be minimized in a variety of ways. The goal is to produce a situation in which the subjects respond spontaneously without worrying about the correctness of the response. This feeling can be minimized somewhat by having the subject respond anonymously so that the experimenter will not know how she behaved in the situation. Unfortunately, this does not solve the problem. Most subjects want to impress not only the experimenter, but also themselves. They want to think of themselves as good people and therefore do what they can to behave in the right way. As long as a subject is thinking about these considerations, it is virtually impossible to eliminate this kind of bias, though the procedure described in Box 2–3 may work.

Another tactic is not to tell subjects they are being observed. We could observe how white salespeople in a store treat black and white customers on a particularly busy, hard day compared to an easy day. If frustration leads to aggression, the salespeople should be nastier on the hard day, and even more so to blacks than to whites if that aggression is directed at people of the two races differentially. Or experiments can be set up so that the crucial measure is taken after the subject thinks the experiment is over.

Yet another tactic is to use unobtrusive or so-called nonreactive measures, in which the subject does not know that a measure is being taken. As a measure of hostility, we could observe how near from a black or white person the subject sits when entering the room.

Jones and Sigall (1971) devised an ingenious procedure for minimizing subject bias. The general idea was to construct a situation in which subjects would give their true opinions, feelings, and attitudes regardless of what the experimenters wanted or might think of them. In other words, the situation was constructed to make the subjects ignore any concerns they might have had about being nice to the experimenters, impressing them, or even looking good to themselves. To the extent that the subjects were able to respond honestly, the situation was designed to elicit their real opinions.

The method was to tell the subjects that they were hooked up to what was essentially a fancy lie detector that could tell their true opinions from a variety of physiological measurements. Electrodes were attached to the subjects' arms and legs. A very impressive-looking piece of machinery with moving dials stood in the room emitting all sorts of whirring noises. The machine actually measured nothing. The subjects were then asked to respond to a few questions just to check on the machine's accuracy. These questions were selected to make it appear as if the subjects' true feelings could be known, but actually the experimenters knew them from a questionnaire they gave the subjects earlier. Thus the subjects discovered that the machine did, in fact, give the right answers. Then the subjects were asked to respond to other questions, including the ones the experimenters were really interested in. Under these circumstances, the subjects had no reason to lie and so gave honest answers, even if the answers were unpleasant or uncomfortably revealing.

Perhaps the most obvious and common tactic is simply not to let the subject know what our hypothesis is. The study must be designed carefully so that it is difficult for the subject to figure out what our intention is. We do not inform the subject about our hypotheses until the study is complete. We embed our crucial measures in the midst of others that deal with other topics. All these techniques reduce the possibility that the dependent measure reflects the subject's view of what is socially desirable more than his or her natural inclination.

RESEARCH ETHICS

During the late 1950s and early 1960s, many people became concerned about the ethics of research on human subjects. Some of the concern stemmed from the discoveries of Nazi atrocities during World War II, such as the dangerous and often fatal experiments carried out by doctors in concentration camps on unwilling camp inmates. Some of it stemmed from the discovery of medical experimentation of dubious ethicality in this country, such as the notorious Tuskegee case. In 1932, the United States Public Health Service began a 40-year experiment on 399 poor and semiliterate blacks in Alabama who had syphilis. The goal was to trace the effects of syphilis on untreated males over many years. The men were told they were being treated, but in fact they never were, despite the fact that penicillin had become available in the 1940s and was highly effective against the disease. Even by 1972, treatment was still withheld from the survivors as the study continued.

Some of the concern also focused on experiments that involved deception or potential psychological harm to subjects. The Milgram experiment on obedience described in Box 2–4 received much criticism because of its deception. His subjects genuinely thought they were hurting another person, just as the Tuskegee patients thought they were being treated. The ethical issue is that the subjects were induced to commit seemingly dangerous acts toward another person without being informed about the real nature of the experiment. The study violated **informed consent**: The subject did not

---

BOX 2–4
The Tendency to Obey

When thousands of Germans obeyed orders to send Jews to the gas chambers, were they simply acting in the way people normally act? Or was this behavior an example of some pathology in their own individual personalities, or in the German people as a whole? Stanley Milgram (1963) believed that their actions reflected a normal human tendency to obey the orders of legitimate authorities, even when it means hurting innocent people. He conducted an experiment to try to demonstrate this. Like the Hartmann (1969) experiment presented earlier, it was described to the subjects as a study of the effects of punishment on memory. Two subjects, (one was actually a confederate of the experimenter) participated at a time. The real subject was told he would be the "teacher," and the other subject (the confederate) would be the "learner." Whenever the "learner" made an error, the subject was to punish him by shocking him. The subject was given a "shock generator," with 30 clearly marked levels ranging from 15 to 450 volts. The label "Danger: Severe shock" appeared at the 375 volt level; even higher levels of shock were marked "XXX."

As the experiment proceeded, the "learner" would make occasional mistakes, and each time the experimenter would instruct the "teacher" (the real subject) to administer the next highest level of shock. At 300 volts, the learner (who was in a separate room) pounded on the wall. At 315 volts, more pounding was heard. After that, no more was heard. Nevertheless, the "teacher" was told to keep on shocking the learner as though a failure to respond was the same as an error. When the subject finally refused to give any more shock, the experiment ended.

In Milgram's basic experiment (1963), *all* subjects administered at least 300 volts. And 65 percent (26 of 40 subjects) gave the maximum possible shock: 450 volts. A comparable group of college students, given a full description of the experiment, had estimated that on the average subjects would go no further than 150 volts. So Milgram's intuition was correct, and theirs was wrong: Ordinary people would indeed administer very dangerous shocks to perfect strangers, simply on command from a legitimate authority.

The Milgram obedience study. (Copyright 1965 by Stanley Milgram. From the film OBEDIENCE, distributed by the New York University Film Library.)

agree to participate in the study on the basis of adequate information about the procedure.

Such studies raise a number of issues. When are researchers justified in deceiving subjects about the research they are participating in? When is it legitimate to do harmful things to subjects? How far does the right to privacy go when one is a subject of research? Was it ethical for Milgram to deceive subjects into thinking they were really delivering harmful shocks to other people?

These questions led to efforts within professional associations to define ethical behavior. The American Psychological Association, the American Sociological Association, and the American Association of Public Opinion Research all drew up codes of ethics for their researchers. However, the standards were of necessity rather general and therefore ambiguous and compliance was voluntary, so they did not really provide effective protection against abuse.

By the 1960s, the federal government was funding much of the research on human subjects done in the United States. Not surprisingly, many people felt the government should take responsibility for the ethical standards of the research. This raised a number of rather touchy issues. Who should make those judgments? Should government bureaucrats dictate the procedures to be used by every researcher all over the country, setting up an authoritarian and cumbersome system that might stifle free inquiry? Or should the foxes be guarding the henhouses—should the researchers themselves be allowed to make their own judgments, at the risk of permitting some unscrupulous investigators to harm subjects? The solution finally agreed upon in the late 1960s was to have a committee of researchers at each research institution review all proposed research using human subjects. This institutional review board would be responsible for ensuring that all research using human subjects would be conducted according to a set of general principles laid down by the federal government's Department of Health and Human Services.

These general principles include three requirements for each research project. First, it must obtain the subject's *informed consent* to participate in the research. The subject must voluntarily agree to participate, without any coercion. And the subject must understand what the participation involves. Second, *risks* to subjects must be *minimized*; that is, the research procedures must "not unnecessarily expose subjects to risk." And third, the *risks* to the subjects must be *balanced* by the expected *benefits* of the research, either to the subjects themselves or to society at large. In social psychology, of course, unlike medical research, there are usually no great benefits to the subjects themselves. The justification for the research is usually in terms of the benefits obtained by enlarging knowledge about human behavior.

Informed Consent

"Participation by subjects should be voluntary and based on informed consent to the extent that is consistent with the objectives of the research." Ordinarily, individuals should not be subjected to research unless they have agreed to it. Whenever possible, this agreement should be given after they have heard exactly what is going to take place during the course of the study. The researcher has an obligation to tell potential subjects as much as possible about the study before asking them to participate. The federal regulations are quite specific about the exact nature of this informed consent. It must be written out, and the subject must sign an informed consent form. The form must describe the research procedures, identify any risks and/

or benefits of the research, specify that refusal to participate or withdrawal during the research can be done without penalty, and indicate to whom inquiries or complaints can be addressed.

These requirements sound quite reasonable, but many create some problems for social psychologists. As we have just seen, it may be important not to tell subjects the true purpose of the study, to avoid biasing their responses. Even in the simplest research, subjects are rarely told the specific hypotheses that are being tested.

Several of the studies we discussed in this chapter did not provide fully informed consent, and it is hard to see how they could have. Darley and Latané did not tell their subjects in advance that a confederate would feign a seizure in order to determine whether or not the subject would rush to help. Knowing that the confederate was not really having a seizure in the Darley-Latané study or that he was not in fact being shocked for making a "mistake" in the Milgram study would certainly influence how much the subject helped or obeyed orders. It is hard to imagine either study being valid if the subjects had really given full "informed consent." Imagine what would have happened if Darley and Latané had told their subjects the study concerned bystander intervention, and they were testing to see if the subject would help in an emergency!

Some people believe that deception of any kind is unethical in psychological research. They feel it demeans the subjects and should never be used. A more moderate position endorsed by most research psychologists is that deception should not be used if at all possible, or used only after considering its possible harmful effects. Subjects, however, should always have *volunteered* to be in the study. Perhaps they need not necessarily be told everything that will happen, but they should know that they are in an experiment and should have freely given their permission. In other words, only someone who has given informed consent or consent based on trust should be exposed to potentially distressing conditions.

And subjects should always be *debriefed*; that is, the purposes and procedures of the experiment should always be explained to them afterward. They should be given an opportunity to ask questions, express their feelings, and generally recover from any upset the experiment has caused. After his debriefings, Milgram found that 84 percent of his subjects were glad to have participated.

Minimal Risk

Another key research guideline is to minimize potential risks to the subjects. **Minimal risk** means that the risks anticipated in the research are no greater "than those ordinarily encountered in daily life." What are the kinds of risk sociopsychological research can pose?

One of the most important is the invasion of *privacy*. An individual's right to privacy must be respected and cherished. As a president's panel on privacy and behavior research stated, every individual must be allowed to "decide for himself how much he will share with others his thoughts, his feelings, and the facts of his personal life." Although privacy is a complex matter, certain guidelines can be observed.

Clearly some areas are more sensitive than others. The most sensitive are matters that could affect one's legal status or one's job, such as information about illegal behavior, sexual behavior, alcohol or drug use, or health-related matters. People are generally private about their income, partly because the Internal Revenue Service has strong feelings about that income, and some legal clout. Religious and political feelings are considered private by many people, though many others have no hesitation about expressing them to one and all. How people behave when they are angry, frustrated, or scared can also be quite personal. Research designed to obtain such information must carefully observe the guidelines on privacy.

On the other hand, public behavior, or events on the public record, do not have to be protected as carefully. Births, marriages, and deaths are all on the public record. Anyone can go to the local courthouse and look up who, when, and how in all those cases. In contrast, surgical or other medical procedures are private. A woman's giving birth is public, whereas her having an abortion is private. Whether someone crosses the street when the light is red or smokes cigarettes is relatively public information. Almost anyone can obtain it merely by watching the individual's behavior in public.

Threats to privacy, like all the risks involved in social psychological research, can change over time as the society itself changes. For example, people are much more willing to discuss details of their sexual relationships now than they were a generation ago. Similarly, a generation ago cancer was a disease to be kept private at all costs. Obituaries would describe someone as having died from "a long illness" or "a lingering illness," but never from "cancer." The subject's privacy must be protected, but we must also remember that standards of privacy must be adjusted as people's needs for privacy change with time.

One of the most important ways of protecting privacy is through maintaining the confidentiality of the data. Perhaps we are conducting a study of status relationships within an organization, and we wish to obtain a secretary's candid perceptions of her relationship with her boss. It is vital that we guarantee her the boss will not have access to those perceptions. If we conduct studies like Milgram's obedience experiment or the Darley-Latané bystander intervention, we must guarantee subjects that their responses will be confidential. It would be a gross violation of privacy to publicize which subjects obeyed or failed to help, because of the embarrassment that could result. Responsible researchers today protect confidentiality carefully, usually by having the person participate in the study anonymously, by replacing the subject's name with a code number on all records, and by keeping all data in a secure place, such as a locked file cabinet.

The other main category of risk in social psychology experiments comes from stresses of various kinds. Some are fairly obvious. Fear can be created in the laboratory, and at times can build up to fairly high levels. A classic case is the study by French (1944). A group of subjects were put in a room at the top of an old building at Harvard, ostensibly to discuss a problem. Soon after the experimenter left, smoke began coming under a door in the room. The subjects soon discovered that all the doors were locked, and at this point most presumably became quite frightened. However, they did not take this kind of situation lying down. Several groups included varsity football players, and they broke down the door, terminating the experiment. Other groups managed to break into the closet from which the smoke was pouring and discovered the smoke machine. Still others convinced themselves it was an experiment and calmly went about discussing the problem, ignoring the smoke that was beginning to fill the room.

Other stresses may be less obvious. Some studies may threaten the individual's self-respect. As we will see in Chapter 5, many studies in recent years have been focused on the causal explanations, or attributions, that people make for their own successes and failures. To do such studies frequently requires that success or failure be experimentally manipulated. A gratuitous failure experience in a psychology experiment is no fun. Similarly, neither the Milgram obedience study nor the Darley-Latané bystander intervention study threatened the subject physically. But the person who later finds that he willingly obeyed orders that might have killed an innocent person, or who is confronted with the fact that he was unwilling to go to the aid of a person who was having a life-threatening seizure, may well lose some self-respect. It would not be surprising if some subjects became resentful about having been deceived into participating in studies that confronted them with unpleasant truths about themselves.

How much risk should a subject be exposed to? The first and most important principle is once again informed consent. If at all possible, the subjects must be allowed to make that decision for themselves, based on adequate information. The situation is like the decision people face about what surgical procedure to undergo: Ultimately, the decision must be in the hands of the patient, but it must be as informed a decision as possible.

But if it is not always possible to fully inform a subject in a social psychology experiment about the exact nature of the study, the investigator or the institutional review board must make a decision about how much risk is allowable. Then a second rule of thumb comes into play: The risks faced in the research should be no more severe than those the person is likely to encounter in normal life. Being threatened with an injection may be frightening, but it is a usual occurrence—we all get injections. In contrast, being threatened with isolation for five hours is also frightening, but it is not a usual occurrence—most people never face this threat. So we would be more hesitant about deceiving a person about isolation than about a harmless injection.

Finally, another general rule many researchers and review boards use in evaluating risk is that the subjects should leave the study in essentially the same state of mind and body in which they entered. That is, participation in the study should have no substantial effect of any kind that carries over once the subject has finished. Another way of stating this is that the study may be pleasant, interesting, and enjoyable, or mildly unpleasant, boring, or tedious—but the subjects' state of mind, knowledge of themselves, and general attitudes should not be altered by the experience. This guideline, if followed closely, would ensure that subjects would not have been exposed to excessive risk.

SUMMARY

1. Although we all know a great deal about social behavior from our daily observations and experience, some of our impressions are incorrect. Systematic research is necessary to be certain which of our intuitions are right and which are wrong.

2. There are two types of questions with which to begin research. One kind is directly related to an existing theory. Theoretical research is designed to test the theory, to compare two theories, or to assess the limits and exceptions to a theory. Nontheoretical research starts with a general question that is not directly related to a theory and tries to discover new relationships or test a hunch or intuition.

3. A second distinction among types of research is between basic and applied. Basic research deals with fundamental questions, general principles, or theories. Applied research is directed toward answering a question related to a specific problem in the world—such as how to reduce prejudice, sell toothpaste, or design housing.

4. There are two main types of research designs in social psychology—experimental and correlational. Correlational research asks whether two or more variables are related. If one variable is high, is the other also high? Or is the other consistently low? Correlational research can deal with a great many variables at once, and can investigate factors that cannot usually be manipulated in the laboratory, such as very high fear, poverty, or social class.

5. Correlational research usually does not allow strong causal inferences. We cannot always be certain if A caused B, B caused A, or some third, unknown variable caused both. In experimental research, subjects are randomly assigned to situations that differ only in specific deliberately varied ways. If there is any difference in behavior, it is due to that variable. This provides control over the situation and allows unambiguous causal statements.

6. Research can be done in the laboratory or in field settings. The former provides more control, but the latter is closer to the real world and often permits a greater range of intensity in the variables studied.

7. The most common sources of data are systematic observations of behavior, self-report, and the use of archives.

8. In designing an experiment, the key questions are how to manipulate the independent variable and how to measure the dependent variable. Great care must be taken to avoid the effects of bias. The experimenter can affect the results, even unintentionally, or subjects can give results they think are "correct" but are not what they would have done spontaneously.

9. Social psychologists face many ethical problems in doing research. They must be careful to guard the safety of subjects, to respect their privacy, and to ensure that their research produces no harmful effects on anyone involved. Current guidelines emphasize obtaining informed consent to whatever extent possible.

10. Ethical considerations impose considerable restrictions on scientists, but they need not prevent legitimate research. With sufficient ingenuity and care, researchers can study virtually any problem and still safeguard the privacy and well-being of their human subjects.

SUGGESTIONS FOR ADDITIONAL READINGS

ARONSON, E., BREWER, M., & CARLSMITH, J. M. 1985.   Experimentation in social psychology. In G. Lindzey & E. Aronson (eds.), *The Handbook of Social Psychology, 3rd Edition*, Reading, Mass.: Addison-Wesley. The generally accepted mainstream treatment of experimentation in social psychology.

BOWER, R. T., & DE GASPARIS, P. 1978.   *Ethics in social research: Protecting the interests of human subjects.* New York: Praeger.

COOK, T. D. & CAMPBELL, D. T. 1979.   *Quasi-experimentation: Design and analysis issues for field settings.* Chicago: Rand McNally. The use of nonexperimental techniques in field situtations is becoming increasingly important. This presents the state-of-the-art thinking about how to design and interpret such studies.

HYMAN, H. H. 1972.   *Secondary analysis of sample surveys: Principles, procedures, and potentialities.* New York: John Wiley & Sons. A clear and straightforward explanation of how to use archival data, with many interesting examples.

JONES, E. E., & SIGALL, H. 1971.   The bogus pipeline: A new paradigm for measuring affect and attitude. *Psychological Bulletin, 76,* 349–64. This article presents the technique discussed in Box 2–3.

JONES, J. H. 1981. *Bad blood.* New York: Free Press. A fascinating historical account of the ''Tuskegee case'' that revolutionized protection of human subjects.

WEBB, E. J., CAMPBELL, D. T., SCHWARTZ, R. D., & SECHREST, L. 1966.   *Unobtrusive measures: Nonreactive research in the social sciences.* Chicago: Rand McNally. An engaging description of many clever techniques for collecting data without letting people know you are doing it. Often not very ethical, but they minimize subject bias!

3

PERSON PERCEPTION

A murder trial hinges on the testimony of one key witness. The jury members' belief in this witness will determine their decisions. The impression they form of her in her brief appearance in the courtroom will determine whether the defendant goes to jail or stays free. They examine her face, her features, her clothes, the quality of her voice, and her answers, trying to decide what kind of person she is.

Two freshmen destined to be roommates arrive at college and meet for the first time. Each one's personality—how easy each one is to get along with, how nice each is—will have an enormous effect on the other's life. In the first few minutes of their meeting, each tries to form an impression of the other, because they know they will be spending a great deal of time together during the year. How late does each one stay up studying at night? What kind of music does the other like? How loud? How does each feel about parties in the room? They try to find out as much about each other as they can.

Our knowledge of and expectations about others are determined first of all by the impressions we form of them. A glance at someone's picture or at an individual passing on the street gives us ideas about the kind of person he or she is; even hearing a name tends to conjure up images of what its owner is like. When two people meet, if only for an instant, they form impressions of each other. With more contact, they form fuller and richer impressions that determine how they behave toward each other, how much they like each other, whether they will associate often, and so on.

People use whatever information is available to form these impressions of others—to make judgments about their personalities or hypotheses about the kinds of persons they are. In this chapter we deal with this process, which is called **person perception:** how we make first impressions, what biases affect them, what kinds of information we use in arriving at them, and how accurate our impressions are.

FORMING IMPRESSIONS

People tend to form extensive impressions of others on the basis of very limited information. Having seen a person or even a photograph for only a few minutes, people tend to make judgments about a large number of that person's characteristics. Although ordinarily individuals are not overly confident of opinions formed in this way, they are generally willing to estimate another's intelligence, age, background, race, religion, educational level, honesty, warmth, and so on. They will also tell us how much they think they will like the person if they can get to know him or her better and how much they like him or her at the moment.

Evaluation: First Impressions

The most important and powerful aspect of first impressions is **evaluation.** Do we like or dislike this person? How much do we like or dislike him or her? Our immediate impression may be composed of other dimensions; he or she may seem friendly, talkative, and helpful. But all these specific traits are fundamentally tied to the question of whether we like or don't like him or her.

Put more formally, the evaluative dimension is the most important of a small number of basic dimensions that organize these unified impressions of people. This was shown in work by Osgood, Suci, and Tannenbaum (1957) on the so-called *semantic differential.* In their study, subjects were given a list of trait pairs and asked to indicate which trait particular persons and objects fell closest to. The list consisted of such trait pairs as happy-sad, good-bad, strong-weak, and warm-cold, and the items the subjects had to place ranged from mothers to boulders. For example, the subject had to rate whether "mothers" fell closest to "happy" or "sad," and so on. Osgood and his associates then ana-

lyzed the responses to see if any clusters emerged that could be considered basic dimensions on which all things had been described.

Three underlying dimensions accounted for most of the ratings: *evaluation* (good-bad), *potency* (strong-weak), and *activity* (active-passive). Once a particular person or object was placed on these three dimensions, little additional information could be gotten from getting additional ratings of it. In other words, once we know that someone rates "mother" as very good, moderately strong, and somewhat passive, we learn little more about her perceptions of "mother" by asking for additional ratings. These researchers thus concluded that evaluation was the main dimension underlying such perceptions, with potency and activity also playing some lesser role. Once we place someone on this dimension, much of the rest of our perception of him or her falls into place. A favorable or unfavorable impression in one context, at one meeting, extends to all other situations and to other seemingly unrelated characteristics.

Much other research has supported the hypothesis that evaluation is the most important

Delta Air Lines

How confident is this couple likely to be about their impression of the woman? What aspects of her life and personality would they feel confident about?

underlying dimension of person perception. Rosenberg, Nelson, and Vivekananthan (1968), for example, found that people evaluated others in terms of their separate task-related or *intellectual* qualities, and their interpersonal or *social* qualities, at least some of the time. However, this distinction does not alter the basic point: People think primarily in terms of liking and disliking when they perceive other people.

Overall Impressions

THE AVERAGING MODEL Suppose you've just met someone, and you notice that she is neat, tall, dark-haired, attractive, flirtatious, and "preppy" in dress. Or you meet someone else who is a premed, deeply religious, a tennis expert, an extrovert, and engaged to be married. How do we put such separate pieces of information together into simple overall impressions?

Psychologists have two main views on this matter, one emphasizing learning and the other cognitive factors. The learning approach, in its simplest form, suggests that people combine information in a rather mechanical, simple-minded fashion, without thinking about it much. Just as a pigeon or a rat develops a habit rather mechanically, without seeming to interpret or give the experience meaning, so a person forms an impression without reinterpreting or analyzing available information very much. If we receive mainly favorable ideas about a person, we develop a favorable impression of that person. If we hear mainly unfavorable or lukewarm things, we develop that kind of impression instead.

As applied to impression formation, this learning approach has evolved into an **averaging principle** (Anderson, 1965). Here is how it works: Suppose Susan has just met her blind date, John. She quickly perceives that he is witty, intelligent, and courteous—but very short and poorly dressed. She processes this information in terms of how positive or negative she thinks those traits are. Suppose that she were asked to indicate her degree of favorable or unfavorable evaluation of those traits on a scale from +10 (very positive) to −10 (very negative). She might feel that being witty or intelligent are extremely favorable qualities and assign them the maximum value each (+10); that being courteous is quite favorable (+4); that being very short is somewhat unfavorable (−5); and that being poorly dressed is very unfavorable (−9). Now she combines these traits to form an overall evaluation of John. The averaging model suggests the person would receive an overall evaluation that was approximately an average of the five traits—that is, he would be considered moderately positive (+2). This is shown in Table 3–1.

THE ADDITIVE MODEL   A variant of the averaging model is an *additive model*. It holds that people integrate separate pieces of information

by adding scale values rather than averaging them. The major difference occurs when the person is confronted with two pieces of information on the same side of zero, one more extreme than the other. Supposing Susan liked John very much (+6), but then she learned something new about him that was only mildly favorable, such as that he is "cautious" (+1). According to the averaging theory, she should like him a little *less* as a result, because the average (+3.5) is lower than the original evaluation (+6). According to the additive theory, she should like him more, because adding any additional positive information to an already positive impression should make it even more favorable.

Norman Anderson, in a series of careful and precise experiments (1959, 1965), produced strong evidence to support the averaging model. He found that when a piece of information that is only moderately favorable was combined with a previous very favorable impression, the overall evaluation did not increase and could even decrease. Similarly, two strongly negative traits produced a more negative evaluation than two strongly negative plus two moderately negative traits.

As a result of further research, Anderson proposed a refinement that predicts impression formation even more accurately—the weighted averaging model (1968). According to this model, people form an overall impression by averaging all traits but giving more weight to those they feel are important. For example, an administrator interviewing scientists as candidates for a laboratory job would probably weigh "intelligent" more heavily than "attractive"; but someone hiring an actor for a television commercial might reverse that priority. An administrator interviewing candidates for a job as a counselor in a rape crisis center might give "warmth" more weight than either intelligence or attractiveness. This body of research as a whole indicates quite convincingly that the best way to account for impression formation is the weighted average principle, though it is probably not the only principle at work.

Table 3–1 Susan Sizes Up Her Blind Date, John	
INDIVIDUAL TRAITS	SUSAN'S EVALUATION
Witty	+10
Intelligent	+10
Courteous	+4
Very short	−5
Poorly dressed	−9
Overall impression	+10/5 = +2.00

Consistency

Evaluation also introduces distortions and inaccuracies in several different ways. One is that people tend to form evaluatively consistent characterizations of others, even when they have only a few pieces of information. We have a tendency to view others in a way that is internally consistent. Since evaluation is the most important dimension in person perception, it is not surprising that we tend to categorize people as good or bad, not as both. The other person is not seen as both honest and dishonest, warm and frightening, considerate and sadistic. Even when there is contradictory information about someone, he or she usually will be perceived as consistently good or bad, likable or dislikable. The perceiver distorts or rearranges the information to minimize or eliminate the inconsistency. This may also happen when people perceive objects, but it is particularly strong in person perception.

Following from this basic evaluation, we may go on to perceive other traits as consistent with it. If a person is likable, she should also be attractive, intelligent, generous, and so on. If she is bad, she should be sneaky, ugly, and inept.

This tendency toward consistency is called the halo effect. The stimulus person is seen as likable or not very likable, and all other qualities are perceived as consistent with this decision. This is called the **halo effect** because one who is labeled "good" is surrounded with a positive aura, and all good qualities are attributed to him or her. The converse (what should be called a "negative halo" or a "forked-tail" effect) is that one who is labeled "bad" is seen as having all bad qualities.

A good illustration of these effects is provided in a study by Dion, Berscheid, and Walster (1972). In this study, subjects were given pictures of people who were physically attractive, unattractive, or average. The subjects then rated each on a number of characteristics that had nothing to do with attractiveness. As you can see in Table 3–2, the attractive people were rated highest and the unattractive people lowest on almost all characteristics. Just because someone looked good and therefore had one positive trait, that person was perceived as having other positive traits; conversely, those who looked bad were perceived as having other bad traits.

An interesting question is just how far this halo effect goes. A number of studies have ex-

Table 3–2
The Halo and Forked-Tail Effects Illustrated by Ratings of Attractive, Unattractive, and Average Persons

TRAIT ASCRIPTION[a]	ATTRACTIVE STIMULUS PERSON	AVERAGE STIMULUS PERSON	UNATTRACTIVE STIMULUS PERSON
Social desirability of personality	65.39	62.42	56.31
Occupational status	2.25	2.02	1.70
Marital competence	1.70	.71	.37
Parental competence	3.54	4.55	3.91
Social and professional happiness	6.37	6.34	5.28
Total happiness	11.60	11.60	8.83
Likelihood of marriage	2.17	1.82	1.52

[a]The higher the number, the more socially desirable, the more prestigious an occupation, and so on, the stimulus person is expected to possess.
Source: Dion et al. (1972).

Table 3–3 Mean Sentence Assigned, In Years			
	DEFENDANT'S ATTRACTIVENESS		
OFFENSE	ATTRACTIVE	UNATTRACTIVE	CONTROL
Swindle	5.45	4.35	4.35
Burglary	2.80	5.20	5.10

Source: Sigall and Ostrove (1975).

plored its boundaries with respect to physical attractiveness. It is one thing to expect a beautiful woman to be warm (who wouldn't be, if everyone were always reacting to you as if you were wonderful?), but quite another to expect her to be highly intelligent, innocent of any crime she might be accused of, or especially qualified for high political office.

In fact, the halo effect for physical attractiveness has been shown to generalize into a number of areas that are quite irrelevant to physical beauty. For example, Landy and Sigall (1974) presented male subjects with essays on the role and effects of television on society. The essays were supposedly written by the women whose pictures were attached to them. The women were either attractive or unattractive. Some essays were written well (clear, grammatical, organized) and some poorly (ungrammatical, spelling errors, clichés). The subjects were instructed to rate the quality of each essay. The essay written by the more attractive woman was rated better than the essay written by the unattractive woman, regardless of whether the essays were objectively good or bad.

Other studies have found that attractive people are treated more leniently when they do something wrong. Dion (1972) found that transgressions committed by attractive children were viewed less harshly by adults than the same acts committed by unattractive children. Similarly, Landy and Aronson (1969) found that members of a mock jury sentenced an unattractive defendant to more years in prison than they did an attractive defendant, given a crime described in exactly the same terms. Moreover, in two dif-

ferent studies they found that killing an attractive victim brought a longer sentence than killing an unattractive victim.

But, as with all things, the attractiveness-based halo effect has its limits. Sigall and Ostrove (1975) hypothesized that jurors would actually be *more* punitive toward a beautiful defendant if her offense were somehow directly related to her attractiveness. So they gave mock jurors the details of a case, along with a picture of the defendant. The charge was one of burglary, which could have almost nothing to do with the defendant's beauty, or swindling, which is something a beautiful woman might use her looks to get away with. Verifying this hunch about connecting crime to attractiveness, a control group, not shown the photographs but given the case materials, did in fact rate the swindler as probably more attractive than the burglar. And attractiveness did reduce the burglar's sentence, as in the studies cited above. But the beautiful swindler was given a somewhat harsher sentence than the unattractive one. The results are shown in Table 3–3.

In some cases, the halo effect may be based on some irrational need to have a consistent impression, such as punishing unattractive children more than attractive children for minor misbehavior. But at other times it may have a more realistic basis. Attractive people may in fact develop more pleasing personalities over time, because their self-esteem is constantly being enhanced and their self-confidence built up. Attractive people are likely to go further occupationally, because they do in fact get promoted faster, and so on. Indeed, Goldman and

Lewis (1977) showed that more attractive people have more social skills. In their study, college men phoned a woman student they had never met. The two students chatted for five minutes, and then they each rated their phone partners for social skills. The more attractive students were rated as having greater social skills, even by partners who had never met them and had only talked with them on the phone, and therefore had no direct way of knowing whether they were physically attractive or not.

In these examples, we have described halo effects that result from physical attractiveness. But halo effects can result from anything that produces a positive impression. A person can be regarded favorably because of being an outstanding athlete, a great scholar, a powerful business executive, or a warm family member. There will be a tendency to misperceive all that person's characteristics as favorable to make them consistent with the overall impression. Similarly, there is an unfortunate tendency to see a person with some shortcomings as negative in other areas as well. It is common to perceive an overweight person, or one with a physical handicap, or one who comes from an unpopular nationality as having many other negative characteristics as well. These are all examples of a general tendency to develop impressions that are evaluatively consistent.

Positivity Bias

We have been emphasizing the importance of evaluation in person perception, but we have not said much about whether positive or negative evaluations are most common. In fact, however, positive evaluations of other persons are much more common than negative ones. For example, in one study students rated 97 percent of their professors in college favorably (that is, above "average" on a rating scale), despite all the mixed experiences students have in their college classes (Sears, 1983). This tendency for positive evaluations of other people to outnumber negative evaluations has been called

the *leniency effect* (Bruner & Tagiuri, 1954) or the **positivity bias** (Sears, 1983). Similarly, public opinion polls show that individual political leaders are consistently approved of more often than they are disapproved of (Sears, 1982). In Gallup polls done in the United States since the mid-1930s, about three-fourths of the specific persons asked about were liked by more people than disliked them. When an impression changes, it generally tends to become more favorable rather than more unfavorable, everything else being equal (Sears & Whitney, 1973).

There are some plausible hypotheses about why people are evaluated so leniently. One stems from what Matlin and Stang (1978) call the *Pollyanna principle*. They suggest that people feel better if they are surrounded by good things, pleasant experiences, nice people, good weather, and so on. Even when their houses are falling down, they are sick, neighbors are terrible to them, and the weather is dismal, they will evaluate their situation favorably. The result: Most events are evaluated "above average" most of the time; pleasant events are thought more common than unpleasant ones; good news is communicated more frequently than bad news; and pleasant words are recalled more accurately than unpleasant ones.

Sears (1983), on the other hand, contends there is a special positivity bias in our evaluations of other human beings which he describes as the *person-positivity bias*. People feel some similarity to any other person they evaluate, and therefore extend them a more generous evaluation than they do more impersonal objects. According to this view, the person-positivity bias operates only in evaluations of individual people, and it should not show up as strongly when impersonal objects are being evaluated.

In testing this idea, Sears confronted the problem that people and objects are so different it is hard to compare them. You could compare evaluations of one's mother with evaluations of a rock, but they differ in so many other ways it would be hard to attribute any difference in evaluation just to the fact that one is a person and the other an impersonal object. To try to make this person versus object comparison in a fair way, Sears turned to evaluations of professors. At UCLA, students routinely fill out a standard form for evaluating their classes that includes comparable items for the evaluation of the instructor (a person) and for the evaluation of the course (an impersonal object): What is your overall rating of the instructor, and What is your overall rating of the course? Presumably, both ratings concern approximately the same experience—a specific course. But the course rating concerns mostly impersonal aspects of the class, such as books, exams, and class meetings. The instructor ratings concern only individual teachers.

Confirming the person-positivity bias, 97 percent of a sample of UCLA professors were rated positively (above "average"). And the personal stimulus, the professor, was rated higher than the impersonal object, the course, in 74 percent of the cases (in 7 percent they were equal, and 19 percent of the time the course was rated higher). So perhaps when we evaluate specific, concrete human beings with whom we can identify and empathize, we give them a special break.

The Cognitive Approach

Up to this point, we have described person perception as dominated by two assumptions: (1) The process of impression formation is viewed as rather mechanical and tends simply to reflect the nature of the stimulus person. (2) The process is seen as dominated by feeling or evaluation, rather than by thought or cognition. Both assumptions have their roots in a learning theory approach. That impression formation mechanically reflects available information about the stimulus person resembles a simple learning theory analysis of how a white rat learns to turn right rather than left in a T maze. If the rat is given food pellets on the right side and is shocked on the left side, it will learn to turn right without great analysis or distortion of the realities of the situation.

A simple averaging theory also assumes that the process of impression formation is primarily evaluative. All information is immediately reduced to some evaluation. "Friendly" is just a +5, "strong," just a + 3, and "dull," just a − 3. This too resembles a simple learning theory, in that the environment is treated as consisting mainly of rewards and punishments. We learn to like and approach good things and dislike and avoid bad things.

Although there is much value in these two assumptions, they do oversimplify the process. We do not just take in a literal copy of the environment. We do not perceive people as disconnected bits of flesh and clothing and movement and sound, though that is literally what they consist of. We are active, organizing perceivers. We take in information selectively, then organize it into a meaningful **gestalt** that makes sense out of the full input. Each piece of information is taken as an aspect of a coherent whole, rather than as simply another isolated trait to be averaged into the overall impression. The major implication for impression formation is that processing is not mechanical, but involves an attempt to perceive some coherent *meaning* in the stimulus object.

Thus people are seen as trying to develop meaningful impressions out of *all* the information they have about another person (or event, or whatever), rather than just averaging in each separate element separately. This is what lies behind the old saying that "the whole is greater than the sum of its parts." The perceiver does not just consider each separate piece of information in isolation, but tries to come to an impression about the person as a whole. This has a number of specific implications.

CONTEXT Assume perceivers are trying to arrive at a meaningful impression of whole persons, rather than just to absorb each new piece of information separately. Their understanding of any new piece of information will depend in part on the context. The meaning of "intelligent" in the context of knowing that a person is a "warm, caring therapist" will probably be quite positive. But the meaning of "intelligent" when the person is otherwise a "cold, ruthless Russian spy" will probably be more negative; it makes the person seem even more dangerous. To predict the impact of new information, we need to know the context, because that influences its meaning.

Considerable research has shown that context does indeed influence the impact new information has on an existing impression. But how context effects are produced is a matter of some debate. For Asch (1946), working mainly out of the cognitive approach, the whole is more than a mechanical average of its parts. Perceivers create a meaningful whole out of whatever information is given, and the whole will change with different information. So any given attribute will have different meaning if it is placed in a different context. Wearing only a bikini has quite a different meaning in a symphony concert hall than it does on a summer beach, and would be evaluated quite differently, even though it, and both contexts, are all quite pleasant.

Asch says a new attribute undergoes a **shift of meaning** when placed in a new context. "Intelligence" in a cold, ruthless person could be threatening, potentially hostile, and destructive. In a warm, caring person, "intelligence" might be expected to contribute to empathy, to insight, and to the ability to give to another person.

Anderson (1966), on the other hand, consistent with his averaging approach, suggests that the influence of the context on the value of the new attribute can be predicted by just averaging in its value along with the value of the new information. In this example, suppose "intelligent" is a +2 when it is considered all by itself. And suppose the joint value of "cold, ruthless, Russian spy" is −4. In this context, the contribution of "intelligent" to the overall impression would be an average of the two, or about −1. On the other hand, if the value of "warm, caring" is +4, you can readily see that "intelligent" would come in around +3 in that context. Anderson describes this effect of context as a *generalized halo effect.* As you can see, he does not assume much deliberate thought; the new attribute merely mechanically absorbs some of the good or bad feelings associated with the context.

A good bit of research has been done on these two explanations for context effects. One way to approach the controversy is to determine whether in fact a given trait has a different meaning in different contexts. Hamilton & Zanna (1974; Zanna & Hamilton, 1977) found that the connotations of a particular trait changed when placed in different contexts. For example, in a positive context the word "proud" bore the connotation of "confident." In a negative context, it connoted "conceited." Similarly, Wyer (1974) found that the evaluations of these connotations also reflected the context. To use this example, the connotation ("conceited") of the original trait ("proud") implied by a negative context itself bore a negative evaluation. Such studies show that contextual effects are partly determined by a shift-of-meaning phenomenon.

CENTRAL TRAITS A second potential difference concerns whether or not certain traits imply more about an individual than others. The averaging approach simply assumes that all traits are plugged into the process at whatever value they have. The perceptual-cognitive approach assumes that some traits are inherently more meaningful than others. For example, the pair of traits "warm-cold" appears to be associated with a great number of other characteristics, whereas the pair "polite-blunt," under most circumstances, is associated with fewer. Traits that are highly associated with many other characteristics have been called **central traits.**

In a classic demonstration of their importance, Asch (1946) gave subjects a description of an individual that contained seven traits—intelligent, skillful, industrious, warm, determined, practical, and cautious. Other subjects were given exactly the same list except that "cold" was substituted for "warm." Both groups were then asked to describe the individual and to indicate which of various pairs of traits he or she would be most likely to possess. The portraits that resulted were very different: Substituting "cold" for "warm" made a substantial change in subjects' impression of the other person. In another condition, instead of the "warm-cold" pair, Asch used "polite-blunt." He found that substituting "polite" for "blunt" made considerably less difference in the overall picture formed by the subjects.

A later study by Kelley (1950) replicated this result in a more realistic setting. Students in psychology courses were given descriptions of a guest lecturer before he spoke. The descriptions included seven adjectives similar to those Asch used; half the students received a description containing the word "warm," and the other half were told the speaker was "cold"; in all other respects the lists were identical. The lecturer then came into the class and led a discussion for about twenty minutes, after which the students were asked to give their impressions of him. The results are shown in Table 3–4. As in the Asch study, there were great differences between the impressions formed by students who were told he was warm and those who were told he was cold. In addition, those students who expected the speaker to be warm tended to interact with him more freely and to initiate more conversa-tions with him. The different descriptions affected not only the students' impressions of the other person, but also their behavior toward him.

The averaging model has been adapted to handle such phenomena. Its weighted-averaged version assumes that some traits are more important than others, and therefore are weighed more heavily. Presumably warmth is one of these. Most of the time, it is very important to us whether someone is warm or cold, and perhaps not very important whether they are good jumpers or not. So we weigh very heavily any information about warmth or coldness in coming to an overall impression, and give little weight to information about jumping ability. This example also illustrates Asch's point about how context influences meaning. In the context of a party, "warm-cold" is probably quite a central trait, because it is so important to whether we enjoy the person or not. But in the context of a basketball game or Olympic tryouts, "warm-cold" may not be very central, and jumping ability may be weighed much more heavily.

THE NEGATIVITY EFFECT Another exception to the averaging principle is that people weigh negative information more heavily than positive information in arriving at a complete impression. That is, a negative trait affects an impression more than a positive trait, everything else being equal (Fiske, 1980). This has been called the **negativity effect.** It follows that a positive impression is easier to change than a negative one (Hodges, 1974). People are more confident of evaluations based on negative traits than of those based on positive traits (Hamilton & Zanna, 1972). And it also follows that the averaging principle does not hold for negative traits quite as well as it does for positive traits.

This difference is particularly noticeable with the more extreme negative traits. They seem to have a "blackball" effect: One extremely negative trait produces an extremely negative impression, no matter what other traits the person possesses (Anderson, 1965). When we are told that a prominent public leader is "a crook," our

Table 3–4		
Effect of "Warm" and "Cold" Descriptions on Ratings of Other Qualities		
	INSTRUCTIONS[a]	
QUALITY	WARM	COLD
Self-centered	6.3	9.6
Unsociable	5.6	10.4
Unpopular	4.0	7.4
Formal	6.3	9.6
Irritable	9.4	12.0
Humorless	8.3	11.7
Ruthless	8.6	11.0

[a]The higher the rating, the more the person was perceived as having the quality.
Source: Adapted from Kelley (1950).

evaluation of him becomes quite negative, regardless of what else we know about him. If we are told he is "impatient," we will just average that mildly negative quality in with whatever else we know about him.

The main explanation for this negativity effect is based on the figure-ground notion discussed in Chapter 1. As we noted in the discussion of the person-positivity bias, positive evaluations of other people are much more common than negative evaluations. Negative traits, being more unusual, are therefore more distinctive. In a simple perceptual sense, then, a negative trait is *figural*; it stands out the way an unusual deformity or bright clothing or something of great size stands out. People may simply pay more attention to those negative qualities and give them more weight.

ACCURACY OF JUDGMENTS

How accurately do people usually perceive others? One implication of these various evaluative and cognitive biases is that person perception must not be very accurate. On the other hand, people must be reasonably accurate in order for society to function as smoothly as it does. After all, we interact with other people hundreds of times every day, and these interactions usually require fairly accurate judgments of others. Since most interactions proceed without serious difficulties or mistakes, person perception must be fairly accurate.

People seem to perceive external, visible attributes fairly accurately. It is generally no more difficult to judge the height of a person than it is to judge the height of a bookcase, a car, or a camel. The same is true of weight, skin color, or style of clothing. We make these kinds of judgments about the external attributes of all objects, and we make them fairly accurately. And it is fairly easy to make judgments about somebody's social role, as long as the appropriate cues are provided. The man in the blue suit with the gun strapped to his side is a police officer, and we treat him accordingly. The woman in a business suit with a briefcase rushing down a platform toward a train is obviously a commuter in a hurry to get to work, and we get out of her way to make it easier for her to catch the train. The contexts in which we see the people enable us to make accurate assumptions about their roles.

But person perception becomes more difficult when we try to infer *internal states*—feelings, emotions, and personalities. The bookcase obviously has none of these; the car has them only in advertisements and fantasies; perhaps the camel has them, but we usually do not worry about camels. However, we do attempt to judge the internal states of human beings. We look at people and perceive them as angry, happy, sad, or frightened. We form an impression of another person and think of her as warm, honest, and sincere. We also make judgments about such internal characteristics as the person's attitudes toward various issues. We guess whether she is a Republican or a Democrat, religious or nonreligious, an environmentalist or not.

Judgments of such internal states as emotions, personality traits, and attitudes are often extremely difficult. The person's internal state cannot be observed directly—it must be inferred from whatever cues are available. Therefore, the question of accuracy focuses primarily on the judgments individuals can make of internal states, and on the cues used to make these judgments.

Recognition of Emotions

Much of the work on the accuracy of person perception has focused on the recognition of

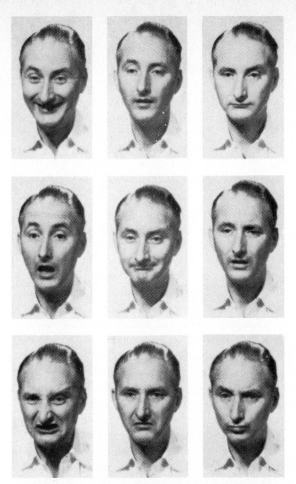

FIGURE 3–1 Examples of stimuli used in the study of the perception of emotions. The photographs illustrate expressions posed to portray the emotions listed. (You might try to identify them before looking at the key below.) Top (left to right): Glee, passive adoration, complacency. Middle: Amazement, optimistic determination, dismay. Bottom: Rage, mild repugnance, puzzlement.

emotions, on whether a person is happy or afraid, horrified or disgusted. The basic procedure is to present a subject with a stimulus representing another person and ask the subject to identify the other's emotion. For some studies, trained actors portrayed a number of different emotions, and pictures were taken of their ex-

pressions. One picture was chosen for each emotion. These were then shown to subjects, who were asked to indicate what emotion was depicted. Some of these pictures are shown in Figure 3–1. Other studies have used real people or disembodied voices.

Given this wide range of techniques, it is perhaps not surprising that the results have also been varied. Early studies seemed to indicate that people could not judge emotions in facial expressions at better than a chance level. Later studies have shown that people can discriminate among the major groups of emotions, even if they cannot discriminate very well between each individual emotion. Woodworth (1938) suggested that emotions can be arranged on a six-point continuum, with the ease of distinguishing between any two emotions being related to the distance between them on this continuum. This generated a number of such studies. They generally agree on finding people expressing seven categories of emotions. The seven groups are:

1. Happiness, joy
2. Surprise, amazement
3. Fear
4. Sadness
5. Anger
6. Disgust, contempt
7. Interest, attentiveness

People seem to be quite good at distinguishing emotions in categories that are three, four, or five points apart—they rarely confuse happiness with disgust or surprise with contempt. People have a particularly easy time distinguishing pleasant from unpleasant emotions in others' faces (again indicating the importance of the evaluative dimension in person perception). But they find it almost impossible to discriminate emotions in the same category or only one group away.

Considerable research has been done on judging more permanent personality traits, such as dominance-submission or need for affiliation. This work is more discouraging, for a number of reasons. First, biases may influence observers.

Second, it is very difficult to measure personality traits, so there is a problem in identifying the proper criteria. A third and even more serious problem is, according to some influential psychologists (such as Mischel, 1979), any given personality trait only influences behavior consistently in a fairly limited range of situations. That is, we may have unique, idiosyncratic dispositions that make us regularly react in our own distinctive way to any given situation, but these may not be very constant from one set of situations to another. It may therefore be more useful to think of personality traits as holding in some fairly limited set of situations, rather than to think of traits that hold in all situations.

For example, it used to be that psychologists would talk about a *general* trait of honesty or dishonesty, and thus describe a person as "honest" or "dishonest." The implication of Mischel's work, however, is that we are better advised to generalize about the person's honesty only within more limited classes of situations. We know a man who frequently cheats at pool or when he is playing golf; he often seems to replay poor shots without giving himself a penalty. But he is scrupulously honest in his dealings with co-workers and subordinates. Should we describe him as generally a "somewhat dishonest person"? Or are we better off saying that he is honest in professional situations and cheats at competitive games?

The problem this raises for the accuracy of person perception is that if personality traits are limited to certain classes of situations, they become more difficult for observers to judge accurately. The observers would need to perceive both the person's tendencies and the situation accurately. As we will see in Chapter 5, observers have a tendency to ascribe general personality traits to people, ignoring the fact that people may behave quite differently in different classes of situations.

For all these reasons, social psychologists believe that people are more accurate in judging a person's emotions than stable personality dispositions.

Universal Emotional Expressions

Why might people be reasonably accurate in judging others' emotions? One reason might be that all people use the same facial expression for expressing a given underlying emotion. Perhaps we all smile when we feel happy, frown when we are worried, and so on. In 1872, on the basis of his evolutionary theory, Charles Darwin proposed that facial expressions universally conveyed the same emotional states. Such universal signals would have great survival value for Homo sapiens. Darwin's argument was that universal expressions have evolved because they allow us to communicate our emotions and thereby control others' behavior. For example, if one animal shows an angry or threatening face, others may behave more submissively, which allows the first animal to win the encounter without risking an actual fight.

In fact, virtually all species of Old World monkeys and apes have been found to use facial gestures to signal dominance or submissiveness. Differing eyebrow positions seem to be crucial: typically, the brows are lowered on dominant or threatening individuals and raised on submissive or receptive individuals (Keating et al., 1981). The evolutionary argument is that there may be a link between the facial expressions used by subhuman primates to communicate with, and control, other species members, and those used by humans for the same purpose. If so, presumably the same link between emotion and facial expression would exist among humans across all (or most) cultures.

Are there such universals in humans? Do we have particular facial expressions or body postures for each emotion? Does everyone who is feeling a particular emotion have the same facial expression? Or is it possible that one person's expression of disgust is another person's expression of contentment? The link between lowered-brow expressions and dominance in nonhuman primates suggests a possible similar link in human beings. To test for this, Keating et al. (1981) had people from each of a number of countries in Europe, Africa, North and South America, and Asia pose with brows lowered, and then again with brows raised. The researchers also tested for a link between perceptions of smiling and happiness because a number of studies had suggested a link between primates' grins (or grimaces) and communicating submissiveness. On the other hand, there was some evidence that among humans, smiling was related to happiness. So they had people pose with a smile or with mouth relaxed. The only differences between poses was brow or mouth position. The subjects were presented with pictures of the model from their own country and asked, in their native language, to judge the pose for dominance and happiness. Keating found that nonsmiling and lowered-brow poses were generally associated with dominance, especially among the most Westernized peoples. Smiles were identified with happiness.

These findings parallel those from other studies in the West in which lowered brows are identified with anger, assertive behavior, working on competitive tasks, and dominance. Raised brows are associated with social deference in a number of ways: with children's fleeing during disputes, with perceptions of fear or surprise, and as a signal inviting social contact. Smiles (see Box 3–2) are generally associated with greeting, approval-seeking behavior, and happiness or joy (Keating et al., 1981). It is possible, then, that the analog to the human smile is the primate submissive grin. When an ape grins it means submission. Perhaps there is an evolutionary link to the human tendency to express sociability and submissiveness in the same manner.

An even tougher test of the universality of particular emotional expressions was a study conducted with people from a remote part of New Guinea who had never lived in any West-

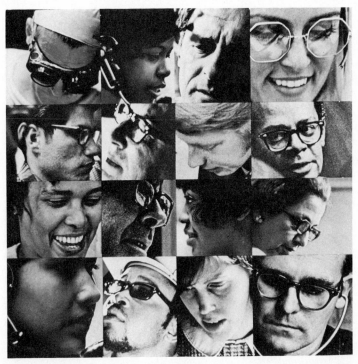

Can you tell what emotions these people are feeling? What cues do you use in trying to decide?

What's in a Smile?

Smiling might be thought always to reflect the underlying emotion of happiness or joy. Anything that makes people happy ought to make them smile. Smiling might also be a communicative act—it might have little to do with the person's underlying emotion, but might instead be a gesture of friendliness. Kraut and Johnston (1979) observed a large number of people in ordinary interaction to test this contrast. They found that bowlers smiled when engaging in social contact, such as looking at their friends, but not when avoiding social contact, such as looking at the ground. However, their smiling was only weakly related to happiness; they smiled 30 percent of the time after a spare or a strike, and 23 percent of the time otherwise. In another set of observations, the researchers checked whether the smiling of pedestrians is caused by being with friends, and therefore by engaging in social interaction, or by the happiness caused by good weather. As this table shows, the weather had very little effect. Being with friends, however, had a strong effect. So it would seem that smiling is part of social interaction—a technique of communication—more than an intrinsic sign of happy emotions.

	PERCENTAGE OF PEDESTRIANS SMILING	
	GOOD WEATHER	BAD WEATHER
Social interaction	61%	57%
No interaction	12	5
Source: Kraut & Johnston (1979).		

ern settlement or government towns, had seen no movies, understood neither English nor Pidgin, and had never worked for a Caucasian. Presumably these people had had no visual contact with conventional Western facial expression of emotions. Each was given a brief story depicting an emotion, such as for "sadness," "His child has died, and he feels very sad." Then the participant was given one photograph Western observers overwhelmingly agreed depicted that emotion, and two pictures depicting other emotions. On the average, both children and adults chose the "correct" picture more than 80 percent of the time (Ekman & Friesen, 1971). This does not prove there are no cultural differences in the facial expression of emotion, but it does provide evidence of universals that transcend cultural boundaries.

In particular, happiness, sadness, anger, and disgust can be detected with high levels of agreement both within and across cultures. Fear and surprise were often confused with each other (Ekman & Oster, 1982).

There are some qualifications, however. Cultures do differ substantially in *amount* of emotional expression that is customary. Swedes tend to be relatively impassive; Italians are quite expressive. Sometimes social norms forbid honest expression—we are supposed to conceal disgusted reactions to someone with a terrible deformity, or anger at being belittled by our superior at work. Still, the level of consensus on the meaning of facial expressions is impressive, given the fact that most of these studies have used photographs and hence provide no information about context.

NONVERBAL COMMUNICATION

If you think about it, you will realize that you make judgments about another person's emotional state on the the basis of more than facial expression. If studies show that perceivers are not perfectly accurate in detecting emotions from facial expressions, what other cues do they use? And if they use a wider range of cues, do they become more accurate? What about other internal states, such as attitudes or intentions, or personality traits or lies? What are the ways in which people communicate internal states in general, and what cues do observers use in detecting them?

Generally speaking, people communicate information about themselves through three main channels. The most obvious is *verbal communication*, the content of what a person says. The other channels are nonverbal and provide a whole set of much subtler cues. *Nonverbal communication* is the sum of the ways in which we transmit information without using language. This communication comes to us through a *visible channel*, which includes such expressive behaviors as facial expression, gesture, posture, and appearance, and a *paralinguistic channel,* what is left in the speech signal when the content has been removed, such as the pitch, amplitude, rate, voice quality, and contour of speech.

The visible and paralinguistic channels have generated a good bit of enthusiasm among researchers and they do prove informative to perceivers. As research has progressed, a wide variety of different nonverbal cues have been identified, and observers seem to get quite different kinds of information from them. However, as helpful as they can be, nonverbal communications provide no magic clues to another person's internal states. Perceivers usually require other information about a person.

The Visible Channel

Some of the main nonverbal cues of the visible channel are expressed through distance, gesture, and eye contact.

DISTANCE   In general, the more friendly and intimate a person feels toward another, the closer he or she will stand. Friends stand closer than strangers (Aiello & Cooper, 1972); people who want to seem friendly choose smaller distances (Patterson & Sechrest, 1970); and people who are sexually attracted to each other stand close (Allgeier & Byrne, 1973). Although most people do not think much about personal space, we are all aware that standing close is usually a sign of friendship or interest. It may be one of the most important and easiest ways of telling someone you have just met that you like him or her. The other person is immediately aware of your interest, and if he or she is not interested, will generally move away to make that clear.

GESTURES   In recent years many popular books have been published on the subject of **body language.** These books suggest that you can tell exactly what someone is thinking or perfectly interpret what they say merely by observing their bodily movements and posture. An open

People are able to interpret each other's gestures quite easily when they are familiar and in a known context.

Ken Karp

palm is an invitation, crossed legs are defensive, and so on. Clearly bodily gestures and posture carry information. There are straightforward, direct gestures and very subtle ones. Many bodily movements are generally accepted and convey specific information or directions—the gestures for "stop" and "come" are examples, as are pointing and gestures for "sit down," "yes," "no," "go away," "goodby." Various obscene gestures have well-known meanings. In a sense, all these gestures are a sign language.

But gestures have meaning mainly when observers and participants understand the context, and especially when they understand the culture. An open palm is not always an invitation: Putting a hand up with palm out means "stop," not "go"; the reverse gesture, with the palm in and the fingers moving toward the body, means "come" or "enter." No one has constructed a reliable dictionary of gestures. Popular books on body language are usually not based on scientific research and should be read with healthy skepticism. The meaning of gestures depends on the context, or the person doing the action, on the culture, and probably on other factors also.

EYE CONTACT   Eye contact is an especially interesting form of nonverbal communication. As with other forms, the meaning of eye contact varies greatly and depends on the context. But in nearly all social interactions eye contact does communicate information.

At the minimum, eye contact indicates interest or lack of it. Hollywood movies often have a couple staring into each other's eyes to portray love, affection, or great concern. Certainly we are all familiar with eye contact held for a long time as a means of demonstrating attraction for someone. An otherwise casual conversation can become an expression of romantic interest if one of the speakers maintains eye contact. Conversely, avoiding or breaking the contact is usually a sign that the person is not interested. Indeed, when someone does not make eye contact during a conversation, we tend to interpret this as an indication that he or she is not really involved in the interaction. No matter how attentively someone answers questions, nods at appropriate times, and carries on the conversation, lack of eye contact means he or she is not interested in what we are saying.

But there are obvious exceptions to this general principle. Someone who is conveying bad news or saying something painful may avoid eye contact. Lack of eye contact can sometimes mean the person is shy or frightened. When people have feelings they are embarrassed about, they do not like to be the focus of a direct gaze. In a study by Ellsworth and colleagues (1978), female college students were told they would have to discuss questions "about rather intimate personal areas of your life, things that college students usually do not like to talk about." Each student then had to wait with a confederate who stared directly at her 75 percent of the time, or just glanced at her once. By far, most subjects preferred the gaze-averting confederate. Other subjects who were not expecting an embarrassing conversation did not. The direct gaze apparently threatened the embarrassed women.

Moreover, eye contact can be used more actively, to threaten. In another experiment, someone stared at a subject who was in a position to act aggressively toward the starer. Subjects who were stared at were less aggressive than when there was no staring (Ellsworth & Carlsmith, 1975). Apparently prolonged eye contact can be interpreted as a threat and causes people to escape or act in a conciliatory manner. We all can probably remember teachers who have used this technique very effectively on us.

It is perhaps not surprising that eye contact can have two seemingly contradictory meanings—friendship or threat. In both cases, eye contact indicates greater involvement and higher emotional content. Whether the emotion is positive or negative depends on the context; the nonverbal cues themselves have no fixed meaning.

Paralanguage

Variations in speech other than the actual words and syntax, or **paralanguage,** carry a great deal

Teri Leigh Stratford

Eye contact leads to quite accurate inferences in contexts people understand well.

of meaning. Pitch of the voice, loudness, rhythm, inflection, and hesitations convey information. Parents can often tell whether their baby is hungry, angry, or just mildly cranky by how it cries. Dogs bark in different ways, and each means something different to someone familiar with the animal. And, of course, the significance and meaning of adult speech depend in part on these paralinguistic factors.

A simple statement such as "You want to move to Japan" can mean entirely different things depending on emphasis and inflection. Say it aloud as a flat statement with no emphasis, and it sounds like a mere statement of fact. Say it with an inflection (rising voice) at the end, and it questions the wisdom of going to Japan; you are expressing doubt that it is a good place to move to. Say it with added emphasis on the first word and it turns into a question as to whether or not the person addressed is qualified; you are raising doubts about whether or not the person is capable of getting along in such a foreign country. The short phrase "I like you" may indicate almost anything from mild feeling to intense passion, depending on its paralinguistic characteristics.

These variations are often crucial in conveying emotion. In fact, they are so important that they often must be added to written language. To show that someone thought Japan was an unlikely choice, the sentence might read, " 'You want to move to Japan?' he said with disbelief." To describe the feeling behind a statement of liking, one might write, " 'I like you,' she murmured passionately." Without these paralinguistic clues, the statements are hard to interpret.

One of the difficulties in studying paralanguage (and most other kinds of nonverbal behavior) is that the cues have no fixed meaning. We all agree on the meaning of words. We all know what "Japan" refers to, and with some variations we know that when someone says he "likes" you, he is making a statement of positive feelings. But people differ considerably in the meanings they attach to paralinguistic cues. For some people, a pause may be for emphasis; for others, it may mean uncertainty. Higher pitch may mean excitement or lying; loudness can be anger, emphasis, or excitement. The particular meaning depends on the context. It is hard to interpret what is communicated when a speaker talks louder at you: If the person makes a fist, it is anger; if the person hugs you, it is affection. It also depends on individual habits and characteristics.

Multiple Channels

Which of these three channels of communication—verbal, visible, and paralinguistic—provides the most information about a person's real emotions? Many writers in recent years have speculated that observers weigh nonverbal cues most heavily and tend almost to disregard verbal communication. For example, Birdwhistell (1970) says that no more than 30 to 35 percent of the social meaning of a conversation is carried by the words. Mehrabian (1972) estimated that only 7 percent of the communication of emotion was accomplished by the verbal channel, 55 percent was accomplished by the visible channel, and 38 percent by the paralinguistic channel. Other writers have gone even further, arguing that the visible channel dominates in the communication of emotion; that is, "video" in-

formation is more important than "audio" (DePaulo et al., 1978).

The question of which channels are taken most seriously becomes particularly important when the observer is receiving conflicting cues from different channels. How do you interpret your girlfriend's feelings when she says she loves you but moves away from you and won't look at you? The verbal and visible channels of her communication seem to conflict. What if your roommate shouts at you at the top of her lungs that she is really *not* mad at you, *at all*, for breaking her favorite coffee cup? Shakespeare said, "Methinks she doth protest too much." Conflicts across channels ought to be particularly important in interpreting apparently deceptive communications. In such cases, is nonverbal, and especially visible, communication truly relied on most heavily, as some of these researchers suggest?

Only recently have such claims been subjected to rigorous tests. In one of the clearest of such studies, Krauss et al. (1981) presented subjects with videotapes of the 1976 televised debate between the two candidates for vice-president, Walter Mondale and Robert Dole. The debate started pleasantly, but turned rather heated and rancorous. The researchers selected 12 passages for each speaker, half of which seemed to display positive emotions and half negative. Then each subject was presented these passages in one of four conditions: (1) audiovisual—the standard videotaped version; (2) verbal only—a written transcript as published in the *New York Times*; (3) video only—with the audio channel turned off; and (4) paralinguistic—the audio track only, but with content filtered out so that speech was unintelligible, while nonverbal features such as pitch, loudness, rate, and so on were preserved.

The full audiovisual condition provided all three channels of communication; the other three provided, respectively, only verbal, visible, and paralinguistic information. The basic question was which of the latter three yielded responses most similar to those obtained from the full, audiovisual version. Presumably that would show which individual channel communicated the most information about the speakers' true emotions.

The written transcript turned out to be critical for detecting whether positive or negative emotions were being expressed; that is, verbal information was most important, contrary to speculations about the importance of nonverbal communication. To see if the same finding would hold with communication more typical of students' daily lives, Krauss et al. did a second experiment presenting subjects with undergraduates' responses to affectively loaded questions ("Who is the person in your life you like most? Describe what he/she is like and your reaction to that person") under the same four conditions as in the debate study just described. The results were very similar: The actual written transcript of the person's comments carried the most weight in determining perceptions of the person's feelings. The data from these studies are shown in Table 3–5.

In both studies, the visible channel made little contribution to observers' judgments. Paralinguistic information did contribute to judgments of the potency and activity levels of the speakers' presentations. That is, observers who were given only the unintelligible soundtrack gave the same kinds of judgments about energy levels as did those given full audiovisual information. The implication is that paralinguistic information, like eye contact, can be sufficient to detect energy and involvement, even if it is not sufficient to detect the particular kind of emotion expressed.

A follow-up study by Apple and Hecht (1982) found that paralinguistic information could be particularly useful in detecting sadness. They had speakers deliver sentences that varied in the kind of emotion they presented: happiness, sadness, anger, or surprise. No visual cues were provided, and the verbal content of the sentence was screened out from the recording. Listeners were able to identify the sadness sentences quite readily, but they could identify the others at only slightly better than chance levels. The authors speculate that sadness is expressed through distinctive paralinguistic cues (slow, soft, low-pitched speech), whereas the other emotions are expressed with more energetic cues that easily confuse the listener.

Table 3–5
Importance of Various Channels of Information in Judgments

	VERBAL ONLY	VIDEO ONLY	AUDIO FILTERED	TOTAL
Study 1 (vice-presidential debaters)				
Dimension of judgment				
Evaluation	51.8[a]	2.2	8.8	63.8
Potency	3.4	29.6	45.1[a]	78.1
Activity	0.1	36.8	5.2	42.1
Study 2 (undergraduates)				
Dimension of judgment				
Evaluation	88.4[a]	0.9[a]	0.9	90.2
Potency	32.5[a]	0.7	5.6[a]	38.8
Activity	25.3[a]	0.4	8.5[a]	34.2

[a] $p < .05$.
Note: The entry is the percentage of variance in judgments of full audiovisual communication that was accounted for by each individual channel. Rows do not sum to 100 percent because factors other than these three channels account for some of the full-channel judgment process.
Source: Adapted from Krauss et al. (1981), pp. 316–7.

In general, then, nonverbal cues—paralinguistic or visible—are not very precise guides, by themselves, to emotional feelings in others. There is nothing magically or unambiguously communicative about nonverbal cues. Most can communicate a variety of messages depending on the context. A touch on the arm by an attractive acquaintance means something quite different from the same touch made by a derelict in a subway station. Being tapped on the shoulder by your boss may mean something still different. A smile on the face of a bully as he moves in on a helpless prey means something quite different from the smile on a friend's face when he or she sees you walking across the campus. Nonverbal cues can be informative, but only when they are solidly embedded in a familiar context, when we know the role of the other person, have some notion of his or her general goals, know the norms for the situation, and so on. When we do not have a known or familiar context, as in a first visit to a foreign country, we frequently feel lost and can make little sense of nonverbal cues.

THE PROBLEM OF DECEPTION

A particularly important area of conflict between verbal and nonverbal cues is judging when people are lying or otherwise trying to deceive observers. Police, judges, and jurors are constantly trying to learn the truth from people who try to mislead them.

Nonverbal Leakage

As might be expected from our discussion of nonverbal communication, one important theory is that people will give away deception through nonverbal cues even when they are successful in lying verbally. Ekman and Friesen (1974) argue that people attend more to what they are saying than to what they are doing with their bodies. If they are trying to deceive someone, for example, they may lie verbally in a calm way, but reveal their true emotions through nonverbal cues. In Ekman's terms, there is **nonverbal leakage.** True emotions "leak out" even if the person tries to conceal them. A student may say she is not nervous about a test, but will bite her lower lip and blink more than usual, actions that often indicate nervousness. A young man waiting for a job interview may attempt to appear calm and casual, but will cross and uncross his legs continually,

straighten his tie, touch his face, play with his hair. As a result, he will in fact come across as a nervous wreck.

Liars often betray themselves through paralinguistic expressions of anxiety, tension, and nervousness. It sometimes is possible to tell when someone is lying by noting the pitch of the voice. Several studies (Ekman et al., 1976; Krauss et al., 1976) indicate that the average (or more technically, fundamental) pitch of the voice is higher when someone is lying than when he or she is telling the truth. The difference is small, and one cannot tell just by listening. But electronic vocal analysis reveals lying with considerable accuracy. In addition, shorter answers, longer delays in responding, more speech errors, and more nervous, less serious answers all are characteristic of people perceived as liars or of people instructed to tell lies (Apple, Streeter, & Krauss, 1979; Kraut, 1978; Zuckerman, DePaulo, & Rosenthal, 1981).

The concept of "leakage" implies that some nonverbal channels "leak" more than others because they are less controllable. Several studies (Zuckerman, De Paulo, & Rosenthal, 1981) have found that the body is more likely to reveal deception than the face. Paralinguistic cues can also "leak" because , like the body, tone of voice is less controllable than facial expression.

Zuckerman, Larrance, Spiegel, and Klorman (1981) have found that senders were better able to modify (suppress and exaggerate) facial expressions than tone of voice. The "leakage" hypothesis proposes, then, that when people are trying to conceal something, it may "leak" out in bodily gestures and paralinguistic cues.

Accuracy of Detection

Perceivers do quite consistently perceive deceptive messages as somewhat less truthful than truthful messages. Across dozens of studies, deception accuracy usually exceeds chance, but rarely by an impressive margin (De Paulo et al., 1982). Not surprisingly, people can detect the fact of lying better than they can figure out the nature of the liar's true feelings. For example,

they have trouble distinguishing deceptive communication from genuinely ambivalent messages.

In one study, De Paulo et al. (1982) had senders record messages about people they genuinely liked and disliked, either telling the truth or telling the opposite, and then had them record messages about people they had genuinely mixed feelings about. These messages were, as in the other studies discussed in this section, presented to observers through different channels. They found that observers were not able to distinguish mixed messages from deceptive messages. Perhaps people are able to distinguish true expressions of positive or negative feelings from everything else, but are not able to isolate deception itself—all they know is that the person does not sound wholeheartedly positive or negative.

Rick Smolan, Stock, Boston

Leaning forward and gazing into the other's eyes usually implies strong attraction. We would be surprised if he were not in love, or at least, very fond of the person facing him.

BOX 3–3
Detecting Smugglers at the Customs Gate

How good are ordinary people at detecting lying? What cues do they use in detecting it? One of the most realistic and complete studies was conducted by Kraut and Poe (1980). They induced airline travelers to try to smuggle some "contraband" past an interview with a real U. S. Customs inspector. The participants were people who happened to be waiting for an airline departure in Syracuse, New York. Some were randomly selected to serve in the "smuggler" condition, and were given contraband, such as small pouches of white powder or miniature cameras, and told to hide them on their persons. They were offered a prize of up to $100 for being able to smuggle the contraband successfully past the customs inspector. Others were randomly selected to be in the "innocent" condition, and were given no contraband. The whole interaction of passenger and inspector was videotaped. To determine what special nonverbal behaviors were displayed by people actually engaged in deception, each passenger's behavior with the inspector was coded by other judges for many of the visible and paralinguistic variables of nonverbal communication we have been discussing: grooming, postural shifts, relaxed posture, smiling, gaze avoidance, speech errors, response latency, response length, evasiveness, nervousness, and difficulty in answering. Each interaction was also played back to observers who attempted to identify which of the passengers were "smugglers" and which were not.

There were no discernible systematic differences in behavior between the innocent and smuggling passengers. If the "smugglers" were "leaking" their deceptiveness, they were not doing so consistently via the nonverbal behaviors coded. Not surprisingly, then, neither the real customs inspectors nor the observers who later viewed the videotapes were successful in picking out the "smugglers" from the "innocent" passengers. This finding suggests that observers have limited ability to detect deception in a real life situation.

Despite this lack of accuracy, there was strong consensus among observers on who the actual smugglers were. So the next question became this: What cues were the observers using that allowed them to come to such a high level of consensus about smuggling behavior, and yet that proved to be of such little value? Observers also showed considerable consensus on the specific cues associated with "smuggling." Decisions to search a passenger were strongly associated with the person's apparent nervousness, giving short answers, and shifting the body more. Nervousness in turn was associated with taking a long time to answer a question and avoiding eye contact with the inspector. So there were a number of verbal and nonverbal cues observers thought were associated with "smuggling," but they were incorrect; no systematic differences actually existed between smuggling and innocent passengers in actual behavior, either verbal or nonverbal.

In short, neither professional nor untrained observers could accurately determine whether or not a traveler was lying. And in fact the lying and honest travelers did not differ in any way that could be coded in terms of verbal and nonverbal behavior. Yet the judges came to a striking level of consensus. And their perceptions could be accounted for by a relatively limited set of overt cues displayed by the passengers. All this is consistent with the notion that the observers shared a clear stereotype about how smugglers behave. Yet in this case it seems to have been inaccurate. As indicated in the text, observers are somewhat more sensitive to deception in controlled laboratory situations. Even in those situations, however, they still are not terribly accurate, though they are very confident about being able to detect it, and have many ready explanations for their skills.

The Giveaways

What cues do observers use to discover deception? Is the leakage hypothesis correct? Is the body less controllable than the face, and do people catch deception primarily through nonverbal bodily cues? Or is the voice an even leakier channel than the body? It may be that the tone of voice—pitch, loudness, speed, and so forth—is even more difficult to control than the body, even when the person can control the content of verbal communication.

Most of the research shows that all these cues help a little to trap a potentially deceptive communicator. But they are really useful only when the observer also has access to the content of the person's speech. A typical study is one done by Zuckerman, Amidon, Bishop, and Pomerantz (1982). They had "senders" describe either a target person they liked (a "liked target") or someone they disliked (a "disliked target"), and they did so in one of three modes: "truth," in which they conveyed their true feelings; "concealment," in which they tried to conceal their true feelings; and "deception," in which they tried to communicate feelings opposite to those they really had. The "receivers" did not know the senders' true feelings, or which mode the sender was instructed to use.

The crucial comparison is between the channels in which receivers were then given these communications: full audiovisual (face plus verbal content), full audio only (verbal content, no face), visual plus filtered speech (face, no verbal content), or filtered speech only (no verbal content, no face). The question was how access to the face, to verbal content, and to paralinguistic cues affected observers' ability to detect whether the sender really liked or disliked the target.

The results showed that either face or tone of voice added significantly to ability to detect deception. This can be seen in Table 3–6. The receivers were significantly able to distinguish a liked from a disliked target when given only filtered speech, without being able to see the face or hear any verbal content (as indicated by the fact that they perceived the truly liked target as liked +.31 more, on the average, than the truly disliked target). Second, adding access to the face significantly increased detection of the sender's true feelings, as indicated by the fact that face plus filtered speech is higher (+.74) than filtered speech only (+.31), even when verbal content was not available. Both channels are somewhat "leaky," then, in the sense that both communicated significantly to the receiver about a possibly deceptive sender's true feel-

Table 3–6
Accuracy of Perception of Communicators' True Feelings about Target Person

	VERBAL CONTENT	
	AVAILABLE	NOT AVAILABLE
Face present	+.85	+.74
Face absent	+.84	+.31

Note: The entry is the perception of communicator's true feeling about the liked target minus the perception of communicator's true feeling about the disliked target, each rated on a nine-point scale.
Source: Adapted from Zuckerman et al. (1982), p. 353.

ings, even when the receiver could not understand the content of the communication.

The main finding, however, is that accuracy is greatest when verbal content is available. The table shows the highest accuracy in the left-hand column, with verbal content available. Moreover, adding visual nonverbal cues helps the perceiver very little when verbal content is available (+.85 is almost identical to +.84). So in this study, as in most others, we find good evidence for the "leakage" hypothesis: People can detect deception significantly through nonverbal cues, such as the face, filtered speech, or the body, as described by Zuckerman, DePaulo, & Rosenthal (1981) and Ekman and Friesen (1974). We have little reason yet to say that the face is more or less leaky than tone of voice or body. But it is quite clear that the best cues of all by far are those that come from hearing full speech, whether or not we can also see the person. That is, the best guide to deception is hearing what a person has to say—which includes both the content and paralinguistic cues.

SUMMARY

1. People tend to form highly consistent impressions of others, even with very little information.
2. The evaluative dimension is the most important organizing principle behind first impressions. People seem to decide first how much they like or dislike another person, then ascribe characteristics to them that fit this pleasant or unpleasant portrait.
3. There are two rival points of view about how people process information about other people: The learning approach, which has people essentially averaging information in a quite mechanical manner; and the Gestalt approach, which has people forming more coherent and meaningful impressions.
4. Various identifiable perceptual biases distort our judgments of others, such as the halo effect (we tend to think a person we like is good on every dimension), and the positivity bias (we tend to like most people, even some who are not so likable).
5. Our judgments of other people are not always very accurate. In particular, we have a hard time judging people's emotions from their facial expressions. We can tell fairly easily if the emotion is a positive or a negative one, but we have difficulty telling which positive or negative emotion is being experienced. Nevertheless, there do seem to be some universal connections across cultures between certain emotions and certain facial expressions.
6. We use a wide variety of cues in arriving at impressions of people, including physical appearance, verbal behavior, and nonverbal cues. Nonverbal communication includes cues from both the visible channel (such as facial expressions, gestures, and posture) and the paralinguistic channel (cues in speech when the content has been removed, such as the pitch, rate, and delays of speech).
7. A person's verbal communication is probably the single most important source of information about them. However, visible and paralinguistic information make an important additional contribution, particularly when the content helps us to interpret their meaning.
8. Deception "leaks" out in numerous nonverbal ways, such as nervous gestures or high-pitched and rapid speech. Observers can usually detect deception at slightly better than chance levels, but they need all three channels of communication to do so effectively.

SUGGESTIONS FOR ADDITIONAL READING

ANDERSON, N. H. 1965. Averaging vs. adding as a stimulus-combination rule in impression formation. *Journal of Experimental Psychology, 70,* 394–400. This gives the flavor of averaging research, using trait adjectives about hypothetical stimulus persons.

ASCH, S. E. 1946. Forming impressions of personality. *Journal of Abnormal and Social Psychology, 41,* 258–90. This is the classic statement of the Gestalt approach to impression formation, and indeed to social perception in general.

EKMAN, PAUL (Ed.) 1982. *Emotion in the human face.* (2nd ed.). New York: Cambridge University Press. The best treatment of how people judge emotions from facial expressions.

HALL, EDWARD T. 1966. *The hidden dimension.* Garden City, N.Y.: Doubleday. An original statement by one of the pioneers in the study of nonverbal communication.

KRAUSS, R. M., APPLE, W., MORENCY, N., WENZEL, C., & WINTON, W. 1981. Verbal, vocal, and visible factors in judgments of another's affect. *Journal of Personality and Social Psychology, 40,* 312–320. An interesting and careful analysis of how people combine cues from different channels to arrive at impressions.

MEHRABIAN, A. 1972. *Nonverbal communication.* Chicago: Aldine. A useful summary of research on nonverbal communication.

SCHNEIDER, D. J., HASTORF, A. H., & ELLSWORTH, P. C. 1979. *Person perception* (2nd ed.). Reading, Mass.: Addison-Wesley. A paperback that pursues the material in this chapter in more detail.

4

SOCIAL COGNITION

As indicated in the last chapter, we have so far described person perception as dominated by two assumptions. First, the process of impression formation is rather mechanical. Second, the process is dominated by feeling or evaluation, rather than by thought or cognition. Although there is much value in these two assumptions, they do oversimplify the process. We do not just take in a literal copy of the environment, no matter whether we are perceiving people or things. Each piece of information is taken as an aspect of a coherent whole, rather than as simply another isolated trait to be averaged in to the overall impression.

The focus on evaluation, though central to impression formation, is also incomplete. It ignores cognitive processing mechanisms. Although human beings clearly have a greater capacity for processing information than other animals, it is not infinite. We can absorb only a limited amount of the stimulation we are bombarded with every minute; and when we need to retrieve it from our memory, we cannot get it all back in a flash. So any analysis of person perception must start out by acknowledging our limited processing abilities.

We might be described as lazy perceivers (McGuire, 1969), or somewhat more charitably as **cognitive misers** (Taylor, 1981a). When we perceive other people, we try to cut corners and save effort. We do not try to perceive or remember all possible bits of information; we do only what is necessary to get a clear impression of what is going on.

This emphasis on cognitive process is one of the main approaches to social psychology. In the context of person perception it is called *social cognition,* because it studies cognitive processes focused on social stimuli, mainly persons and groups. At the core of the social cognition approach is the view that person perception is a cognitive process: People are actively organizing perceivers, not passive receptacles; they are motivated by the need to develop coherent and meaningful impressions, not just likes and dislikes.

And our limited processing capacities lead to the use of a series of cognitive shortcuts. These can produce efficiencies in processing, but they also can produce biases and errors. The social cognition approach is a supplement to the simpler, more mechanical processes described earlier. It asks what else is going on besides the simple judgment of liking or disliking.

Here we will discuss four of the general ideas that have been developed in research on social cognition, beginning with the simplest. (1) Processing of information about people involves perceiving some coherent *meaning* in the stimulus object. As we have already seen in the last chapter, the central thrust of the cognitive approach has been to find exceptions to a simple averaging principle reflecting more complex cognitive processing.

(2) Perceivers tend to pay special attention to the most *salient* features of the perceptual field rather than giving equal attention to everything. That is, figural people, or figural aspects of a particular person, get more attention than does the background. On a rainy day, our attention is drawn to the police officer in the middle of a crowded intersection, because he or she is wearing a bright orange raincoat and all the other colors in the intersection are drab. And our

attention is drawn to the raincoat, rather than to the cap, face, or boots.

(3) We organize the perceptual field by *categorizing* or grouping stimuli. Of course everything we see, hear, smell, or feel is a little different from everything else, but we do not perceive them that way. Rather, we tend to see each separate stimulus as part of a category or group; a Porsche as a car, a person wearing a white lab coat as a doctor, and a motion with the foot as a kick, even though each of these may have features that make them quite different from other cars, doctors, or kicks.

(4) We perceive stimuli as part of some kind of *structure*. Each separate stimulus tends to be related to others in time, space, and a causal flow. We see a downhill skier as part of a broader context: She is in a ski race, so she begins skiing when the starter gives the order; she skis between the flags down the hill; and she stops when she crosses the finish line. All we literally see is a young woman in motion, but that is part of a much more complex cognitive structure which includes our knowledge of the rules of slalom racing and our impression of her grace, agility, and power. In other words, we spontaneously embed the individual stimulus in a broader structure of knowledge.

SALIENCE

People are sensitive to many cues in others, and use these cues to form impressions. But clearly people do not use all the cues available to them. According to the **figure-ground principle,** people direct their attention to those aspects of the perceptual field that stand out. In impression formation, the salient cues will be utilized most heavily. If a student appears in a wheelchair the first day of class, everyone else in the room is likely to form an impression that is most heavily influenced by the fact of the person's physical handicap. Clothing, hair style, and perhaps even age, race, and sex will all be secondary.

What Makes a Cue Salient?

What determines the **salience** of one cue as opposed to another? A number of clearly specifiable objective conditions make cues stand out. *Brightness, noisiness, motion,* or *novelty* are the most powerful conditions, according to Gestalt principles of object perception (McArthur & Post, 1977). A man in a bright red sweater stands out in a crowded classroom, and the sweater is his most salient feature. The student who gets up shouting in the middle of a lecture and leaves the room draws our attention because she is noisy and moving, and almost everything else in the classroom is quiet and stationary. A student in white robes and a turban is a novel stimulus, and we may notice few of the other people in a classroom.

So, anything that makes a cue objectively *unusual* in its context makes it subjectively more salient, more likely to be attended to, and more heavily utilized. A novel cue is unusual in the time dimension; it is unlike anything that preceded it and so attracts our attention. Openly gay men and lesbians were novel in the early 1970s, and so were punk rockers in the late 1970s. Impressions of them were heavily influenced by their sexual preference and colored hair, respectively. Loud noises are unusual in sound, and their distinctiveness attracts attention; we probably notice very little else about a waiter who drops a tray in a restaurant. We are more likely to describe a redhead in terms of hair color than we would a brunette, because red hair is more unusual.

Another way to make the same point is to think of the *extremity* of a cue in its normal dis-

What stimuli are most salient in this picture? What makes them salient?

tribution in the population. The wheelchair, exciting behavior, white robes, red sweater, and red hair are all extreme in the normal distribution of paraphernalia, classroom behavior, clothing, and hair color.

How Does Salience Affect Perception?

Salience has a number of consequences for person perception. If you think about people as "cognitive misers," you will see that they are always trying to get the most accurate and meaningful impressions of people and events around them by expending the least cognitive effort. One of their most valuable shortcuts is to respond to the most salient stimuli without trying to process all the information they could possibly obtain. So, salient behaviors draw more attention than do subtler, less obvious ones (McArthur, 1981). Second, salience influences perceptions of causality in that more salient

people are seen as having more influence over their social context. The student who sits in front of the class and asks an occasional question is more likely to be perceived as dominating the discussion than the student who sits in the back and talks just as much.

Third, evaluations of salient people are more extreme than evaluations of less salient people. Taylor et al. (1977) ran a series of experiments in which they varied the "solo" status of black group members; some groups had an even mixture of white and black members, other groups had only one black member. The "solo" black was clearly more salient than blacks in the evenly divided groups. A pleasant black group member was evaluated more favorably when "solo" than when in an evenly divided group, and an unpleasant one was evaluated more negatively.

Last, salience increases the coherence of an impression (Taylor, 1981b). If the salient person is a member of a stereotyped group, such as "drug addict," he or she will be seen as possessing all the stereotyped attributes of that group, such as having criminal tendencies, weak moral character, slovenly manner and dress, a lack of honesty, and so forth.

Salient stimuli draw the most attention; they are seen as the most causally powerful; they produce the most extreme evaluative judgments; and they produce more consistency of judgment. These effects have been called "top of the head" effects by Taylor and Fiske (1978) because they seem to occur simply at the level of the direction of attention. That is, they occur because they focus the perceiver's attention one way or another, not because they involve any very deep changes in thinking. As might be expected, therefore, they seem to be strongest when the stimuli are sufficiently interesting and exciting to attract the perceiver's real attention. The salience of different stimuli matters more when the perceiver is responding to exciting conversations, such as humorous debates, than when he or she is responding to stiffer, more formal and boring situations (McArthur, 1981). But the effects appear to be rather general. They seem to occur on important issues as well as unimportant ones (Taylor et al., 1979; Borgida & Howard-Pitney, 1983).

The Case of Vividness

So far we have been considering salience in terms of the perceptual unusualness or extremity of a stimulus. Some researchers have extended the idea of salience to include the notion of *vividness:* "Information may be described as vivid, that is, as likely to attract and hold our attention and to excite the imagination to the extent that it is (a) emotionally interesting, (b) concrete and imagery-provoking, and (c) proximate in a sensory, temporal, or spatial way" (Nisbett & Ross, 1980, p. 45). Vivid stimuli might be especially influential for a variety of reasons: They might be more readily noticed, easier to remember, easier to visualize, and/or their greater emotional impact might make them particularly important. For example, opposition to the Vietnam war in its later stages is often ascribed to its vivid presentation. It was "the television war": People could watch all the horrors in living color in their living rooms. This more vivid presentation of the Vietnam experience, compared to the blander reporting of past wars in the printed press, is said to have created a greater public reaction.

But there is little evidence that vividness in fact has any special power in impression formation. Many studies of its effects have been done, but only rarely have vivid messages been more powerful (Taylor & Thompson, 1982). Why salience should have such reliable effects while vividness does not remains something of a puzzle. Salience is usually defined more clearly and precisely, in terms of such objective characteristics of the stimulus as novelty, intensity, and change; vividness has a looser definition, which could lead to less clear results.

CATEGORIZATION

Perceivers do not respond to salient stimuli in isolation; they immediately and spontaneously perceive them as part of some group or category. We do not see that unshaven, dirty, disheveled man in the park with worn-out shoes and a couple of old shopping bags as just another human being; we immediately categorize him as a derelict. When we go to a basketball game, we usually categorize people right away into members of one or another of five social groups: players on one team or the other, referees, cheerleaders, and spectators. The **categorization** or grouping process is immediate, spontaneous, and does not take any time or thought, any more than you need to think about what category of objects your pencil belongs to.

Categorizing People

At the crudest level, we categorize on the basis of natural similarities in appearance. We tend to assign people to the category of "men" or "women" on the basis of their physical characteristics, usually their secondary sex characteristics, and culturally defined differences in appearance (hair length, makeup, type of clothing). The same is true of assigning people to other social groupings such as racial categories, as illustrated by the story of Lize Venter (see Box 4–1).

Recent research suggests a more precise answer, however. The crucial similarity is between the object being categorized and a typical or ideal example of the category, called a *prototype* (Cantor & Mischel, 1977). For example, a dog would be a more prototypical mammal than would be a whale, because most species of mammals have body hair, move on four legs, and live on land. So most people would probably decide whether or not an unfamiliar animal was a mammal by comparing it to a dog, not to a whale.

What are the consequences of categorization? It speeds information-processing time, as the "cognitive miser" idea suggests. For example, Brewer et al. (1981) presented subjects with photos of people in three different categories, "grandmother," "young woman," and "senior citizen," along with verbal labels clearly identifying their category. Then they presented the subjects with additional information about each target person, and measured how long the subjects took to incorporate the information

---

BOX 4–1
Where Does Lize Fit?

The Union of South Africa categorizes all people into one of three groups: White, Colored, or Black. All persons of mixed blood are included in the Colored category. This categorization determines much of the pattern of the person's life. Blacks are forbidden to vote; they must go to all-black schools; they generally must leave their familes in the countryside if they go to the cities to work; they cannot marry or have romantic or sexual relationships with persons in the other categories, and so on.

Lize Venter was a two-week-old infant found in a field, and her parents were unknown. The authorities were unable to decide which category to place her in, since she was light-skinned and her face showed no definable racial characteristics: "She's cute, that's all I can say," one nurse was quoted as saying. The problem arose because the hospital wished to put her out for adoption. But what kind of a family should she go to? If she were Colored, she could not be adopted by a white family, would have to live in a nonwhite area, and would be forbidden to marry or have sexual relations with a white. If she were determined to be white, the same prohibitions would hold in reverse. As an orphan, she was entitled to public assistance from the government. But since the public assistance services were also segregated by category, no agency would handle her case until a decision had been made about her category. Ultimately a decision would be made by the Department of Internal Affairs, and that decision would determine much of Lize's future life.

Source: Los Angeles *Times*, July 27, 1983.

---

into their impressions. Information consistent with the prototype of the category ("kindly" for "grandmother") was processed faster than information inconsistent with it (such as "aggressive" for grandmother).

Categorizing simplifies and makes processing easier, of course. The other side of the coin is that it can lead to misperception. Oversimplification can hide some of the person's unique characteristics. For example, Taylor and her colleagues (1978) had college students listen to a tape of a small group discussion and simultaneously observe slides that purportedly pictured the group members. The tape-slide show depicted six men discussing a publicity campaign for a play. Three of the men were white, and three were black. At the end, the students were given a list of the suggestions made during the discussion and asked to identify which discussant had made each suggestion. Categorization led to misperception. They mistakenly credited discussants with the suggestions made by others of the same race, but not with those made by discussants of the opposite race. That is, the observers made more mistakes within a race than between races. Apparently, as they watched the show, they categorized the suggestions as being made by a black or by a white discussant, rather than remembering which individual made the remark. Such categorizations certainly are unfair when they lead us to overlook the unique characteristics of a particular person.

Intergroup Discrimination

Numerous studies show that the mere act of categorization can produce discrimination when it involves categorizing people into "us" (an ingroup) and "them" (an outgroup). That is, even a completely arbitrary categorization of people as being in one group as opposed to another leads to discriminatory behavior. Once a person feels he belongs to a group, the person tends to favor other group members at the expense of nonmembers (or members of other groups). This tendency can be seen in more favorable evaluations of ingroup members than outgroup members, or in more favorable allocation of rewards to ingroup members. Favoritism can be observed even when the basis for group membership is purely arbitrary and even when the person gets little or nothing tangible from the group.

Perhaps the simplest demonstration of this *minimal intergroup discrimination* effect comes from a series of studies by Henri Tajfel and his colleagues (1971). In these studies, students were brought into a laboratory and divided into two groups on the basis of some arbitrary procedure. In one typical study, they were divided into two groups supposedly on the basis of their preferences between the two modern painters Klee and Kandinsky (though in fact they were assigned randomly to the two groups). They had no actual interaction with fellow group members (the ingroup) or members of the other group (the outgroup), but they were asked to evaluate all individuals in the experiment and distribute some rewards to them. The general finding was that participants evaluated positively and rewarded ingroup members at the expense of outgroup members.

You might think that the subjects would feel some special liking for ingroup members because they were supposedly selected for their similar tastes in art, and similarity is a strong determinant of liking, as we will see in Chapter 8. But later experiments made it clear to the subjects that their assignments to groups were completely random, and they shared no common characteristics with other ingroup members. Locksley et al. (1980) assigned subjects to be a Phi or a Gamma by having them pull a lottery ticket out of a can, with the same results: Subjects allocated significantly more rewards to ingroup than to outgroup members.

The point is that mere categorization leads to ingroup favoritism and discrimination against the outgroup, even when there are no selfish gains to be made, any especially pleasurable interaction with the ingroup, or any especially unpleasant interaction with the outgroup. These subjects were not allowed to reward themselves, and they could not be rewarded by other ingroup members. They had no interaction with members from either group. The purely cognitive act of categorization, apart from any other factors, was enough to promote different responses to ingroup and outgroup.

SCHEMA

A still more complex organization of cognition is called a **schema.** This refers to an organized, structured set of cognitions, including some knowledge about the object, some relationships among the various cognitions about it, and some specific examples (Taylor & Crocker, 1981). We might, for example, have a schema of a "preppie," a WASP college student who wears alligator shirts and khaki pants, buys clothes from L. L. Bean, is partial to pink and kelly green, sports Oxford cloth button-down shirts with madras ties, and likes to sail and jog and play tennis. This "preppie" schema would probably not include going bowling, wearing Caterpiller Tractor caps, driving a 1970 Chrysler Imperial, or having a beer belly.

The content of a schema can be almost anything—a theory about a type of person, a conception of the self, an attitude, a stereotype about a group, perceptions of a ritualized type of event.

What all schemas have in common is not their content, but their structural characteristics and the effects these have on processing. Schemas help us process complex bodies of information by simplifying and organizing them. They can help us remember and organize details, speed up processing time, fill in gaps in our knowledge, and help us interpret and evaluate new information. As we will see, such preexisting cognitive structures organize the processing of new information. Our perceptions of new information are biased to make them consistent with what we already know. If we think someone is "warm," for example, we are more likely to talk to him and interpret his behavior as re-

flecting that warmth. All this is pretty abstract, but some examples should help to illustrate.

Types of Schemas

Schemas can be about different things. There are *person schemas,* which are structures about people. They can focus on particular people. For instance, you may have a schema about Abraham Lincoln. It might include such elements as his being deliberate, honest, serious about his duties, and concerned for oppressed people. This would be a schema if in your view these qualities were all related to one another in President Lincoln, in the sense that you perceive them all as aspects of his basically decent and conscientious personality, not unrelated traits he just happened to display from time to time.

Another version of a person schema is a schema you have about yourself, or a *self-schema.* A self-schema describes the dimensions along which you think about yourself. For example, Markus (1977) investigated the extent to which people had schemas of themselves as independent or dependent by determining whether or not they would apply to themselves such adjectives as "individualistic," "unconventional," "assertive," "cooperative," "timid," or "moderate."

You may be very concerned about maintaining and displaying your own independence by refusing to take money from your parents for college, doing your own laundry, not asking your roommate for help with your math, and so on. Or you may be more interested in dependent relationships and think a lot about ensuring security for yourself by surrounding yourself with people you can depend on, like your brother, girlfriend, doctor, minister, and so on. You could do both, perhaps with some conflict and ambivalence. In any of these cases, you would have a strong self-schema concerning the independence-dependence dimension. On the other hand, you may just not think of yourself very much in connection with that dimension, in which case you would not be thinking schematically in these terms. You would be described as *aschematic* on the dimension of independence-dependence.

Person schemas can also focus on particular types of people. For example, our schema of an "extrovert" might include such elements as "spirited," "outgoing," "enthusiastic," and "self-assured" (Cantor & Mischel, 1977). Sometimes this type of schema is described as an **im-**

Many group stereotypes have been broken in recent years.

A.T.&T. Co. Photo Center

plicit personality theory because it seems to be a theory about what traits go with what other traits, and which ones do not go together. On overhearing someone say that Suzi is "spirited," the person would infer that she was probably outgoing and self-confident even in the absence of any other information about her. An implicit personality theory, then, is this web of presumed relationships among traits.

Other schemas focus on groups. The most familiar is the group **stereotype,** which attributes specific traits to a particular group of people. An early study by Katz and Braly (1933) found white college students checking "superstitious," "lazy," and "happy-go-lucky" as the most common traits of blacks, and "scientifically minded," "industrious," and "stolid" as most common for Germans. Such stereotypes would be schematic if each perceived trait was part of a coherent underlying structure about the group.

You might expect a student who is in the Beta fraternity to act like other Betas, or a black football player to act like other black football players, or people from Boston or Texas or Iran to resemble one another. All these involve having a particular schema for the personality and behavior of members of a group. (We will take up stereotypes in some detail in Chapter 13.)

Then there are *role schemas.* These represent the organized, abstract pictures we have of people in a particular role, such as cowboy, professor, receptionist, or devoted lover. Sometimes these schemas are unrealistic. If our schema for "devoted lover" includes elements such as always understanding, always supportive, never angry, never childish, and always concerned first with the other person's happiness, we could be in trouble. Not too many people will live up to that schema.

Similar problems sometimes arise between college students and faculty when each has an unrealistic schema for the other's role. A faculty member's schema about the student role might include constant interest and attention to the course, while the student's schema for professor might include endless patience and consideration. But students sometimes are sick or distracted by other problems in their lives and unable to pay attention in class. Faculty members may have arguments with their spouses and therefore behave irritably toward innocent students.

People also have schemas for events, or standard series of events. Sometimes such schemas are called *scripts* (Abelson, 1976). A script is a standard sequence of behavior over a period of time. One script might be called "ordering for a group in a Chinese restaurant." Everyone sits down, and the waiter brings the menus. Several people talk at once, giving their favorite dishes, while others say they never know what to have and would someone else just please decide. Then people go through the menu section by section, haggling over which soup to have, bargaining away their favorite beef dish (which no one else wants) for sweet and sour pork (which at least one ally does), and finally appointing the most self-confident and brash person to communicate the whole negotiated package to the waiter.

We could generate similar scripts for other ritualized series of events, such as having a baby, taking a shower, taking a final exam, or playing a basketball game. The essence of a script is in its boundedness in time, its causal flow (early events cause later ones), and in its being a simple, coherent, perceptual unit.

Natural Contours

Like categories, schemas follow the natural contours of the information we receive. But schemas are not just passive reflections of the information environment. The person must actively organize the information into a more abstract cognitive structure. One way of triggering this organizing cognitive activity in an experiment is to tell subjects to form a coherent impression (as opposed to having them simply try to remember the separate bits of information they have been exposed to). We would expect that under such conditions, people would form organized impressions that reflect the underlying structure of the input information; that is, they would form a schema that follows the natural contours of the information that is given.

Hoffman, Mischel, and Mazze (1981) demonstrated this by experimentally varying the traits underlying descriptions of stimulus persons presented to subjects. Each subject was presented with 25 short behavioral episodes (about three sentences each) concerning a particular target person. Each episode was chosen to illustrate one of five traits (such as dishonesty or generosity), so over the set of 25 episodes, each trait was emphasized in 5 episodes. One episode intended to illustrate the trait of dishonesty had the target person looking through her friend's purse and stealing some amphetamine pills. Then the subjects were told either that they would have to present an impression of the target person ("impression-set") or recite the details of the episodes they had read ("recall-set"). Finally, they were asked to organize the episodes into clusters.

The "impression-set" subjects tended to organize the episodes along the lines of the underlying traits, and gave labels to the clusters that corresponded to those underlying traits. In this example, the impression-set subjects would have clustered the information around the trait of dishonesty and labeled the cluster accordingly. In short, when the subjects tried to organize information about a stimulus person into a coherent impression, they began to think schematically about the target person and therefore to organize their thinking along the lines of dimensions actually underlying the target's personality. As shown in Table 4–1, the "impression-set" led subjects to organize their impressions around the traits built into the episodes, and to label the categories in their impressions according to these built-in traits. People with a "recall set" did not organize their impressions nearly as tightly around these built-in traits.

Event schemas, or scripts, are also formed

Tim Carlson, Stock, Boston

Peter Menzel, Stock, Boston

Although it is usually a mistake to assume that appearances tell us much about people, it is difficult to avoid forming very different impressions of the two people pictured here.

Table 4–1		
The "Impression Set" Leads People to Organize Impressions in Terms of the Objective Contours of a Stimulus Person's Personality		
	MATCH OF IMPRESSIONS TO BUILT-IN TRAIT CATEGORIES[a]	PERCENT OF CATEGORIES LABELED WITH BUILT-IN TRAITS
Impression set	28.17	65%
Recall set	7.17	17

[a]Range 0–50, hi = greater match.
Source: Hoffman, Mischel, & Mazze (1981), pp. 216, 218.

along natural contours. Human behavior might be thought to occur in a continuous and uninterrupted flow; indeed, it has been referred to as a "behavior stream." But people cannot absorb everything at once. They tend to perceive behavior in coherent, meaningful chunks of action that are marked off by **breakpoints** (Newtson, 1976). For example, imagine watching an outfielder break into a run at the sound of the bat hitting the ball; he dashes to the outfield wall, leaps up, catches the ball, lands on his feet, sets for a throw, and then throws the ball to the third baseman to stop the baserunner. Newtson argues that we perceive such a flow of activity as a sequence of separate behaviors, not as one continuous act. Breakpoints occur between the separate actions and mark where one ends and another begins.

Breakpoints are inherent in any stream of behavior; they are not imposed on it by the perceiver. To identify these breakpoints, Newtson had subjects watch a film and push a button to indicate when they think one segment has ended and another has begun. This method is quite reliable: Perceivers agree on where certain breakpoints occur in films of someone in action, and they perceive the same breakpoints again when shown the film five weeks later. It also seems quite easy and comfortable for subjects to do. All this argues that the breakpoints occur naturally within the flow of behavior in a given scene.

When do breakpoints occur? Some ingenious research has tied them to changes in behavior,

specifically to changes in the movement of different parts of the body (Newtson, Engquist & Bois, 1977). Breakpoints also occur when the state of objects associated with the person changes. For example, breakpoints would be perceived when a baseball's trajectory is suddenly interrupted by the outfielder's glove, when it disappears from view, or when it suddenly flies through the air back toward the infield. Breakpoints convey the most information about a sequence of behavior. When the breakpoint moments of a film are presented to subjects as still photos, in order, they convey the story almost as well as the full movie itself. People also seem to remember the breakpoints better than any other moments during the sequence.

The more general point, then, is that we do not simply swallow the other person's behavior whole when forming an impression. Rather, we absorb meaningful, structured chunks of it. The chunking process is partly imposed on the flow of behavior by the perceiver's own experiences, expectations, and needs. And partly the chunks reflect real changes within the behavioral sequence.

Hierarchical Organization

One other feature of schemas is that they often have some hierarchical organization. They may have some abstract and general elements, and some more concrete, specific ones.

Suppose we had a schema of "cocktail party." We know that cocktail parties usually are held in the later afternoon or evening, usually in someone's home. They have a number of guests and usually a host and a hostess; they have some food and a lot of alcoholic drinks (all of which are more likely to be prepared and served by the host and hostess than by the guests). Normally the people interact by standing and talking to each other rather than by watching some common event (like a singer) or sleeping or running in circles. In short, we have a clear, well-developed, somewhat abstract picture in our minds about a "cocktail party." It has a standard sequence, a number of elements, and clear causal interrelationships among them.

At a more specific level, the schema might well have different categories of cocktail parties, all of which would be clearly distinct. For example, a wine-and-cheese party held at the opening of an art gallery would be clearly different from the weekly Saturday night bashes at the country club, where all the local businessmen and their wives get together and drink too much and get loud and sloppy, or from a formal diplomatic reception at a foreign embassy. At a still more specific level, our schema might include several specific parties we have attended. All told, we might have a hierarchical schema of "a cocktail party" that would include a general, abstract concept covering all kinds of cocktail parties, some more specific subtypes of cocktail parties, and some particular parties we have gone to.

Individual Differences

Of course people may have different schemas about the same matter. Others may not think schematically about something at all; that is, they may be aschematic. Some schemas are widely shared. One very general example is suggested by the finding discussed earlier, that two types of evaluative dimensions underlie most impressions—the social and intellectual.

This suggests that most perceivers share a common implicit personality theory—namely, that social qualities such as "helpful," "sincere," and "popular" go together, and that intellectual qualities such as "scientific," "determined," and "reliable" go together. Similarly, many racial and ethnic stereotypes are widely shared.

On the other hand, as might be expected, people also have their own personal schemas, in addition to whatever they share with people like them. For example, one person might mainly describe others in terms of their degree of sense of humor and warmth, whereas someone else might consider these characteristics relatively unimportant and instead be concerned with assessing the individual's diligence and religiosity.

Different groups of people will also have quite different schemas about behavioral sequences. Experts will pick up finer segments of behavior than will novices. A veteran baseball coach will perceive more separate acts in an outfielder's play than will a foreigner attending his first baseball game. The spectator will simply think, "The player made a nice catch." The coach, on the other hand, will think, "Did he get a good jump on the ball? How fast is he? How is his timing? Was he ready to throw right away?" Newtson's research shows that when people are instructed to make finer distinctions, they develop more confident impressions of the stimulus person. Put another way, the more breakpoints we perceive in a person's stream of behavior, the more information we receive and the stronger and clearer the impressions we develop.

Groups of people may differ in their schemas. One rather interesting case concerns the theories ordinary people hold about intelligence. It turns out that college students have schemas for intelligence that relate it closely to academic intelligence, whereas nonstudents (people interviewed in supermarkets and a railroad station) saw it as more closely related to everyday intelligence, more concerned with practical problem-solving ability, social competence, and so on (Sternberg et al., 1981).

SCHEMATIC PROCESSING

Advantages

Schemas are important because they help us process an enormous amount of information swiftly and economically. Indeed, schemas make processing more efficient in several different ways. They help us interpret new information, draw valid inferences from it, and evaluate whether or not we agree with it. They help us fill in gaps in our knowledge by suggesting what is likely to be true. And they help us prepare for the future by structuring our expectations about what is likely to happen. These advantages of schematic processing have been demonstrated in a wide variety of studies (see Fiske & Taylor, 1984, and Taylor & Crocker, 1981, for reviews).

A schema can aid recall. Memory often works best when we can bring back some schematic representation of past events or people, because the schema will bring many details along with it. For example, Cohen (1981) presented subjects with a videotape of a woman and her husband. Half were told that the woman was a librarian, and half that she was a waitress. Some of the features of the woman fit the schema of a librarian (as measured separately), such as wearing glasses, eating salad, drinking wine, and playing the piano. Others fit the schema of a waitress, such as having a bowling ball in the room and no bookshelves, and eating a chocolate birthday cake. Later the subjects were asked to recall the details of the videotape. They remembered the schema-consistent details better, no matter whether recall was assessed immediately or a week later.

Moreover, as indicated earlier, schematic processing can be triggered simply by the attempt to form an impression of another person. Hamilton (1981) found that subjects who were instructed to form an impression of the stimulus person, and thus were operating under an "impression-set," recalled more information about the stimulus person than did "memory-set" subjects, who were just told to try to remember as much as they could. Presumably the impression set induces perceivers to use various "person-relevant schemas" that help them organize and recall material better.

But schema-inconsistent material is not always poorly recalled. Sometimes it is remembered much better than things that are simply irrelevant to the schema (see Brewer, Dull, & Lui, 1981). This may be because it is difficult to learn material that does not fit neatly into a schema (Fiske & Taylor, 1984).

Speed of processing is often increased by a relevant schema. Markus (1977) contrasted subjects with self-schemas as being independent or as being dependent people with subjects who had neither schema. She then read them sentences about certain independent or dependent behaviors. People with self-schemas were able to indicate more quickly than those with none whether or not the behavior was typical of them. The Brewer et al. (1981) study of reactions to photographs of elderly and young women described earlier yielded similar results: Processing time was much longer for schema-inconsistent than consistent information. But not all research finds that schemas speed processing up. In some cases, evoking a schema slows things down by introducing a more complex mass of information (Taylor & Crocker, 1981).

As shown in Figure 4–1, recall was considerably greater for statements that were either clearly consistent or clearly inconsistent with the prototype the subjects had been given. When the statement neither fit nor violated the prototype, it was hardest to remember.

A schema can help us fill in missing information when there are gaps in our knowledge. If we read about a policeman but it says nothing

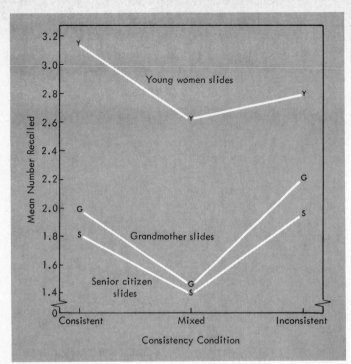

FIGURE 4–1
Recall of statements consistent or inconsistent with the prototype. The entry is mean number of correctly recalled statements. (From Brewer, Dull & Lui, 1981, p. 667.)

about his clothing, we imagine him to be wearing a blue uniform. We imagine a nurse to be warm and caring, and a queen to be rather aloof and haughty. Missing information is filled in by adding schema-consistent details, even when we must invent them. Schemas also help us interpret new information. For example, when a pediatrician diagnoses a child as having mumps, it enables her to make a whole series of other inferences with confidence: how the child got the disease, what symptoms should be present, what the course of the disease will be, what treatment is best, and so on. To a person with no schema for mumps, none of this would be possible. The problem would just seem mysterious. Schemas allow confident inferences about matters that would otherwise not be clear. Box 4–2 gives an example.

Schemas also provide normative expectations for what should happen. These expectations in turn can determine how pleasant or unpleasant we find a particular situation. Suppose an Anglo student with a fine record applies to medical school but is rejected and replaced

with a Hispanic student with an inferior record. This violates the Anglo student's expectations and is likely to make her quite angry. The same would apply to blacks who have worked hard to become educated but still are unable to find jobs at their level of expertise. This sense of deprivation relative to expectation has been cited as one of the causes of ghetto riots and other forms of social insurrection (Sears & McConahay, 1973).

Some Liabilities

All these advantages of schematic processing have their accompanying disadvantages. The tendencies to accept new information only if it fits a schema, to fill in gaps in thinking by adding elements that are schema-consistent, to apply schemas even when they do not fit very well, and to be unwilling to change schemas, all can be liabilities. We can easily be misled by oversimplifications. Structuring tends to make us

Ken Karp

A.T.&T. Co. Photo Center

A schema allows us to make sense of an otherwise bewildering situation.
What sense would these pictures make to someone who had never heard of
baseball? or of award ceremonies in Western civilization?

blind to inconsistencies; simplification leads easily to the problem of oversimplification; and abstraction can lead us away from concrete realities.

There are so many familiar examples of the dangers of stereotyping that it hardly seems necessary to labor the point. Everyone knows that people frequently behave in ways contrary to the stereotype generally held about their groups, so schematic processing can lead the perceiver to some dangerously false inferences about individual members of the group. (We

Learning from History

A number of writers have observed how political leaders often apply "the lessons of history" when arriving at decisions about foreign policy. The "lessons" they apply frequently turn out to be analogies from events that occurred in their formative years (Jervis, 1976). John F. Kennedy was very impressed during his years in college, in the late 1930s, by the British blunder of appeasing Hitler at Munich.

In 1938, British and French leaders held a highly publicized meeting with Adolf Hitler at Munich, Germany, to discuss his desire to expand the borders of Germany. They arranged a compromise with him that allowed the Germans to take over the Sudetenland, the region of Czechoslovakia closest to Germany. The British prime minister returned to London, triumphantly announcing that they had insured "peace in our time." In just a few short months, of course, Hitler invaded Poland and Belgium, not in the least bit satisfied by the territory he had been given at Munich.

The "lesson of Munich" was that dictators need to be confronted and stopped or they will continue to make inroads. Kennedy applied this "Munich schema" to the civil wars in Southeast Asia in the early 1960s, and came to the conclusion that America needed to stand up militarily to the Communists there, or other "dominos" would fall, just as they had in Europe after Munich. In contrast, a "Vietnam schema" has become common since the end of that war. It describes the dangers to the United States of becoming involved in faraway civil wars and nationalist, anti-imperialist revolutions in the Third World.

The power of such schemas to dictate preferences about current foreign policy is illustrated in an experiment by Gilovich (1981). He presented two hypothetical case studies of a small democratic country threatened by an aggressive, totalitarian neighbor. They differed only in having salient Munich-like, pre-World War II symbols as opposed to those associated with Vietnam. The first case study mentioned in passing Winston Churchill Hall, "blitzkrieg," boxcars, and FDR; the second case study mentioned Dean Rusk Hall, chinook helicopters, small boats, and LBJ. Otherwise the two cases were the same, and clearly hypothetical. Subjects given the irrelevant allusions to pre-World War II events were more likely to support intervention than were those given the Vietnam allusions. Exactly the same facts could be interpreted in two quite different ways, with very different implications, depending on whether the irrelevant cues had induced them to apply their Munich or their Vietnam schemas.

will discuss these issues in somewhat more detail in Chapters 12 and 13.)

Implicit personality theories can also lead to errors, since there is a strong tendency for people to infer from the presence of one trait the presence of others. Knowing someone is intelli-gent causes most people to expect the person also to be imaginative, clever, active, conscientious, deliberate, and reliable. Knowing someone is inconsiderate leads most people to expect him or her also to be irritable, boastful, cold, hypercritical, and so on. These inferences are not derived logically from the given trait; they are based on assumptions about personality. Intelligence does not necessarily denote activity, nor does inconsiderateness denote irritability. The tendency to make these assumptions is sometimes called the *logical error,* because people see certain traits as going together and assume that someone who has one of them also has the others.

The examples given earlier of "learning from the past" (see Box 4–2) illustrate some of the deficiencies of schematic processing. Applying "the lessons of Munich" may be quite inappropriate in Third World countries such as Lebanon, El Salvador, and Vietnam, where wars are caused by ancient tribal, religious, and class conflicts, and anticolonial nationalism. This "lesson of Munich" was that dictators are always trying to expand their territories, so free nations must stand up to them and not permit any expansion. This theory had by the early 1960s evolved into the very similar "domino theory" of Communist expansion, which held that communism was advancing around the globe, and every time one nation fell to communism, its neighbor became endangered. According to this theory, it was dangerous for us to allow even one nation to fall under Communist domination. As the conflict in Vietnam wore on, however, it became clearer and clearer that the war there was not a pure conflict between the free world and Communist expansionism.

It also involved the ancient desire of the Vietnamese to be free of any foreign domination, whether Chinese, French, or American. And it involved considerable hostility toward the corrupt political regime with which we had allied ourselves in South Vietnam. In later conflicts, the "lesson of Munich" has also prevented foreign policy decision-makers from seeing clearly the strength of longstanding religious rivalries in Lebanon, which made Russian-American conflicts almost incidental to the tremendous violence of the Lebanese civil war. In Central America, the "lesson of Munich" similarly blinds many Americans to the terrible inequality and corruption in some Central American nations, which has led to strongly supported local revolutionary movements. Whether or not the Russians and Americans were involved, those revolutions would have much local support.

So schematic processing has the advantage of speed and efficiency and of making events comprehensible and predictable. It has the disadvantage of leading to wrong interpretations, inaccurate expectations, and inflexible modes of response. But even this resistance to *dis*confirmation can sometimes prevent irrational and destructive change. If you have a strong schema about your star pitcher's ability and about the role of chance variations in baseball, you will not bench him just because he loses the first three games of the season. And if your schema for intense relationships includes occasional fights, you will not split up from your boyfriend just because you have a fight two nights in a row.

SUMMARY

1. The social cognition approach to social perception describes people as forming coherent, meaningful impressions that incorporate everything they know about the stimulus person.
2. Our attention is particularly drawn to perceptually salient stimuli, such as those that are bright, moving, novel, or unusual. Salient stimuli have a disproportionate influence over our impressions, and they can distract us from more valid information.
3. We tend automatically to categorize persons and their attributes. The categories usually reflect natural similarities in appearance.
4. Categorization eases the processing of complex social experiences but it can lead to oversimplified perceptions, such as in group stereotyping.

5. Cognitive structures called schemas help us organize information about the social world. Schemas make information processing more efficient and speedy, aid recall, fill in missing information, and provide normative expectations. However, they sometimes fill in erroneous information or lead us to reject good but inconsistent evidence. They sometimes result in biased impressions.

SUGGESTIONS FOR ADDITIONAL READINGS

BREWER, M. B. 1979. In-group bias in the minimal intergroup situation: A cognitive-motivational analysis. *Psychological Bulletin, 86,* 307–324. A carefully reasoned analysis of the cognitive approach to stereotyping.

FISKE, S. T., & TAYLOR, S. E. 1984. *Social Cognition.* Reading, Mass.: Addison-Wesley. An up-to-date, extremely thorough treatment of all the research on social cognition.

MCARTHUR, L. Z., & POST, D. L. 1977. Figural emphasis and person perception. *Journal of Experimental Social Psychology, 13,* 520–535. A clever demonstration of the importance of salience in person perception.

NEWTSON, D. 1976. Foundations of attribution: The perception of ongoing behavior. In J. H. Harvey, W. J. Ickes, & R. F. Kidd (Eds.), *New Directions in Attribution Research, Vol. 1.* Hillsdale, N.J.: Erlbaum. A clearly presented description of an ingenious research program documenting how people perceive the stream of behavior in the world around them.

NISBETT, R., & ROSS, L. 1980. *Human inference: Strategies and shortcomings of social judgment.* Englewood Cliffs, N.J.: Prentice-Hall. An elegant and outspoken treatment of social cognition, especially cognitive biases in person perception.

TAYLOR, S. E., & FISKE, S. T. 1978. Salience, attention, and attribution: Top of the head phenomena. In Berkowitz, L. (Ed.), *Advances in Experimental Social Psychology, Vol. 11.* New York: Academic Press, pp. 249–88. The many ways in which salience affects person perception.

5

ATTRIBUTION

Imagine you are standing on a curb on a rainy day and a car whips past you, splashing dirty water from the gutter all over you. You might explain the driver's behavior in one of two ways. He could have been driving in the lane close to the curb because traffic was heavy and he had no choice. If so, you might feel forgiving and do nothing. Or he might have been doing it because he gets a kick out of splashing pedestrians. Then you would be likely to feel angry and want to retaliate against the driver. You might shout or wave a fist.

How do we form judgments about internal states in other people that we might need to know about, such as motives, personality, emotions, and attitudes? We do not have direct information about such internal states. We only have access to limited external cues such as facial expressions, gestures, what the person says about his or her internal state, what we remember about his or her behavior in the past, and so forth. So we must make such inferences on the basis of the indirect information given by external cues.

Making inferences about internal states is part of a more general process of explaining the behavior of other people and of ourselves, which is called making causal **attributions.** This is the process by which people arrive at causal explanations for events in the social world, particularly for actions they and other people perform. When someone says something that hurts our feelings, we ask ourselves why it happened. Sometimes we conclude it was caused by some relatively permanent internal state, such as the person's having a long-standing grudge against us. We might decide it was due to temporary in-

ternal states, such as having a stomach ache or being in a bad mood. Or perhaps it was due to external pressures, such as trying to show off in front of fraternity brothers. But whatever our explanation for the behavior, we must infer it from a few external cues; we do not have direct access to the true cause.

Causal attributions in turn determine our own feelings, attitudes, and behavior. According to

Expectations about the future are often very important and are influenced by our attributions about past events.

Weiner (1982), for example, anger usually results when something negative happens to us, and we perceive it as being under someone else's control. That is the case if we assume the driver could have been driving further from the gutter. We feel angry if the driver could have avoided splashing us, but not if it was the only lane and there was no choice.

Pity arises when a negative event happens to someone else and no one could have controlled it. You feel pity for a cerebral palsy victim; no one could have prevented the handicap. Pride results from perceiving one's own efforts as the cause for a success. You feel pride when you work on a term paper and get an A. But if the professor gives an A to every paper, even some poor ones, you will no longer feel that pride.

Our expectations about the future are influenced by our attributions for past events. We are likely to expect future successes if we attribute our past successes to ability (Weiner, 1979). If we attribute our As in high school English to a natural talent for literary analysis, we will be more optimistic about similar successes in our college career. But if we attribute these past As

to teachers who were easy graders, we are not likely to expect such high grades later on. Dweck (1975) has shown that training children to make internal attributions for their behavior—training them, for example, to explain successes and failures as resulting from the amount of effort they put forth—can make them work harder in the future.

Our attributions for events in the political arena can also influence our political attitudes. Feldman (1983) has shown that blaming blacks' poverty on discrimination and other failures of environment is associated with support for special government aid to blacks. Blaming their poverty on laziness and unwillingness to get appropriate job training is associated with opposition to government aid.

In these and numerous other ways, our understanding of the causes of behavior are crucial mediators of our reactions to the social world. Our reactions to other people—liking, aggression, helping, conformity, and so on—frequently depend on our interpretation of their behavior. So causal attributions have become a major focus of research.

BASIC PRINCIPLES

Although there are different approaches to the attribution process, they rest on a common set of basic principles called *attribution theory*. These concern the entire process of making causal attributions: what motivates people to generate causal explanations, how they decide which particular cause is most important, and the biases in attributional processes that prevent people from arriving at accurate causal explanations. Let us start by considering the most basic of these attributional principles.

Heider's Naive Psychology

Theorizing about attributions began with Fritz Heider (1958). He was interested in how peo-

ple in everyday life figure out what causes what. Like most in the cognitive tradition in social psychology, he proposed two strong motives in all human beings: the need to form a coherent understanding of the world, and the need to control the environment.

One of the essentials for satisfying these motives is the ability to predict how people are going to behave. If we cannot predict how others will behave, we will view the world as random, surprising, and incoherent. We would not know whether to expect reward or punishment for our work performance, a kiss or punch in the jaw from a friend.

Similarly, to have a satisfactory level of control of our environment, we must be able to predict others' behavior. To avoid an accident, we need to be able to predict that the big truck will not suddenly make a U turn into our front bumper. To control our diet, we need to be able to count on getting a club sandwich when we order it in a restaurant, rather than suddenly being presented with an entire roast pig.

To be able to predict how others are going to behave, we need some elementary theory of human behavior. Heider proposed that everyone, not just psychologists, searches for explanations for other people's behavior. He called the result a **naive psychology**—that is, a general theory of human behavior held by each ordinary person.

Dimensions of Causality

LOCUS OF CAUSALITY   The central issue in most perceptions of causality is whether to attribute a given act to *internal* states or to *external* forces. That is, what is the "locus of causality"? You have asked the young woman who sits next to you in lecture to go out to a movie this weekend, but she has said she is busy. What is the "real" cause of her refusal? It could be due to some internal state, such as her lack of attraction to you or her interest in doing something else. Or it could be due to some external factor, such as that she really does have some other obligation. *Internal attributions* include all causes internal to the person, such as moods, attitudes, personality traits, abilities, health, preferences, or wishes. *External attributions* would include all causes external to the person, such as pressure from others, money, the nature of the social situation, the weather, and so on. So is this young woman really busy (an external attribution), or has she just decided that she is not interested in dating you (an internal attribution)?

A student who is failing a course wants to know whether it is because she is not smart enough or doesn't work hard enough (internal causality), or because the professor's lectures are ambiguous, the text is too difficult, or the tests are unfair (external causality). Debates rage in school board meetings, academic conventions, courtrooms, and legislative halls about whether black children do less well in school than white children because of inferior native endowment or low motivation (internal causality) or because of racial discrimination, insensitive middle-class white teachers, inferior facilities, and unstimulating peer groups (external causality).

So the major question is whether to make an external or an internal attribution for the stimulus person's behavior. External attributions ascribe causality to anything external to that person, such as the general environment, some other person being interacted with, role constraints, possible rewards or punishments, luck, the specific nature of the task, and so on. Internal causes include personality traits, motives, emotions, moods, attitudes, abilities, and effort.

STABILITY OR INSTABILITY   A second dimension of causality is whether the cause is *stable* or *unstable*. That is, we need to know whether or not the cause is a relatively permanent feature of that external environment or of the internal dispositions of the person. Some external causes are quite stable, such as rules and laws (the prohibition against running a red light, or against breaking the throwing arm of an overly successful opposing quarterback), occupational roles (professors are called upon to give lectures year in and year out), or the difficulty level of certain tasks (it is always hard to hit a curveball, and always easy to get our daughter to laugh by tickling her).

Some external causes are quite unstable: the weather has a lot of influence over whether we spend Saturday out shopping or at home reading, but the weather varies a lot. Sometimes Fernando Valenzuela gets every pitch where he wants it, and sometimes his control is not so good and his pitches go where they are easier to hit. So the batters' success is controlled by an unstable, external cause. Certain jobs vary a good bit in the external demands they place on the jobholder. Being a general places quite different external forces on a person in wartime than in peacetime, and even quite different demands depending on the sector of combat.

Internal causes can also be stable or unstable. Woody Allen almost always has a genius for making funny remarks; his talent for humor is quite stable. On the other hand, Hamlet is famous for his lack of stable resolve about what to do with his stepfather. Some baseball players are legendary for going on hot streaks and then becoming enmired in terrible slumps; on the average they are quite talented, but the talent seems quite unstable.

In other words, causes can consist of any combination of these two dimensions. An illustration is Weiner's typology for simple achievement tasks, shown in Table 5–1. A student's success or failure at a particular task could be attributed to one or more of four possible causes: ability, effort, luck, and task difficulty. And these causes fall quite neatly into the four categories, as the table shows.

CONTROLLABILITY   A third general dimension of attributions is *controllability,* according to Weiner (1982). We perceive some causes as within the individual's control and others as beyond their control. Perceived controllability or uncontrollability can coexist with any combination of locus of control and stability. For example, an unstable internal cause like effort is generally seen as controllable; a student can try to work hard, or can decide not to. A stable internal cause like ability is less often perceived as within the person's control. A "born genius" or

How might many observers explain the successes of these two students?

someone who is "gifted" with "native talent" is assumed not to control that ability. Sometimes, though, ability is perceived as controllable. Some highly successful people are perceived as having developed their abilities through long and patient hard work. Similarly, luck is sometimes seen as controllable—"she makes her breaks"—though more often as uncontrollable. In short, it is easy to think of virtually any combination of the three basic dimensions of causal attribution.

These three are the most logical dimensions of causal attribution. They also seem to be the ones people use most frequently in explaining outcomes. Studies asking college students to account for others' exam performances, or for their own high school achievement experiences, show that causal explanations tend to rest on these underlying dimensions (according to factor analyses conducted by Meyer, 1980, and Meyer & Koebl, 1982).

Table 5–1
Classification Scheme for the Perceived Causes of Achievement Behavior

| | LOCUS OF CONTROL | |
STABILITY	INTERNAL	EXTERNAL
Stable	Ability	Task difficulty
Unstable	Effort	Luck

Source: Weiner (1974), p. 6.

When Are Attributions Made?

When do people engage in this process of asking "why?" Though human beings are supposedly a curious species, they do not go around asking why about everything that happens. They do not wake up in the morning and ask why the sun comes up, why the boxer on TV is wearing gloves, or why the bus they are riding in is still stopped while the red light has changed to green. Most natural events and human acts probably do not inspire much cognitive effort to search out the correct causal attribution. As we saw in the last chapter, human beings tend to be miserly with their cognitive resources; they take many shortcuts and avoid cognitive work in a wide and creative variety of ways. What are the conditions under which we do undertake the search for causes?

People tend to be especially curious about causality when something unexpected or unusual happens. Explanations for the sun's and moon's movements are sought more around the time of an eclipse than normally. Newspaper readers, government officials, and social scientists want answers when there is a sudden, unexpected outburst of racial violence or student unrest than when things are humming along as usual. Lau and Russell (1980) found that unexpected outcomes of World Series and college and professional football games relative to pre-game gambling odds generated considerably more causal explanation per inch of newsprint in the sports columns than did expected outcomes. Journalists focused on attributions most when a big favorite was upset, or won only narrowly.

Bad, painful, unpleasant events also inspire a search for causal attributions. Taylor found (1982) that 95 percent of her sample of cancer victims made attributions about the cause of the disease. Among their family members, for whom the disease was presumably less painful, only 70 percent did so. Bulman and Wortman (1977) poignantly document the efforts of paraplegics crippled by spinal cord injuries to analyze why it happened to them. Most of the injuries were the result of unavoidable accidents, but still the victims wanted some more definite explanation. The assassination of John F. Kennedy inspired not only the Warren Commission's official explanatory effort, but a number of amateur investigations. In intimate relationships, conflict triggers both partners to search for the causes of the problem (and often to exchange competing explanations; see Orvis, Kelley, & Butler, 1976).

Both the unpleasantness and the unexpectedness of an event work independently to motivate the search for attributions. Wong and Weiner (1981) have shown that people are most likely to ask why an event happened when it is both negative and unexpected. They gave subjects four hypothetical situations depicting expectedly or unexpectedly passing or failing a midterm test, and then asked: "What questions, if any, would you ask yourself?" Questions about the causes of the outcome ("Why did this happen?") were most common with unexpected failure.

Two Simple Principles

How do we arrive at attributions? Attribution theory begins with two simple principles: the principle of covariation and the discounting principle. According to Heider, the principle of **covariation** means that we tend to look for an association between a particular effect and a particular cause across a number of different conditions. If a given cause is always associated with a particular effect in many different situations, *and* if the effect does not occur in the absence of that cause, we attribute the effect to that cause. The cause always covaries with the effect; whenever the cause is present, so is the effect; and whenever the cause is absent, so is the effect. Suppose your roommate gets grouchy and complains about everything right before exams, but is quite pleasant the rest of the time. Do we conclude that she is a grouch in general—that is, that she has a generally grouchy personality? Probably not. Instead, we would attribute her complaints to the tensions associated with exams, rather than to her being generally a short-tempered person. Her grouchiness is almost always associated with exams and does not occur in the absence of exams, so we attribute it to exams, not to her personality.

This principle of covariation is, of course, exactly the same as the scientific method scientists use. A scientist also arrives at a judgment of causality by seeing that a particular factor is associated with a particular effect across a number of different conditions. If scientists find, for example, that objects invariably fall from higher elevations to lower elevations, no matter whether they are feathers or cannonballs, no matter whether they dropped from the top of a building or waist height, they conclude there is a general causal factor—namely, gravity. As naive psychologists, ordinary people observe the behavior of others and look for regular, invariant effects that follow a particular stimulus. In that way, they arrive at an attribution.

The other main principle in making causal attributions is what Kelley calls the **discounting principle:** "the role of a given cause in producing a given effect is discounted if other plausible causes are also present" (1972, p. 8). That is, we make less confident attributions, and are less likely to attribute the effect to any particular cause, if more than one cause is likely. An insurance salesperson is very nice to us and offers us coffee, but we may not be able to make a confident attribution about why he or she is so friendly. We could attribute the behavior to a real liking for us. More likely, we may discount that possible cause and attribute the behavior partly to the salesperson's wanting our business. On the other hand, if the person knows we have no money to buy insurance we may not do any such discounting, because the desire for business is no longer a plausible cause.

ATTRIBUTIONS ABOUT OTHERS

These theoretical principles are usually applied to attributions about the behavior of other people. The most important question is this: When do we infer that others' actions reflect real dispositions, such as traits, attitudes, moods, or other internal states? When do we assume that others are simply responding to the external situation? Or, putting the contrast the way it is normally put, when do we make a *dispositional* as opposed to a *situational* attribution?

We know that people do not always say or do what they really believe. A prisoner of war may say things contrary to his real attitudes. Or a boy may try to act cheerful and happy in school the morning after his girlfriend has jilted him. On the other hand, sometimes a POW expresses real, heartfelt criticism of his own nation's war effort. This certainly happened in Vietnam with some American soldiers and airmen. And the boy may have some genuine sense of relief if the affair had been depressing him for a long time. So how can we tell when a person's actions are a true reflection of their internal attitudes or other dispositions?

The discounting principle suggests that we would first consider whether or not any plausible external forces might have led the person to misstate his or her true attitude. For example, was someone holding a gun to the person's head? If so, an external attribution might be made. In the absence of such plausible external forces, however, external causes would be discounted, and an internal attribution would be made: The person must really hold the attitude he says he does.

A number of studies have shown that the discounting principle operates when perceivers are trying to determine another person's true attitude. Jones and Harris (1967) presented subjects with essays written by other students, in four conditions: The essays supported Fidel Castro or opposed him and were supposedly written on an assigned side or with free choice of position.

With the free choice conditions, observers readily inferred that the writer's expressed opinion was the same as his or her true underlying attitude. The pro-Castro and anti-Castro speeches were seen as reflecting underlying pro- and anti-Castro attitudes, respectively. The subjects discounted the possibility of external causality, given the presence of free choice. Data from their two very similar experiments are shown in Table 5–2.

On the other hand, when the writer was described as having no choice of position (strong external forces), observers still generally felt the written position reflected the underlying attitude, but they were less sure that this was so.

In other words, the discounting principle suggests that we typically give some weight to external forces when they are evident. In this Jones and Harris study, observers were more likely to make an external attribution for attitudes toward Fidel Castro expressed in an essay when the writer had no choice about what position to write. Observers apparently partially discounted the possibility of an internal attribution (that the writer actually believed the position taken in the essay), given clear external pressure.

Table 5–2 Attitude Attributed to Writer		
	SPEECH DIRECTION	
CONDITION	PRO CASTRO	ANTI CASTRO
Experiment 1		
Choice	59.6[a]	17.4
No choice	44.1	22.9
Experiment 2		
Choice	55.7	22.9
No choice	41.3	23.7

[a]A high score indicates a pro-Castro position attributed to the writer.

Source: Jones and Harris (1967), pp. 6, 10.

A second factor is our *expectancy* about the individual's true underlying attitudes, based on any information we might have about the person. Usually we know more about the person than just this one statement of attitude. We might have heard the person speaking about this issue before, or we might have heard him or her speaking about other related issues. Either kind of additional information might give us some expectations that help us make a confident attribution in the current case. We know our friend has long been a supporter of black liberation movements in South Africa. So when we have dinner with her parents and see her nodding agreeably at her parents' conservative statements, we nevertheless infer that she is a strong supporter of the movement and make an external attribution for her nodding. We have past information about her attitudes on this issue that gives us an expectancy about what she really believes. We use that information, along with our perception of her current overt behavior (which seems to be somewhat anti-movement) and the external forces (she does not want to get into an argument with her parents), to give us a confident attribution.

In general, as this example suggests, we are likely to make more of an external attribution when people depart from a customary pattern of behavior. Kulik (1983), for example, had subjects watch videotapes of male students in conversation in two different settings. The students behaved in a consistently extroverted, consistently introverted, or inconsistent manner in the two episodes. The subjects were most likely to make a situational attribution for the second episode when it was inconsistent with the first episode.

Kulik calls this a "confirmatory attribution": People adopt attributions that confirm whatever prior expectation or schema they have about others. If people act in a way consistent with our prior schemas about them, we believe the behavior is dispositionally caused. If they behave in a new and different way, we believe it is situationally caused. This need to confirm a prior schema is strong enough that it occurred even in this study, when the schema was based on nothing more than a very brief videotaped exposure to the person (see also Crocker et al., 1983).

A second general source of expectancies about others' attitudes comes from our knowledge of their attitudes on other issues. Even if we had never heard our friend talk about black liberation movements in South Africa, we might have a pretty clear expectation about how she feels based on conversations about other topics, such as revolutions in Central America, special admissions for minorities, and so on.

To test this, Jones and associates (1971) did an experiment much like the earlier Jones-Harris study, but this time directly varying additional information about attitudes on other issues held by the essay writer. The writer again either had or did not have free choice about the position taken in the essay. As in the Jones and Harris study, choice led to more confident internal attributions. When the position taken in the essay was expected from the writer's other attitudes, the observers made confident internal attributions, even when the writer had had no choice of position. Put another way, observers felt that overt behavior corresponded to a true underlying attitude (1) when there were no obvious external forces (the free choice condition), *or* (2) when the overt position was consistent with expectancies about the writer's overall sociopolitical attitudes, even given strong external forces.

In general, then, observers do attribute overt behavior to internal dispositions in the absence of clear external forces, or when they have other information about past behavior that allows them to discount the role of the external forces.

ATTRIBUTIONS ABOUT THE SELF

One of the most interesting hypotheses in attribution theory is that people arrive at perceptions of their own internal states in the same way as they arrive at perceptions of others' states. This idea derives from the general assumption that our own emotions, attitudes, traits, and abilities are often unclear and ambiguous to us. We have to *infer* them from our own overt behavior and from our perceptions of the environmental forces surrounding us.

The approach suggests that in self-perception, just as in the perception of others, we search for invariant associations of causes and effects and use the discounting principle to divide up responsibility about various plausible causes. If we perceive strong external forces pushing us in the direction of our own behavior, we are more likely to come to a situational attribution. In the absence of clear external forces, we assume that a dispositional attribution is more correct. This approach has generated a good deal of research on the self-perception of attitudes, motivation, and emotion.

Attitudes

Psychologists have long assumed that people figure out their own attitudes by *introspection*, by reviewing the various cognitions and feelings in their consciousness. Bem (1967) argued instead that we receive only minimal and ambiguous internal cues to our attitudes, just as we have no direct access to the internal cues in others. If so, we must infer our own attitudes by observing our own overt behavior. When we observe our own behavior in a situation with no strong external forces, we assume we are simply expressing our own true attitudes and make an internal attribution. In contrast, when there are strong external pressures on us to do something (such as having been assigned a particular position in a debate), we perceive our statements to be externally caused.

In other words, we learn about our own attitudes by observing how we behave in environments with different external pressures in them, not by introspecting to see how we feel. Bem does not hold that people never use internal evidence, just that to a surprising degree people rely on the external evidence of their overt behavior, and the conditions under which it occurs, to infer their own true attitudes.

To test Bem's self-perception theory, we would need to manipulate an individual's perception of his behavior while holding other factors constant (such as the actual behavior and the pressure of the environment). Then we could determine whether the person's perception of his own behavior determined his perception of his own attitudes. To test this, Salancik and Conway (1975) cleverly manipulated subjects' descriptions of their own religious behavior: Some were asked if they "occasionally" read a religious newspaper or magazine, attended a church or synagogue, or consulted a minister about personal problems. Many students had engaged in at least these minimal religious acts, so students in this condition reported lots of religious behavior. Others were asked if they "frequently" did each of these things. Since most college students do not do them "frequently," students in this condition reported very little religious behavior.

Since the two groups were randomly selected, they were presumably in fact almost exactly the same in actual behavior. But because of these differences in the wording of the questions, the first group of subjects described themselves as engaging in quite a variety of religious behaviors, while the second group described few religious acts. And sure enough, when later asked about their own overall religious attitudes in the form of the question "How religious are you?" the first group, which had been induced to describe themselves as engaging in more religious behaviors, said they were more religious in general.

Motivation

A similar idea has been applied to the self-perception of motivation. The idea is that performing a task for high rewards will lead to an external attribution—I did it because I was paid so well for it. Performing the same task for minimal reward will lead to an internal attribution—I couldn't have done it for that small amount of money I got, so I must have done it because I really enjoyed it. This leads to the paradoxical prediction that minimal rewards will lead to the greatest intrinsic interest in a task because the person attributes performance to intrinsic interest, not to extrinsic reward. Put another way, **overjustification** for engaging in an activity undermines intrinsic interest in the activity.

The earliest demonstration of overjustification varied whether or not nursery school children were given awards for engaging in a task (playing with felt-tip pens) which they enjoyed doing anyway (Lepper, Greene, & Nisbett, 1973). Some children were told they would get a "Good Player Award" with a gold star and ribbon if they would draw pictures with a felt-tip pen for a few minutes. Other children were not told about any award. All the children then did the drawing, and the first group was given their awards. A few days later, all the children were observed in a free-play situation with felt-tip pens provided. The children who had been given the awards spent half as much time drawing as the no-award children did. Their intrinsic interest in drawing had been undermined by the extrinsic reward.

This finding has been repeated in many contexts since then. Kunda and Schwartz (1983), for example, asked subjects to help record material for a blind student for payment or without payment. Later they were asked how morally obligated they would feel to help others in a number of ways, including reading school work to a blind student. Those given no money felt significantly more obligated.

If extrinsic rewards for engaging in pleasurable tasks reduce intrinsic interest, then external threats that prevent engaging in specific behaviors ought to increase interest. For example, the stricter the penalty for using an illegal drug, the more attractive the drug should seem to be. Here people attribute their avoidance of the activity to the threat, not the unpleasantness of the activity itself. Wilson and Lassiter (1982) found some evidence for this hypothesis, when they varied threatened punishment for cheating.

The same reasoning would also suggest that the overjustification effect would be increased when external rewards are made more salient (Ross, 1975) and decreased when the real initial interest in the activity is made more salient. In an experiment to test this latter point, Fazio (1981) had children play with magic markers, and then later varied whether or not they were shown photos of themselves engaging in this highly pleasurable task on the earlier occasion. Otherwise the experiment closely resembled the Lepper et al. (1973) study described above. For the children shown those photos of their earlier play, initial intrinsic interest in playing with the magic markers was highly salient, so extrinsic rewards had little undermining effect. They knew they had really enjoyed the magic markers, so they attributed their later play to their own pleasure, not to the reward.

The implications of this research are important. Rewards can sometimes backfire: Instead of encouraging people, they can actually turn them away from activities they would otherwise enjoy. And punishments may make a forbidden activity seem all the more attractive, though there is less evidence on this point.

Emotions

Traditional theorists of emotion proposed that we recognize what we feel by considering our physiological state, our mental state, and the external stimulus causing these states. But recent evidence indicates that many emotional reactions are biochemically similar. We can distinguish high arousal from low arousal, but not various types of emotion. For example, it is hard to tell the difference between intense jealousy and intense love. So we need other information to identify our own emotions.

Stanley Schachter (1962) has taken a self-perception approach to emotion. He suggests that perceptions of our emotions depend on (1) the degree of physiological arousal we experience and (2) the cognitive label that we apply, such as "angry" or "happy." To arrive at a cognitive label, we review our own behavior and the situation. If we feel physiologically aroused and are laughing at a comedy show on television, we might infer that we are happy. If we are snarling at someone for shoving us on a

Courtesy of Special Olympics

The participation of these handicapped youngsters in the Special Olympics clearly evokes strong emotions in both the participants and spectators. What do you think the dominant emotions are? How do you think they are influenced by the perceived causes of these youngsters' behavior?

crowded street, we might infer that we are angry. In each case, our behavior and our interpretation of the situation provide us with the cognitive label that allows us to interpret our internal experience of emotional arousal. Like Bem's theory of self-perception, this point of view again emphasizes the ambiguity of internal states, and therefore that self-perception is highly dependent on perceptions of overt behavior and of the external environment.

LABELING AROUSAL Schachter and his colleagues conducted a number of studies based on the idea that high degrees of physiological arousal give rise to a search for an appropriate attribution. If a plausible attribution exists for the arousal, it will be accepted. If no such attribution exists, the person will search the environment for something that could have caused the arousal. Whatever the environment provides as an explanation will also provide the label for the emotion.

If you suddenly felt yourself to be very physiologically excited but did not know why, you would do a quick search to try to discover the cause. If you suddenly remembered that someone had just insulted you, you might label your arousal as anger at that person, and explain it that way. Although this sounds very conscious and deliberate, it all probably happens in a flash, so that we may not even be aware of going through this process. The key ideas, then, are that arousal is undifferentiated and leads to a search for explanation, that we frequently adopt whatever explanation the environment offers most readily, and that we use that explanation to provide a specific label for our emotion.

In the first of these experiments, Schachter and Singer (1962) gave subjects an arousing drug, epinephrine, which produces physiological arousal generally associated with emotions. Some of these subjects were told that the drug would produce a noticeable physiological arousal, such as more rapid heartbeats, and others were not. Some of the aroused people could thus attribute their internal state to the drug,

whereas others had no ready explanation. All subjects were then placed in a situation in which a confederate of the experimenter pretended to be experiencing a particular emotion. Half the subjects were exposed to someone behaving in a euphoric, elated way; he made paper planes and flew them around; started a small game of basketball using crumpled papers and an old wastebasket; sang, danced, hopped around, and in general presented a zany, lightheaded attitude. The other half were exposed to an angry confederate who made nasty remarks, had an unpleasant expression on his face, muttered to himself, and generally presented a disgruntled, annoyed impression.

Those who had been aroused by the drug and had not been informed of this (the "no-explanation" condition in Table 5–3) became more euphoric in the euphoria condition and more angry in the anger condition than the other subjects. When they were aroused without any plausible cause, the subjects presumably interpreted their arousal as being caused by the situation. What was the nature of that situation? Perhaps the clearest clues to that lay in the confederate's behavior. If he behaved in a euphoric manner, it must be a situation generating euphoria. If he behaved angrily, it must be one generating anger. Consistent with this logic, the "no-explanation" subjects tended to act happy when the confederate was euphoric, and angry when he was angry.

But when aroused subjects could attribute their arousal to the drug (in the "informed" condition), they were relatively unaffected by the other person's behavior. They knew their physiological state was due to the drug and therefore did not interpret it as emotional arousal. The procedure and results of this experiment are shown in Table 5–3.

The key element here is that when subjects were both aroused and placed in a situation with no other attribution (the "no-explanation" condition), they "caught" the salient emotion from the external situation. That is, in the absence of any alternative, they attributed their arousal to the situation's capacity for producing

Table 5–3
The Schachter-Singer Experiment

| | SEQUENCE | | | | |
| | STEP 1 | STEP 2 | STEP 3 | STEP 4 PRESUMED ATTRIBUTION FOR OWN AROUSAL (UNMEASURED) | STEP 5 OWN BEHAVIOR (MEASURED) |
CONDITION	GIVEN AROUSING DRUG	TOLD IT WOULD BE AROUSING	CONFEDERATE'S BEHAVIOR		
No explanation	Yes	No	⎧ Euphoric or angry ⎫ in all cases ⎩ ⎭	Situational	Euphoric or angry
Informed	Yes	Yes		Drug	Calm
No arousal	No	No		None	Calm

Source: Adapted from Schachter and Singer (1962).

either euphoria or anger and they acted in a more euphoric or angry way. In the "informed" condition, where arousal was explicitly attributed to the drug, no such emotion was experienced. Nor was it in a control condition with no arousing drug provided.

What was important for the experience of emotion was first of all the *arousal*, and second the *cognitive label* or the attribution made for the arousal. When the experimenter provided a label attributing the arousal to the drug, the subjects acted as if they experienced no particular emotion. When they did not know the drug was responsible for their arousal, they took their cues about the emotions from the external environment.

One implication of this reasoning is that internal arousal states are so ambiguous that they can be attributed to any plausible stimulus. Whichever emotion is experienced therefore depends more on available plausible causes than it does on the nature of the actual internal sensations. Even fake internal sensations should be sufficient, given an external cause that can supply a plausible label. Valins (1966) tested this idea by giving random false feedback to subjects about their own arousal.

He presented heterosexual male subjects with slides of nude females and after each slide provided faked feedback through earphones to the subject about his own heart rate. After some

slides, subjects heard increased heartbeats, which they thought were their own; after others, they heard decreased heartbeats; and after still others, they heard what they thought were irrelevant sounds. Valins found that subjects rated the nudes accompanied by the supposedly changed heartbeat as the most attractive.

After the experiment was over, subjects were allowed to take some slides home. They mostly took slides that had been associated with the fake feedback about changed heartbeat. Presumably they had searched the environment for a plausible cause for the change in their heartbeats, found the slides of the nude females to be a reasonable cause, and therefore labeled their arousal as sexual. This was evidence that people infer their own emotions from the perception of arousal (in this case, faked changes in heartbeat) and a plausible external cause (in this case, pictures of nudes).

Another example illustrates how readily people ignore real internal cues when there is a plausible external cause. Cantor, Zillman, and Bryant (1975) had heterosexual male subjects ride an exercycle vigorously enough to reach a high level of physiological arousal. Physiological arousal based on this kind of exercise tends to last longer than the person realizes. A few minutes later, the subjects no longer felt aroused, but objective indicators of arousal showed they were. Female nudes shown at this point were rated as more attractive than those rated immediately after the exercise (when they presumably attributed their arousal to the exercise) or at a still later point (when there was no remaining arousal to be wrongly attributed to the nudes).

MISATTRIBUTION   In the "informed" condition of the Schachter-Singer experiment (Table 5–3), subjects evidently agreed with the experimenter that the pill was a plausible cause of their arousal. They reacted as if the pill, not the situation, had influenced them. Nisbett & Schachter (1966) extended this reasoning. They proposed that if people could be induced to attribute arousal to a drug that had really caused it, perhaps they could also be persuaded to misattribute arousal caused by the environment to a neutral pill.

To do this, they gave all subjects an ordinary sugar pill. Experimental subjects were told the pill would produce physiological symptoms, such as hand tremors and palpitations; control subjects were told it would produce only nonphysiological symptoms. Finally, all subjects were administered painful electric shock. The hypothesis was that the experimental subjects would attribute their physiological reactions after the shock to the pill rather than to the shock itself, and so would think the shock would hurt less. The control subjects, having no basis for an attribution to the pill, would blame their reactions on the shock itself. And indeed it was found that these control subjects found the shock more painful than did the experimental subjects. A number of these **misattribution** studies have been done, and they generally share the same basic idea: If people can be persuaded

---

BOX 5–1
A Pretty Day Can Make for a Happy Life

People can base self-perceptions about enduring internal states on temporary moods. Schwarz and Clore (1983) showed that people evaluated their lives as a whole as more happy and satisfying on sunny days than on rainy days. Using telephone interviews, they asked people: "What we are interested in is people's moods. . . . could you just answer four brief questions? First, on a scale of 1 to 10, with 10 being the happiest, how do you feel about your life as a whole? . . . All things considered, how satisfied or dissatisfied are you with your life as a whole these days? And, how happy do you feel at this moment?" Half the respondents were called on sunny spring days, and half on rainy spring days. The higher the number, the happier they said they were. As the table shows, they were happier at the moment on sunny days, and evaluated their "lives as a whole" as happier and more satisfying. Their momentary mood influenced their self-perception of stable internal states.

	WEATHER	
	SUNNY	RAINY
Happiness of mood at moment	7.5	5.4
Happiness of life as a whole	7.4	5.0
Satisfaction with life as a whole	6.6	4.9

Source: Adapted from Schwarz and Clore (1983), pp. 519–520.

---

to misattribute their negative emotional states from the real external causes to some other, more neutral cause, the level of emotional distress associated with the real external cause will diminish.

SOME LIMITATIONS   The most extreme forms of this self-perception viewpoint would seem to argue that we get almost no information about our own attitudes and emotions by introspection; outside observers know as much about our own internal feelings as we do. This is almost surely too extreme.

First of all, this self-perception process works mainly when there is a good bit of ambiguity or uncertainty about our internal states. People do have attitudes that endure and are not based entirely on current behavior. They do not decide about whether or not they like steak on the basis of whether or not they have recently eaten steak. They have real feelings toward steak and it is those feelings that determine their responses. Israelis have certain attitudes about Nazis, and bigots have certain attitudes about minorities, which they are quite clear about regardless of their most recent behavior. When we are slapped in the face, we do not have to wait to see if we strike back to know if we are angry. When our boyfriend says he no longer loves us, we know we feel hurt no matter whether tears come or not.

If a male subject is shown a whole series of beautiful nude females, it may be fairly easy to alter his preferences among them based on false feedback. But it strikes us as unlikely that the same subject, shown a nude Miss July and a nude hippopotamus and given false feedback that his heartbeat had accelerated more for the hippo, will seriously think he desires the hippo and will want to take her slide home.

A second limitation is that this self-perception process seems to work best when people do not care very much about what response they make. When it really matters, people seem to monitor their own attitudes and emotions more carefully, and are less influenced by external cues. To test this idea, Taylor (1975) ran an experiment like the Valins nude-slides study—except that this time *female* college students were presented with pictures of full-face color photographs of clothed *male* graduate students. She first had each of the women rate these pictures for attractiveness. Then the subject was given false feedback about her physiological reactions to one of the slides by overhearing a confederate saying that she (the subject) had reacted more strongly to that slide than to any other slide. Half the time this false feedback concerned a slide the subject had already rated as highly attractive, and half the time it concerned a slide of a man the subject had rated as only medium in attractiveness. According to the self-perception idea, this false high-arousal feedback ought to boost ratings of the attractiveness of the slides linked to false feedback.

False feedback changed initial attitudes significantly only when no future meeting was expected; that is, when the ratings were not very important. In general, people probably use external cues to determine their own attitudes most often under conditions of low involvement. When the subjects actually expected they might meet the stimulus person, they evidently paid closer attention to their own true feelings and were not much influenced by the false feedback.

When these "misattribution" or "reattribution" studies were first done, they gave some promise of providing a new therapeutic tool for dealing with disruptive anxieties, fears, depressions, low self-esteem, and other seemingly neurotic emotions. A variety of other studies have tried to apply reattribution therapies to public speaking anxiety, test anxiety, depression, and other unwanted emotions (Storms & Nisbett, 1970, Valins & Ray, 1967). The general technique was to try to get the person to reattribute anxieties to less threatening sources. However, the effects have been short-lived, unreliable, limited to weak anxieties, or so slight as to be unimportant (see Fiske & Taylor, 1984; Harvey & Weary, 1981, for reviews). So the technique is probably not powerful enough for therapeutic purposes.

THE NAIVE SCIENTIST

By and large, research findings do seem to follow the pattern described by the covariation and discounting principles. People do seem to review what information they have about their own behavior, or the behavior of others, and attribute it to internal or external causes, depending on the information available. If there is strong evidence of internal dispositions, an internal attribution is made. If there is evidence of no internal causes or just weak ones, with evidence of strong external forces, an external attribution is made.

Harold Kelley has generated the most formal and comprehensive analysis of attribution, which he calls the *covariation model*. As indicated earlier, the principle of covariation states that "The effect is attributed to that condition which is present when the effect is present and which is absent when the effect is absent" (1967, p. 194). But Kelley goes beyond that to specify that people use three specific types of information to arrive at causal attribution. They check to see whether or not the same effect occurs across: (1) **stimulus objects,** (2) **actors** (persons), and (3) **contexts.** This is perhaps easiest to grasp with a simple example. Suppose our friend Mary shows up at work one day and tells us that she went to a local nightclub the night before. She tells us the show featured a comedian. She laughed hysterically at his jokes, and in fact thought he was the funniest thing she had heard in years. We should definitely go see him.

We want a causal attribution for her hysterical laughter. If the cause was that the comedian really is very funny, we should follow her advice. But if it was just something unusual about Mary, or about the situation that night, we would not be so likely to go. That is, we try to decide whether her behavior is caused by something specific to the stimulus object (the comedian), to the actor (Mary), or to the context (the people she was with, the drinks, etc.).

Kelley suggests that we would search for an attribution by checking each dimension in turn. This involves answering three questions for ourselves: (1) Is the behavior specific to a particular stimulus object? Does Mary always laugh at *any* comedian, or did she really laugh unusually hard only at this one? (2) Is the behavior specific to a particular actor? Have we heard the same report from others, or is Mary the only one who laughed at this particular comedian? (3) Is the behavior specific to a particular context or occasion? Did she laugh each night she went to see this comedian, or did she only laugh the night there was a packed house and she was with her best friend and had one more drink than usual?

Kelley's theory suggests that people use all three of these kinds of information in trying to arrive at a causal attribution: (1) *Distinctiveness* information. Does the person act in this manner only in regard to this stimulus object, and not in regard to other objects? Is Mary's reaction distinctive to this particular object? (2) *Consensus* information. Do other people act in the same way in this situation? Did other people like this comedian as well? (3) *Consistency* information. Does this person consistently react the same way at other times or in other situations? Did Mary react this way to this comedian on only this one occasion?

Kelley hypothesizes this process occurs when we attribute a given effect to a given cause. We quickly review our store of information along these three dimensions. The review may be implicit and automatic rather than deliberate and conscious, but still we review what we know.

For an external attribution to be made—that is, for the comedian's comic ability to be the true cause of Mary's laughter—all three tests have to be passed in the appropriate manner: high distinctiveness, high consensus, and high

Table 5–4
Why Did Mary Laugh at the Comedian?

| CONDITION | AVAILABLE INFORMATION | | | MOST COMMON ATTRIBUTION |
	DISTINCTIVENESS	CONSENSUS	CONSISTENCY	
1	High—she didn't laugh at anyone else.	High—everyone else laughed too.	High—she always laughs at him.	Stimulus object: The comedian (61%)
2	Low—she always laughs at comedians.	Low—hardly anyone else laughed.	High—she always laughs at him.	Person: Mary (86%)
3	High—she didn't laugh at anyone else.	Low—hardly anyone else laughed.	Low—she has almost never laughed at him.	Context: (72%)

Source: Adapted from McArthur (1972).

consistency. Her reaction has to be distinctive to this comedian and not to others; other people have to like the comedian; and she has to like the comedian consistently in this and other situations.

For an internal attribution to be made—that is, for her laughter to be attributed to her general disposition to laugh at anything—low distinctiveness, low consensus, and high consistency must hold. She laughs at all comedians, no one else does, and she laughs in all places and at all times.

McArthur (1972) made the first systematic study of Kelley's predictions. She gave subjects a simple hypothetical event, varied the kind of consensus, distinctiveness, and consistency information available to them, and then measured their attributions. The three main predictions and the results are shown in Table 5–4, using this same example. The first condition is the

same and promotes an attribution to the object itself, since it passes all three tests. Everyone else was also laughing, Mary didn't laugh at any of the other performers, but she always laughed at this one. So he must be a funny comedian. Mostly, the subjects saw it that way too; given this pattern of information, 61 percent attributed her reaction to the comedian (the other 39 percent made other attributions).

The second condition leads the observer to make a person attribution: Mary laughs at any comedian and always laughed at this one—but hardly anyone else did. Mary must be a laugher (86 percent). The third condition leads us to think there is something special about the context: she didn't laugh at anyone else, she has almost never laughed at him before, and hardly anyone else laughed. Something unique must have happened. And 72 percent did attribute her laughter to the particular circumstances.

COGNITIVE BIASES

Attribution theory, in this version, describes an essentially rational, logical process. In fact, Kelley draws an analogy between the person in the street who tries to arrive at causal attributions for everyday events and the systematic scientist who applies the scientific method to achieve

causal explanations for natural events. In that form, attribution theory assumes that people process information in a rational way, that they are fairly objective in assessing information and in combining it to produce a conclusion.

However, as we saw in the last chapter, people tend to be intellectually lazy (or at least cognitively miserly). It is unlikely that they spend most of their waking moments diligently trying to ferret out the causes of things. Moreover, since psychologists themselves have such a struggle unraveling the causes of human behavior, ordinary people can hardly be expected to do much better. Furthermore, people are far from being logical and rational. Indeed, most of this book, and most of psychology, is devoted to studying the irrational aspects of human behavior. For that reason, we now turn to several biases that have been identified in attributional processes. We begin with a consideration of various cognitive processes that derive from the tendencies to respond more to salient or figural stimuli than to background stimuli, and to simplify perception by developing meaningfully structured impressions.

Salience

One way we simplify cognitive processing is to overreact to *salient* stimuli. This bias leads us to perceive the most salient stimuli as the most influential ones. If something is in motion, or colorful, or loud, or novel, we are likely to see it as the main cause of whatever else is changing in the environment. The person who is running down the street is seen as causing the bank alarm system to go off. The loud thunderclap is perceived as causing people to scurry for cover. The woman in the red dress is thought to cause people's heads to turn.

Sometimes the most salient stimuli are in fact the strongest causes of people's behavior, so such attributions would then be accurate. Bias arises because the most perceptually salient stimuli often dominate causal explanations even when they are not actually the most powerful causes.

In a most elegant way, Taylor and Fiske (1975) tested this simple idea: whatever is perceptually salient will be seen as the dominant cause. Two confederates served as "actors." They engaged in a conversation, facing each

other. The ordinary subjects were "observers" sitting behind the confederates or next to them. Each actor thus had observers sitting behind him and facing him. Clearly, the actor and his behavior would be more salient for those who faced him than for those who sat behind him. But both actors ought to be equally salient for the observers sitting to the side, equidistant from the two actors.

This arrangement is illustrated in Figure 5–1. The confederates held a standardized five-minute conversation, chatting as if they had just met. They exchanged information about majors, common job plans, home towns, family, extracurricular activities, and the like. The conversation was carefully monitored to make sure that roughly the same conversation occurred in all experimental groups.

Then the subjects were asked for their causal perceptions: How much had each confederate set the tone of the conversation, determined the kind of information exchanged, and caused the

FIGURE 5–1 Seating arrangements for actors and observers, with arrows indicating visual orientation. (Adapted from Taylor & Fiske, 1975, p. 441.)

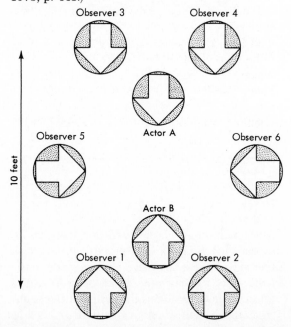

Table 5–5
Mean Ratings of Causal Role Attributed by
Observers to Each Actor as a Function of the
Observer's Seating Position

| | ACTOR | |
OBSERVER'S POSITION	A	B
Facing actor A	20.25	15.54
Center	17.51	16.75
Facing actor B	12.00	20.75

Source: Taylor and Fiske (1975), p. 441.

other actor to behave as he did? The results are shown in Table 5–5. It shows that the more perceptually salient actor (the confederate the subject faced) was given the dominant causal role, and that the less salient actor (the one the confederate sat behind) was seen as less influential. Subjects sitting equidistant from both confederates saw both as about equally potent. Thus actor A was seen as most powerful by those facing him (observers 1 and 2), while actor B was seen as most powerful by those facing *him* (observers 3 and 4)—even though all subjects in reality were observing exactly the same interaction (and one in which both actors contributed about equally, according to unbiased observers 5 and 6 in the center).

The finding that perceptual salience induces exaggerations of a person's causal role turns out to be quite general. To show this, McArthur and Post (1977) presented subjects with videotapes of getting-acquainted conversations, manipulating the visual salience of the actors in various ways. In one study, the salient actor was seated in a bright light, while the nonsalient actor was seated in a dim light. In another, the salient actor was seated in a rocking chair, while the other sat still. In the other studies, the salient actor wore a brightly patterned shirt rather than a solid gray one, or was of a different sex than the other in the conversation. In all these cases, the salient actor's behavior was attributed more to dispositional causes than was the nonsalient actor's behavior.

Robinson and McArthur (1982) found the same thing using audio rather than visual salience: The louder of two unseen speakers was perceived as the most causally dominant, even though the difference in loudness was only 75 to 70 decibels. Taylor and her colleagues (1979) found the same thing even under conditions they thought would reduce the importance of salience: When the perceiver was distracted, when impressions were assessed after a delay, when the conversation itself was very interesting, and when the perceivers themselves were involved in the discussion.

Overattributing to Dispositions

One consequence of this bias is that we are too likely to explain others' behavior as resulting from such dispositions as their general personality traits or their attitudes, while we tend to overlook the importance of the situation they are in. When we ask for information from a clerk at a window in the college administration building and he seems impersonal, brusque, and unhelpful, we think he is a cold, unfriendly person. We tend to ignore the fact that he must have scores of such brief encounters with anonymous complaining students each day. It probably is his particular job situation, rather than his personality, that is most likely to make him act brusquely. Overattribution to dispositions, and underestimation to situations, is so common

BOX 5–2
The Perceived Power of the "Solo"

Some of the most salient people in our society are the "solos"—the one black astronaut in a news conference, the only woman engineer in an office, the one white starting in a professional basketball game, and so on. If mere perceptual salience is responsible for biasing observers' perceptions of causal importance, one would think these "solo" individuals would be perceived as having an exaggerated causal role in their social settings. To test this, Taylor, Fiske, Close, Anderson, and Ruderman (1977) set up group discussions that were all white, had one black, or were evenly divided in race. Their discussion was presented via tape recording, and exactly the same tape was used in all cases. However, each speaker was identified with a still slide as he spoke, and in this way the race of the speakers was varied. Observers of this mixed-media discussion rated the speakers for amount of contribution to the discussion. The "solo" black stood out as talking more and being more influential than did the same speaker in either of the other contexts, where his race did not make him so salient because he was portrayed as just one black in a group that was racially evenly divided, or as a white in an all-white group.

that Ross (1977) calls it **the fundamental attribution error.**

Salience is the most likely explanation for this attributional bias. According to Heider, "Behavior . . . has such salient properties that it tends to engulf the field"; that is, we pay so much attention to the person's behavior that we tend to ignore the situation in which it occurs. The behavior becomes figure and stands out against the surrounding ground of the situation.

We have already seen one example of this fundamental error in the Jones and Harris (1967) study of attributions about the attitudes of people writing essays on Fidel Castro. You may remember (and it can be seen in Table 4–3) that essay writers taking a pro-Castro position were regarded as truly much more pro-Castro than were writers taking an anti-Castro position, even when the writer had no choice about which position to take in the essay. Observers much underestimated the strength of the external situation (that is, the lack of choice about what position to take), and much overestimated the role of internal dispositions (the writer's true position on Castro) in trying to explain the position taken in the essay.

This is an important finding, because it illustrates the principle that causal attributions for the behavior of others are biased in the direction of overemphasizing dispositions and underemphasizing environment. Quite a number of later studies have been done to determine whether this Jones and Harris result is typical, and almost all have found substantially the same thing. Some have tried to generalize the finding to perceptions of personality traits, as well as to perceptions of attitudes. For example, Miller, Jones, and Hinkle (1981) repeated the same general procedure, this time assigning subjects to write an essay designed to convince a reader that they were introverted, or an "extraverted" essay. Because each of the subjects also wrote one of the essays, they knew no choice was involved. They *still* overestimated the role of dispositions: They still thought the "introverted" essays were written by people who were more introverted.

All in all, it appears that the tendency to take speakers' positions as their true attitudes seems amazingly resilient, even in conditions when it should be easy to make an external attribution: when speakers have no choice, are unenthusiastic, give weak arguments, and are simply reading somebody else's speech. As long as the target person is presenting the material visually or orally, the behavior still seems to engulf the field. Only under the most extreme situational constraints, and with very weak arguments delivered in drab, written form, does the phenomenon disappear, and do observers finally accept the causal role of external forces (see Snyder & Jones, 1974; Schneider & Miller, 1975; Miller, 1976).

Why do we do this? Why do we resist information about external constraints? As we have seen in the previous section, salience leads to the perception of causality. Thus the essay writer, rather than the situation, is seen as the primary causal factor. Jones (1979), following Heider, contends that people and their actions form a natural perceptual and cognitive unit. They are in a "unit relation." We think of the two as indivisible. It is *"the person's* action," not an independent event that temporarily seems to be in the same physical space as the actor. It is very hard to break a unit relation by detaching the two perceptually. So we naturally connect people to their acts, and perceive the people as the main cause of their own behavior.

Actors versus Observers

One of the most interesting twists in the fundamental attributional error is that it holds for observers, but not apparently for actors perceiving their own behavior. Actors instead seem to overemphasize the role of external factors. For example, some parents set fairly restrictive rules for their adolescent children, such as that they can go out on dates during weekends only; they have to be home at a certain hour; they can watch television only during certain hours; and so on. How is this rule-making interpreted? The

BOX 5–3

How to Seem Smart

One ingenious use of this fundamental attribution error made observers considerably overestimate other students' general knowledge. Ross, Amabile, and Steinmetz (1977) set up pairs of Stanford students in a quiz situation. One was a "questioner," and the other a "contestant." In the experimental condition, each questioner was allowed to make up ten "challenging but not impossible" questions on any subject he or she wanted and then pose them to the contestant. Both then rated themselves and their partner for general knowledge.

The questions that were made up were indeed fairly difficult (e.g., on the order of "What is the capital of New Mexico?"), and contestants only got four of ten right, on the average. But the important finding was that contestants vastly overestimated the questioner's knowledge. Contestants rated the questioners as extremely well informed by comparison to themselves, while questioners rated both as about equal, as shown below.

The fundamental attribution error occurs when observers take overt behavior too seriously and ignore the situation. These contestants apparently thought the questioners were really well informed since they had known the answers to seemingly hard questions. They ignored the artificiality of the situation—that is, the questioners were able to make up any question they liked and were obviously likely to make up questions they knew the answers to.

RATING MADE BY	RATING[a] OF:	
	QUESTIONER'S KNOWLEDGE	CONTESTANT'S KNOWLEDGE
Questioner	53.5	50.6
Contestant	66.8	41.3

[a]High = more knowledgeable on a 100-point scale.
Source: Ross, Amabile, and Steinmetz (1977).

"observers," the adolescents, frequently perceive these rules as dispositionally caused: The parents are mean, authoritarian, arbitrary, and old-fashioned. The "actors" themselves, the parents, are often more likely to explain their behavior in terms of the situation: They are just doing what is best for their children, living up to the role of the parent, or responding to the rebelliousness and irresponsibility of the children themselves.

How do both sides interpret it if the adolescents repeatedly violate the rules? The "observers," this time the parents, interpret it dispositionally: The adolescents are rebellious, bad, irresponsible, and so on. The "actors," this time the adolescents, interpret their own behavior as situationally caused: The party was fun so they didn't want to leave, the parents' rules are unreasonably strict, the parents misunderstand them, and so on. In short, observers overestimate dispositional causes, actors overestimate situational ones. Both groups are causally explaining the same behavior, but with quite different attributions.

This **actor-observer bias** (Jones & Nisbett, 1972) has proved to be one of the most widely researched of the various attributional biases. In one of its earliest demonstrations, Nisbett et al. (1973) asked male students to write a paragraph on why they liked the woman they dated most, and why they had chosen their major. Then they were asked to answer the same questions as if they were their best friend. Responses were scored for the extent to which the behavior was attributed to the actor's disposition (e.g., I need someone I can relax with, or I want to make a lot of money) or externally, to aspects of the woman or major (e.g., chemistry is a high-paying field). The subjects gave external reasons for their own behavior much more than for another person's behavior. And there was some tendency, though it was not as strong, to give more dispositional reasons for a friend's behavior.

Jones and Nisbett offer two explanations for this difference in attributions. One is that the participants have access to *different information* and therefore naturally come to different conclusions. Actors have access to much more historical information about their own behavior in different situations than the usual observer. With all this inside information about how their own behavior has varied across situations, actors should be more likely to attribute it to the unique characteristics of each particular situation, rather than perceiving themselves as behaving uniformly due to some general predisposition. This would be the covariation model explanation.

The other explanation, and the one pursued by most researchers, is that the difference is due mainly to *different perspectives,* with the key factor again being differences in salience. The observer is naturally focused on the actor. This special salience of the actor leads the observer to overattribute the actor's behavior to dispositions, as we have already seen. This is "the fundamental attributional error." But the actor is not looking at her own behavior. She is looking at the situation—the place, the other people, their expectations, and so on. The actor's own behavior is not as salient to herself as it is to an observer who is watching her. For this reason, the actor will see the situation as more salient and therefore more causally potent. In short, for the observer, the actor's behavior engulfs the field, and so it becomes perceived as the major causal force. For the actor, the environment rather than behavior is most salient, and *it* engulfs the field and becomes the main causal explanation.

Storms (1973) succeeded in showing that this differential perspectives idea could explain the actor-observer difference. He reasoned that if difference in attributions was simply due to a difference in perspective, it could be reversed by reversing point of view. If the actor's own behavior was videotaped and played back to him, he ought to perceive himself as the most salient object in the field and ascribe causality to his own dispositions. If the observers see a videotape from the actor's perspective, they will see more of the situation to which the actor is responding, rather than just focusing on the actor, and so they ought to ascribe more causality to the situation rather than simply seeing the actor's dispositions as the major cause.

To test this hypothesis, Storms also set up a situation in which two strangers (the actors) meet to get acquainted. Sitting at the other end of the table from them were two observers watching their conversation, each assigned to watch a different actor. Both actors were videotaped. Then the interaction was played back on videotape for all four participants. One actor's behavior was shown and the other's was not (the experimenter said one camera had not worked). One actor saw himself, which should have increased dispositional attributions; the other actor saw the same thing that he had seen during the conversation, the other actor. So he should respond just as he had earlier. Similarly, one observer saw a videotape of the actor to whom *his* actor has been responding, and therefore should have been more attuned to the situational forces operating on his actor. The other observer saw a repeat of the same thing he had seen earlier, so he should also respond as he had earlier.

The results of this experiment are shown in Table 5–6. The first column shows that perceptions of the conversation itself, without any videotape replay, yielded the standard actor-observer difference: Observers were more likely to give dispositional attributions (4.80) than the actors were (2.25). The second column shows what happened when everyone saw a videotape of the interaction, but from exactly the same perspective as the one in which they had viewed the original interaction. Again the standard actor-observer difference emerged: Observers made more dispositional attributions (4.90) than the actors (0.15) did, as expected, because neither had changed perspective. The crucial condition was the one in which the videotaped replay reversed the perspectives. This is shown in the right-hand column of Table 5–6. When the actors saw their own behavior played back, their attributions became much more dispositional (6.80). And when the observers watched a videotape replay of the situation to which their actor had been responding, they generated much more situational attributions for their own actor's behavior (1.60).

This experiment confirms the basic prediction of Jones and Nisbett, that under normal circumstances actors make more situational attributions and observers make more dispositional attributions. But it also suggests that this difference occurs because of different perceptual orientations or points of view. That is, they are receiving different current information from their respective perceptual fields. When this perceptual orientation is reversed, so are the causal attributions.

Regan and Totten (1975) added another wrinkle to this same idea. They found that if the observer adopted a more empathic attitude and tried to think or see things the way the actor did, the observer would see the world the same way the actor does. That is, when the observers had the normal observer set, they were inclined to give more dispositional than situational attributions. However, under instructions to empathize with the actor this reversed slightly. The situational attributions became more prominent, presumably just as they would have been for the actor herself. Similarly, observers who merely anticipate engaging in the same actions start giving actorlike attributions—that is, they start to use the situation to explain the actor's behavior, just as the actor does (Wolfson & Salancik, 1977). Presumably they are empathizing and identifying with the actor, and are already starting to see things from the other perspective.

These studies give good evidence that the actor-observer effect can be produced merely by the different points of view actors and observers have. Does this invalidate the differential-

Table 5–6
Tendency to Give Dispositional Rather than Situational Attributions[a]

ATTRIBUTION	NO VIDEOTAPE	VIDEOTAPE— SAME ORIENTATION	VIDEOTAPE— NEW ORIENTATION
Actors' attributions for own behavior	2.25	0.15	6.80
Observers' attributions for actor's behavior	4.80	4.90	1.60

[a]The higher the number, the more dispositional relative to situational attributions.
Source: Adapted from Storms (1973), p. 169.

information hypothesis? Probably not. It is more likely that each is most important under different conditions. In general, when historical factors or internal states are crucial determinants of behavior, actors will have better information and will probably be more accurate attributors. But when the behavior itself or the external situation is salient, the differential-perspective theory will account better for differences between actors' and observers' attributions (Monson & Snyder, 1977).

Underusing Consensus Information

One safeguard against the fundamental attributional error ought to be consensus information. With high consensus, we should make a situational attribution. If we know that almost everyone responds the same way to a given entity in a given context, a dispositional attribution ought to be quite unlikely. For example, if we know that almost everyone thinks calculus is difficult, we should not attribute Kenneth's trouble with calculus to low ability or effort. We should attribute it to a difficult situation.

But people tend to underuse consensus information. Kelley's covariation model assumes that consensus, distinctiveness, and consistency information will all be used about equally. None of these three is regarded as inherently more informative than any other. Yet experiments comparing them have found that people do not use consensus information as much. For example, in trying to explain why Mary laughed at the comedian, it makes little difference to most observers whether other people laughed at him or not. Instead, they respond mainly in terms of Mary's own past history—whether she always laughs at this comedian or not, and whether she laughs at all comedians or not. Consistency and distinctiveness information get used, but people tend not to pay much attention to consensus information (McArthur, 1972; Nisbett & Borgida, 1975; Ruble & Feldman, 1976; Wells & Harvey, 1977).

Not only do people frequently ignore available information about others' behavior, but they imagine that everyone responds the way they do. They tend to see their own behavior as typical. In an early demonstration of this so-called *false consensus effect,* students were asked if they would walk around their college campus for 30 minutes wearing a large sandwich board with the message "Eat at Joe's." Some students agreed, others refused. But both groups estimated that about two-thirds of the other students on the campus would make the same choice they did. Both groups clearly could not be right (Ross, Greene, & House, 1977).

When are people most likely to ignore information about others in forming causal attributions? That is, when are they most likely to ignore consensus information? When people have direct sensory experience with the object in question, they seem more likely to trust their own experience than reports of how others feel. Feldman and co-workers (1976) showed subjects videotapes of a person choosing their favorite of several pictured items. Immediately after this choice, four other people visible within camera range were asked whether or not they liked that object best too. They all responded positively that they did (high consensus) or negatively (low consensus). Then the subjects were asked to explain the original person's choice.

From Kelley's model, high consensus should lead to an attribution to the stimulus object: If everyone likes Apple computers, they must be excellent computers. Low consensus should lead to a person attribution: If only one person likes anchovy pizzas, it must be a special quirk. So Feldman et al. also varied whether the subjects were also shown the same pictures of the objects as shown to the actor, or not. The results showed that consensus information had little effect when the subjects had direct information about the object in question.

People also tend to ignore new consensus information when they already have plenty of experience about how others feel and behave. They may depend on their own sense of others' feelings, rather than take an experimenter's report of social consensus. Higgins and his colleagues (1982) showed children videotapes of other children choosing among pictures of animals, cars, cartoon characters, and colors. This provided consensus information about others' choices. But this consensus information was much less influential in children's attributions when it came from their own agemates than when it came from children of other ages. Presumably the reason is that the subjects had a pretty good sense already of how their own agemates would react to these objects, so they tended to ignore the rather minimal information given in the videotape. But they were less likely to have a good sense of how children of other ages would react, so they used the videotape to help them with that.

Finally, in some situations everyone is likely to do the same thing, because idiosyncratic personal values are not very relevant. Almost everyone would prefer a new Mercedes-Benz 450SL to a ten-year-old Ford Pinto. But in other situations, idiosyncratic values are more important. Whether you would prefer to go to an all-Beethoven orchestra concert or to a boxing match probably will depend more on your own taste than it will on the fame of the conductor or the expertise of the boxers. And not surprisingly, consensus information proves to have less effect when choices are made so strongly on the basis of personal taste.

In a study by Gilovich (1983), students ignored consensus information on the question of whether they would prefer to watch gymnastics or a track and field meet because they assumed such choices are quite personal and idiosyncratic. They took consensus more seriously on a choice between buying stock in IBM or Exxon, since the objective characteristics of which stock was the better investment presumably would determine most people's decisions.

Are people being "irrational" in ignoring consensus information in these situations? It does seem they are throwing away good information when they ignore consensus just because they too happen to have seen a picture of the object in question, as in the Feldman et al. (1976) study. Perhaps the salience of the object placed the other judges in the background. But it would have been informative to know how everyone else looking at the object felt about it.

It would seem irrational if we disregarded the reports of all our friends who have seen a particular movie, and instead decided about it on the basis of a short preview. On the other hand, it seems quite reasonable that 4-year-olds would have a pretty good sense of what 4-year-olds would like, and would therefore disregard a videotape of a few of them. And it would seem reasonable to disregard consensus on matters of personal taste. So, as we suggested earlier, the Kelley covariation model is a good starting point for determining whether people are arriving at reasonable attributions or not. But it cannot be the final test.

MOTIVATIONAL BIASES

A second general class of biases arises from people's efforts to satisfy their own needs and motives. The cognitive biases were analyzed as if people had only one kind of need—the need to have a coherent, clear understanding of their environments. This is a characteristic operating assumption of the cognitive viewpoint, as we indicated in Chapter 1. But in reality people have many other needs—for love, revenge, self-esteem, prestige, material goods, and so on. Quite a lot would be left out of our account if these factors were ignored. And they prove to play a substantial role in biasing causal attributions.

Self-Serving Biases

Perhaps the most common motivational bias in the attribution process is the **self-serving bias.** This term describes attributions that glorify the ego or defend self-esteem. Perhaps the simplest example is that we tend to attribute our successes to internal causes such as our own ability, hard work, or general goodness. We tend to blame our failures on external factors like bad luck, an oppressive political structure, a nagging wife or sexist husband, bad weather, and so on. For example, college students attributed A and B grades in three examinations in a semester course to internal factors such as ability and effort, whereas they attributed C, D, and F grades to external factors such as test difficulty and bad luck (Bernstein et al., 1979).

In numerous experimental studies, subjects have been given a success or a failure experience and then asked to explain the outcome. Others have had subjects try to teach a student something while manipulating the ''learner's'' success or failure. Either way, most subjects attribute their successes to internal causes and their failures to external ones (see Bradley,

1978; and Zuckerman, 1979, for careful reviews).

The same self-serving bias is often applied to groups with which one is identified. Sears and McConahay (1973) reported on interviews with people in Los Angeles done shortly after the massive rioting by blacks in Watts in 1965. People tended to give explanations that exonerated their own group from blame. As Table 5–7 shows, blacks who were arrested overwhelmingly blamed the rioting on the miserable situation blacks found themselves in, and on the justifiable hostility and desire for revenge those conditions produced. Most blacks in the community who were neither arrested nor for the most part involved in the rioting came to the same conclusion—the causes lay in a stable, bad, external situation. Whites, on the other hand, were more likely to blame chance external factors or bad individual rioters.

This difference in attributions for the rioting had great political significance, of course. If the real causes lay in bad local conditions, as the blacks said, then those conditions should be changed. This would indicate developing government programs that would help blacks in

Table 5–7
What Do You Think Caused the Watts Riots?

| PERCEIVED CAUSES | BLACKS | | WHITES |
	ARRESTEES	COMMUNITY SAMPLE	COMMUNITY SAMPLE
Stable external (grievances about society, pent-up hostility)	85%	64%	34%
Unstable external (weather, accident, chance happening)	8	11	28
Stable internal (Communists, criminals, agitators)	2	9	29
Don't know, no answer	6	17	10
	101%[a]	101%[a]	101%[a]

[a]Rounding error.
Source: Adapted from Sears & McConahay (1973), p. 160.

Wonderful Winners and Victimized Losers

A homey example of the self-serving bias comes from interviews by Kingdon (1967) with the winning and losing candidate in each of thirty-three races in Wisconsin for U. S. senator, U. S. congressman, state senator, state assemblyman, and five statewide offices. They were asked a series of questions about why they thought they had won or lost. The winners thought the most important factor was the characteristics of the candidates! The losers downplayed that factor and blamed the outcome on party label (the voters just voted a party line against my side). Some of the results are shown in the table below. In addition, the losers blamed their loss on the voter's ignorance: 70 percent of the losers said the voters were "not informed," compared to 32 percent of the winners.

For "wins" throughout their careers, 75 percent of the respondents emphasized matters within their control: "their hard work, personal service to constituents, matters of campaign strategy, building a reputation, and publicizing themselves." For their "defeats," 90 percent of the respondents emphasized matters beyond their control, "the party makeup of the district, the familiar name or other unbeatable characteristics of the opponent, national and state trends, lack of money, or other uncontrollable circumstances" (p. 141).

Comparison of Winners and Losers on Perceived Causes of Election Outcomes		
MOST IMPORTANT CAUSES	WINNERS	LOSERS
Characteristics of the Candidates	62%	35%
Election Issues	17	7
Party Label	21	59
	100%	101%[a]

[a]Rounding error.
Source: Kingdon (1967).

terms of housing, health, jobs, education, and so on. If the true causes lay in some fluke, such as hot weather, nothing need be done. If malicious agitators or criminals were responsible, a harsh "law and order" policy might be appropriate. Stable external attributions supported liberal policies; unstable external or stable internal attributions gave ammunition to political conservatives.

The same self-serving bias emerges from an analysis of players' and coaches' postgame explanations for the outcomes of World Series and college and professional football games (Lau & Russell, 1980). Internal attributions (as opposed to external) were made by 80 percent of the winners and 53 percent of the losers. The winning manager of one World Series game made an internal attribution, saying that his star player "had done it all." A losing player explained the same outcome externally: "I think we've hit the ball all right. But I think we're unlucky."

MOTIVATIONAL INTERPRETATIONS Self-serving biases have been interpreted in several ways. Perhaps the simplest and most obvious is that such self-serving attributions give the person more self-esteem. We feel better about ourselves if we think we are responsible for our successes and blameless in our failures. Several kinds of evidence indicate that esteem maintenance is indeed an important factor. When people have success experiences, internal attributions give them a more positive feeling both in terms of a more positive mood and higher self-esteem than do external attributions such as task ease or chance. So it is to the subject's advantage, in terms of self-esteem, to claim the credit for success internally rather than sharing it (McFarland & Ross, 1982).

Self-serving biases are even stronger on tasks with heightened ego involvement. As a task becomes more personally important, people are more motivated to bias their attributions to protect bruised egos (Miller, 1975). Furthermore, self-serving biases are stronger for actors than for observers, presumably because the emotional stakes are greater for the actor (Snyder, Stephan, & Rosenfield, 1976). As would be expected, therefore, observers instructed to empathize with the actor also show the self-serving bias. Gould and Sigall (1977), for example, asked subjects to empathize with the target person: "While you are watching him, picture to yourself how he feels. . . . try to forget yourself." Then they learned the target person had succeeded or failed at a task. With empathy, subjects attributed the target person's success to internal factors and his failure to external factors.

All these findings indicate that self-serving biases are enhanced as the emotional stakes of

Being overpaid for one's work can undermine intrinsic interest in it. Relative to other professionals, classical musicians are usually paid poorly and even research scientists are usually not paid lavishly. How do you think their payment affects their interest in their work?

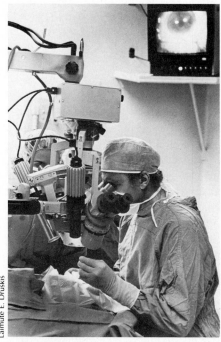

Laimute E. Druskis

Ken Karp, Sirovich Senior Center

the task outcome increase; that is, as success or failure becomes more important to the individual. So there is substantial evidence that the needs to bolster self-esteem, and to protect oneself from losses in self-esteem, are at least partially responsible for self-serving biases in attribution.

COGNITIVE INTERPRETATIONS   Some authors (Miller & M. Ross, 1975; Nisbett & L. Ross, 1980) suggest there might be cognitive instead of motivational reasons for the self-serving bias. For instance, perhaps the subjects in these experiments have been much more used to success than to failure experiences (high school and college students receive few Fs) and therefore failure comes as a surprise to them. Experiences consistent with past experience should lead to an internal attribution: If I always perform this way, then my latest performance must be due to something about me; therefore my success must be internally caused. On the other hand, if my performance departs from what I expect from past experience, it must be due to this new situation; therefore my failure must be situationally caused. In Kelley's terms, a success would be high consistency information and would provoke an internal attribution. Failure, being low consistency information, would provoke an external attribution. People might show a pattern of attributions that would appear to be self-serving, but that have simply been made for cognitive reasons, without ego enhancement being a factor at all.

One problem with this argument is that most people do not have universally successful experiences. Their judgment of their success is normally determined by some subjective level of aspiration, not by some absolute standard. For example, most college students do not regard getting a C or D as a success experience, even though it is a passing grade. Some even feel disappointed by a B. Most people have had many experiences they regard as failures, and it is doubtful that their past history leads them to expect success most of the time.

The question then becomes this: Do self-serving biases disappear with such expectancies for success or failure held constant, as this cognitive interpretation would suggest? An experiment by Ross and Sicoly (1979) tested that in a clever way. First they put subjects through a task that supposedly measured their "social perceptiveness." The subjects were led to believe they had either succeeded or failed at the task. Since this was a novel task, the experience determined their expectancies for further success or failure. A critical variation was therefore introduced at this point: An observer randomly told the subject she bore either more or less personal responsibility for the outcome. That is, the observer told the subject that the outcome was more internally caused, or more externally caused, than the subject had claimed.

No matter which it was, this new information was equally unexpected, since it departed by the same amount from the subject's judgment as already expressed. So expectancy was held constant. Finally, the subject was asked how accurate this new feedback was. Ego-enhancing feedback (internal attributions for successes, and external for failures) was judged to be considerably more accurate than ego-deflating feedback. Self-serving biases, therefore, are present even when expectancies are held constant.

IMPRESSION MANAGEMENT   Yet a third possibility is that self-serving biases may simply serve a self-presentation or impression-management function. That is, we may not really misperceive the causes of our outcomes at all. But when asked, we try to persuade other people we are responsible for our successes and blameless in our failures, because then they will have a higher opinion of us.

Bradley (1978) has argued that many of the studies showing self-serving biases can be reinterpreted in this vein. In partial support of this view, Orvis (1977) found that people in intimate relationships argued publicly for more self-serving explanations of their conflicts than they thought were probably true. In discussions with their partner, they would frequently blame the partner for their conflicts more than they privately thought was justified.

But this tendency to be especially self-serving in public pronouncements does not explain away all instances of self-serving biases in attributions. People really believe their own self-serving propaganda. A number of studies have shown that people exhibit self-serving biases even under very private conditions, when it is unlikely they are trying to impress other people. For example, Greenberg et al. (1982) and Schlenker et al. (1983) found self-serving biases even when subjects thought the experimenter did not know how they performed. Riess et al. (1981) found them even when subjects were hooked into the "bogus pipeline" (see Box 2–3), an apparatus that supposedly would detect any lies.

In general, self-serving biases are not merely "fronts" for impression management, though they probably serve that function on occasion. There seems to be quite a strong tendency for attributions to be biased by self-esteem needs, especially in the case of taking credit for good events and avoiding blame for bad ones. But the confirmation or disconfirmation of expectancies is also an important factor in our attributions for success or failure. When something surprising happens, we need a new explanation. At this point, all three interpretations remain viable. Indeed, probably all have some validity.

The Illusion of Control

We have seen how people tend to distort the social world perceptually into a more orderly, organized, predictable, and sensible thing than it really is. They do it in many ingenious ways, using first impressions, schemas, scripts, attributional biases, and a wide variety of other cognitive mechanisms. But people do not only perceive the world as more orderly than it really is. They also distort it in more *controllable* directions as well. They systematically overestimate

their own control over events, and underestimate the role of chance or uncontrollable factors.

Langer (1975) has called this the **illusion of control.** Calling it an illusion may be a little strong; it is more like a systematic bias of modest magnitude than a total lack of contact with reality. But such a bias has been demonstrated in some interesting ways.

The typical experiment has led subjects to exaggerate their control over chance outcomes. For example, Wortman (1975) put two different marbles in a can and told subjects that each marble stood for a different prize. Some subjects were told which marble stood for the prize they wanted, and some were not. Then subjects either chose a marble or were given one, without being allowed to see which marble was which. There was no conceivable way they could actually control the outcome. Nevertheless, when they knew in advance which marble stood for the prize they wanted and were allowed to choose a marble, they thought they were more responsible for the outcome than when they were just given a marble. They had the illusion of control.

Another version of this illusion is that people consistently exaggerate their own contribution to shared activities. Ross & Sicoly (1979) did several studies of married couples' estimates of relative contributions to joint activities, college basketball players' estimates of their own roles in recent games, and recent college graduates' estimates of their own contribution to their bachelors' theses. In each case, people exaggerated their own contributions.

Thompson and Kelley (1981) found the same thing: Each member of a couple consistently claimed he or she took more than half the responsibility for such joint activities as carrying the conversation when the two of them were alone, waiting for the other person, resolving conflicts, being sensitive to the other's needs. It should be noted that this overestimate of one's own role was not limited to socially desirable activities. Each member of the couples also overestimated his or her role in causing arguments. In all cases, people seem simply to exaggerate their own control in activities shared with others.

"A JUST WORLD" The illusion of control implies that people have more control over their fates than they in fact do. One consequence of this illusion is the tendency to blame the victim. A person who is involved in a traffic accident must have been driving carelessly. Victims of theft are perceived as having brought it on themselves by not taking adequate security precautions (Tyler & Devinitz, 1981). A woman who is raped must have been acting in a provocative manner and brought it on herself. Even the victims blame themselves. For example, many rape victims blame themselves for being raped; they see themselves as having behaved in the wrong way, such as hitchhiking or leaving their apartment window unlocked (Janoff-Bulman, 1979). Minorities who are discriminated against are often seen as being too pushy, unmotivated, or passive and are believed to alienate people with their demands; they therefore are seen as deserving their fates. Earthquake, tornado, hurricane, and flood victims are believed to have shown insufficient preparedness.

There are many accounts of the guilt experienced by survivors of disasters and accidents, or by bereaved family members. They frequently dwell on the period before the incident, thinking of some way they could have averted the tragedy. They desperately imagine ways they could have controlled what is usually uncontrollable (Wortman, 1976). In short, people are presumed to control their environments and are seen as getting what they deserve, and deserving what they get.

To explain such observations, Lerner (1965) has offered the notion that we believe in a **just world:** Good people get good outcomes, and bad things happen to bad people. The key idea is that observers attribute chance events to the victims' moral dispositions. That is, instead of making the seemingly obvious attribution to luck, the fates, or some other aspect of the situation, people make an attribution to the victim's moral character. Thus, I blame you for being a lousy driver because someone ran a red light and hit you at an intersection on the way to campus. To test this notion, Lerner ran several laboratory experiments in which victims were picked at random to be given electric shock. The subjects tended to denigrate them, as if the victims were morally responsible for their misfortunes.

Lerner interprets these indications of a belief in a just world as reflecting a need to believe we can control events, much like the illusion of control. To protect this sense of control, we blame people for the bad things that happen to them. If people in general are responsible for any disaster that befalls them, presumably we ourselves can avoid personal disaster by acting properly. One unfortunate consequence of the tendency to see the world as a just place, as Lerner (1980), Ryan (1971), and others have pointed out, is that it provides a justification for the oppression of society's victims. If people themselves are responsible for the fact that they are sick, poor, or disabled, there is no need for the rest of us to help them.

CONTROL: AN ADAPTIVE ILLUSION? What happens when this sense of control is threatened? Suppose a woman student is followed by a strange man one night on the way home back to her dormitory from the library. She has always felt safe in this well-lit part of the campus, but suddenly she feels alone and very vulnerable. He finally comes close to her and grabs her arm and tries to pull her off the path. She breaks away and runs to the dormitory, panic-stricken. She arrives there safely. But after this episode, she no longer feels safe walking at night alone on that path. She has lost her sense of control; something bad can happen to her at any moment, no matter what she does. How do people who have lost the illusion of control respond?

Reactions vary all the way from seeking information (Swann & Stephenson, 1981), to pain, increased reactivity to stress, and declines in performance (Glass & Singer, 1972), anger or hostility (Brehm & Brehm, 1981), or hopelessness and apathy (Abramson et al., 1978). But a major response is the attempt to restore control. Even when people get cancer, a disease that is among the most difficult to control and whose causes are very poorly understood, they try to regain a sense of mastery in a variety of ways. Taylor (1983, p. 1164) reports these efforts to restore control among women afflicted with breast cancer:

[Where the cancer came from] was an important question to me at first. The doctor's answer was that it was a multifaceted illness. I looked over the known causes of cancer, like viruses, radiation, genetic mutation, environmental carcinogens, and the one I focused on very strongly was diet. I know now why I focused on it. It was the only one that was simple enough for me to understand and change. You eat something that's bad for you, you get sick.

Another woman said:

I felt that I had lost control of my body somehow, and the way for me to get back some control was to find out as much as I could. It really became almost an obsession.

And one spouse described his wife:

She got books, she got pamphlets, she studied, she talked to cancer patients, she found out everything that was happening to her, and she fought it. She went to war with it. She calls it taking in her covered wagons and surrounding it.

Indeed, a number of psychologists feel that a strong sense of control over oneself and one's life is extremely adaptive—even if it is based in part on illusion: "Far from impeding adjustment, illusion may be essential for adequate coping" (Taylor, 1983, p. 29).

For example, Bulman and Wortman (1977) interviewed 29 paraplegics in a rehabilitation institute who had been disabled in accidents ranging from being shot to being tackled in a football game. They were each rated by a nurse and a social worker on how well they were coping with the accident, in terms of accepting the reality of the accident and attempting to deal positively with the paralysis. The more they blamed another person and the less they blamed themselves for the accident, the worse they coped. The authors suggest that "the ability to perceive an orderly relationship between one's behaviors and one's outcomes is important for effective coping" (p. 362).

A similar phenomenon is what Seligman (1975) has called **learned helplessness.** When people feel a lack of control over the environment, they begin to lose motivation and performance deteriorates. Seligman contends it can lead to depression and even to death. It was first noted in experiments on animals. After the animals had been given shocks they could not escape for some length of time, they later proved unable to learn how to escape, even when it was possible to do so. In contrast, animals who initially were allowed to escape from the shock by pressing a bar later had no trouble learning a new response that would help them escape. It is as if the initially helpless animals just give up.

A typical learned helplessness experiment on humans is very similar. Subjects are given problems to work out and then given feedback about their performance that has nothing to do with how well they did. In this sense, the problems are insoluble. The outcomes have been externally caused and are seemingly random. The subjects learn they have no control over the problems; they have learned they are helpless. When tested later on easier problems, they prove much less successful than subjects for whom the original feedback was contingent on performance—that is, those for whom the environment had been predictable and controllable.

This learned helplessness model has been extended to the general problem of depression. The basic idea is that attributing negative events to internal, stable, and global factors—that is, to large, internal, uncontrollable factors—leads to depression (Abramson, Seligman, & Teasdale, 1978). I got a C rather than an A on that math midterm because I am terrible at math and always will be. The young man I went out with last week never called me back because I am just not attractive to men and never will be. Once we begin making such attributions, we go on to avoid exerting control in situations where we might in fact be effective. I decide not to go to the post-midterm review session run by the math TA because I think my situation is hopeless. In reality, I might learn from my mistakes and do better the next time. When my neighbor in French class asks me out for coffee, I say I'm busy because I'm convinced he won't like me when he gets to know me. In reality, he seems pretty interested and might be quite receptive.

An example of how such internal, stable, global attributions for negative events produce depressive affect comes from a study by Metalsky et al. (1982). They found students who were biased initially toward making such attributions showed bigger jumps in depressive affect after getting a poor grade on a midterm than did students who normally made external or less global attributions. In another example, Peterson et al. (1981) found that blaming one's enduring *character* rather than one's own *behavior* (that is, making more global attributions) was associated with more depressive symptoms in female college freshmen.

Much of the research on learned helplessness has found it to be associated with depressive moods and symptoms. Similarly, the "illusion of control" may be an important element of nondepressed moods. Alloy, Abramson, and Viscusi (1981) found that normal women in general, or depressed women who had just undergone an experimental mood-elating experience, showed the same kind of illusion of control we discussed above. In contrast, little illusion of control was found among depressed women in general, or normal women whose mood had been experimentally depressed.

However, there is no strong evidence that such attributions are a central cause of serious clinical depressions; they may be symptoms rather than causes of such disorders. Nevertheless, the learned helplessness model is a provocative one, and it has generated much intriguing research.

Obviously an illusion of control is not always adaptive—for example, it may not be helpful in an environment one cannot control at all. And self-blame may have quite detrimental effects on coping (also see Taylor, 1983). But in many instances, this sense of personal control, even if an illusion, may be quite adaptive.

WHY THE ILLUSION OF CONTROL? A number of phenomena described in this chapter have been seen to reveal a pervasive bias toward perceiving internal or dispositional control of behavior. The fundamental attribution error overestimates internal control. Work on the illusion of control, the just world, and learned helplessness all documents how people prefer to believe in internal control, and in fact are disrupted psychologically when they are forced to face their own helplessness and the randomness of much that affects their lives.

Why this bias toward internality? One possibility has been considered above. Perhaps, at a simple perceptual level, actors and observers alike tend to see an act as so thoroughly connected to the actor (in what Heider called a "unit relation") that they cannot easily attribute it to some external cause (Jones, 1979).

Another possibility is that all human beings share a strong emotional commitment to the feeling of free will, and to feeling that they are free to act any way they choose. The illusion of choice or of control may be crucial to our motivational systems and feelings of well-being, for some adaptive reasons deriving from natural selection (Brehm, 1966; Monson & Snyder, 1977). Perhaps it is only the belief in internal control that keeps us actively trying to manipulate our environment, which in turn is crucial for survival.

A third possibility is that this bias toward internal attribution is a cultural norm particularly characteristic of Americans. Many observers have noted how dedicated Americans are to individualistic values, to the beliefs that individual people can control their own destinies, are responsible for their outcomes, and so on. Some studies have shown that American students best like people who give internal attributions, especially those who so attribute their failures (Carlston & Shovar, 1983; Jellison & Green, 1981). The Horatio Alger myth is one of our hardiest: Poverty is due to the laziness and stupidity of the poor, wealth to the genius and hard work of the successful. Inkeles (1983), for example, reports that when Americans are asked to explain why one person has succeeded and another failed, despite having the same skill and training, 1 percent invoke fate or God's will. But in six developing countries he found luck or fate was the explanation of about 30 percent.

This individualism has been traced back to America's Protestant heritage (see, for example, McClelland, 1964; Sears & McConahay, 1973; Sniderman & Brody, 1977). More interdependent cultures emphasize the collective and interpersonal causes of events, and not so much the free acts of individuals (Sampson, 1977).

The tradition in the United States, on the other hand, is that individuals stand on their own two feet. Most Americans do not think of themselves as part of a larger social whole, such as an extended family or church or community. For example, in the United States, the decision to marry is supposed to be the free choice of the persons involved and is based on romantic love. In many other cultures, such decisions are made collectively by family or kinship groups because marriages are thought to affect the whole community. So it remains for further research in other cultures to determine whether this emphasis on dispositions, free will and choice, and personal control is limited to our culture, with its strong tradition of Protestant individualism, or is a more general human characteristic.

SUMMARY

1. Attribution theory is concerned with how ordinary people explain social events. The most common causal attributions explain behaviors as internal or external to the person, stable or unstable, and controllable or uncontrollable.
2. Theorists begin from the assumption that people are strongly motivated to explain the events around them. They do so by looking for invariance; that is, which causes are regularly associated with which effects. And they use a discounting principle; that is, to the extent that several causes are plausible, they will spread their explanations among them.
3. Kelley's theory suggests that people base their attributions on three kinds of information: distinctiveness (is this the only situation in which the person does this), consensus (would other people do the same thing in that situation), and consistency (does the person always do this in this situation).
4. Other people's personality traits and attitudes are normally inferred from their overt behaviors by considering the external forces operating on them at the time. If these forces are strong, attributions are shared between external and internal causes. If these forces are weak, internal attributions are made.

5. Attribution theory can be applied to self-perception as well as to the perception of others. That is, the same principles may account for how we infer the causes for our own acts and how we infer the causes for others' acts.
6. The internal cues we receive from our own emotional arousal states are more ambiguous and undifferentiated than has commonly been assumed in the past. Consequently, we infer both the nature and degree of our own emotional arousal by an attributional process that relies on evidence about our own behavior, external indications of our arousal states, and environmental conditions.
7. To some extent, we infer our own attitudes from our own behavior, particularly when we are not especially involved in our attitudes and when they have little consequence for our future lives.
8. In its purest form, attribution theory describes a logical, rationalistic mechanism for arriving at causal explanations. But several systematic biases have been discovered.
9. In general, people ascribe more causality to internal dispositions than they should and less to external forces. This has been called the fundamental attribution error. It is particularly true for

observations of other people's behavior. Self-perceptions may indeed be biased in the opposite direction and overattribute causality to external forces. In both cases the bias seems due mainly to the relative salience of the behavior and of the situation.

10. People are quite heavily influenced by the need to give explanations that support or protect their own self-esteem; they do so by externalizing blame or taking credit for success.

11. People seem to need the illusion of control over their environments. Their perceptions exaggerate their own level of control, and they become emotionally disturbed when they feel they have no control. They believe in a just world in which people get what they deserve, seemingly based on the assumption that people can control their own outcomes.

SUGGESTIONS FOR ADDITIONAL READING

FRIEZE, I. H., BAR-TEL, D., & CARROLL, J. S. (Eds.). 1979. *New approaches to social problems.* San Francisco: Jossey-Bass. Applications of attribution theory to a wide variety of social problems.

HARVEY, J. H., ICKES, W., & KIDD, R. F. (Eds.). 1976, 1978. *New directions in attribution research.* Vols. 1 and 2. Hillsdale, N.J.: Erlbaum. Essays on almost every facet of attribution research by almost everyone who has made a major contribution to it.

KELLEY, H. H. 1967. Attribution theory in social psychology. In David Levine (Ed.), *Nebraska symposium on motivation.* Lincoln: University of Nebraska Press. Still the best and most coherent basic statement of attribution theory.

KELLEY, H. H., and MICHELA, J. L. 1979. Attribution theory and research. *Annual Review of Psychology,* 31, 1–79. An excellent recent review of the whole attribution tradition, coauthored by one of its principal originators.

JONES, E. E., KANOUSE, D. E., KELLEY, H. H., NISBETT, R. E., VALINS, S., & WEINER, B. 1972. *Attribution: Perceiving the causes of behavior.* Morristown, N. J.: General Learning Press. An influential early collection of theoretical statements on attribution theory. Includes excellent chapters on the actor-observer effect, self-perception, negativity, and others.

6

ATTITUDES

What makes someone a Republican or a Democrat, a conservative or a liberal, a Protestant or a Catholic? Why are some people anti-Semitic, others antiblack, and still others not prejudiced at all? Why do people decide that one toothpaste is best or that cigarette smoking is dangerous? What determines whether or not someone will change her mind about toothpastes or cigarettes? How can we convince Republicans to vote for a Democrat? How can we prepare our own supporters to resist the propaganda put out by the other party's candidates? If our friend decides smoking is bad, what will make her actually quit doing it? These questions form the basis for the extensive work on attitude formation and change, which has been a central core of social psychology in the United States for many years.

In 1937, in the first text mainly devoted to experimental studies in social psychology, Murphy, Murphy, and Newcomb wrote: "Perhaps no single concept within the whole realm of social psychology occupies a more nearly central position than that of attitudes" (p. 889). Although interest in this problem has probably declined somewhat in recent years, social psychologists have devoted more time in the past fifty years or so to the study of attitudes than to any other topic.

DEFINING ATTITUDES

Each of the traditional definitions of **attitudes** contains a slightly different conception of what an attitude is or emphasizes a somewhat different aspect of it. G. W. Allport (1935) proposed that "an attitude is a mental and neural state of readiness, organized through experience, exerting a directive or dynamic influence upon the individual's response to all objects and situations with which it is related" (p. 810). Because this definition was much influenced by the learning tradition, it also emphasized how past experience forms attitudes. For the same reason, it viewed an attitude primarily as a set to respond in a particular way, and emphasized its behavioral implications.

In contrast, Krech and Crutchfield (1948, p. 152), who were strongly committed to a cognitive perspective, defined an attitude as "an enduring organization of motivational, emotional, perceptual, and cognitive processes with respect to some aspect of the individual's world." Notice that they omit any reference to the origins of the attitude and instead are concerned with current subjective experience. Note also that they emphasize organization; they view the person as a thoughtful and actively structuring organism. And finally, note there is no mention of overt behavior. The cognitive tradition emphasizes the person's subjective experience.

The Three Components

Today, the most common definition combines elements from both approaches. An attitude toward any given object, idea, or person is an enduring orientation with cognitive, affective, and behavioral components. The *cognitive* component consists of all the cognitions the person has about that particular attitude object—the facts, knowledge, and beliefs concerning the object. The *affective* component consists of all the person's affects or emotions toward the object, especially evaluations. The *behavioral* component consists of the person's readiness to respond or tendency to act regarding the object.

Consider a student's attitude toward nuclear weapons. The cognitive component might include some information about their size, mode of delivery, the number of warheads on a missile, and some beliefs about which countries probably have them, their destructive potential, and the likelihood of their being used. The affective component would include the person's feelings, which in this case might be dominated by a strong negative evaluation, mixed perhaps with some fear or even dread of nuclear destruction. The behavioral component refers to the student's tendencies to act with respect to nuclear weapons, such as a tendency to sign petitions and march in protest against the deployment of nuclear missiles, to vote against candidates supporting missiles, and so on.

This is the definition of attitudes that most social psychologists share today and the one we will use here. The thing to remember is that any attitude toward a particular attitude object has these three different components or aspects. The components are distinguished for analytic convenience because they follow somewhat different principles. They are not always consistent with each other; indeed, questions about that consistency have led to some of the most interesting research in the area.

Consider another example of an attitude, shown diagrammatically in Figure 6–1. The figure shows our friend's attitude toward smoking

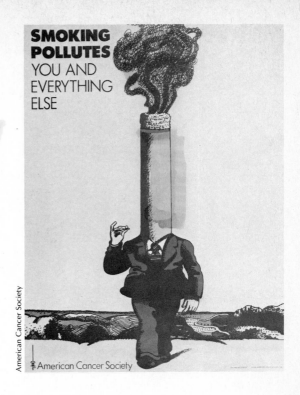

SMOKING POLLUTES YOU AND EVERYTHING ELSE

American Cancer Society

🜲 American Cancer Society

cigarettes. The focus of the whole attitude is on the attitude object, in this case smoking cigarettes. Surrounding the object are the various elements perceived as relevant. Some of these are people, such as parents or roommates; others are personal states such as one's own smell; and others are simple attributes of the object itself, such as its price or taste. This whole cluster of cognitions and their link to the main attitude object, then, constitute the cognitive component of an attitude.

Next there is the **affective,** or evaluative, **component.** The separate cognitive elements themselves have positive or negative feelings connected to them, and the central attitude object does too. In Figure 6–1 positive and negative evaluations of the elements and central object are indicated by plus and minus signs, respectively. The evaluations of the related ob-

FIGURE 6–1 Schematic representation of an attitude toward smoking cigarettes. The core object is surrounded by a cluster of cognitions, which are all related to it. The signs refer to the affective components of her overall attitude toward smoking and her affects toward the separate cognitions she associates with smoking. A positive sign refers to a positive or favorable affect and a negative sign to a negative or unfavorable affect.

jects are shown in the boxes. Her negative feelings about smoking come from the dislike her roommate and parents have for smoking, its bad taste and smell, and her feelings that smoking is dangerous and too expensive. To be sure, she likes studying to go easier, and to be relieved of some social discomfort. Still, the affective component of her attitude toward the central object, smoking, combines evaluations of all these separate cognitions. And she plainly has a strong negative evaluation of cigarettes. She dislikes and is afraid of them. This is shown in the diagram by the minus sign in the central circle. The affective component of the attitude, then, can be thought of as consisting of all the affects toward the central object and toward the separate cognitions linked to the attitude object in question.

Cognitive Complexity

One feature of many attitudes is cognitive complexity. We have a great many thoughts and beliefs about the object. They may not all be factually correct, but the cognitions are numerous. In Figure 6–1 we have shown only a few of the cognitions an individual could have regarding cigarettes. And a number of other factors are not included in the structure. For example, each cognition can vary in importance (e.g., the fact that cigarettes are expensive is probably less important than the fact that they are linked to lung cancer). The attitude can get quite complex and include a great many cognitions that vary in the nature of their relationship to the core and in their evaluative component. This figure is an oversimplification of many attitudes in real life.

Just think of the Pandora's box opened up by the fact that these cognitions are related to one another and to many others, rather than existing in a vacuum. The thought that cigarettes help studying is meaningful only when an attitude toward studying is considered. And then attitudes toward studying can bring in attitudes toward parents, teachers, a future career, and so on. The real cluster would contain all the person's thoughts in connection with cigarettes.

Evaluative Simplicity

Most attitudes tend to be as evaluatively simple as they are cognitively complex. Even though our friend has many cognitions about smoking, her evaluation of it is relatively simple: Smoking alienates her roommate and parents, tastes bad, smells bad, is expensive, runs the risk of lung cancer—and helps her study late at night. Almost all the attributes or consequences of smoking are negative, and so is her overall attitude. This pattern is quite common: The multitude of cognitions exists in people's minds and may have some influence on them, but by and large, the evaluative components of their attitudes are much simpler.

There have been many demonstrations of the evaluative simplicity of most attitudes. As noted in Chapter 3, our impressions of other people quickly tend to become evaluatively consistent. No matter how much we know about them, we tend generally to like or to dislike them. Even at the more remote level of attitudes about public affairs, where people often do not have much information, their attitudes are quite consistent, at least on the most important issues (Kinder & Sears, 1985).

When they vote for Ronald Reagan for president, for example, people tend to support him on most economic and defense issues, feel that he has performed well as president, perceive him as sharing their own positions on the issues, and perceive him as having generally desirable personality traits. On racial issues, white Americans tend to have highly interrelated attitudes. If they are opposed to affirmative action programs, they are also likely to be opposed to busing of schoolchildren for integration, and so on (Sears, Hensler, & Speer, 1979).

This evaluative simplicity is extremely important. For example, both police officers and drug users know a great deal about drugs, have much complex information about them, and understand a variety of interrelationships between drugs and other aspects of the world. And each of these pieces of information to some extent influences their general feelings toward drugs and has a substantial effect on their behavior. Knowing what drugs look like, how much they cost, where they can be obtained, the difference among various kinds, and so on, affects the activities of both users and narcotics squad.

Nevertheless, the relatively simple evaluative component of the attitude is the major determinant of behavior. Although the details of users' and police officers' behavior toward drugs is influenced by the knowledge they have, the general direction of their behavior is influenced primarily by their overall evaluation—

whether they consider drugs to be positive or negative.

Another difference between the cognitive and affective components of an attitude is that it is usually much easier to change the cognition. Think about the difference between "attitudes" and beliefs in "facts." Attitudes have an evaluative or emotional component that beliefs in facts do not have.

A scientist believes that it is 252,710 miles to the moon or that human beings have 46 chromosomes. She also has a complex collection of other beliefs about the moon and chromosomes. But under most circumstances, she does not have any emotional feelings toward either—she does not think the moon is good or bad. She does not like or dislike chromosomes. In contrast, she has a collection of "facts" about Ronald Reagan or poison gas, but she also *does* have emotional feelings about these.

As a result, facts and attitudes function differently. Attitudes, once established, are much more resistant to change than beliefs in "facts." The scientist who believes that humans have 46 chromosomes in most cases has no strong commitment to that belief or strong feelings about it one way or the other. Not so many years ago, scientists were convinced that humans had 24 chromosomes. Then somebody discovered that there were 46. Those who originally believed we had 24 probably changed their belief quite readily when they saw the evidence. Certainly high school and college biology students, who were in no way involved in the controversy, changed their "knowledge" almost instantaneously.

This is different from the way people react when their attitudes are concerned. Attitudes are more complicated in this respect than facts. People do not change their attitudes without putting up a fight and being exposed to a considerable amount of pressure. The presence of the evaluative component seems to change the dynamics considerably; it makes the attitude-change process much more difficult. One reason for this is that the evaluation of an attitude object can persist long after the content that produced it is forgotten, as Anderson and Hubert (1963), among others, have shown. The affective component is more durable and central than the cognitive component.

Attitudes and Behavior

The third component of an attitude concerns behavioral tendencies. Suppose we have persuaded our friend that smoking contributes to lung cancer and heart disease, so the cognitive component is in place. She now feels that smoking is bad, so the affective component is in place. But will she stop smoking? That is, will her behavioral component fall into line? Much research in social psychology suggests that actual behavior is often inconsistent with attitudes, and that people seem to be able to live quite comfortably with the inconsistency. Many smokers do believe smoking is bad for your health, and many do not like the taste of nicotine. But it is hard for them to give up. Their smoking behavior is not controlled by their negative evaluations and cognitions about smoking.

So the behavioral component of an attitude is not always consistent with the affective and cognitive components.

The opposite causal link between attitudes and behavior is of interest. Overt behavior can control the evaluative and cognitive components of attitudes. People can behave in a certain way, and their attitudes may fall into line. Perhaps our friend gets pregnant and gives up smoking because her doctor says it would be bad for the unborn baby, her husband is worried about the baby, and her friends criticize her for jeopardizing the baby's health. For nine months, she stops smoking. She may gradually become convinced that smoking is bad not just for baby but for Mama, she may learn to dislike the smell and taste of nicotine, and she may learn new facts about the dangers of smoking. By the time her baby is born, she may have a repertoire of antismoking cognitions and negative evaluations of smoking. So the relationships between the cognitive and affective components of an attitude, on the one hand, and overt behavior, on the other, can go in either direction. In the last half of this chapter we will discuss these causal relationships.

THEORIES OF ATTITUDES

Now that we have a general view of an attitude, we can consider the theoretical frameworks within which attitudes have been studied. The main theoretical approaches outlined in Chapter 1 have been applied in one form or another to research on attitudes just as with other areas of social psychology. The learning approach sees attitudes as habits, like anything else that is learned; principles that apply to other forms of learning also determine the formation of attitudes. The incentive theory holds that a person adopts the attitude that maximizes his or her

gains. Each side of an issue has its costs and benefits, and the individual will adopt the side on which the net gains are greater. Finally, the cognitive approach asserts that people seek harmony and consistency in their attitudes, and between attitudes and behavior. It particularly emphasizes acceptance of attitudes that fit into the person's overall cognitive structure. These approaches are not necessarily contradictory or inconsistent. They represent different theoretical orientations and differ primarily in the factors they emphasize when explaining attitudes.

Learning

The learning approach is most closely associated with Carl Hovland and others at Yale University (1953). The basic assumption behind this approach is that attitudes are learned in much the same way as other habits. People acquire information and facts; they also learn the feelings and values associated with these facts. A child learns that a certain animal is a dog, that dogs are friends, that they are good; finally, he learns to like dogs. He learns both the cognitions and affects of an attitude. And he learns them through the same processes and mechanisms that control other kinds of learning.

This means that the basic processes by which learning occurs should apply to the formation of attitudes. The individual can acquire information and feelings by the process of *association*. Associations are formed when stimuli appear at the same time and in the same place. If a history teacher, a parent, or a television reporter shows us a mean-looking military man in a storm-trooper uniform and says the word *Nazi* in a hostile tone, we form an association between negative feelings and the word Nazi. Conversely, we may be exposed to positive things that can become associated with the U.S. Marines: a friend says they are good, or we see a movie in which they are doing something heroic.

Many of the studies described in the chapter on person perception illustrate this association process. For example, Norman Anderson (1965) conducted experiments in which he listed a number of attributes of a person and then asked subjects to state their impression of that person. As you will remember from Chapter 3, the subject's final attitude was roughly an average of the listed characteristics (warm, friendly, intelligent, ambitious, courageous, and so on). The subject learned to associate those characteristics with the stimulus person. By doing so, the subject also associated their values with the person. The subject likes the stimulus person because the very positive values of "warm" or "friendly" are associated with him. The subject learned an attitude toward the stimulus person by a process of association, acquiring both a cognitive component (the specific characteristic of the stimulus person) and an affective component (the resulting evaluation of the person).

This process of association leads to attitudes toward things as well as toward people. Individuals learn the characteristics of a house, a coun-

Association with the highly respected *New York Times* may get votes.

BOX 6–1
Things Go Better with Coke
(Or Maybe It's Pepsi. . . .)

In one study supporting the direct-reinforcement process in attitude formation, college students were given peanuts and Pepsi-Cola while they read a series of four persuasive communications on different topics; others read the same communications but were given nothing to eat or drink (Janis et al., 1965). The students who had received a reward (a Pepsi) while reading were more positively influenced on all four topics than were those who had not received one, as shown in the table below.

TOPIC	EXPERIMENTAL CONDITION	
	WITH FOOD AND DRINK	WITHOUT FOOD OR DRINK
Cure for cancer	81%	62%
Size of armed forces	67	43
Moon shot	55	30
Three-D movies	67	60

Source: Adapted from Janis et al., 1965, p. 184. Entry is percent of subjects' changing attitudes in advocated direction minus percent changing in opposite direction.

try, an idea, a bill pending in Congress, or anything else. An attitude consists of that knowledge plus the associated evaluative component. The simplest factor in attitude formation is thus the associations the object has.

Learning can also occur through *reinforcement.* If you take a class in psychology, and get an A in it and enjoy it, the act of taking psychology classes is reinforced and you will be likely to take more in the future. Similarly, if you say that psychology is really interesting and your friends all agree with you and support you, positive attitudes toward psychology are reinforced.

Finally, attitudes can be learned through *imitation.* People imitate others, particularly if those others are strong, important people. One of the most important sources of basic political and social attitudes in early life is the family. Children are likely to imitate their parents' attitudes. In adolescence, they are likely to imitate

peers' attitudes. They often find they have learned contradictory values from different people and are under great stress to resolve the conflicts. Later, many students find that friends, teachers, and books in college confront them with ideas and values different from those they had previously learned.

Association, reinforcement, and imitation are the major mechanisms in the learning of attitudes. As a result, learning theories have dominated the research on the *acquisition* of attitudes. The learning approach to attitudes is relatively simple: It views people as primarily passive. They are exposed to stimuli, they learn by means of one learning process or another, and this learning determines the person's attitude. The final attitude contains all the associations, values, and other bits of information the individual has accumulated. A person's ultimate evaluation of a person, object, or idea depends on the number and strength of the positive and negative elements learned.

Incentives

The incentive theory views attitude formation as a process of weighing the pros and cons of various possible positions and then adopting the best alternative. A student might feel partying is fun, and exciting, and her friends like to do it. These considerations give her a positive attitude. But she knows her parents don't want her just to party while she's in college, and it interferes with her studying, and she wants to go to law school. These considerations give her a negative attitude toward partying. According to incentive theory, the relative strengths of these incentives determine her attitude.

One popular version of the incentive approach to attitudes is **cognitive response theory** (Greenwald, 1968; Petty, Ostrom, & Brock, 1981). This theory assumes that people respond to a communication with some positive or negative thoughts (or ''cognitive responses''), and that these thoughts in turn determine whether or not the people change their attitudes as a result of the communication. Suppose you listen to a televised speech by a senator in which she advocates cutting government medicare payments to the elderly. If you say to yourself, ''But what about retired people on small pensions, or people who can't support themselves, like the handicapped, or the poor? Somebody has to support those people, and government programs are about the only way to do it.'' These negative cognitive responses would mean you are unlikely to be persuaded by the speech.

But if you said to yourself, ''That's right! Taxes are too high and those programs are probably just paying for extravagant hospital costs and people should be bearing some of their own medical payments anyway!'' you are likely to come to the speaker's support. The key assumption of the cognitive response viewpoint is that people are active processors of information who generate cognitive responses to messages, rather than being mere passive recipients of whatever messages they happen to be exposed to.

Another common version of incentive theory is the **expectancy-value approach** (Edwards, 1954). People adopt positions that would lead to the most probable good effects, and reject positions that are likely to lead to bad effects or unlikely to lead to good effects. Put more formally, this approach assumes that in adopting attitudes, people try to maximize the value of the various expected outcomes. Suppose you are trying to decide whether to go to your friend's party tonight. You would try to think of the various possible outcomes (dance, drink beer, not study for your midterm tomorrow, meet someone interesting), the values of those outcomes (somewhat enjoy the dancing and drinking beer and meeting someone interesting, might be somewhat hungover, and will get a very bad grade on the midterm), and the expectancy of those outcomes (certain to dance and to get a terrible grade, but unlikely to meet anyone new at a small party).

Taking both expectancy and value into consideration, it's time to start studying: A certain terrible grade is not balanced by a little fun dancing and drinking beer. Putting the expectancy-value theory more formally, people try to maximize subjective utility. The subjective utility of any given position is the product of (1) the *value* of a particular outcome, and (2) the *expectancy* that this position will produce that outcome.

Both versions of the incentive approach are similar to the learning approach in that the attitude is determined more or less by a sum of the positive and negative elements. One difference is that incentive theories ignore the origins of the attitude, and consider only the current balance of incentives. Another difference is that the incentive theories emphasize what people have to gain or lose by taking a particular position. Whether or not their friends would like them, how enjoyable the experience is, etc. are the critical considerations. When there are conflicting goals, people adopt the position that maximizes their gains. The result is that it treats people more as deliberate, calculating, active decision-makers. In contrast, the learning approach treats people more as passive reflectors of the environment and therefore as less rational and deliberate.

Cognitive Consistency

Another major framework for studying attitudes emphasizes **cognitive consistency.** The cognitive consistency approach grows out of the cognitive tradition; it depicts people as striving for coherence and meaning in their cognitive structures. This approach includes a number of somewhat similar theories. They differ in some important respects, but the basic notion behind them is the same: They all assume that people seek consistency among their cognitions.

An individual who has several beliefs or values that are inconsistent with one another strives to make them more consistent. Similarly, if his cognitions are consistent and he is faced with a new cognition that would produce inconsistency, he strives to minimize the inconsistency. Trying to maintain or restore cognitive consistency is the primary motive.

BALANCE THEORY   There are three main variants on the cognitive consistency idea. The first is **balance theory,** which involves consistency pressures among the affects within a simple cognitive system (Heider, 1958). Such a system consists of two objects (one of which is often another person), the relationships between them, and an individual's evaluations of them.

There are three evaluations: the individual's evaluation of each of the objects and of the relationship of the objects to each other. That is, one person's (P, for person) feelings about another person, (O, for other) and both their feelings about an object (X, for some thing). For example, consider a student's attitude toward a teacher and both their feelings about abortion. If

we limit ourselves to simple positive-negative feelings, there is a limited number of combinations of these elements. They are diagrammed in Figure 6–2 with the symbols P, O, and X standing for the student (person), teacher (other), and abortion (attitude object), respectively. The arrows indicate the direction of the feelings. A plus sign means a positive affect, and a minus sign means a negative one. The first diagram shows that the student likes the teacher and that they both support abortion.

The notion of balancing forces comes originally from Gestalt theories of perceptual organization. As we have noted, people try to achieve "good form" in their perceptions of others, just as they try to achieve "good form" or "good figures" in their perceptions of inanimate objects. Balanced relations between people "fit"; they "go together"; they make a sensible, coherent, meaningful picture. The main motive pushing people toward balance is trying to achieve a harmonious, simple, coherent, and meaningful view of social relationships. So a balanced system is one in which you agree with a liked person or disagree with a disliked person. Imbalance exists when you disagree with a liked person or agree with a disliked person. That is, the system is balanced only when either one or three of these relationships is positive.

On the left side of Figure 6–2 are four possible balanced situations—situations in which the relations among the elements are consistent with each other. When the student likes the teacher and both support abortion, the system is balanced. It is certainly consistent when two people who like each other like the same things; their relationship is harmonious because they both agree. If the student likes the teacher and both dislike abortion, balance (harmony) also exists. Neither likes abortion, and they are united in opposition to it. Finally, if student and teacher disagree about abortion, but the student dislikes and would not want to have much to do with the teacher anyway, there is no conflict.

The imbalanced systems have an odd number of negative relations. These occur when the

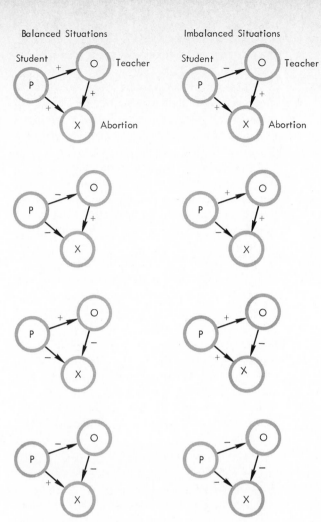

Balanced Situations   Imbalanced Situations

Student   O   Teacher   Student   O   Teacher
P   P
X   Abortion   X   Abortion

FIGURE 6–2
The balance model of
liking. There are eight
possible configurations
of two people and an
object. According to
the model, the
imbalanced structures
tend to become
balanced by a change
in one or more
elements.

student and the teacher like each other but disagree, or dislike each other and agree, about
abortion. The inconsistency lies in the fact that
we expect those we like to have similar likes
and dislikes to ours and those we dislike to have
different likes and dislikes.

The second assumption of the balance model
is that imbalanced configurations tend to
change toward balanced ones. It is this assumption that gives the model its importance. Imbalanced systems produce pressures toward attitude change and continue this pressure until
they are balanced. That is, the systems on the

right side of the figure will change toward becoming like those on the left.

The change can occur in many ways. Balance theory uses a *least effort principle* to predict the direction of change. People will change
as few affective relations as they can and still
produce a balanced system. Any of the relations
may be altered to produce balance. For example, if the student likes abortion but the teacher
does not, and the student likes the teacher, balance could be produced in several ways. The
student could decide that she really does dislike
the teacher, or that she actually dislikes abor-

tion. Alternatively, she might distort reality by misperceiving that the teacher really supports abortion. Which mechanism is chosen depends on the ease of using it and on the individual doing the changing. The important point is that various possibilities exist.

Research on balance theory has generally supported these predictions: People do adjust imbalanced systems toward balance, and in ways that minimize the number of changes that must be made. But balance pressures seem to be much weaker when you dislike the other person than when you like him or her. Newcomb (1968) calls such situations "nonbalanced" rather than "imbalanced." His idea is that we simply do not care very much whether

The memorial for Vietnam Veterans on the Mall in Washington, D.C. is simple but extremely moving emotionally. What cognitions do these people experience, do you think, as they read name after name of the Americans who died in Vietnam?

Marc Anderson

we agree or disagree with someone we dislike; we just cut off the relationship and forget about the whole thing.

Aside from this, perhaps the main value of this research is that it describes the notion of cognitive consistency in extremely simple terms and provides a convenient way of conceptualizing attitudes. The balance model makes it clear that in a given situation there are many ways to resolve an inconsistency. It focuses our attention on one of the most important aspects of attitude change—the factors that determine which of the various modes of resolution are adopted.

COGNITIVE-AFFECTIVE CONSISTENCY   A second version of the consistency approach is that people also try to make their cognitions consistent with their affects. That is, our beliefs, our "knowledge," our convictions about the facts of the matter are determined in part by our affective preferences, and vice-versa. The idea that information determines our feelings is pretty obvious. If we know that a dictator has imprisoned and murdered most of his opponents, we don't like him.

The more interesting version of cognitive-affective consistency is that our evaluations influence our beliefs. Suppose a voter develops a strong negative affect toward the new governor because all his friends at work voted against him, but doesn't really know anything about him. Consistency theory suggests he will acquire the cognitions necessary to support that negative evaluation. In other words, the voter acquires the cognitions consistent with his affective preferences.

Rosenberg (1960) provided a striking demonstration of the cognitive changes created by a change in affect toward an attitude object. He obtained from white subjects a comprehensive description of their attitudes toward blacks, racial integration, and the whole question of relations between blacks and whites. He then hypnotized the subjects and told them that their attitude toward blacks moving into their community was the opposite of what it had previously been. If the subject had previously been strongly against integrated housing, he was told he now was in favor of it (or vice-versa). That is, Rosenberg changed the subject's affect toward integrated housing.

The important point is that he changed their affects without supplying any new cognitions or changing any old ones, since he did it by hypnotic induction. The subjects were then awakened from their hypnotic trance and questioned about their current attitudes about blacks and integration.

Rosenberg found that the change he had produced under hypnosis in this one affect was followed by many dramatic reversals in the subjects' cognitions relevant to integration. For example, the subjects who had originally been opposed to integrated housing came to believe integration was necessary to remove racial inequality, that it was necessary to maintain racial harmony, that it was the only fair thing to do, and so on. These ramifying changes tended to reduce the imbalance that had resulted from the induced change. As the theories of cognitive consistency would predict, the pressures toward reducing inconsistency resulted in a variety of cognitive changes once affect had been changed.

This process is important because many attitudes are acquired as strong affects without many supporting cognitions. A child who likes the Democrats because her parents vote Democratic needs to rationalize that favorable affect later on by acquiring pro-Democratic cognitions. Citizens are supposed to grow up patriotically, supporting their own country, even though they love it mainly by virtue of having been born in it; they must come up with most of the supporting cognitions later on.

DISSONANCE THEORY   A third variant of the cognitive consistency approach is that attitudes will change in order to maintain consistency with overt behavior. Its main expression is cognitive dissonance theory, first proposed by Leon Festinger (1957). As originally proposed, dissonance theory focused on two principal sources of attitude-behavior inconsistency: the effects of making decisions, and the effects of engaging in counterattitudinal behavior.

A decision usually creates some inconsistency, because the behavior of deciding means you have to give up something desirable (all the things you decided not to do) and accept something partially undesirable (even the best choice usually has some flaws). When you engage in counterattitudinal behavior, such as working at a boring job (maybe because you need the money) or taking an uninteresting class (maybe because it is required), inconsistency is produced between your attitudes and your behavior. Such inconsistencies are described as producing cognitive dissonance, which may be reduced in a number of different ways. The most interesting way is to change attitudes so they are no longer inconsistent with behavior. We will discuss this theory in a later section of this chapter, spelling out its predictions and describing some of the ingenious research it has led to.

ATTRIBUTION THEORY   Attribution theory has also been applied to attitude-behavior inconsistencies. Psychologists usually assume that people figure out their own attitudes by reviewing the various cognitions and affects in their consciousness. However, as we saw in the last chapter, Bem (1967) has argued that people know their own attitudes not by inspecting their insides, but by inferring them from their own behavior and their perceptions of the situation.

The implication is that a person's changing of her behavior may lead to the person's inferring that her attitudes have changed as well. If I suddenly find myself studying biochemistry every night, I infer I must really like it. We will discuss research related to this idea in a later section.

ATTITUDES AND BEHAVIOR

Now it is time to consider the impact of attitudes on behavior. Originally it was simply assumed that people's attitudes determined their behavior. A person who favors a certain politician is likely to vote for him; if she likes marijuana she is likely to smoke it; if she is prejudiced against blacks, she is unlikely to send her child to a school in which blacks are in the majority. A great deal of the interest in attitude change, which we will discuss in the next chapter, has come from the assumption that attitudes do affect behavior.

And yet we know of many instances in which behavior does not follow from attitudes. How many times have you seen people smile and say how pleased they are to meet someone when you know they are bored stiff or hate them? The Watergate tapes revealed just how far President Nixon's public behavior departed from his private attitudes. Do attitudes in fact control behavior?

The degree of influence of attitudes over behavior has become one of the important controversies in attitude research. In a classic study, LaPiere (1934), a white professor, toured the United States with a young Chinese student and his wife. They stopped at 66 hotels or motels and at 184 restaurants. Although at the time in the United States there was rather strong prejudice against Orientals, all but one of the hotels and motels gave them space, and they were never refused service at a restaurant. Sometime later, a letter was sent to the same motels and restaurants asking whether they would accept Chinese as guests. Of the 128 establishments replying, 92 percent said they would not. That is, the Chinese couple received nearly perfect service in person, but nearly universal discrimination in the subsequent letters.

LaPiere, and many after him, interpreted these findings as reflecting a major inconsistency between behavior and attitudes. Almost all the proprietors behaved in a tolerant fashion, but they expressed an intolerant attitude when questioned by letter. A similar inconsistency between intolerant verbal attitudes and tolerant overt behaviors was found by Kutner, Wilkins, and Yarrow (1952). A group of two white women and one black woman was seated in all eleven restaurants they entered. But later they telephoned for reservations for a group that included blacks and were refused by six of the restaurants.

Part of the controversy centers on how typical these early studies were. Wicker (1969) conducted one widely cited review. He looked at studies testing for consistency between attitudes and behavior in the areas of race relations, job satisfaction, and classroom cheating. Summarizing 31 separate investigations, Wicker concluded: "It is considerably more likely that attitudes will be unrelated or only slightly related to overt behavior than that attitudes will be closely related to actions."

Yet this conclusion has been widely criticized as underestimating attitude-behavior consistency. Indeed, later studies show much higher degrees of consistency than Wicker reported. In one study, a large sample of Taiwanese married women was asked "Do you want any more children?" In the subsequent three years, 64 percent who had said "Yes" had a live birth, whereas only 19 percent who had said "No" had a child.

Another example is voting behavior. Kelley and Mirer (1974) analyzed large-scale surveys conducted during the four presidential election campaigns from 1952 to 1964. Voters' partisan attitudes, as revealed in preelection interviews, were highly related to actual voting behavior: 85 percent of the respondents showed a correspondence between attitude and behavior, despite the fact that the interviews took place over a two-month span prior to election day. Moreover, most (84 percent) of the inconsistencies occurred for persons whose attitudes showed only weak preferences for either candidate or party.

Such studies led a later careful review to the following conclusion: "Most attitude-behavior studies yield positive results. The correlations that do occur are large enough to indicate that important causal forces are involved, whatever one's model of the underlying causal process may be" (Schuman & Johnson, 1976, p. 199). But everyone acknowledges there is substantial variation across different situations in just how consistent attitudes and behavior are. In recent years, the major research effort has gone into trying to determine the conditions that yield greater or lesser degrees of consistency.

Strength of the Attitude

One set of important conditions affecting consistency is whether the attitude is a *strong* and *clear* one. Inconsistencies can come from weak or ambivalent attitudes. As mentioned, Kelley and Mirer (1974) found that most attitude-vote inconsistencies came from voters with conflicted or weak attitudinal preferences to start with. Similarly, consistent behavior may not follow when the affective and cognitive components of the attitude conflict (Norman 1975).

Anything that contributes to a strong attitude should increase attitude-behavior consistency. One factor certainly would be how much we are forced to rehearse and practice our attitude. Fazio et al. (1982) show that when people have to think about and express their attitudes, their behavior becomes more consistent with the attitude, presumably because this helps to strengthen the attitude.

Having direct personal experience with an issue gets us to think and talk about it more than if it is remote to us. So one hypothesis has been that we will have firmer attitudes about an atti-

tude object when we have direct experience with it than when we only hear about it from someone else, or read about it. If we have firmer attitudes about it, they should also be especially consistent with relevant behaviors.

Regan and Fazio (1977) showed this with students at Cornell University during a severe housing shortage. Many freshmen had to spend the first few weeks of the fall semester in temporary housing, usually a cot in a dormitory lounge. Unlike students assigned immediately to permanent housing, they had direct personal experience with the shortage. While all this was going on, the researchers measured both sets of students' attitudes toward the crisis and their interest in possible behavioral actions, such as signing and distributing petitions, or joining committees to study the crisis. These attitudes and behavior were much more closely related for the students with direct personal experience with the crisis ($r = .42$) than they were for students with only second-hand experience, such as talking to friends or reading about it in the student paper ($r = .04$). Fazio and Zanna (1981) present several other examples of the strong relationship of behavior with attitudes based on direct current experiences.

Past direct experience with an issue should also strengthen attitudes, and thus increase the power of one's attitudes over one's behavior. Manstead et al. (1983), for example, studied predictors of whether mothers would breast-feed or bottle-feed their babies. They found mothers' own attitudes were a better predictor of their choices if they had already had children and had personal experience with feeding an infant. First mothers' behavior depended relatively more on other people's judgments, and less on their own attitudes.

Another source of attitude strength presumably comes from having some vested or selfish interest in the issue. Sivacek and Crano (1982) found support for this notion using the issue of the minimum drinking age. A ballot proposition in Michigan in 1978 would have raised the legal age from 18 to 21. Presumably students under

21 had more of a selfish interest in the issue than did older students. Indeed, attitudes toward the proposal were considerably more tightly correlated with behavior (volunteering to call voters) among these with a vested interest than among the disinterested.

There are of course other reasons why attitudes are strong. But these examples illustrate the general point: Any substantial attitude-behavior relationship depends in part on the attitude itself being a strong one.

Stability of the Attitude

Another critical point is that attitudes may change over time. The attitude held by a person some months or years ago will certainly not affect behavior as much as the person's current attitude. One would not expect to find a close relationship between a college girl's attraction to a boy and her dating behavior with him if her attraction is measured when she is a freshman, and her behavior when she is a senior. Therefore, consistency between attitudes and behavior ought to be maximum when they are measured at about the same time. Kelley and Mirer (1974) found that errors in predicting the vote declined quite rapidly as the preelection interviews got closer to election day.

Partly these longer time intervals diminish the attitude-behavior correlation because attitudes change. But the person and the situation change in other ways as well. For example, a woman might continue not to want to have a child, but her husband may threaten her with divorce if she does not agree to have children.

The longer the interval between measuring the attitude and measuring the behavior, the more such unforeseen contingencies might have arisen. Indeed, in this study, longer time delays in behavior measurement led to worse predictions of behavior by attitudes, quite aside from attitude change. So, when assessing whether or not someone "does what he says," make sure you don't try to hold him to something he said two years ago! Things may have changed.

Relevance of Attitudes to Behavior

The more *specifically relevant* attitudes are to behavior, the more they will be correlated. Attitudes vary quite a bit in how relevant they are to the act in question. LaPiere's asking a proprietor about his feelings about Orientals in general is plainly not as relevant as asking about his attitudes toward this particular Chinese couple (who happened to be quite well-dressed and dignified). In general, behavior tends to be more consistent with attitudes specifically relevant to it than with very general attitudes that apply to a much larger class of potential behaviors.

Several studies have asked people whether they believe in God or consider themselves religious, and then noted whether the subjects attended church. Typically there was only a weak relationship between the answers to those two questions and church attendance, (e.g. Wicker, 1971). But attending church is not necessarily perfectly relevant to a belief in God or even to being religious. Many people who believe in God and even consider themselves religious do not attend church. They may not like organized religions or just wish to practice their religious beliefs privately.

Other people may not consider themselves very religious, but attend church for a variety of reasons having nothing to do with religion. That may be their one social outing of the week. Thus, it is not surprising that the answers to these two questions do not relate directly to church attendance. On the other hand, if people were asked whether they thought attending church was a good idea, presumably the relationship to actual church attendance would be much stronger because that attitude would be more directly related to the behavior.

This point is clear in a study of the predictors of oral contraceptive use (Davidson & Jaccard, 1979). Attitudes toward using "the pill" in the next two years correlated .57 with actual behavior, but attitudes toward birth control *in general* correlated only .08 with the use of oral contraceptives in the next two years. This is

Table 6–1

Correlations of Attitude Measures Varying in Specificity with Behavior (Use of Birth Control Pills during a Two-year Period)

ATTITUDE MEASURE	CORRELATION WITH BEHAVIOR
1. Attitude toward birth control	.083
2. Attitude toward birth control pills	.323
3. Attitude toward using birth control pills	.525
4. Attitude toward using birth control pills during the next two years	.572

Source: Davidson & Jaccard (1979).

shown in Table 6–1. Schwartz (1978) found the same to be true with regard to volunteering to tutor blind children: Attitudes toward the specific behavior predicted it very well, even over several months' or years' time, but attitudes toward altruistic acts in general did not. Similarly, Weigel, Vernon, and Tognacci (1974) found that very general environmental attitudes were not significantly related to willingness to engage in various actions on behalf of the Sierra Club, but attitudes specifically toward the Sierra Club were (a correlation of .68).

Salience of Attitude

In most situations, several attitudes may be relevant to behavior. Cheating on college examinations might be determined by lax attitudes about honesty or by a strong desire to get into law school. "White flight" behavior, putting one's child in a private school to avoid integrated schools, might be determined by attitudes about racial equality or the quality of education in integrated schools. A school superintendent's decision about letting a gay rights sympathizer address a high school assembly might be dictated by his favorable attitude toward the general principle of free speech or by his distaste for gays.

So one important determinant of attitude-behavior consistency should be the salience of whatever relevant attitude we are interested in.

The consistency between intolerant attitudes and discriminatory behavior will probably be fairly low if the person has another attitude in mind at the time of her action. Perhaps her restaurant has so little business she cannot afford to turn anyone away. Her serving a Chinese couple may be consistent with the attitude salient to her at the moment, which is making some money, and inconsistent with the attitude she is not thinking about, her ethnic prejudice.

As a general matter, then, when a specifically relevant attitude is made particularly salient, it is more likely to be related to behavior. Snyder and Swann (1976) assigned subjects to a mock jury situation and gave them a sex discrimination case. In one condition subjects' attitudes about affirmative action were made salient by instructing them to take a few minutes before the case to organize their thoughts on affirmative action. In the "not salient" condition, subjects were not given any warning that affirmative action was involved. When attitudes were made salient, they were highly related to jurors' verdicts in the case. But attitudes about affirmative action were not closely related to verdicts when they had not been made salient.

As you might expect, salience is particularly crucial when the attitude is not a very strong one. When the attitude is very strong, presumably it does not have to be brought very forcefully to the person's attention to be strongly related to behavior. Borgida and Campbell (1982) studied students during a campus parking shortage at the University of Minnesota. Some students were more directly affected by the shortage than others, because they usually drove to campus and either spent a long time looking for a parking place, or got a lot of parking tickets. The researchers exposed some students in each group to a conversation that included complaints about the parking situation and was intended to make attitudes about parking more salient. Others heard a conversation on summer job plans and the merits of racquetball. It turned out that the conversation including the parking issue enhanced the consistency of attitude and behavior (willingness to sign a full-page ad in the campus newspaper) only for students with little real interest in or experience with the issue, for whom the attitude was presumably not very strong.

Situational Pressures

Whenever people engage in overt behavior, they can be influenced both by their attitudes and by the situation. When situational pressures are very strong, attitudes are not generally likely to determine behavior as strongly as when such pressures are relatively weak. This is easy to see in the LaPiere study. Well-dressed, respectable-looking people asking for rooms are hard to refuse, despite feelings of prejudice against their ethnic group. The external pressures are even stronger when the law requires letting rooms to anyone who asks.

A similar dramatic impact of situational pressures on attitudes can be seen in a study of teenage marijuana smoking (Andrews & Kandel, 1979). Attitudes toward marijuana (whether or not it should be legalized, whether use causes physical harm) correlated about .50 with actual marijuana use. But situational forces, in this case peer pressure (as indexed by the number of friends using marijuana), had an effect several times greater.

The relative effects of attitude strength and situation may change from one setting to another. In another study, teenagers' attitudes toward

drinking beer, hard liquor, and wine were the best predictors of frequency of actual drinking of them, but only at parties. At home, actual drinking behavior was better predicted by perceptions of their parents' positions toward drinking, a situational force (Schlegel et al., 1977). Obviously these predictions are not independent. Your friends probably influence your attitudes; you pick friends partly on the basis of attitude similarity; and your own attitudes influence your perceptions of your parents' views.

The Reasoned Action Model

These findings suggest that the theory that attitudes determine behavior is too simple. Sometimes they do and sometimes they do not. The question is, when do they? A related question is how rationally people behave. Do their actions follow logically from their attitudes?

Perhaps the most influential effort to generate and test a simple model of attitude-behavior links is Fishbein and Azjen's "theory of reasoned action" (1975; Azjen & Fishbein, 1980). It is an attempt to specify what factors determine attitude-behavior consistency, starting with the assumption that people behave fairly rationally. The model is diagrammed in Figure 6–3.

The Azjen-Fishbein model has three steps:

1. It predicts that a person's behavior can be predicted from intention. If a woman says she intends to use birth control to avoid getting pregnant, she is more likely to do so than is someone who does not intend to.
2. Behavioral intentions can be predicted from two main variables: the person's attitude toward the behavior (does she think birth control is a good and desirable step for her?) and her perception of what others think she should do (does her husband want her to? What about her church, and her mother?).
3. Attitudes toward the behavior are predicted using the familiar expectancy-value framework. Attitude is a function of how good the outcomes of the behavior will be, considering how likely each

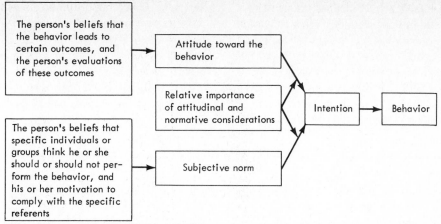

Note: Arrows indicate the direction of influence

FIGURE 6–3 The reasoned action model of factors determining a person's behavior. (From Azjen & Fishbein, 1980, p. 8.)

outcome is. It also provides predictors of the "subjective norm," in terms of the person's beliefs about others' preferences and his or her motivation to comply with them.

This model has been widely used. A simple example is a study by Manstead et al. (1983) predicting whether pregnant women would wind up breast-feeding or bottle-feeding their babies. From prenatal questionnaires the researchers measured behavioral intentions (did the woman intend to breast-feed?), attitude toward the behavior (for example, did she believe that breast-feeding establishes a closer mother-baby bond, and how important is that bond?), and subjective norm (what did the woman's husband, mother, closest female friend, and doctor prefer, and how motivated was the woman to follow their wishes?). The researchers found the model was very successful in predicting later behavior. The correlation of these various attitudes with actual postbirth breast-feeding was .77, which is quite high.

Bentler and Speckart (1981) also used the model quite successfully to predict college students' exercise, dating, and studying behavior over a two-week period. Similar findings have been reported by Ajzen and Fishbein (1980)

and their numerous collaborators on a wide variety of behaviors, such as weight loss, consumer choices, voting behavior, women's occupational choices, and so on.

The model appeals to many social psychologists because it makes people seem reasonable and restores attitudes to a central place in determining behavior. Of course no model is perfect. What are some of the difficulties with this one? The role of behavioral intention is one source of problems. Sometimes "behavioral intention" is not, as measured, very different from "attitude toward the behavior," so it does not add very much to our understanding to bring it in as a separate factor. Asking a pregnant woman whether she intends to breast-feed her baby or not may be almost the same thing as asking her whether she thinks it is a good idea or not. .

In some studies, the model does pretty well without referring to behavioral intention at all (Bentler & Speckart, 1981). Sometimes attitudes have effects on behavior apart from their effects on behavioral intention (Manstead et al., 1983). A number of factors we have mentioned but that are not in the model determine the closeness of the link between behavioral intention and behavior, such as the time interval between the two, their relevance to each other, and so on. Prior behavior also influences future behavior, above and beyond attitudes. How a woman fed her first child influences how she will in fact feed her second, no matter what she or all her friends and family members think is right (Manstead et al., 1983). People are to some extent creatures of habit.

With these reservations, this theory clearly has value in helping to understand the role attitudes play in determining behavior. In general we believe a great deal of evidence now supports the idea that attitudes affect behavior. It seems correct to say that attitudes always produce pressure to behave consistently with them even though other pressures also affect behavior.

COGNITIVE DISSONANCE THEORY

We have been discussing attitude-behavior consistency in terms of the conditions under which attitudes determine behavior. Another possibility is that we have the causal order backward. People's attitudes may be rationalizations for the things they have already done. The person who has given up smoking through a long and agonized process becomes the most obnoxious critic of anyone else who smokes. The newlywed couple expecting the birth of an unplanned baby abandon their ambivalence about having children and broadcast their great delight at the prospect. The military commander who commits his troops to a chancy mission that turns out to be a disaster, costing thousands of casualties, now resolutely declares he was certain he was right all long, and would not change his tactics in any way if he had it to do all over again.

All these examples depict a process in which a person's behavior is followed by substantial attitude change. It also assumes pressure toward consistency between attitudes and behavior, but in a far less flattering manner than the theory of reasoned action. It says that people's behavior controls their attitudes no matter how unthinking the behavior was, rather than that people deliberately and reasonably act on the basis of their thinking.

Most of the research on this problem was originally inspired by the theory of **cognitive dissonance** (Festinger, 1957). Like several other theories we have discussed, cognitive dissonance theory assumes there is a pressure toward consistency. Although it can be applied to inconsistencies between any cognitions, dissonance theory has dealt most creatively with inconsistencies between behavior and attitudes. It has dealt with two particular kinds of behavior-attitude inconsistencies, those produced by making decisions, and those produced by engaging in attitude-discrepant behavior.

Dissonance creates psychological tension, and people feel pressured to reduce or remove it. Dissonance operates much like any other drive: if we are hungry, we do something to reduce our hunger; if we are afraid, we do something to reduce our fear; and if we feel dissonance, we do something to reduce it also. We want to restore consistency, or *consonance.*

The main way of reducing dissonance, if the behavior cannot be revoked or changed in some way, is to change one's attitude. The pacifist who joins the Marines may decide that he does not believe in pacifism any more. Or he may change his attitude about the Marine Corps. Instead of thinking Marines are all killers, he may conclude that the surest way to avoid war is to have a strong military.

Postdecision Dissonance

One behavior that almost always arouses dissonance is decision making. Whenever we must decide between two or more alternatives, whatever choice we make is to some extent inconsistent with some of our beliefs. After we decide, all the good aspects of the unchosen alternative and all the bad aspects of the chosen alternative are dissonant with the decision. If we decide to buy a Mercedes-Benz instead of a Pinto, the Mercedes' speed and stylishness, and the Pinto's crampedness and homeliness, are consonant with the decision. But the Mercedes' price and its expensive repairs, and the inexpensiveness of the Pinto, are dissonant with it.

This dissonance can be reduced by changing our evaluations of the chosen and unchosen alternatives. Increasing our evaluation of the chosen alternative reduces dissonance, because everything positive about it is consonant with the decision. Dissonance can also be reduced by lowering the evaluation of the unchosen alternative. The less attractive it is, the less dissonance should be aroused by choosing the other. Therefore, after people make decisions, there is a tendency for them to increase their liking for what they chose and to decrease their liking for what they did not choose.

A study by Brehm (1956) demonstrated this effect. College women were shown eight products, such as a toaster, a stopwatch, and a radio, and were asked to indicate how much they would like to have each of them. They were then shown two of the eight products and told they would be given whichever they chose. After the objects were chosen and the subjects received the one they selected, they were asked to rate all the objects again. As shown in Table 6–2, on the second rating there was a strong tendency for the women to increase their evaluation of the item they had picked and to decrease their evaluation of the other item.

A no-dissonance control group (shown on the bottom line in the table) shows that the effect was due primarily to dissonance reduction. These women made the first rating but, instead of next choosing between two items and receiving their preference, they were simply given one of the products they had rated high. When they rerated all the products, they showed no tendency to increase the evaluation of the object they owned. This demonstrated that the reeval-

Dissonance is starting to build up already, as people make their purchase decisions.

uation was not simply due to pride of ownership —making the decision was the critical factor.

The tendency toward reevaluation is particularly strong when the two alternatives are initially rated close in attractiveness. Suppose you are trying to choose between a Ford and a Toyota, and you initially much prefer the Ford. You would have little difficulty deciding and little dissonance afterward. There are few reasons why you should have made the opposite choice and therefore little dissonance. Since there is little dissonance, there should be relatively little change in your evaluations of the two alternatives. On the other hand, if the Ford and the Toyota were close in your estimation before the decision, it should arouse a great deal of dissonance. The more reason you had for choosing the Toyota, the more dissonance is aroused by picking the Ford. Thus, when two alternatives are close in attractiveness, a great deal of dissonance is aroused. After the decision is made, there should be greater reevaluation of the two alternatives.

Brehm tested this notion also. He gave some women a choice between a product they had ranked high and one they had ranked only one point below it. Other women were given a choice between a high-ranked product and one that was, on the average, two and one-half points below it. As shown in Table 6–2, the two conditions differed considerably in the amount of dissonance reduction they produced after the choice.

When the products were far apart initially (the low-dissonance condition), there was a total of .37 scale points of dissonance reduction; when the products were quite close (the high-dissonance condition), there was a total of .85 scale points of dissonance reduction. As the theory predicts, the closer the alternatives to begin with, the more dissonance aroused by the decision and the more attitude change after the decision is made.

Dissonance is often created when, having committed ourselves strongly to a course of action, we find the results inconsistent with what we expected. This was the reaction of a group who predicted the end of the world. They thought the world was going to end on a particular day but that they would be saved by a spaceship from outer space. The group kept to itself, avoided publicity, and in general was quiet about its beliefs. When the fateful day arrived and passed without the world being destroyed, they were initially greatly shaken.

Their response, however, was not to give up their beliefs and return to normal life. This would not have reduced the dissonance caused

CONDITION	RATING OF CHOSEN OBJECT	RATING OF UNCHOSEN OBJECT	TOTAL DISSONANCE REDUCTION
High dissonance (objects initially rated close)	+.32	−.53	+.85
Low dissonance (objects initially rated far apart)	+.25	−.12	+.37
No dissonance (gift with no choice)	.00	na	.00

Table 6–2
Dissonance Reduction Following a Decision

Note: The entries in the first two columns are the mean changes in evaluation of the chosen and unchosen objects from before to after the decision. The difference between the two is the total amount of dissonance reduction, shown in the third column.
Source: Brehm (1956).

by all the effort they had put into their plans. Instead, they decided that the day was put off but that the end of the world was still coming soon. In addition, they changed their style considerably. Instead of being quiet and avoiding publicity, they argued that their efforts had postponed the end of the world. And they became much more active in trying to get new supporters (Festinger, Riecken, & Schachter, 1956). Presumably, this helped reduce their dissonance by showing that their original beliefs were basically correct and that, in fact, more and more people were accepting these ideas. Part of the appeal of cognitive dissonance theory is that it often makes counterintuitive predictions. In this case, common sense might suggest that the group give up after its prediction failed so miserably. But dissonance theory predicts that this disproof would lead them not to abandon the theory, but to argue it even more forcefully. And that was just what happened.

Attitude-Discrepant Behavior

The other situation to which the theory of cognitive dissonance has been most often applied is that of **attitude-discrepant behavior.** When an individual holds a belief and performs an act inconsistent with it, dissonance is produced. The pacifist who joins the Marines feels dissonance. He can reduce this dissonance by changing his attitude on pacifism.

Whenever people perform attitude-discrepant behavior, they should experience some dissonance and there should be a tendency for their attitudes to change. Note this assumes that the other element in the situation (the knowledge that they performed the behavior) does not change readily. They have, in fact, performed the act and would find it difficult to convince themselves that they did not. Most of the pressure must be relieved by changing the attitude.

BOX 6–3
Role-Playing and Attitude Change

An impressive example of the attitude-changing effects of engaging in discrepant behavior was provided by Irving Janis. In his work on convincing people not to smoke (Janis & Mann, 1965), cigarette smokers playacted the role of someone who has lung cancer. The subjects became extremely involved in their roles—they looked at X-rays, pretended they were talking to the doctor, playacted their response to the news that they had cancer, imagined themselves waiting for the operation and finally undergoing it, and so on. It was an intense, emotionally arousing experience for them. Janis reported that subjects who went through this experience were more likely to be successful in giving up cigarette smoking than were people who did not participate in such intense role playing.

In a follow-up survey six months later (Mann & Janis, 1968), a large percentage of the people in this condition were still not smoking cigarettes. The subjects who had engaged in less intensive playacting were considerably less successful in giving up smoking. Apparently, the intensive role-playing was an unusually effective persuasive device. This study is just one of a number that show active playacting, or role-playing, to be highly effective in producing attitude change.

BARELY SUFFICIENT INCENTIVES   The most interesting prediction from dissonance theory concerns the effects of incentive on attitude change. On the one hand, there has to be enough incentive to make the person commit the counterattitudinal act. People normally do not act in a way contrary to their attitudes unless there is some reason to do so. So imagine the person as being subjected to a certain level of pressure to perform the attitude-discrepant act. The pressure has to be enough to produce the act.

The next question is what determines how much attitude change will occur. The more dissonance aroused, the more attitude change will be necessary to reduce it. The amount of dissonance aroused depends on just how inconsistent the behavior is with the person's attitudes. If there is great pressure on the individual to perform the discrepant act it is consistent with the decision and does not produce much dissonance. If the pacifist is warned he will be jailed if he does not join the Marines, or if he had

been unemployed for a year and this was the only job he could get, he will experience little dissonance about joining up.

In short, there has to be enough pressure on the person to make him commit the counterattitudinal act. Yet beyond that level, the more pressure is exerted, the less the dissonance, and thus the less the attitude change. The optimal level of pressure is thus a *barely sufficient* amount—enough to produce the behavior, but not enough to prevent dissonance arousal.

POSITIVE INCENTIVES   Perhaps the simplest way to get people to perform attitude-discrepant behavior is to pay them money. Some minimum payment is necessary to get the person to perform it. But beyond that minimal positive incentive, the more money someone is paid for performing an attitude-discrepant act, the less dissonance should be produced if he performs it. So paradoxically, after a certain point, the *more* money the person is paid, *the less* he will change his attitude to justify having done it.

Well, the incentive *does* have to be sufficient to produce the attitude-discrepant behavior!

Suppose you are offered a menial summer job but the pay is extremely good. There is no dissonance and so there is no pressure to reevaluate the job. But suppose you work at a low wage, say $3.50 an hour. Then dissonance is created, which you might reduce by reevaluating the job. Perhaps you start to think that it is an educational experience, or that you meet very interesting people, or that you have plenty of freedom to do other things. The idea is that the *more* original pressure to perform the act (that is, the more consonant cognitions), the *less* the pressure to change your attitudes to make them consistent with the action.

The best early example of this point is found in a study by Festinger and Carlsmith (1959). Volunteers for an experiment worked on an exceedingly dull task. After they had completed it, the experimenter said he needed their help because his usual assistant could not be there that day. He said he was studying the effect of pre-

conceptions on people's performance on a task. He was studying several groups of subjects who were told good things about the task ahead of time, bad things, or nothing.

The next subject was supposed to receive favorable information about the task before performing it. The experimenter asked the subject whether he would be willing to do this for him. All he would have to do is stop the next subject as he was coming into the room, talk to him briefly about the experiment, and tell him that the task was an exceedingly enjoyable one. In other words, he was supposed to pretend to be a regular subject who was just completing the experiment and to lie to the next subject about the dull task by saying that he had found it enjoyable.

At this point, the key experimental manipulation was introduced. Some subjects were told the experimenter would pay them $1 for helping, and others were told they would be paid $20. Virtually all the subjects agreed to the arrangement and proceeded to describe the task to the next subject as very enjoyable. There was also a control group, the members of which were not asked to lie. Soon afterward, the experimenter had all the subjects indicate how much they had actually enjoyed the task. Dissonance about telling the lie could be reduced by

Table 6–3
Amount of Attitude Change Resulting from Attitude-Discrepant Behavior

| | DEPENDENT VARIABLE | |
CONDITION	ENJOYMENT OF TASK	WILLING TO PARTICIPATE IN SIMILAR EXPERIMENTS
$1 reward	+1.35	+1.20
$20 reward	− .05	− .25
Control	− .45	− .62

Note: Entry is the amount of attitude change in each condition. A positive number indicates greater enjoyment of the task or greater willingness to participate in similar experiments

Source: Adapted from Festinger and Carlsmith (1959).

changing attitudes about the task—that is, by deciding that the task was quite enjoyable.

The key comparison was between the $1 and $20 conditions (Table 6–3). Those who were paid $1 rated the task more positively than those who were paid $20. This is what dissonance theory would predict. The larger amount of money served as an additional reason for performing the task; therefore it was a consonant element in the situation and reduced the overall amount of dissonance. The less dissonance, the less attitude change.

This was an extremely influential experiment. It supported the surprising prediction that liking for a disagreeable task would actually be greatest when the person was paid least to do it.

BOX 6–4
Cold Cook, Great Grasshoppers

Another positive incentive we might have for engaging in a discrepant act is how much we like the person who is trying to get us to do it. If your best friend asks you to do something—lend him ten dollars, drive him to the airport, help him cheat on an exam—there is a considerable amount of pressure to agree. If someone you dislike asks you, you are under considerably less pressure. Under most circumstances, it is more difficult to refuse a friend. Thus, if you do something for someone, there should be more dissonance if you dislike the other person than if you like him. This, in turn, means that performing a discrepant act for somebody you dislike should produce more attitude change than performing the same act for someone you like.

This effect was demonstrated in a study (Zimbardo et al., 1965) in which subjects were persuaded by two different kinds of experimenters to eat grasshoppers. In one condition, the experimenter was pleasant, casual, relaxed, and friendly. He presented his arguments in an offhand manner and did his best to be as attractive as possible. In the other condition, the experimenter was cold, formal, somewhat aggressive, and rather forbidding. In general, he did everything he could to be unpleasant. After the subjects who had chosen to eat the grasshoppers had done so, they indicated how much they liked them.

The analysis in terms of dissonance is straightforward. If a subject chose to eat the grasshoppers, dissonance existed if he disliked them. This dissonance could be reduced by making his evaluation of the grasshoppers more positive. To the extent that he liked the experimenter and was eating the grasshoppers as a favor to him, he had additional justification for performing the discrepant behavior. Therefore, the more he liked the experimenter, the less dissonance would exist and the less need he would have to decide that he really liked the grasshoppers.

The results were consistent with this analysis. Subjects who ate the grasshoppers when there was a nasty experimenter liked the grasshoppers more than those who ate the grasshoppers when there was a pleasant experimenter. The pleasant experimenter provided justification, which reduced the dissonance and therefore made it less necessary to reevaluate the grasshoppers.

Many similar experiments have been conducted. Some have used other kinds of positive incentives, such as the amount of justification for performing a boring task (Freedman, 1963). Others have explored the particular conditions under which dissonance-reducing attitude change is most likely to occur. We will discuss several of these; many of them use the same general procedures as the Festinger-Carlsmith study.

THREATS In principle, threats or negative incentives ought to work exactly the same way as positive incentives. One way to try to get people to perform disliked acts is to threaten them with punishment. If they do not pay their income taxes or do their homework, they are penalized. Threats are also used to prevent people from doing things. If people drive too fast, steal cookies from the cookie jar, play with a forbidden toy, or sniff cocaine, they may be punished. The severity of the possible punishments varies enormously. They may get a mild reprimand, miss dessert, be fined $100, spend five years in jail, or even face execution. Assuming the threat of punishment is strong enough to produce the desired behavior or suppress the wrong behavior, greater threat should produce less attitude change.

In experiments by Aronson and Carlsmith (1963) and Freedman (1965), children were shown a group of toys and then forbidden to play with one of them. They were threatened either with mild or with severe punishment if they played with that particular toy. Under these circumstances, if they obeyed and did not play with the toy, dissonance was aroused. The attitude "I would like to play with that toy" is dissonant with the behavior of not playing with it. On the other hand, the behavior of not playing with the toy is consonant with the perceived threat of punishment. Therefore, the *less* severe the threat, the more dissonance it provided.

If the children did not play with the toy, we would expect the dissonance to produce some change in their attitude toward it. A convenient way to reduce the dissonance would be to decide that the toy was not attractive. This would make their attitude less dissonant with their behavior. The greater the dissonance aroused, the more changes of this sort should occur. And because the greater the threat, the less the dissonance, there should be more attitude change with lower threats. Thus, the children would experience more attitude change when the mild threat was used to prevent them from playing with the toy than when the severe threat was used.

In these experiments, none of the children played with the toy, regardless of whether they were threatened with mild or severe punishment, because both threats were strong enough to prevent them. In the two studies, the children either rerated the toys at this point, or were given another opportunity to play with the toy several weeks later. The results of the two experiments are shown in Table 6–4. It can be seen that the children reduced their evaluation of the

Table 6–4
Effect of Severity of Threat on Forbidden Behavior

CONDITION	PERCENTAGE DEVALUING FORBIDDEN TOY[a]	PERCENTAGE NOT PLAYING WITH FORBIDDEN TOY[b]
Mild threat	36	71
Severe threat	0	33

Note: The entry shows the percentage of subjects in each condition showing dissonance-reducing attitudes or behavior.
Source: [a]Aronson and Carlsmith (1963); [b]Freedman (1965).

forbidden toy more and were less likely to play with it later on under mild threat than under severe threat. The greater dissonance in the mild-threat condition was reduced by devaluing the toy or deciding it was wrong to play with it.

Other Conditions for Dissonance

We have identified two general situations in which our behavior may change our attitudes: making decisions and engaging in attitude-discrepant behavior. Attitude change depends on the magnitude of dissonance, and dissonance theory specifies the conditions under which more or less dissonance will be created. Two of these conditions are minimal positive incentives or minimal threats. What are some of the other factors necessary for dissonance-reducing attitude change to occur?

IRREVOCABLE COMMITMENT An interesting aspect of the effect of decisions is that the reevaluation appears only when the result of the decision is certain. If you have taken the Mercedes on a lease-purchase agreement and can get most of your money back if it breaks down, the threat of expensive repairs will not create as much dissonance as if there was no turning back. One key, therefore, to attitude change as a dissonance-reducing mechanism is maintaining the person's commitment to the decision or behavior. As long as the person feels irreversibly committed to that course of action, dissonance promotes attitude change. But if the person feels he can get out of the decision if it works out badly, or he can do it half-heartedly, or he may not have to go through with it at all, dissonance will not be present, and no attitude change may occur. Little dissonance will be created by paying $4,000 tuition if you know you can drop your classes anytime before finals and get most of it refunded.

FORESEEABLE CONSEQUENCES A related point is that people must feel they could have anticipat-

ed the consequences of their behavior. There should be nothing dissonant about making a choice or performing an act that turned out badly as long as there was no way for the individual to foresee this negative outcome.

If someone decides to walk to class on the left side of the street rather than the right side, and as she walks along a brick suddenly falls off a roof and hits her on the head, this is a terrible misfortune. But (if she lives), she should not experience dissonance. "I chose to walk on the left side of the street" is not dissonant with "a brick hit me on the head." For all intents and purposes, the two cognitions are not relevant to each other. On the other hand, if she knew that there was some chance that she would get hit on the head, perhaps because in the last week three other people had been hit on the head by bricks, dissonance probably would be aroused.

Goethals, Cooper, and Naficy (1979) predicted that *foreseeable* consequences, even if unforeseen, would produce dissonance and attitude change; only unforeseeable consequences would not. They had students at Princeton record speeches favoring the doubling of the size of the freshman class. That was a disagreeable possibility to the subjects, given Princeton's reputation as a relatively small, elite college. The possible negative consequence was that the speech might help bring about that undesirable change. Some (foreseen consequences) were told the speech might be given to the board of admissions, which was considering such an increase; others (foreseeable consequences) that it would be given to some other groups, but they were not named. Still others (unforeseeable consequences) were not told of any further use of the speech. After the speech was recorded, all were told of the negative consequences: their counterattitudinal speech would be given to the board of admissions.

Under what circumstances did the subjects change their attitudes in the dissonance-reducing direction of their speech? It turned out that either foreseen or foreseeable consequences promoted attitude change, in line with the notion that either can produce dissonance.

CHOICE Another major contributor to dissonance is the feeling of choice about the behavior. If you feel you freely and of sound mind chose the Mercedes, you will have dissonance to reduce afterward. But often we do not feel much sense of choice about what we do. Maybe the salesperson talked us into signing a contract and writing a check before we knew what was happening. Or maybe our old car had been wrecked and this was the only new one available. Without the feeling of choice, there is no dissonance.

Similarly, attitude-discrepant behavior creates dissonance only when the behavior is freely chosen (or at least the person feels it is freely chosen). This is shown quite clearly in two experiments by Linder, Cooper, and Jones (1967). Students wrote an essay that disagreed with their opinions. Some subjects were made to feel they had a choice about whether or not they wrote the essay; others were given no choice. Half the subjects in each condition were paid $2.50, and half were paid $0.50. The amount of attitude change in the four conditions for the two experiments is shown in Table 6–5.

With free choice, the typical dissonance effect appeared. There was more change with less reward. With no choice, the dissonance effect did not obtain. There was more change with greater reward.

RESPONSIBILITY FOR CONSEQUENCES The importance of perceived choice is that it brings with it perceived responsibility for all consequences, whether or not it is "logical" to feel responsible for them. As we saw in the last chapter, people tend to make internal attributions whenever behavior is committed under free choice, and assign moral responsibility for behavior that is internally caused. A series of studies has shown the crucial role of this feeling of responsibility for dissonance arousal.

Even unforeseen negative consequences provoke dissonance, as long as the decision maker feels responsible for the consequences. If he feels no responsibility for the outcome, there is no dissonance regardless of how disastrous the

| Table 6–5 | | |
| The Effects of Incentive and Choice on Attitude Change | | |
CONDITION	FREE CHOICE	NO CHOICE
Experiment 1:		
$0.50 incentive	2.96	1.66
$2.50 incentive	1.64	2.34
Experiment 2:		
$0.50 incentive	3.64	2.68
$2.50 incentive	2.72	3.46

Note: The figures are ratings on a scale from 1 to 7. The higher the figure, the greater the attitude change.
Source: Adapted from Linder, Cooper, and Jones (1967).

result. If he does feel responsible, then dissonance occurs whether the consequence could reasonably have been foreseen or not. Pallak and his colleagues designed a series of studies to illustrate this point. In the first one (Pallak, Sogin, & Van Zante, 1974) a boring task was reevaluated in a more favorable direction, consistent with dissonance reduction, even when the negative consequences (learning that the task was just wasted time) were not known until after the task was completed—as long as the subject completed it under high perceived choice. In later work (Sogin & Pallak, 1976), they pinpointed the dissonance effect as depending on an internal attribution. If the negative consequences came about because of something the subject felt responsible for, a dissonance reevaluation would take place whether the effects were foreseen or unforeseen.

So the critical question regarding unforeseen negative consequences is whether or not the individual *feels* her own prior behavior was responsible for them. That is why perceived choice is so important. When people choose something that works out badly, they feel responsible for the outcome, and it creates dissonance.

These, then, are the main preconditions for cognitive dissonance, and for the attitude change that results from taking decisive action: minimum incentives, irrevocable commitment and foreseeable consequences, perceived choice, and personal responsibility for the consequences. This is a somewhat narrower set of conditions than originally proposed by dissonance theorists. Both postdecisional dissonance and dissonance inspired by attitude-discrepant behavior are not as common as had been believed in the earliest versions of dissonance theory. But they do occur fairly reliably, given this restricted set of circumstances.

SELF-PERCEPTION THEORY

Cognitive dissonance theory originally inspired this research on the effects of behavior on attitude change, and for a number of years provided the only theoretical interpretation of these findings. However, in 1967 Bem offered another interpretation in terms of self-perception theory. As we saw in the last chapter, he argued that many of our attitudes are based simply on our perceptions of our own behavior and/or the circumstances in which this behavior occurs.

If we eat oranges and somebody asks us how we feel about oranges, we say to ourselves, "I just ate oranges; nobody forced me to eat them; therefore I must like oranges." Accordingly, we tell the person we like oranges. Similarly if we vote for a Republican in a free election, we assume that we have Republican attitudes; if we go to church, we assume that we are religious; and so on.

It is easy to see how this might apply to attitude-discrepant behavior. A subject is paid one dollar to tell someone that a particular task was very enjoyable. When the subject is subsequently asked how enjoyable he himself thought the task was, he says to himself, "I said that the task was enjoyable and I was paid only one dollar. One dollar is not enough to make me lie, so I must really think that the task is enjoyable." On the other hand twenty dollars perhaps is a sufficient amount to tell a lie. So the subject then might say to himself, "The reason I said it was enjoyable was to get the $20; I didn't really believe it."

Thus this self-perception explanation makes the same predictions as dissonance theory: The more the subject is paid to make the discrepant statement, the less he will believe it. Similar explanations can be offered for virtually all dissonance phenomena. The major difference is not in the predictions, but in the interpretations. The two theories offer radically different views of attitudes and of the way in which behavior influences attitudes.

The more traditional view of attitudes reflected in dissonance theory is that they are enduring, learned predispositions. When people engage in counterattitudinal behavior, they suffer from unpleasant tensions that can be relieved only by giving up their attitudes. Dissonance theory describes people as stubbornly resisting change. They have to be lured and cajoled into a very particular set of circumstances in which they finally feel so involved and committed they must change. Bem's self-perception theory suggests that people's expressions of attitude are "top of the head" phenomena, rather casual verbal statements. People have no great stake in their attitudes; rather, they seem simply to be trying to cooperate with a curious questioner by giving a plausible answer, without strong conviction or feelings.

Conditions for Self-Perception

Dissonance theorists at first reacted with horror to Bem's reinterpretation. The very original, painstakingly created, and ingenious experiments they had done were now being seriously misinterpreted as reflecting some alien process. Their initial response was to try to design experiments that would disprove Bem's interpretations. This proved to be surprisingly difficult. Today, social psychologists assume that both processes occur on some occasions. The real question is this: Under what conditions is one more likely to occur than the other?

The self-perception process should be most likely to occur when people's own attitudes are vague and ambiguous. It would not be surprising if we should arrive at an attitude about a new and unfamiliar laboratory task on the basis of our perceptions of our behavior in the experimental situation. It would be more surprising if we were to use self-perception to figure out our attitude about our favorite foods, like beer or pizza or broiled lobster. We do not need to feel ourselves salivate or watch ourselves devour every last morsel to know that we love those things; we know that when we think about them.

Chaiken and Baldwin (1981) tested the hypothesis that self-perception theory works only when people do not possess well-defined prior attitudes. They first separated subjects with strong, consistent attitudes toward ecology and the environment from those with relatively inconsistent attitudes. Then they put all subjects through the procedures developed by Salancik and Conway (1975) and described in the last chapter. Briefly, this involved manipulating subjects' perceptions of their own behavior by asking some subjects whether or not they do something "on occasion," and others whether or not they do it "frequently."

If the self-perception process works, the variation in perceptions of one's own behavior should result in parallel differences in self-perceived attitudes. People who say they "litter on occasion" should perceive themselves as having anti-environmental attitudes. Those who say they do not "litter frequently" should perceive themselves as having pro-environmental attitudes. These attitudes were measured on items concerning nuclear power, solar energy, outlawing nonreturnable soft drink bottles, aerosol cans, and so on.

The hypothesis, that the self-perception process would work only for those without strong and well-defined prior attitudes, was quite strongly supported. This can be seen in Table 6–6. Among the subjects whose prior attitudes were highly consistent, the manipulation of self-reported environmentalist behaviors had no significant effect on attitudes, as shown in the top row. However, among those with relatively inconsistent attitudes, the manipulation had the large effect predicted by Bem's self-perception theory: People who had been induced to describe their behavior as pro-environment perceived themselves as being more pro-environmental in their attitudes than did those induced to describe their behavior as more anti-environment.

The conclusion (Chaiken & Baldwin, 1981, p. 8) was that "the self-perception account of attitude expression holds primarily for individuals who do not possess well-defined prior attitudes toward the target attitude object. . . ." Later research has developed this conclusion. Well-defined prior attitudes might not be available because the individual has relatively few

	INDUCED REPORTS OF BEHAVIOR AS:	
PRIOR ENVIRONMENTALIST ATTITUDES	PRO-ENVIRONMENT	ANTI-ENVIRONMENT
High consistency	9.00	9.68
Low consistency	11.33	8.25

Table 6–6
Self-Perceived Environmentalist Attitudes

Note: The entry is mean score on a pro-environmental scale.
Source: Adapted from Chaiken and Baldwin (1981), p. 6.

prior beliefs, or has had relatively few prior experiences with regard to the issue (Wood, 1982). Or it might be because the person has no immediate sensory data relevant to the issue—as, for example, never having tasted the food products one is trying to decide between (Tybout & Scott, 1983). Under the opposite conditions, in which people do have well-defined prior attitudes, we might expect the dissonance rather than the self-perception process to be more important.

Is Dissonance a Drive?

Another line of attack on this controversy between these theoretical positions involves the contention that dissonance is uncomfortable, that it acts as a drive much like hunger, and that the person does what she can to reduce this discomfort. Bem's analysis would not expect attitude-discrepant behavior to arouse discomfort or drive. Fortunately, this difference between the theories is directly testable.

One implication of the misattribution studies discussed in the last chapter is that subjective arousal states can be reduced to the extent that the person attributes them to other stimuli, such as a pill. This observation can help us determine whether dissonance is a subjective arousal state or not.

The theoretical reasoning is this: Dissonance is supposed to occur when one writes an attitude-discrepant essay under high-choice conditions. But if dissonance is really an aroused internal drive, we should be able to reduce it either by reattributing the drive to a pill, or by changing attitudes to restore consistency. Telling subjects they have been given an arousing pill therefore ought to substitute for attitude change. But attitude change should occur when the subject cannot reattribute her reactions to an external cause such as a pill. The Bem self-perception analysis assumes that dissonance-producing situations arouse no drive. If that analysis is correct, the presence or absence of a plausible external cause like a pill is irrelevant.

The dissonance-as-drive idea holds that no attitude change should occur if arousal can be attributed to some cause other than inconsistency. To test this, Zanna and Cooper (1974) gave subjects a pill; in one condition they were told the pill would make them feel tense, in the other, that it would make them feel relaxed. Subjects were then induced to write counterattitudinal essays under either high- or low-choice conditions.

Subjects who were told they would feel tense because of the pill showed no dissonance effect—that is, high choice produced no more attitude change than low choice. When the subject could attribute arousal to the pill there was presumably no dissonance, and therefore no dissonance-produced difference in attitude change. However, when they were told the pill would just make them feel relaxed, the high-choice condition produced more attitude change in the direction of the essay than did the low-choice condition, in line with the usual dissonance effect. That is, when the subject could not attribute arousal to the pill because it was supposedly a relaxation pill the dissonance effect occurred, presumably because the person still felt aroused. This gives additional evidence for supposing that dissonance effects do depend on some kind of physiological arousal mechanism, which can be eliminated or reduced if the subject can attribute arousal to some extraneous stimulus.

The general principle appears to be that situations involving commitments or counterattitudinal acts create tension under the conditions described: choice, foreseeable negative consequences, minimal external pressure, and so on. Attitude change as a response depends on having no other way to reduce the tension—by blaming it on external pressure, a drug-induced state (especially if unpleasant; see Higgins et al., 1979), or by revoking the behavior. And the two processes probably work best in different arenas: dissonance theory with more controversial, involving issues; and self-perception theory with more vague, uninvolving, minor, novel issues.

SUMMARY

1. Attitudes have a cognitive (thought) component, an affective (feeling) component, and a behavioral component.
2. People often have cognitively complex attitudes. However, like personality impressions, attitudes tend to be organized around the affective (or evaluative) dimension and to be evaluatively simple.
3. The learning approach views attitudes as learned by association, reinforcement, and imitation. The incentive approach views attitudes as the products of cost-benefit calculations by the individual. Cognitive consistency theories view people as attempting to maintain consistency among their various attitudes, between their affects and cognitions toward a given object, and between their attitudes and behavior.
4. It is usually assumed that behavior arises from attitudes, but considerable research questions how consistent the two are with each other. Now it appears that behavior is consistent with attitudes only under certain conditions: strong, clear, specific attitudes, and with no conflicting situational pressures.
5. Dissonance is most commonly created by the individual's behavior. Dissonance arises following decisions and following behavioral acts contrary to the individual's attitudes.
6. Dissonance can be reduced in a variety of ways. If the behavior itself cannot be revoked, the most important alternative is attitude change to reduce attitude-behavior discrepancies.
7. Postdecisional dissonance is greatest when people remain committed to their decisions for a long time, if they have free choice in their decisions, if the consequences of the decisions are known in advance and are certain, and if they feel responsible for the consequences.
8. Dissonance following attitude-discrepant behavior depends upon barely sufficient incentives to commit the behavior. These incentives can be either minimal threat or minimal promised reward. The maximum dissonance following attitude-discrepant behavior occurs with minimum incentive, negative consequences of the act, and clear personal responsibility for the consequence.
9. Alternative explanations for these dissonance effects have been generated by attribution theorists. When people have rather vague, undefined attitudes, behavioral acts may lead to fresh self-perceptions of attitudes, thus leading to attitude-behavior consistency through an attribution rather than a dissonance-reduction process.

SUGGESTIONS FOR ADDITIONAL READING

ABELSON, R. P., ARONSON, E., McGUIRE, W. J., NEWCOMB, T. M., ROSENBERG, M. J., & TANNENBAUM, P. E. 1968. *Theories of cognitive consistency: A sourcebook.* Chicago: Rand McNally. An extensive compilation of papers on almost every version of consistency theory, by almost everyone who ever wrote about it. Its nickname is TOCCAS.

AJZEN, I. & FISHBEIN, M. 1980. *Understanding attitudes and predicting social behavior.* Englewood Cliffs, N.J.: Prentice-Hall. A succinct treatment of the "theory of reasoned action," applying it to such social problems as obesity and weight loss, family planning, career choices, and voting behavior.

BEM, D. J. Self-perception theory. 1972. In L. Berkowitz (ed.), *Advances in experimental social psychology, Vol. 6.* New York: Academic Press. The clearest and best statement of the self-perception approach to attitudes.

COLLINS, B. E., & HOYT, M. F. 1972. Personal responsibility for consequences: An integration and extension of the "forced compliance" literature. *Journal of Experimental Social Psychology, 8,* 558–93. A good example of an experiment that attempts to maximize the conditions for dissonance arousal.

DAVIDSON, A. R., & JACCARD, J. J. 1979. Variables that moderate the attitude-behavior relation: Results of a longitudinal survey. *Journal of Personality and Social Psychology, 37,* 1364–76. A sophisticated state-of-the-art study of attitudes and behavior.

FESTINGER, L., 1957. *A theory of cognitive dissonance.* Stanford, Calif.: Stanford University Press. The original statement of cognitive dissonance theory. It is elegant in its simplicity, and offers plausible speculations about a broad range of psychological phenomena.

KIESLER, C. A., COLLINS, B. E., & MILLER, N. 1969. *Attitude change: A critical analysis of theoretical approaches.* New York: Wiley. A good overview of the several different approaches to attitude theory covered in this chapter.

7

ATTITUDE CHANGE

What makes a person vote for a Democratic candidate in one election and switch to his Republican opponent in the next election? Why did so many Americans change their anti-German and anti-Japanese attitudes during World War II to supportive attitudes a few years later? Why do people change their attitudes toward long hair, or miniskirts, or neckties, in such short periods of time?

A major answer is that our attitudes are influenced by other people, in particular by mass communications in television, radio, newspapers, and books. Corporations pour millions of dollars into advertising aimed at convincing us that last year's skirts are too long or too short, that our old cars are passé and should be replaced at once, and so on. Political candidates spend sizable fractions of their campaign budgets to buy TV time and put much energy into figuring out how to get additional free exposure. Although we may not think of it in the same way as advertising, the government, schools, and other social institutions also seek to shape and change attitudes. Public debates over the content of school textbooks and school prayer suggest that many people are concerned about the messages being presented by our public institutions. This chapter analyzes the attitude change that results from mass communication.

A MODEL OF PERSUASION

Much of the research on mass communication and attitude change began with a program organized by Carl Hovland at Yale University shortly after World War II.

Figure 7–1 presents a model based largely on Hovland's but simplified and changed to bring it more in line with recent work in this area.

There must be a *communicator* who holds a particular position on some issue and is trying to convince others to hold this position. To do so, this person produces a *communication* designed to persuade people that the position is correct and to induce them to change their own positions in the direction of this one. Such a communication is presented in a given *situa-* *tion*. These constitute the external stimuli—the source, the message, and the surroundings.

Similarly, the *target* individual is no blank slate. Each person comes to a situation with prior attitudes and predispositions that will influence his or her openness to the message. A television viewer may hate all beer, or drink a different brand, or distrust all television commercials, and so be unresponsive to persuasion. Or the person may be a heavy beer drinker with no strong brand preference and be quite amused by the ad.

Part of the story of mass communications, then, is knowing the independent variables that affect persuasion. But to fully understand the ef-

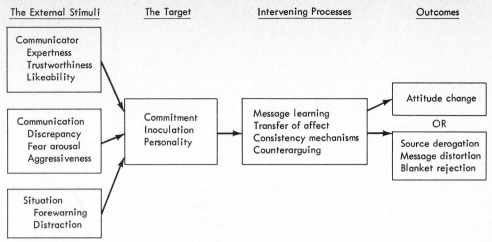

| The External Stimuli | The Target | Intervening Processes | Outcomes |

Communicator Expertness Trustworthiness Likeability			
Communication Discrepancy Fear arousal Aggressiveness	Commitment Inoculation Personality	Message learning Transfer of affect Consistency mechanisms Counterarguing	Attitude change OR Source derogation Message distortion Blanket rejection
Situation Forewarning Distraction			

FIGURE 7–1 Model of the persuasion situation.

fects of mass communications, we must also understand the underlying social-psychological processes. In Chapter 6 we touched on the best-known theories of attitude change, which have grown out of the general learning, incentive, and cognitive approaches. So another goal of this chapter is to describe the underlying processes that determine how these communicator, communication, situation, and target factors affect attitude change. Finally, there are many possible effects of a persuasion attempt other than attitude change. The viewer may wind up thinking the communicator is a fool rather than believing the message. The viewer may miss the message altogether; he or she may think the beer commercial was trying to sell T shirts. So we need to consider other outcomes as well.

In this chapter we will examine each element of this general model in detail. We begin by considering the psychological processes that underlie attitude change. We then review research on how characteristics of the communicator, the message, the target, and the situation affect attitude change.

Steve Kagan, Photo Researchers, Inc.

Dan Rather is one of the best-known communicators on American television. What characteristics does he have that help make him a credible and persuasive souce of information?

The External Stimuli

The *communicator* is one of the first things we notice in a mass communication situation. Some communicators are authoritative, like our strict high school geometry teacher or a scientist being interviewed on public television about her research on African apes. Others may be more humorous, like the weekend touch football players who urge us to buy a particular beer from their sweat-stained vantage points in a crowded bar. Others may not seem like communicators at all, like the friend we ask for advice about where to buy a formal skirt and sweater for an upcoming job interview. Whatever the nature of the person delivering the message, he or she is a crucial ingredient in its persuasive success.

In the typical attitude change situation, individuals are confronted with a *communication* in favor of a position different from the one they hold. They may have a negative attitude toward capital punishment and someone tells them that it really deters crime; they may be Democrats listening to a Republican campaign speech; they may be smokers reading the Surgeon General's report linking lung cancer to cigarette smoking. The discrepancy between the individual's attitude and the attitude expressed in the communication places some pressure on the person to resolve the discrepancy.

But mass communications always reach the individual in a context. Part of that context involves the external *situation* around the person, such as whether he or she has been forewarned of what the communicator will say or how distracted the person is at the moment. Someone watching a football game briefly interrupted by a beer commercial may be dazzled by a horde of joking retired professional athletes, some flirting with attractive women. But this person is in quite a different situation from the one who has deliberately tuned in to watch a hated political candidate argue for some disagreeable position; the latter is ready and waiting, forewarned and undistracted.

Processes of Attitude Change

It would be impossible to keep track of all the factors that can affect attitude change if they were not organized in some way. The theories

described at the beginning of the last chapter are the most commonly cited efforts to account for behavior in the area of attitudes. But not all of them have been useful in explaining research results. Here we will emphasize four somewhat more specific versions of those theories that have proved helpful in understanding the results of studies on attitude change. These are message learning, transfer of affect, consistency mechanisms, and counterarguing.

LEARNING THE MESSAGE   Perhaps the most obvious idea is that learning the message is crucial in attitude change. If the person learns the message, change will follow. If this were true, the key question would be what increases or decreases learning. For example, expert communicators might be very effective because people want to remember what they have said, and complex messages would be ineffective because they are difficult to learn.

Surprisingly, however, actually learning the message is much less important than we might expect. To be sure, it is vital that the listener know what position is being advocated. If the president is advocating military aid to a Central American nation, the listener must learn that and not think the president wants to send toys to Norway. But beyond this learning of the communicator's basic position, additional learning of the details of the message seems not to affect attitude change very much one way or the other. In other words, beyond some necessary minimum, message learning has turned out to be relatively unimportant in determining the success of persuasion. It seems to be enough for people to get the general conclusion of the message. Whether or not they get the details is not terribly important, since at that point other processes seem to matter more (see McGuire, 1969).

TRANSFER OF AFFECT   People may simply transfer the affect or evaluation between two objects that are associated. Imagine a television commercial for an automobile. To persuade you to have a positive attitude toward the automobile the car is associated with many other positive objects. We are not simply shown a sleek car and told how powerful, quiet, and comfortable it is. While the message is being delivered, we are shown beautiful women, handsome men, and lovely children, with perhaps some graceful horses or cute dogs in the background. Or the car may be endorsed by a famous athlete or movie star. Presumably, all this beauty, fame, and popularity will become associated with the car, thus increasing our positive feelings toward the car and the likelihood that we will buy it. In other words, people simply transfer their feelings about one object (beautiful people) to another (the car). This idea comes from the association version of learning theory discussed earlier.

To test this **transfer of affect** notion, Lorge (1936) presented American students with the following message: "I hold that a little rebellion, now and then, is a good thing, and as necessary in the political world as storms are in the physical." Subjects agreed with the message when it was attributed to Thomas Jefferson, and disagreed with it when it was attributed to Lenin. Lorge argued that the positive affect associated with Jefferson made the message more positive when it was attributed to Jefferson, while the negative affect associated with Lenin had the opposite effect—in either case a simple transfer of affect. Later research has supported this idea in a wide variety of contexts.

CONSISTENCY MECHANISMS   A third approach derives from consistency theories and emphasizes that inconsistency produces psychological tension.

Suppose you have just voted for your state's new governor, and she comes out in favor of some changes you really do not like, such as increased tuition and reduced student aid for the state universities. You are faced with an inconsistency between your support for the governor and her endorsement of positions you oppose. According to the consistency theories, this inconsistency should be uncomfortable for you and lead you to change. You may change your

attitudes about tuition and student aid, or you may change your attitude about the governor, but some change is required if consistency is to be restored.

In general, a communication causes some pressure toward change when it is discrepant from the recipient's original position. Consistency theories suggest the pressure can be reduced in a variety of ways. If the recipient changes her attitude, reducing the discrepancy, then this pressure ought to be reduced. Most research on attitudes has concentrated on this mechanism for restoring consistency. The emphasis on so-called alternative modes of resolution is one of the important contributions of Carl Hovland's model of attitude change and of the cognitive consistency models, as we will see below in discussing alternative responses to the communication.

COUNTERARGUING   You read a story in the student newspaper about a proposal to ban all students from driving their cars to campus because of severe parking and traffic problems surrounding the campus. You think this is a bad idea. Right off the bat you can think of some serious problems the proposal would create. You know students who live in a town thirty miles from campus; how could they get to school? The local bus service goes to some neighborhoods where students live but not to others, and it is too far for those students to walk or bike. Some women students have labs or work in the library until very late at night, and it might be risky for them to walk or hitchhike home at that hour. You have friends who work off campus, and you cannot see how they could make their classes and get to their jobs on time if they used the bus. All in all, you see a lot of arguments against the ban.

Sometimes the recipient can resist by considering and actively attempting to refute the arguments. He can engage in a debate and attempt to demonstrate to himself that his own position has more merit than the other one. This debate can be implicit or explicit, verbal or nonverbal, perhaps even conscious or unconscious. He can argue against the discrepant communication, produce evidence to support his own position, show how the other side is illogical or inconsistent, and in general do anything he can to weaken the impact of the communication. To the extent that he is able to do this, the pressure to change should be reduced. This counterarguing mechanism differs from the consistency mechanisms, which describe a person who resists persuasion, but who does not deal with the merits of the arguments.

Cognitive response theory is the main statement of this counterarguing view. As described in the last chapter, it depicts the recipient as responding to the communication with a series of thoughts about it. These cognitive responses determine the person's overall response to the message. But attitude change will depend on how much and what kind of counterarguing the message triggers. Conversely, persuasion can be produced by interfering with the counterarguing process. If the person cannot think of any good counterarguments, or can be distracted from thinking of them while listening to the message, the communicator has a better chance.

This process describes the recipient as actively relating the new arguments to prior attitudes and beliefs. In so doing, the person rehearses her own attitudes and considers the details of the communication. The problem with this mode of resolution is twofold: Usually recipients are rather lazy, and communicators are more motivated. Most people, most of the time, are not very motivated to analyze the pros and cons of complex arguments.

Moreover, persuasive messages are usually designed to be difficult to reject on purely logical grounds. The authors of the communication naturally present as strong a case as they can and are generally better informed on the topic than the recipients. Therefore, although arguing against the discrepant communication is a rational mode of resolution, it is often difficult to employ.

These, then, are four simple ideas to keep in mind about why attitude change occurs: message learning, transfer of affect, the consistency mechanisms, and counterarguing.

The Response

The implication of the consistency approach is that many different responses can occur in a communication situation. Usually the communicator intends to produce attitude change in the members of the audience. This means that affects, cognitions, and behaviors regarding the attitude object would all change. The used car salesman on late-night television wants us to feel that his cars are the best; to believe that they are the cheapest and most reliable used cars in town; and he wants us to come out and buy one the next day. All three components of an attitude would change, if attitude change were complete.

But one major problem for the communicator is to maximize the likelihood that targets will choose attitude change as their mode of resolution and to minimize or eliminate the use of other modes. Therefore, one of the critical factors in any attitude-change situation is whether or not other modes of resolution are present and, if they are, the extent to which they are used. We need to consider how the person can resist persuasion and still reduce the pressure created by a discrepant communication. Therefore, before discussing attitude change in detail, we will describe briefly the most important alternative responses the individual can make.

DEROGATING THE SOURCE Someone who is faced with a discrepant communication can reduce the inconsistency by deciding that the source of the communication is unreliable or negative in some other way. If we look at the balance model described earlier, we see there is nothing inconsistent about disagreeing with a negative source. In fact, people expect to disagree with a negative source.

Such an attack on the source of a communication is common in politics, informal debates, courtroom trials, and practically every kind of adversary proceeding. The defense attorney in a trial tries to discredit the damaging witness when she cannot rebut his evidence. The politician calls his opponent a communist or a fascist or some other name when he finds it difficult to argue on the issues themselves.

This device is extremely effective because it not only eliminates the threat from the current argument, but also makes all future arguments from the opponent much less powerful. When an opponent has been discredited, anything he or she says carries less weight. Thus, attacking the source of the communication is an effective way of reducing the pressure produced by a discrepant communication.

DISTORTING THE MESSAGE   Another type of resolution is distorting or misperceiving the communication to reduce the discrepancy between it and one's own position. The Surgeon General says it is extremely dangerous to smoke because smoking has been shown to be a significant cause of lung cancer. The confirmed smoker reads this message and decides that the Surgeon General is recommending a decrease in smoking but that the evidence on lung cancer is not yet conclusive.

Smokers can do this by grossly misperceiving the article when they read it, by distorting the article in memory, or perhaps by reading only part of the article and reconstructing the rest of it in their minds. However they accomplish it, the result is the same—the message becomes considerably less discrepant.

Alternatively, the person may exaggerate the communication to make it ridiculous. Many environmentalists want to slow down the development of undeveloped lands and restrict the building of pollution-causing plants and buildings. Developers and many other businesspeople naturally oppose these restrictions. It is fairly common for them to distort the positions taken by environmentalists to make those positions appear so unreasonable no thinking person

would ever support them. They might argue that environmentalists want such extreme restrictions that no factories could operate in the area at all.

Hovland has suggested that message distortion follows certain rules. When a discrepant position is quite close to that of the audience, they perceive it as closer than it actually is. This is called **assimilation**. When it is quite far away, they perceive it as farther away than it is. This process is called **contrast**. We will discuss the conditions for these misperceptions later; for now it is enough to note that either could reduce the inconsistency in an attitude change situation.

BLANKET REJECTION   A discrepant communication is inconsistent with one's prior attitude, so the most primitive (and perhaps most common) mode of resolution is simply to reject the communication. Rather than refuting the arguments on logical grounds or weakening them by attacking their source, individuals simply reject arguments for no apparent reason.

A typical response by a smoker to a well-reasoned, logical attack on cigarette smoking is to say that the arguments are not good enough to make her stop. She does not answer them; she just does not accept them. When someone who believes in capital punishment is shown overwhelming evidence that it does not deter homicide, he tends to be unconvinced. He shrugs off the evidence, says he does not believe it, and continues to maintain his position. So it often takes more than a good argument to convince people of something.

With these in mind, we can turn to a consideration of the independent variables that increase or decrease the amount of attitude change produced by a persuasive communication. Following the model in Figure 7–1, these factors are divided into several classes: those involving the communicator, the communication itself, the surrounding environment extraneous to the communication and the participants, and the characteristics of the targets.

This man quite plainly has not accepted the communication. Which one or more responses, has he probably had instead of attitude change?

THE COMMUNICATOR

You strike up a conversation with the secretary in the Psychology Department office. She tells you that the word processing machines the department has been using for a year or two are always breaking down, and are out of service as often as they are in service. Your mechanic tells you you are lucky to have bought your car when you did, because the same model from the previous model year was a real lemon; it had a lot of bugs that were not worked out until the next year. The campus policeman advises you not to walk down a particular poorly lit walkway late at night; there have been reports of harassment of women students in that area. In all these cases, you are inclined to go along with these observations, because you are confident all these people are knowledgeable about these matters.

One of the most straightforward and reliable findings in attitude change is that the more favorably people evaluate the communicator, the more they are apt to change their attitudes. This follows from any of the cognitive-consistency models. If the teacher says abortion is immoral but the student thinks it is a basic women's right, the system is unbalanced. She can reduce the imbalance by changing her attitude toward abortion and agreeing with her teacher. In contrast, if someone she dislikes has an attitude different from hers, there is no imbalance and no pressure to change.

Thus, the more favorably people evaluate the source of a discrepant communication, the more likely they will be to change their attitude. But there are several ways in which a communicator can be evaluated favorably, and not all of them yield exactly the same results.

Research on this phenomenon began with "the prestige effect." This was illustrated in the work of Lorge on transfer of affect. It simply compared the effectiveness of favorably evaluated authorities like Jefferson with that of unfavorably evaluated authorities like Lenin in a crude manner, without attempting to specify the exact characteristics making up "prestige." Later work narrowed this concept to **credibility,** which consisted primarily of two factors: expertness and trustworthiness (Hovland & Weiss, 1952). However, the mechanisms by which these two factors influenced attitude change turn out to be somewhat different, so it subsequently became important to make that distinction.

Expertness

The effect of expertness (though described more generally by the researchers as credibility) was demonstrated in a study by Hovland and Weiss (1952). Subjects heard communications concerned with four issues: the advisability of selling antihistamines without a prescription, whether the steel industry was to blame for the steel shortage, the future of the movie industry in the context of the growing popularity of television, and the practicality of building an atomic-powered submarine.

Each communication came from either a high- or low-credibility source. For example, the communication on atomic submarines was supposedly from J. Robert Oppenheimer, a noted physicist, or from *Pravda,* the Russian newspaper. The results indicated that communications attributed to high-credibility sources produced more change than those from low-credibility sources.

In another study (Aronson, Turner, & Carlsmith, 1963), subjects were told they were in an experiment on esthetics and were asked to evaluate nine stanzas from obscure modern poems. They then read someone else's evaluation of one of the stanzas they had not liked very much. The communication argued that the poem was better than the subject had indicated.

The crucial variable was that the communication was supposedly from T. S. Eliot, the famous poet, or Agnes Stearns, who was described as a student at Mississippi State Teachers College. After reading the communication, the sub-

jects reevaluated the poems. There was more change with the high-credibility communicator than with the low-credibility one.

These effects of expertness are fairly straightforward and reasonably noncontroversial. An interesting question, not yet answered, is how far an expert in one field can transfer the influence of his expertise to other fields. If T. S. Eliot, who was respected in the field of poetry, had taken a stand on politics or education, would his opinion have carried more weight and produced more attitude change than that of someone less well known? The question of the transferability of prestige is an open one and should be more fully investigated in the future.

Trustworthiness

Regardless of the expertise of the communicator, it is extremely important for the listener to believe the communicator is unbiased. Someone may be the world's greatest expert on poetry, but we would not be influenced by her writing reviews of her own poetry or of poetry written by a friend of hers. We would not be concerned about her ability to write accurately; we would be concerned about her objectivity and therefore her trustworthiness. If she is perceived as having something to gain from the position she is advocating or if she is taking that position for personal reasons, she would be less persuasive than someone perceived as advocating the position for entirely objective reasons.

One way for communicators to appear trustworthy is to argue in a disinterested manner for positions contrary to their self-interest. Consider a situation in which a district attorney and a criminal are each making statements about whether or not law enforcement agencies should be strengthened. Normally the district attorney should be seen as much better informed and more prestigious, and therefore be more persuasive. And in a study by Walster, Aronson, and Abrahams (1966), that is exactly what happened—as long as the speaker was advocating more power for law enforcement agencies.

With that position, the district attorney was much more persuasive than the convicted criminal, as shown in Figure 7–2. But what if the criminal takes a position against his own self-interest, and argues in favor of strengthened law enforcement? As shown, the criminal becomes quite persuasive, and indeed even matches the persuasive power of the district attorney.

So one way to become more trustworthy, and therefore have more influence, is to argue against your own interest. The criminal may really be repentant and feel that society needs stricter law enforcement so that people like him cannot get away with crimes. The head of the state taxpayers' association may really believe that taxes need to be raised, or else the schools will deteriorate so badly that people in the state will be worse off. A union leader may feel that an immediate wage increase is a bad idea because it would damage the financial standing of the company. People often argue against their own self-interest, for a variety of reasons, and it usually makes them more persuasive when they do.

When we want to predict an audience's judgments of a speaker's trustworthiness, an attributional analysis is suggested. The audience's judgments must be based on the attributions about the causes of the speaker's statements: Is she taking that position because she knows the facts of the matter, or because she hopes to get something out of it? Or is it because the position fits her own prejudices and biases? For example, when an American president says the Soviet Union is responsible for the latest guerrilla movement in Central America, we try to figure out whether he is saying that because his strong anti-communist biases lead him to see Russian subversion behind every rebellion anywhere in the world, or because he has information that points specifically to Russian involvement in this case.

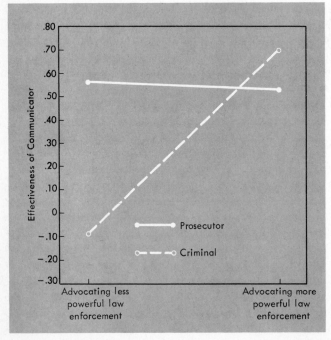

FIGURE 7–2
Effectiveness of communicators when advocating positions for and against one's own self-interest. (Walter, Aronson, & Abrahams, 1966, p. 333.)

Three attributions are possible. The communicator's statement may simply reflect the truth. Its causes may lie in reality. Second, his statement may be biased even though he is reporting his attitudes honestly and faithfully. He may not have enough information to know the real facts, or he may have been misinformed by others, or his own prejudices may have blinded him to the truth. In short, he may be reporting his own attitudes quite truthfully, but they do not square with the realities of the subject matter. This is called *knowledge bias* (Eagly, Wood, & Chaiken, 1978).

Third, he may have really accurate and truthful underlying beliefs, but he may not communicate them to other people in an accurate and honest way. This is called *reporting bias.* Reporting bias could happen for any number of reasons, since people frequently have strong incentives to take a public position they do not really hold. A politician running for reelection, an applicant at a job interview, or a person on a first date all have strong incentives to engage in some reporting bias. But whichever of these three attributions is made, the cause attributed to a communicator's statement should make an important difference in judgments of trustworthiness, and thus in the audience's willingness to agree with his or her position.

So a key factor in trustworthiness is making attributions to reality rather than to the communicator's biases or other dispositions. When do we make attributions to an individual's dispositions? As we saw in Chapter 5, observers are especially likely to make dispositional attributions when the actor's behavior is consistent with expectations based on past behavior. So we are more likely to attribute a conservative president's statements about Central America to his dispositions when his statements fit those biases than when they do not. If he claims the Russians are behind some guerrilla action, that is consistent with our expectations about him, so we tend to attribute it partially to his dispositions. If he says the rebellion is a genuine nationalistic movement with no Soviet involvement, we are

likely to attribute it to some evidence he has.

In short, when a communicator says something contrary to expectations, the audience is more likely to make an attribution to evidence rather than disposition. The communicator is perceived as more trustworthy and should produce more attitude change. This sequence has been examined in several recent studies, such as that by Wood and Eagly (1981). They had a male communicator give communications supporting or opposing pornography. To set up prior expectations about his general political philosophy, subjects had earlier been given a short autobiographical statement by the speaker that described his general attitudes about freedom of speech, abortion, and religion. His later communication about pornography could then be seen as consistent or inconsistent with his general political views.

As Table 7–1 shows, when his message confirmed expectations about him, it was more likely to be attributed to his background and less likely to be attributed to factual evidence: He was perceived as more biased, and he produced less opinion change. Note that expectancy confirmation had no effect on message comprehension: The mechanism responsible for the trustworthiness effect on attitude change here is the attribution, not learning.

Liking

As consistency theories suggest, people change their attitudes to agree with those of the people they like. Anything that increases liking ought also to increase attitude change. For example, physical attractiveness increases liking; Chaiken (1979) has shown that students rated by other students as physically attractive were also more persuasive communicators.

Similarity is another important basis of liking; people tend to be influenced more by those who are similar to them than by those who are different. For example, Brock (1965) conducted

Table 7–1
What Effects Follow When a Communicator Confirms or Disconfirms Expectations about the Communicator's Position?

EFFECTS	EXPECTATIONS	
	CONFIRMED	DISCONFIRMED
Attributions		
To source's background	11.81	6.40
To factual evidence	10.39	11.84
Communicator bias	9.35	7.43
Message comprehension	2.36	2.08
Opinion change	1.56	2.51

Note: A high score indicates more of the effect; e.g., more attribution to the source's background.
Source: Adapted from Wood and Eagly (1981), p. 254.

an experiment in the paint department of a retail store. Salesmen were taught to vary how similar they said their own paint use was to that of a customer. The more similar salesman was more effective than the dissimilar salesman in getting buyers to change their minds about the brand of the paint they wanted to purchase.

Similarity also increases influence because we assume people with backgrounds like our own share our general values and perspectives about things. Suppose someone is similar to us in terms of national, economic, racial, and religious background. If he then says that he doesn't like a particular new movie, we would probably assume he made this judgment on the same bases we would. Accordingly, his judgment tends to carry considerable weight. Thus, in terms of both increased liking and shared perspectives, the greater the similarity between the source and recipient of a discrepant communication, the more attitude change.

Reference Groups

One of the strongest sources of persuasive pressure is a group to which an individual belongs. The group can be as large and inclusive as all American citizens or the middle class or a labor union. It can also be a much smaller, more specialized group, such as a college fraternity, the Elks Club, a group of friends, or an extended family.

The opinion of the group can be an extremely persuasive force. If the Young Republicans endorse a particular candidate, there is a tendency for all the members of the club to feel she is a good candidate. If our friends tell us they are in favor of student activism or like a particular movie, we probably are convinced by them. If most of the members of a fraternity think initiations are a good idea, the others will probably agree with them.

The reasons why reference groups are so effective in producing attitude change are those we have just discussed: liking and similarity. If people value a group, it is a highly credible, highly esteemed source of communication. When the group says something, each member tends to trust it and believe the message.

In addition, because they consider themselves members of the group, they tend to evaluate themselves in comparison with it. In essence, the group serves as the standard for their own behavior and attitudes. They want to be similar to the other members. When the other

Groups have a variety of techniques for making membership salient; uniforms and other visible emblems are among them. This group's political norm is also quite clear: vote for Mario Cuomo for Governor of New York.

Ken Karp

members express a particular opinion, each member thinks his or her own opinion wrong if it is different. Only when the opinion is the same as the group's is it correct or "normal." Therefore, they tend to change their opinion to make it agree.

Attachment to the group can also serve to prevent somebody from being influenced by a communication from an outside source. If the group agrees with the individual's opinion, they provide that person with strong support. Consider a member whose fraternity believes strongly in initiations. He may occasionally be exposed to an attack on initiations from someone outside the fraternity. Whenever this happens, knowing that his group agrees with him makes it easier for him to resist persuasion.

This dual effect of groups—changing a member's opinion to make it coincide with the group's opinion and supporting a member's opinion so he or she can resist persuasion from outside—depends to some extent on how strong the individual's ties are to the group. The more people want to be a member of it and the more likely they value it, the more they will be influenced by the group's beliefs.

Kelley and Volkart (1952) demonstrated the effect of attachment to the group on members'

resistance to outside influence. A communicator attempted to change some Boy Scouts' opinions on various issues away from their troop's norms. The more the Scouts valued their membership in the troop, the less effect the communicator had on their opinions.

Another way of demonstrating the effect of groups is to show how changes in the group's norms can pull people away from their own old positions. Kelley and Woodruff (1956) played subjects a tape recording of a speech arguing against their group's norm—they were education students, and the speech argued against "progressive education." The speech was interrupted periodically by applause which the experimenters attributed to faculty members and recent graduates of the college in one experimental condition ("members' applause"), or to an audience of college-trained people in a neighboring city, interested in community problems related to education ("outsiders' applause").

Attitude change toward the speech was much greater in the "members' applause" condition. This gives additional evidence of the power of groups in producing or blocking attitude change; in this case, subjects confronted with an apparent change in their group's norm were likely to change their own attitudes to fit the group's new position.

Communicators versus Messages

Many of these communicator effects are no doubt due to a simple transfer of affect process; any conclusion that is associated with a favorably evaluated source itself becomes more favorably evaluated. But it is not enough to leave it at that. Sometimes a source's conclusion will be accepted simply because an expert or otherwise favorably evaluated source stated it, regardless of the arguments. On other occasions the arguments themselves are important. What is the difference between these situations? Several factors seem to be important.

One is whether the favorable evaluation of the source stems from the source's expertness or likability. Good arguments are critical to an expert's persuasiveness, but may not be terribly important for a nonexpert who is liked. Norman (1976) tested this idea by using two sources: an unattractive expert and an attractive nonexpert. Since the topic was the number of hours of sleep required per night by the average person, the expert was a professor of physiological psychology who had just coauthored a book on sleep; the nonexpert was a twenty-year-old college student.

Their pictures and other personal information were also presented. The student was an attractive, athletic young man recently elected to the student government, whereas the professor was middle-aged and not very attractive. In each case, half the subjects received extensive arguments on why people should cut down on their sleep, while the other half received the simple statement that they should cut down. The addition of arguments significantly increased the expert's persuasiveness, but it did not affect the amount of attitude change produced by the attractive nonexpert.

BOX 7–1
The Medium Affects the Messenger

The communication medium also affects the source's effectiveness. A visual or even an audio communication provides many nonverbal cues to the recipient. As we saw in Chapter 3, these nonverbal cues can be very important in determining impressions of a person. So, not surprisingly, they also turn out to be quite important in determining a communicator's persuasiveness. Chaiken and Eagly (1983) have shown that communicator likability is much more important in visual or audio communications, where such nonverbal information about the communicator is available. In written communication, however, where only verbal information is available, the message content is relatively more important.

They varied likability by having the communicator praise or derogate the students, faculty, and overall institutional quality of the university the students were attending (the University of Toronto). Then he delivered a persuasive communication supporting a change to the trimester system on videotape, audiotape, or via a written transcript. The students' opinions about the trimester system were indicated afterward. As the table below shows, the communicator's likability contributed to opinion change only in the video or audio versions, where nonverbal cues about him were available.

Additional evidence pointed to the conclusion that communicator attributes are central in video and audio, and message factors relatively more important in written communications. The students' cognitive responses were also measured after the communication. There were more cognitive responses about the communicator in the videotape than in the written condition, but no difference in the number of message-oriented thoughts. Furthermore, in the audio and video conditions, opinion change was related to the favorability of communicator-oriented thoughts. In the written condition, opinion change was related to the favorability of message-oriented thoughts.

The implication is that simple transfer of affect processes were most important in the video (and to a lesser extent audio) situations, whereas the message-oriented counterarguing process was crucial in written communication. In other research, these investigators have shown that written communications have a greater advantage over video or audio communication as the arguments get more complex, presumably because the written medium does induce a message-oriented or counterarguing mentality (Chaiken & Eagly, 1976).

Opinion Change as a Function of Source and Medium		
	COMMUNICATOR	
	LIKABLE	UNLIKABLE
Videotape	4.87	0.48
Audiotape	4.82	1.47
Written	3.66	3.43

Note: The entry is the mean amount of attitude change on a 15-point scale.

Source: Adapted from Chaiken and Eagly (1983), p. 246.

Finally, consistency mechanisms are also critical to communication effects. In general, any characteristic of communicators which implies they know what they are talking about (are experts), are being honest (have no ulterior motive), or are likable increases the effectiveness of the communication. Since derogation of the communication source is a major way of avoiding attitude change, these variables relating to the communicator are extremely important.

Any disliking of the communicator or lack of trust in his or her competence or credibility makes it relatively easy to reject the message by attacking the source. In this way, targets free themselves from the pressure of worrying about the complex details of the message itself.

THE COMMUNICATION

But what about the actual content of the message? Advertisers try to sell a particular product; is it any good or not? Politicians try to get elected; are they actually qualified for the job or not? Your friend tries to get you to go to a particular party with her; will it actually be a good party or not?

Of course, it is easier to sell something good. Crest became the best-selling toothpaste in part because it really did offer protection against cavities; the automobile became popular because it was a useful product; and some political candidates are more qualified than others. Given a particular product or opinion to sell, however, a number of variables in the communication itself have important effects on the amount of attitude change produced.

Discrepancy

As noted earlier, a major source of pressure for attitude change comes from the **discrepancy** between the target's initial position and the position advocated by the communication. The greater the discrepancy, the greater potential pressure to change. If the typical person needing eight hours of sleep per night hears a distinguished health scientist say that only six hours are necessary, the individual's attitude is under some pressure; if the communication argues that only four hours are really necessary, there is much more pressure.

With more discrepancy, more change is required if the pressure is to be reduced. As might be expected, therefore, within a wide range, there is more attitude change with greater discrepancy (Hovland & Pritzker, 1957).

However, the effect of discrepancy on pressure and amount of change is not always this simple. There is more pressure with greater discrepancy, but it does not always produce more change. There are two complicating factors. First, as discrepancy becomes quite great, the members of the audience find it increasingly difficult to change their attitudes enough to eliminate the discrepancy. Moreover, an extremely discrepant statement tends to make individuals doubt the credibility of the source. So at high levels of discrepancy, the pressure tends to be reduced more by source derogation than by attitude change. In other words, source derogation rather than attitude change is chosen as the mechanism for restoring consistency.

Suppose a person hears the scientist say that eight hours of sleep are not really required. If the scientist's message is at low discrepancy, and says that six hours are adequate, the person is likely to be somewhat influenced. There would be some pressure on her to change her opinion in the direction of the scientist's, and if the scientist presented a fairly persuasive argument, the person would probably do so. In this situation, it is difficult to reject a credible communicator but easy to change one's opinion the little bit required to reduce the discrepancy.

As the discrepancy becomes extreme, however, it becomes much harder for individuals to reduce the pressure by changing their opinion. It is extremely difficult for the person who thinks eight hours are required to decide that only four hours will do. The person then starts to doubt the communicator's credibility. She begins to think that the scientist does not know much about real human beings.

Two factors thus operate as discrepancy increases: Attitude change becomes more difficult, and rejection of the communicator becomes easier. The result is that attitude change generally increases with greater discrepancy up to a point, and then declines if discrepancy increases still further. As discrepancy increases, attitude change increases, but only up to a point (e.g., Freedman, 1964; Eagly & Telaak, 1972).

Greater credibility, however, should allow communicators to advocate more discrepant positions with success, because they will not be rejected as easily. If one deeply respects the scientist who says that four hours of sleep is enough, it is harder to decide he does not know what he is talking about. Therefore, the greater the credibility of the communicator, the higher the level of discrepancy at which the maximum change occurs. Similarly, a lower-credibility source makes rejection relatively easy and the maximum point occurs at lower levels of discrepancy.

These effects of discrepancy and credibility are nicely illustrated in a study by Bochner and Insko (1966), as shown in Figure 7–3. They had a Nobel Prize winner (high credibility) and a YMCA instructor (low credibility) give messages regarding the number of hours of sleep the average person requires per night. Each subject received one message from one source. Some subjects received a message saying eight hours were required, others a message saying seven hours were required, and so on. Since the great majority of subjects initially thought eight hours was correct, these messages varied in discrepancy accordingly; zero discrepancy for the eight-hour message, one-hour discrepancy for the seven-hour message, and so on.

As you can see, there was more change at moderate levels of discrepancy than at higher levels. In addition, as expected, the optimal level of discrepancy was greater for the high-credibility source. The YMCA instructor did best by

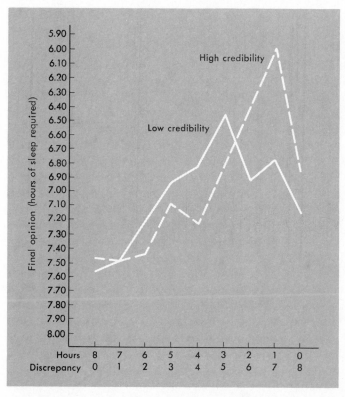

FIGURE 7-3
Opinion change produced by high- and low-credibility communicators at various levels of discrepancy. (Bochner and Insko, 1966.)

advocating three hours of sleep, but the high-credibility source got the maximum attitude change by arguing that only one hour was really necessary. Even so, the high-credibility source still could at best reduce the subjects' attitudes only from an average of eight hours per night to an average of about six.

Thus, the level of credibility does not change the basic inverted-U relationship between discrepancy and attitude change, but it does change the point at which maximum change occurs. The more difficult it is to reject the communicator, the greater the discrepancy at which maximum change occurs. This example illustrates both how an interplay of forces determines which mode of resolution is adopted in a given situation, and how the use of one mode implies less use of another.

Another example of alternative modes of resolution concerns how discrepancy affects misperception of the message. Discrepant positions that are close to the individual's are often seen as closer than they actually are (assimilation), whereas those that are far away are seen as farther away than they are (contrast). Exaggerating the closeness of a discrepant position makes it easy to change enough to reduce the small discrepancy, or it may eliminate change by making the two positions essentially identical. Exaggerating the remoteness of a position makes it easier to attack the credibility of the person advocating it (Hovland, Harvey, & Sherif, 1957).

Fear Arousal

Arousing fear is one of the most natural ways of trying to convince someone to do something. A mother tells her young son he will be run over if he crosses the street without her. Religious leaders frighten their followers with threats of eternal damnation and suffering. Political candidates warn that if their opponents are elected, the economy will be ruined, people will starve, and war will break out. Environmentalists warn of mass deaths from cancer, chemicals in our vital organs, and dying fish in polluted lakes and streams. Opponents of environmental improvements warn of rising unemployment.

All these arguments could be made on a nonemotional basis, but they usually are based on the arousal of great fear. Given a particular argument in favor of a position, how does the amount of fear aroused affect the success of the argument?

The original study in this area was conducted by Janis and Feshbach in 1953. They showed high school students a film that emphasized the importance of brushing one's teeth three times a day, after every meal. The film described the dangers of not doing this and explained the advantages of good dental care. High fear was aroused by showing pictures of badly decayed teeth and gums, closeups of diseased teeth, mouths in which the gums had pulled away from the teeth, and so on. In the mild fear condition, subjects saw less dramatic and less frightening pictures. And in the no-fear, or control, condition, the subjects saw no pictures of diseased teeth.

The subjects in the high fear condition reported being more impressed by the presentation and agreeing with it more. However, a week later it was found that the subjects in the no-fear condition had changed their behavior more than had subjects in either of the fear conditions. The authors concluded that the maximum effect was produced by the persuasive arguments without the fear-arousing slides.

Many of the experiments done after that early study have produced the opposite result, however. For example, a series of experiments conducted by Howard Leventhal and his colleagues at Yale University have shown that the arousal of fear tends to facilitate both attitude and behavior change. In one study (Dabbs & Leventhal, 1966), college students were urged to get inoculations for tetanus. The disease was described in detail—it was pointed out how serious it was, that it was often fatal, and that it was easy to catch.

In the high fear condition, the descriptions of the disease were extremely vivid, the symptoms were made very explicit, and everything was done to make the situation as frightening as possible. In the second condition, a moderate amount of fear was aroused; and in the third, very little. In addition, the students were told that the inoculation was extremely effective and that it gave almost complete protection against the disease. Students were then asked how important they thought it was to get the inoculation and whether or not they intended to get one. The university health service, which was nearby, recorded how many of the students went for inoculations during the next month.

The findings (Table 7–2) are straightforward and impressive. The greater the fear aroused, the more the subjects intended to get shots. Perhaps more important, higher fear induced more subjects to go to the health service and receive inoculations. Thus, fear arousal not only produced more attitude change, but also had a greater effect on the relevant behavior.

Various other studies have used such issues as automotive safety, atom bomb testing, fallout shelters, and dental hygiene to study the effects of fear. Under most circumstances, fear arousal seems to increase the effectiveness of a persuasive communication (Higbee, 1969; Leventhal, 1970).

On the other hand, Janis (1967) argues that the relationship between fear and attitude change depends on the level of fear involved. He holds that at low levels greater fear produces more attitude change, but that at some point the fear becomes too intense, arouses defensive mechanisms, and thereby produces less change. This would explain some seemingly contradictory results from studies that involved different amounts of fear.

For example, high fear normally has had its strongest effects in experiments on tetanus, which is a simply prevented disease and rarely scares people much. However, high fear arousal is less often successful on lung cancer and smoking, probably because lung cancer causes too much fear and is too difficult for a lifelong smoker to prevent. Janis has reanalyzed a number of experiments in these terms, and although not all the data fit this model, most of the results appear to be consistent with it.

Even more specific theories about the conditions under which fear is effective have been developed by Leventhal (1970) and others (Rogers & Mewborn, 1976); these rest generally on an expectancy-value approach and view the individual as somewhat more cognitive and rational than does the Janis model. These theories take into consideration the character of the feared event, the person's vulnerability to the feared event, and the effectiveness of the recommended measures. They try to predict the special conditions under which fear will influence attitude change.

For example, fear should increase attitude change if highly effective measures are recommended, but not if there is little or no remedy. These theories can also account for some of the

Table 7–2
Effects of Fear Arousal on Attitudes and Behavior

CONDITION	INTENTION TO TAKE SHOTS[a]	PERCENTAGE TAKING SHOTS
High fear	5.17	22
Low fear	4.73	13
Control	4.12	6

[a]The figures are ratings on a scale from 1 (lowest) to 7 (highest).
Source: Adapted from Dabbs and Leventhal (1966).

data, though it seems clear that people do not always calculate the most rational response in these situations.

To sum up, the evidence indicates that under most circumstances arousing fear increases the effectiveness of persuasive communications. But arousing too much fear may be disruptive. Causing people to be too frightened can make them either so paralyzed that they are unable to act or so threatened that they tend to deny the danger and reject the communication. At moderate levels, however, it appears that fear-arousing arguments are more effective in producing attitude change than arguments which arouse little or no fear.

Aggression

The learning approach suggests that motive arousals would lead to attitude change only when accepting the message will reduce the arousal. If fear is aroused by seeing gruesome pictures of tetanus victims and I accept the communicator's position and go to get a tetanus shot, my fear is reduced. Attitude change depends on reducing arousal. The same should be true of **aggression.** Arousal of aggression should lead to attitude change only when the listeners can reduce their aggression by accepting the new attitude. Political leaders would be able to produce attitude change by stirring up their followers' aggression—but only if they provide

their followers with something to hate, like a convenient enemy or scapegoat, so the listeners can express their aggression.

A study by Weiss and Fine (1956) tested this hypothesis, that aggression arousal produces attitude change only when the communication is an aggressive one. Some subjects were put through an annoying, frustrating experience designed to make them feel aggressive. Other subjects had the opposite experience—they had a pleasant, satisfying experience. Then both groups were exposed to a persuasive communication that took a lenient attitude toward juvenile delinquency, or one that took a punitive position. The experimenters hypothesized that the subjects who had been made to feel aggressive would be more likely to accept the punitive communication, because the punitive message would provide aggressive subjects with a way of expressing their aggression. The lenient message would be more likely to satisfy the relatively nonaggressive needs of the nonaggressive subjects.

The results were in line with these expectations—the aggressive subjects were more influenced by the punitive communication, and the nonaggressive subjects were more influenced by the lenient one. So personal frustrations might make a person more vulnerable to persuasive communications advocating military action, attacks on minorities, or harsh treatment of dissidents, but probably they would not increase susceptibility to such nonaggressive appeals as charity campaigns.

THE TARGET

Even after a message from a particular source has reached the target, the problems of attitude change are not over. The effects of an ad for environmental protection may be quite different for the owner of a strip coal mine than for a suburban university professor. Characteristics of the target and the target's experience affect her reaction to the message.

Commitment

The ultimate impact of a persuasive message depends in great part on the strength of the target's **commitment to an attitude.** Several factors affect strength of commitment. One is action taken on the basis of the attitude, as we saw in Chapter 6. If a person has just bought a house, she is more committed to the belief that it is a fine house than if she had not yet bought it. As a homeowner, she will probably not be very open to hearing that the house is not a very good one.

Second, public statements of the attitude produce more commitment. Someone who has just told all his friends that he thinks smoking is bad for health and is an evil, dirty habit is more committed to this attitude than if he had kept his thoughts to himself. Changing his attitude is harder if he expressed it publicly because then the change would involve admitting to his friends he was wrong. Whenever changing an attitude would cause the individual to give up more, suffer more, or change more of his other attitudes or behaviors, his commitment to his initial attitude increases and makes it more difficult for him to change it.

Third, freely choosing a position produces a greater feeling of commitment than being forced. In a study on this problem (Freedman & Steinbruner, 1964), subjects were given information about a candidate for graduate school and asked to rate him, under circumstances of either high or low choice. The subjects were made to feel that they had made up their own minds and freely selected the particular rating or that they had virtually nothing to do with the decision and had been forced to select the rating.

The subjects were then exposed to information that strongly contradicted their initial rating and were allowed to change the rating if they desired. Those who had made the first rating with a feeling of free choice changed less than those in the low-choice condition. Strong commitment reduces the amount of attitude change produced by a discrepant persuasive communi-

cation. Greater commitment makes it harder for the individual to change an attitude and means that he or she is more likely to use other modes of resolution instead.

The exact mechanism by which commitment increases resistance is still not very clear. Greater commitment makes people give more counterarguments when they are confronted with discrepant information (Petty & Cacioppo, 1979), but it is not clear whether they are necessary to this added resistance to change.

The joint effects of commitment and discrepancy on attitude change are similar to those of credibility and discrepancy. Commitment to an initial position also shifts the amount of discrepancy at which maximum attitude change occurs, but in the opposite direction. The harder it is to change one's attitude, the lower the discrepancy at which rejection of the source starts to substitute for attitude change. Therefore, the greater the commitment, the lower the discrepancy at which maximum attitude change occurs (Freedman, 1964; Rhine & Severance, 1970).

Inoculation

In the aftermath of the Korean war, William McGuire and others became very interested in reports of "brainwashing" of American prisoners of war by Chinese Communists. A number of POWs had given public speeches denouncing the American government, and several said publicly that they wished to remain in China when the war was over, rather than return to the United States. McGuire speculated that some soldiers might have been vulnerable to influence because they were being attacked on matters they were quite inexperienced and ignorant about—they had never been forced to defend the United States against the sophisticated attacks used against them by the Chinese.

McGuire hypothesized that another source of resistance to change in the target comes from past experience with the issue. He and his associates conducted a series of experiments on the effects of giving people experiences designed to increase their ability to resist persuasion. He pictured the individual faced with a discrepant communication as being like somebody attacked by a virus or a disease. The stronger the persuasive message (virus), the more damage it would do; the stronger the person's defenses, the better able he or she is to resist persuasion (disease).

There are two different ways of strengthening someone's defense against a disease. We can strengthen his body generally, by giving him vitamins, exercise, and so on; or we can strengthen his defenses against that particular disease by building up antibodies. McGuire argued that these two approaches are also applicable to the influence situation.

To begin with, he identified a number of *cultural truisms*—opinions so universally held in our society that they are almost never subjected to any kind of attack. One example is the belief that it is good to brush one's teeth after every meal. Probably almost everybody in the United States believes that this is basically a good idea in terms of dental health. And most people have never heard anything to the contrary. Thus, someone holding this opinion is like an individual who has never been exposed to the smallpox germ. He has never been forced to defend himself from attack so has never built up any defense against attack.

One procedure that strengthens resistance is to build up the person's opinion directly by giving her additional arguments supporting her original position. McGuire called this a *supportive defense*. If she believes it is good to brush her teeth three times a day, she is shown a study by the United States Public Health Service which shows that people who do so have fewer cavities than those who brush their teeth less often or not at all. Giving individuals this kind of support for their position does, in fact, somewhat increase their resistance to subsequent persuasive communications.

A different approach is to strengthen the individual's defenses against persuasion. McGuire argued that, as with diseases, the most effective way of increasing resistance is to build up defenses. If people are given mild cases of smallpox that they are able to fight off, their bodies produce antibodies which in the future provide an effective and strong defense against more powerful attacks. Similarly, if a particular opinion has never been attacked, it is extremely vulnerable because no defenses have been built up around it. When such an opinion is suddenly subjected to persuasive pressure, the individual does not have a set of defenses, and the opinion tends to be relatively easy to change. However, if the opinion has been attacked and the individual has successfully defended herself, she should be able to resist later attacks because she has built up a relatively strong defensive system.

In other words, McGuire argued that it is possible to **inoculate** individuals against persuasive attacks just as we can inoculate them against diseases. This is accomplished by weakly attacking the individual's attitude. The attack must be weak, or it would change the attitude and the battle would be lost. To be certain this does not occur, the target is helped to defend herself against the mild attack. She is given an argument directed specifically at the attack or is told that the attack is not very good and she should be able to refute it.

The key study by McGuire and Papageorgis (1961) used both the supportive and inoculation methods to build up defenses. There were three groups of subjects: One group received support for their position; one group had their position attacked weakly and the attack refuted (the inoculation condition); and the third group received neither procedure. Afterward, all groups were subjected to a strong attack on their initial position. Table 7–3 shows how much each group changed as a result of this final attack. The supportive method helped subjects resist persuasion a little—the group receiving support changed a little less than the group that had no preparation. But the inoculation method helped a great deal; subjects receiving this preparation changed much less than the other subjects.

One implication would be that supportive

Table 7-3
The Effects of Supportive or Inoculation
Defenses on Resistance to Persuasion

CONDITION	AMOUNT OF ATTITUDE CHANGE
Supportive defense	5.87
Inoculation defense	2.94
Neither	6.62

Source: Adapted from McGuire & Papageorgis (1961).

defenses are best when the target simply needs to be taught specific arguments. The inoculation defense would be better when the target has to be stimulated to thinking up her own defensive arguments. Consistent with this view, later research has shown that support tends to be particularly effective when the subsequent attack contains arguments similar to the content of the supporting arguments, but it is relatively ineffective when new arguments are used. In contrast, inoculation is effective even when the attack includes new arguments (McGuire, 1964).

The specific mechanism by which inoculation operates is not yet clear. Cognitive response theory is perhaps most often used to explain these results. It suggests that in refuting the mild attack, the individual uses and therefore exercises all her defenses. She prepares arguments supporting her own position, constructs counterarguments against the opposing position, derogates the possible sources of opposing views, and so on. This would make each of the defensive mechanisms stronger and would provide the individual with a more effective position.

Personality Factors

Some people are generally more persuasible than others, regardless of the issue involved or the type of influence being attempted. Experiments have been conducted (Hovland & Janis, 1959) in which subjects were exposed to persuasive communications on a variety of issues with different types of appeals and arguments and in different persuasion situations. They indicated that subjects who were highly persuasible under one set of conditions tended to be highly persuasible under others.

The effect is not very strong; it explains only a small percentage of the total variance. But considering the diversity of the situations and issues studied, the consistency found offers convincing support for the existence of the trait of general persuasibility.

One fairly consistent finding has been that subjects with low self-esteem tend to be more persuasible than those with high self-esteem. The standard explanation is that low self-esteem people place a low value on their opinions, just as they do on everything else about themselves. Since they do not value their own opinions, they are less reluctant to give them up and are more likely to change them when they are attacked.

It also might seem that individuals with high intelligence would be less persuasible than those with lower intelligence, because of greater critical ability. Research has not generally supported this assumption. On the average, people of high intelligence are persuaded just as much as people of low intelligence. However, there is reason to believe that intelligence does have some effect on the kinds of persuasive appeals that are most effective. People of high intelligence are influenced less by inconsistent and illogical arguments than are people of lower intelligence, and the latter may be influenced less by complex, difficult arguments (Eagly & Warren, 1976). It is important to note that the lack of an overall correlation between intelligence and persuasibility does not necessarily mean that intelligence is entirely unrelated to the influence process. Rather, it indicates that the relationship is complex.

Other than these few factors, there is little to support hypotheses about how personality affects persuasibility. There have been many suggestions (authoritarianism, richness of fantasy), but the evidence is rather weak at the moment.

THE SITUATION

The factors described thus far have concerned the communicator, the message, and the target. Yet mass communications usually are delivered within a broader context in which other things are happening, and these also often prove to have decisive effects on the success of persuasion attempts.

When we watch a political candidate's television commercial in an election campaign, we know that she is running for election; her statement is not a dispassionate, academic one. Most people watch television news in the midst of all the hubbub of family members returning home from work, talking to each other, making dinner, children shouting and screaming, and so forth. We watch commercials for new cars during the halftime of football games, in the midst of getting up to get another beer, going to the bathroom, and making sarcastic comments about the commercials with our friends. These situations all are likely to influence the success of attempts at persuasion. Let us now consider some of the most important situational variables in attitude change.

Forewarned Is Forearmed

If someone is told ahead of time that she is going to be exposed to a discrepant communication on an issue she cares strongly about, she is better able to resist persuasion by that message. In a study by Freedman and Sears (1965), teenagers were told ten minutes beforehand that they were going to hear a talk titled "Why Teenagers Should Not Be Allowed to Drive." Other teenagers were not told about the talk until just before the speaker began. Under these circumstances, those who had the warning were less influenced by the talk than were the others. In some way, the warning enabled them to resist this very unpalatable message.

This is certainly a plausible finding, and it seems to be believed by many people in the business of persuasion. For example, we often hear an advertisement on radio or television with no warning that this is going to be an advertisement. Instead, the station sneaks in the ad before we are fully aware of what it is. A similar although more altruistic example is the dentist who warns us that something is going to hurt. He seems to feel that we will be better able to withstand the pain if we are warned. In fact, there is some experimental evidence that subjects who are warned ahead of time that they are going to receive an electric shock report it hurts less than do subjects who are not warned.

All this sounds plausible and reasonable, but why does it occur? Why does a ten-minute warning help people resist persuasion? It is important to keep in mind that all the subjects know the speaker disagrees with them—the only difference is that some people know it ten minutes ahead of time and others know it only just before the speech. The greater resistance shown by those with the longer warning is due to some mechanism that operates during those minutes between the warning and the speech.

Most likely, as with the inoculation procedure, the individual's defenses are in some way exercised and therefore strengthened. Although there is little evidence to demonstrate directly how these defenses are strengthened, the individual probably uses all the maneuvers and tactics we discussed previously. She may anticipate the arguments that will come from the opponent and try to make up counterarguments. Indeed Petty and Cacioppo (1977) have shown the delay period between warning and exposure to the communication allows subjects to generate more counterarguments, though they had no way of being certain that anticipatory counterarguing was responsible for the increased resistance.

Listeners also probably use derogation of the discrepant source. The person who has been through the inoculation procedure has plenty of opportunity to derogate the opponent. Similarly, the forewarned person has ten minutes to convince himself that the communicator is unreliable, prejudiced, and misinformed.

In other words, the individual who is warned (or who has just experienced a mild attack) is like a fighter who has prepared for a match. He has been through training, so when the fight comes, he is in better shape and able to meet his opponent. He also spends time convincing himself that his opponent is not very good and that he, himself, is great. This makes him more confident and better able to do his best.

All this work has been done on situations in which the recipient was strongly committed to a position discrepant from the communicator's. When the listener is not very committed to a position, though, warning turns out to have the opposite effect—it actually facilitates attitude change. When the person is unlikely from the start to cling very tightly to the original attitude, the warning seems to operate as a cue to propel her along the road she was destined for sooner or later anyhow.

For example, Apsler and Sears (1968) hypothesized that warning would actually facilitate attitude change among subjects who were not personally involved in the topic, whereas it would have the usual effect of blocking change among highly involved subjects. They gave subjects a persuasive communication advocating replacement of professors by teaching assistants in many upper-division courses, a change opposed by almost all subjects. Some subjects were told the change would come quickly, in time to affect their own education (high involvement); others were told it was several years off and would not affect them (low involvement).

Forewarning helped block change among the highly involved subjects, just as it had among the teenagers who were highly involved in the issue of teenage driving in the Freedman and Sears experiment. However, it facilitated

Forewarned is forearmed (except when you like fast cars anyway): She surely was forewarned of the position he would advocate. Does that help her resist persuasion? Or was her position not very discrepant from his to begin with?

Table 7–4
Forewarning Increases Attitude Change with Low Involvement

| | MEAN ATTITUDE CHANGE | |
CONDITION	HIGH INVOLVEMENT	LOW INVOLVEMENT
Warning	1.5	2.4
No warning	1.8	0.7
Effects of warning	−0.3	1.7

Note: $n = 20$ in each cell. The larger the score, the greater the amount of change in the advocated direction on a 16-point scale.
Source: Apsler and Sears (1968), p. 164.

change in the low-involvement condition. This is shown in Table 7–4.

These two effects of warning frequently can be detected even before the subject receives the communication. The highly committed person seems to begin to resist even before she is exposed to the communication, while the uncommitted person seems to moderate his stand. In one experiment, subjects highly committed to their initial position became more extreme (and presumably more resistant to change) when warned of a debate, while weakly committed subjects became more moderate (and presumably more receptive to change) (Sears, Freedman, & O'Connor, 1964).

Cooper and Jones (1970) have shown that these anticipatory changes are due to the subjects' expectations of exposure to the communications and their likely effects, rather than just to the knowledge of their existence. Weakly committed subjects changed when warned of forthcoming exposure to the communication, but not when told that such a communication existed without any implication of forthcoming exposure.

There are still some controversies surrounding the exact nature of these responses to warning. For example, we do not know whether the increased resistance of highly committed persons is based on real thought and anticipation of arguments, increased blanket rejection of the

communication, or source derogation. Forewarning does inspire more counterarguing, but that could just be a byproduct of a stubborn refusal to give in.

And some researchers suggest that the anticipatory attitude change among the uncommitted may be more apparent than real. That is, it may just be done to avoid looking like a compliant person, and may not be genuine. Finally, we do not mean to give the impression that all these maneuvers are done deliberately. Rather, people tend to think about the issue a little, go over some of the points in their minds, and in this way prepare for exposure. As far as we know, the process is all quite casual and almost accidental. But the effects are clear.

Distraction

In parts of our discussion, we have described the individual as actively fighting the persuasive message. People whose opinions are attacked usually try to resist changing especially when they are committed to their attitudes. They counterargue, derogate the communicator, and generally marshal all their forces to defend their own positions. One important implication of this is that the ability to resist persuasion is weakened by anything that makes it harder to fight the discrepant communication. In particular, distracting attention from the battle may enable the persuasive message to get through.

A study by Festinger and Maccoby (1964) demonstrated this effect of **distraction.** Subjects listened to a speech against fraternities while watching a film. For some of the subjects, the film showed the person making the speech. For others, the film was "The Day of the Painter," a funny, somewhat zany satire on modern art. Presumably, those watching the irrelevant film were more distracted from the antifraternity speech than those watching the person speak. Subjects who initially disagreed with the speech (who were in favor of fraternities) were more influenced in the distraction than the nondistraction condition. Taking the subjects' minds off the speech increased its effectiveness.

Enhanced persuasion with mild amounts of distraction appears to be a reliable finding. Petty and Brock (1981) reviewed 22 separate studies on the topic and found some increased persuasion with distraction in all but two of them. Much of this work has been guided by a cognitive response approach. As might be expected, therefore, distraction does not facilitate attitude change under all conditions. Distraction should increase persuasion only when it interferes with an otherwise effective counterarguing process. Petty, Wells, and Brock (1976) have shown that distraction fosters attitude change more when the message otherwise easily generates many counterarguments.

So distraction would help persuasion much better on a familiar issue on which we know our own arguments (against a person advocating racially segregated schools) than on an issue we do not have ready arguments about (on some technical issue). It seems to work best when the communications are highly discrepant and on very involving topics, presumably because these inspire the most vigorous counterarguing. And it works best with high-credibility sources, because they are the most threatening and therefore trigger the most counterarguing (Petty & Brock, 1981).

In any case, the effect must depend on the right amount of distraction. An usual, there is a conflict between getting the message through and getting it accepted. Obviously, too much distraction prevents the persuasive message from being heard at all and reduces its effectiveness to zero. If the person is totally focused on something else, none of the message can get through. The idea is to get the position through but inhibit counterarguing.

Advertisers may want to distract television viewers from the main point of commercials by irrelevant pictures and action. They do not, however, want to have the irrelevancies so fascinating that the message is lost. Having a beautiful woman in the background during a soap commercial may help sell soap; having her in the foreground may help; but having her in the foreground singing so loudly that the commercial can barely be heard would certainly reduce the effectiveness of the ad. Distraction may work under some conditions, but it is important that the distraction not be too great, or the effect will be reversed.

ATTITUDE CHANGE OVER TIME

So far we have focused on immediate responses to one-shot communications—that is, under what conditions does a televised speech, radio ad, or conversation with a friend *immediately* produce attitude change? In many cases, however, we want to know how attitudes change over time. We especially want to know the effects of repeated exposure to a message and what effects are likely to last when the exposure ends.

Repetition

Consider your reaction to seeing the same potato-faced athletes in a TV commercial downing the same brand of beer at the same bar week after week. Does the repetition reinforce your association between that brand of beer and the athletes? Or do you just get sick of the commercial and tune it out?

Much research by Zajonc (1968) and others shows that familiarity based on repetition increases liking, as we will see in Chapter 8. This would imply repetition should generally increase attitude change. With persuasive communications, however, repetition apparently increases attitude change only up to a point. Cacioppo and Petty (1979) presented students with communications containing eight different arguments on increasing university expenditures (see Figure 7–4). Each communication was presented one, three, or five times. They found agreement increased with more exposure up to a point and then fell off.

This inverted-U function occurred whether the communication advocated a position that was "desirable" and low discrepancy for students, arguing for an increase in the luxury tax, or an "undesirable" high-discrepancy one arguing for an increase in tuition. Cacioppo and Petty also found that high levels of repetition produced fewer favorable and more unfavorable thoughts, consistent with the notion that boredom sets in after a certain point. Exactly where this point occurs, or how much is "too much,"

FIGURE 7–4 The effects of discrepancy and message repetition on agreement. (Adapted from Cacioppo & Petty, 1979, p. 100.)

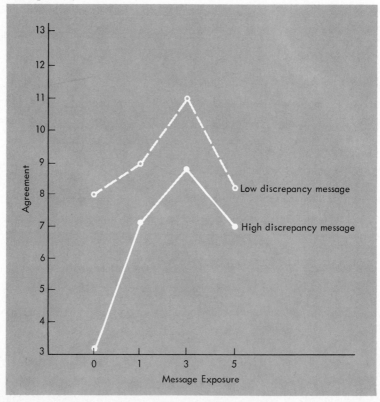

is not known. It probably depends on the pleasantness and novelty value of the stimulus, and the time intervals involved. In any case, there is clearly a limit to the value of repetition.

Spontaneous Attitude Change

Attitudes apparently get stronger the longer people hold them. Tesser (1978) has done a series of studies that find thinking about an attitude object tends to make the attitude more extreme. So if you spend more than the usual amount of time thinking about your best friend you will probably like her better, whereas if you think about your enemy more often, you will probably dislike her even more. According to Tesser, people review and rehearse their cognitions, and consistency pressures move them toward more evaluatively consistent clusters.

In thinking about your best friend, you might remember additional good qualities or enjoyable experiences you shared. And you might reinterpret some of your less pleasant memories to excuse your friend's behavior. The same could happen with your enemy: You would lengthen your list of offenses and find seamy motives for her apparently good and generous acts. Because the process by which thinking makes the attitude more extreme requires generating additional cognitions and reinterpreting existing ones, it should be at its strongest with an established schema rather than with an attitude having little cognitive depth.

Attitudes also spontaneously move toward logical consistency over time, even in the absence of explicit pressure to think about them. McGuire (1960, 1981) has investigated the so-called *Socratic effect,* by which people arrive at logical conclusions simply from being asked about a set of premises. You will recall that Socrates was able to lure his students into very sophisticated and correct conclusions just by asking them leading questions, even when they were sure they did not know the ultimate answer he was driving at.

McGuire shows that the same process occurs spontaneously with ordinary people. He has shown that asking questions about the premises and conclusions of logical syllogisms makes them become more consistent over time. For example, if you believe that gasoline supplies are likely not to increase and that people are not likely to reduce their consumption, then over time you are likely to come to expect shortages, even in the absence of any direct evidence of them. In McGuire's research the increased consistency of the conclusions occurred no matter whether the subjects had been asked about the premises ten minutes or seven days ahead of time.

Persistence of Attitude Change

A last question concerns the persistence of attitude change over time, once it has been induced by a communication. It seems clear that, in general, memory for the details of an argument decays with time in a way resembling an Ebbinghaus forgetting curve—that is, decreases are rapid at first, then diminish later on. In general, though, the persistence of attitude changes is not necessarily dependent on retention of the details of arguments. A good bit of research finds memory for arguments of only secondary importance (McGuire, 1969). Other events that occur after the communication are of much greater significance.

One important factor may be whether or not the recipient is later reminded of important cues other than the arguments themselves, such as the credibility of the source. Kelman and Hovland (1953), for example, manipulated source credibility and found the usual difference on an immediate posttest: The high-credibility source had produced more attitude change. Three weeks afterward, the credibility difference was gone. The low-credibility source's message was, by then, just as effective. The original credibility difference could be reinstated, however, if the subject was reminded of the original source of the message.

This is shown in Figure 7–5. As you can see,

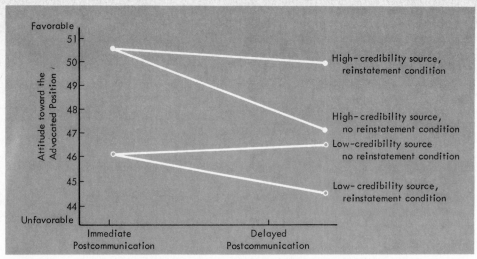

FIGURE 7–5 Attitude change measured immediately and three weeks after the communication. (Kelman & Hovland, 1953. Graph adapted from Petty & Cacioppo, 1981, p. 91.)

immediately after the communication, the difference between high- and low-credibility sources was very large. Three weeks later, it had disappeared in the "no reinstatement" conditions. However, when subjects were reminded of the original source, the credibility difference reemerged. The authors reasoned that people forget the source of a message more readily than the arguments, so without reinstatement the credibility of the source no longer matters after a while.

This study led to some controversy and considerable research. If attitude change increased because the association of message with low-credibility source was forgotten, the *discounting cue* hypothesis would suggest that reinstating this degrading association would kill off that gradual increase in attitude change. The idea is that various cues surrounding a message indicate to the recipients whether or not they should disregard the message. Low credibility of the source may be one such cue, as would be any other indication that the arguments are misinformed or biased. If these cues are forgotten over time attitude change may actually in-

crease, a phenomenon known as *the sleeper effect.*

Cook and Flay (1978) and others (see Petty & Cacioppo, 1981, p. 92) have concluded that such sleeper effects are likely to happen primarily when discounting cues originally followed the message. When the discounting cue follows the message, the recipients will have already listened to the arguments and taken them seriously. If they hear the discounting cue before the message, the recipients will probably not even pay attention to the message and there will be no memory of the arguments to take over when they have forgotten the low-credibility source.

Low credibility is not the only discounting cue. Attitude change may also be artificially suppressed by warning the recipient about the communicator's intent. People tend to become stubborn when they feel the source is trying to persuade them. But over time, such people seem to show increased attitude change, presumably as the discounting cue (persuasive intent) is forgotten (Watts & Holt, 1979).

Another determinant of persistence, and probably the most important, is the kind of so-

What are the special efforts that this man has made to enhance his credibility? Look closely at the diplomas and see if their actual prestige value corresponds with your first snap impression of his background.

cial support given the person after exposure to the communication. The best example is New-comb's (1963) study of the long-term changes in political attitudes of young women attending Bennington College in the 1930s. Most became considerably more liberal while they were in college. Persistence depended on the environment they established after graduating. Those surrounded by liberals stayed liberal; those surrounded by conservatives "regressed" to their precollege conservatism. We will discuss this study in more detail in Chapter 14.

If there is a lesson in all this, it may be that there is no such thing as a free lunch in the day of a persuader. A low-credibility source may get a message through, but the message is always vulnerable to its weak auspices' becoming salient again. Or, one may momentarily trick a person into changing by failing to warn her, but with time the persuasive impact will be lost. And a message can temporarily change people's attitudes, but it needs to be consistent with their long-standing values, and with those of their friends, if it is going to endure. So it is a good idea to be skeptical of reports of sudden, dramatic changes. Unless they are supported by evidence, friends, and basic values, such changes are likely to be short-lived.

Concluding Comment

Many factors affect attitude change. Some act by appealing to a person's reason, by increasing the trust in the communication, strengthening the persuasive message, and, in general, determining how much the individual believes what is being said. An attempt to influence someone's opinion need not, however, be done in an entirely logical, unemotional, cognitive situation. The situation may, and often does, involve strong motivations, appeals to deep-seated needs, and a great many factors extraneous to the logical arguments contained in the message itself.

An entirely rational, cognitive person would be influenced only to the extent that the arguments presented were logically sound. But since there are few entirely rational beings, motivational and emotional factors are also important in determining the effectiveness of a persuasive communication.

As research on attitude change has developed, there has been some change in theoretical emphasis along these lines. Much of the early research was guided by some version of a transfer of affect or rote learning approach, which treated people as rather emotional and reflexive. Most popular now are cognitive theories that place relatively little emphasis on affect and emotion. Cognitive response theory suggests that people change their attitudes not in some unthinking, emotional way, but as a result of the thoughts they have about the content of the communication. We vote against the conservative incumbent because we disagree with her positions on the issues, and when we hear her speak we make up arguments against her underneath our breath. The theory of reasoned action suggests that people act on their beliefs in quite a reasonable way: If people believe they should do something, and think it is the socially approved thing to do, they will do it.

Of course the study of attitude change will always produce a variety of views of human beings, because people are quite various and no one simplified theory will always be correct. But the trend in studying attitude change, like the trend in the study of social perception, has been away from models based on emotion and rote learning and toward models stressing cognitive processes and rational thinking.

SUMMARY

1. A useful model of the attitude change situation classifies possible influences on the target in terms of communicator, communication, and situational and target variables.
2. The major mechanisms by which people resist persuasion include refutation of the communicator's arguments, simple blanket rejection of the message, derogating the communicator, and distorting the message.
3. The target's evaluation of the source of the communication is one of the most critical factors in the success of a persuasion attempt. More attitude change is likely if the source is viewed as credible, trustworthy, and is generally liked by the target. A reference group with which the target identifies is another potent source of influence.
4. The most important aspect of the communication is how far its position differs from that already held by the target—that is, its discrepancy. The more discrepant the communication is, the more influence it has—up to a point, when it starts to fall off again. The point at which it falls off depends on source credibility and the target's commitment to this initial opinion. With high credibility and/or low commitment, the fall-off point occurs at higher levels of discrepancy.
5. Generally speaking, attitude change increases with greater fear arousal. But at very high levels of fear, when the message becomes too threatening or disruptive for the person, fear-arousing communications may become ineffective.
6. The degree of commitment to an opinion is a critical determinant of persuasion. With higher commitment, there is less persuasion.
7. A person can become inoculated against persuasion by being exposed to weak versions of the forthcoming persuasive arguments, and learning to combat them.
8. Forewarning of the position to be advocated tends to increase resistance to change when the listener is highly committed to a very discrepant position. But with weak commitment, forewarning can help to get the persuasion process started, and attitude change occurs even before the full communication is heard.
9. Distraction can help create persuasion by reducing the listener's defenses against very discrepant messages.
10. Repetition of a message is important if attitude change is to be maintained. Too much repetition leads to boredom and lessened support for it, however. Similarly, reinstatement of helpful cues associated with the message, such as high credibility of the communicator, will help attitude change to persist.

SUGGESTIONS FOR ADDITIONAL READING

HOVLAND, C. I., JANIS, I. L., & KELLEY, H. H. (1953). *Communication and persuasion.* New Haven, Conn.: Yale University Press. The original presentation of the best program in experimental studies of attitude change. Much of the rest of the work described in this chapter springs from work originally presented here.

LEVENTHAL, H., & NILES, P. (1964). A field experiment on fear arousal with data on the validity of questionnaire responses. *Journal of Personality,* 32, 459–79. An ingeniously designed, realistic field experiment conducted at the New York City Health Exposition, on the effects of fear arousal regarding smoking and lung cancer.

McGUIRE, W. J. (1984). The nature of attitudes and attitude change. In G. Lindzey & E. Aronson (eds.), *Handbook of social psychology,* 3rd ed., Vol. 2. Reading, Mass.: Addison-Wesley. The most complete review of attitude research and theory.

PETTY, R. E. & CACIOPPO, J. T. (1981). *Attitudes and persuasion: Classic and contemporary approaches.* Dubuque: Wm. C. Brown. A fine brief and contemporary treatment of research on attitude change, though written rather technically.

PETTY, R. E., OSTROM, T. M., & BROCK, T. C. (Eds.). (1981). *Cognitive responses in persuasion.* Hillsdale, N.J.: Erlbaum Associates. A useful and complete application of the cognitive response approach to many of the problems in attitude change presented in this chapter.

8

INTERPERSONAL ATTRACTION

Humans are basically social animals. Think for a minute about how you spent your time yesterday. What were you doing at 9 A.M.? at noon? at 4 P.M.? at 8 P.M.? Chances are that you spent much of your day in the company of other people, whether at home, at school, or at work. In one carefully controlled study of time use, Larson and his colleagues (1982) asked a sample of adults and a sample of teenagers to carry electronic pagers for a week. At random times from early morning to late evening, the researchers activated the pager, sounding a beep that signaled participants to fill out a short questionnaire describing what they were doing and whether they were alone or with others. As shown in Table 8–1, teenagers spent 74 percent of their waking hours with someone else; for adults, the average was 71 percent. People were most likely to be with others when they were at school or work. They were most likely to be alone when they were doing household tasks, taking a bath, listening to music, or studying at home.

For most people, the tendency to affiliate—the desire to be with other people—is quite strong. What are the origins of human affiliation? The earliest roots are to be found in infancy, when infants form strong attachments to one or more adults. This attachment relationship has been described as the child's first love affair.

ATTACHMENT IN CHILDHOOD

Infants become attached to the person with whom they interact most often and most lovingly. This is usually the mother, although it could be anyone with whom the infant has regular contact. By attachment we mean that an infant responds positively to specific people, wants to spend time with them, feels better when they are close, seeks them out when frightened, and so on. Attachment is typically a two-way process, so parents usually become attached to their children.

Infant attachment develops in steps (Ainsworth, 1973). Initially, newborns respond indiscriminately to people. Within a few weeks or months, however, they become able to distinguish between familiar people and unfamiliar ones, and begin to respond accordingly. With familiar people, infants smile and vocalize more, are more easily comforted, and show more concern about the person's leaving. At about six months, clear-cut attachment develops. Now infants actively seek to stay close to the attachment person and protest if the person leaves. As the infant's physical capacities mature, the child calls to the attachment person, crawls after him or her, or climbs on the person's lap. So from a very early age, infants tend to affiliate and express preferences about whom they want to be with.

Attachment serves two major functions for

Table 8–1
How People Spend Their Time

| | ADOLESCENTS | | ADULTS | |
ACTIVITY	ALONE	WITH OTHERS	ALONE	WITH OTHERS
At Home				
Housework	6.7	5.6	5.4	8.6
Self-care (bathing, etc.)	2.1	0.5	2.2	1.2
Studying (adolescents only)	3.5	1.4	—	—
Eating	0.6	3.1	0.7	2.4
Socializing (includes by phone)	2.6	5.4	—	3.8
Watching television	2.0	3.9	2.2	5.1
Personal reading	2.0	1.4	1.5	1.4
Doing hobbies and art	0.7	0.5	0.3	0.2
Idling, listening to music	1.8	2.5	2.4	3.3
All at home activities	20.0	24.3	14.7	26.0
At Work or School				
Working at work	1.6	2.2	5.9	20.9
In class (adolescents only)	—	15.6	—	—
Other activities at work or school	1.2	13.5	3.6	11.5
All at work or school activities	2.8	31.3	9.5	32.4
In Public				
In transit (on bus, etc.)	1.3	3.3	2.9	3.6
Other practical activities	1.2	6.2	0.8	1.1
Leisure	0.6	9.0	1.2	7.9
All public activities	3.1	18.6	4.9	12.6
TOTAL TIME (Alone + With Others = 100 percent)	25.9	74.1	29.1	70.9

Note: The table shows what percentage of the time people reported that they were alone or with others doing each specific type of activity. For instance, adolescents reported spending 6.7 percent of their time alone doing housework.

Source: Adapted from Larson et al. (1982).

children (Shaver & Klinnert, 1982). First, children derive a sense of security from being with the attachment person. When children are frightened or confronted with unfamiliar situations, they turn to this person for comfort and reassurance. Infants show less distress when a stranger approaches if they are being held by their mothers than if they are several feet away from the mother. A second function of attachment is to provide information about the environment. When children are uncertain about how to respond to a novel situation, they look to their attachment person for guidance.

In one study (Klinnert, 1981), for instance, in-fants aged 12 to 18 months were put in a play room with their mothers and presented with such novel stimuli as a large remote-controlled spider, a remote-controlled dinosaur, and a life-size model of the Incredible Hulk's head. When one of these strange objects first appeared, most children looked questioningly at their mothers. If the mother (following instructions from the researcher) showed fear, the child usually moved toward the mother. If the mother showed pleasure and smiled, the child moved toward the new toy. Nonverbal cues from the mother guided the child's response.

Children's attachment has been explained

An infant's intense gaze shows her fascination with her father. At just a few weeks of age, babies begin to form strong attachments to their parents.

both by innate biological factors and by learning. The biological view (see Bowlby, 1969) emphasizes the survival value of attachment for the child. Human infants are helpless creatures who need to be taken care of, protected, fed, and kept warm. When children are old enough to move around, it is important that they not wander too far from their parents because they might get into dangerous situations or simply get lost. Attachment was adaptive in human evolution because it ensured that children got the attention they needed to survive.

The biological explanation of attachment holds that certain behaviors and responses of the infant and parent are "wired in" genetically, and that these cause the attachment to form. The infant's ability to suck and the mother's ability to provide breast milk are one example of biologically based responses. Further, all infants cry, and almost all parents tend to come when their babies cry. Crying is a distress signal parents find difficult to ignore. If babies did not cry, it would be extremely hard for parents to know when help is needed, and so parents would not appear as regularly. Similarly, infants are genetically disposed to smile and tend, once they can distinguish among people, to greet

their parents with a smile. The parents respond with pleasure to this greeting. Thus, the parent is drawn to the baby by the smiles, while the baby becomes attached because the parent comes in response to crying and in order to receive those smiles.

According to the biological view, the development of attachment is a two-way process. Both parent and child play a role. Clearly, if the parent for some reason is not drawn to the child and does not come when it cries or like to see it smile, then the child may not become attached. But some children do not elicit attachment. They do not cry normally or do not stop crying when held; they do not smile; they do not react to the presence of the adult. This behavior makes it much harder for the parent to become attached to the child (Bell, 1968).

A second explanation is that attachment is due to learning and follows all the usual rules that govern the learning of any behavior. The child becomes attached to the parent because the parent feeds and comforts the child; the parent becomes attached to the child because the child rewards the parent. Many of the behaviors described above may be involved. For example, when the child cries, the parent comes because he or she knows that crying usually means the child needs something. The parent arrives, gives the child food or changes a diaper. The child stops crying.

Both have been reinforced by the interaction: The child feels better because it is no longer hungry or uncomfortable; the parent feels good because the child has stopped crying. Similarly, the parent is reinforced by the child's smile. As we all know, almost nothing is more rewarding than having a baby smile at us, especially if the baby favors us with more smiles than it gives to others. So the child learns to love its parent if the parent provides the attention and care it needs. And the parent learns to love the child if the child responds to this care with positive reinforcements in the form of smiles, hugs, lack of crying, and so on.

Both the biological and learning approaches probably contain much truth. Clearly, many innate behaviors of the child contribute to the formation of attachment. The child does not have to learn to cry or smile or feel good when comforted; all these inborn responses are important for producing an attachment bond between parent and child. On the other hand, there is no question that seeing a child smile or hearing it stop crying in response to your presence is reinforcing, and that without this reinforcement you might not develop a strong attachment to a child. Indeed, in unusual cases where a child does not respond to a parent's presence, attachment may not develop. So one could say that certain innate behavior patterns help produce attachment, and that the mechanism by which they operate is through mutual reinforcement of parent and child.

Work on attachment raises the possibility that the tendency to affiliate is, at least in part, biologically based. As a species, humans may be disposed to form emotional attachments to those with whom they interact regularly and to feel more comfortable and secure in the presence of these people. It seems likely that the capacity for emotional attachment that first appears in infancy continues throughout life, as we form bonds to close friends, lovers, and children.

OUR DIVERSE SOCIAL NEEDS

As we grow up, our social needs become more complex and diverse. We affiliate to have fun, to get help, to share sexual intimacies, to feel powerful, to get approval, and so on. Researchers have tried to identify the broad range of social needs that relationships can satisfy.

Laboratory Studies of Affiliation

One of the earliest research approaches to understanding affiliation used controlled laboratory experiments to test specific hypotheses about factors that increase or decrease the tendency to affiliate. The model for much of this research came from an influential series of studies conducted in the 1950s by Stanley Schachter (1959). He began with the plausible hypothesis that adults, like infants, affiliate to reduce fear. Thus, if we randomly assign adults to a condition where they will experience either high or low fear, we should observe significant differences in their desire for human company.

To test this idea, Schachter recruited women undergraduates. When subjects arrived for the study, they were greeted by an experimenter in a white laboratory coat, surrounded by electrical equipment of various sorts. The experimenter introduced himself as Dr. Gregor Zilstein of the Department of Neurology and Psychiatry, and he explained that the experiment concerned the effects of electric shocks. To make some subjects more afraid than others, the experimenter used two different descriptions of the electric shock.

In the high-fear condition, instructions described the shocks in ominous tones. Subjects were told: "These shocks will hurt. . . . In research of this sort, if we're to learn anything at all that will really help humanity, it is necessary that our shocks be intense. . . . These shocks will be quite painful but, of course, they will do no permanent damage." By continuing at some length in this vein, Dr. Zilstein communicated the notion that the subject was in for a very frightening and painful experience.

In the low-fear condition, by contrast, every attempt was made to make the subject feel relaxed and to minimize the severity of the shocks. For example, the subjects were told: "I assure you that what you will feel (electric shock) will not in any way be painful. It will resemble a tickle or a tingle more than anything unpleasant." Thus, although both groups of subjects were told that the experiment would concern electric shock, one group expected a painful and frightening experience, whereas the other group expected a mild and unthreatening experience. When questioned, women in the high-fear condition were indeed more afraid.

Following the arousal and measurement of fear, Dr. Zilstein told the subjects there would be a 10-minute delay while he prepared the equipment. He explained that there were a number of other rooms in which the subjects might wait—comfortable rooms with armchairs and magazines. The experimenter then said it had occurred to him that perhaps some people would prefer to wait alone; others might prefer to wait with other subjects in the experiment, and for these there was a classroom available. Each was asked to indicate whether she preferred to wait with others, alone, or had no preference. She was also asked to indicate the strength of her choice. In this and most subsequent experiments on the topic, the choice and rating of the intensity of subjects' desire to affiliate were the basic measures of the affiliation.

The results of Schachter's study are shown in Table 8–2. The answer to the question of whether highly fearful subjects want to affiliate more than subjects with low fear is "yes." The greater the fear, the greater the tendency to affiliate. Subsequent studies have confirmed this finding. Research has also shown that fear must be distinguished from other stressful situations that may actually decrease affiliative tendencies. For instance, if we are confronted with a situation that is not only stressful but also embarrassing, we may prefer to avoid other people.

This point was demonstrated by Sarnoff and Zimbardo (1961). Their study included high- and low-fear conditions plus a new condition designed to arouse "oral anxiety." In the high oral anxiety condition, men were asked to perform a series of embarrassing tasks, such as sucking on baby bottles and rubber nipples. The

Table 8–2
Effect of Fear on Affiliation

	WAITING PREFERENCE				MEAN STRENGTH OF AFFILIATION TENDENCY (Scale from −2 to +2)
CONDITION	TOGETHER	DON'T CARE	ALONE	TOTAL	
High fear	62.5%	28.1%	9.4%	100.0%	.88
Low fear	33.0	60.0	7.0	100.0	.35

Source: Adapted from Schachter (1959).

results were that men in the high-fear condition were eager to affiliate, but men in the embarrassing high oral anxiety condition preferred to wait alone.

Given that fearful people usually want company, just what is it that they expect to get from being with others? What is the psychological process involved? Two possibilities have been investigated. The first is the mere presence or distraction hypothesis: Fearful people affiliate to take their minds off their problems. In this case, it should not matter very much who they affiliate with—almost anyone will do. In contrast, *social comparison theory* suggests that people affiliate to compare their own feelings with those of others in the same situation. When we are in a new or unusual situation and are uncertain about how to react, we turn to others as a source of information. In this case we should be interested in affiliating only with people who are confronted with the same situation.

Several studies have tested these two possibilities, and results consistently support the social comparison hypothesis. In one study (Schachter, 1959), for example, women subjects were exposed to a high-fear condition. Some subjects were given a choice of waiting alone or waiting with other women taking part in the same study. The other subjects were given a choice of waiting alone or with women students who were waiting to see their faculty advisor. As social comparison theory would predict, the fearful women in this study preferred to wait with others in the same situation, but not with others in a different situation. As Schachter has concluded: "Misery doesn't love just any company, it loves only miserable company."

Social comparison theory is helpful in understanding why fearful people want to affiliate. But the theory is actually much broader in scope. As described by Leon Festinger (1954), the theory has two basic ideas:

1. People have a drive to evaluate themselves.
2. In the absence of objective nonsocial criteria, we evaluate ourselves by comparison with other people.

All of us want to know how good we are at the things we care about. Am I a good tennis player, a talented writer, a graceful dancer, a loyal friend? Sometimes we can evaluate ourselves on objective criteria. If we get a perfect score on an exam, we know we are doing very well. But most of the time there is no convenient standard, so we turn to other people to help us evaluate ourselves. This is especially true when feelings and emotions are involved. Should I enjoy eating chocolate-covered grasshoppers, or laugh at the comedian's dirty jokes, or be afraid of the huge but harmless snake? Knowing how others are responding helps to clarify and evaluate our own thoughts and feelings.

Thus, both Schachter's laboratory experiments on affiliation between strangers and studies of parent-child attachment emphasize that affiliation is linked to fear and to uncertainty. At any age, affiliation is likely to be most beneficial if we can associate with someone who is both sympathetic and knowledgeable.

Satisfying Our Needs

In recent years, theorists have attempted to classify the major types of benefits people receive in relationships (House, 1981). One analysis of affiliative needs has been proposed by Robert Weiss (1974). He identified what he called six basic "provisions of social relations"—important things relationships provide for individuals:

- *Attachment* is the sense of security and comfort provided by our closest relationships. As children we are usually strongly attached to our parents; as adults we may experience this intimacy with dating partners, spouses, or other close friends.
- *Social integration* is the sense of having shared interests and attitudes that is often provided by relationships with friends, co-workers, or teammates. Such relationships offer companionship and give a sense of belonging to a community.
- *Reassurance of worth* is provided when people support our sense of being a competent and valued person.

- *A sense of reliable alliance* involves knowing that there are people who will assist us in times of need. When emergencies arise, we often turn to our families for help.
- *The obtaining of guidance* is provided by counselors, teachers, doctors, friends, and others to whom we turn for advice and information.
- *The opportunity for nurturance* occurs when we are responsible for the well-being of another person. Taking care of someone provides us with a sense of being needed and important.

This analysis of specific social needs highlights two major points about human affiliation. First, the rewards of companionship are many and diverse. We could undoubtedly add many other social needs to Weiss's list. Second, this approach emphasizes that no single relationship can fulfill all our affiliative needs. A love relationship may provide a sense of attachment, but not a sense of belonging to a community. Our neighbor may water our plants while we're out of town, but not provide the sympathetic ear we want in a close confidante. A rich and healthy social life requires a network of social relations capable of satisfying all these varied needs. Those whose relationships fail to satisfy essential social needs suffer the pain of loneliness.

LONELINESS: UNSATISFIED SOCIAL NEEDS

Few people escape the misery of loneliness. As a child, you may have felt lonely when you started in a new school, moved to a new town, or went away to summer camp. As a young adult, you may have suffered the loneliness that follows breaking up with someone you once loved. Life is filled with social transitions that disrupt personal relationships and set the stage for loneliness. For many people, the social challenge of going to college creates feelings of loneliness, as noted in Box 8–1.

Loneliness versus Aloneness

Loneliness and aloneness are not the same. **Loneliness** refers to the subjective discomfort we feel when our social relations lack some important feature. This deficit may be quantitative: We may have no friends, or fewer friends than we want. Or the deficit can be qualitative: We may feel our relationships are superficial, or less satisfying than we would like. Loneliness goes on inside a person and cannot be detected simply by looking at someone.

In contrast to subjective feelings of loneliness, aloneness is the objective state of being apart from other people. Aloneness can be pleasant or unpleasant. If you're stranded on a dark street with a stalled car, being by yourself may be distressing. But solitude can also offer many rewards (Suedfeld, 1982). Religious leaders go off on solitary quests to seek spiritual inspiration. Writers and musicians frequently do their best work alone, away from the distractions of social interaction. In daily life, we may crave time alone to study for an important test, read a good book, or think over a problem. Even living alone can be a positive experience involving accomplishment and independence.

There is no inevitable link between aloneness and loneliness: We can be happy alone or lonely in a crowd. Nonetheless, people are somewhat more likely to feel lonely when they are alone. For example, in the time use study by Larson described earlier, people felt lonelier when they were alone than when they were with others. A closer look at the data revealed, however, that this pattern resulted primarily from being alone on Friday or Saturday night. People did not feel particularly lonely if they

The misery of time alone is seen in this young man's sense of loneliness and rejection. The pleasures of time alone are seen in this young woman's romp at the beach.

were alone during the week while shopping or studying. But being alone on a weekend evening when personal preference and social norms suggest you should be out with friends was a major impetus to loneliness.

The Experience of Loneliness

In national surveys (such as Bradburn, 1969), roughly one American in four says he or she has felt "very lonely or remote from other people" in the past two weeks. Loneliness can range from fleeting twinges of discomfort to severe and persistent feelings of intense misery (Peplau & Perlman, 1982).

DURATION OF LONELINESS Sometimes loneliness is caused by a life change that takes us away from friends and intimate relationships. So-called situational loneliness occurs when a person has had satisfying relationships until some specific change takes place in his or her life. Sit-

uations that commonly cause loneliness include moving to a new town, going away to school, starting a new job, being separated from friends and loved ones while on a trip or in the hospital, or ending an important relationship through death, divorce, or breaking up. People usually recover from situational loneliness and reestablish a satisfying social life, although this is obviously more difficult in some situations than in others. We may make friends at our new job in a few months, but take a year or more to get over the ending of a love relationship.

Some people suffer from loneliness for many years, more or less independent of changes in their lives. They are experiencing chronic loneliness. Such individuals might describe themselves as a "lonely person," rather than someone who is in a lonely period of life. Perhaps 10 percent of American adults suffer from severe and persistent loneliness.

TYPES OF LONELINESS Robert Weiss (1973) has distinguished two types of loneliness, based on the specific social provision that a person lacks.

BOX 8–1
Loneliness on Campus

For many students, the excitement of beginning college is mixed with the temporary loneliness of leaving friends and family, and anxiety over building a new social life. One student commented:

> Coming to a large university such as this was a big change for me. After being voted in high school "Best Personality" and "Most Popular," I had to start over. Seeing nothing but strangers was rather difficult at first, but I find myself getting used to it.

To learn about the social transition of going to college, Carolyn Cutrona, Daniel Russell, and Anne Peplau conducted a study of entering students at UCLA. Participants in the study were contacted during their first few weeks on campus and then seven months later in the spring (Cutrona, 1982). At the start of the school year, 75 percent of new students had experienced at least occasional loneliness since their arrival on campus. More than 40 percent reported that their loneliness had been moderate to severe in intensity. Fortunately, most students were able to cope successfully with the adjustment to college. By spring, only 25 percent were still lonely.

How did students who overcame their loneliness differ from those who remained lonely throughout their first year at college? The most striking difference was found in their attitudes. Students were more likely to recover from loneliness if they began the school year with positive expectations that they would be successful in making friends and if they felt good about themselves and their personality. In other words, optimism and high self-esteem were significant ingredients in creating a satisfying social life at college.

Students living at home with parents were no more lonely than students living in a dorm on campus. Successful and unsuccessful students reported about the same frequency of such activities as joining clubs, playing intramural sports, going to parties, or talking to strangers in classes. Both groups were also equally likely to report efforts to improve their appearance and social skills or to find new ways to meet people.

But there may be more subtle differences in the behavior of students who do and do not recover from loneliness. Jones (1982) observed that lonely college students interacted in a more self-focused way than did the nonlonely. For instance, in a conversation with a new acquaintance, lonely students asked fewer questions about the other person, made fewer statements focusing on the other, and responded more slowly to comments by the partner. Lonely people tended to be more negativistic and self-absorbed and were less responsive to others. Other research (Solano, Batten, & Parish, 1982) suggests that lonely college students may be atypical in their patterns of self-disclosure, either pouring out their heart to someone they've just met or revealing unusually little about themselves. The researchers suggest that these inappropriate disclosure levels may interfere with the development of close relationships.

BOX 8–2
Children of Divorce

Divorce, once an unusual event, is now common, and most divorces today involve families with children. Divorce affected less than 15 percent of children born in 1955. Today, that percentage has doubled. It has been estimated that a third of the children born in the 1980s will experience a parental divorce before they reach age 18 (Bane, 1976). Researchers are only beginning to understand the many ways that divorce can affect children (Longfellow, 1979). One possibility is that children of divorce may be more vulnerable to loneliness as they become adults.

In a large survey of Americans, Rubenstein and Shaver (1982) found that adults whose parents had divorced were more likely to be lonely, especially if the divorce occurred before the person was 6 years old. Perhaps surprisingly, the death of a parent during childhood was not related to adult loneliness. To explain these findings, Shaver and Rubenstein (1980) turned to the work on parent-child attachment discussed earlier in this chapter. They suggested that the loss of a parental attachment relationship through divorce influences children in two major ways.

First, children often blame themselves for the divorce. Although it is an irrational belief, many children believe that they have in some way caused their parents' marriage to end. This tendency seems especially strong among preschool children, whose cognitive development is immature and self-focused (Wallerstein & Kelly, 1975). If children are older at the time of the divorce, they are usually better able to understand that the divorce was not their fault. The legacy of this self-blame can be persistent low self-esteem— an enduring belief that one is unlovable and unworthy of affection. Studies of adults (Peplau & Perlman, 1982) show a clear link between low self-esteem and loneliness. The person who lacks self-confidence may be less willing to take risks in social situations and may subtly communicate a sense of unworthiness to others. This, in turn, may set the stage for poor social relationships and for loneliness.

Rubenstein and Shaver also speculate that children of divorce may come to see other people as rejecting and unreliable. If a child perceives a parent as unresponsive or frustrating, the child may develop a more generalized view of people as untrustworthy and of relationships as undependable. Such a "model" or image of relationships established in childhood may persist into adulthood, making it harder for the individual to form rewarding relationships. Consistent with this idea are data showing that children of divorce have more negative and less trusting views of other people (Shaver & Rubenstein, 1980). This problem may be greater for children of divorce than for children whose parents die. In divorce, children usually continue to see the noncustodial parent, and may regard each visit as an opportunity to entice the parent to return. When the parent leaves at the end of the visit, the child may perceive that he or she has been rejected still again.

The possibility that childhood experiences in the family influence loneliness in adulthood is intriguing, and an important topic for additional research. We should be cautious, however, not to overstate the impact of childhood events on later loneliness. Many children of divorce have gone on to create close and satisfying relationships as adults. Further, greater awareness about the potential effects of divorce may enable divorcing parents to help their children cope more effectively with this major life transition.

Emotional loneliness results from the absence of an intimate attachment figure, such as might be provided for children by their parents or for adults by a spouse or intimate friend. **Social loneliness** occurs when a person lacks a sense of social integration or community that might be provided by a network of friends or co-workers.

It is possible to experience one type of loneliness without the other. A young couple who get married and move to Alaska to seek adventure and high-paying jobs may not feel emotional loneliness—they have each other. But they are likely to experience social loneliness until they make friends and start feeling a part of their new community. A young widow may feel intense emotional loneliness after the death of her husband, but continue to have many social ties to family and friends.

No segment of society is immune to loneliness, but some people are at greater risk than others (Peplau & Perlman, 1982). Certain childhood experiences may predispose individuals to loneliness. As noted in Box 8–2, children who lose a parental attachment relationship because of death or divorce may be more vulnerable to loneliness as adults.

Married people are less likely to be lonely than others. It is interesting to note, however, that some married people—18 percent in one large study—do feel lonely. Married people might be lonely because they lack friends or because their marriage is not personally satisfying. Loneliness is more common among the poor than the affluent. Good relationships may be easier to maintain when people have the time and money for leisure activities and entertaining.

Loneliness is related to age. Popular stereotypes depict old age as a time of great loneliness. But research shows that loneliness is highest among teenagers and young adults, and lowest among older people. In one large survey (Parlee, 1979), 79 percent of people under age 18 said they were sometimes or often lonely, compared to only 53 percent of those 45 to 54, and 37 percent of those 55 and over. Researchers have not yet determined the reasons for this age pattern. In part, there may be a "generation gap," with young people being more willing to talk about their feelings and acknowledge loneliness than are their parents. It is also true, however, that young people face a great many social transitions, such as leaving home, living on their own, going to college, or taking a first full-time job—all of which can cause loneliness. As people get older, their social lives may become more stable. Age may also bring greater social skills and more realistic expectations about social relations.

Several personality factors have been linked to loneliness (Peplau & Perlman, 1982). Lonely people tend to be more introverted and shy, more self-conscious, and less assertive. Lonely people often have low self-esteem, and in some cases have poor social skills. Loneliness is also associated with anxiety and depression. Several of these personality factors can be both a cause and a consequence of loneliness. For example, people with low self-esteem may be less willing to take risks in social settings, making it harder for them to form friendships and increasing their chances of loneliness. On the other hand, the experience of being lonely for a long time may lead a person to see him or herself as a social failure and so cause a drop in the person's self-esteem.

Having examined some of the many reasons why people affiliate, we now turn to a new question. Why are we attracted to some individuals and not to others?

BASIC PRINCIPLES OF INTERPERSONAL ATTRACTION

You're sitting in the first meeting of a seminar on English literature, listening to the discussion with one ear and sizing up your new classmates. You've taken an instant dislike to one rather pompous man who seems bent on dominating the conversation. Whenever he opens his mouth, you and the woman sitting across from you exchange knowing glances and smiles. She seems to be friendly, and you decide to talk to her during the coffee break. As your eyes travel around the seminar table, you think about each student, making mental notes about who you like and who you don't like.

We saw in Chapter 3 that the major dimension of first impressions is evaluation. Why is it that we like some people and not others? What determines who will become our friends? Perhaps the most general answer is that we like people who reward us and who help us to satisfy our needs. Learning theories and incentives theories both offer explanations of the specific mechanisms through which rewards influence liking.

REINFORCEMENT   A basic principle from learning theory is *reinforcement*. We like people who reward us in one way or another. One important type of reward is social approval, and many studies have shown that we tend to like people who evaluate us positively. In one experiment (Aronson & Linder, 1965), subjects went through a series of brief interactions with a confederate who was posing as another subject. After each interaction, the subject overheard an interview between the confederate and the experimenter in which the confederate gave his impressions of the subject.

In one condition, the confederate was quite flattering and said at the beginning that he liked the subject; he continued to make positive statements about the subject after each interview. In another condition, the confederate was critical. He said he was not sure that he liked the subject much and gave fairly negative descriptions of him. He continued being negative throughout the study. Afterward, the subjects were asked how much they liked the confederate. The results are shown in Table 8–3. As expected, subjects liked the confederate significantly more if he said positive things about them than if he was negative in his evaluations.

SOCIAL EXCHANGE   This perspective proposes that our liking for another person is based on our assessment of the costs and benefits the person provides us. According to *social exchange theory,* we like people when we perceive our interactions with them to be profitable—that is, when the rewards we get from the relationship outweigh the costs. Thus, we may like Allen because he's interesting and funny and overlook the fact that he is perpetually late. Social exchange theory also emphasizes that we make comparative judgments, assessing the profits we get from one person against the profits we get from another.

ASSOCIATION   A useful principle from classical conditioning is *association:* We come to like people who are associated with good experi-

---

Table 8–3
Liking in Response to Another's Evaluation

CONDITION	LIKING
Positive evaluation by confederate	6.4
Negative evaluation by confederate	2.5

Numbers are ratings on a scale from −10 to +10.
Source: Adapted from Aronson and Linder (1965).

Christa Armstrong, Photo Researchers, Inc.

A shared family background is often an important basis for interpersonal attraction. Here, a family reunion brings together three generations to celebrate their common ancestry.

ences and dislike people who are associated with bad experiences (Clore & Byrne, 1974). A demonstration of this effect comes from a study by May and Hamilton (1980). They were interested in the impact of pleasant versus unpleasant background music on interpersonal attraction. They first determined which type of music college women liked most (rock music) and least (avant-garde classical music). They then had other women students rate photographs of male strangers. While the women made their ratings, they heard rock music, avant-garde classical music, or no music. The results were clear-cut. Women rated the men least favorably when their photos were associated with disliked music and most favorably when they were associated with enjoyable music. The idea is that liking for someone can be influenced by a conditioned emotional response to events arbitrarily associated with that person.

This association notion is important. Yet, as with so much that occurs with people, its very truth and simplicity should not blind us to other processes that may reverse it on occasion. For instance, someone with whom you spend a very painful or stressful time may wind up a close friend, even though by association the person should make you think of pure misery. For example, Kenrick and Johnson (1979) put subjects in a situation that involved very noxious, unpredictable bursts of loud noise. Subjects' liking for each other increased even though they hated the experience. Sometimes shared misery creates a sense of solidarity that forms the basis for friendship.

With these general principles in mind, we now turn to research on more specific factors that influence interpersonal attraction. Four powerful determinants of liking are personal qualities of the other individual, similarity, familiarity, and proximity. As we discuss each of these important factors, we will also note occasional exceptions—special cases that differ from the general pattern.

PERSONAL CHARACTERISTICS

Just what is it that makes us like one person more than another? There is no single answer to this question. One person may find red hair and freckles irresistible; another may dislike them intensely. Some of us prize compassion in our friends; others value intelligence. Individuals vary in the things they find most rewarding in other people. There are also large cultural differences in those personal qualities considered socially desirable. Many Americans equate feminine beauty with being thin, but other societies consider plump women the most attractive. Researchers have sought to identify some of the general characteristics associated with liking in our society.

Some years ago, Norman Anderson (1968b) compiled a list of 555 adjectives that are used to describe people. He then asked college students to indicate how much they would like a person who had each of these characteristics. A sample of these adjectives is given in Table 8–4. There seemed to be general agreement among the students in this study on which characteristics were desirable and undesirable. One of the most striking results was that for students in the 1960s, sincerity was the most valued trait. Of the eight top adjectives, six—sincere, honest, loyal, truthful, trustworthy, and dependable—related to sincerity in one way or another. Similarly, the adjectives rated lowest included liar and phony.

Two other themes that emerged in the list of

Table 8–4
Likableness of Personality Traits

HIGHLY LIKABLE	SLIGHTLY POSITIVE TO SLIGHTLY NEGATIVE	HIGHLY DISLIKABLE
Sincere	Persistent	Ill-mannered
Honest	Conventional	Unfriendly
Understanding	Bold	Hostile
Loyal	Cautious	Loud-mouthed
Truthful	Perfectionistic	Selfish
Trustworthy	Excitable	Narrow-minded
Intelligent	Quiet	Rude
Dependable	Impulsive	Conceited
Thoughtful	Aggressive	Greedy
Considerate	Shy	Insincere
Reliable	Unpredictable	Unkind
Warm	Emotional	Untrustworthy
Kind	Bashful	Malicious
Friendly	Naïve	Obnoxious
Happy	Restless	Untruthful
Unselfish	Daydreamer	Dishonest
Humorous	Materialistic	Cruel
Responsible	Rebellious	Mean
Cheerful	Lonely	Phony
Trustful	Dependent	Liar

Source: Adapted from Anderson (1968b).

highly likable traits were personal warmth and competence. These correspond to the two fundamental dimensions of liking proposed by Zick Rubin (1973). According to Rubin, the key components of liking are affection and respect. Affection stems from the way another person treats us, and is experienced as emotional warmth and closeness. Respect is based on admiration for a person's desirable characteristics and competence. Both warmth and competence have been the topic of psychological research.

PERSONAL WARMTH   In Chapter 3 we described research showing that warmth is a central trait affecting our first impressions of another person. What is it that makes one person seem warm and friendly, while another comes across as cold and unfriendly? One clue comes from a series of experiments by Folkes and Sears (1977). These researchers suggested that people appear warm when they like things, praise them, and approve of them—in other words, when they have a positive attitude toward people and things. In contrast, people seem cold when they dislike things, disparage them, say they are awful, and are generally critical.

In this research, subjects read or listened to interviews in which the interviewee was asked to evaluate a long list of things such as political leaders, cities, movies, or freshman courses. Sometimes the interviewees expressed predominantly positive attitudes—they liked most of the politicians, cities, movies, or courses. In other cases, the interviewees expressed mainly negative attitudes. As predicted, subjects liked the interviewees more if they were positive rather than negative in their attitudes. Folkes and Sears concluded that the explanation lay in the greater warmth communicated by the positive attitude, because other analyses showed that the liking effect was not due to any greater perceived intelligence, knowledge, or similarity of attitudes on the part of the positive interviewees.

COMPETENCE   In general, we like people who are socially skilled, intelligent, and competent. The particular type of competence that matters most depends on the nature of our relationship with the person: We are attracted to friends who are good conversationalists, to mechanics who are good at fixing cars, to professors who are interesting lecturers, and so on. Competent

Erika Stone, Photo Researchers, Inc.

Beauty is often an advantage in social relations. Other things being equal, attractive people tend to be liked more than people considered less physically attractive.

BOX 8–3
Beauty by Contrast: It All Depends

Television presents a world largely populated by beautiful people—adorable children, sexy young women, men with rugged good looks, and so on. Even TV news reporters are coached to improve their clothes and physical appearance. Social critics argue that these idealized images create unrealistic standards few of us can attain. Critics note that even the actors and actresses we see on the screen do not look nearly as attractive in real life, without the help of makeup artists, wardrobe experts, flattering lights, and other props. Do these media beauty standards actually influence how we react to people in everyday life?

To find out, Douglas Kenrick and Sara Gutierres (1980) designed a clever field study. College men were contacted in their dorm either before or after they had watched "Charlie's Angels," a popular TV show starring three very beautiful young women. To reduce response bias, the men were not told they were in an experiment. Two college students (confederates of the researchers) approached groups of men sitting in a dorm lounge and asked them to help settle a personal debate about how pretty a particular young woman was. The men were shown a photo of the woman and were asked to write their ratings of her beauty secretly, so they wouldn't be influenced by each other. The woman had previously been rated by other college men as being of average attractiveness, about 4 on a 7-point scale.

As predicted, men who had just watched three lovely actresses for an hour rated this typical woman as less attractive than did men who had not seen the TV show. The same researchers replicated this effect in two more laboratory studies. In both, exposure to a photo of a highly attractive woman led to lower attractiveness ratings of an average-looking woman by both male and female subjects. All three studies found a "contrast effect": The average-looking person was seen as less attractive because of the extreme beauty of the recent comparison stimulus.

Michael Kernis and Ladd Wheeler (1981) took this research one step further by asking when the contrast effect occurs and when, as noted in the text, an opposite "radiating effect" occurs. They hypothesized that the relationship between the average-looking person and the beautiful person makes a difference. They designed a laboratory experiment so that subjects saw two people, a target person of average attractiveness and a comparison person of either above-average or below-average looks. As a further variation, these people were sometimes presented as being strangers and sometimes as being friends.

The two relationship conditions (stranger and friend) produced opposite results. When the two people were thought to be strangers, a contrast effect occurred. The average-looking target person was rated less favorably when paired with a very attractive stranger. But when the two people were believed to be friends, a radiating effect occurred. The target person was rated more favorably when seen with a very attractive friend, and less favorably when seen with a very unattractive friend. The contrast effect was apparently offset by other influences leading subjects to assume that someone with a beautiful friend was somehow more attractive. Gender did not affect these patterns: The same results were found regardless of whether the subject and the people being evaluated were male or female.

We need to be cautious in applying these findings to real-life situations. These studies involved ratings of strangers. As people learn more about each other, the effects of physical attractiveness may change. Just when contrast and radiating effects occur in interactions with friends and lovers is an important question for future research.

people are usually more rewarding to be with than inept people.

An interesting exception to the competence-leads-to-liking principle is the case of someone who is a little "too perfect" for comfort. A study by Aronson, Willerman, and Floyd (1966) demonstrated this effect. Participants listened to a tape recording of a student who was trying out for a College Quiz Bowl team. In one condition, the candidate gave an outstanding performance and answered nearly every question correctly. In a second condition, the candidate gave a mediocre performance. As an added twist to the experiment, after the tryout was over, the candidate was sometimes heard to spill coffee on his suit.

The results showed the usual competence-leads-to-liking effect: The outstanding candidate was liked better than the mediocre one. However, the outstanding candidate was liked even better when he made a minor blunder or "pratfall" than when his performance was flawless. Apparently spilling coffee served to "humanize" the brainy student and so made him more likable. In contrast, the blunder only detracted from the evaluations of the mediocre applicant. He was liked less when he spilled coffee than when he didn't.

PHYSICAL ATTRACTIVENESS One of the first things we notice about a person is appearance.

Other things being equal, people considered attractive are liked more than people considered unattractive. For example, Walster et al. (1966) conducted a "computer dance" in which students were randomly assigned to each other as dates for the evening. The researchers secretly made ratings of the physical attractiveness of each participant. At the end of the evening, students were asked to rate how much they liked their assigned partner. Liking was closely related to the person's physical attractiveness. Both men and women who were considered attractive were liked more.

One reason for the strong influence of appearance is the halo effect discussed in Chapter 3. We tend to assume that people who are physically attractive also have other desirable characteristics, such as being warm or having a pleasant personality. A second factor is the so-called radiating effect of beauty. People may find it rewarding to be seen with a particularly attractive friend or date because they think it will enhance their own public image. Indeed, studies have shown that both men and women are rated more favorably when they are accompanied by an attractive romantic partner or friend than when they have an unattractive companion (see Kernis & Wheeler, 1981; Sheposh, Deming & Young, 1977; Sigall & Landy, 1973). For an interesting exception to the radiating effects of beauty, see Box 8–3.

SIMILARITY

Another basic factor in interpersonal attraction is similarity. We tend to like people who are similar to us in attitudes, values, interests, background, and personality. There is much truth to the old adage that "birds of a feather flock together."

Research Findings

One of the first demonstrations that similarity leads to friendship was done by Theodore Newcomb (1961). He took over a large house at the University of Michigan and offered male undergraduates free housing in return for taking part in his research. Before the students arrived, they filled out various questionnaires about their attitudes and values. Newcomb controlled the assignment of roommates so that some had very similar attitudes and others had very dissimilar attitudes. He then intervened very little during the semester. The results showed that roommates with similar preacquaintance attitudes generally liked each other and ended up as friends; dissimilar roommates tended to dislike each other and did not become friends.

Attraction through similarity has been the focus of much research. In a series of experiments, Donn Byrne (1971) and his associates examined attitude similarity. To rule out other factors such as appearance or personality that might influence liking, Byrne developed the *phantom-other technique*. In these studies, participants fill out questionnaires describing their own attitudes. Then they read questionnaires allegedly filled out by a stranger.

In actuality, there is no other person. Experimenters deliberately select the answers to be either very similar, moderately similar, or dissimilar to the person's own answers. Subjects are then asked how much they think they would like this other person. The results of these studies have shown that attitude similarity strongly determines liking. The more similar the attitudes, the greater the anticipated liking. This effect has been demonstrated with very diverse groups including children, college students, medical patients, job trainees, and alcoholics.

The importance of similarity extends well beyond attitudes. Similarity in ethnic background, religion, politics, social class, education, and age all influence attraction. Kandel's (1978) study of the friendships of 2,000 high school students illustrates this point. Each student identified his or her "best friend in school" and completed questionnaires about his or her own background and attitudes. Most best friends were similar in gender, year in school, age, and race. Best friends also tended to be similar in their school grades and their attitudes toward drug use.

In dating and marriage, the tendency to choose similar partners is called the **matching principle.** It is unusual for an ardent feminist to date a sex-role traditionalist, or for an orthodox Jew to date a fundamentalist Christian. Dating partners and spouses tend to be relatively matched in their physical and social characteristics. For example, one study of dating couples (Hill, Rubin, & Peplau, 1976) found that partners tended to resemble each other in age, intelligence, educational plans, religion, physical attractiveness, and even height. They were also matched in their attitudes about sexual behavior and sex roles. Furthermore, couples who were most similar in background at the beginning of the study were most likely to be together one year later.

Explaining the Similarity Effect

Why should similarity be so important in interpersonal attraction? There are two major explanations (Rubin, 1973). First, similarity is usually rewarding. People similar to us will tend to agree with our ideas and bolster our confidence in the rightness of our views. In contrast, it is unpleasant to have someone disagree with us, criticize our beliefs, and challenge our taste and judgment. Similar values and interests provide the basis for sharing enjoyable activities with another person, whether this be picketing a nuclear power plant or going to a prayer meeting.

A second explanation for the similarity-liking connection comes from cognitive balance theory, described in Chapter 6. According to this theory, people strive to maintain harmony or consistency among their attitudes, to organize their likes and dislikes in a balanced way. To like someone and at the same time to disagree with that person about fundamental issues is psychologically uncomfortable. We maximize cognitive balance by liking those who support our views and disliking those who disagree.

Social Desirability versus Similarity

At this point, you may have noticed an apparent contradiction in our discussion. We are attracted to people who have the most socially desirable qualities. We might all prefer to date someone who is beautiful, rich, and famous! But in reality, most of us wind up with partners who resemble ourselves. Our abstract ideals are brought down to reality by the constraints of social life.

Research on physical attractiveness illustrates this process. We saw earlier that people usually like handsome men and beautiful women more than less attractive persons. But actual dating partners tend to be matched in physical appeal, with beautiful women dating handsome men, while average-looking men date average-looking women (Hill et al., 1976; Murstein, 1972; White, 1980). For instance, Folkes (1982) studied members of a video dating service. As part of the service, members watch videotaped interviews of potential dates, and then decide about asking the other person out. Folkes rated members on physical attractiveness and inter-

viewed them about whom they had contacted for a date. She found that both men and women were most likely to pursue a relationship with someone similar to themselves in physical attractiveness. Only the most attractive people sought dates with the most attractive partners.

The matching principle can be explained by the expectancy-value theory of decision-making discussed in Chapter 1. The theory proposes that people consider not only the reward value of a particular choice (here, a potential date's attractiveness), but also the expectancy of being successful with this choice (here, actually going out with the person). The implication is that people will pursue the most attractive possible partner only if the probability of being rejected is fairly low.

In real life, however, the most socially desirable people are most in demand, and so the chance of rejection is usually high. Expectancy-value theory argues that people will go for the most desirable person they can realistically expect to get. People therefore tend to select someone roughly similar to themselves in attractiveness. Support for this view comes from an experiment by Shanteau and Nagy (1979). They presented women students with pictures of men varying in attractiveness. The photos were accompanied by labels indicating how likely the man would be to go out on a date with them. The women's choices were affected by both attractiveness and the probability of rejection.

Limits to the Similarity Effect

Although similarity usually leads to liking, there are exceptions to this general pattern. Sometimes similarity is threatening. If someone much like us has a heart attack or suffers from some other unfortunate fate, we may worry that we are also vulnerable and so we may prefer to avoid that person. This point was demonstrated by Novak and Lerner (1968). In a variation of the Byrne "phantom other" study, subjects read a questionnaire completed by another student whose attitudes were either very similar or dissimilar to their own. The researchers also led students to believe that this other person was either emotionally disturbed or normal.

In the "disturbed" condition, the other person had written at the end of the questionnaire: "I don't know if this is relevant or not, but last fall I had a kind of nervous breakdown and I had to be hospitalized for a while. I've been seeing a psychiatrist ever since. As you probably noticed, I'm pretty shaky right now." In the "normal" condition, no such information was added. For subjects confronted with a normal person, attitude similarity increased liking as usual. For subjects confronted with an emotionally disturbed person, attitude similarity *decreased* liking; people were more eager to avoid the other person if he was similar than if he was different.

Another point is that differences between people are sometimes very rewarding. Few of us want to associate with clones, people who are identical to us in virtually every respect. The joys of friendship include stimulation and novelty—learning about new ideas and coming to appreciate the rich variety of human experience. Research suggests that we may be most open to the rewards of differentness when we feel that another person accepts us. In one study, Walster and Walster (1963) hypothesized that college students would be more willing to associate with dissimilar strangers if they knew in advance that the strangers would like them. Subjects could choose to participate in a discussion group with people who were very similar to themselves (introductory psychology students) or with people who were very dissimilar (psychologists, factory workers).

Before making their choice, some students were told that people in all groups were disposed to like them; others were told that group members were disposed to dislike them. When students were assured of being liked, they greatly preferred to be with dissimilar people. When students thought they might be disliked, they wanted to talk to similar others. A feeling of acceptance may be a prerequisite for appreciating differences.

Another advantage of differentness is that it enables us to divide tasks according to people's distinctive skills and interests. In planning a group camping trip, it is convenient to have one person who knows about tents and equipment, someone else who can plan for meals, and a third person who knows the area and can pick a good campsite. In a traditional marriage, where the wife is the "homemaking expert" and the husband is the "breadwinning expert," the spouses' roles are different but complementary. When we say that "opposites attract," we are often referring to role relationships such as these, where people with different skills and knowledge contribute to a shared enterprise. However, most cases of complementarity require that partners have *similar* values and goals—such as a desire to spend a weekend camping in the wilderness or shared beliefs about how to organize married life.

FAMILIARITY

A third factor in liking is familiarity. Consider, for example, Parisians' reactions to the Eiffel Tower. When it was first constructed, they were outraged and thought it was hideous, a blot on the landscape of their beautiful city. Today it is a beloved monument, and has even come to symbolize Paris. Familiarity has bred liking.

The Mere Exposure Effect

This turns out to be a quite general phenomenon in interpersonal attraction. Simply being exposed frequently to a person can increase our liking for that person. This **mere exposure effect** has been demonstrated by Robert Zajonc and his associates (Moreland & Zajonc, 1982; Zajonc, 1968). In one study, Zajonc showed college students pictures of faces. Some of the faces were shown as many as 25 times, others only once or twice. Afterward, subjects indicated how much they liked each face and how much they thought they would like the person pictured.

The results are presented in Figure 8–1. The more often the subjects had seen a face, the more they said they liked it and thought they would like the person. The same result has been found for repeated exposure to actual people (Saegert, Swap & Zajonc, 1973).

Another ingenious demonstration of the familiarity effect involves people's reactions to their own faces. Faces are not perfectly symmetrical; maybe our left eye is a little higher than the right, our smile is a little crooked, our hair is parted on the right instead of the left, and so on. Our friends see our face as it looks to an outside observer. But we see a different face—the mirror image of the one our friends see. Here the right eye is higher, the part is on the left, and so on.

According to the mere exposure hypothesis, our friends should prefer our face from the perspective they are used to, and we should prefer our mirror image. Mita, Dermer, and Knight (1977) showed just that. They photographed college women and showed these pictures to the women and their friends. Some pictures were true prints and others were made from reverse negatives (what we would see in the mirror). The women themselves preferred the mirror image (by 68 to 32 percent). Their friends, however, preferred the true prints (by 61 to 39 percent). Each liked best the face that he or she had seen the most.

LIMITS ON EXPOSURE There are some limits on the mere exposure effect. Exposure is most effective in enhancing liking for a person or object that is initially perceived as pleasant or at least neutral, but not as strongly negative. To make this point, Zajonc uses the example of repeatedly seeing a particular man in handcuffs. After a while, we become convinced he really is a criminal. Perlman and Oskamp (1971) tested this idea by presenting subjects with pictures of people presented positively (as scientists), neutrally (dressed in a sports shirt), or negatively (in a police lineup). They found that repeated exposure to positive and neutral pictures increased liking, but had no effect on negative pictures. The results are shown in Figure 8–2.

Another exception to the familiarity-liking connection occurs when two people have conflicting interests, needs, or personalities. As long as they see little of each other, the conflicts are minimized. They may not particularly like each other, but they have little reason to dislike each other. When contact is increased, however, the conflicts are exaggerated and aggravated. Un-

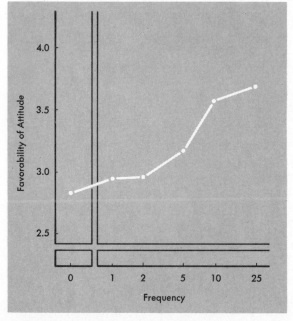

FIGURE 8–1 The relationship between frequency of exposure and liking. Subjects were shown photographs of different faces and the number of times each face was shown was varied. The more often the subjects saw a particular face, the more they said they liked the person pictured. (Adapted from Zajonc, 1968.)

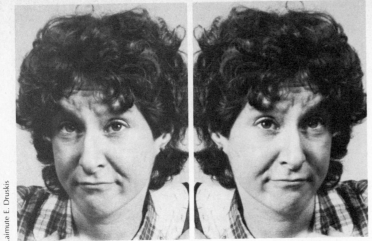

Because the human face is not perfectly symmetrical, the way we see our own face in the mirror differs subtly from the way other people see us during interaction. The left photo shows a woman as her friends view her. The right photo is a "reverse image" that shows the woman as she appears to herself. Research shows that people like best the face that they have seen most often.

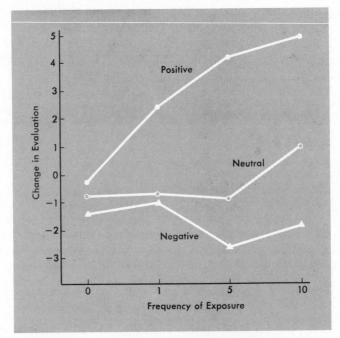

FIGURE 8-2 Mean change in evaluation of stimulus persons, as a function of frequency of exposure and picture content (positive, neutral, or negative). Positive scores indicate a positive shift in evaluations. (Adapted from Perlman and Oskamp, 1971.)

Political Advertising: Does Mere Exposure Work?

One application of the mere exposure principle is in political advertising. Millions of dollars are spent annually on campaigns designed to influence voters. Candidates with more money can clearly buy more ads, but does this increased exposure actually attract more voters?

Grush, McKeough, and Ahlering (1978) proposed that political ads work only under limited conditions—namely, when there are many candidates (so voters would have difficulty identifying any one candidate without ads), when there is generally high exposure (all candidates have many ads), and when candidates are previously unknown (so candidates are not overexposed). Under other conditions, the researchers predicted that voting would be influenced by how well known candidates were before the campaign even began, with the advantage going to officeholders who are already familiar to voters.

To test these predictions, they investigated the 1972 primary elections for the U.S. Senate and House of Representatives. All their predictions were confirmed. The amount of money spent by candidates on advertising was the best predictor of success *only* in races with unknown candidates who did not currently hold a major state office and when all candidates spent a good deal on advertising. Otherwise, the best predictor of success was the winner's precampaign visibility, based on being an incumbent, holding a highly visible public office, or having a famous name. Interestingly, advertising was the best predictor of victory in only 19 percent of the races studied. There appear to be fairly severe limits on when the mere exposure effect works in real-life politics.

der these circumstances, they may dislike each other even more as a result of frequent contact.

A third limitation is that a lot of repetition causes bordeom and satiation. There is probably some optimal level of exposure to maximize liking, depending on the people and the situation. For an application of this to politics, see Box 8-4.

How Familiarity Works

Why does familiarity increase liking? Repeated exposure undoubtedly improves our recognition of someone, and this may be a helpful first step in coming to like them. As people become more familiar, they also become more predictable. The more we see the new neighbor in our apart-

ment building, the more we learn about her and the better we can predict how she will behave in the elevator and the laundry room. As a result, we feel more comfortable in her presence.

As people become more familiar, we may also assume them to be more similar to ourselves. In a recent study, Moreland and Zajonc (1982) showed college students a photo of a male college student once a week for four weeks. Some people saw the same man each week; others saw a different photo each week. Subjects were also asked to indicate their own attitudes on a variety of issues, and to guess the attitudes of the person in the photo. With repeated exposure, subjects came to rate the person in the photo as more similar to themselves and as more likable than before.

PROXIMITY

Probably the best single predictor of whether two people are friends is how far apart they live. If one of them lives in Brazil and the other in China, it is almost certain they are not friends. If one lives in Chicago and the other in Phoenix, or even if they live on opposite sides of the same city, it is unlikely they are friends. In fact, if two people live only 10 blocks apart, it is much less likely that they are friends than if they live next door to each other.

Proximity Studies

Some years ago W. H. Whyte (1956) studied friendship patterns in Park Forest, a newly built suburban town. Almost everyone moved to this community at about the same time. Because all the houses were similar, residents had chosen their homes and neighborhoods pretty much by chance. There were no "better" areas, no cheap houses. It was almost as though a large group had been randomly assigned to houses.

Whyte tracked the social activities of residents by reading the social column in the local newspaper. Almost everyone at a baby shower lived within a few blocks of one another, and al-

most everyone who lived in the area was there. The same was true on the other side of town at a weekend barbecue. In the whole town, there were practically no friends who did not live near one another. Similarly, most people who lived close together became friends.

The same proximity effect occurs on a smaller scale in apartment buildings and dormitories. A study by Festinger, Schachter, and Back (1950) investigated friendship patterns in Westgate West, a large apartment complex. Westgate had 17 separate two-story buildings, each containing 10 apartments (5 on a floor). The layout is shown in Figure 8–3.

The apartments were almost identical. More important, residents did not choose where they were to live; they were given apartments as the apartments became vacant. In other words, like Park Forest, Westgate came close to being a field experiment with residents randomly assigned to a condition.

All the residents were asked, "Which three people in Westgate West do you see socially most often?" The results are shown in the graph in Figure 8–4. It is clear that residents were most friendly with those who lived near them.

People on the same floor mentioned their next-door neighbor more often than their neigh-

FIGURE 8–3 Floor plan of Westgate West. All the buildings in the housing development had the same layout. In the study, functional distance was defined simply as the number of doors away two people lived—the differences in distance measured by feet were ignored. (Adapted from Festinger, Schachter, and Back 1950.)

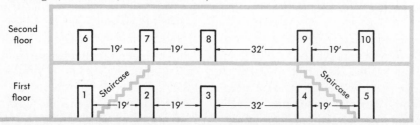

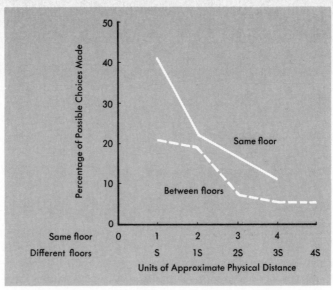

FIGURE 8–4 The relationship between functional distance and liking. The distance between people on the same floor and on different floors was closely related to friendship patterns—the closer two individuals lived, the more likely they were to be friends. Living on different floors (bottom line) reduced the likelihood of friendship because functional distance was increased. (Adapted from Festinger, Schachter, and Back 1950.)

bor two doors away and their neighbor two doors away more often than their neighbor at the other end of the hall. Of next-door neighbors, 41 percent were chosen, whereas only 22 percent of those two doors away and 10 percent of those at the end of the hall were chosen. In actuality, the physical distances involved were very small. People who lived next door were 19 feet apart (in the case of the two middle apartments, 32 feet apart), and the maximum distance between two apartments on one floor was only 88 feet. But these distances, only a few extra seconds in walking time, were important factors in determining friendships.

In addition, people who lived on different floors (the bottom line of the graph) became friends much less often than those on the same floor even when the physical distance between them was roughly the same. This was probably because it takes more effort to go up or down stairs than to walk down a hall. Thus, people on different floors were in a sense farther away than those on the same floor. The investigators referred to this as *functional distance,* meaning that the probability people would meet was determined by the design of the apartment house plus actual distance. The closer people lived, as measured by either physical or functional distance, the more likely they were to be friends.

Another demonstration of the proximity effect comes from a study done at the Training Academy of the Maryland State Police (Segal, 1974). Trainees were assigned to seats in classrooms and to dormitory rooms by name in alphabetical order. Thus, the closer their last names were alphabetically, the more likely they were to spend time in close proximity, both in and out of the classrooms.

After six months, each trainee was asked to name his closest three friends on the force. To an astonishing degree, the trainees' friends turned out to be those with names near theirs in the alphabet. On the average, each person chosen as a friend was only 4.5 letters away from his chooser in the alphabet. So the mere fact of being assigned to a room and sitting closer dictated friendship choice, despite an intensive training period in which all trainees became well acquainted.

Why Proximity Causes Liking

The proximity effect incorporates many of the factors we have already seen are important in interpersonal attraction. First, proximity usually increases familiarity. We see our next-door neighbor more often than the person down the street. This repeated exposure, in and of itself, can enhance liking. Second, proximity is often linked to similarity. Although the citizens of Park Forest did not select their neighbors, people who decided to live in that community tended to start out with things in common. They all had enough money to afford nice homes, they wanted to live in suburbia, and so on. Over time, Park Forest neighbors developed other points of shared interest, as they gossiped about the noisy teenagers down the block or complained about the pothole in their street. In other words, we often choose to live and work with people who resemble us, and our geographical closeness further enhances our similarities.

A third factor is that people who are physically close are more *available* than those who are distant. Obviously, we cannot like or be friends with someone we do not know! We choose our friends from people we know. The ready availability of people close by also affects the balance of rewards and costs of interacting, a point emphasized by social exchange theory. It takes little effort to chat with a neighbor or to

The social life on these dormitory terraces shows the importance of functional distance. Although the entrances to these rooms may be quite far apart, the terraces bring people together and allow the formation of friendships.

Rick Smolan, Stock, Boston

ask about bus service to the airport. Even if a neighbor's company is only moderately pleasant, we come by it "cheaply"—and so may find it profitable. In contrast, long-distance relationships require time, planning, and money. When good friends move apart, they often vow to keep in touch regularly. But most find that their contacts dwindle to an occasional birthday phone call or Christmas card.

A fourth explanation of the proximity effect is based on cognitive consistency. It is psychologically distressing to live or work side-by-side with someone we dislike, and so we experience cognitive pressure to like those with whom we must associate. One formulation of this theory was proposed by Fritz Heider (1958). He distinguished between *unit relations* and *sentiment relations.* People or objects that "belong together" comprise a unit. Most people would perceive me as having a unit relationship with my cat, with my car, with my sister, and with my roommate. Proximity is a common basis for unit relationships. Sentiment relations involve feelings—liking or disliking between the person and the other. Do I like my sister or my roommate? The basic idea of Heider's **balance theory** is that we strive to maintain balance between our sentiment and unit relations. More specifically, we are motivated to like those we are connected to, and to seek proximity with those we like.

When does the desire to balance unit relations with sentiment relations affect liking? The most obvious case is when we are in a unit relation with someone we dislike. Then our positive unit relation is unbalanced by our negative sentiment relation. Suppose you arrive at college to meet your assigned roommate and instantly dislike him or her. To try to balance your unit relation with your sentiment relation, you have two options. You can avoid the roommate as much as possible and try to move to another room. Or you can reevaluate the roommate, trying to see some good qualities, to avoid conflicts, to make the best of the situation.

The issue comes down to which of these relations, unit or sentiment, you are able to

change. Often it is nearly impossible to break off the unit relation. Your dorm counselor may insist that you cannot change roommates until the term ends. Therefore you experience pressure to increase your liking.

Tyler and Sears (1977) demonstrated this effect experimentally. Women in this study first met a person who was quite obnoxious. This person (secretly a confederate of the experimenter) forgot the subject's name, snapped gum, blew smoke in her face, claimed the subject was saying silly things, and did not look at the subject when she talked. This was done to establish a negative sentiment relation. Next, the experimenter told the subject that she would spend another 40 minutes talking to the obnoxious person (creating a unit relation with the unpleasant person), or she would spend 40 minutes talking to someone else. Finally, the subject was taken into a separate room to fill out a questionnaire which, among other things, asked how much she liked the confederate. As shown in Table 8–5, liking for the obnoxious person increased with anticipated interaction.

Other studies have also shown that the anticipation of interaction increases liking. In one study (Berscheid et al., 1976), college students agreed to let the experimenters organize their dating life for a period of five weeks. Then the subjects saw videotapes of various people, separated at random into those described as future dates and those as people they would not date. Prospective dates were liked significantly better. More generally, if we know that we are going to interact with someone in the future, we tend to

Table 8–5 Effect of Anticipated Interaction on Liking	
Pleasant stimulus person	−1.56
Unpleasant stimulus person	+3.78

Note: Entry is greater (or lesser) liking for stimulus person when anticipating further interaction, as compared to no further interaction.
Source: Adapted from Tyler and Sears (1977).

play up the person's positive traits and ignore or minimize the negative ones. A desire for cognitive balance motivates us to like our neighbors, roommates, and others in close proximity.

There are, of course, exceptions to the proximity-liking connection. Sometimes no amount of cognitive reevaluation will convince us that the rude secretary in our office is really nice or that our bratty kid sister is really a little angel. Proximity is most likely to foster attraction when the people involved have similar attitudes and goals. Indeed, when there are initial antagonisms or conflicts between people, increased proximity and contact may actually intensify negative feelings.

Research has shown that similarity, familiarity, and proximity are powerful forces in interpersonal attraction. To give a complete account of the processes of interpersonal attraction, we have noted various exceptions to these patterns. But these minor exceptions should not obscure the importance of the general principles involved.

These factors are not only causes of liking, but consequences as well. Proximity causes liking, but once we like someone, we often take steps to ensure that we will be close to them in the future. First-year roommates may be thrown together by chance. But if their proximity leads to friendship, they will probably ask to live together the following year. Similarity can work in the same way. Similarity may bring two people together in the first place, but as their friendship continues and they share ideas and experiences, they tend to become even more similar because of their association. Similarity is both a cause and a consequence of liking.

SUMMARY

1. Most people spend most of their waking hours in the company of others. This tendency to affiliate begins in childhood, when infants form strong attachments to the significant adults in their lives. The attachment process is affected by both biology and learning.

2. Adults have diverse social needs. Laboratory experiments have shown that affiliative tendencies are strongest when people are afraid or uncertain. Weiss and others have attempted to classify specific social needs, such as a need for attachment, for social integration, or for guidance.

3. Loneliness is the subjective discomfort we feel when our social relations are lacking in some important way. Loneliness can range from a temporary state resulting from a change in our social life to a chronic and enduring condition. Weiss has distinguished emotional loneliness, caused by the lack of an attachment relationship, from social loneliness, caused by the lack of social integration.

4. We like people who reward us and who help us to satisfy our needs. Three important principles affecting interpersonal attraction are reinforcement, social exchange, and association.

5. People differ in the qualities they most value in others. In general, we tend to like people who are sincere, warm, competent, and physically attractive. Being seen with a beautiful date or friend may have a "radiating effect," causing others to evaluate us more favorably. Sometimes, however, being associated with a very attractive stranger leads to a "contrast effect": A person of average attractiveness suffers by comparison with a particularly beautiful other.

6. We tend to like people who are similar to us in attitudes, values, interests, background, and personality. In dating and marriage, the tendency to select similar partners is called the "matching principle." The importance of similarity can be explained in terms of rewards, cognitive balance, and the expectancy-value theory of decision-making.

7. Familiarity also enhances liking. If a person or object is initially evaluated as neutral or mildly positive, repeated exposure usually increases liking.

8. A final factor in attraction is proximity. People who are physically close to us tend to be more familiar and are often, coincidentally, similar to

us in background or interests. Social exchange theory suggests that people close by are more available for interaction, and so the costs of a relationship are usually less. According to cognitive balance theory, we may experience psychological pressure to like those with whom we must interact.

SUGGESTIONS FOR ADDITIONAL READING

AINSWORTH, M. D. S., BELHAR, M. C., WATERS, E., & WALL, S. 1978. *Patterns of attachment.* Hillsdale, NJ: Erlbaum. Presents research and theory on human attachment behavior.

BERSCHEID, E., & WALSTER, E. H. 1978. *Interpersonal attraction* (2nd ed.). Menlo Park, CA: Addison-Wesley. A readable paperback that provides an excellent introduction to the topic.

BYRNE, D. 1971. *The attraction paradigm.* New York: Academic Press. Describes Byrne's program of research on attitude similarity and liking.

HUSTON, T. L. (Ed.) 1974. *Foundations of interpersonal attraction.* New York: Academic Press. Leading experts review major theories of interpersonal attraction.

HUSTON, T. L., & LEVINGER, G. 1978. Interpersonal attraction and relationships. *Annual Review of Psychology,* 29, 115–156. A comprehensive review of attraction research up to that date.

PEPLAU, L. A., & PERLMAN, D. (Eds.) 1982. *Loneliness: A sourcebook of current theory, research, and therapy.* New York: Wiley-Interscience. An up-to-date survey of research findings and strategies for helping lonely people.

9

CLOSE RELATIONSHIPS

The tender attachment of parent and infant, the good-humored rivalry of tennis partners, the finely-tuned cooperation of astronauts on a space mission, the passion of a love affair—the variety of human relationships is immense. We experience our strongest emotions in relationships: the pleasures of love, the pain of rejection, the anger of conflict. Some relationships are freely chosen; we usually pick our friends and lovers. Other relationships are thrust upon us by fate, when we are assigned to a particular first-grade teacher, a college roommate, or a therapist at the counseling center. But from birth to death, relationships are at the core of human experience.

Social psychologists try to see beneath the great variation in human relationships to discover general principles of how people behave in them. This chapter presents concepts and theories about relationships and explores such key issues as power, self-disclosure, and love.

DEFINING A RELATIONSHIP

When two people are in a relationship, their lives are intertwined: What each does influences the other. The specific ways people can influence each other are very diverse. Another person can make us feel happy or sad, tell us the latest gossip or criticize our opinions, help us to get something done or get in our way, make us laugh or keep us awake at night worrying, give us advice or tell us off, bring us presents or make us spend money. As these examples illustrate, influence in relationships involves feelings, beliefs, and behavior. The defining feature of a relationship is that two people have mutual influence on each other, that they are interdependent (Kelley et al., 1983).

A model of pair **interdependence** developed by Levinger and Snoek (1972) is shown in Figure 9–1. The model shows two people, P and O, in increasing stages of interdependence.

At one extreme, the two people are completely unaware of each other and are unrelated in any way. They are at the point of *zero contact.*

The stage of *awareness* exists when one person notices or learns something about another, but no direct contact has taken place. We often form impressions of people from observing their appearance and behavior. Sometimes we learn about another person from a third party, as when a friend arranges a blind date and tells us about the date before we actually go out. Awareness can be unilateral (as shown in Figure 9–1 by the one-way arrow from P to O), or bilateral, when two strangers glance at each other across a room. The awareness stage can be quite important. If we form a favorable impression of another person, we often take the initiative to interact with them. Indeed, people sometimes have very intense experiences in the awareness stage, as when fans develop passionate feelings for rock singers and movie stars they have never met.

The next level of relatedness is *surface contact*. Here, two people begin to interact, perhaps by talking or exchanging letters. Surface contact is the beginning of interdependence, and hence the beginning of a relationship. When we exchange small talk with a friendly supermarket checker or chat with the passenger next to us on an airplane, we are engaging in surface contact. These interactions are usually brief; the topics of conversation are superficial; the impact people have on each other is limited;

FIGURE 9–1 A model of pair interdependence. (Adapted from Levinger & Snoek, 1972, p. 5.)

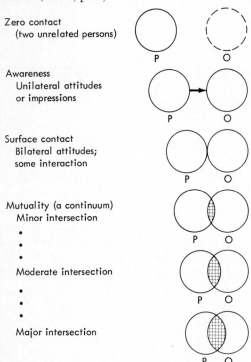

Zero contact
(two unrelated persons)

Awareness
Unilateral attitudes
or impressions

Surface contact
Bilateral attitudes;
some interaction

Mutuality (a continuum)
Minor intersection

·
·
·

Moderate intersection

·
·
·

Major intersection

and the contact is often defined by specific social roles. Many relationships never develop beyond this stage of minimal interdependence.

As the degree of interdependence increases, the pair moves to the stage of *mutuality*. Levinger and Snoek conceptualize mutuality as a continuum from lesser interdependence (shown by little overlap in the circles in Figure 9–1) to extensive interdependence (shown by much overlap). An example would be the increasing mutuality experienced by people who go from being casual acquaintances to becoming best friends.

We define a relationship as close if it involves much interdependence. All close relationships, whether with parents, a best friend, a teacher, or a spouse, share several basic characteristics (Kelley et al., 1983). First, they usually involve frequent interaction that continues over a relatively long period of time. Second, close relationships include many different kinds of activities or events. In a friendship, for example, people discuss many different topics, and generally share a wide range of activities and interests. This contrasts with superficial relationships focused around a single activity or topic.

Third, in close relationships, the influence between people is strong. We may quickly forget a snide remark from a salesclerk, but agonize for weeks about a comment made by our best friend. We may be momentarily grateful for the help offered by a bus driver, but benefit daily from the cooperativeness of our roommate. Further, when two people are highly interdependent, they have the potential for arousing strong emotions in each other. We like to think of our close relationships as source of positive feelings of love, caring, and concern. But it is also true that our strongest emotions of anger, jealousy, and despair are likely to occur in our closest relationships.

Neil Goldstein

Barbara Rios, Photo Researchers, Inc.

Myron Wood, Photo Researchers, Inc.

From childhood to old age, close relationships with loved ones, friends, and colleagues are at the core of human experience.

Dick Lee, U.S. Census Bureau.

A SOCIAL EXCHANGE PERSPECTIVE

The most influential perspective on social relationships is social exchange theory (Blau, 1964; Burgess & Huston, 1979; Kelley & Thibaut, 1978). This perspective analyzes the rewards and costs partners give and receive in relationships. The theory proposes that we select those partners we think are best able to reward us, a point that was emphasized in Chapter 8. The theory also states that we try to arrange our interactions to maximize our own rewards.

In order to receive rewards, however, we must also give them. For instance, as children we learn a general rule or **norm of reciprocity:** We are expected to reward those who reward us. If people help us, we feel obligated to help them (Gouldner, 1960). If we invite someone to dinner, we expect that person to return the invitation in the future. Social interaction can thus be viewed as a process of exchange between partners.

Rewards and Costs

A *reward* is anything a person gains from a relationship, such as feeling loved or getting financial assistance. What is rewarding for one person may be of little value for someone else. A useful analysis of the rewards of close relationships was proposed by Foa and Foa (1974), and is shown in Figure 9–2.

They identify six basic types of rewards: love, money, status, information, goods, and services. These can be classified along two dimensions. The dimension of *particularism* concerns how much the value of a reward depends upon who provides it. The value of love, or more specifically of such things as hugs and kisses, depends very much upon who they come from. Thus love is a particularistic reward. In contrast, mon-

ey is useful regardless of who it comes from; money is a nonparticularistic or universal reward. When we say that a relationship is very special to us, we often mean that it provides us with unique or particularistic rewards that we cannot get elsewhere. The dimension of *concreteness* captures the distinction between tangible rewards—things you can see, smell, and touch—and nonconcrete or symbolic rewards, such as advice or social approval.

Costs are the negative consequences that occur in a relationship. A relationship might be costly because it requires a great deal of time and energy, because it entails much conflict, because other people disapprove of the relationship and criticize us for it, and so on. A further cost of relationships is that they may deprive us of the opportunity to do other rewarding activities: If you spend the weekend skiing with a friend, you do not have the time to study or visit your family.

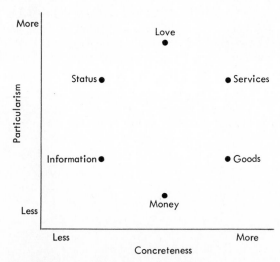

FIGURE 9–2 Rewards people exchange. (Adapted from Foa, 1971, p. 347.)

Evaluating Outcomes

Social exchange theory assumes that people keep track of the rewards and costs of a particular relationship. People seldom do this very explicitly; we do not typically make lists of the good and bad things about a relationship. Nonetheless, we are aware of the costs and rewards involved. In particular, we focus on the overall *outcome* we get in a relationship—that is, whether on balance the relationship is profitable for us (rewards outweigh costs), or whether we are experiencing an overall loss (costs outweigh rewards). People do not necessarily evaluate relationship outcomes very consciously or systematically, but the basic process is reflected in such statements as "I'm really getting a lot out of this relationship" or "I don't think our relationship is worth it anymore."

People use several standards for evaluating relationship outcomes. The simplest standard is whether the relationship is profitable or costly. Also important are comparisons we make between relationships, assessing how one relationship compares to others we have been in or that we know about. Thibaut and Kelley (1959) have emphasized two main comparison standards.

The **comparison level** reflects the quality of outcomes a person believes he or she deserves. This baseline standard undoubtedly differs from one type of relationship to another: We have different standards for a platonic friendship than for a love relationship. Our comparison level reflects our past experiences in relationships. For example, we may consider whether a current dating relationship is as good as those we have had in the past.

We may also compare a relationship to those we have seen in movies, heard about from friends, or read about in pop psychology books. The comparison level is our personal belief about what constitutes an acceptable relationship. Our comparison level may change as we have new experiences.

A second major standard is the **comparison level for alternatives.** This involves assessing how one relationship stacks up against other relationships that are currently available. Is our current dating partner better or worse than the other people we could readily be going out with right now? Even if a relationship is profitable in absolute terms, we may leave it if a *more* profitable alternative becomes available. In contrast, if our relationship is the best we think possible, we may stay in it, even if the profits are small. Our dependence on a relationship is based on our perceptions of the relationship as a unique source of rewards not available elsewhere.

Coordination of Outcomes

A key fact about relationships is that one person's outcomes are interlinked with the outcomes of the partner. Consider a young married couple deciding how to spend the money they just received from their income tax refund. The wife would like to spend the money for a new sofa; the husband would like to buy a video recorder. Since the couple has a limited amount of money available and cannot afford both the sofa and the VCR, they must coordinate their use of the funds and resolve their conflicting interests.

They might solve the problem in one of several ways. They might decide to spend the money on a trip—neither person's first choice, but an alternative that is attractive to both. Or, they might decide to take turns, buying the sofa this year and the VCR next year. Coordinating outcomes is a basic issue in relationships (Thibaut & Kelley, 1959).

How easy or difficult it is to coordinate outcomes in a relationship depends on how much the two people share the same interests and goals. When partners like to do many of the same things and value the same activities, they will have relatively few coordination problems. In such cases, they are said to have *correspon-*

dent outcomes, because what is good for one is good for the other, and what is bad for one is bad for both (Thibaut & Kelley, 1959).

When partners have different preferences and values, they have *noncorrespondent outcomes,* and are therefore more prone to conflicts of interest and coordination problems. One reason similarity is such a powerful factor in relationships is that similar people usually have fewer problems of coordination, and so may find it easier to develop a mutually rewarding relationship.

Of course, even well-matched partners experience conflicts of interest from time to time. When this occurs, the partners must negotiate a settlement. Common solutions are to select a less preferred alternative that is acceptable to both or to take turns. Another possibility is to make an explicit exchange of some sort: I'll watch you play soccer if you'll come with me to the ballet.

Settling conflicts of interest by negotiation is at best a time-consuming activity and at worst, a source of arguments and bad feelings. Over time, partners often develop rules or **norms** about coordinating their behavior. Neither spouse may like to take out the garbage or pay the bills, but they may agree that he will do one if she will do the other. Shared norms reduce the need for continual negotiation to arrive at coordinated behavior patterns.

In many types of relationships, cultural rules prescribe certain coordinated patterns. In a traditional marriage, for example, it may be predetermined that the wife should do the housekeeping tasks and the husband should have a paying job. **Social roles** are clusters of rules about how people should behave in a particular type of relationship. Roles contain established solutions for some of the problems of coordination the participants are likely to encounter. In some relationships, such as traditional marriage or doctor-patient interactions, social roles provide fairly specific guidelines for action. In other relationships, such as between same-sex friends, cultural rules are much less explicit.

When social guidelines are vague or in the process of change, individuals have greater freedom of action, but must put more effort into coordinating interaction successfully. Today, traditional sex roles are being questioned. As a result, a young dating couple may hesitate as they approach a doorway, trying to decide if the man should open the door or not. They may pause uncomfortably after a dinner out, waiting to decide whether to split the bill or have the man pay for both.

We can contrast the process of *role-taking,* in which people act out conventional cultural roles, and the process of *role-making,* in which people develop their own shared norms for social interaction (Turner, 1962). In close relationships, both processes operate. People adopt conventional guidelines about what friends, lovers, and relatives should do, but they also improvise and create their own solutions to problems of interdependence.

Fair Exchange

People are most content when their social relations are fair. We don't like to feel exploited by others, nor do we usually like to take advantage of others. Equity theory, an offshoot of social exchange theory, focuses on fairness in relationships (Greenberg & Cohen, 1982; Walster, Walster & Berscheid, 1978).

Equity theory has three basic assumptions:

1. People in relationships try to maximize their outcomes.
2. Dyads and groups can maximize their collective rewards by evolving rules or norms about how to apportion rewards fairly to everyone concerned.
3. When individuals perceive that a relationship is inequitable, they feel distressed and take steps to restore equity.

Considerable research has been amassed showing that people do seem to behave along the lines predicted by equity theory.

People use various rules for determining

Barbara Rios, Photo Researchers, Inc.

Learning to share with friends is an important step in understanding principles of fairness in social relations.

whether or not a relationship is fair. Consider the case of two teenage boys trying to decide how to divide a chocolate cake. They might decide to "share and share alike," using the *equality* rule that everyone should receive equal profits. Research suggests that people are more likely to use the equality principle when they are friends rather than strangers (Austin, 1980). Children are more likely than adults to use the equality rule, perhaps because it is the simplest principle (Hook & Cook, 1979).

The boys might instead use the principle of "to each according to need," the idea that the *relative needs* of the people should be taken into account. By this rule, one boy might get a larger piece of cake if he was especially hungry, or if he hadn't had cake in a long time. This principle is illustrated by a family that spends most of its income to care for a seriously ill child who needs expensive medical treatment.

A third fairness rule is *equity,* that each person's profits should be proportional to their contributions. Here, the boy who contributed more to the cost of buying the cake, or who had exerted greater effort by baking the cake himself, should be entitled to a larger portion. In this view, equity exists when:

$$\frac{\text{outcomes of person P}}{\text{contributions of person P}} = \frac{\text{outcomes of person O}}{\text{contributions of person O}}$$

Both people receive the same ratio of outcomes to contributions. This is the fairness rule that has been the focus of equity research.

Research has supported several specific predictions from equity theory (Greenberg & Cohen, 1982; Walster et al., 1978). It has been shown, for example, that when relationships are not equitable, the partners feel distressed. Interestingly, it is not only the underbenefited (exploited) person who feels distress, but also the overbenefited person who receives more than he or she deserves.

There is also evidence that people will try to restore equity when they perceive a relationship to be unfair. A person can do this by restoring *actual equity:* For example, a husband might agree that he hasn't been doing his share of the housework and do extra work to compensate. Sometimes, however, individuals use cognitive strategies to alter their perception of the relationship, thus restoring *psychological equity.* The husband might distort reality and argue that he really has done a fair share of the work.

Whether people restore actual or psychological equity depends on the costs and benefits associated with each particular alternative. Much of the research on equity has come from laboratory studies of strangers interacting for short periods of time. More recently, however, studies are beginning to show that equity considerations also influence close relationships (see Kidder, Fagan, & Cohn, 1981; Walster, Walster, & Berscheid, 1978; Walster, Walster, & Traupmann, 1978).

Satisfaction and Commitment

Two of the things people most want to know about close relationships are how to make them "good" and how to make them "last." In more technical terms, we are concerned with the personal satisfaction we get in a relationship, and with the degree of commitment we and our partner have to continuing the relationship. There are important differences between satisfaction and commitment (Berscheid & Walster, 1978; Kelley, 1983).

In an "empty-shell marriage," for example, spouses feel little love for each other but stay together because of religious principles, concern for the welfare of their children, or fear of loneliness. They are committed, despite low satisfaction. Or consider the case of a college woman who loves a man intensely, but recognizes that he does not return her passion. Despite her love, she may realize that a continuing commitment is not in her best interests and so end the relationship to seek a more compatible mate.

Satisfaction depends on the profits we receive from the relationship. However, our evaluation of the quality of a relationship is based not only on the absolute level of profits, but also on our comparison level. How favorably does this relationship compare to our hopes and expectations? Perceptions of fairness also affect satisfaction: Even if a relationship provides many benefits, we will not be fully satisfied if we perceive that we are being treated unfairly. Lopsided relationships in which one person gives more—or gets more—than the other are not unusually as satisfying as balanced exchanges.

Commitment refers to all the forces, positive and negative, acting to keep an individual in a relationship. People who are strongly committed to a relationship are likely to stay together "through thick and thin," "for better or for worse." Positive forces of attraction are one determinant of commitment. If we like another person, enjoy that person's company, and find it easy to get along, we will be positively motivated to continue the relationship. Social exchange theory emphasizes, however, that commitment is also based on negative forces or constraints that make it costly for a person to leave a relationship.

One barrier to leaving a relationship is a lack of alternatives. We may dislike our boss and regret having to interact daily, but continue the relationship because we need the salary and can't find another job. We may date someone who falls below our comparison level because he or she is the only eligible person we know. If we are dependent on a relationship to provide things we value and cannot obtain elsewhere, we are unlikely to leave. In more technical terms, commitment is closely related to our comparison level for alternatives.

The investments we have made in a relationship are another factor influencing commitment (Rusbult, 1980; 1983). *Investments* can include time, energy, money, emotional involvement, shared experiences, sacrifices for a partner, and so on. To invest much in a relationship and then find it unrewarding can arouse cognitive dissonance, and so we may feel psychological pressures to see the relationship in a positive light and downplay its drawbacks (Rubin, 1973). The more we have put into a relationship, the more costly it would be for us to leave. One of the many costs of divorce is dividing the joint property a couple has accumulated together. The greater our investment, the more committed we are to a relationship.

Empirical research has demonstrated the importance of these exchange considerations for satisfaction and commitment (Levinger, 1979; Rusbult, 1983). For example, in a study of dating relationships, Rusbult (1980) explicitly tested an exchange model. College students completed detailed questionnaires assessing the rewards they got from their dating relationship (such as the partner's attractiveness and intelligence, the couple's ability to coordinate activities) and the costs (such as conflict or the partner's embarrassing behaviors). Participants also described the quality of the best available alternative to their current relationship, and indicated how much they had invested or "put things into" the relationship.

Finally, they completed several measures of satisfaction and commitment. Consistent with exchange theory, the strongest predictors of satisfaction were rewards and costs; investments and alternatives did not affect satisfaction. The most satisfied people reported many rewards and few costs. In contrast, commitment was affected by satisfaction, investments, and alternatives. People felt most committed when they were satisfied with the relationship, had invested a lot, and had relatively undesirable alternatives.

In many relationships, satisfaction and commitment go hand in hand. As a young couple discovers the special rewards of their developing relationship, they take steps to build commitment. They may stop dating other people, exchange presents, and forego other activities to be with each other. As their affection blossoms into love, they may take public actions to demonstrate their feelings and to build a future together.

A wedding ceremony, buying a home together, having children—these investments in the relationship are usually based on love, and further serve to build commitment. If the couple encounters difficult times of conflict and disagreement, their commitment may provide the motivation to "work to improve the relationship" and to rekindle their love. But satisfaction and commitment are not inseparable. We sometimes find ourselves stuck in unsatisfying relationships, and we sometimes avoid commitment despite strong attraction.

Conflict

Conflict, the process that occurs when the actions of one person interfere with the actions of another, is common in close relationships (Peterson, 1983). In one national survey (Gurin, Veroff, & Feld, 1960), 45 percent of married people said they had had "problems getting along with each other." In a study of 1000 engaged couples, Burgess and Wallin (1953) found that about 80 percent had had disagreements. Indeed, conflict occurs even in couples who are very satisfied with their relationship. Gurin et al. found that 32 percent of people who rated their marriage as "very happy'" nonetheless reported having had conflicts.

The potential for conflict increases as two people become more interdependent. As interactions become more frequent and cover a more diverse range of activities and issues, there are more opportunities for disagreement. Braiker and Kelley (1979) found that conflict was usually quite low during casual dating, but increased significantly for serious dating relationships. Couples can apparently fight about almost anything, from politics and religion to work and money, from how to spend their time to how to divide household chores. Gottman (1979) found 85 different kinds of conflict among young married couples!

Braiker and Kelley (1979) have suggested that specific conflict problems can be grouped into three general categories:

- *Specific behaviors.* Some conflicts focus on specific behaviors of a partner, such as getting drunk at a party or forgetting to pick up milk at the grocery store. One partner's actions are costly to the other, such as interfering with their studying. Or a partner fails to provide rewards desired by the other, perhaps by refusing to do something that the other wants.
- *Norms and roles.* Some conflicts focus on more general issues about the rights and responsibilities of partners in a relationship. Conflicts of this sort might concern a failure to live up to promises, a lack of reciprocity, or neglect of some agreed-upon task. Thus one spouse might complain that the partner is not doing a fair share of the cooking.
- *Personal dispositions.* People frequently go beyond specific behaviors to make attributions about the intentions and attitudes of their partner. One person might complain that the partner is lazy, inconsiderate, or lacks self-discipline.

BOX 9-i
Breaking Up: When Love Affairs End

The high divorce rate reminds us that relationships begun with love do not necessarily last forever. Why do these romantic relationships end? The most obvious answer is that one or both partners grow dissatisfied with the relationship. But social exchange theory emphasizes that another important factor is the investments partners have made in the relationship and the alternatives available to them.

How do lovers respond when problems arise in their relationship? Rusbult and Zembrodt (1983) identified four common response patterns, based on people's descriptions of their experiences in romantic relationships:

- *Voice:* A person voices the problems, tries to compromise, seeks help from a counselor, tries to change the self or the partner, or more generally works to improve the relationship.
- *Loyalty:* A person responds more passively by waiting, hoping, or praying that things will improve with time.
- *Neglect:* A person reacts by spending less time with the partner, ignoring the partner, treating the partner badly, or "just letting things fall apart."
- *Exit:* A person ends the relationship by leaving.

As social exchange theory predicts, how a person responds to dissatisfaction is affected by characteristics of the relationship (Rusbult, Zembrodt & Gunn, 1982). College students in this research were more likely to have used relationship-promoting responses of voice and loyalty when they had been satisfied with the relationship before problems arose, when their investments in the relationship were high, and when they had poor alternatives. In contrast, students were most likely to end the relationship when their preproblem satisfaction was relatively low, their investments were low, and they had good alternatives.

A longitudinal study of dating relationships provides more evidence for the impact of exchange factors on breakups. Rusbult (1983) recruited college students who were in a dating relationship and had them fill out questionnaires about the relationship at several times during the school year. She compared three groups: the stayers, the leavers, and the abandoned.

The *stayers* were students whose relationships continued throughout the year. Over time, their relationship became more rewarding; their costs also increased, but only slightly. The perceived quality of alternatives decreased, and their investments in the relationship increased. Not surprisingly, their perceived commitment also increased. The *leavers* were those students who personally ended their relationship. During the time prior to breakup, their rewards increased only slightly, but their costs increased greatly. The quality of their alternatives increased, and they reported putting less into the relationship. The *abandoned* were those students whose partner ended their relationship. Prior to the breakup, their satisfaction with the relationship increased very little. Although their alternatives declined during this period, they continued to invest as much in the relationship as did the stayers. Rusbult suggests that the abandoned experienced entrapment. Because of their poor alternatives, they remained committed to (and trapped in) a relatively unsatisfactory relationship until the partner ended it.

Further evidence for the importance of exchange factors comes from a longitudinal study of college dating couples by Hill, Rubin and Peplau (1976). They found that relationships with an imbalance of involvement were significantly more likely to end than were relationships in which both partners were equally involved. It was most common for the less involved partner to end the relationship. But in a minority of cases, it was actually the more involved person who, sensing that the partner did not reciprocate the strong attraction, ended the relationship.

There are two sides to every breakup, a point emphasized by Hill, Rubin and Peplau. Very few breakups were truly mutual, with both partners deciding at the same time to end the relationship. Over 85 percent of students reported that one partner wanted to end the relationship at least somewhat more than the other. However, partners did not always agree about who was the leaver and who was the rejected lover. Each partner tended to say that he or she was the one who wanted to end the relationship. This self-bias may make it easier to accept and cope with the breakup. Both women and men felt freer, happier, less depressed, less lonely, but more guilty when they perceived that they were the one to initiate the breakup.

One other interesting finding in the Hill, Rubin, and Peplau study was that breakups were not randomly distributed throughout the academic year. Instead, breakups peaked in September, December-January, and June. Factors external to the relationship such as graduation may have contributed to some breakups. In other cases, vacations may have made it easier to call off a relationship that was already in trouble. It is probably easier to say "Let's date others during the summer," rather than to say, "I'm bored with you and want to end our relationship."

According to Braiker and Kelley, these three types of conflict reflect the fact that couples are interdependent at three levels. At the behavioral level, partners have problems of coordinating specific activities. At the normative level, they have problems negotiating rules and roles for their relationship. At the dispositional level, they disagree about each other's personality and intentions.

This last type of interdependence arises because partners are important sources of validation for our self-image. Conflicts can easily arise if a person thinks of him or herself as kind and considerate, but has a partner who insists he or she is really self-centered and rude. Conflicts may escalate as partners use specific problem behaviors to make more general attributions about each other's character.

In close relationships, events are often open to different interpretations (Kelley, 1979). Consider a husband who does not give his wife a present on their wedding anniversary. The wife may consider this an insult and complain about it to her husband. The husband may see his actions differently and try to justify them to his wife. In such situations, people tend to explain their own and their partner's behaviors differently, consistent with the actor-observer attributional bias discussed in Chapter 4 (Kelley, 1979; Orvis, Kelley & Butler, 1976).

The complaining person tends to attribute the event to the partner's negative characteristics. The wife might insist, "You forgot our anniversary because you don't really love me anymore." Her motivation may be to punish the husband's misconduct or to challenge him to show he really does care. In contrast, the person who performed the act tends to excuse the behavior ("I meant to buy you something but I was preoccupied with a big deadline at work"), or to justify the action ("I thought we agreed not to spend money on each other"). The husband's explanations are an attempt to exonerate himself from blame and to keep the event from disrupting the relationship.

Conflict can help or harm the development of a relationship, depending on how it is resolved. Conflict can provide an opportunity for clarifying and changing expectations about the relationship and conceptions of the self and the partner. Lovers' quarrels allow lovers to test their own and their partners' dependence on the relationship, to discover the depth of their feelings for each other, and to renew their efforts to create a satisfying relationship. On the other hand, because conflicts arouse strong emotions, they may not provide the best setting for constructive problem-solving. The escalation of conflict and the trading of personal insults is unlikely to benefit a relationship.

Beyond Exchange

Social exchange principles help us understand different types of relationships, ranging from interactions among co-workers to lifelong marriages. Most people recognize that exchange influences casual relationships, but may resist the idea that exchange factors also govern our most intimate relationships. It is certainly unromantic to suggest, as did sociologist Erving Goffman (1952), that "A proposal of marriage in our society tends to be a way in which a man sums up his social attributes and suggests that hers are not so much better as to preclude a merger or a partnership in these matters" (p. 456).

Social psychologist Zick Rubin (1973) voiced the common concern about exchange theory:

> The notions that people are "commodities" and social relationships are "transactions" will surely make many readers squirm. Exchange theory postulates that human relationships are based first and foremost on self-interest. As such, it often seems to portray friendship as motivated only by what one person can get from another and to redefine love as a devious power game. . . . But although we might prefer to believe otherwise, we must face up to the fact that our attitudes toward other people *are* determined to a large extent by our assessments of the rewards they hold for us. (p. 82)

It may be helpful to remember that although exchange theory borrows terminology from economics, the rewards and costs involved are often very personal and unique: An adorable smile and shared secrets are as much a part of exchange theory as money and fur coats. In long-term relationships, patterns of reciprocity and exchange become complex. In our most intimate relationship we may develop a sense of unity or "we-ness" so we perceive benefitting a loved one as a way of benefitting ourselves. Exchange principles may not tell the whole story of close relationships, but they do play an important part.

POWER

On their third date, Carol and John go to a movie and then to John's apartment. John opens a bottle of wine and turns on soft music. As he sits next to Carol on the sofa, John strokes her back, hoping they'll make love for the first time tonight. Carol senses John's intentions, but doesn't feel ready for sex with him. She inches a little farther away on the couch, and starts talking about a newspaper review of the movie they saw.

Partners in a relationship often have different preferences for their joint activities and may try to influence each other in order to accomplish their own goals. **Social power** refers to a person's ability to influence deliberately the behavior, thoughts, or feelings of another person (Huston, 1983). Social psychologists are interested in how people influence each other and in the resulting balance of power in a relationship.

Six Bases of Power

Think for a moment about all the possible ways you might try to get a friend to do something you wanted. You might first use fairly subtle, nonverbal tactics—hinting about your desires and hoping the friend will go along. Or you might try a more explicit approach, promising to do something special for the person if he or she does what you want now. Or you might get huffy, and tell the person you aren't sure he or she really cares for you if he or she is not willing to do such a little thing.

A useful way to classify influence strategies such as these is provided in a model developed by Raven and his colleagues (French & Raven, 1959; Raven & Rubin, 1983). They identified six distinct bases of power, each reflecting a different type of resource a person might use to influence someone.

LEGITIMATE AUTHORITY   Sometimes one person has the right or authority to ask another person to act a certain way. In most families, parents feel they have the right to tell their young children when to go to bed, and children usually feel obligated to comply. Children may try to renegotiate bedtime rules or ask to make an exception for a special occasion, but they usually accept the parents' authority to make rules.

Social roles such as parent-child, teacher-student, supervisor-employee often dictate the legitimate rights and responsibilities of people in a relationship. When someone deviates from agreed-upon rules, we feel we have the right to remind them of their obligations. A prerequisite for effective legitimate authority is that both people agree about the norms in their relationship.

REWARDS   Another basis for power is the ability to provide positive outcomes for another person—to help that person accomplish a desired goal or to offer a valued reward. Sometimes people make explicit bargains: A father might promise to take his daughter to the zoo if she cleans up her room. Often there is no explicit contract, but rather a general awareness that rewards are reciprocated in the relationship: If I do what you want now, you'll be more likely to do what I want later.

COERCION   Coercion can range from actual physical force to threats of punishment or subtle signs of disapproval. After trying futilely to convince a young child to take a nap, a parent may simply place the struggling child in the crib, walk out, and close the door. Or a spouse may threaten divorce if a mate refuses to go into marriage counseling.

Rewards and coercion are not exact opposites. To obtain rewards, people are motivated

A three-year-old copies the gestures of his brother and friends. According to Raven's model of power, identification is a type of social influence.

to make their "good" behavior known. In contrast, the target of coercion may do what the influencer wants, but only so long as he or she is being watched. Coercion may lead to secrecy rather than actual compliance.

EXPERTISE   Special knowledge, training, and skill are sources of power. We defer to experts and follow their advice because we believe their special knowledge will help us achieve our goals. If a trusted doctor advises us to take three little green pills daily for an allergy, we are likely to comply whether or not we understand what the pills will do. We may unquestioningly accept a friend's suggestion about a new recipe for homemade ice cream because we know that the friend is a gourmet cook with specialized knowledge.

INFORMATION   We often try to influence people by giving them information we think will suggest the right course of action for them. A child might get her mother to serve dinner later than usual by telling her there will be a special educational program on TV during the regular dinner time. A friend might convince us to go to a concert by informing us that our favorite group is performing. In these cases, the influencer is

not an expert. Rather, it is the content of the message that produces the desired effect. If friends try to settle a conflict using information power, their discussion might appear somewhat like a rational debate over specific information and details of the situation.

REFERENT POWER   A basis of influence with special relevance to close relationships is referent power. This exists when we admire or identify with someone and want to be like them. In such cases we may voluntarily copy their behavior or do what they ask, because we want to become more similar to them. In everyday life we may not think of identification as a type of influence, but it can be very effective. A young child who looks up to an older brother and tries to imitate his mannerisms and adopt his interests is an illustration.

The six bases of power describe the major types of social influence. People usually have more than one basis of power at their disposal. For example, a mother may be able to influence her child because the child identifies with the mother (referent power), because the mother has useful information, and because the mother is generous in her affection (rewards). For a discussion of power strategies used by dating couples, see Box 9–2.

BOX 9-2
Come-Ons and Put-Offs: Power in Sexual Encounters

How do young lovers try to influence each other to have or to avoid sexual intercourse? To find out, Naomi McCormick (1979) asked college students to imagine that they were alone with an attractive dating partner whom they had known for a few weeks. They had "necked," but had not yet had sexual intercourse. In one question, students were asked to describe in their own words how they might influence this partner to have sexual intercourse. In a later question, they were asked to indicate how they would avoid having sex with a "turned on" date. These essays were then coded for the particular power tactics used.

When their goal was to have sex with the partner, both men and women said they were most likely to use indirect strategies of seduction. One student wrote: "First of all I would put on some soft music and offer some wine, then I would start kissing gently and caressing [the person's] body, then I would give a massage with oil" (p. 199). The use of body language (sitting closer, touching the partner) and of changing the environment (putting on music, dimming the lights) were common. Some students said they would emphasize the nature of their relationship: "I would tell my date that we have a very strong, close relationship and that it is time to express it through sexual intercourse."

Tactics for *avoiding* sex were usually more direct. The favored approach by both men and women was to emphasize that it was too early to have sex. Others proposed using logic or information—for example, telling the partner that they were concerned about pregnancy or that they weren't in the mood for sex. Some suggested using body language (moving farther away) or manipulating the interaction by changing the conversation. A few would invoke moral principles.

McCormick was interested in whether men and women report using different power tactics in sexual encounters (McCormick & Jesser, 1983). In the study described above, where students were asked to imagine how they might hypothetically try to seduce or reject a partner, few sex differences were found. Both men and women approached seduction similarly, and both proposed similar ways to reject a sexual advance. In actual dating, however, the situation is rather different.

A consistent finding from this and other studies is that men and women usually have different sexual goals in a dating situation. It is more often men who are the sexual initiators trying to seduce their partner, and women who are the limit setters trying to avoid sex. Despite changing sexual attitudes and the women's movement, this traditional role-playing persists in the early stages of dating.

Thus when people are asked what strategies they have actually used in sexual encounters, women usually report tactics for avoiding sex, and men report tactics for having sex. Similarly, when people are asked how others have typically tried to influence them, women report being the targets of attempted seductions, and men report having been turned down.

The Balance of Power

In some relationships, both partners are equally influential. In other relationships, there is an imbalance of power with one person making more of the decisions, controlling more of the joint activities, winning more of the disagreements, and generally being in a position of dominance. What factors determine whether or not a relationship is equal in power? (See reviews by Rollins & Bahr, 1976; Scanzoni, 1979.)

NORMS As we saw in the discussion of legitimate power, social norms can dictate patterns of influence in a relationship. When a teenager takes a part-time job at a fast-food restaurant, he expects to take orders from the boss and to follow company regulations. It is generally understood that subordinates follow instructions from their superiors—at least in job-related matters.

In heterosexual dating and marriage, social convention has traditionally conferred greater authority on men. Until recently, for example, state laws gave husbands legal control over all family property and permitted husbands, as the "head of the household," to decide where the family should live. More informally, women were taught to "look up to" the man they married and to defer to his wishes (Bernard, 1972).

Today, some people are rejecting these traditional power norms as outdated and unfair. Instead, they believe that dating and marriage relationships should ideally be equal in power (egalitarian). In one study (Peplau, 1979), 87 percent of college men and 95 percent of college women said that ideally both partners in a dating relationship should have "exactly equal" influence in the relationship.

RELATIVE RESOURCES Norms are not the only determinant of the balance of power. Social exchange theory (see Blau, 1964) proposes that the relative resources of the two partners also affect their relative power. A resource is anything that "can be used to satisfy or frustrate needs or move persons further from or closer to

their goals" (Huston, 1983, p. 206). Rewards, coercion, information, expertise, and referent power are all personal resources.

The prediction from exchange theory is that when partners are imbalanced in their resources, the person who has more resources will have more power. In dating or marriage, the partner who earns more money, has more education, has a more prestigious job, is more physically attractive or socially desirable, and so on has a power advantage. To the extent that it is men who pay the bills, have the "more important job," and are believed to be more knowledgeable about life decisions, equality in male-female relations may be hard to achieve. As women gain greater resources, however, we may expect to see more equal-power relationships (Scanzoni & Scanzoni, 1976).

THE PRINCIPLE OF LEAST INTEREST Exchange theory proposes that another determinant of power is the relative dependency of the two partners on the relationship, based on their comparison level for alternatives. In some relationships, both partners are equally attracted and committed, and this tends to build power equality. In other relationships, one partner cares more about continuing the relationship, and this sets the stage for an imbalance of power.

Sociologist Willard Waller (1938) called this the "principle of least interest": The less interested partner in a relationship has greater power. An implicit bargain is struck in which the more interested and dependent person defers to the other's wishes in order to ensure that the relationship will continue. An illustration of this principle is provided by Margaret, an unpopular young woman who had an affair with an older man:

> I accepted his structuring of our relationship. When he chose to deal in wit rather than in real information, I followed suit. When he acted casual about sex, so did I. I wanted something real from him. . . . Even when I knew this was impossible on my terms, I went ahead with it in his way. . . . I didn't back off, because I thought the potential was there, and a dateless summer had taught me

that opportunities didn't come up all that often. (Cited in Goethals & Klos, 1970, p. 283)

Ultimately, relationships based on lopsided dependencies are likely to prove unsatisfactory to both partners. We would expect such relationships to change toward more equal involvement or to end.

A study of college-age dating couples found that the balance of involvement was a strong predictor of power (Hill, Rubin & Peplau, 1976; Peplau, 1979). There was a significant link between perceiving an imbalance of involvement and an imbalance of power, with the less interested partner being seen as having greater power. Further, in a one-year follow-up, couples who initially reported an imbalance of involvement were significantly more likely to have broken up than couples who were equally involved. In sum, equal power is most likely in relationships if social norms favor equality, if partners have comparable personal resources, and if partners are equally dependent on the relationship for valued rewards.

In traditional marriages, all three of these factors tipped the balance of power in favor of male dominance. Women were supposed to defer to their husband's authority, controlled fewer resources, and were relatively more dependent on marriage for financial support. Today, however, marriages in which the husband is the undisputed head, with near-total control of decision-making, are rare (Huston, 1983). But are most male-female partnerships totally equal in power? This question is surprisingly hard to answer.

In long-term relationships, power is difficult to assess precisely, and partners frequently disagree in their assessments of the balance of power (Huston, 1983; Peplau, 1979). For instance, one partner might say that the relationship is egalitarian because both partners share fully in day-to-day decisions about their joint activities. The other partner might agree that daily decisions are shared, but give more weight to a few major decisions in which one person was especially influential.

Power in close relationships is, to some extent, in the eye of the beholder. Precise statistics about the proportions of equal-power, male-dominant, and female-dominant relationships are not available. A common pattern in research on dating and marriage is for many people to say that their relationship is equal, a large minority to say it is male-dominant, and a small percentage to say it is female-dominant (Scanzoni & Scanzoni, 1976).

SELF-DISCLOSURE

Self-disclosure is the sharing of intimate feelings and information with another person. Self-disclosure can be both descriptive and evaluative (Morton, 1978). In descriptive disclosures, we reveal facts about ourself that might otherwise be unavailable to a listener—the kind of work we do, where we live, how we voted in the recent election. In evaluative disclosures, we reveal our personal opinions or feelings—that we like the other person, that we feel guilty about being overweight, that we hate getting up early in the morning.

Self-disclosure can serve many different functions. Derlega and Grzelak (1979) have proposed five possible reasons for self-disclosure:

1. *Expression:* Sometimes we talk about our feelings to "get them off our chest." After a hard day at work, we may eagerly tell a friend just how angry

we are at our boss and how underappreciated we feel. Simply being able to express our feelings is one reason for disclosure.

2. *Self-clarification:* In the process of sharing our feelings or experiences with others, we may gain greater understanding and self-awareness. Talking to a friend about a problem can help us to clarify our thoughts about the situation.

3. *Social validation:* By seeing how a listener reacts to our self-disclosures, we get information about the correctness and appropriateness of our views. Other people may reassure us that our reactions "seem perfectly normal"—or that we're "blowing things out of proportion." In either case, listeners provide useful information about social reality.

4. *Social control:* We may reveal—or conceal—information about ourselves as a means of social control. For instance, we may deliberately refrain from telling things about ourselves to protect our privacy. We may emphasize things we think will make a favorable impression on our listener. In extreme cases, people may deliberately lie to exploit others, as when an imposter claims to be a lawyer but has actually had no legal training.

5. *Relationship development:* The sharing of personal information and confidences is an important way to begin a relationship and move toward increasing levels of intimacy. For young lovers, self-disclosure may have moved from initial exchanges of background information to the discovery of shared interests to the first expression of "I love you."

Altman and Taylor (1973) proposed a model of relationship development that gives a central role to self-disclosure. They call the process of attaining interpersonal intimacy **social penetration.** As shown in Figure 9–3, they believe that social penetration occurs along two major dimensions of breadth and depth.

As relationships develop from superficial to intimate, people disclose increasingly more personal things about themselves. We might willingly talk with a stranger about our preferences in food and music, talk with a casual acquaintance about our attitudes on politics and religion, but reserve for close friends discussions of our personal relationships or fears in life. Relationships also develop from narrow to broad, as

FIGURE 9–3 The breadth and depth of self-disclosure is represented as "wedges" into the personality and experience of the person. For strangers, the wedge is narrow and superficial. For a close friend, the wedge is deeper (more intimate) and broader in the range of topics disclosed. (Adapted from Altman and Haythorn, 1965, p. 422.)

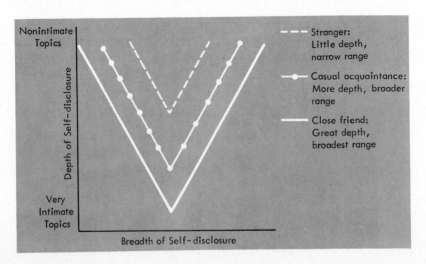

BOX 9-3
Silent Men and Talkative Women?

Stereotypes depict men as "silent types" who keep their feelings to themselves, and women as "talkers" who freely tell confidences. As one wife complained about her husband, "He doesn't ever think there's anything to talk about. I'm the one who has to nag him to talk" (cited in L. Rubin, 1976, p. 124). How accurate is this traditional stereotype about gender differences in self-disclosure?

In *same-sex* relationships, women do indeed disclose more than men, on average (Cozby, 1973). Throughout adult life, women are more likely than men to have an intimate, same-sex confidant, and to emphasize the sharing of personal information. In a recent study of college students (Caldwell & Peplau, 1982), for example, women were more likely than men to say that they enjoy "just talking" to their best woman friend, and to indicate that talking helped form the basis of their relationship. In contrast, college men emphasized sharing activities with their best male friend.

In *opposite-sex* relationships, however, gender differences are much less clear-cut. In general, heterosexuals disclose more to spouses than to anyone else. The most common pattern is for both spouses to reveal at equal levels, with some couples sharing a lot and others disclosing relatively little (see Komarovsky, 1967). The norm of reciprocity encourages partners to disclose at comparable levels.

It seems that young Americans today expect more self-disclosure in their intimate relationships than did earlier generations. Rands and Levinger (1979) asked college students and senior citizens to describe relationships characteristic of 22-year-olds of their own generations. They found that today's young people expect pairs to be more expressive, to do more things together, and to disclose both positive and negative feelings more openly than the young people of two generations ago. Studies also find that younger dating couples today usually do disclose at quite high and equal levels (see Rubin, Hill, Peplau, & Dunkel-Schetter, 1980). It should be noted, however, that when exceptions to this equal-disclosure pattern ooccur, it is usually the man who discloses less.

The fact that men and women often disclose at equal levels of intimacy does not mean that they necessarily reveal the same kinds of personal information. One study (Hacker, 1981) of college students found that in male-female relationships, women were more likely to reveal their weaknesses and to conceal their strengths; men showed a reverse pattern of disclosing their strengths and concealing their weaknesses. Another study (Derlega, Durham, Gockel, & Sholis, 1981) found that men disclosed more on "masculine" topics such as when they had been aggressive or had taken risks; women disclosed more on "feminine" topics such as when they felt childlike or were sensitive about their appearance.

Rosenfeld (1979) investigated why people sometimes avoid disclosure. For both sexes, the most important reason was concern about "projecting an image I do not want to project." However, men also expressed concerns about losing control over another person; women expressed concerns about providing information that might be used against them and about hurting the relationship.

In general, research does not support the stereotype that all men are inexpressive. In heterosexual dating and marriage, men and women usually disclose at similar levels. Sex differences are most pronounced in same-sex relationships, with women friends showing a strong preference for talking, and men friends showing a greater interest in sharing activities.

over time people discuss a wider range of topics and share more diverse activities. These phases of relationship development are shown in Figure 9–3 as "wedges" that one person makes into the personality and life experiences of another.

Self-Disclosure and Liking

Liking is an important cause of self-disclosure. People reveal much more to spouses and best friends than to co-workers and casual friends. The more interesting question is how the act of self-disclosing affects liking. One view might be that self-disclosure is inherently rewarding, and "the more the better." Research generally supports a different view, however, that we like people most whose self-disclosure is appropriate to the situation (Derlega & Chaikin, 1975).

Altman and Taylor (1973) argued that self-disclosure leads to liking only if it is carefully paced. It must be slow enough that it does not become threatening to either person. If it races ahead prematurely into areas of great personal intimacy, it will arouse anxiety and defensiveness. Someone who "comes on too strong, too fast" will be disliked.

An illustration of this effect comes from a study by Kaplan and colleagues (1974). They varied both the formality of the interaction setting and the intimacy of the subject's own self-disclosure. College men came to a laboratory to be interviewed in one of three contexts. One was highly formal: The paneled and carpeted room was decorated with management and business journals, and the interviewer was supposedly a business student. In the medium-formality condition, the room was stocked with psychotherapy literature and the interviewer

was supposed to be a student in clinical psychology. In the low-formality condition, the room contained marital counseling and sexology literature, and the interviewer was a "human relations" student learning how to do sexual counseling.

The interviewer asked the subject questions that were highly intimate ("How often do you masturbate?" and "Would you describe anything you dislike about your mother?") or nonintimate ("What are the kinds of movies that you like to see?" and "How many hours of sleep do you need to feel your best?") Ratings of attraction to the interviewer were obtained in an unusual way: After every question, the subject pressed a button indicating liking, ostensibly to give an ongoing measure of the "interviewer's" performance. The results are shown in Figure 9–4.

Liking for the interviewer was highest in the informal setting with nonintimate questions—that is, for a quite modest level of social penetration between these two complete strangers. Liking was least for the formal-context interviewer asking intimate questions. Clearly, this person was probing at too deep a level too fast. His demands for intimate self-disclosure were especially inappropriate given his own formality. In sum, we are most apt to like someone whose own disclosures and requests for us to disclose are appropriate to the situation and the nature of the relationship.

Reciprocity

Consistent with social exchange theory, there appears to be a norm of reciprocity for self-disclosure. If someone tells us something personal,

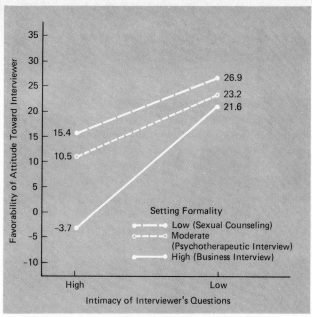

FIGURE 9–4 Interview setting formality and liking. (Adapted from Kaplan, Firestone, Degnore, & Morre, 1974.)

we usually feel obligated to respond with a comparable revelation. A gradual process of mutual self-disclosure, paced over time, spurs the growth of a relationship.

Altman and Taylor proposed that we like best people who disclose at about the same level of intimacy as we do. Someone who discloses more intimate personal details than we do threatens us with a premature rush into intimate territory, and we may want to put on the brakes. If we are disclosing at a more intimate level than the other person, we are left feeling vulnerable or foolish.

There is much evidence that reciprocity in self-disclosure is a key factor in liking. In the Kaplan study, the formal interviewer asked for extremely intimate self-disclosure, but provided none in return. And he was not liked. A more direct test of the reciprocity idea would involve experimentally manipulating the intimacy level of both persons' self-disclosures.

Chaikin and Derlega (1974) videotaped two actresses' improvising a first-acquaintance encounter in a school cafeteria. Each actress did this in two ways: at a high and at a low level of self-disclosure. Then the experimenters presented the performances to subjects in each of the four combinations of self-disclosure: both women high in self-disclosure, both low, high-low, or low-high.

In the high self-disclosure case, one woman told immediately of her relationship with her boyfriend "Bill," who was her first sexual partner, and of her parents' reactions; the other woman's high-intimacy disclosures concerned her mother's nervous breakdown and hospitalization, her fighting with her mother, and the possible divorce of her parents. In the low self-disclosure cases, the women talked about the problems of commuting to school, where they went to high school, the courses they were taking, and so on.

Self-disclosure ranges from a casual chat with strangers to the shared intimacies of long-time friends.

The main finding is that liking for both women was higher when they disclosed at the same level of intimacy than when they were at different levels. Breaking the reciprocity norm led to less liking, but for different reasons. The woman who disclosed too little (relative to the other) was thought cold, whereas the more intimate norm breaker was thought maladjusted.

Demands for reciprocal intimacy of self-disclosure seem to be especially strong in two circumstances. Early in a relationship, we expect reciprocity for *nonintimate* disclosures. If you tell the stranger next to you in the lecture hall that you like this course, she is supposed to reciprocate with her reactions to it. In this opening stage of a relationship, there is no norm for reciprocity about intimate matters. If she suddenly changes the subject and tells you about her parents' rancorous divorce, you do not feel obligated at all to tell her anything intimate about your life. Indeed, her revelation may seem inappropriately intimate, since she is a complete stranger.

Later in the development of a relationship, reciprocity about *intimate* details becomes important. Suppose you sit next to her for several weeks, then go to the campus coffeehouse after the first midterm. If you start telling her about your doubts about your ability in school, and your worry that maybe you should have gone to an easier college, you are putting yourself out on a limb. It is important that she make some reciprocal gesture, to show that she is interested in having a closer relationship too. If, in the midst of your disclosures about your secret fears, she suddenly starts talking about the weather, you may feel hurt and want to pull back to a less intimate level. Reciprocity is important for supporting tentative moves toward a closer relationship.

People generally do not reciprocate sudden intimate disclosures by strangers. For example, Rubin (1975) found that people waiting in an airport responded *less* intimately to a student who provided intimate disclosures and then asked for reciprocation than to a student who provided more impersonal material. Their reluctance is partly due to feeling pressured into reciprocity, or "reactance" against loss of freedom. Archer and Berg (1978) found telling recipients it was perfectly all right to say anything they wanted—and thereby removing the pressure to reciprocate—made them feel much freer to reciprocate with intimate disclosures.

A more gradual approach to self-disclosure is more conducive to reciprocity. For example, Davis (1976) set up an acquaintance exercise in which two people took turns disclosing to each other. He found that the average intimacy level increased throughout the exercise, as might be expected from our discussion of social penetration. More important for the reciprocity norm, he found that both the average level of intimacy and the rate of increase of intimacy were closely matched between partners. As one person became more intimate, or slowed down, so did the other.

In a later study, Davis (1977) allowed the two discussion partners to talk more explicitly between turns about their feelings about the interaction itself. The intimacy of each partner's disclosures was still matched over the entire discussion, but the reciprocity norm was relaxed a little. Apparently they did not feel that both sides of every exchange had to be equally self-disclosing; instead, they came to a rough overall agreement that allowed an exchange to be unbalanced temporarily.

Also, with more explicit discussion of the disclosure process itself, the two partners became more equal in taking the initiative. There was less tendency for one person to take the lead, with the other following. Finally, because of the explicit attention to the process, they reached a more intimate level of disclosure more rapidly.

LOVE

Love and romance have long been a favored topic for poets and songwriters. Only recently have researchers used the scientific tools of psychology to study love systematically. Before turning to the research findings, we might set the mood by considering this newspaper story of young love:

On Monday, Cpl. Floyd Johnson, 23, and the then Ellen Skinner, 19, total strangers, boarded a train at San Francisco and sat down across the aisle from each other. Johnson didn't cross the aisle until Wednesday, but his bride said, "I'd already made up my mind to say yes if he asked me to marry him." "We did most of the talking with our eyes," Johnson explained. Thursday the couple got off the train in Omaha with plans to be married. Because they would need to have the consent of the bride's parents if they were married in Nebraska, they crossed the river to Council Bluffs, Iowa, where they were married Friday.

This account may remind you of such starstruck lovers from literature as Romeo and Juliet. But have you personally ever experienced this rather magical love at first sight?

When Averill and Boothroyd (1977) asked university students how closely their own most intense love experience corresponded to this romantic model, only 40 percent said there was a strong resemblance. Another 40 percent said they had never experienced anything at all like this story, and the rest thought their most intense love relationship bore only a partial similarity to this one. This range of answers highlights one of the dilemmas of love researchers— how to capture the essential features of love, and at the same time depict the diverse experiences of people in love.

Love versus Liking

One of the first researchers to study romantic love was Zick Rubin (1970, 1973). He was interested in the connection between love and liking. One view is that love is merely a very intense form of liking. According to this unidimensional view, our positive feelings of attraction range along a continuum from mild liking to strong liking to mild love to strong love. A contrasting view, and the one Rubin favored, is that liking and love are qualitatively distinct and represent two different dimensions. This view seems consistent with folk wisdom that we can like someone a great deal, but not be in love with him or her—and that we can feel passionate love for someone we do not totally like or respect.

To study this issue, Rubin first compiled various statements that people thought reflected liking and other statements that people thought reflected love. These included such things as idealization, trust, sharing emotions, believing someone is intelligent, and tolerating the other's faults. Next Rubin asked several hundred college students to rate how characteristic each of these statements was of their feelings toward their boyfriend or girlfriend and toward a nonromantic friend of the other sex. Rubin believed that if love and liking are distinct, some statements would characterize a romantic partner but not a friend. The results of this first study supported the idea that love and liking are distinct.

Based on these findings, Rubin constructed two separate paper and pencil tests, a Love Scale and a Liking Scale. Each scale consists of nine statements. A sample liking statement is "I have great confidence in _____'s good judgment." Respondents rate each statement on a nine-point scale from strongly disagree to strongly agree.

To collect further evidence that these scales were measuring somewhat different attitudes, Rubin recruited 182 dating couples at the University of Michigan. Both members of each couple filled out detailed questionnaires about their relationship and also participated in lab experiments. Rubin's results supported the distinction between love and liking. For example, he found that although students rated their dating partner and best friend equally on the Liking Scale, they rated their boyfriend or girlfriend much higher on the Love Scale.

In an experimental session, Rubin found that couples who scored high on the Love Scale spent more time making eye contact than did low scorers, confirming the idea that lovers often gaze into each other's eyes. Those with high love scores were more likely to say that they and their partner were in love. Strong lovers also gave a higher estimate of the probability of eventually marrying the partner.

If a follow-up study six months later, Rubin examined whether love scores were related to staying together versus breaking up. Strong lovers were more likely to stay together, but only if they were also high in "romanticism," the belief that true love conquers all. Taken together, these and more recent data suggest that although love and liking are related experiences, there are important qualitative differences between the two.

The Experience of Romantic Love

Research has begun to identify the various thoughts, feelings, and behaviors that are associated with romantic love (Kelley, 1983). Most of the information we have about love comes from studies of young adults in our society. The experience of love is quite different in other cultures and at other historical times (Hunt, 1959). We need to be cautious about generalizing from current findings to "all lovers."

THOUGHTS OF LOVE   Rubin's Love Scale conceptualizes love as an attitude we have toward another person, as a distinctive cluster of thoughts about the loved person. Rubin identified three main themes reflected in his scale items. One theme, which Rubin called attachment, is a sense of need and urgency. A sample statement is "It would be hard for me to get along without _____." These statements reflect a person's awareness of their dependence on the other to provide valued rewards.

A second theme concerns caring for the other person, as illustrated in this item: "I would do almost anything for _____." A desire to promote the other person's welfare and to be responsive to his or her needs is a central idea. The third theme emphasized trust and self-disclosure. These ideas of love contrast with the Liking Scale, which concerns beliefs that the other person is likable, intelligent, well-adjusted, and has good judgment.

A study by Steck, Levitan, McLane and Kelley (1982) investigated the relative importance of various components of the Love Scale to people's perceptions of how much someone is in love. College students read several Love Scale questionnaires, each with a different pattern of responses. Students indicated how much love the person who completed each questionnaire felt for the partner. By manipulating responses to specific questions, the researchers created different versions of the scale that had the same total score, but differed in the importance given to needing, caring, and trust.

Results showed that perceptions of how much a person loved a partner were more strongly influenced by the degree of caring than by needing. In other words, if two men both scored moderately on the Love Scale but one emphasized how much he cared for his girlfriend and the other indicated how much he needed his girlfriend, the caring person was seen as loving more. The person who showed great need but not great care was rated as showing "attraction" but not "love." In judgments of love, trust was given much less importance than either caring or needing. In ratings of friendship, however, trust was the most important factor.

BEHAVIORS OF LOVE   In assessing whether someone loves us, we usually depend not only on their words, but also on their actions. If someone professes love but forgets our birthday, goes out with other people, criticizes our appearance, and never confides in us, we may doubt their sincerity. Swensen (1972) asked people of different ages what behaviors they thought were most closely associated with love for a romantic partner or spouse. The answers fell into seven categories or types of love behaviors:

1. Verbal statements of affection, such as saying "I love you."
2. Self-disclosure.
3. Nonmaterial signs of love, such as showing interest in the person's activities, respecting his or her opinions, or giving encouragement.
4. Communicating nonverbally such feelings as happiness and relaxation when the other is present.
5. Material signs of love, such as giving presents or doing tasks to help the other person.
6. Physical expressions of love, such as hugging or kissing.

7. Showing a willingness to tolerate the other and to make sacrifices to maintain the relationship.

Swensen found that many of these romantic love behaviors were also seen as signs of love for parents, siblings, or same-sex friends.

In a more recent study, King and Christensen (1983) identified specific events that indicated how far a heterosexual dating couple had progressed toward marriage. In most cases, the college couples in their research went through a predictable sequence of events moving toward greater commitment. Events that usually occurred early in the development of a relationship included spending a whole day together and calling the partner by an affectionate name. At a later stage, partners started referring to each other as "boyfriend" and "girlfriend," and received invitations to do things together as a couple. A further development was to say "I love you" and to date each other exclusively. A common next step was to discuss living together or marriage, and to take a vacation together. Events indicating greatest progress included living together or becoming engaged. Although couples varied in how far their relationship had developed and in the speed with which they moved toward permanence, most couples followed a similar sequence of key events.

FEELINGS OF LOVE One feature that often distinguishes romantic love from friendship is the experience of physical symptoms. According to popular songs, a lover's heart skips a beat now and then, the lover loses sleep and has trouble concentrating. To investigate this matter, Kanin, Davidson, and Scheck (1970) asked 679 university students to rate the intensity of various feelings they had had during their current or most recent love experience.

The most common reactions were a strong feeling of well-being (reported by 79 percent of students) and great difficulty concentrating (reported by 37 percent of students). Other reactions included "floating on a cloud" (29 percent), "wanted to run, jump, scream" (22 percent), feeling "nervous before dates" (22 percent), and feeling "giddy and carefree" (20 percent). Strong physical sensations such as cold hands, butterflies in the stomach, or a tingling spine were reported by 20 percent and insomnia by 12 percent of students.

Researchers also found differences between the love experiences of women and men, with women being more likely to report strong emotional reactions. Dion and Dion (1973) found a similar sex difference: Women more often reported feelings of euphoria associated with love. Whether these results reflect actual sex differences in the experience of love or women's greater willingness to disclose such feelings is not known.

Research has identified some of the thoughts, feelings, and behaviors Americans commonly associate with love. But studies also find that individuals differ in their specific love experiences. This suggests that there are distinct types of love. In the next section, we examine two major models of love. For a more detailed look at ways people define love, see Box 9–4.

Passionate Love and Companionate Love

Passionate love has been described by Berscheid and Walster as "a wildly emotional state: tender and sexual feelings, elation and pain, anxiety and relief, altruism and jealousy coexist in a confusion of feelings" (1978, p. 177). Emotions play a central role in passionate love. People are swept off their feet by uncontrollable passions that draw them irresistibly toward the loved person.

The physiological arousal that fuels the passion of this type of love can have many sources. Sexual desire, the anxiety of possible rejection, the excitement of getting to know someone, the frustration of outside interference, the anger of a lover's quarrel—all may contribute to the strong emotions experienced in passionate love. Berscheid (1983) has suggested that the uncontrollable quality of passionate love provides a conve-

BOX 9–4
Definitions of Love

When people say "I love you," they can mean very different things. How would you personally define love?

Researchers have identified six different ways in which people commonly define love (Lasswell & Lobsenz, 1980; Lee, 1973). These love styles are idealized types; each individual may define love in a way that combines more than one style:

- *Romantic love.* Love is an all-consuming emotional experience. Love at first sight is typical. Physical attraction is essential to love. A romantic lover might agree that, "At the first touch of his/her hand, I knew that love was a real possibility."
- *Possessive love.* The possessive lover is emotionally intense, jealous, obsessed with the beloved. The possessive lover is highly dependent on the beloved, and therefore fears rejection. Preoccupation with the loved one swings quickly from peaks of joy to valleys of despair. The possessive lover might agree, "When my lover doesn't pay attention to me I feel sick all over."
- *Best friends love.* Love is a comfortable intimacy that grows slowly from companionship, mutual sharing, and gradual self-disclosure. A best friends lover is thoughtful, warm, and companionate. He or she might agree that "The best kind of love grows out of a long friendship."
- *Pragmatic love.* According to Lee, this is "the love that goes shopping for a suitable mate, and all it asks is that the relationship work well, that the two partners be compatible and satisfy each other's basic or practical needs" (1973, p. 124). The pragmatic lover is logical and thoughtful in selecting a suitable partner, and seeks contentment rather than excitement. The pragmatic lover might agree that "It makes good sense to plan your life carefully before you choose a lover."
- *Altruistic love.* This style of love is unconditionally caring, giving, and forgiving. Love means a duty to give to the loved one with no strings attached, with no expectations of reciprocity. Altruistic love is expressed through self-sacrifice, patience, and faith in the beloved. An altruistic lover might agree that "I try to use my own strength to help my lover through difficult times, even when he/she is behaving foolishly."
- *Game-playing love.* This person plays at love as others play games: to enjoy the "love game" and to win it. In game-playing love, strategy is important, and commitment is to be avoided. The game-player may have several relationships going at once. No relationship lasts for long, usually ending when the love partner becomes boring or too serious. A game player might agree that "Part of the fun of being in love is testing one's skill at keeping it going and getting what one wants from it at the same time."

The two general models of love discussed in the text can be seen as combinations of several specific love styles. Passionate love is often a mix of romantic and possessive love. Companionate love combines being best friends and being pragmatic.

To study these love styles empirically, Lee (1973, 1977) and other researchers have developed techniques to assess how individuals rate on each of the six types. The statements given above are from a love questionnaire developed by Lasswell & Lasswell (1976). Research has found at least preliminary support for the idea of distinct love styles. Individuals are rarely a "pure" type, but instead may score high on two or three styles, or may be moderate in some styles and low in others.

Gender differences in love styles have emerged in several studies (Hatkoff & Lasswell, 1979; Hendrick et al., in press). In general, men are more likely to be romantics who believe in love at first sight or game players who enjoy the thrill of the chase. Women are more likely to adopt a best friends or pragmatic approach to love.

Intrigued by these findings, researchers have freely speculated about the possible reasons for sex differences in love styles (Rubin, Peplau & Hill, 1981). The most common explanation concerns the social and economic context of mate selection. As sociologist Willard Waller (1938) explained, "A man, when he marries, chooses a companion and perhaps a helpmate, but a woman chooses a companion and at the same time a standard of living. It is necessary for a woman to be mercenary" (p. 243). Men, it is argued, can afford to be more frivolous and passionate in love.

nient justification for lovers to engage in behaviors they might otherwise consider unacceptable—such as an extramarital affair. The lovers' defense is that they "couldn't stop" themselves.

Another element of passionate love is preoccupation with the other person. The lover is obsessed with thoughts of the new love. There is a tendency to idealize the loved person, to see the person as wonderful and perfect in every way. Passionate love is often said to strike suddenly and fade quickly. This type of love is intense, but fragile.

Companionate love has been defined as "the affection we feel for those with whom our lives are deeply intertwined" (Berscheid & Walster, 1978, p. 177). This is a more practical type of love that emphasizes trust, caring, and tolerance of the partner's flaws and idiosyncrasies. The emotional tone of companionate love is more moderate; warmth and affection are more common than extreme passions.

Kelley (1983) suggests that companionate love develops slowly as two people build a satisfying relationship. He also speculates that companionate love is more common in equitable relationships where partners perceive that they are benefitting in equal measure from the partnership. Companionate love is believed to provide an enduring basis for long-term relationships.

The models of passionate and companionate love represent different images of the experience of love. People differ in their beliefs about which type of love is the better or truer form. The contrast between passionate and companionate love raises interesting questions about the experience of emotions in close relationships.

Why might it be that the early stages of a romantic relationship are usually characterized by extreme emotions, whereas the later stages are marked by emotional tranquility and moderation? Berscheid (1983) has suggested that over time, the novelty and surprise of the relationship wear off. Idealization of the partner confronts the reality of human imperfection. The couple develops routine ways of interaction, and life together becomes more settled.

However, Berscheid also suggests that as a relationship continues over time and interdependence grows, the *potential* for strong emotion actually increases. The greater our dependence on another person, the greater the possible influence of the partner in our lives. But, paradoxically, because long-term couples learn to coordinate their activities successfully, the actual frequency of strong emotions is usually fairly low.

The latent potential for strong emotion may emerge occasionally, however. When partners are separated because of travel or illness, they often have intense feelings of loneliness and desire. Another situation that can arouse strong emotions in a long-term relationship is the threat posed by a partner's involvement with another person.

Jealousy occurs when a person perceives a real or potential attraction between the partner and a rival (White, 1981). A husband's discovery that his wife is having a sexual affair with someone else would be an example. Jealousy is likely to be a mixture of fear and anger based on threats to the person's self-esteem and to the relationship. According to Berscheid (1983), jealousy should be greatest when the person is highly dependent on the partner and when the person perceives that the threat is a serious one. Although empirical research on jealousy is still quite new, there is some evidence linking jealousy with both dependence and insecurity (Buunk, 1982; Pines & Aronson, 1983; White, 1976).

The study of close relationships is a field of growing interest in social psychology. Researchers in this area hope to gain a better understanding of how relationships actually work. Ultimately, greater knowledge may help people to create more satisfying relationships.

SUMMARY

1. A relationship exists when two people are interdependent—that is, when each person influences the other. We call a relationship close if there is frequent interaction involving many different kinds of interaction and strong mutual influence.
2. The most influential analysis of relationships comes from social exchange theory. In this view, people are concerned with the outcomes (rewards and costs) they receive in a relationship. People use several standards to evaluate their relationship outcomes including a general "comparison level" and a "comparison level for alternatives." When two people are in a relationship, their individual outcomes are in some measure interdependent, and so partners try to coordinate their activities to maximize their joint profits.
3. People care whether their relationships are fair. Three major rules of fairness are equality, relative needs, and equity. Equity exists when each person's outcomes are proportional to their contributions to the relationship. According to equity theory, when individuals perceive inequity in a relationship, they feel distress and take steps to restore equity.
4. Commitment refers to all the forces, positive and negative, that keep a person in a relationship. Positive factors include satisfaction, liking, and love. Negative factors are barriers that make it costly for someone to leave a relationship. Two important barriers are the lack of alternatives and the investments a person has made in a relationship.
5. Social power refers to a person's ability to influence deliberately the behavior, thoughts, or feelings of another person. Raven and his colleagues identified six different bases of power: legitimate authority, rewards, coercion, expertise, information, and referent power. The balance of power concerns whether partners have equal power or whether one partner is dominant. Three determinants of the balance of power are norms, the relative resources of the partners, and the "principle of least interest."
6. Self-disclosure is the sharing of intimate feelings and information with another person. There is a norm of reciprocity for self-disclosure, so partners tend to disclose at similar levels of intimacy. In the formation of a relationship, we are most apt to like someone whose disclosures are appropriate to the situation.
7. Psychological research on romantic love is relatively new. Rubin has shown that liking and love are qualitatively distinct. Although the two often go together, it is possible to like someone a lot without loving them, and to love a person with-

out fully liking them. Theorists have suggested that it is useful to distinguish between passionate love (the exciting and emotionally charged experience some people experience early in a love relationship) and companionate love (the deep affection, trust, and caring a person feels for a long-term partner).

SUGGESTIONS FOR ADDITIONAL READING

ALTMAN, I., & TAYLOR, D. A. 1973. *Social penetration: The development of interpersonal relationships.* New York: Holt, Rinehart & Winston. A thoughtful analysis of the development of intimate relationships, with emphasis on self-disclosure.

BURGESS, R. L., & HUSTON, T. L. (Eds.). 1979. *Social exchange in developing relationships.* New York: Academic Press. Leading experts use exchange theory to discuss such topics as the initiation of relationships, conflict, and breakups.

DUCK, S., & GILMOUR, R. (Eds.) 1981. *Personal relationships 1.* New York: Academic Press. The first volume in a series of edited books that present theories, research, and literature reviews on all aspects of relationships.

HENDRICK, C., & HENDRICK, S. 1983. *Liking, loving, and relating.* Monterey, CA: Brooks/Cole. A basic introduction to the field written for undergraduates.

KELLEY, H. H., et al. 1983. *Close relationships.* New York: W. H. Freeman. A team of psychologists provide a professional-level analysis of the nature of close relationships, including such topics as interaction, development, emotion, power, roles, conflict, and commitment.

RUBIN, Z. 1980. *Children's friendships.* Cambridge, MA: Harvard University Press, A delightful paperback about how young children learn to be friends.

WALSTER, E., & WALSTER, G. W. 1978. *A new look at love.* Reading, MA: Addison-Wesley. Intended for nonprofessional readers, this paperback offers a lively discussion of romantic love.

WALSTER, E., WALSTER, G. W., & BERSCHEID, E. 1978. *Equity: Theory and research.* Boston: Allyn and Bacon. A clear presentation of equity theory and how it applies to various types of relationships.

10

AGGRESSION

When we think of aggression and violence, most of us probably think first of crimes committed by one individual against another. As the 1980s began, the United States was experiencing over 20,000 murders per year, over 75,000 rapes, and over 600,000 assaults—in reported crimes alone. The murder rate in the United States far exceeded that in most other civilized countries. New York City had 22 murders per 100,000 population and Los Angeles 18, but London had less than 2, and New Delhi only 0.1. The murder rate was 10 times as high in New York City and Los Angeles than it was in London, and 200 times as high as it was in New Delhi. The murder rate was over double in 1980 what it had been in 1960, and the assault rate was four times as high.

We probably also think of war. There were over 50 wars in the 1970s, almost all in Third World countries—those most oppressed by poverty, disease, and all manner of other problems. Each year, the nations of the world spend over $500 billion on military forces, or about $170 for every man, woman, and child on the globe.

But the greatest threat to humankind comes from the threat of nuclear war. By the early 1980s, the United States had over 1000 intercontinental ballistic missiles (ICBMs). The nuclear warhead on each Titan II missile has the explosive power of 9 million tons of TNT—the equivalent of 700 Hiroshima bombs. If the United States or the Soviet Union were to launch an ICBM, it would take about 30 minutes to reach the other nation. Experts estimate that of those 30 minutes, about 10 would be required to communicate word of the attack throughout the entire command structure of the targeted nation, including getting word to the chief of state. The American president or the Soviet premier would thus have about 20 minutes to decide whether or not to retaliate—and in any event, at least one nation would be devastated.

A surprising number of small children are subjected to real brutality, even from their parents and often even in quite affluent, comfortable life circumstances.

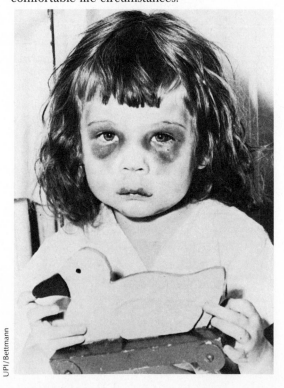

UPI/Bettmann

This is violence and aggression on a global scale, but in fact most violence is committed against people closest to us—against those in our own families, our spouses, children, and brothers and sisters.

According to a recent national survey (Straus, Gelles, and Steinmetz, 1981), each year 16 percent of all married persons engage in some act of physical violence against their mate, ranging from throwing something to using a knife or a gun on them. Straus et al. estimate that about 2 million Americans have at one time or another beaten up their spouses (and husbands and wives do so with about equal frequency), and another 1.7 million have used a knife or gun on their mates.

A great many parents commit surprising levels of violence against their own children. The same study showed that 13 percent of the parents had hit their child with an object in the previous year, 58 percent had slapped or spanked their child, and 3 percent had threatened their child with a gun or knife sometime in the child's life. The authors estimate that about 1.5 million children are physically injured by their parents each year. The most violence in families occurs between siblings. In a given year, 40 percent of all children hit their own siblings with an object, and 16 percent beat up their sibling.

Because people frequently treat one another so badly, even destructively, social psychologists have done a great deal of research to try to understand the violence people do to each other, usually under the general heading of research on aggression.

DEFINING AGGRESSION: THREE DISTINCTIONS

Although it might seem that everybody understands what aggression is, there is considerable disagreement about how to define it. Let us make three important distinctions here. The first is whether we should define aggression simply in terms of *hurtful behavior,* or whether we need to take into consideration whether the person has *hurtful intentions.* The simplest definition of aggression, and the one favored by those with a learning or behaviorist approach, is that aggression is any behavior that hurts others. The advantage of this definition is that the behavior itself determines whether or not an act is aggressive.

Unfortunately, this definition ignores the intention of the person who does the act—and this factor is critical. If we ignored intent, some actions intended to hurt others would not be labeled aggressive because they turned out to be harmless. Suppose an enraged man fires a gun at a business rival, but the gun turns out to be unloaded. The act is harmless because firing an unloaded gun is not dangerous. Despite the fact that the man was enraged and was trying to kill someone, he was not being aggressive because no actual harm was done.

Ignoring intention can also produce the opposite error—calling some acts aggressive that are not, by the usual meaning of the term. If a golfer's ball accidentally hits a spectator, has the golfer committed an aggressive act? She has in fact caused somebody a great deal of pain, but surely no one would believe the golfer was being aggressive. Similarly, criminal law provides exceptions for acts that are painful but intended to help the victim, such as surgery performed by physicians.

Intentions have a central role in our judgments about aggression in another way. People are particularly motivated to make causal attributions when others' actions are painful to them. People should therefore be especially likely to search for an attribution when they are the victims of aggressive acts.

One of the first attributions people make about aggression is of the person's intent. If a person tries to hurt someone, we ordinarily consider her to be aggressive; if she is not trying to cause harm, she is not being aggressive.

Thus, we will define **aggression** as any action that is *intended* to hurt others. This conception is more difficult to apply, because it does not depend solely on observable behavior. Often it is difficult to know someone's intention.

But we will accept this limitation because we can define aggression meaningfully only by including intent.

A second major distinction is also needed, between **antisocial** and **prosocial** aggression. Normally we think of aggression as bad. After all, if an aggressive act results from an intent to hurt another person, it must be bad. But some aggressive acts are good. We applaud the police officer who shoots a terrorist who has killed in-

---

BOX 10–1

Who Are the Worst Aggressors?

Because prosocial aggression obeys the law, and antisocial aggression does not, we usually think antisocial aggression is worse. But which is in fact the most destructive?

Something you might give some thought to: How common are these various types of aggression? Most of the terrible atrocities seem to have been committed as official acts of government. The murder of 6 million European Jews by the Nazis in World War II was by official order of the German government. The murder of more than 3 million Cambodians in the mid-1970s by the Pol Pot regime was by government order. Widespread torture of and violence against dissidents, such as that uncovered by Amnesty International in repressive regimes in Argentina, Chile, El Salvador, Iran, and the USSR, has all been by government order. The mass suicides at Jonestown in Guyana in 1979 occurred by order of the cult's leader, Jim Jones, and the norms of the cult were that everyone had to obey the leader.

The irony is that all these atrocities are examples of *prosocial* aggression. Each was committed by the legitimate leadership of the nation or group, and supposedly for the broader social good. The Nazis claimed the noble goal of "purifying" the German race, leaders in Argentina and other nations wanted to restore "law and order," and so on.

Sanctioned aggression too can open the doors to much cruelty and barbarism. Consider the near extinction of the American bison; although it was not caused by government order, it was certainly legal and was encouraged by the economic system.

In contrast, there are, relative to these mass atrocities, few individual murders in any society at any given time. How much antisocial aggression do you see in everyday life? Is the most serious problem of civilized societies prosocial aggression or antisocial aggression? Crime is a major problem in the United States today. Yet the Founding Fathers felt in some respects that unrestrained governments as well as unrestrained private citizens could be extremely dangerous. The Bill of Rights is a partial response to that fear. What do you think?

---

nocent victims and is holding others hostage. The question is whether the aggressive act violates commonly accepted social norms, or supports them.

Unprovoked criminal acts that hurt people, such as assault and battery, murder, and gang beatings clearly violate social norms, so they are described as antisocial. But many aggressive acts are actually dictated by social norms, and therefore are described as prosocial. Acts of law enforcement, appropriate parental discipline, or obeying the orders of commanders in wartime are regarded as necessary.

Some aggressive acts fall somewhere between prosocial and antisocial, and we might label them **sanctioned aggression.** This includes aggressive acts that are not required by social norms, but that are well within their bounds. They do not violate accepted moral standards. A coach who disciplines a disobedient player by benching him or her is usually thought to be well within his rights. So is a shopkeeper who in self-defense hits someone who is criminally assaulting him, or a woman who strikes back at a rapist. None of these acts is required of the person, but they fall within the bounds of what is permitted by social norms.

A third distinction is between *aggressive behavior* and *aggressive feelings,* such as anger. Our overt behavior does not always reflect our internal feelings. Someone may be quite angry inside, but make no overt effort to hurt another person. Society discourages and condemns most forms of aggressive behavior, and indeed can exist only if people control their aggressive feelings most of the time. We cannot have people hitting other people, breaking windows, or acting violently whenever they feel like it. Society places strong restraints on such expression; and most people, even those who feel angry much of the time, rarely act aggressively.

We need to consider both the factors that increase anger and the restraints that may prevent it from being translated into aggressive action. We thus have two separate questions—what produces angry feelings and what produces aggressive behavior?

SOURCES OF ANGER

An aggressive feeling is an internal state that cannot be observed directly. We all experience anger, and virtually everyone at one time or another would like to hurt someone else. Indeed, most people report they feel at least mildly or moderately angry anywhere from several times a day to several times a week (Averill, 1983, p. 1146).

But these feelings are not necessarily expressed openly. Aggressive impulses must be studied largely by asking individuals how they are feeling or by inferring the existence of their internal state from physiological measures or behavior, neither of which is a reliable indicator. Nevertheless, there has been a considerable amount of research on the factors that arouse anger.

Attack

One of the most common sources of anger is being attacked or bothered by another person. Imagine that you are waiting at a red light, and the driver of the car behind you blows the horn just as the light turns green. Or imagine that you are reading a newspaper, and someone unexpectedly pours a glass of water down your neck. Or, finally, imagine a student's reaction when he expresses an opinion in class and someone else disagrees with him and says he is stupid to hold such an opinion. In all these cases, someone has done something unpleasant to someone else. Depending on how the injured person takes it, he or she has been annoyed or attacked. It is extremely likely that the person will become angry and feel aggressive toward the source of the attack. Similarly, aversive stimulation of a wide variety of other kinds produces aggression. For example, people exposed to foul odors, irritable cigarette smoke, and disgusting scenes show increased aggressive feelings (Berkowitz, 1983).

People often respond to attack with retaliation, in an "eye for an eye" fashion (Baron, 1977). This was shown clearly in an experiment by Greenwell and Dengerink (1973). Male college students were placed in a competitive task with a fictitious opponent. Each was allowed to shock the other. They received information, supposedly from this person, indicating that (1) their opponent was intentionally raising the level of his shock settings over trials or that (2) he was deliberately maintaining those shocks at a constant, moderate level. For half the subjects within each of these groups, the strength of the shocks received actually *did* increase; for the others, it remained constant.

The results indicated that the opponent's intentions were more important in determining the subjects' own shock settings than was the strength of the actual shocks they received from this person. The apparent motives or intentions behind another person's actions—especially when these are potentially provocative—may often be far more important in influencing our tendency to aggress against him or her than the nature of these actions themselves.

This can produce an escalation of aggression. Gang warfare often starts out with a few insults and ends up in murder, as depicted so clearly in Shakespeare's *Romeo and Juliet* or the musical *West Side Story*. One of the consequences of this retaliatory tendency is that domestic violence breeds more domestic violence. Many cases of family violence involve not one aggressor and one victim, but a pattern of mutual violence within a married couple or between parents and children (Straus et al., 1981, chap. 5).

Frustration

A second major source of anger is **frustration.** Frustration is the interference with or blocking of the attainment of a goal. If one wants to go somewhere, perform some act, or obtain something and is prevented, we say that person is frustrated. One of the basic tenets in psychology is that frustration tends to arouse aggressive feelings.

The behavioral effects of frustration were demonstrated in a classic study by Barker, Dembo, and Lewin (1941). Children were shown a room full of attractive toys but were not allowed to enter it. They stood outside looking at the toys, wanting to play with them, but were unable to reach them. After they had waited for some time, they were allowed to play with them. Other children were given the toys without first being prevented from playing with them. The children who had been frustrated smashed the toys on the floor, threw them against the wall, and generally behaved very destructively. The children who had not been frustrated were much quieter and less destructive.

This effect of frustration may also be seen in broader perspective in society at large. Economic depressions produce frustration that affects almost everyone. People cannot get jobs or buy things they need and are greatly restricted in all phases of their lives. The consequence is that various forms of aggression become more common.

Evidence of this was presented by Hovland and Sears (1940) and confirmed by Mintz (1946). They found a strong relationship between the price of cotton and the number of blacks lynched in the South during the years 1882 to 1930. When cotton prices were high, there were few lynchings; when prices were low, the number of lynchings was relatively high. A drop in the price of cotton signified a depressed period economically. This depression

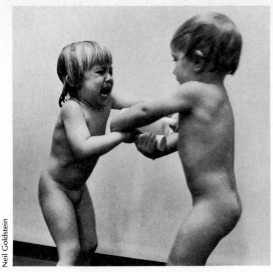

A common source of frustration occurs when someone tries to take something away from you. Sometimes our anger is so intense that we are oblivious to our surroundings.

produced frustration, which in turn led to more aggression. An extreme manifestation of the increased aggression was the increase in lynchings.

The survey of family violence we referred to before (Straus et al., 1981) found that the most commonly reported source of conflict in American families is housekeeping. Families argue and fight endlessly about what and how much to clean, about the quality of food served, about taking the trash out, mowing the lawn, and fixing things. These authors report that one-third of all American couples say they *always* disagree about housekeeping. Close behind are conflicts about sex, social activities, money, and children, in that order (p. 157).

Some families have higher levels of frustration than others, for reasons that are easy to understand. There is more family conflict, and more domestic violence, in working-class than in middle-class families. There is also more in families with unemployed breadwinners or with especially large numbers of children (Straus et al., 1981). Of course, many working-class families with large numbers of children and marginal economic situations are loving, relatively conflict-free, and free of domestic violence. But on the average, these life stresses lead naturally to greater frustration, and ultimately to more violent incidents.

These examples illustrate the typical effect of frustration, but the original statement of the relationship between frustration and aggression was in more absolute terms. Dollard, Doob, and others at Yale began the work on this problem. They asserted that "*aggression* is always a consequence of frustration. . . . the occurrence of aggressive behavior always presupposes the existence of frustration and, contrariwise, the existence of frustration always leads to some form of aggression" (Dollard et al., 1939, p. 1). It appears now that neither *always* in these assumptions is correct. Although frustration usually arouses anger, there are circumstances when it does not; increased anger may not always lead to more aggressive behavior. And, as we will see below, factors other than frustration can also produce aggressive behavior.

The Role of Attributions

For an event to produce anger and aggressive behavior, the key is that the victim must perceive the attack or frustration as intended to harm. This is easily understood in terms of attribution theory. If the victim attributes the frustration to unavoidable circumstances, then it will not create so much anger. But if there are no such justifying external forces and an internal attribution is made, the anger is much greater.

In Weiner's (1982) terms, anger is most likely when the attack or frustration is perceived as under the personal, *internal* control of the other person. For example, we would expect more anger among newly unemployed workers if they have been fired by a boss who said she did not like them than if they were laid off because a recession forced the entire plant to shut down.

Averill (1983) did a survey of occasions on which people felt angry. In 59 percent of the

Instinct Theories of Aggression

It has been proposed by Freud, McDougall, Lorenz, and others that humans have an innate drive or instinct to fight. Just as they experience physiologically based feelings of hunger, thirst, or sexual arousal, so too it is argued that they have an innate need to behave aggressively. Although there are no known physiological mechanisms connected with aggressive feelings as there are for the other drives, they argue that aggression is a basic drive.

It is true that many subhuman animals respond aggressively to certain stimuli whenever they appear and that these responses appear to be instinctive. If two male Siamese fighting fish are put in the same tank, they immediately attack and fight until one is badly mauled or dead. The presence of another male is sufficient to produce this aggressive behavior in each one. The aggression seems to be triggered automatically by the other's presence and was obviously not learned.

There are countless other examples of similar reactions. Animals certainly do a great deal of fighting. They fight for food, to protect their territory, to defend their young, and so on.

But our definition of aggression as requiring the intent to harm may not be appropriate to much of this behavior. A lion that chases and kills a buffalo obviously intends to harm the buffalo. On the other hand, as far as we know, the killing is not done in response to anger or with intent to cause suffering. The lion must hunt for food and the buffalo happens to be its natural prey. The lion kills to satisfy hunger, not to satisfy some aggressive drive. Fighting for mates and for territory also seems to be motivated by sexual drives or the need for food.

The work by ethologists on animal behavior is fascinating. It indicates that many species respond instinctively to specific cues and have many instinctive drives. It does not, however, provide evidence concerning humans. Although some ethologists continue to be convinced that all animals have instinctive aggressive drives, most psychologists now dispute this. Among animals relatively low on the phylogenetic scale, instinct plays an important role in producing aggression, but there seems little reason to believe that humans have instinctive impulses toward aggressiveness.

episodes, anger was a response to an act perceived as voluntary and unjustified; 28 percent of the time, to a potentially avoidable accident or event; and only 2 percent of the time to an unavoidable accident or event.

The result is that arbitrary or unjustified frustrations produce more anger and aggressive behavior than nonarbitrary ones. If the frustration is perceived as being unintended, justified, miti-gated by extenuating circumstances, or accidental, apparently it does not make people as angry, and they are less likely to be aggressive. A teacher who prevents the class from taking a trip to the zoo is frustrating their wishes. If she explains that the trip is a bad idea because rain is expected, less anger will be aroused than if she says she just doesn't feel like going. A good reason for frustration minimizes aggressive feelings. Thus retaliation following an attack is most likely when the attack is perceived as unjustified (Dyck & Rule, 1978).

A good example concerns the effects of heat. Common sense certainly tells us we are more irritable and susceptible to becoming aggressive when it is too hot. Folk wisdom tells us that it is the heat of ghetto summers ("a long hot summer") that is partly responsible for riots and crime. But high heat is normally not something we perceive as resulting from an intent to harm us.

And a series of rather careful experiments has shown that heat, by itself, does not increase hostility or aggressive behavior. Nor does it make angry people any more likely to aggress. In fact, the opposite tended to happen: heat (averaging 94° vs. averaging 73°) tended to diminish the aggressive behavior of subjects angered by a confederate (Baron & Bell, 1975, 1976a). Presumably, under oppressive heat an angry person attributes the anger to the environment, rather than to an annoying confederate. And the person may attribute the anger-arousing behavior by the confederate to the heat, and for that reason react less angrily to the confederate's apparently justified annoyance.

Attribution theory also suggests that other kinds of emotional arousal can sometimes be misperceived as anger. The notion follows from Schachter's two-factor theory of the self-perception of emotions discussed in the chapter on attribution. Arousal stemming from any number of sources might promote aggressive behavior, as long as it is labeled as anger. For example,

vigorous exercise seems to increase aggressiveness when it occurs in a situation that seems to call for anger.

Zillmann and Bryant (1974) did a study that varied nonspecific arousal by having the subject pedal a bicycle ergometer for one minute (high arousal) or thread nickel-size disks with off-center holes onto a plastic-coated wire (low arousal). Verbal attack by a confederate was also varied, on the assumption that such verbal attacks would help the high-arousal subjects mislabel arousal stemming from their energetic exercising as anger. Finally, the subject was allowed to deliver loud, painful noises to the confederate.

As is shown in Table 10–1, the highest aggression was delivered in the high-arousal attack condition. The subjects who were attached and exercised subsequently behaved more aggressively than when the exercise was not included. But the *least* amount of aggression occurred with exercise and no attack, presumably because the aroused subject then had no basis for labeling the arousal as anger. Similar findings have been obtained from arousals due to loud noises (Geen & O'Neal, 1969) or competitive behavior (Rocha & Rogers, 1976).

So even arousal that is apparently irrelevant to aggressiveness or anger can increase aggressive behavior, provided it occurs in a situation where arousal may plausibly be labeled as "anger." Arousing any kind of drive or emotion may produce aggression if the person somehow misattributes the arousal as stemming from anger, rather than from exercise, the game, the film, or whatever else is in fact arousing that in-

---

Table 10–1
Painful Noises Delivered to Confederate

	ATTACK	NO ATTACK
High arousal (exercise)	126.5	58.0
Low arousal (no exercise)	90.1	75.0

Note: The entry is the mean level of painful noise delivered by the subject to the confederate in each condition.
Source: Adapted from Zillmann and Bryant (1974), p. 789.

dividual. With aggression, then, as in so many other contexts discussed in Chapter 5, the person's attribution is a key to response to frustration.

A lot of annoying things happen to us all the time, of course, and only some of them come attached with "intent-to-annoy" attributions. This is not to say that we *never* feel angry unless there is some intent to annoy. Inanimate objects can create a great deal of anger: flat tires, snowdrifts, leaky faucets, burnt scrambled eggs, and rocks on which one stubs one's toe are not usually ascribed the human property of trying to harm us (though there are exceptions to everything). What it does suggest is that many frustrations and annoyances will make us much less angry when no intent to harm is present.

LEARNING AGGRESSIVE BEHAVIOR

Attack and frustration tend to make people feel angry, and these angry feelings constitute one important determinant of aggressive behavior. But people often feel angry and behave peacefully, or at least are not overtly aggressive. In one survey, people reported engaging in overt physical aggression on only 10 percent of the occasions when they felt angry, expressed verbal aggression 49 percent of the time, and engaged in various kinds of nonaggressive calming activities 60 percent of the time (Averill, 1983). Indeed, people typically did *not* behave aggressively when they felt angry, though they usually felt some urge to do so. This is shown in Table 10–2.

It is also possible for people to act aggressively without *feeling* angry. So the factors that control aggressive behavior are as important as those that arouse anger in the first place. The problem is like the attitude-behavior problem discussed in the chapter on attitudes. Attitudes control behavior to some extent, but other factors play a role as well.

The main mechanism determining human aggressive behavior is *past learning.* A newborn infant expresses aggressive feelings quite impulsively. Whenever it is the least bit frustrated, whenever it is denied anything it wants, it cries in outrage, flails its arms, and strikes out at anything within range. In the earliest days of life, an infant does not realize that other people exist and therefore cannot be deliberately trying to harm it. When the infant does discover the existence of others, it continues to vent its rage and probably directs much of it toward these people.

But by the time the individual is an adult, this once savage, uncontrolled animal has his or her aggressive impulses under firm control and aggresses only under certain circumstances, if at all. This development is primarily due to learning. We learn habits of behaving aggressively in some situations and suppressing anger in others, to aggress against some kinds of people (like siblings) and not others (like police), and in response to some kinds of frustration and not others. These habits are crucial to our control of our own aggressive behavior.

Reinforcement

One major mechanism by which this learning occurs is reinforcement. When a particular behavior is rewarded, an individual is more likely to repeat that behavior in the future; when it is punished, he or she is less likely to repeat it. Just as a child learns not to track mud onto a rug, so he learns not to express aggression. He is punished when he punches his brother, throws stones at the girl next door, or bites his mother, and he learns not to do these things. He is re-

Table 10–2
How Do People Respond When They Feel Angry?

RESPONSE TYPE	FELT THE IMPULSE TO ACT AGGRESSIVELY	ACTUALLY ACTED AGGRESSIVELY
Direct aggression		
Verbal or symbolic aggression	82%	49%
Denial or removal of some benefit	59	41
Physical aggression or punishment	40	10
Indirect aggression		
Telling a third party in order to get back at the instigator (malediction)	42	34
Harming something important to the instigator	25	9
Displaced aggression		
Against a nonhuman object	32	28
Against a person	24	25
Nonaggressive responses		
Engaging in calming activities	60	60
Talking the incident over with a neutral party; no intent to harm the offender	59	59
Talking the incident over with the offender without exhibiting hostility	52	39
Engaging in activities opposite to the instigation of anger	14	19

Note: Entry is the percent of episodes during which the person felt angry (*n* = 160), when the person felt like or actually engaged in the behavior indicated or the specific times they felt angry. For example, out of all times the respondents felt angry, 82% of the time they felt like engaging in verbal aggression, and 49% of the time they actually did so.
Source: Adapted from Averill (1983), p. 1148.

warded when he restrains himself despite frustrations, and he learns this also.

For example, in one study (Geen & Pigg, 1970) subjects were verbally reinforced ("that's good," "you're doing fine") for shocking a confederate. Other subjects in a control group shocked the confederate but were not rewarded. The reinforced subjects gave considerably more intense shocks than did nonreinforced subjects. We could give many other examples making the same point: Aggressive acts are to a major extent learned responses, and reinforcement is a major facilitator of aggression.

Imitation

Imitation is another mechanism that shapes a child's behavior. All people, and children in particular, have a strong tendency to imitate others. A child watches people eat with a fork or listens to them talking and tries to do the same. After a while, the child also uses a fork and talks. This imitation extends to virtually every kind of behavior, including aggression. A child observes other people being aggressive or controlling their aggression, and copies them. The child learns to aggress verbally—to shout at people, to curse, and to criticize—and not to resort to violence—not to punch people or throw stones or blow up buildings.

The child also learns when, if ever, each of these behaviors is permissible. At certain times one should not aggress even verbally (such as when one disagrees with one's parents), but at others, any kind of aggression is not only allowable but even necessary (such as when one is being attacked). Thus the child's own aggressive behavior is shaped and determined by what he or she observes others doing.

An experiment by Albert Bandura and his co-workers (Bandura, Ross, & Ross, 1961) illustrated this imitative learning of specific, aggressive behaviors. Children watched an adult play with tinker toys and a Bobo doll (a 5-foot, inflated plastic doll). In one condition, the adult began by assembling the tinker toys for about a minute and then turned his attention to the doll. He approached the doll, punched it, sat on it, hit it with a mallet, tossed it in the air, and kicked it about the room, all the while shouting such things as "Sock him in the nose," "Hit him down," "Pow." He continued in this way for nine minutes, with the child watching. In the other condition, the adult worked quietly with the tinker toys and ignored the doll.

Some time later, each child was frustrated mildly and then left alone for twenty minutes with a number of toys, including a 3-foot Bobo doll. The children's behavior was rated as shown in Table 10–3. They tended to imitate many of the actions of the adult. Those who had seen the adult act aggressively were much more aggressive toward the doll than those who had witnessed the adult working quietly on the tinker toys. The first group punched, kicked, and hammered the doll and uttered aggressive comments similar to those expressed by the aggressive adult.

The key theoretical notion in these experiments is that children learn specific aggressive responses by observing others perform them. It therefore follows that such vicarious learning should be increased when the adult's behavior is reinforced, and when the situation promotes

Table 10–3
Aggression by Children Witnessing Violent or Neutral Model

| | AMOUNT OF AGGRESSION | |
CONDITION	PHYSICAL	VERBAL
Violent model	12.73	8.18
Neutral model	1.05	0.35

Note: The entry is the mean amount of physical or verbal aggression children administered to the Bobo Doll after watching the type of model indicated.
Source: Based on Bandura, Ross, and Ross (1961).

identification with the adult model. So in these Bandura experiments, there was more imitative aggression (1) when the model was rewarded, (2) with a model of the same sex as the child, and (3) when the child had had a previous nurturant relationship with the model (when the model was a friend or teacher of the child).

The children in this situation learned to attack a certain type of doll. They might also attack the same kind of doll in a different situation, and perhaps a different kind of doll, as well. Just how far this would extend—whether or not they would also punch their siblings—is not clear; but it is clear that they would be somewhat more likely to attack some things than they were before. Through the process of imitation, these children showed more aggressive behavior.

Children do not imitate indiscriminately—they imitate some people more than others. The more important, powerful, successful, and liked the other people are, the more a child will imitate them. Also, the people they see most often are the ones they imitate most. Parents fit all these criteria, and they are the primary models for a child during the early years. Since parents are both the major source of reinforcement and the chief object of imitation, a child's future aggressive behavior depends greatly on how parents treat the child and on how they themselves behave.

This joint dependence on the parents for reinforcement and imitation produces an interesting consequence. Punishing a child for acting aggressively might be considered an effective method of teaching the child not to be aggressive, but it often produces the opposite effect. Punishment should make the aggressive behavior less likely in the future. The child learns that she will be punished if she hits her sister, so she avoids the punishment by not hitting her. More generally, she will not be aggressive whenever she expects to suffer for it. She will not ordinarily start a fight with someone who is certain to beat her; she will not start a fight, even if she can win it, if she expects to be severely punished for it afterward. Parents are aware of this simple relationship and employ it to stop children from fighting.

As far as the parents are concerned, this tends to have the desired effect. A child who is punished for fighting does tend to be less aggressive—at home. Home is where the risk of punishment is greatest and therefore where the threat of punishment has the strongest inhibiting effect. Unfortunately, the situation is quite different when this child is out of the home. A child who is punished severely for being aggressive at home tends to be more aggressive outside (Sears, Whiting, Nowlis, & Sears, 1953).

The explanation for this effect is that the child imitates the parents' aggressive behavior. When she is in a situation in which she has the upper hand, she acts the way her parents do toward her. They are aggressive and so is she. The punishment teaches her not to be aggressive at home, but it also teaches her that aggression is acceptable if she can get away with it. Regardless of what parents hope, children will continue to do what their parents do as well as what they say.

One form of imitative aggression that is important in crime and in crowd behavior is **contagious violence.** The French sociologist Tarde introduced the idea of contagious violence when he noted that news of a spectacular crime in one community produced imitative crimes. He pointed out that lurid news stories about the Jack the Ripper murders inspired a series of fe-

male mutilation cases in the English provinces (Tarde, 1903). Police in this country have at times offered similar observations. In 1966, Richard Speck murdered 8 nurses in Chicago in July, and Charles Whitman shot 45 people from the University of Texas Tower in August. In November, Robert Smith, an 18-year-old high school senior, walked into an Arizona beauty school and shot 4 women and a child. He told police he had gotten the idea for a mass killing from the news stories of the Speck and Whitman outbursts.

Many other illustrations of apparently contagious violence can also be cited. Berkowitz (1970) found evidence for an increase in violent crimes (murder, rape, aggravated assault, and robbery) following the 1963 assassination of President John F. Kennedy. Phillips (see 1983) found that highly publicized suicides (suicides presented on the front page of the newspaper) provoke suicidal acts, such as fatal single-vehicle auto accidents or noncommercial airplane crashes. Similarly, heavyweight championship prize fights are followed by a rise in the homicide rate, whereas Super Bowl games are not. Presumably the publicity given these suicides and prize fights induces imitative acts in a contagious manner.

Social Norms

A third aspect of the learning approach is that we learn the general norms of our society that regulate when and how it is appropriate for any of us to aggress. It is all right to yell at a child who hits you on the playground, but not to yell at a teacher who marks your spelling as incorrect. People learn whether or not to aggress as a habitual response to certain cues. If such aggression-eliciting cues as being hit are present in the situation, anger is more likely to be converted into aggression (Berkowitz, 1965). But if aggressive-suppressing cues are present, anger is not likely to produce aggressive behavior.

Which cues are associated with expressing aggression, and which are associated with suppressing it, is regulated in a very fine-tuned manner by the **social norms** we are all taught for specific situations. We learn that it is all right to honk at someone stopped at a green light but not a red light. An American soldier will shoot a German in March 1945, while World War II was on, but not in December, after the war was over. An argument will lead to a brawl in a bar or on a playing field but rarely in an office building. A schoolboy will get into a fight with another boy but rarely with a girl or with a crippled child. Of course, some aggressive behavior is impulsive, and some is inappropriate to the situation. But the most impressive thing is how much aggressive *behavior* is controlled by the very complex, and often subtle, social norms developed by every human culture or subculture. Therefore it must also be controlled by cues that inform us about the norms for the situation we are in.

What we learn are the social norms concerning the expression of aggression. Sometimes these norms apply to the whole society; for example, we all generally share the view that it is wrong to kill another person, except under fairly extreme conditions (self-defense, executions).

We learn norms about prosocial aggression, where aggression is the appropriate behavior. In one national survey, 77 percent regarded slapping or spanking a disobedient 12-year-old as "normal," and 71 percent as "good" and 70 percent as "necessary" (Straus et al., 1981). Similarly, 71 percent supported the use of capital punishment in cases of murder (Blumenthal et al., 1972, p. 108).

We also share norms about sanctioned aggression, which are situations that permit but do not require aggression. For example, 60 percent "strongly agreed" that "a man has the right to kill another man in a case of self-defense," and 58 percent agreed that "a man has the right to kill a person to defend his house" (Blumenthal et al., 1972).

Most of the time we all agree on what is appropriate and what is inappropriate aggression. Occasionally we do not agree. In the 1960s, many blacks rioting in protest of discrimination and deprivation felt quite justified in their aggression, whereas most whites felt quite the opposite (Sears & McConahay, 1973). Members of youth gangs may feel retaliatory killings are justified, whereas most other people would disagree. Members of the Johnson and Nixon administrations felt the mass killings of North

Ken Karp

Complex social norms regulate aggression: The norms that regulate aggression in a civil disobedience protest are very complex indeed, but they have become quite predictable and everyone seems to share them and understand them. The protestors must be passive and nonviolent, while the police are supposed to be firm, make arrests, but not physically harm nor verbally abuse the protestors. When either side breaks these rules, they tend to get into trouble.

Vietnamese were justified because of the threat of communism, whereas antiwar protestors called them war crimes.

But such dramatic instances of disagreement should not obscure the consensus almost all humans share about the vast majority of aggressive acts. Unprovoked aggression against an innocent victim is wrong. Killing is wrong except in certain very clearly specified cases. Aggressive acts in the service of social control, by duly authorized authorities, are permissible within certain boundaries. All over the world, and in all cultures, there is broad agreement on such general principles.

Understanding the differences among antisocial, sanctioned, and prosocial aggression depends on knowing what the relevant social norms are. The distinctions are sometimes quite subtle. But individuals must learn them in order to function effectively in society. Those who never control their aggression will not be allowed to remain free; those who never use ag-

---

BOX 10–3

The Anger of the "New Urban Blacks"

The 1960s witnessed an outbreak of violence by black people that had no real precedent in American history. Yet blacks were in most ways better off than they had been since being forcibly brought to this country as slaves two centuries earlier.

Sears and McConahay (1973) analyzed this change as being due to changes in blacks' learning concerning expressed aggression. They identified a new generation of blacks, brought up in northern cities in the post-World War II era, as having been socialized to a new set of norms. They called them the "new urban blacks," to compare them with the previous generation of blacks, who had mainly been brought up in the rural and small town South of pre-World War II days.

The "new urban blacks" had grown up in the urban North, an environment whose formal norms were racially egalitarian, unlike the earlier generation, which had grown up in the formally racially segregated old South. Moreover, the postwar era saw the desegregation of many major institutions, such as the armed services, educational institutions, and professional sports. Finally, the era of civil rights protest, in the late 1950s and early 1960s, provided models of aggressive blacks demanding their rights.

The "new urban blacks" were better educated, more politically sophisticated, took more pride in being black, and were more politically disaffected. Most important, they had more aggressive feelings about racial issues by the time of the ghetto riots. They were more sympathetic to the use of violence in achieving political aims, and more demanding of their rights.

As a result, they themselves showed higher rates of active participation in ghetto riots than did older, southern-reared blacks. Sears and McConahay concluded that the new ghetto norms promoted both more angry impulses and more overt aggression on the part of young blacks.

gression are probably worse off than those who use it at appropriate times. The critical problem in socialization is not how to teach children never to aggress, but how to teach them when aggression is appropriate and when it is not. The impressive thing is how well almost all people do learn these complex norms. Almost everyone can tell us when aggression is all right and when it is not. The few who cannot make at least the broad distinction are thought insane and are not held responsible for their actions.

Deindividuation

Normally people's behavior is fairly tightly regulated by social norms. An interesting exception occurs in mob behavior. The sociologist LeBon (1896) observed that people in crowds often feel free to gratify "savage, destructive" instincts. He felt that the reasons lay in two characteristics of people in large crowds: invincibility and anonymity. "The individual forming part of a crowd acquires . . . a sentiment of invincible power which allows him to yield to instincts." Moreover, "a crowd being anonymous, and in consequence irresponsible, the sentiment of responsibility which always controls individuals disappears entirely" (p. 30). More recently, Zimbardo (1969) described this phenomenon as **deindividuation,** and suggested it leads to unrestrained behavior. A number of factors associated with being in a crowd might produce deindividuation: anonymity, diffused responsibility, size, activity, a novel un-

---

BOX 10–4
The Baiting Crowd

Leon Mann (1981) applied the notion of deindividuation to a well-known phenomenon called "the baiting crowd," in which a crowd has gathered at the base of a tall building where a person is threatening to commit suicide by jumping from a ledge or window. Frequently members of the crowd begin to yell at the person to jump, a phenomenon Mann called "the baiting crowd." He relates a number of well-known incidents, such as a night in New York in 1938 when thousands of persons waited, some for eleven hours, until a man jumped from a seventeenth-floor hotel ledge. From newspaper listings of suicides and suicide attempts in the 1960s and 1970s, he found 21 cases in which crowds had gathered to observe someone threatening to or succeeding in committing suicide by jumping from a building, bridge, tower, or cliff. In 10 cases, the crowd had taunted and urged the victim to jump.

What had produced a baiting rather than a nonbaiting crowd? The main factors were those that might be expected to produce deindividuation. Baiting was more common when people were more anonymous, being in larger crowds (over 300 people), involved in episodes that occurred at night, or in crowds at some distance from the victim (not on the same level or on adjoining roofs or windows). They were also more likely to bait the victim in longer episodes, when the crowd became larger, more irritable, and developed some crowd intensity.

structured situation, arousal due to noise, and fatigue.

Deindividuation will be discussed in more detail later in the chapter on groups. But it is important for aggression as well. A good example is Watson's (1973) analysis of the factors associated with extreme forms of aggression in warfare carried out by primitive peoples. The most extreme violence was carried out by peoples who used such deindividuating devices as masks, face and body paint, and special garments.

Closer to home, Prentice-Dunn and Rogers (1980; Rogers & Prentice-Dunn, 1981) have done several experiments to test whether these deindividuating factors do in fact lead to more aggressive behavior. They used a modification of the sham-learning situation described in Chapter 2. Students were told they were to shock another student in a learning experiment. The subject became the "teacher" and a confederate became the "learner." Then the "teacher" was supposed to punish the "learner" for errors with electric shock. In a "deindividuating cues" condition, subjects were not addressed by name; they were told the experimenter would not know what shock intensities they chose; they were told they would not meet or see the victim. The experimenter took full responsibility for the victim's well-being, and the room was dimly lit. In contrast, in an "individuating cues" condition, the subjects wore name tags, were addressed by their first names, and the experimenter took keen interest in the shock intensities selected. Subjects were told that they would meet the victim after the experiment and that the victim's well-being was the subjects' responsibility. The room was well-lit.

As expected, this manipulation created significant differences in a number of subjective dimensions of deindividuation, such as a lack of feeling of inhibition, and lack of concern for the victim's, experimenter's, and other group members' reactions. In both experiments, deindivid-

uation led to significantly greater shock being administered.

Instrumental Aggression

Instrumental aggression occurs when a person uses aggression to attain some practical goal by hurting others. Some people are paid killers or paid assassins; they kill for money, not because of anger. Sometimes young thugs mug people in big cities not because they are angry, but to steal money. Slave-trading Europeans committed many acts of violence against eighteenth- and nineteenth-century Africans not out of anger, but for commercial motives. National leaders take their countries to war with adjoining nations not out of anger, but because they want to acquire territory, raw materials, or a better defensive position. In all these cases, aggressive behavior is committed simply as a way to attain other valued goods, and not because of angry feelings.

One particularly important form of instrumental aggression stems from what LeVine and Campbell (1972) have called **realistic group conflict.** Sometimes two groups are in a situation in which they are competing for the same scarce resources. For example, one quite common analysis of antiblack prejudice in the South in the earlier part of this century blames it on realistic group conflict. At that time, the South was relatively impoverished, depending heavily on cotton and tobacco farming, and with relatively little industry. Jobs were few and far between. As a result, working-class whites were in direct competition for these scarce jobs with blacks, most of whom were unskilled laborers and poorly educated. According to this theory, the conflicts between these two groups helped perpetuate racial prejudice, and contributed to discrimination against blacks in employment, since whites had much greater economic and political power. In short, sometimes anger is the main motive, and sometimes it is not.

REDUCING AGGRESSIVE BEHAVIOR

Aggressive behavior is a major problem for human societies. Individual crimes and large-scale social violence are extremely damaging and harmful both to individual well-being and to the general social fabric. Freud viewed aggressive instincts as central dilemmas for social control in every society. Human beings have the capacity for great anger and for very destructive behavior. All societies expend much energy simply to control this tendency toward violence. So it is vital to understand how to reduce aggressiveness.

Whether or not somebody aggresses in a particular situation is determined by three variables: (1) the strength of the person's angry feelings, which in turn is determined partly by the degree of frustration or attack that produced them, and partly by the extent to which the individual's interpretation of this frustration produces feelings of anger; and (2) the tendency to express the anger, which in turn is determined by what the person has learned about aggressiveness in general, and by the nature of this situation in particular; and sometimes (3) violence

is committed for other, more instrumental reasons.

This analysis suggests some of the ways in which aggressive behavior can be reduced: (1) Frustration can be reduced. (2) People can be taught not to aggress in a particular situation, or can be taught to restrain aggressiveness in general. For example, children are taught not to fight in the classroom, and indeed are taught to be careful about really hurting each other in general. But any solution has its own risks and unintended consequences. So let us look systematically at the possible techniques for reducing aggressive behavior.

Punishment and Retaliation

It seems obvious that the fear of punishment or retaliation should suppress aggressive behavior. The kind of rational people described earlier by incentive theories would certainly include such future consequences in their calculations about aggression, and avoid behaving aggressively if

One of the dangers of aggressing when you are angered by others in traffic is that they will retaliate.

DeSazo-Rapho, Photo Researchers, Inc.

punishment seemed likely. Indeed, Bond and Dutton (1975) and Wilson and Rogers (1975), both using the shock-learning technique (see Chapter 2), found reduced aggression when the subject was told that the roles would later be reversed, so he (or she) would be in the position of being shocked.

Consistent with these findings, younger children are consistently more likely to be victims of domestic violence than older children because they are weaker and less likely to retaliate (Straus et al., 1981, p. 69). But as a general matter it turns out not to be so simple. For one thing, children who are frequently punished for being aggressive turn out themselves to be more aggressive than normal (Sears, Maccoby, & Levin, 1957). Perhaps it is because they model themselves on an aggressive parent. Perhaps it is because frequent punishment, like any attack, generates a lot of anger itself. In any case, punishment of children's aggressiveness does not result in a simple inhibition of their aggressive behavior.

A second problem is that fear of punishment or retaliation seems to spark *counteraggression.* People who are attacked have a tendency to retaliate against their attackers, even when retaliation is sure to provoke more attacks. One series of studies set up a situation in which subjects could avoid further attacks by responding to a first attack with nonaggression. But they did not; they continued to counteraggress following the first attack, even if it brought more attacks on them (Deverink, Schnedler, & Covey, 1978). It seemed that the subjects just wanted to get back at their tormentors, even when this deepened their own trouble. Many lives have been lost on battlefields (and in palaces) because national leaders have felt that "national honor" demanded counteraggression, even though it almost guaranteed further retaliation and bloodshed.

The effects of anticipated punishment or retaliation are not simple. Sometimes they simply suppress aggression, as the person quite rationally wants to avoid future pain. But sometimes the threats are simply interpreted as attacks, and inspire even more aggression. Even if punishment, or threat of retaliation, were usually temporarily effective in suppressing direct aggression, it is too expensive to be a general solution to the problem. There are too many people in too many places for all to be monitored constantly. As it is, many people who commit serious crimes, such as murder, are never caught and punished. It is simply impossible to depend on external controls to minimize violence, and anyway we would not want a society with such repressive control of individual citizens' behavior. So the threat of punishment or retaliation cannot be a general solution to the problem of violence.

Reducing Frustration

A better technique may be to reduce the potential for attack and frustration. All societies, to one degree or another, try to ensure some level of equality of access to the necessities of life, such as food, clothing, shelter, and family life. A major reason is to avoid large-scale violent disruptions of daily life from especially frustrated groups. For example, after the ghetto riots of the 1960s, the Kerner Commission recommended a sweeping set of social changes to improve the treatment of blacks in America, on the assumption that reducing their frustration would reduce the chance of further rioting.

Similarly, most societies make some provision for collective police protection so that ordinary people are not continually subject to attack from bandits or otherwise violent persons. This helps to reduce the chances for widespread violence in two ways: People are protected, and they are not themselves goaded into retaliation. In the nineteenth century, life on the frontier in the United States was often lived without benefit of such tight community control over attack. The result was that people were quite vulnerable to attack and sometimes responded with retaliatory vigilantism.

Efforts to reduce instrumental aggression must focus on the underlying causes of the ag-

BOX 10–5
The Social Heredity of Domestic Violence

This tendency for punishment to make the target even more aggressive—whether it occurs because of modeling or because of increased anger—passes aggressiveness down from one generation to the next, as well. Of the married men who had seen their parents attack each other, 35 percent had hit their own wives in the past year; of those who had not seen any such violence between their parents, only 11 percent had hit their own wives. The same held for wives: 27 and 9 percent, respectively, had hit their own husbands (Straus et al., 1981, p. 100). Men and women who had been physically punished as children were much more likely to be violent themselves toward their families in adulthood. Violent parents pass their own violent tendencies on to the next generation—and conversely, nonviolent parents pass their own more peaceful tendencies on. This relationship between family violence experienced in growing up, and marital violence engaged in as an adult, is shown quite clearly in the following figure.

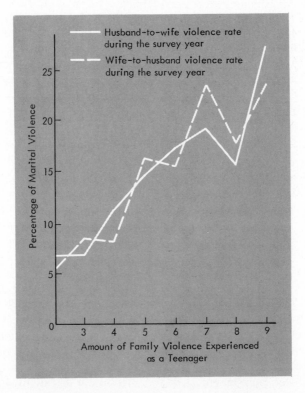

Marital violence in survey year by amount of family violence experienced as a teenager. (Straus et al., 1980, p. 112.)

gression as well as on the overt behavior itself. We avoid war not only by training political leaders to inhibit their aggressive impulses, by trying to make them less angry, or by threatening them with retaliation. We also avoid war through patient diplomatic efforts to reduce real conflicts.

Some societies, particularly those organized around socialist philosophies, make a particular effort to minimize the frustration of their citizens. Capitalist societies, on the other hand, tend to accept some frustration as part of the price of freedom. The evidence is that socialist societies generally do provide more economic equality. There is, of course, much debate about other costs of that equality in terms of overall productivity, individual freedom, and so on. But even the nations most conscientiously dedicated to the public's well-being cannot eliminate all individual frustration.

There always will be conflict between parents and children, or between co-workers or schoolmates; no one ever will have exactly what and as much as he or she wants to eat when he or she wants it; some people will never be able to achieve what they would like; some people will always be dissatisfied with the things their mates do, and so on. That is the nature of life. So while forward-looking societies are wise to try to minimize as much large-scale frustration as they can, they can never completely eliminate frustration, or probably even come close. So other techniques for minimizing violence are necessary.

Learned Inhibitions

Another technique to reduce aggression is for people to learn to control their own aggressive behavior, whether or not they are in danger of being punished. Just as people learn when aggression is desirable or permissible, so too they must learn when aggressive behavior must be suppressed. There are two general lessons people learn: to suppress their aggressive behavior in general, and to suppress it in specific situations.

The general learned inhibition of aggression can be called **aggression anxiety** (or *aggression guilt*). The person feels anxiety when nearing an aggressive response. Like a burnt child approaching a stove, the person then backs off and suppresses the urge to aggress. Not everyone has equal amounts of aggression anxiety, of course. Women have more than men do. Children reared in middle-class homes tend to have more than children reared in lower-class homes. Parents who use reasoning and withdrawal of affection as disciplinary techniques produce children with more aggression anxiety than parents who use high degrees of physical punishment (Feshbach, 1970).

We also learn anxiety about expressing aggression in certain very specific situations. All through our lives we are learning and relearning "the ropes," the norms of our social environments. Students learn not to curse their professors to their faces, and professors learn not to throw things at their students. We learn that it is all right to yell and scream at our children, but that it is not all right to beat them up. We can kill animals for sport or food, but we cannot kill each other or someone's pet animal. We all possess a great many finely graded distinctions about what is and what is not permissible aggression. These learned inhibitions represent the most potent controls of human violent behavior we have; no police force could ever be numerous enough, far-sighted enough, or quick enough even to come close to them.

These learned inhibitions are triggered by cues that tell us what kind of a situation we are in—one that calls for expression, or one that calls for suppression, of aggression. Do pain cues trigger these inhibitions? What about a potential victim's reaction? Signs of a victim's distress sometimes do arouse, vicariously, a similar negative emotional state in the aggressor: He or she identifies with the victim, has empathy for the person's suffering, and inhibits further attack. Still, since the intent of aggression is to hurt, the signs of pain in another person might simply reinforce the aggression, and increase it still further.

To test these possibilities, a number of studies have been done varying the pain cues transmitted by victim to aggressor. Baron (1971a), using the shock-learning technique, transmitted the supposed physiological reactions of the shock victim to the subject in the form of a "pain meter." This registered either high or mild levels of pain. The subject was angered in two ways: by having his own initial efforts at solving a problem criticized by the confederate, and by having the confederate shock him. But pain cues reduced further aggression, whether the subject had been angered or not. Then Baron (1971b) varied attitude similarity of subject and victim, on the assumption that the subject would not feel much empathy with a very dissimilar person. Even here pain cues led only to decreased aggression.

Finally, Baron (1974) suggested that pain cues might increase aggression if higher levels of anger were used. This time, instead of just giving the confederate instructions to shock the subject to induce anger, the experimenter told the confederate he could shock the subject or deliver light flashes. The confederate then shocked the subject, totally incensing the person and arousing high levels of anger, as planned. This time pain cues did increase further aggression, at least in the angry condition. In general, then, signs of a victim's suffering inhibit further aggression, except in cases of extreme anger, when they are taken as signs of successful hurting.

For such reasons, the phenomenon of *dehumanization* is thought to increase aggression against victims who are far away or anonymous to their attackers. For example, it was thought that it was easier to bomb North Vietnamese from the great heights of a B-52, or to order troops into battle from the distance of Washington, D.C., than to attack at closer, more personal range. Having the victim distant or anonymous supposedly makes aggression easier, because the pain cues are absent. Conversely, making the victim more human to the point that the attacker empathizes with the person's suffering, should reduce aggression.

Displacement

What happens to aggressive feelings when, for one reason or another, they cannot be expressed against the cause of the anger? People are often frustrated or annoyed by someone but unable to retaliate against that person—the person may be too powerful, not available, or they may be too anxious and inhibited to do it. In such a situation, they are likely to express aggression in some other way, one of which is called **displacement**—that is, expressing aggression against a substitute target.

When a man forbids his son to go to the movies on a school night, the boy feels angry and aggressive. He cannot attack his father because his father is too strong and because there are social inhibitions against it. Also, doing so would probably make it less likely that he would be permitted to go to the movies in the future. So he vents his rage on someone else. He has a wide range of people available. There is his mother, his older brother, his older sister, his younger brother, and a boy his own age who lives next door. The question is, what determines which of these people he will select and how much aggression he will express?

The basic principle of displacement is that the more similar a target is to the original source of frustration, the stronger will be the individual's aggressive impulses toward that target. In this case, the boy's aggressive impulse is strongest toward his father and gets weaker as the target toward whom it is directed becomes less similar to his father. It is not very strong toward his dog, for example. But the boy's anxiety operates in much the same way as his anger. Just as his impulse to hurt the source of frustration generalizes to other people, so does his anxiety about attacking the source. The more similar the person is to this source, the stronger the anxiety felt toward him or her.

An important characteristic of displaced aggression is that the anxiety declines faster with increasingly dissimilar targets than does the aggressive impulse. This is shown in Figure 10–1. As long as the anxiety is stronger than the aggressive impulse, the individual will restrain him or herself; when the tendency to aggress becomes stronger than the anxiety, the individual will express aggression. As a result, aggressive behavior is most likely to occur against a person moderately dissimilar from the original target—someone similar enough to draw some anger, but dissimilar enough to be associated with relatively little anxiety.

In this case, the boy's younger brother may be just dissimilar enough to the father that the boy is not afraid of him and similar enough that the aggressive impulse is still quite strong. So because the boy is unwilling to hit his father, he makes a nasty comment to his brother.

In general, therefore, displaced aggression is most likely to be directed toward targets who are perceived as weaker and less powerful. One

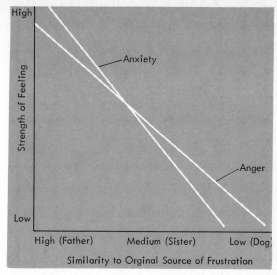

FIGURE 10–1 Displaced aggression.

When children are punished by their parents, they sometimes take out their feelings of aggression on dolls or other surrogate objects.

BOX 10-6
Fear of Black Retaliation Makes Whites' Aggression Indirect

One interesting line of research has shown how whites' aggression toward blacks becomes more indirect and covert when blacks later will have the opportunity to retaliate. The Donnersteins placed white subjects in the sham-learning situation, in which the "learner" was a black confederate. Then they tested how much the subject shocked the confederate, depending on whether their roles would later be reversed or not. Presumably, if the roles would reverse later on, the black might retaliate against the white.

In several such studies, the Donnersteins (1972a, 1972b, 1975) found that potential retaliation markedly reduced the direct aggression performed by whites against blacks. In this teacher-learner situation, direct aggression was indexed by the intensity of the shock delivered by the subject when the confederate made an "error."

Indirect aggression was measured by setting the shock machine at one particular intensity, so the subject had no control over intensity, and then telling the subject he had to deliver shock for every error, so the subject had no control over whether to shock or not. But the subject did control the duration of shock; he could give either a quick one or a long one. The long one was a relatively disguised form of aggression; after all, the subject was just following instructions by giving the shock!

And potential retaliation actually increased such indirect, relatively covert, disguised forms of aggression. So the black potential for retaliation against a white aggressor does indeed seem to reduce the white's direct aggression—but it increases, instead, subtle and indirect forms of aggression.

Finally, it is interesting to note that all these effects occurred for black targets and not for white. Apparently the threat of black retaliation for white aggression is most potent.

example comes from a learning situation in which women were insulted and angered by a co-worker and then were instructed to punish a child for errors (Berkowitz & Frodi, 1979). They tended to give the most punishment to children who were physically unattractive or who stuttered. These children were more likely to be the targets of displaced aggression than more attractive children or those who spoke normally.

The dimension along which similarity is determined need not be as simple as the one in our example. For example, many adolescents tend to have feelings of anger against their parents. Parents are the source of power in the family, they are the authority, and they must in-

evitably frustrate their children's wishes to some extent. In some cases, this anger is expressed directly against the parents. In many cases, however, it is displaced to other people who represent authority. School administrators, trustees, teachers, the government, and so on fit the criterion and become likely objects for aggression.

Or, displacement may occur along a dimension of response similarity as well as along a dimension of target similarity. The adolescent boy may become surly and uncooperative rather than overtly belligerent. It creates less anxiety, but also expresses less anger. This kind of response is not a direct act of aggression in response to frustration; rather, it is displaced to subtler, more covert forms. In fact, there is a term for people who habitually resort to such indirect forms of aggression: the *passive-aggressive personality*.

Catharsis

One final idea is that angry feelings can be reduced simply by expressing the aggression. Freud called this process **catharsis.** In commonsense language, it involves "letting off steam" or "getting it out of your system." The core of the catharsis notion is that when people feel aggressive, committing aggressive acts should reduce the intensity of their feelings. This, in turn, should make them less likely to act aggressively afterward. If someone annoys us by honking a horn at us, we feel angry. If, at the next traffic light, we find ourselves behind that car and honk at it, this should reduce the anger.

Freud's version of the catharsis theory presupposed that we always have a reservoir of instinctual aggressive energy within us. No matter what the situation is, we have a certain amount of aggressiveness that we need to "get off our chest." The problem with this view is that it predicts aggressive behavior will always reduce anger, because that reservoir is always with us. Some empirical evidence contradicts this: Aggressive behavior increases aggressiveness in nonangry people; they have built up steam instead of letting it off (Doob & Wood, 1972; Konecni, 1975).

A later version came from the frustration-aggression hypothesis which assumed that aggressive drives are not instinctual, but are instigated by situational factors like frustrations and attacks. The implication was that aggressive behavior would produce catharsis only for those people who were angry to start with. Since there is no permanent reservoir of aggressive energy in this theory, catharsis would reduce aggressiveness only for those people in whom it had been built up through frustration or attack.

Some early research on physiological arousal supported this view. Two studies (Hokanson, 1961; Hokanson & Burgess, 1962) found that aggressive behavior decreased angry feelings, as indexed by physiological arousal. In these studies, subjects were insulted by a low-status person, which increased their blood pressure, indicating increased physiological tension. Presumably they were angry. Some of the subjects were then given an opportunity to deliver shocks to the experimenter who had annoyed them; some were not given this opportunity. Being allowed to express aggression resulted in lower blood pressure among those who were angry.

DIRECT AGGRESSION   Later research has found, however, that catharsis is successful in reducing aggression only when an angry person has expressed that anger directly against his or her frustrator. A typical demonstration is in an experiment by Konecni and Ebbesen (1976). First, the subject was insulted. She did an anagram task with the confederate, who finished her own problems quickly and then proceeded to insult the subject, criticize her for being so slow, and express doubts about her intellectual ability. Then some subjects were given the opportunity to aggress against the confederate, while others were not.

Using a variant on the standard sham-learning situation, the subjects were required to deliver loud blasts of noise to the confederate each time she made an error. Control subjects did not send any noise to the confederate. The dependent variable involved a "creativity test" in which all subjects were given a two-button box, one labeled "good" and the other "noise." The subject could administer either reward or punishment, depending on her feelings.

The results clearly showed that delivering blasts of noise at the confederate reduced a subsequent tendency to do so. A similar study by Doob and Wood (1972), using shock rather than noise, found essentially the same thing: When the subjects were angered by a confederate, catharsis resulted from giving shocks to the confederate.

However, relying on this kind of direct retaliatory catharsis as a way of reducing aggression is risky because it may have a number of undesirable side effects. There is the possibility of **disinhibition.** We all control our anger fairly tightly most of the time. But if it is once released, particularly when it seems to be socially approved, we may relax our inhibitions about further hostilities. So expressing aggression may lead to even more aggression.

Geen and Quanty (1977) cite the reaction of a man who killed four people: "He said . . . he had a funny feeling in his stomach but after the first [killing] . . . it was easy" (p. 29). Aggression may be reinforced if it relieves emotional tension (as it appears to). Then reinforced behaviors would tend to recur more frequently. And aggressive behavior also may provide practice and cues for further aggression that would not have been present without it.

Another risk is that within any given sequence of behavior, aggression seems to escalate rather than to decline, as we indicated above in discussing the effects of retaliation. That is, catharsis seems to reduce aggression only when there is some break in the action, a change in the victim, or some change in the mode of expression of aggression. This has been a common finding with the Buss aggression machine, which has been used in so many experiments. As the experiment goes on, the "teacher" almost always gives increasingly strong shocks to the "learner," no matter what conditions they are in.

Goldstein, Davis, and Herman (1975) found the same thing with verbal responses, using the same teacher-learner situation. The subject was given a list of standard verbal responses from which to choose, depending on whether the "learner" had made an error or not. The subject tended to give more and more intense punishments for errors. For example, if the subject first responded to an error with "That's no good," he later would escalate with "You're a jerk," through "I never met anyone as dumb as you," to "Stupid son of a bitch." So if you get into a fight, it is likely that the fighting will increase your aggression toward your opponent rather

than decrease it. The authors suggest this *escalation phenomenon* may be the same thing that happens in the "battered child" syndrome, in which the level of violence just seems to keep increasing.

INDIRECT AGGRESSION   Given the hazards of directly expressing aggression against a frustrator or attacker, what about the possibility that more indirect expressions of aggression might produce catharsis? Aristotle felt that watching tragedy could produce catharsis, because the audience could vicariously experience the actors' emotions. Freud developed the same idea by hypothesizing that people could reduce their aggressive impulses through aggressive fantasy, such as in violent daydreams, cruel jokes, or writing stories. If such indirectly expressed aggression truly did cathart aggressive energy, aggressive behavior might be reduced without all the negative side effects we have enumerated.

An early study of the possible effects of **fantasy aggression** was conducted by Seymour Feshbach (1955). First, most of the subjects were angered by being insulted in class by their instructor. Then half the subjects were allowed to express aggression on a fantasy task—responding to four cards from a projective test that showed ambiguous pictures for which the subjects were to make up stories. The other half of this group did not respond to the cards. Afterward, their aggressiveness toward the instructor was measured. The insulted subjects who were given the opportunity to express aggression on the fantasy task were somewhat less aggressive on the final measure than the insulted subjects who did not do the fantasy task.

However, fantasy aggression may not be an especially reliable way to reduce aggressiveness either. Freud felt that hostile humor could serve as an indirect mechanism for releasing aggressive energy. When we are angry and hear someone tell a hostile joke (like a hostile ethnic joke), we vicariously engage in the expression of hostility and should no longer feel so angry ourselves. To test this idea, a number of studies have aroused various degrees of anger, presented hostile (or unhostile) jokes to the subjects, and then measured their subsequent aggressiveness.

The catharsis theory predicts that the angered subjects will show less aggression after being shown hostile jokes than after being shown nonhostile jokes, because the hostile jokes help to siphon off their anger. Research testing this hypothesis has produced generally inconsistent results, though humor does seem to distract people from their frustrations and annoyances (Mueller & Donnerstein, 1977), and generates responses incompatible with aggressive behavior, such as laughter (Baron & Ball, 1974).

The question of fantasy aggression is also relevant to the hot political issue of whether violence on television or in the movies affects aggressive behavior. If watching a crime movie actually reduced our aggressiveness, it would be quite an important matter, so we will discuss this issue in some detail in the next section. But from the above findings our suspicion must be that vicariously experienced aggression against some neutral person is generally not especially cathartic. Watching a boxing match may not really do much about the fact that your girlfriend is going out with your rival at that very moment, and it apparently would not be likely to do much to relieve your anger either.

Evidence that modes of expressing aggression other than physical acts produce catharsis have also been sought. One is *displaced aggression;* that is, aggression against someone other than your tormentor. Another is *vicarious aggression* against your tormentor; that is, aggression actually committed by someone else. A third is *verbal* rather than physical aggression. In these cases, there are some studies that find cathartic effects (e.g., Konecni and Doob, 1972; Bramel, Taub, & Blum, 1968), but other studies that do not (see Geen & Quanty, 1977). In fact, the rates of various kinds of aggression turn out to be relatively highly correlated.

For example, couples that were in the highest quarter of the population in verbal aggression had extremely high levels of physical violence against each other: 56 percent had engaged in at least one violent episode within the past year. Couples in the lowest quarter on verbal aggression very rarely were physically violent—only 0.5 percent had had a violent incident in a year (Straus et al., 1981). So in married couples, verbally "getting it off your chest" is not associated with peace and harmony, but with later outbreaks of even more serious violence.

At the moment, social psychologists simply do not know whether or not such alternative modes of expressing anger produce a cathartic reduction in aggressive behavior, and if they do, what additional conditions would be necessary for them to do so regularly. In any event, catharsis does seem to reduce the expression of aggression fairly reliably only when (1) the person is angry, and (2) is able to express aggression in a fairly direct manner, and (3) is able to express aggression against the person who he or she perceives as responsible for the anger—the attacker, annoyer, or frustrator. These are fairly stringent limitations on the catharsis effect.

MEDIA VIOLENCE: THE POLITICAL ISSUE

It is an understatement to say that in recent years movies have begun to portray a great deal of violence. Fighting, beating, killing, and murder have always been common in Westerns and gangster movies. But the level of violence has risen over time. Content analyses show a long-term trend dating from the early 1930s of increasing violence in films shown in theaters (Comstock, 1982). And movies in the 1970s escalated the amount of carnage as well as its vividness. People did not just die at a distance or clutch their stomachs and fall slowly to the ground. In these movies they actually bled and suffered; the bullet wounds gaped; blood pumped rhythmically from victims' bodies, rather than slowly staining their clothes.

Television has also used quite a bit of violence in its programming. With the exception of talk, variety, doctor, and comedy shows, virtually all original programming for prime time television, as well as shows designed specifically for children, involve violence in one form or another. Westerns, police, gangsters, and spy shows, and most television movies include a full complement of fighting, shooting, and killing. Saturday morning cartoons feature more of the same. Although the violence on television is much less explicit and vivid than that in the movies, it is remarkably pervasive.

It is certainly widely assumed that such media violence stimulates people to aggressive behavior. For example, in 1983 the chief of the California state prisons adopted a policy of preventing "any movie that glorifies sick violence" after he discovered that the movie *The Texas Chainsaw Massacre* had been shown at the men's prison in Chino (*Los Angeles Times,* June 29, 1983). There is some evidence that the crime rate in American cities increased more than usual right after television was introduced, soon after World War II (Hennigan et al., 1982).

But as we have seen, aggression is a very complex behavior. Mere exposure to films may not have much effect on it one way or the other. The catharsis theory would even predict that violent films might reduce aggression. So we explore this question in some detail, especially since this has become one of the more controversial areas of the application of social psychological research.

The Surgeon General's Report

The politics of media violence have become very important. Congressional concern about violence on television began to be expressed in hearings as early as 1952. As a result of congressional action, an enormous amount of money was made available for research on media violence in the late 1960s. A report was finally prepared for the Surgeon General of the United States Public Health Service, which had administered the research grants. This report concluded, rather cautiously, that:

> [There is] a preliminary and tentative indication of a causal relation between viewing violence on television and aggressive behavior; an indication that any such causal relation operates only on some children (who are predisposed to be aggressive); and an indication that it operates only in some environmental contexts (Surgeon General's Scientific Advisory Committee on Television and Social Behavior, 1972, p. 11).

This report immediately came under harsh attack, partly because some of the members of the committee that prepared it had been representatives of the television networks, and it was felt (quite understandably, but not necessarily accurately) that they therefore could not be disinterested scientific observers (Cater & Strickland, 1975).

Most of the criticism held that the commission had underestimated the effects of media violence. The report led to the preparation of a number of briefer reviews, which arrived at widely differing conclusions (contrast Comstock, 1975, with Kaplan & Singer, 1976, for example). Nevertheless, the mid-1970s saw considerable further political action on this question. By 1975, the American Medical Association had passed a resolution against television violence, and the National Parents and Teachers Association had mounted an active campaign to reduce it. The Federal Communications Commission set aside early-evening "family viewing hours" to minimize the amount of violence children would be exposed to.

Ten years later, the Surgeon General again asked the behavioral science community to evaluate the effects of televised violence. This time the reviewing committee was dominated by academic researchers active in the effort to assess the effects of televised violence. They came up with two findings in particular. One was that there had been no reduction in violence on television since the late 1960s, despite all the controversy. Indeed, among the most violent programs on television were weekend shows aimed at children. Second, "the consensus among most of the research community is that violence on television does lead to aggressive behavior by children and teenagers who watch the programs. . . . A causal link between televised violence and aggressive behavior now seems obvious" (National Institutes of Mental Health, 1982, p. 6).

This report met with much approval from many researchers in the field, who had long since become persuaded of the success of this conclusion. The networks issued more skeptical reports. For example, ABC said the conclusions were "unsubstantiated when subjected to scientific analysis" (Walsh, 1983). We might be tempted to dismiss such statements because the networks have a financial stake in having free rein over their own programming. But self-interest does not necessarily mean their statements are unjustified. Nor can we safely assume that social scientists who do research in the area are necessarily unbiased; they may have quite strong preconceptions about the dangers of media violence. So telling the good guys from the bad guys may not be as simple as it might seem.

MEDIA VIOLENCE: THE RESEARCH EVIDENCE

What is the evidence on the effects of media violence? Basically three types of studies have been done: laboratory experiments, correlational surveys, and field experiments. It is perhaps useful to look at all three, both because all can help us understand this particular research question, and because they provide good examples of how different kinds of research get applied to a practical problem.

Laboratory Experiments

Various social psychological theories would argue that violence on television or in the movies increases aggression among those who watch it. Bandura's imitation theory, for example, suggests that it would lead the viewers to engage in imitative aggression. Other learning theories would suggest that media violence presents cues that trigger habitual aggressive responses among viewers. Yet the catharsis theory makes exactly the opposite prediction; it predicts that watching aggression or violence done by others will actually reduce anger among those who are feeling angry. Which is correct?

The strongest early proponent of the catharsis theory in situations involving observed aggression was Seymour Feshbach. He did a pioneering experiment (1961) in which angered and nonangered subjects were shown either a violent boxing film or a neutral film. Measures of aggression taken after the film showed that watching the boxing film lowered the aggressiveness of angered subjects, supporting the catharsis prediction. Observing others involved in aggression seemed to be a way of working through angry feelings, thereby reducing anger and aggressive behavior. But this one demonstration of catharsis stands as an exception in the large body of laboratory studies done on aggression. Practically all the other laboratory studies have shown that watching others' violence actually increases subsequent aggressive behavior. These studies have typically followed one of two procedures.

The imitation experiments done by Bandura using a Bobo doll, as described earlier, represent one type. The point of these experiments was to demonstrate that young children can learn aggressive behavior by imitating the aggressive behavior of adults. Preschool-age children were mildly frustrated, and then they observed an adult batting a Bobo doll around. When the children themselves were placed in the room with the doll, they repeated many of the aggressive behaviors performed by the adult.

A second common type of laboratory experiment has involved showing a brief film embodying violent physical aggression to college students who had either been angered (typically by insult) or not angered. The dependent variable has usually been shock supposedly administered to a confederate, in the standard sham-learning situation. Many of these studies used a seven-minute clip from a boxing film starring Kirk Douglas called *The Champion* (e.g. Berkowitz, 1965). Viewing the violent film generally produced more attacks on a confederate whether or not the subject himself had previously been attacked (e.g., Geen & O'Neal, 1969).

When subjects were told to identify with the winner of the boxing match, they displayed more aggression than did subjects who were told to identify with the judge or were not given any instructions about how to watch. Similarly, in another study the confederate was described as a boxer or as a speech major. A confederate named "Kirk" got more shocks than one named "Bob" after seeing Kirk Douglas play the boxer who got beaten up in the film (Berkowitz & Geen, 1966). When the film presented justified aggression, by presenting the loser of the boxing match in an unfavorable light, more aggression was displayed (see Berkowitz & Rawlings, 1963; Berkowitz & Geen, 1967).

In short, the more similar the subject to the filmed aggressor, or the confederate to the film victim, or the more justified the film violence, the more behavioral aggression shown by the subject. The vast majority of these laboratory experiments have shown that observing aggression provokes greater aggressive behavior, not less. The catharsis effect rarely occurs. Whether one describes the effect as imitating, stimulating, activating, or triggering aggression, the result is the same: In these laboratory experi-

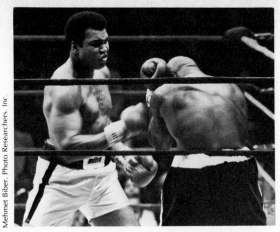

Mehmet Biber, Photo Researchers, Inc.

Relative to other kinds of violence on television, boxing matches are short, mostly composed of sanctioned violence, and depict little that is not violent. However, Muhammed Ali was renowned for his humor, especially his humorous poems, and for a well-publicized protest against the Vietnam War which cost him his world heavyweight championship.

ments, observing aggression produces heightened aggressive behavior.

External Validity

Nevertheless, it is quite a long step from such typical laboratory studies to the real-life situations to which we might want to generalize. These laboratory experiments must be judged, therefore, in terms of their **external validity** (Campbell & Stanley, 1963). External validity asks the question of *generalizability*. Do these laboratory findings hold up in other situations, with other populations, other measures, and other ways of manipulating the same variables? Most important, do they hold up in the real-life situations we are most concerned about?

One way to approach the question of external validity is to see how closely the real-life situation to which we most want to generalize matches the experimental situations we have been studying. The concern about media violence has been expressed most about television, since it is piped free into the home and exposure is virtually uncontrolled (and nearly uncontrollable). Mostly the concern is that male adolescents (who are most responsible for violent crimes) will watch a great deal of violent television, then go out and commit violent crimes.

But these laboratory experiments differ in some very important ways from this real-life situation. Consider the independent variables. The segments presented to subjects are normally very brief, and they are almost entirely composed of a single violent episode, like a few rounds from a boxing match, or an adult beating up a Bobo doll.

In contrast, the normal child in real life spends up to four hours a night watching television and sees a number of different programs. Each program contains quite a mixture of romantic stories, humor, altruistic behavior, heroism, ordinary conversation, and all sorts of other human acts having nothing to do with violence. Even violent cops-and-robbers programs have humor, romantic entanglements, loyalty between cops, scenery, and other nonviolent matters. So instead of the brief, concentrated dose of exposure to violent models typical of experiments, television in real life presents children with a varied diet of all manner of possible behaviors to copy.

Laboratory experiments differ even more from real life in the dependent variable. In virtually all experiments, the subject engages in aggression that is fully sanctioned, and often even prosocial. The Bobo doll experiments involve sanctioned aggression. Children know it is perfectly all right to hit the Bobo doll; nobody will disapprove of them or think they are bad for doing it. Indeed, experiments that show the model being punished for hitting Bobo have produced markedly reduced imitative aggression. Other experiments have used a variant of the sham shock-learning machine. The subject is told she is in a learning experiment and is supposed to punish the victim for errors. This is prosocial aggression. The subject has been instructed to shock the confederate to help increase scientific knowledge.

The concern about aggression in real life, in contrast, focuses exclusively on antisocial aggression. We are worried about unprovoked assaults, armed robbery, assault and battery, rape, and murder. The concern is about the media causing too much antisocial aggression, not too much sanctioned or prosocial aggression.

Laboratory measures of aggression differ from real-life violence in several other ways. There is normally no possibility of retaliation; indeed, where there is, aggression is reduced. Often the aggressive task is fun, novel, and a game; one writer has described Bobo-beating as "solitary aggressive play." A 5-year-old playing with what is obviously a new toy is a far cry from a gang of teenagers holding up a gas station and shooting the manager.

Finally, in these experiments the aggression measure is taken immediately after exposure to the film because any delay would obviously reduce the effect of the film. In fact, it is hard to imagine a seven-minute film clip having an effect that would last more than a couple of hours. Several studies have shown that the effects can wear off within a matter of minutes. But in real life, the boy does not rush out of his living room with a knife and attack the first person he sees. Most crime is committed quite a long time after the person has watched television. People who are roaming the streets are not home watching television; in fact, we might all be safer if they were.

So the external validity of these experiments is open to some question: (1) The film itself tends to be brief and to be composed of pure violence, rather than containing the broad mixture of themes customary in most drama; (2) the viewing situation is controlled and socially isolated, providing few distractions from the violence; (3) the subject's response is measured immediately after the film; (4) the "aggressive" behavior measured is usually prosocial or sanctioned aggression, with the subject knowing he or she is doing no harm to anyone or at least being directly told by the experimenter to perform the "aggressive" response; and (5) there is no likelihood of retaliation. The important point is that all these special conditions of laboratory experiments have themselves been shown to increase aggression. They are likely to present an exaggerated portrait of the aggression inspired by violent films. So to generalize more confidently to real-life situations, we probably need to turn to studies done under conditions that more nearly resemble real life.

Correlational Surveys

One solution to the problem of external validity is to conduct **correlational** surveys to determine whether the children who watch the most violent television are also the ones who are the most aggressive. If they were, the causal interpretation might still be open to question; personal aggressiveness might lead children to watch more violent television, rather than vice versa, or some third variable might produce both a preference for watching violent television and higher levels of personal aggressiveness. But if the correlation between the two was zero, it would be much harder to make a case for the causal role of media violence. So the results from correlational surveys would be valuable, even if not decisive.

Many studies have used children's self-reported television preferences to measure their actual television viewing. Aggressive behavior has been assessed using ratings by peers about how aggressively the children behave. Correlations between the two vary quite widely. In some studies (Eron et al., 1972; Eron, 1982; Huesmann, 1982), there are modest but significant correlations (of around .2), even when viewing preferences are measured some years earlier than the aggression. In other studies, using very similar measures, the correlations are weaker, and generally nonsignificant (Milavsky et al., 1982). Presumably neither set of measures is perfectly reliable. On the average, the correlations tend to be rather weak but usually positive. Moreover, they lend themselves to a variety of causal interpretations. So the correlational studies do not provide strong evidence for a causal role of media violence in producing aggressive behavior in real life.

Field Experiments

A third approach to studying the media-aggression link uses experiments that come closer to matching real-life conditions. To do this, we would want to maintain the experimental variation of exposure to violent, as opposed to neutral or nonviolent, films. But we would want to do it in the context of something more closely resembling the normal media diet of adolescents, and then observe their aggressive behavior in ordinary, day-to-day situations. Such studies are called **field experiments,** because they are done in the individual's natural situation, or in "the field." Only a few major field experiments have been done. The first was conducted by Feshbach and Singer (1971).

Boys in private boarding or state residential schools were randomly assigned to two groups: One group watched largely aggressive television programs such as "Gunsmoke" and "The FBI," while the other group was limited to nonaggressive programs such as the "Ed Sullivan Variety Show" and "Bachelor Father." The boys watched only shows on the designated lists and could watch as much as they wanted as long as they spent at least six hours a week watching television. Various measures of aggressiveness were given before and after the six-week viewing period, and both peers and adult supervisors also rated the boys' aggressiveness.

The results showed that boys in the state schools who watched aggressive programs actually became less aggressive. They engaged in fewer fights and argued less with their peers. The effect was the same but somewhat weaker for the boys in the private schools. This study thus indicates that, at least under some conditions, observing television violence under ordinary conditions might actually decrease aggressive behavior. The explanation offered for this effect follows from the catharsis notion. The children identified with both the heroes and the villains in the programs, and vicariously expressed some of their aggressive feelings.

On the other hand, it must be noted that the effect could be due to the fact that boys who were limited to the nonaggressive programs might have been annoyed because they were not allowed to watch their favorite television shows. A very similar study by Wells (1973) found that violent versus nonviolent television diets made very little difference. Despite these complications, these studies do attempt to test how ordinary television affects aggressiveness, and they do suggest that the effect may not be to increase it.

Three other studies were done in minimum-security penal institutions for juvenile offenders in the United States and Belgium (Leyens et al., 1975; Parke et al., 1977). After a week of observation, the boys in some living cottages were shown violent movies (*Iwo Jima, Bonnie and Clyde*), while boys in other cottages were shown neutral films (*Lily, Daddy's Fiancée*). In the Belgian study, two cottages saw an aggressive film every night for a week, and two saw a neutral film every night. In the first U.S. study, one cottage watched a violent film every night for a week, and another saw a neutral film. In the second U.S. study, one cottage saw a violent film each night for five nights, and another saw a neutral film; a third cottage saw one violent film one night, and the last cottage saw just one neutral film on one occasion. Then the boys' behavior was observed for an additional week.

These studies found little evidence that violent films increased aggressiveness. The Belgian study found an increase in overall aggressiveness immediately after the film for one cottage but not the other, though even this increase had disappeared by the next day. The first American study also found a greater increase in aggressiveness immediately after violent than nonviolent films, but the second found little difference, and neither found any cumulative or lasting effects of exposure.

Friedrich and Stein (1973) put nursery school children on a diet of twelve violent cartoons (*Batman, Superman*), or prosocial entertainment (*Mister Rogers*) or neutral films (e.g., about nature) for a period of four weeks. They were carefully observed by trained observers. They had three measures of aggression, and five others of good classroom behavior (rule obedience, delay tolerance, task persistence, cooperation, and prosocial behavior). The groups differed significantly on at most two of these eight measures, so the effect of the filmed violence cannot have been very great.

A somewhat different set of studies was done by Milgram and Shotland (1973). They prepared special versions of a prime-time television show—"Medical Center"—that included illegal (but nonviolent) acts. Three different versions of the episode were prepared. For example, in one, the protagonist smashes several charity-drive collection boxes, steals the money, and escapes to Mexico. Subjects viewed the program in a theater, and then were offered a free radio if they would show up at a downtown office a week later. At the office, there was a sign saying there were no more radios, and there was a charity donation box containing some money, including a $1 bill sticking partway out. Concealed TV cameras coded whether or not the subject took the dollar. Viewers of different versions did not differ. Seven experiments were done in this general style, and none showed any effect of viewing illegal acts.

Each of these studies has its flaws. As was pointed out before, in the Feshbach-Singer and the Wells studies, the adolescent boys in the nonviolent conditions were deprived of their normal favorite programs. This frustration could by itself have increased their aggressiveness, thus eliminating any possible differences between the violent and nonviolent conditions.

The Leyens, Parke and associates studies used group-viewing situations in dormitories where boys in prison had been living together for some time. This was perhaps a little like watching movies in a fraternity (except with juvenile delinquents instead of college boys), and it evidently stimulated a good bit of rowdiness during and right after the movies. But this rowdy-group context is not the usual one for TV viewing in the home. The Milgram-Shotland studies were at the mercy of the idiosyncrasies of their specific versions of "Medical Center," and in most cases so little stealing emerged that it would have been hard for anything at all to influence it enough to be detectable.

But all studies in social science are flawed. It is a myth that a perfect study can be devised. The minute we patch up one problem, another emerges (often created by the patch, in fact). The way to come to a conclusion about an important area of research is to look at the pattern of the data. The effects of these violent versus nonviolent TV field experiments are not very dramatic. Feshbach and Singer get diminished aggression from the violent diet, but only in one set of schools. The studies by Wells, Friedrich, and Stein, and Milgram and Shotland show no strong results. Parke and colleagues find increased aggression in some cottages, but it does not last and may be an effect more of group contagion than individual arousal. Milgram and Shotland get no differences in seven experiments. So it is difficult to see a very powerful effect of movie or TV violence on aggressive behavior leaping out at us from these field studies. Rather, observed violence in movies or television seems not to affect aggressive behavior much in these real-life situations, one way or the other.

Sexual Violence

So far, our discussion of the effects of media violence has focused on films that show murders, beatings, and other gruesome forms of aggression. A related area of interest concerns the effects of sexually explicit materials on aggressive behavior. Does pornography, and perhaps especially violent erotica, increase sex crimes, antisocial behavior, or aggression more generally? The interest in this question derives partly from a concern that sexual content in films, books, and magazines makes men more violent toward women. But as a theoretical question it bears on the same underlying processes as the effects of witnessed aggression: the stimulation of violent behavior by media content.

In the late 1960s, President Lyndon Johnson appointed a Commission on Obscenity and Pornography. After a careful review of the research evidence, the committee reported (1970) that it could document no antisocial effects of pornography. The growing availability of pornography in the United States and Europe was not associated with a rise in sex crimes (relative to other crimes). Juvenile delinquents seemed to have no more experience with pornography than did their peers. The early background of sex offenders was generally sexually repressive and restrictive, not permissive. Antisocial aggression among young men is more heavily influenced by peers than by the media. This report therefore suggested that early socialization and peer influence, rather than pornography, were the key factors in antisocial sexual aggression.

As might be expected, the matter did not rest there. Politically conservative and religious groups immediately attacked the commission's conclusions. Later, feminists too criticized these conclusions, arguing that some types of pornography degrade women and do encourage sexual violence (see Diamond, 1980; Lederer, 1980).

Feminists emphasized a distinction between acceptable erotica and violent or coercive pornography. For example, Gloria Steinem, the feminist editor of *Ms. Magazine,* said: "Look at any photo or film of people . . . really making love . . . there is usually a sensuality and touch and warmth. . . . a sense of shared pleasure. [But] look at any depiction of sex in which there is clear force, or an unequal power that spells coercion. It may be very blatant, with weapons of torture or bondage, wounds and bruises, some clear humiliation. . . . there is no sense of equal choice or equal power" (1980, p. 37). Feminists argued that aggressive pornography had increased sharply during the 1970s. This opened the possibility that the commission's findings were limited to the effects of "soft core'' or nonaggressive pornography, and were not applicable to ''hard core'' or violent pornography.

Such observations have led to a resurgence of research on the possible effects of violent pornography on aggressive behavior (see Malamuth & Donnerstein, 1982). The central question is whether or not aggressive pornography produces more behavioral aggression than either nonaggressive pornography or nonsexual violence alone. That is, is there something special about the *mixture* of violence and sexual themes that triggers unusual levels of aggression against women? There is particular concern about pornography that depicts violent or coercive sex and that shows the female victim as enjoying the experience, since this is thought to be one stereotype which may incite men to rape.

As might be expected, depictions of rape produce more aggressive fantasies than do mutually consenting versions of a sexual encounter (Malamuth, 1981). And men become more sexually aroused when women are depicted as consenting in a sex scene than when they are shown as abhorring the experience. Numerous studies have also shown that viewing violent sexuality produces more accepting attitudes about violence against women. It also leads to accepting such myths as that women often enjoy being raped or being forced to perform various sexual acts. For example, Malamuth and Check (1981) compared the effects of viewing the films *Swept Away* and *The Getaway,* both showing women as victims of erotic and nonerotic aggression, with those of viewing more neutral films. The more aggressive films increased males', but not females', acceptance of violence against women. This study was particularly useful because the viewing students' attitudes were measured in regular class sessions, so they were not aware of being subjects in an experiment. In these several ways, then, view-

---

BOX 10–7
Legislating against Pornography: The Issues

Feminist activists argue that if pornography is harmful, the victims must have some legal recourse. A city ordinance passed by the city council in Minneapolis in early 1984 was based on just this legal theory. Its supporters believed that pornography is central to "creating and maintaining the inequality of the sexes . . . just being a woman means you are injured by pornography." They defined pornography as "the sexually explicit subordination of women" in one or more of nine specific ways, such as presenting women who "experience sexual pleasure in being raped or mutilated." The ordinance would have allowed any woman who was the victim of sexual violence to sue magazine publishers or movie theater operators, and indeed it would have been possible for any woman to sue those involved in distributing and selling pornography. The ordinance was finally vetoed by the mayor, a man with a long history of commitment to liberal causes, partly because of his concern about the violation of free speech. Such a proposal raises a number of issues that are worth thinking about. How clear is the evidence that pornography does harm to women in general? What are the permissible limits on free speech? Should men who contribute indirectly to sexual violence be held responsible for it?

ing violent erotica seems to induce more sexually aggressive fantasies and attitudes.

The key, though, is whether or not violent pornography increases behavioral aggression. The best studies have used films and some variant of the sham teacher-learner aggression procedure. A confederate makes the subject angry (or does not), the subject is exposed to some erotic pictures, literature, or films, and then is assigned to the teacher role with instructions to shock that confederate. Donnerstein's aggressive-erotic (1980) film contained black and white scenes in which a man with a gun forces himself into a woman's home and coerces her into having sexual intercourse with him. The Donnerstein-Berkowitz (1981) version depicts a young woman who comes into view, apparently to study with two men. They have been drinking, and she is forced to sit between them and drink. They then tie her up, strip her clothes off, slap her around, and rape her.

A number of such studies have shown that violent pornography produces more such aggression than does nonviolent pornography (see Malamuth & Donnerstein, 1982; Donnerstein, 1980; Donnerstein & Berkowitz, 1981).

However, this comparison of violent and nonviolent pornography adds little to the laboratory experiments on media violence discussed above. It shows that viewing violent films produces more aggression than viewing nonviolent films, in laboratory experiments. It does not deal with the possibly unique effects of witnessing *sexual* violence. More relevant to this point is a study comparing males viewing this aggressive pornographic film with males who viewed an aggressive but *non*pornographic film (Donnerstein, 1983). In the latter film, the woman is tied up and slapped around, but there is no nudity or even simulated sexual activity. The two films were perceived as similar in aggressiveness, but quite different in sexuality. When subjects were angered by a female and then viewed the aggressive pornography film, they gave more intense shocks to a confederate than in any other condition.

Other Possible Effects of Media Violence

The potential role of media violence is not limited to imitative aggression, however. A number of other questions can readily be raised. Why is there so much violence in movies and television? Is it because of some compelling interest viewers have in violent content? Furthermore, watching violence may have effects other than allegedly stimulating violent behavior. We may become so accustomed to the sight of violence that it no longer offends us or shocks us. On the other hand, being confronted at close range with the vicious things that people do to each other may make us more resolved than ever to turn this into a peaceful world.

It was argued that the comprehensive television coverage of the Vietnam war (the "first televised war") hastened public condemnation of the war and ultimately helped remove our armed forces from it. Some observers fear that even nonviolent erotic literature, pictorial magazines, and movies provide yet another stimulant to violence, especially against women. In all these cases, research is so preliminary as only to be suggestive. But it is perhaps worth seeing what can be said at the moment about these other possibilities.

PUBLIC INTEREST IN VIOLENCE   Is violence especially interesting and exciting to people? Apparently not for its own sake. Violent programs do not get markedly higher ratings than nonviolent programs (Comstock, 1982, p. 109). Diener and De Four (1978) did content analysis ratings of television programs for violence, drama, humor, and action. Then they correlated these qualities with the relative popularity of various programs. They found humor and action were crucial determinants of popularity, but violence was not.

Angry, aggressive people may prefer more violence in their films, however. Fenigstein (1979) induced subjects to have aggressive fantasies or to behave aggressively using the sham teacher-learner procedure, and found they were more likely to want to watch film clips that featured violence, such as rioting at a rock concert, fist fights, and so on.

DESENSITIZATION TO VIOLENCE Media violence is also thought by some observers to desensitize viewers to any later real-life violence. The argument is that when you watch people being killed and maimed and beaten up on television, you become accustomed to the sight of violence, and it therefore no longer upsets you as much. Ultimately, it is argued, you yourself will be more willing to hurt other people, or at least you will be less likely to step in to prevent violence in real life.

The argument implies a two-stage sequence. It first suggests that the constant sight of media violence reduces our emotional response to it later in the real world. Then, second, this lower emotional responsivity should reduce our tendency to stop aggression in real life. There is a little evidence of at least short-term reductions in emotional arousal. Physiological arousal during violent films was reduced by exposure to a prior eleven-minute excerpt from a television police series (Thomas et al., 1977), or among children who are especially heavy television viewers (Cline, Croft, and Courrier, 1973). But it is not yet clear that such exposure reduces the tendency to help stop aggression.

SPORTS EVENTS Some people argue that sports events help spectators relieve their everyday frustrations by allowing them to yell, cheer, boo, and root for their favorite teams. Sports events, they say, are cathartic because they allow people to reduce their tensions in a vicarious, playful manner that hurts no one. Others argue that the moblike atmosphere of sports events reduces people's inhibitions to aggression or leads them to imitate aggressive behavior (particularly in violent sports like hockey, boxing, and football).

Sometimes terrible violence occurs after sports events. In Guatemala in 1977, for example, soccer fans of the losing team attacked the fans of the winning team with machetes and hacked five persons to death (Arms, Russell, & Sandilands, 1979).

To test whether sports events increase aggression in spectators, Goldstein and Arms (1971) and Arms and associates (1979) gave spectators paper-and-pencil tests of hostility before and after a football game, a hockey match, a professional wrestling match (all having a high degree of physical aggression), and a gymnastics meet and a swimming meet (neither of which present much aggression). On some tests, watching violent sports seemed to increase irritability and hostility more than did watching the nonviolent ones. However, the effects were not very marked.

NONVIOLENT EROTICA Exposure to nonviolent erotica turns out to increase violent behavior, at least under one set of limited conditions: when subjects are angry to start with; the erotic materials are extremely explicit, realistic, "hardcore" pornography; and the predominant affect experienced by the subject is negative (disgust or distaste).

For example, Donnerstein (and Barrett, 1978; Donnerstein and Hallam, 1978) had his confederates shock male subjects. Then he showed them some hard-core black-and-white stag films depicting oral and anal intercourse and female homosexuality. Such subjects shocked the offending confederate more than did nonangered subjects, or subjects shown no film or a neutral wildlife documentary. Similar findings were reported by Jaffe et al. (1974), who used highly explicit literary passages (though their subjects were not first angered).

However, almost any form of erotica less explicit than "hard-core" or "blue movies" seems not to increase aggression, and indeed often actually *reduces* aggression below normal levels (that is, below the levels of no-film or neutral-film control groups). For example, viewing still colored pictures of nude women or of sexual intercourse tended to reduce aggression below normal levels (Baron & Bell, 1977; Donnerstein et al., 1975). In at least one case, this reduction was greatest for previously angered subjects (Zillmann & Sapolsky, 1977).

There is some debate about why nonviolent erotica has such different effects. One possibility is that the "hard-core" material may itself be rather frustrating, because it is too arousing for the etiquette of the psychological experiment situation. Or, the more common, milder "soft core" material may be distracting from the original anger-arousing provocation by the confederate. Most likely, though, the more "hard core" material is inherently not very pleasant to most subjects. Indeed White (1979) has shown that college students find pictures of same-sex masturbation or mutual oral-genital contact much less pleasant than more common forms of pictorial erotica, such as conventional intercourse and lovemaking.

And he argues, rather persuasively, that erotica decreases aggression when it produces positive feelings, though it may increase aggression somewhat when it produces a negative effect. So presumably any erotic materials that depict sex in an ugly, disgusting way would be more likely to inspire aggression than would materials that are more artistic, and/or present acts the subjects themselves feel comfortable looking at. Indeed, he argues that any such pleasurable experience, whether or not it concerns sex, would have the same aggression-suppressing effect.

Conclusions

The effects of media violence have become one of the most passionate and most political of research topics in social psychology. Some researchers work for the television networks, and their conclusions are suspected (rightly or wrongly) of being influenced by the networks' interests in absolving themselves of any blame for violence in our society. On the other hand, many academic researchers approach the topic with a passionate desire to expose what they regard as a serious social ill, and it is hard to imagine that their research is any more disinterested.

But the real question is not what biases the researchers approach the topic with, because few scientists are ever completely free of some preconception or another. The major question is how the evidence really stacks up.

We have discussed three different methods of researching the effects of media violence. Laboratory studies seem quite generally to show that observed violence increases aggressive behavior. But these studies have been conducted in such a way that they may not be especially applicable to real-life instances of antisocial violence. For the reasons given earlier, we do not have much confidence in generalizing from these laboratory studies to crime in the streets.

Most correlational surveys find a modest positive association between children's liking for violent television programs and various indicators of their behavioral aggression. However, these relationships are never very strong, and in some of the best studies are not even statistically significant.

The field experiments we have described come much closer to realistic replicas of real life. They have presented the typical movie and television fare of the day to male adolescents living in their normal life situations (though most of these have been in boarding schools, rather than living at home with their parents). They have measured genuine interpersonal aggression in a free, unconstrained atmosphere. However, these studies have generally shown that media violence has little or no systematic effect on interpersonal aggression. Some show a modest, temporary increase in aggression. Others show a debatable decrease in it. But on balance there is no major impact one way or the other. Therefore, it seems correct to say that at the moment the field experiments also show media violence having little impact.

From a policy point of view, the question is whether the evidence is strong enough to urge the suppression of certain kinds of entertainment programs in order to reduce crime and violence. There are social conditions we all know are important in producing violence, such as unemployment, racial prejudice, poor housing, poor medical care (especially for people with mental health problems), the widespread availability of guns and alcohol and illegal drugs, a highly mobile population that does not settle into tight little self-policing communities, and parental indifference to the welfare of their children, among many other things. It seems to us that, at most, television and the movies could contribute only a small amount above and beyond such large social factors.

And we must be very careful about censorship of any kind. Today the government might decide that it is illegal to depict a knifing on television; tomorrow some censor may decide that it is illegal to depict an adulterous act, because people might imitate that; and the next day a censor may decide that it is illegal to depict pro-test demonstrations. Once the principle of censorship is accepted, it becomes harder and harder to draw the line.

So it is no idle academic matter, this business of the effects of media violence on interpersonal aggressiveness. We should recognize that no matter how passionately we feel about the issue, we must be cautious about taking a stand before we have sufficient evidence. It is fair to say that most psychologists today believe TV violence does generally increase aggressiveness. In our opinion, however, the actual empirical evidence is weak and has not shown a role of media violence in increasing crime. At this time there would seem not to be sufficient positive evidence to justify imposing restrictions on entertainment programs.

SUMMARY

1. Aggression is defined as an action that hurts another person, and that is perceived as intended to do so.
2. Aggressive acts can be antisocial, prosocial, or merely sanctioned, depending on whether they violate or conform with social norms.
3. Aggressive feelings, or anger, need to be distinguished from aggressive behavior.
4. The major determinants of anger seem to be attack and frustration.
5. Frustrations that are not attributed to intent on the part of the frustrator do not create as much anger. Generalized, nonspecific arousal states can result in experienced anger if they are accompanied by the appropriate cognitive labels.
6. Aggressive behavior has as its major determinants angry feelings and the learning of aggressive responses. This learning can take place through direct reinforcement of aggressive responses or through imitation.
7. Social norms are crucial in determining what aggressive habits are learned.
8. Fear of punishment or retaliation can reduce aggressive behavior. However it may sometimes result instead in covert aggression, or actually increase aggression over the longer run.
9. Learned inhibitions of aggression are the most important control over it. Anxiety can be associated with the expression of aggression in general, or with its expression in quite specific contexts. Most people reduce their aggression when they see signs of pain in others. Such inhibitions can also result in the displacement of aggression to other innocent parties, and to the scapegoating of members of minority groups.
10. Direct aggression against an attacker or frustrator can reduce aggressive feelings through the process of catharsis. However, this too depends on perceiving the tormentor as the responsible agent.
11. Observed aggression generally increases aggression in laboratory studies, whether they are done with small children, adolescents, or adults. It is especially potent in increasing aggression when the model is rewarded or when the observed victim is similar to the target of the subject's own aggression.
12. Field experiments of televised or movie violence, on the other hand, have not generally shown that it increases aggressive behavior in real-life settings. Therefore the laboratory studies of observed aggression may not generalize to real-life situations. The evidence that media violence contributes to violence and crime in our society is still rather indirect.

SUGGESTIONS FOR ADDITIONAL READING

BANDURA A. (1973). *Aggression: A social learning analysis.* Englewood Cliffs, N.J.: Prentice-Hall. The definitive statement by the most influential spokesman for the social learning and imitation approach to aggression.

BARON, R. A. (1977). *Human aggression.* New York: Plenum Press. A thorough, readable, comprehensive treatment of aggression from a social-psychological perspective.

COMSTOCK, G., CHAFFEE, S., DATZMAN, N., McCOMBS, M., & ROBERTS, D. (1978). *Television and human behavior.* New York: Columbia University Press. A conscientious review of research on the effects of television, concerning aggression, politics, advertising, and other areas.

DOLLARD, J., DOOB, L., MILLER, N. E., MOWRER, O. H., & SEARS, R. R. (1939). *Frustration and aggression.* New Haven: Yale University Press. The original statement of the theory that frustration breeds aggression. As well as discussing their laboratory experiments, it ranges far into the larger social manifestations of aggression, such as criminality, war, and fascism.

FREUD, S. (1955). *Civilization and its discontents.* London: Hogarth Press, first published 1930. The classic exposition of how civilization must deal with aggressive instincts. One of Freud's most brilliant and influential critiques of society.

NATIONAL INSTITUTE OF MENTAL HEALTH. (1982). *Television and behavior: Ten years of scientific progress and implications for the eighties.* Rockville, Md. This is the follow-up report on the effects of television, following all the research done in the ten years since the Surgeon General's original report. It is a useful summary, though influenced by the authors' own perspectives.

SEARS, D. O., & McCONAHAY, J. B. (1973). *The politics of violence: The new urban blacks and the Watts riot.* Boston: Houghton-Mifflin. A social-psychological analysis of the causes of ghetto riots.

SURGEON GENERAL'S SCIENTIFIC ADVISORY COMMITTEE ON TELEVISION AND SOCIAL BEHAVIOR. (1972). *Television and growing up: The impact of televised violence* (Report to the Surgeon General, U.S. Public Health Service, U.S. Department of Health, Education, and Welfare, Publication NHSM 72-9090). Rockville, Md.: National Institute of Mental Health. This was the report that created such furor.

11

ALTRUISM AND PROSOCIAL BEHAVIOR

On January 21, 1984, 11-year-old Timothy Diakis ran to the burning apartment next door to rescue his 83-year-old neighbor. Awakened from sleep and clad only in his underwear, the young boy crawled on his hands and knees through the smoke-filled apartment to reach the bedroom where the woman he called "Grandma" was trapped. He pulled her to the floor where a few pockets of air remained, and then tried desperately to lead her to safety. As they made their way toward the exit, they faced flames creeping down the hallway. Overcome by smoke at last, Timothy and Sarah Sherman lapsed into unconsciousness just as fire engines arrived. Firefighters wearing protective masks and clothing ultimately rescued both and rushed them to a nearby hospital. Sarah suffered minor injuries, but Timothy spent months in the hospital undergoing skin grafts for severe burns. Firefighters say Sarah would have died had the youngster not rushed in and dragged her at least part way to safety. When newspaper accounts

Charles Cocaine, Photo Researchers, Inc.

The bravery of firefighters risking their lives to save others contrasts vividly with scenes of people ignoring the plight of those in need of help.

an Lukas, Photo Researchers, Inc.

of the story reported that the family had no medical insurance, readers moved by the boy's altruism sent more than $50,000 in donations to help pay his expensive medical bills.

Acts of altruism and public generosity such as this stand in stark contrast to stories of public apathy to the plight of victims. In Chapter 1 we recounted the tragic story of Kitty Genovese, a young woman stabbed to death on a city street while at least 38 people watched and did nothing. There are countless stories of this sort. People are beaten, raped, robbed, and killed while those who could give assistance stand by. Clearly, humans are capable of helping or ignoring others in distress. Why do people sometimes help another? And why, sometimes, do they fail to give badly needed assistance?

BASIC DEFINITIONS

Before trying to answer this question, let us be clear about what we mean by altruism and prosocial behavior. **Altruism** refers to an act performed voluntarily to help someone else when there is no expectation of receiving a reward in any form (except perhaps a feeling of having done a good deed). By this definition, whether or not an act is altruistic depends on the intentions of the helper. The stranger who risks his own life to pull a victim from a burning car and then vanishes anonymously into the night has performed an altruistic act.

Prosocial behavior is a broader category: It includes any act that helps or is designed to help others, regardless of the helper's motives. Many types of prosocial behavior are not altruistic. For example, if you give a hefty contribution to your boss's favorite charity in the hope of making a favorable impression and getting a raise, you are not acting altruistically in the pure sense. Prosocial behavior ranges over a continuum from the most selfless acts of altruism to helpful acts motivated entirely by self-interest (Rushton, 1980). We will focus on the altruistic end of the scale—situations where the immediate rewards for helping are minimal.

THEORETICAL PERSPECTIVES

Our understanding of altruistic behavior has benefitted from three broad theoretical perspectives. Some theorists have emphasized the historical roots of this behavior. Sociobiologists propose that a predisposition to help has become part of our genetic, evolutionary heritage. A contrasting historical view is that rules about helping others in need have developed as part of the history of human civilization. A second approach proposes that helping is affected, sometimes subtly, by basic principles of reinforcement and modeling. The third perspective, decision-making, focuses on the processes that influence our judgments about when help is needed. It also emphasizes the weighing of costs and benefits in the decision to give help.

Historical Roots

Prosocial behavior is not an invention of the twentieth century. Two contrasting analyses of historical forces that may have encouraged altruism are offered by sociobiology and social evolution.

BOX 11–1
Prosocial Behavior Is Part of Everyday Life

Prosocial behavior is a part of daily life, a fact documented by much psychological research. Helping activities can be seen even in young children. Strayer, Wareing, and Rushton (1979) observed children ages 3 to 5 at play in a university preschool. On average, each child engaged in 15 helpful acts per hour, ranging from giving a toy to another child, comforting an upset friend, or helping a teacher.

In a midwestern American city, over half of women shoppers were willing to give 40 cents for bus fare to a university student who explained that his wallet had "disappeared" (Berkowitz, 1972). In New York City, most pedestrians responded positively to requests for help from a passerby. Eighty-five percent of New Yorkers gave the time of day, 85 percent gave directions, and 73 percent gave change for a quarter (Latané & Darley, 1970). In another study on the streets of New York, 50 percent of people who found a wallet that had been "lost" mailed it back to its owner (Hornstein, Fisch, & Holmes, 1968).

Prosocial behavior even occurs on city subways. When a passenger (actually a researcher) fell down with an apparent knee injury, 83 percent of those in the subway car offered assistance (Latané & Darley, 1970). In another subway study, a researcher pretending to be physically disabled repeatedly fell down and always received help (Piliavin, Rodin, & Piliavin, 1969).

In all these examples, people show a willingness to be helpful, even to strangers. We seem to help or respond to appeals for ordinary or small favors very easily.

SOCIOBIOLOGY Scientists have long observed prosocial behavior among animal species. Charles Darwin (1871) noted that rabbits will make noise with their hind feet to warn other rabbits of predators. In termite hives, the soldier termites will defend a nest against an intruder by putting themselves in front of the other termites and exposing themselves to danger (Wilson, 1971). Many soldiers die so that others may live and the nest survive. Some varieties of baboon have a characteristic pattern of responding to threats (Hall, 1960). The dominant males take the most exposed positions, and may even rush at an intruder. As the tribe moves away from the threat, the males risk their own safety by remaining to protect the rest of the group.

Dolphins show a fascinating pattern of rescuing injured peers. Since dolphins are mammals, they must breathe air to survive. If an injured animal sinks below the surface, it will die. Several observers have reported that dolphins will aid an injured companion. In one case (Siebenaler & Caldwell, 1956), a dolphin was stunned by an explosion in the water. Two other adults came to its aid by holding the animal afloat until it recovered and was able to care for itself.

Among many animals, parents will sacrifice themselves when their young are threatened. An impressive example is the female nighthawk, which responds to a potential attack on her young by flying from the nest as if she had a broken wing, fluttering around at a low level, and finally landing on the ground right in front of the intruder but away from the nest (Armstrong, 1965; Gramza, 1967).

This portrait of animals helping and sacrificing for each other runs counter to the dog-eat-dog, survival of the fittest image that some people have of the animal kingdom. Indeed, the existence of altruism has posed a problem for evolutionary theorists: if the most helpful members of an animal species sacrifice themselves for others, they will be less likely to survive and pass along their genes to the next generation by having offspring. How then does a biological predisposition to act altruistically persist among animals or humans (Hoffman, 1981)?

To understand the paradox, we need to review some basic ideas in **sociobiology.** This relatively new field uses evolutionary theory to explain social behavior in animals. Any genetically determined trait that has high survival value (that helps the individual survive) will tend to be passed on. This happens because the individual with the trait is more likely to survive than one without the trait and so produces more offspring, each of whom will tend to have the trait and will in turn be more likely to survive and reproduce, and so on. Eventually, individuals with genes that carry this trait will grow more numerous than those without those genes, and will come to dominate the species.

Giraffes with genes that give them longer necks are better able to reach scarce food; they produce more young giraffes than those who have shorter necks. After many generations, we have giraffes with very long necks. However, necks that are too long are awkward; these animals tend to die out. The species thus comes to be dominated by animals whose necks are just long enough for them to reach the food. Of course, this process takes many generations, and sometimes the environment changes in the meantime and a trait that was useful at one time becomes less useful later. But the principle that useful characteristics dominate less useful ones generally holds.

This principle is easy to understand when it involves individual survival. Obviously, if an animal lives longer and is healthier, it will produce more healthy young and its genes will be carried on. Sociobiologists such as Edmund Wilson (1975) suggest that the same principle can also apply when the particular individual's own survival is threatened by its genetically determined behavior.

In the case of altruism, the tendency to help others has high survival value for the individual's genes, but not necessarily for the individual. Imagine a bird that has fathered six chicks. Half of the genes in each chick come from the father. Together, the six chicks have three times as many of the father's genes as he does himself. If the father sacrifices himself to save the chicks, his particular gene pool is still ahead of the game. Similar analyses can be done for other relatives who have varying percentages of the individual's genes.

Sociobiologist Robert Trivers (1971) has argued that only mutual or *reciprocal altruism* is biologically based. In his view, the potential costs of altruism to the individual are offset by the possibility of receiving help from others. But such a system of mutual help giving is threatened by potential "cheaters" who accept help but offer none in return. To minimize cheating, natural selection may have favored a disposition to feel guilt and a tendency to enforce mutual helping through social means such as punishing those who do not follow group rules.

One good feature of the sociobiological approach is that it leads to testable predictions. For example, animals should be most altruistic to those who are genetically most closely linked to themselves. They should be more helpful to immediate family than to distant relatives or strangers. The theory also predicts that parents will behave more altruistically to healthy offspring than to unhealthy ones who are less likely to survive. A further prediction is that mothers will be more altruistic to their offspring than will fathers. The reasoning here is that males have the biological potential to sire a great many offspring and so can perpetuate their genes without investing much in any one infant. Females can produce only a relatively small number of offspring, and so must help each of these young to thrive to ensure the survival of the mother's genes.

The idea that altruism is a genetically determined part of "human nature" is quite controversial. To date, research has largely been conducted with animals other than humans. Just how well the theory applies to people is still an open question. What this perspective suggests, however, is that self-preservation may not be the overwhelming motive that we sometimes think. Biological dispositions to aggression may coexist with biological dispositions to altruism.

SOCIAL EVOLUTION Critics of sociobiology argue that social factors are much more important than biology in determining prosocial behavior. Donald Campbell (1975) suggests that genetic evolution may help explain a few basic prosocial behaviors such as parents' caring for their young, but that it does not apply to more extreme instances of helping a stranger in distress. Such cases are better explained by what Campbell calls *social evolution*—the historical development of human culture or civilization. In this view, human societies have gradually and selectively evolved skills, beliefs, and technologies that promote the welfare of the group. Because prosocial behavior is generally beneficial to society, it has become part of the social rules or norms. Three norms in particular may be most important for prosocial behavior: social responsibility, reciprocity, and social justice.

A **norm of social responsibility** prescribes that we should help others who depend on us. Parents are expected to care for their children, and social agencies may intervene if parents fail to live up to this obligation. Teachers are supposed to help their students, coaches to look after team members, and co-workers to assist each other. The religious and moral codes of many societies emphasize the duty to help others. Sometimes this obligation is even written into the law.

The state of Minnesota recently enacted a statute requiring that "Any person at the scene of an emergency who knows that another person is exposed to or has suffered grave physical harm shall, to the extent that he can do so without danger or peril to himself or others, give reasonable assistance to the exposed person." Laws are one way of emphasizing to people that they have a responsibility to help. Later in this chapter we will review studies documenting the fact that an increased sense of personal responsibility does indeed increase the likelihood of an individual's giving assistance.

The **norm of reciprocity** says that we should help those who help us. Several studies (Berkowitz, 1968; Wilke & Lanzetta, 1970) have shown that people are more likely to help someone from whom they have already gotten aid. A study by Regan (1968) illustrated this idea that favors are reciprocated. College students were tested in pairs, one partner actually being a confederate of the experimenter. The study was described as dealing with perceptual and esthetic judgment. The subjects were put in separate rooms, shown a series of pictures, and asked to rate how much they liked each picture. After they had rated one series of pictures, there was a short break. The subjects were told they could do what they wanted as long as they did not talk about the experiment.

At this point, the confederate got up, left the building, and returned several minutes later carrying two bottles of Coke. He handed one to the subject, saying "I asked him [the experimenter] if I could get myself a Coke and he said it was okay, so I brought one for you, too." The subject took the Coke, and the experimenter gave them a second series of pictures to rate. In another condition, the experimenter went out, returned with two Cokes, and handed one to the confederate and one to the subject, saying: "I brought you guys a Coke." In the third condition, no Coke was given to the subject.

After the second series of pictures was rated, there was another short break, during which the confederate asked the experimenter (loud enough for the subject to hear) whether he could send a note to the subject. The experimenter said that he could as long as it did not concern the experiment. The confederate then wrote the following note:

> Would you do me a favor? I'm selling raffle tickets for my high school back home to build a new gym. The tickets cost 25 cents each and the prize is a new Corvette. The thing is, if I sell the most tickets I get 50 bucks and I could use it. If you'd buy any, would you just write the number on this note and give it back to me right away so I can make out the tickets? Any would help, the more the better. Thanks. (Regan, 1968, p. 19)

The measure of helping was how many tickets the subject agreed to buy. The results are shown in Table 11–1. When the confederate gave the subject a Coke and then asked him to do a favor, there was considerably more helping than when the experimenter gave the subject a Coke or when no Coke was given. Helping in the latter two conditions did not differ appreciably.

The reciprocity norm seems to be quite strong and has been shown to operate in many cultures (Gergen et al., 1975). The strength of feelings of obligation is influenced by factors in the situation. For example, Greenberg and Frisch (1972) found that a larger favor was reciprocated more often than a smaller one. People's attributions about the motives of the helper also matter. Returning a favor is more likely when the original help was perceived to be given intentionally and voluntarily. Goranson and Berkowitz (1966) found that subjects who had been helped by someone tended to repay that specific person, but were not especially likely to offer aid to someone else.

Human groups also develop **norms of social justice,** rules about fairness and the just distribution of resources. One common fairness principle is equity. According to this principle, two people who make equal contributions to a task should receive equal rewards. If one receives more than the other, the people will feel pressure to try to restore equity by redistributing the rewards. The short-changed person obviously feels aggrieved. The more interesting fact is that even the person who receives more than a fair share may give some to the person who got too little. And a third person, observing the unfair

Table 11–1 Effect of Doing a Favor on Helping	
CONDITION	MEAN NUMBER OF TICKETS BOUGHT
Confederate gave Coke	1.73
Experimenter gave Coke	1.08
No Coke	.92
Source: Adapted from Regan (1968).	

Animals other than humans also help each other. Here, one monkey is grooming another, perhaps because it expects to be groomed in return.

one member of a team, given more than his partner, tended to give some of the money to the partner in order to make their rewards more equitable. In addition, the overrewarded partner often chose to play a different game when assured that this would result in a more equal division of the rewards. In other words, not only did he give away some of his own money to produce a more equitable division, but he also changed the situation to avoid producing more inequity.

These three norms—social responsibility, reciprocity, and social justice—are common in human societies. They provide a cultural basis for prosocial behavior. Through the process of socialization, individuals learn these rules and come to behave in accord with these guidelines for prosocial behavior.

Learning to Help

A second perspective on prosocial behavior emphasizes the importance of learning. In growing up, children learn their society's norms about helping. At home, at school, and in the community, adults teach children that they should help other people. You can probably remember times when you were praised for being helpful, or chided for forgetting to help when you should have. Two general learning principles discussed in earlier chapters are again important here. People learn to help through *reinforcement,* the effects of rewards and punishment for helping, and *modeling,* observing others who help.

Studies show clearly that children will help and share more when they are rewarded for their prosocial behavior. For example, 4-year-olds were more likely to share marbles with another child when they were rewarded with bubblegum for their generosity (Fischer, 1963). A study of sixth-grade girls (Midlarsky, Bryan, & Brickman, 1973) showed the impact of seeing a helpful model. Girls played a special pinball machine to win chips that could be exchanged for

situation, might be tempted to give to the one who suffered. Everyday acts of "helping the less fortunate" such as donating to a charity seem to be motivated by a desire to create a more equitable situation.

Numerous studies have demonstrated that overbenefitted people will act to restore equity when they can (Walster, Walster, & Berscheid, 1978). In several experiments (Berscheid & Walster, 1967), subjects played a game in which one person, through no fault of her own, lost a lot of money or trading stamps while the partner won a good deal. At the end of the game, the winner (the real subject) was given an opportunity to give some of the money to the partner who lost. There was a strong tendency to give some of the winnings to the loser, even though they had been won legitimately. In contrast, in a condition where both partners had equal winnings, there was little tendency for the subject to give any winnings to the other player.

In another study (Schmitt & Marwell, 1972),

candy and toys. Before her own turn came, each girl watched an adult model play the game.

In one condition, a selfish model put all the chips she won into a jar labeled "my money." In another condition, a charitable model put some of her chips into a jar labeled "money for poor children." Regardless of condition, the model then urged the girl to think about the poor children who would "love to receive the prizes these chips can buy." Results showed a clear effect of modeling. Girls who had seen a charitable model donated an average of 19 tokens to the poor, compared to only 10 tokens given by girls who saw the selfish model.

Another study (Rushton & Teachman, 1978) combined both modeling and reinforcement. First, a helpful adult model was used to get boys to behave altruistically by giving some of the tokens they won at bowling to an orphan named Bobby. Then the model rewarded the child for his generosity ("Good for you." "That's really nice of you.") or punished him ("That's kind of silly for you to give to Bobby."). There was also a no-reinforcement condition in which the adult said nothing. As Figure 11–1 shows, children who were rewarded gave more to Bobby on later trials than did children who were punished.

Two weeks later, when children again played the same game and were reminded about Bobby, the effects of the earlier reward or punishment still influenced how much they gave to Bobby.

Modeling is also a strong promoter of prosocial behavior in adults, as a study of adult blood donors clearly showed. In this clever experiment (Rushton & Campbell, 1977), female college students first talked to a friendly woman (actually a confederate of the researchers) as part of a study of social interaction. The researchers arranged things so that as the two women left the interaction study, they passed a table set up in the corridor, staffed by people asking for blood donations. Half the time, the confederate immediately volunteered, modeling prosocial behavior. In another condition, the confederate stepped aside to talk to someone else.

The effects of the model's behavior were striking. A helpful model led 67 percent of subjects to pledge to donate blood, compared to only 25 percent of subjects who saw no model. More impressive were data on whether the women actually followed through on their pledges to give blood. None of the women in the no-model condition actually gave blood, but

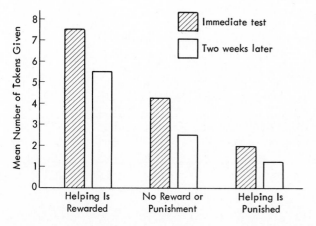

FIGURE 11–1
Effects of reward and punishment on giving tokens to an orphan. (Adapted from Rushton & Teachman, 1984, pp. 322–325.)

BOX 11–2
Lassie to the Rescue

Can children's television shows influence prosocial behavior? Research suggests that they can. In one study, 3- to 5-year old children were exposed to one of three television diets for a four-week period (Stein & Friedrich, 1972). In an aggressive condition, children watched Batman and Superman cartoons. In a prosocial condition, they watched episodes from "Mister Roger's Neighborhood." In a neutral condition, they watched scenes such as children working on a farm. At the end of the testing, children who had seen prosocial programs showed an increase in helping relative to children in the other two conditions. A problem with this study, however, was that the programs varied in many ways, such as format, interest level, and educational goals.

To correct these problems, another study (Sprafkin, Liebert, & Poulos, 1975) exposed children to different episodes from the popular children's TV show "Lassie." Half the first-graders in the study watched an episode that focused on Lassie's efforts to keep her puppy from being given away. At the story's climax, the puppy falls into a mining shaft. Unable to rescue the puppy herself, Lassie brings her owner Jeff and his grandfather to the scene. Jeff risks his life by hanging over the edge of the shaft to save the puppy. In the neutral condition, children watched an episode of Lassie that dramatized Jeff's attempt to avoid taking violin lessons. It contained no examples of humans helping a dog, although Lassie was obviously featured in a positive light.

Children watched the TV program individually, and were then given an opportunity to help some puppies, but only at the cost of foregoing personal benefits. A female researcher took the child to another room and showed the child how to play a point game. The more points scored, the better the prize the child would receive. The woman also explained that she had to leave the room briefly, and asked the child to do something for her while she was gone. She said that she was using earphones to listen to some dogs who were in a nearby kennel to make sure they were safe. The child was asked to wear the earphones while playing the game.

If the child heard barking, he or she could help the puppies by pressing a button marked "Help." The researcher left the room and shortly turned on a tape recording in which the dogs began to bark frantically. Would the children give up playing their point game in order to help the dogs? During the 3-minute testing period, most children pressed the Help button at least briefly. But children who had watched the prosocial TV show were significantly more helpful: They helped for 93 seconds compared to 52 seconds for children who had watched the neutral show. This and other studies (Ahammer & Murray, 1979) show that watching helpful models on TV can indeed increase children's prosocial behavior.

Alice Kandell, Photo Researchers, Inc.

When dad helps his son get dressed, he offers a model of helpfulness that the child may learn to copy. Modeling is one major way that children acquire prosocial behavior.

33 percent of those who saw the altruistic model did. Similar evidence of modeling effects has been found in a variety of situations, such as donating money to a Salvation Army kettle at Christmas or helping a stranded motorist fix a flat tire (Bryan & Test, 1967).

Experiments have also shown that adult helping is influenced by reinforcement. In one study (Moss & Page, 1972), individuals walking along the main street in Dayton, Ohio, were approached by an attractive woman who asked how to get to a local department store. After getting instructions, she either rewarded the helper (by saying, "Thank you very much, I really appreciate this") or punished the helper ("I can't understand what you're saying, never mind, I'll ask someone else"). When the naive subject continued walking down the street, he

or she encountered another woman who accidentally dropped a small bag and continued walking as if she didn't know she had lost it. The question of interest was whether the subject would help the woman by returning the bag to her. In the reward condition, 90 percent of people helped; in the punishment condition, only 40 percent helped.

Taken together, these and other studies provide convincing evidence of the power of reinforcement and modeling to shape prosocial behavior. Over time, people learn norms about who they should help when, and develop habits of helping. The childhood origins of prosocial behavior depend largely on external rewards and social approval. For adults, helping can become an internalized value, not dependent on external supports. It can be enough to know that you've lived up to your own standards and to feel the warm glow of having done a good deed.

Deciding to Help

So far, we have discussed general ways in which biological dispositions, social norms, and previous learning experiences can influence helping. But even the most motivated altruist does not offer aid all the time. In any particular situation, the decision to help involves complex processes of social cognition and rational decision-making (see Latané & Darley, 1970; Schwartz, 1977). A person must first notice that something is happening and decide whether or not help is required. If help is needed, the person may consider the extent of his or her own personal responsibility to act. Third, the person may evaluate the rewards and costs of helping or not helping. Finally, the person must decide what type of help is needed, and just how to provide it.

PERCEIVING A NEED It's 2 A.M. and a piercing shriek fills the night air. Some people sleep on, oblivious to all but their private dreams. You wake up with a start. A woman shouts, "Stop it! Leave me alone!" You hear an angry male voice, but you can't quite make out what he's saying. Quickly you ask yourself what is going on—is it merely a noisy lovers' quarrel, or a serious physical attack? Is this an emergency requiring outside intervention?

The crucial first step in any prosocial act is noticing that something is happening and deciding help is required. In some situations, the need is clear: Flood waters are rising in the river in your town and all able-bodied people are needed to fill sandbags to hold back the water; your child has gashed her head playing soccer and needs medical attention. But in many situations, such as hearing screams in the night, it can be difficult to decide. Uncertainty about a situation is a major reason why people sometimes fail to offer assistance (see Clark & Word, 1974; Solomon, Solomon, & Stone, 1978). For example, one study (Clark & Word, 1972) found that when students heard an unmistakable emergency—a maintenance man falling off a ladder and crying out in agony—all of them went to the man's aid. In another condition, where students heard an ambiguous emergency—the sounds of an identical fall but without verbal cues that the victim was injured—help was offered only about 30 percent of the time.

What cues do people use in deciding whether there is an emergency requiring intervention? Research by Shotland and Huston (1979) identified five important characteristics which lead to the perception that an event is an emergency:

1. Something happens suddenly and unexpectedly.
2. There is a clear threat of harm to a victim.
3. The harm to the victim is likely to increase over time unless someone intervenes.
4. The victim is helpless and needs outside assistance.
5. Some sort of effective intervention is possible.

For example, most people considered a drug overdose, a heart attack, a rape in progress, and a car accident with the driver motionless on the ground to be emergencies. People were less certain about whether an emergency existed if there was a power blackout, if a friend said he was miserable and depressed, or if there was a disabled car on the side of a road.

Our interpretation or definition of a situation is a vital factor in whether or not we offer aid. Shotland and Straw (1976) showed that people respond quite differently to an identical fight scene, depending on whether they perceive it as a lovers' quarrel or a fight between strangers. In this study, students came to the psychology department individually in the evening to fill out an attitude questionnaire. While working on the task, the student heard a loud fight break out in the corridor (actually staged by drama students). A woman screamed and pleaded with a man to "get away from me." In a "marriage" condition, where the victim yelled "I don't know why I ever married you," only 19 percent of students intervened. But in a "stranger" condition, where the woman yelled, "I don't know you," 65 percent of subjects intervened either directly or by calling the police. Even though the fights were identical in all respects, subjects perceived the situation as more serious and the woman as more eager for help in the stranger condition.

In a real-life fight where the relationship between people is unclear, onlookers may assume it to be a lovers' quarrel and so decide not to intrude. Perhaps this is unfortunate, but it means that the lack of help is often due to misinterpretation of the situation, not to unwillingness to help.

TAKING PERSONAL RESPONSIBILITY   You're at the beach, lying in the sun. A woman spreads her blanket near yours and turns on her portable radio to a local rock station. After a few minutes she goes for a swim, leaving her radio on the blanket. A bit later a man comes along, notices the radio, snatches it up quickly, and walks off. What do you do? Chances are that you do not try to stop the theft—reminding yourself, perhaps, that it's not your responsibility.

In an experiment re-creating the scene just described (Moriarity, 1975), only 20 percent of people intervened by going up to the thief and demanding an explanation. In a second condition, however, the owner of the radio first approached the person next to her on the beach and asked if they would "watch my things." Once such a commitment had been established, 95 percent of people intervened to stop the thief. When individuals feel personal responsibility, they are significantly more likely to act in a prosocial way.

Another demonstration of the importance of taking personal responsibility comes from a recent field study (Maruyama, Fraser, & Miller, 1982). Groups of children who came to a certain house while trick-or-treating for Halloween were asked to donate candies for hospitalized children. There were three experimental conditions, designed to manipulate the childrens' perceptions of responsibility. In one condition, the woman who greeted the kids made each child responsible for donating candies by putting the child's name on a bag for the candies. In another condition, she made one child responsible for the entire group. In the third condition, no one was given responsibility.

The variations in responsibility had clear effects on the number of candies donated by the children. When each child was individually responsible, the average donation was 5 candies; when one child was responsible for the group, this dropped to 3.3; when no one was responsible, an average of only 2.2 candies per child was given.

Another factor influencing perceived responsibility is competence (Bickman, 1971). We apparently feel a greater sense of obligation to intervene in a situation where we have the skills to help effectively. In one study, for instance (Clark & Word, 1974), participants witnessed a person (actually a confederate) pass out from an electrical shock from malfunctioning equipment. Of participants who had formal training or experience in working with electrical equipment, 90 percent intervened to help; among those with no electrical skills, only 58 percent intervened.

WEIGHING THE COSTS AND BENEFITS According to the incentive theories described in Chapter 1,

people consider the potential gains and losses that will result from a particular action, including helping another person (see Lynch & Cohen, 1978; Piliavin et al., 1981). So a person will act prosocially when the perceived profits (rewards — costs) for helping outweigh the profits from not helping.

Sometimes it is relatively easy to help; at other times, helping may involve considerable costs in time, energy, and complications. If someone asks you for directions, it is easy to stop for a moment and help out if you can. But if you are driving along a highway and see someone stuck at the side of the road, it is much more time-consuming to stop to help. In both situations, the costs will depend in part on whether you perceive any possible threat to your own safety. Does the person needing help look respectable, or is there some chance that you will be robbed? The greater the perceived costs, the less likely you are to help.

There is also some cost to not giving assistance. You may feel guilty about not helping. Other people may see that you have not been helpful, and you will feel badly because they may have a poor opinion of you. You may have a general moral value that says you should help if you can, and not helping will make you feel that you have not been a good person. Thoughts such as these influence whether or not you offer help.

On the other hand, there are benefits to helping which provide positive incentives. The greater the good you perceive you will do, the more likely you are to help. The more the person deserves to be helped, and the more help you are able to give, the better you may feel about offering assistance. For example, Gruder, Romer, and Korth (1978) had a female confederate telephone people and request aid. The woman's story was that her car had broken down and she needed to reach a service station. She had gotten a wrong number, and asked the person to call the station for her. In some cases, she was in great need; in others less. In some cases, her problem was largely her fault because she said she had forgotten to take

BOX 11–3
Avoiding Helping

A request for aid often arouses mixed feelings. On the one hand, people would like to help because it is a nice thing to do. On the other hand, they realize that costs are involved, costs that they would perhaps rather not assume. Indeed, one study (Pancer et al., 1979) demonstrated that people sometimes actively avoid a situation in which they will be asked for help. A table was set up in a passageway. In some conditions it held a box for donations to charity; in others it did not. People tended to walk farther away from the table when donations were requested than when no donations were requested. Similarly, when someone was sitting at the table collecting donations, people avoided it more than when no one was there. And finally, when a handicapped person was sitting at the table, people steered farther away than when the person was not handicapped.

In each case, the stronger the request for aid, the more people avoided the situation. Clearly, helping situations can create conflict, and people tend to minimize this conflict by keeping away. Presumably, it is easier not to donate money when you are far away than when you are close.

George Malave, Stock, Boston

the car in for service even though she knew it needed repairs; in others, it was not her fault—the car had broken down with no warning. People helped more when her need was greater and when she was not at fault, and therefore presumably was more deserving of help.

Several researchers (see Lynch & Cohen, 1978; Morgan, 1978; Morgan & Leik, 1979) have tested this model of helping and have found generally supportive results. It seems likely that cost-benefit considerations do influence helping, at least in some situations. On the other hand, they do not fully explain all helping decisions. The person who instantly rushes into a burning building to save a child is unlikely to have weighed carefully the expected utility of the action. Rather, such acts may be motivated by basic emotions and values having to do with human life, courage, and so on.

DECIDING HOW TO HELP AND TAKING ACTION   A final element in the decision to help is figuring out what type of assistance to offer, and then taking action. Should you intervene directly in the fight outside your door, or act indirectly by calling the police? Should you try to administer CPR to the accident victim, or call the paramedics? Whether a person takes direct action or

We are more likely to intervene in an emergency if we know how to help effectively. By taking a course in cardiopulmonary resuscitation (CPR), these people will have the knowledge to help heart attack victims.

Wil Blanch, dpi

seeks further assistance from someone else depends on many factors, such as the type of aid needed and the expertise or physical size of the potential helper. In emergencies, decisions are often made under great stress, urgency, and sometimes even personal danger. Unfortunately, sometimes well-intentioned helpers are not able to give assistance or may even mistakenly do the wrong thing.

Our analysis of different elements in the decision to help highlights the many reasons why people may fail to give needed assistance. They may not notice that a problem exists, or may misperceive the situation as a trivial problem. They may recognize a need, but not feel personally responsible for helping. They may believe the costs of helping are too great. They may want to help, but be unable to. Or they may hesitate, caught in a state of indecision.

SPECIFIC DETERMINANTS OF PROSOCIAL BEHAVIOR

We turn now to research on more specific factors that influence helping. Social psychological studies have shown that prosocial behavior is affected by characteristics of the situation, characteristics of the potential helper, and characteristics of the person in need.

The Situation

Even the most dedicated altruist is less likely to offer aid in some situations than in others. Research has documented the importance of several situational factors, including the presence of other people, the nature of the physical environment, and the presssures of limited time.

THE PRESENCE OF OTHERS   One of the shocking things about the Kitty Genovese murder is that so many people heard the young woman's screams and yet did not even call the police. Many social commentators interpreted this as a sign of widespread moral decay and alienation in society. Another hypothesis was offered by social psychologists Bibb Latané and John Darley (1970). They proposed that the very presence of so many onlookers may have been a reason for the lack of helping. Those who witnessed the murder may have assumed that others had already called the police, and so may

have felt little personal responsibility to intervene.

To test this idea that the number of witnesses affects helping, Darley and Latané (1968) designed the laboratory study described in Chapter 2. College students who overheard an "emergency" were much more likely to respond if they were alone than if they thought others also knew about the situation. The more people present, the less likely it was that any one individual actually offered help, and the longer the average delay before help was given. Darley and Latané called this the **bystander effect.**

Many studies have replicated this finding in different settings (Latané & Nida, 1981). For example, Latané and Darley (1970) conducted a field study at the Nu-Way Beverage Center in Suffern, New York. The researchers staged a series of robberies. When the salesclerk went to the back of the store to check on something, two husky young men muttering, "They'll never miss this," walked off with a case of beer. The robberies were staged when either one or two customers were in the store. As expected, people who witnessed the crime alone were significantly more likely to report the theft to the clerk than people who were in the store with another customer.

Why does the presence of others sometimes

inhibit helpfulness? The decision-making analysis of prosocial behavior suggests several explanations. One is the *diffusion of responsibility* created by the presence of other people. If only one person witnesses a victim in distress, then he or she is totally responsible for responding to the situation and will bear all the guilt or blame for nonintervention. When others are present, help can come from several people. The responsibility for helping and the possible costs of failing to offer aid are shared. Further, if a person knows that others are present but cannot actually talk to them or see their behavior, as in the Kitty Genovese case, the person may assume that others have already done something to help, such as calling the police. Experiments (Korte, 1971; Ross, 1971) have supported this idea—that it is not the number of people present that is crucial, but the lessened feelings of personal responsibility that can result from being in a group.

A second explanation for the bystander effect concerns *ambiguity* in the interpretation of the situation. The decision-making analysis suggests that potential helpers are sometimes uncertain whether a particular situation is actually an emergency. The behavior of other bystanders can influence how we ourselves define a situation and react to it. If others ignore a situation or act as if nothing is happening, we too may assume that no emergency exists. The impact of bystanders on interpreting a situation was demonstrated by Latané and Darley (1970).

In this experiment, college men sat filling out a questionnaire. After a few minutes, smoke began to enter the room through a vent. Within four minutes, the smoke was so thick it was difficult to see and to breathe normally. When subjects were alone, they usually walked around the room to investigate the smoke, and 75 percent reported the smoke to the researcher within four minutes. In a condition where the real subject was in a room with two confederates who deliberately ignored the smoke, only 10 percent reported the smoke. This result is all the more dramatic because the smoke was very

noticeable and unpleasant. Apparently the calmness of the other people led subjects to define the situation as not dangerous.

A third factor in the strength of the bystander effect is *evaluation apprehension*. If we know that other people are watching our behavior, we may try to do what we think others expect of us and to present ourselves in a favorable light (Baumeister, 1982). In some situations, such as the smoke-filled room, subjects may have feared they would look foolish or cowardly by showing concern about the smoke when others were apparently calm. The desire to avoid the cost of social disapproval inhibited action. In other situations, however, such as witnessing a person become seriously ill, we may assume that intervention is called for; here, the knowledge that others are aware of our actions may facilitate helping (Schwartz & Gottlieb, 1980).

ENVIRONMENTAL CONDITIONS   The physical setting also influences willingness to help. Think for a moment about whether you are more likely to stop to help a stranded motorist on a pleasant, sunny day or a cold, rainy one? On a dark street in a poor section of town, or in a well-lighted affluent area? On a country lane, or in a big city? Much research has documented the impact of environmental conditions such as weather, city size, and noise level on helping.

The effects of weather on helping were investigated in two field studies by Cunningham (1979). In one study, pedestrians were approached outdoors and asked to help the researcher by completing a questionnaire. People were significantly more likely to help when the day was sunny and when the temperature was comfortable (relatively warm in winter and relatively cool in summer). In a second study conducted in a climate-controlled restaurant, Cunningham found that customers left more generous tips when the sun was shining. Other research suggests that people are more likely to help a stranded motorist in sunny rather than rainy weather (Ahmed, 1979) and during the day rather than at night (Skolnick, 1977). In short, weather does make a difference in helping, although psychologists are still debating the exact reasons for this effect.

A common stereotype is that city dwellers are unfriendly and unhelpful, whereas small-town people are cooperative and helpful. Several studies indicate that when it comes to helping strangers in distress, *city size* does make a difference (see House & Wolf, 1978; Korte, 1981). In a recent study, Amato (1983) investigated helping in 55 Australian communities ranging from small villages to major cities. To ensure a diverse sample of prosocial behaviors, five different types of helping were studied. These included a student asking pedestrians to write down their favorite color as part of a school project, a pedestrian inadvertently dropping an envelope on the sidewalk, a request to donate money to the Multiple Sclerosis Society, overhearing a salesclerk give obviously wrong directions to someone, and witnessing a man with a bandaged leg fall to the ground and cry out in pain.

The results of this study are presented in Figure 11–2. On four of the five helping measures,

the percentage of people who helped was significantly greater in small towns than in larger cities. The one exception to this pattern was the lost envelope. It generally brought little helping, and seemed to get more in the largest cities. What should also be kept in mind, of course, is that these studies dealt only with help offered to strangers: There is no reason to believe that city dwellers are any less helpful than small-town people when it comes to helping friends and relatives.

Many explanations for the lesser helpfulness of city dwellers have been offered. These include the anonymity of urban life, the sensory overload experienced by city dwellers who are constantly bombarded by other people, and possible feelings of helplessness from dealing with unresponsive urban bureaucracies and governments. We don't yet know which explanation is most important.

Another environmental factor that can affect prosocial behavior is noise. Starting with the general idea that noise can reduce people's responsiveness to all events in the environment, several researchers have investigated whether noisy conditions reduce the likelihood of help-

FIGURE 11–2 Percentage of people helping, by community size. (Adapted from Amato, 1983, p. 579.)

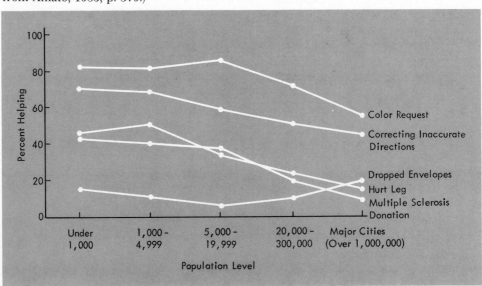

ing a stranger in distress (see Sherrod & Downs, 1974). In one lab study (Mathews & Canon, 1975), for example, it was found that noise decreased the likelihood that students would help a person who had dropped some papers on the floor. When only regular room noise was present, 72 percent of subjects helped, compared to only 37 percent when very loud noise was present. In a field study, the same investigators arranged to have a man wearing a cast on his arm drop some of the books he was carrying from his car. When only typical street noises were present, 80 percent of passersby helped; when a noisy lawn mower was going, only 15 percent helped. The researchers suggested that loud noise causes people to ignore others in their environment and motivates them to leave the situation quickly, thus creating less helpful bystanders.

TIME PRESSURES Imagine that you're walking across campus when a student stops you to ask for help with a fund drive for needy children. Are you more likely to help if you're out for a stroll or if you're late for a midterm exam? Both common sense and research evidence suggest that we are sometimes in too much of a hurry to help.

A clear demonstration of this effect comes from an experiment by Darley and Batson (1973). As part of this study, individual students were asked to walk to another building where they were to give a short talk. Some were told to take their time, that the talk wouldn't begin for several minutes. Others were told to hurry because they were already late and the researcher was waiting. As the subject went from building to building, he encountered a shabbily dressed man slumped in a doorway, coughing and groaning. The question of interest was whether or not the subject would offer assistance.

A further twist to the study was that all participants were theological students. For some, the assigned topic for their talk was the Bible story of the Good Samaritan, about a person who came to the aid of a man who lay injured on the roadside, the victim of robbers. Other students were to talk about a topic not relevant to helping—the sorts of jobs seminary students might pursue after graduation. The results of the study showed that time pressure had a strong impact on helping. In a postexperiment interview all students recalled seeing the victim. But only 10 percent of those in a hurry helped, compared to 63 percent of those who were not in a hurry.

Perhaps surprisingly, the speech topic made no difference. Students about to talk on the Good Samaritan were no more likely to offer assistance than those preparing to talk on jobs. The researchers suggested that time pressure caused some students to overlook the needs of the victim. Another factor may have been a conflict about whom to help—the experimenter or the victim.

The possibility that conflict rather than callousness was at work is supported by a second study (Batson et al., 1978) using a somewhat similar design. When students arrived for this study, they were sent individually to another building to interact with a computer. Some were told to hurry, and others were not. In addition, some were led to believe that their participation was of vital importance to the researcher, whereas others were told that their data were not essential. As the student went from building to building, he encountered a male undergraduate slumped on the stairs, coughing and groaning.

Would the subject help this victim? Results (see Table 11–2) showed that students in a hurry were less likely to help (40 percent) than those with no time pressures (65 percent), but that this was primarily true for subjects who thought their research participation was essential. When subjects thought the researcher was not counting on them, those in a hurry were just about as likely to help (70 percent) as those not in a hurry (80 percent). These results are consistent with the cost-benefit model discussed earlier. Apparently subjects weighed the costs and benefits to both experimenter and victim before arriving at a final course of action.

Table 11–2
Percentage of Subjects Who Offered to Help

	IMPORTANCE TO THE EXPERIMENTER		
TIME PRESSURE	LOW	HIGH	AVERAGE
Low	80%	50%	65%
High	70	10	40
Average	75%	30%	52.5%

Source: Adapted from Bateson et al. (1978), p. 99.

The Helper

Situational factors can greatly increase or decrease the likelihood that people will act in a prosocial way. What these studies also show, however, is that some people offer aid even when situational forces discourage helping, and others fail to help even under the most favorable conditions. Individual differences do exist. In an effort to understand why some people help more than others, researchers have investigated both relatively enduring personality characteristics and more fleeting moods and psychological states.

PERSONALITY FACTORS   Efforts to identify a single personality profile of the "helpful person" have not been very successful. Rather, it appears that specific personality traits dispose people to help in some types of situations, but not in others. For instance, Satow (1975) found that people with a high need for approval were more likely to donate money to a charity than those low in need for social approval, but *only* when others were watching them. Presumably, people high in need for approval were motivated by a desire to win praise from others and so acted more prosocially only when their good deeds would be noticed.

In another study people high in the need to be nurturant were most likely to volunteer to give advice about personal problems to a same-sex high school student (Gergen, Gergen, & Me-

ter, 1972). But nurturance was not related to willingness to counsel someone of the other sex, or to volunteering to help in a research project, or to assist in preparing course materials. In other words, the link between personality and helping depends on the specific trait in question and on the specific type of assistance needed.

Further insights about the people most likely to help come from studies of people who have helped in extreme real-life situations. In one study, London (1970) interviewed Christians who had lived in Europe during World War II and had risked their lives, often repeatedly, to save Jews from Nazi death camps. All these rescuers had a very strong personal sense of morality, and a close identification with a parent who served as a model of moral conduct. One man recalled his mother teaching him that "regardless of what you do with your life, be honest. When it comes the day you have to make a decision, make the right one" (p. 247). Another characteristic of these people was a sense of adventurousness, a willingness to take risks. Finally, many of the rescuers had also felt somewhat apart from others in their community because of their background or values.

MOOD   There is considerable evidence that people are more willing to help when they are in a good mood. For example, people are more likely to help if they have found a dime in a phone booth (Isen & Simmonds, 1978), been given a free cookie at the college library (Isen & Levin, 1972), succeeded on some experimental tasks (Isen, 1970), or listened to soothing music (Fried & Berkowitz, 1979) than if these mood-enhancing events have not occurred. Apparently a warm glow of positive feeling increases the willingness to act prosocially.

There are important limitations to the "feel good" effect, however. First, the effects of positive moods can be quite short-lived—only 20 minutes in one study (Isen, Clark, & Schwartz, 1976). Second, a good mood may actually decrease helpfulness when giving assistance would detract from the person's good mood

Good Samaritans in Action

As the young man drove by a dance hall, he noticed a man assaulting a young woman. As he described it:

> I went over there and I grabbed the dude and I shoved him over and I said lay off the chick. So me and him started going at it. I told him to get out of here, man, look at her, man, the girl's mouth's all bleeding, she got her teeth knocked out, she got a handful of hair pulled out. Everybody was just standing around. (Quoted in Huston, Ruggiero, Conner, & Geis, 1981, p. 17)

Before the police arrived, the men exchanged more blows, one of which broke the intervener's jaw. What motivates this man and other "Good Samaritans" to endanger their own welfare to help a stranger?

Huston, Ruggiero, Conner, and Geis (1981) conducted in-depth interviews with 32 people who had intervened in dangerous crime episodes, such as bank holdups, armed robberies, and street muggings. The responses of these Good Samaritans were compared with a group of noninterveners matched for age, sex, education, and ethnic background. Given the dangerous situations involved, it is perhaps not surprising that the Good Samaritans were significantly taller, heavier, and better trained to cope with emergencies than the noninterveners. All but one of the interveners were men, the exception being an older woman who rescued her 83-year-old neighbor from a knife-wielding attacker. The Good Samaritans were more likely than the noninterveners to describe themselves as strong, aggressive, and principled. And they had more life-saving, medical, and police training.

The results suggested that the interveners were not primarily motivated by humanitarian concern for the victim, but rather acted from a sense of their own ability and responsibility, based on their training and physical strength. The personal qualities that lead someone to stop a crime or mugging may be quite different from those that lead someone to donate money to charity or to help a stranger who collapses from a heart attack. Whether a potential helper intervenes depends on the match between the person's competence, values, and motives, and the requirements of the particular situation.

(Isen & Simmonds, 1978). People in a good mood apparently want to maintain their positive feelings.

The effects of bad moods such as sadness or depression are more complicated, and research results have not been entirely consistent (Cialdini, Baumann, & Kenrick, 1981). If a bad mood causes us to focus on ourself and our own needs, it may lessen the likelihood of our helping someone else (Thompson, Cowan, & Rosenhan, 1980). On the other hand, if we think helping someone else might make us feel better and so relieve our bad mood, we may actually be more likely to offer assistance. A further complication is that the link between feeling bad and helping others is clearer in adults than in children (Cialdini et al., 1981). One reason for this may be that children have to learn, as part of growing up, that helping others is a gratifying act that can improve their own feelings.

GUILT   A psychological state with special relevance to prosocial behavior is guilt, the unpleasant feeling aroused when we do something we consider wrong. A desire to reduce feelings of guilt can lead us to help someone we have harmed, or to get rid of our guilt by doing a "good deed."

Several studies have shown that arousing guilt increases helpfulness (Cunningham et al., 1980). In one study (Freedman, Wallington, & Bless, 1967), the experimenter told the subjects it was extremely important that they not know anything about the test they were going to take, and the situation was set up so that virtually all the subjects said they knew nothing about it. Some of the subjects, however, had been told about the test by a confederate. Thus, these subjects were lying to the experimenter. Telling a lie and thereby perhaps ruining an experiment was expected to arouse guilt. It did. There was almost twice as much compliance among the "liars."

In another experiment by the same researchers, the subjects sat at a table waiting for the experiment to begin. In some conditions, the table was prepared so that the slightest touch would tip it over and scatter index cards, which had been described as needed for somebody's thesis, all over the room. When the subjects tipped the table, they presumably felt responsible and guilty for mixing up the cards. In one control condition, the table was tipped by a confederate. In another, the table was stable and the cards were not scattered. Once again, there was more helping in the guilt condition than in either control condition.

Other studies suggest that guilty people may have conflicting motivations. On the one hand, they want to make up for their bad deeds by helping the victim or doing good for someone else. On the other hand, they also want to avoid confronting the victim, for fear of discovery,

embarrassment, or retaliation. The impact of guilt on helping may be greatest when the guilty person can help without having to confront the victim directly.

An interesting aspect of the relationship between guilt and helping involves the effect of confession. One of the most common assumptions about confession is that it is good for the soul, by which we presumably mean that it is a form of expiation. This, in turn, implies that confession should reduce feelings of guilt. If confession does reduce guilt, it should also reduce helping. Studies by Carlsmith, Ellsworth, and Whiteside (1968) supported this prediction. In the first study, subjects believed they had ruined an experiment because they used information they were not supposed to have. Some were allowed to confess what they had done; others were not given this opportunity; and a third group, who did not think they had ruined the study, served as a control. All the subjects were asked to volunteer for further experiments.

The results are shown in Table 11–3. It is clear that guilt increased helping. Those who used illicit information complied more than those who did not have the information. It is also clear that confessing, which reduced guilt, also reduced helpfulness. Those in the guilt condition who confessed complied little more than those in the control group.

PERSONAL DISTRESS AND EMPATHIC CONCERN
Picture for a moment the sight of people in serious distress: the mangled bodies of victims in a train crash, a starving child in ragged clothes, an

Table 11–3 Guilt, Confession, and Helping	
CONDITION	NUMBER OF HOURS VOLUNTEERED
Guilt	4.33
Confession	2.67
Control	1.92
Source: Adapted from Carlsmith et al. (1968).	

anguished father whose child has disappeared. Witnessing people in need often evokes powerful emotions.

Personal distress refers to our own personal reactions to the suffering of others—our feelings of shock, horror, alarm, concern, helplessness, or whatever. In contrast, **empathic concern** refers to feelings of sympathy and caring for others, in particular to sharing vicariously or indirectly in the suffering of others. The key difference is that personal distress focuses on the self, whereas empathic concern focuses on the victim.

Personal distress motivates us to reduce our own discomfort. We might do this by helping a person in need, but we can also do it by escaping from the situation or ignoring the suffering around us. In contrast, empathic concern can be reduced only by actually helping the person in distress. Since the goal of empathic concern is enhancing the welfare of someone else, it would clearly be an altruistic (not self-interested) source of helping behavior.

Several studies have shown that empathy increases prosocial behavior (Hoffman, 1981). For example, in one study (Toi & Batson, 1982) college students learned of the plight of Carol, another student who had broken both legs in a car accident and was seriously behind in her school work. After listening to a tape-recorded interview with Carol, each subject was asked if she would be willing to help Carol. Empathy was manipulated by varying the listening instructions given to subjects. In a high-empathy condition, subjects were told: "Try to take the perspective of the person who is being interviewed, imagining how he or she feels about what has happened and how it has affected his

Mother Theresa has devoted her life to helping the homeless children of India. She was awarded the Nobel Peace Prize for her humanitarian works.

Calogero Cascio, Photo Researchers, Inc.

or her life." In a low-empathy condition, subjects were told: "Try to be as objective as possible, carefully attending to all the information presented. . . . Try not to concern yourself with how the person being interviewed feels about what happened."

As expected, subjects in the high-empathy condition experienced significantly greater empathy, as reflected in self-ratings of feeling sympathetic, compassionate, and "moved" by Carol's story. Also as predicted, subjects in the high-empathy condition were significantly more likely to volunteer to help Carol than those in the low-empathy condition, even when it would have been easy to avoid helping (71 vs. 33 percent offered to help). Taking the perspective of someone in distress and sharing his or her suffering can be important factors in prosocial behavior.

The Person in Need

As you near the Student Union, someone approaches you and asks to borrow a dime to make a phone call. Are you more likely to help if the person is a clean-cut preppie type or a punk rocker? Would it matter if the person explained that his or her wallet had been stolen or that he or she had forgotten to bring any change to school? Although the true altruist may be blind to everything but the needs of a person in distress, everyday prosocial behavior is often influenced by characteristics of the person in need.

For example, people on a college campus were more likely to give money to the March of Dimes if they were asked for a donation by a paraplegic woman in a wheelchair than if asked by a nonhandicapped woman (Slochower et al., 1980). In another study (Piliavin, Piliavin, & Rodin, 1975), subway riders in New York City saw a man carrying a cane stumble and fall to the floor. Sometimes the victim had a large red birthmark on his face; sometimes he did not. In this situation, the victim was more likely to receive aid if his face was unblemished (86 per-

cent) than if he had an unattractive birthmark (61 percent). In understanding these and other research findings, two themes seem most important: We are more likely to help people we like and think deserve assistance.

HELPING THOSE WE LIKE In Chapter 8 we saw that our initial liking for another person is affected by such factors as physical attractiveness and similarity. Research on prosocial behavior finds that the same characteristics also influence helping. In at least some situations, those who are physically attractive are more likely to receive aid. For example, in a field study (Benson, Karabenick, & Lerner, 1976), researchers placed a completed application to graduate school in a telephone booth at the airport. The application was stamped and ready to be mailed, but had apparently been "lost." To manipulate appearance, the photo attached to the application was sometimes of a very good-looking person and sometimes of a less attractive person. The measure of helping was whether the individual who found the envelope actually mailed it or not. Results showed that people were much more likely to send in the application if the person in the photo, whether male or female, was attractive.

The degree of similarity between the potential helper and the person in need is also important. Some years ago, researchers (Emswiller, Deaux, & Willits, 1971) had confederates dressed as a "hippie" or as a "straight" approach students and ask to borrow a dime. The researchers also used appearance to categorize the potential helpers as "hippie" or "straight." Results clearly showed that people were most likely to help those similar to themselves. For example, hippie men helped a fellow hippie about 77 percent of the time, but helped a straight person only about 32 percent of the time. There is also evidence that helpfulness is greater toward someone who is from the same country rather than a foreigner (Feldman, 1968), and toward someone with similar attitudes (Tucker et al., 1977).

Prosocial behavior is affected by the type of

relationship between people, as everyday experience clearly shows. Whether because of liking, social obligation, self-interest, or empathy, we are more helpful to intimates than to strangers. One study (Bar-Tal et al., 1977) examined college students' expectations about receiving help from parents, siblings, close friends, acquaintances, or strangers. Results indicated that the closer the relationship, the stronger the expectation that help should be given, the less gratitude expressed when help is given, and the more resentment felt if help is refused.

HELPING THOSE WHO DESERVE HELP   Whether a person receives help depends in part on the "merits" of the case. For example, people in a supermarket were more likely to give someone money so they could buy milk rather than cookie dough (Bickman & Kamzan, 1973), presumably because milk is more essential for health than cookies. Passengers on a New York subway were more likely to help a man who fell to the ground if he appeared to be sick rather than drunk (Piliavin, Rodin, & Piliavin, 1969). In both cases, the legitimacy or appropriateness of the request or problem made a difference. Of course, judgments about the importance of a particular need may be strongly influenced by values.

In addition to evaluating the deservingness of the need itself, potential helpers may also make inferences about the causes of the person's need, following the principles of causal attribution outlined in Chapter 5. A teacher might, for example, spend more time helping a student who missed classes because of a death in the family rather than because of a trip to the Carribbean. Several studies indicate that the key causal factor is *personal control:* We are more likely to help someone if we believe the cause of the problem was outside the person's control. For instance, in one study (Meyer & Mulherin, 1980), college students said they would be more willing to lend rent money to an acquaintance if the need arose due to illness (an uncontrollable cause) rather than laziness (a controllable cause).

In another study (Weiner, 1980), students said they would be more likely to lend their lecture notes to a classmate who needed them because of something uncontrollable, such as the professor's being a poor lecturer, rather than something controllable, such as the classmate's not trying to take good notes. If a person could have prevented the predicament by his or her own actions, we are less likely to help. Attributions may also influence how we feel about a person in need. We may feel sympathy and concern for those who suffer through no fault of their own; we may feel anger and disgust toward those who are responsible for their own problems (Meyer & Mulherin, 1980; Weiner, 1980).

Our focus up to now has been on factors that affect whether or not help is given. In the next section we look at helping from a different perspective—that of the person receiving aid.

THE EXPERIENCE OF RECEIVING HELP

Sometimes we react to getting help with happiness and gratitude. The novice swimmer saved from drowning by an alert lifeguard is thankful to be alive and grateful for getting help when it was needed. The student who gets a ride to the airport from a friend is genuinely thankful for the favor. But there are also instances when people react negatively to receiving help. When Dad offers to help his five-year-old get dressed, she may indignantly insist she'd rather do it herself. Welfare recipients may react toward social workers with veiled hostility rather than warmth. Countries receiving millions in U.S. foreign aid complain about American policies and "exploitation" of developing nations. What these examples point out is that receiving help can be a mixed blessing. Several social psychological theories help explain these reactions.

REACTANCE THEORY: LOSS OF FREEDOM According to reactance theory (Brehm, 1966), people want to maximize their personal freedom of choice. Perceived threats to this freedom are experienced negatively, and may lead to efforts to reassert one's independence. So when foreign aid recipients criticize U.S. policies, they may be symbolically proving their independence and reducing feelings of reactance.

Evidence that those who receive aid perceive a substantial loss of freedom comes from a study of welfare recipients (Briar, 1966). Nearly 70 percent of the welfare families surveyed believed they should not complain if a social worker made a surprise visit in the middle of the night, even though they knew this was probably not legal. Most families (67 percent) also said they would feel obligated to get marriage counseling if asked to do so, whether or not they thought it necessary. Intrusions on privacy and personal freedom can easily lead to feelings of hostility toward those providing aid (Gross, Wallston, & Piliavin, 1979).

EXCHANGE THEORY: COSTS OF INDEBTEDNESS Providing help involves an exchange of resources from one person to another. When the exchange of help in a relationship is largely one way, it leads to indebtedness and can create an imbalance of power in the relationship (Worchel, in press). Young adults who receive financial support from their parents may appreciate the assistance, but may also feel that accepting aid gives their parents greater rights to influence their lives.

The exchange perspective suggests that help may be most appreciated when it can be reciprocated, hence maintaining a balance of equity and power in the relationship. Research shows that people are less likely to ask for help when they think they will be unable to repay the aid in some form (Fisher, Nadler, Whitcher-Alagna,

1982). There is also evidence that people like a benefactor more if they are able to make some return for the aid they receive (see Gross & Latané, 1974). In short, lopsided help giving can threaten equity in a relationship, foster power imbalances, and increase negative feelings on the part of the recipient.

ATTRIBUTION THEORY: THREATS TO SELF-ESTEEM Accepting help can have important implications for our self-esteem. If we perceive that people are helping us because they genuinely care about us and our welfare, we may get an ego boost. If accepting aid implies that we are incompetent, unsuccessful, and dependent, help may threaten our self-esteem (Fisher et al., 1982). For instance, people are sometimes reluctant to seek aid from social agencies because they fear humiliation and embarrassment (Williamson, 1974).

According to attribution theory, people are motivated to understand why they need help and why others are offering to give them help. If people can attribute their need to external or uncontrollable forces rather than to personal inadequacies, they will be able to maintain positive self-esteem. Several studies (Fisher et al., 1982; Tessler & Schwartz, 1972) have found that people are more likely to seek help when they can attribute the problem to a difficult situation, rather than to a personal deficiency. It has also been found that help may be easier to accept when the person in need does not have to ask for it explicitly. A year-long study of welfare recipients (Gross, Wallston, & Piliavin, 1979) found that people used more of the social services available if their caseworker initiated contacts than if the family had to initiate contacts. The researchers suggest that people avoid asking for help to protect their sense of pride and self-worth.

We have seen that the experience of receiving help is not always positive. There are times when accepting aid can limit our freedom, diminish our power, and lower our self-esteem. An understanding of these processes helps to explain why people sometimes react negatively or ambivalently toward help givers and why people may prefer not to ask for help even when they badly need it. Social-psychological factors may also explain the popularity of self-help groups, in which people with a common problem work together to help one another. Be-cause self-help groups are run by the people in need, offer opportunities for reciprocal helping, and foster the knowledge that others have the same problem, they may minimize the costs of receiving help.

SUMMARY

1. Altruism is helping someone with no expectation of a reward. Prosocial behavior includes any act that helps or is designed to help, regardless of the helper's motives.
2. Sociobiologists believe that a tendency to help others is part of our human biological makeup. In contrast, the social evolution view is that societies create rules about helping, which include norms of social responsibility, reciprocity, and social justice.
3. Children learn norms about helping by reinforcement and modeling. These social learning mechanisms also affect adults' prosocial behavior.
4. The decision to help is a complex process. The potential helper must perceive that help is needed, take personal responsibility, weigh the costs and benefits, and decide how to intervene.
5. Bystander intervention means coming to the aid of someone in distress. Research shows that peo-ple are less likely to intervene when others are present. This so-called bystander effect may result from a diffusion of responsibility, from other people influencing how an individual interprets the situation, and from evaluation apprehension. Other situational factors that influence helping are weather, city size, noise, and time pressures.
6. People are more likely to be helpful when they are in a good mood, feel guilty about some prior ''bad'' deed they have done, and feel empathy for the plight of the victim. People are also more helpful to those they like and to those they believe deserve help.
7. People sometimes react to receiving help with a mixture of gratitude and discomfort. Receiving help may threaten our sense of freedom, make us feel indebted to others, and threaten our self-esteem.

SUGGESTIONS FOR ADDITIONAL READING

EISENBERG, N. (Ed.) (1982). *The development of prosocial behavior.* New York: Academic Press. A series of articles discuss theory and research about how children learn prosocial behavior.

LATANÉ, B., & DARLEY, J. M. (1970). *The unresponsive bystander: Why doesn't he help?* Englewood Cliffs, N.J.: Prentice-Hall. Reviews the classic studies of bystander intervention conducted by these authors.

PILIAVIN, J. A., DOVIDIO, J. F., GAERTNER, S. L., & CLARK, R. D. (1981). *Emergency intervention.* New York: Academic Press. Reviews research and theory on bystander intervention with an emphasis on cost-reward factors.

WILSON, E. O. (1975). *Sociobiology.* Cambridge, MA: Harvard University Press. A fascinating account by a biologist of how genetic factors may affect behavior. Highly controversial and tough going, but well worth reading.

12

CONFORMITY AND COMPLIANCE

In the 1950s, American college men were virtually all clean-shaven, with short hair. Many had crewcuts. Only farmers wore those jeans as everyday clothing. College women almost invariably had short hair, and dressed in blouses and skirts, with skirt lengths well below the knee. In the late 1960s and early 1970s, college men began wearing long hair. Many grew mustaches or beards. College women rarely wore dresses or skirts (except when they visited their parents). Shoulder-length hair was common, as were sandals or even bare feet. Sweatshirts, sweatpants, sneakers, jogging shorts or pants, designer jeans, and legwarmers were unknown on college campuses. How would you describe dress on college campuses today? Does everyone look the same? What is current fashion?

The heads of totalitarian governments always seem to be trying to control others, to get them to behave in a particular way, especially against their own inclinations. The question of compliance or obedience is relevant to practically every phase of social life. We are constantly being urged to act in some way, and we often do the same to others. We are asked to do homework, obey laws, pay taxes, drive carefully, save energy, give to charity, be courteous, support political movements and candidates, and get dental checkups. The socialization of children consists in large part of getting them to behave in ways that are consistent with the needs, laws, rules, and demands of society.

In every case, some person or organization is trying to get others to perform some action when the others would just as soon not. When someone performs an act because everyone else is doing it, we call it **conformity.** When people do what they are asked—even though they would prefer not to—we call it **compliance** or **obedience.** Conformity might be considered a special case of compliance—giving in to group pressure—but it is an especially important phenomenon we shall consider separately. What factors determine whether the act will be performed? Let us consider conformity first.

CONFORMITY

Because conformity is such a powerful phenomenon, it has proved relatively easy to study in the laboratory. We'll begin our discussion with two classic studies that illustrate how conformity works.

A Guess in the Dark: The Sherif Study

A college student is taken into a darkened room and shown a single point of light. He is told that

Tom Tucker. Photo Researchers, Inc.

These campus couples from the 1950s, 1960s, and 1980s conform to the norms of their peer groups and historical eras in several ways: How many can you identify?

Erwin Kramer, Photo Researchers, Inc.

Susan Rosenberg, Photo Researchers, Inc.

the light is moving and that the task is to estimate how far. In this classic study, Muzafer Sherif (1935) took advantage of a perceptual illusion known as the *autokinetic phenomenon*—a single point of light seen in the dark appears to move even though it is stationary. It appears so to virtually everyone, and it is extremely difficult for the person watching the light to estimate how far it moves. Usually it

seems to move at varying speeds and in different directions.

So subjects in this situation could not be sure of their positions. Not surprisingly, therefore, the subjects' estimates varied enormously: Several people thought the light moved only 1 or 2 inches, whereas one thought it moved as much as 80 feet. (Apparently, this person thought he was in a gymnasium, although actually he was in a small room.) In other words, the distance the light moved was not at all easy to determine. Although the subjects had some idea how far it moved, they were far from certain because they had no guidelines, no background on which to base their estimates.

Then a second person was introduced into this situation, also supposedly a subject who was judging how far the light was moving. This other person was in fact a confederate who had been told to make his estimates consistently lower or higher than those of the real subject. The same procedure was repeated for a number of trials.

Under these circumstances, the subject soon began to make estimates that were more and more similar to those of the confederate. For example, if the subject began by estimating that the light moved between 10 and 15 inches and the confederate said it moved only 2 inches, on the second trial the subject would tend to lower his estimate; on the third trial, he would lower it more. By the end of the series, the subject's estimates were very similar to those of the confederate.

The autokinetic phenomenon had created a situation of great ambiguity. The subject had very little information to work with—only his very uncertain perceptions in a novel and peculiar situation. In contrast, the confederate seemed quite sure of himself, giving consistent estimates over the course of the trials even though he apparently had no more information.

This is a strong demonstration of agreement in the absence of a realistic reason, but it could be argued that it is not completely irrational. There are large differences in individual perceptual ability, and the subjects might have thought the other person was better than they at judging how far a light moved in a dark room. So it would be reasonable to go along with the other person or at least to use the estimates of the other person as a frame of reference within which to make their own judgments. In other words, it may have been that the subjects had reason to conform.

As Plain as Day: The Asch Study

Perhaps conformity occurs only in rather ambiguous situations, then, when people are quite uncertain about what the correct standard of behavior is. This was the way Solomon Asch (1951) reasoned. He thought that if the stimulus situation was clear, there would be little or no conformity. When people consider a clear reality, they will trust their own perceptions and remain independent even when every member of a group disagrees with them. Asch therefore designed an experiment to test this expectation (Asch, 1951).

Five students arrived to take part in a study on perception. They sat around a table and were told they would be judging the lengths of lines. They were shown a white card on which three black lines of varying lengths had been drawn and a second card containing one line. Their task was to choose the line on the first card that was most similar in length to the line on the second card. As shown in Figure 12–1, it was an easy task. One of the lines was exactly the same length as the standard, whereas the other two were quite different from it.

When the lines were shown, the subjects answered aloud in the order in which they were seated. The first subject gave his choice and each of the others responded in turn. Since the judgment was so easy, there were no disagreements. When all had responded, a second set of lines were shown, responses were given, and a third set was produced.

At this point, the experiment seems dull and pointless. On the third trial, however, the first subject looked carefully at the lines as before and then gave what was obviously the wrong answer. In the example in Figure 12-1, he might have said A rather than B. The next subject gave the same wrong answer, as did the third and fourth subjects. When it was time for the fifth subject to respond, he was quite disturbed. It was clear to him that the others were giving wrong answers. He knew that B was the line

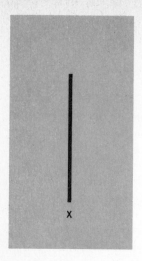
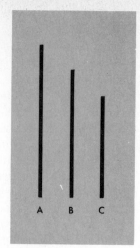

FIGURE 12–1 A representative stimulus in the Asch study. Subjects were shown the four lines simultaneously and asked which line was most similar in length to line X. When a number of confederates unanimously gave the incorrect answer (e.g., C), subjects conformed about 35 percent of the time. (Adapted from Asch, 1951.)

most similar to X. Yet everyone else said it was A.

Under these circumstances many people sitting fifth gave the wrong answer—they agreed with the others even though they knew it was incorrect. In fact, among these college students with good eyesight and presumably sharp minds, the incorrect answer was given about 35 percent of the time. Some subjects never gave the wrong answer, some did all the time; but overall they averaged about one wrong response in three. Of course, in this classic study by Solomon Asch (1951), the situation was staged. The first four "subjects" were confederates of the experimenter and were responding according to a script. But the real subject did not know this and gave the wrong answer rather than disagree with the others.

It is important to keep the unambiguousness of this situation in mind if we are to understand the phenomenon. There is a tendency to think that the conforming subjects are uncertain of the correct choice and therefore are swayed by the majority. This is not the case. The subjects were quite certain of the correct choice and, in control groups with no group pressure, chose

"Well heck! If all you smart cookies agree, who am I to dissent?"

Drawing by Handelsman; © 1972 The New Yorker Magazine, Inc.

correctly 100 percent of the time. When they conform, they are conforming despite the fact that they know the correct answer.

Other studies have found conformity using other physical stimuli, opinion statements, statements of fact, and logical syllogisms. Subjects have agreed that there is no population problem in the United States because 6,000 miles of continent separates San Francisco from New York; that men are 8 to 9 inches taller than women on the average; and that male babies have a life expectancy of only 25 years. In other words, regardless of the type of stimulus and of how clear the correct choice is, when individuals are faced with a unanimous group opinion, the pressure exerted by the majority is strong enough to produce conformity.

These results are very clear. People do conform—even when doing so means contradicting their own perceptions of the world. They do not always accept what the others are saying; in many cases, they continue to believe that their private judgements are correct. Nevertheless, when asked to respond publicly, they give the same incorrect response the others give. This is what we mean by conformity.

WHY DO PEOPLE CONFORM?

Basically, people conform for two major reasons. First, the behavior of other people provides useful *information.* We drive on the right in the USA and on the left in England because others do, and that informs us about how to avoid accidents. Second, we conform to gain social acceptance and to avoid *disapproval.* One of the main reasons we suppress a burp in the middle of a church service is to avoid frowns from those around us.

Lack of Information

Other people are an important source of information. They often know something we do not; by doing what they do, we may gain the benefit of their knowledge. A thirsty traveler at an oasis in the Sahara Desert who sees Arabs drinking from one well and avoiding another would do well to drink from the well they are using.

Similarly, the student in chemistry lab who is uncertain about how much hydrochloric acid to put into the container, and who therefore copies a lab partner, is engaging in an adaptive bit of conformity. These people are doing what someone else is doing because the other has or seems to have information they do not.

Therefore, the amount of conformity based on information is determined by two aspects of the situation: How well-informed are others about what is correct? And how little confidence do we have in our own independent judgment?

TRUST IN THE GROUP   The key factor is whether or not the individual trusts the group's information. In a conformity situation, the individual holds one view and then discovers the group holds an opposing one. The individual wants to give the correct response. Therefore, the more the person trusts the group as a good source of information, the more likely he or she is to conform. If the person thinks the group is always right, he or she will always go along with it, no matter what his or her own opinion. Similarly, if the group has vital information the individual does not have, conformity will be high. The mechanism works this way: The individual decides he or she is mistaken and the group is correct.

One determinant of trust in the group is the expertise of the members. How much do they know about the topic? How qualified are they to give information? The more expert a group is in relation to an individual, the more he or she should trust them and value their opinion. If, in our example concerning thirst in the desert, our traveler sees that the Arabs drinking at the oasis are city dwellers on their first tourist trip to the desert, he or she might be inclined to wonder how much they know and not conform to their example. If they are clearly desert nomads traveling on their usual route, the person would be far more likely to trust them and follow their example.

WEAK CONFIDENCE IN OWN JUDGMENT   The other side of the coin, of course, is that anything that increases the individual's confidence in her own judgment will decrease conformity. One factor that has a powerful effect on confidence and on the amount of conformity is how competent a person feels to make responses. Obviously a question about Sierra Leone's capital would be easier for an expert on Africa than for a social psychologist. If Mary considers herself a math expert, she would be more confident of her answers to math problems than if she were not an expert; this holds even if the problems are quite difficult for her. Someone with good eyes would be more confident about making visual discriminations than someone with bad eyes.

This means you should be able to decrease conformity by making someone feel more knowledgeable about a subject. Sure enough, several studies have demonstrated just this (Mausner, 1954; Snyder, Mischel, & Lott, 1960; Wiesenthal et al., 1976). In Snyder's study, some subjects were given a lecture on art just before being asked to make artistic judgments; other subjects did not hear this lecture. As you would expect, those who felt more expert because they had just heard the lecture conformed less. Anything that increases the individual's confidence in his or her own judgment will reduce conformity, because then the group is not providing superior information.

One factor that influences the individual's feeling of competence is the difficulty of the judgment to be made. The more difficult the judgment, the less confidence the individual

tends to have and the more likely he or she is to conform to others' judgments.

If someone asks us to name the capital of our home state, we know the answer and are sure we know it. Even if four other people gave a different answer, we probably would trust ourselves. We are unlikely to conform because of lack of confidence in ourselves, although we may still conform for the other reasons cited. If we are asked to name the capital of Sierra Leone, we will probably be less certain. If four people disagree with us, we are more likely to trust them and conform.

The Sherif task, for example, was more difficult than the Asch task, and so produced more conformity. Similarly, Coleman, Blake, and Mouton (1958) presented subjects in a conformity situation with a series of factual questions that varied in difficulty. The correlation between difficulty and conformity was .58 for men and .89 for women. That is, the more difficult the item, the more likely the person was to conform to an incorrect but unanimous majority.

Fear of Social Disapproval

A second major reason for conformity is to gain the approval, or avoid the disapproval, of the group. One reason we do not wear garish Hawaiian shirts to church is that the other members of the church will look at us with such great disfavor. Similarly, a child will conscientiously do all her homework and try to get a good grade on exams so that her parents will be pleased with her and give her approval. But a number of different factors determine how this approval and disapproval affect the level of an individual's conformity.

FEAR OF DEVIANCE   The fear of being considered **deviant** is a basic factor in almost all social situations. We do not want to stand out as different; we want to be like everyone else. We want the group to like us, to treat us well, and to accept us. We are afraid that if we disagree with them, they might dislike us, mistreat us, and consider us an outcast. We tend to conform to avoid these consequences.

This fear of being deviant is justified by the group's response to deviance. Someone who does not conform risks grave consequences. When someone disagrees with the rest of the group, various efforts are made to get that person to conform. The most straightforward is trying to convince the person that he or she is wrong and the group right.

This was shown in a study by Schachter (1951), in which three confederates were included in a group. One of them consistently took a position deviant from that of the group, one started deviant and changed, and one took the same position as the group. The rest of the group spent a great deal of time trying to change the position of the two confederates who held deviant positions. They argued with them, presented reasons to support the group position, cajoled, and did whatever they could to change the deviates' stand to agree with the group's.

Being the object of such an intensive campaign is not pleasant. The person feels great pressure to change in order to stop the attacks. The person who changes is accepted and treated like any other member of the group. The one who maintains a deviant position is eventually ignored. In the study, the group liked this person less than someone who agreed with the group, and tended to ostracize and reject him. When the time came to assign jobs, the deviate was never elected to top positions, was never the leader. Instead, he was given the worst jobs.

Similar negative consequences of being deviant were found in a study on aggression by Freedman and Doob (1968). A group of people who had never met before were brought together and given some information about each other. One of them was described as being different from the others, but just how he was different was not made clear. All the groups knew was that his personality was in some way different from theirs.

The group was then asked to choose one

© 1963 Punch; Rothco.

"I fear we must have misread the invitation."

The Hawthorne study: some physical environments make it easy for the group to enforce conformity. How could management have organized this workplace to prevent "binging" or other productivity-reducing types of conformity?

member to take part in a learning study. Whoever was chosen would have the job of responding. Whenever the subject gave an incorrect response, he would receive an electric shock. It was clearly an unpleasant position to be in. The group chose the deviate overwhelmingly for the job of receiving the shocks, or suffering. In another situation, the group had to choose someone to receive a reward of several dollars for taking part in a simple learning study. For this favorable position, the group instead picked an average member. In other words, deviates are selected for painful, bad jobs and not for rewarding, good ones.

A group can also apply punishment directly. A classic study was done at the Hawthorne plant of the Western Electric Company (Homans, 1965). Observations were made of the behavior of a number of workers whose wages depended on their productivity. By working harder and accomplishing more, each worker could receive higher pay. However, the employees had developed their own standards as to the right amount of work to do in a day. Every day, after they had accomplished this

amount of work, they slacked off. By working just this much, they earned a reasonable sum of money and did not have to work hard. Anyone who did work hard would make the others look bad and might cause management to increase its expectation of output.

The group exerted intense pressure on its members to be sure they did not break the rule. To begin with, the group set up a code of behavior. People should not work too much or else they were "rate busters." Nor should people work too little—that would make them "chiselers." In addition, the group devised a method of enforcing this code. Anyone who worked too fast or too slow could be "binged." Binging consisted of giving the deviate a sharp blow on the upper arm. Not only did this hurt, but it was a symbolic punishment for going against the group. Any group member could deliver the punishment, and the person who was binged could not fight back. The punishment had to be accepted and with it, the disapproval it indicated.

Binging is a dramatic example of the kinds of pressure present in all groups that cause members to conform to accepted opinions, values, and behavior. By persuasion, threats of ostracism, direct punishment, and offers of rewards, groups put pressure on individuals to conform.

The strength of the desire not to be deviant varies considerably from person to person and from situation to situation. Some people probably do not feel it at all or even prefer to be deviant; in some circumstances, most people would probably like to be deviant. But for most people in most situations, there is a tendency to avoid it.

The conformity situation is, of course, perfectly designed to raise the individual's fear of being deviant. Everyone is taking one position and she knows that position is incorrect. She is already deviant in her own mind, which is unsettling enough: Why is she out of step? Is there something wrong with her? Then there is the question of the group: The group members all agree and she will stand out if she does not go along with them. By going along with the group, she can at least avoid appearing different to the other people.

The joint effect of lack of confidence in one's own opinion and the fear of being publicly deviant will often cause a person to conform. The strength of these two motives varies considerably depending on the situation, and each of the factors we discuss can be understood in terms of how it affects these basic considerations.

GROUP COHESIVENESS Conformity is also affected by the closeness of the individual's relationship to the group. Do the members feel close to the group or not? How much do they want to be members of the group? The term **cohesiveness** has been used to include all these considerations. It refers to the total sum of the forces causing people to feel drawn to a group and making them want to remain members of it. The more the members like one another, expect to gain from group membership, feel loyalty, and so on, the more cohesive the group is.

Greater cohesiveness leads to greater conformity. The main reason is that when one feels close to other group members, it is more plea-surable for them to approve of us, and more painful when they disapprove of us. In a sense, the stakes of conforming or not conforming are higher when we strongly want to be members of the group. When working for a valuable prize, a group produces more conformity. A group that considers its task important or values itself highly produces more conformity among members than one that puts less value on its task or itself. Moreover, group members conform more in a group with a lot of group spirit.

This increased conformity is due to individuals' reluctance to be deviant. As we saw earlier, being deviant involves the risk of rejection. Someone who is deviant too often or on too important an issue may be mistreated and, in the extreme case, ejected from the group. The more a person cares about the group, the more serious the fear of rejection, and the less likely the person is to disagree. A member of a small group of friends has a tendency to avoid being a minority of one on any issue. Fear of rejection or expulsion is at least one reason for this. If, however, the person no longer likes the group or feels it is restricting his or her social life, this pressure to conform decreases. The worst that could happen is that the person will be thrown out of the group. When this ceases to be a serious threat, there is less reason for conforming and the person feels freer to be deviant.

GROUP UNANIMITY An extremely important factor in producing conformity is the unanimity of the group opinion. A person faced with a unanimous group decision is under great pressure to conform. If, however, a group is not united, there is a striking decrease in the amount of conformity. When even one other person does not go along with the rest of the group, conformity drops to about one-fourth the usual level. This is true when the group is small, and it also appears to hold with up to 15 people. One of the most impressive things about this phenomenon is that it does not seem to matter who the nonconforming person is. Regardless of whether this is a high-prestige, expert figure or someone of low prestige who is not at all expert, conformity tends to drop to very low levels (Asch, 1951; Morris & Miller, 1975).

In one study done when the South was still quite strictly segregated along racial lines, even a black dissenter seemed to reduce pressure on whites to conform. Malof & Lott (1962), put white southern students into the standard Asch situation with unanimous majorities giving incorrect responses. Then, a black student in the group broke the unanimity by disagreeing with the majority. The amount of conformity—for both prejudiced and nonprejudiced subjects—dropped. In fact, the black student disagreeing with the group caused conformity to decrease as much as a white student disagreeing. Apparently, the presence of someone else who disagrees with the majority always makes it easier for people to express their own opinions, regardless of their feelings about the other person.

This reduction in conformity is found even when the other disagreer gives the wrong answer. If the majority says A, another person says C, and the correct answer is B, the subject is less likely to conform than if everyone agreed on one incorrect answer. Simply having some disagreement within the group makes it easier for one person to remain independent despite the fact that no one agrees with him.

In a study by Allen and Levin (1971), subjects in five-person groups were presented with a unanimous majority, or a three-person majority and a dissenter. The dissenter gave the correct answer or gave an answer that was even more incorrect than that of the majority. The subjects were given three different types of judgment tasks—perceptual evaluations such as those used by Asch, information questions such as whether Hawaii was a state, and opinion items for which there was no correct answer but some popular ones. The results are shown in Table 12–1. For all three items, the presence of a dissenter reduced conformity, even when the dissenter was more incorrect than the majority. The effect was strongest for the perceptual items and weakest for the opinion items.

Morris and Miller (1975) showed that the timing of dissent made a difference. When one person dissented after the majority had expressed its opinion, conformity decreased. But when the dissenter answered before the majority, conformity decreased even more. Apparently, when the subjects heard the correct response at the beginning, the majority's incorrect position carried less weight.

The dramatic decrease in conformity when unanimity is broken seems to be due to several of the factors we have already discussed. First, the amount of trust in the majority decreases whenever there is disagreement, even when the person who disagrees is less expert or less reliable than those who make up the majority. Of course, this is in a situation in which the real subject is also disagreeing with the majority. That is, she initially holds an opinion different

Table 12–1
Conformity Produced by Unanimous Majorities, and by Majorities with One Dissenter Who Gives the Correct or an Even More Incorrect Choice

	TYPE OF JUDGMENT		
	PERCEPTION	INFORMATION	OPINION
Unanimous	.97	.78	.89
Dissenter correct	.40	.43	.59
Dissenter more incorrect than majority	.47	.42	.72

Source: Adapted from Allen and Levin (1971).

from theirs, and she discovers that someone else does also. The mere fact that someone else also disagrees with the group indicates that there is room for doubt, that the issue is not perfectly clear, and that the majority might be wrong. This reduces the individual's reliance on the majority opinion as a source of information and accordingly reduces conformity.

Second, if another group member takes the position the individual favors, it serves to strengthen her confidence in her own judgment. As we have seen, greater confidence reduces conformity. A third consideration involves reluctance to appear deviant. When one person disagrees with everyone else, that person stands out and is deviant in both his or her own and the others' eyes. When someone else also disagrees, neither is as deviant as he or she would be alone.

This last result should probably be taken as encouragement to speak one's mind. In the story "The Emperor's New Clothes," for example, the whole crowd watched the naked emperor in his supposedly beautiful new clothes. However, when only one child had the strength to say that the emperor was naked, everyone else found strength to defy the majority. After a while the majority had become the minority and perhaps even disappeared.

Certainly, this is a strong argument for freedom of speech, because it suggests that even one deviant voice can have an important effect as long as there are other people who inwardly disagree with the majority but are afraid to speak up. It may also explain why in totalitarian states and some orthodox religions no dissent is allowed. Even one small voice disagreeing could encourage others to do likewise. After a while, the regime itself might be endangered. The finding that any dissent substantially reduces conformity stands out as one of the most striking aspects of conformity.

GROUP SIZE Suppose there were two people in a room and one of them said it was very warm. If the room was in fact quite cold, the second person would be unlikely to agree with the first. She would feel cold and would assume that the other was mistaken or feverish. If forced to make a public statement on the temperature of the room, she would probably say she thought it was rather cold.

If the room contained five people and four of them said it was warm, the situation would

People usually enforce conforming waiting-in-line behavior very vociferously. What would be the conformists' reactions here if one person broke the line? Two people? How much would it depend on the total number of people in line?

change. Even if one person felt cold, she would be likely to doubt her own perceptions. After all, it is unlikely that all four of the others were feverish or mistaken. If the person were asked how she felt, she might be uncertain enough to agree with the rest. She might say the room was warm and then wonder what was wrong with her. When one person disagrees with you, he or she is feverish; when four others do, you must be sick yourself. Four people tend to be more trustworthy than one, in terms of both honesty and the reliability of their opinions; it is harder to mistrust a group than one person.

A series of experiments has demonstrated that conformity does increase as the size of the unanimous majority increases, at least up to a point. In some of his early experiments, Asch (1951) varied the size of the majority from two to sixteen. As shown in Figure 12–2, he found that two people produced more pressure than one, three a lot more than two, and four about the same as three. Somewhat surprisingly, he found that increasing the size of the group past four did not increase the amount of conformity, at least up to sixteen. He concluded that to produce the most conformity, the optimal group size was three or four.

Using quite a different procedure and a different measure, Milgram and associates (1969) produced quite different results. The situation was very simple. On a crowded street in New York City, a number of people played the old game of looking up to see whether anyone else would look up also. This time it was done as a

FIGURE 12–2 Group size and conformity. (Adapted from Asch, 1951.)

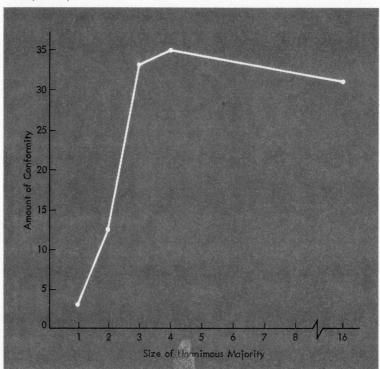

deliberate experiment, and careful observations were made of passers-by.

The confederates stood and looked up at the sixth-floor window of an office building across the street. Either one, two, three, five, ten, or fifteen confederates stood around looking up at the window. The chief measure is what percentage of those who passed by actually stopped and looked up at the window also. When one person was looking up, only 4 percent of the passers-by also looked up; with five confederates, it went up to 16 percent; with ten, it was 22 percent; and with fifteen, it was 40 percent.

A similar increase in conformity as group size increased was found by Mann (1977) in a study of getting in line for the bus in Jerusalem, Israel. When two or four people lined up, there was little tendency for others to join the line. But when six or more were on line, newcomers usually also went on line. The more people there were on line, the more likely it was that other people would join it.

However, research by Wilder (1977) makes it clear that it is not simply the number of people that makes the difference. In this study, subjects heard the opinions of varying numbers of other people. The important difference between this and previous work was that these other people were sometimes expressing their opinions independently and sometimes as members of groups. Some subjects heard the opinions of four people who belonged to one group, some heard the opinions of four people who were members of two different groups, and others heard the opinions of four independent people.

Wilder found that group size had little effect on amount of conformity. The number of independent opinions, from separate groups or from individuals, had a major effect. This may explain why increasing the size of a group above three or four adds little to conformity. Once the group is seen to be acting as a unit, the number of additional individuals within the group does not matter. But adding independent judgments from people outside the group might increase conformity.

COMMITMENT TO AN INDEPENDENT JUDGMENT   A person who is strongly and publicly committed to an independent judgment is more reluctant to conform to a group's contrary judgment. One may risk social disapproval by deviating from the group's position, but it is even worse for everyone to know that you have surrendered your own real judgment just to go along with the group. Hence we can define **commitment** as the total force that makes it difficult to give up a position. Typically, we think of commitment in terms of an individual's feelings of being bound to a position. Does the person feel free to change the opinion or does he or she feel, for some reason, that he or she cannot or should not change it?

There are many ways of producing commitment to an initial judgment. One can write it down, say it aloud in the presence of others, or take any action that establishes the opinion in one's own or others' eyes. In the standard Asch situation, the subject feels little commitment to the initial judgment. He or she has looked at the stimuli and presumably made a judgment, but not communicated it to anybody. The person has not said it aloud, written it down, or in any way made it concrete. So there would be no embarrassment in changing; one would not be admitting that one was wrong or that one was a weak person. There is no reason to stick to the initial judgment except a belief that it is correct. Under these circumstances, maximum conformity occurs.

Once the person expresses the opinion publicly, he or she becomes more committed to it. If others know the initial opinion, they would know that it has changed. The rest of the group might feel that the person is being influenced by group pressure and does not have the courage of his or her convictions, and so on. The individual too would feel this way. But if Jane, for example, has never made her feelings concrete in any way, she can tell herself that her initial judgment was only a first impression, that she was never sure of it, that she changed because she thought it over.

The degree of commitment to a first judgment was varied in a study conducted by Deutsch and Gerard (1955). Some subjects (no-commitment condition) saw the stimuli but did not make a public or private statement of their opinion until they had heard the judgments of the rest of the group. Others made a private commitment by writing their answers on a magic pad before hearing any other responses. (A magic pad is the familiar child's toy that has a piece of cellophane over a layer of graphite. When one writes on the cellophane, it presses into the graphite and the word appears. Lifting the cellophane causes the words to disappear.)

In this weak private commitment condition, the subjects wrote their responses on the pad, heard the other responses, gave their own response, and then erased the pad. In a third condition (strong private commitment), subjects wrote their answers on a sheet of paper they knew was not going to be collected and did not sign it. Finally, there was a public commitment condition. Subjects wrote their response on a piece of paper, signed it, and knew it was going to be collected at the end of the study.

The results are shown in Table 12–2. Clearly commitment reduced conformity. Even the weak private commitment condition, in which the subjects knew no one would ever see what they had written on the magic pad, produced less conformity than the no-commitment condition. The stronger commitments reduced conformity even more. There was no difference between public and strong private commitment, perhaps because the latter produced such strong commitment that conformity was already at a very low level.

COMMITMENT TO NONCONFORMITY A somewhat different type of commitment involves the behavior of conforming itself. Someone who, for one reason or another, does not conform on the first few trials tends to become committed to this nonconforming behavior. Someone who does conform at the beginning tends to get committed to that behavior. An individual can be induced to conform from the start by giving him or her very difficult judgments to make. When the person is subsequently given easier problems, he or she tends to continue to conform. If the person is given easy problems at the beginning and does not conform to the obviously wrong answers of other people, he or she will continue to be independent on later difficult problems.

This is particularly true when responses are public. When others know a subject's response, they know whether or not that person is conforming. This increases commitment to a conformist or independent line. In a face-to-face situation, someone who conforms on early trials continues to conform, and someone who does not conform is generally independent throughout. In a non-face-to-face situation, this effect is less strong. In fact, there is a general tendency for most subjects to conform more on later trials. Commitment, therefore, can be to a particular response (A is the right answer) or a type of behavior (conforming).

	PERCENTAGE OF CONFORMING
Table 12–2 Commitment Reduces Conformity	
COMMITMENT	RESPONSES
None	24.7%
Weak private (magic pad)	16.3
Strong private (written)	5.7
Public	5.7

Source: Adapted from Deutsch and Gerard (1955).

COMPLIANCE AND OBEDIENCE

Conformity is only part of the more general issue with which we started this chapter—how to get people to comply, to do something they would rather not do. Social pressure is one way. As we have seen, a number of factors determine the effectiveness of this pressure. Another way is to reason with the person. Sometimes people will do things they do not want to do just because they have been given information. Students sometimes will read a book just because the professor says it is a good book. Children sometimes will follow good dietary practices just because their parents say it is the right thing to do. But as we all know, it is difficult to get people to do something they do not want to do just by reasoning with them. So we turn to techniques other than social pressure or reasoning.

The Milgram Obedience Study

In the dramatic study by Stanley Milgram (1963) described earlier in Box 2–4, men living in a northeastern city answered a newspaper ad asking for people to participate in a psychology study. They arrived in pairs and were told that the purpose of the study was to investigate the effect of punishment on learning. One of them was selected by chance as the "learner" and the other as the "teacher." The teacher's job was to read aloud pairs of words the learner was supposed to memorize. Each time the learner made a mistake, the teacher was to administer punishment. The teacher sat in front of a large, impressive "shock machine" containing a number of levers, each of which was labeled with the amount of shock it would deliver. The range was from 15 volts to 450 volts. Above the numbers representing voltage were labels describing the severity of the shock: "Slight," "Ex-

treme intensity shock," and "Danger: Severe shock."

The learner was put in a chair in another room. His arm was strapped down to the chair, and electrodes were taped to it. He could not be seen by the teacher or anyone else; they communicated entirely by intercom. Before the testing began, the learner mentioned that he had a slightly weak heart. He was assured by the experimenter that the shocks were not dangerous. Then the experimenter gave the teacher a sample shock, to give him some idea of what the shocks he would be delivering felt like. It was actually fairly severe and hurt considerably, but the teacher was told it was a mild shock.

During the testing, the learner made a number of errors. The teacher told him he was wrong and delivered a shock. Whenever a shock was given, the learner grunted. As the level of shock increased, the learner's reactions became increasingly dramatic. He yelled, begged the teacher to stop shocking him, pounded the table, and kicked the wall. Toward the end, he simply stopped answering and made no response at all. Through all this, the experimenter urged the teacher to continue. "The experiment must go on. It is necessary for you to continue. You must continue." He also said that the responsibility was his, not the teacher's.

Under these circumstances, a large number of subjects dutifully delivered supposedly severe electric shocks. More than half of them continued to the end of the scale and administered the shocks labeled 450 volts. They did this even though the person they were shocking screamed for mercy, had a heart condition, and was apparently experiencing great pain. The "learner" was actually a confederate of the experimenter and did not receive any shocks. All responses, including errors, grunts, and groans, were carefully rehearsed and then tape-recorded to make them identical for all subjects. The "teacher," however, had no way of knowing the situation was staged.

Obedience to Legitimate Authority

The expectations of people in positions of authority are especially likely to produce compliance. The dramatic study by Milgram (1963) strikingly demonstrates this phenomenon. Many people dutifully delivered supposedly severe electric shocks to a man who screamed for mercy, had a heart condition, and was apparently experiencing great pain, simply because an apparently authoritative researcher requested it. Other work has duplicated this research and gotten results similar to those of Milgram. The pressures of the situation, the urging of the experimenter, the lack of perceived choice, and the acceptance of full responsibility by the experimenter made refusal difficult.

Any factors that make individuals feel more responsible for their own behavior or that emphasize the negative aspect of what they are doing will reduce the amount of obedience. In subsequent studies (1965), Milgram has shown that bringing the victim closer to the subject has a substantial effect. In the extreme case, when the victim is placed right next to the subject, compliance decreases dramatically. Tilker (1970) supported this finding and demonstrated that reminding subjects of their own total responsibility for their actions makes them much less likely to administer the shocks.

The results demonstrate that under these circumstances subjects feel enormous pressures from the situation and from demands of the experimenter. Opposed to these feelings are the pressure of responsibility and concern for the welfare of the victim. As long as they can shift the responsibility to the experimenter and minimize in their own minds the pain the victim is enduring, subjects will be highly compliant. To the extent that they feel responsible and are aware of the victim's pain, they will tend to be less compliant.

The phenomenon is even clearer in psychology experiments. Subjects find it extremely difficult to deny the experimenter anything. They have agreed to take part in a study. By doing so they have, in effect, put themselves in the experimenter's hands. Unless the experimenter deliberately frees them from this obligation, the subjects tend to agree to any legitimate request. If a group of subjects are brought into a room and asked to eat dry soda crackers, they will do their best to eat as many as they can. After they have eaten several dozen and their mouths are parched and they are extremely uncomfortable, the experimenter can simply go around and say, "Would you eat just a few more." The subjects will try to cram a few more down. They will do so even though they are given no reason, offered no direct rewards, and threatened with no punishments. Students have been reported to eat huge numbers of crackers in this situation.

The critical factor in obedience is that the person have legitimate authority in that situation, according to the prevailing social norms. Legitimacy refers to the general belief that authority has the right to command obedience to its demands. The experimenter in a white laboratory coat can induce greater compliance in an experiment done in a laboratory, but probably could not do so in a movie theater, because her authority is legitimate only in a scientific context. An airline pilot can induce compliance in an airliner but not in a bar, for the same reason. Not surprisingly, revolutionaries hotly contest the legitimacy of existing political authority because they hope to undermine the populace's level of compliance.

Rewards, Punishments, and Threats

One way to produce compliance is to increase the pressure on individuals to perform the desired behavior by rewards, punishments, or threats. All are standard incentives for getting people to change their behavior. A parent who wants his teenage daughter not to smoke often uses threats. He threatens to deprive her of her favorite TV program, stop her allowance, or give her a beating if she disobeys. He may punish her in one of these ways if she does disobey. Or he may use bribes, and promise her a bigger allowance or extra TV if she obeys.

All these methods—rewards, punishments, or threats—work. A person with acne who is offered $10,000 for giving a testimonial for a skin cream is more likely to agree to have his scarred face appear on television than is one who is offered only $1. Someone who is told that cocaine may cause brain damage is more likely to avoid it than is someone who is told it will give him insomnia (assuming they both believe what they are told). Within limits, the greater the reward, threat, or punishment, the more the compliance.

Compliance can also be affected by modeling and imitation. As with many other behaviors, individuals tend to do what they see others doing. If one person behaves aggressively, the other will also tend to become more aggressive. The same kind of effect occurs with compliant behavior. If the individual witnesses somebody being noncompliant, he or she will tend to be less compliant. This kind of effect has been demonstrated by Bryan and Test (1967), Grusec and Skubiski (1970), and others.

At least for compliance, however, the effects of modeling appear to be somewhat limited. Grusec and Skubiski (1970) showed that to be effective, the model must actually engage in the behavior and not just talk about it. The situation was one in which subjects could share rewards or not share them. There were three conditions—no model, a model who said she would share her rewards but did not actually do it, and a model who did share her rewards. Those subjects who had witnessed a model sharing were more likely to share themselves than those for whom there was no model. But those who merely heard a model say she would share did

not themselves share any more than if there was no model present. In other words, as with many things in life, it appears to be not what the model says that has the effect, but what he or she actually does.

An interesting special case of the use of rewards is the so-called **Hawthorne effect.** One of the most effective ways of exerting pressure on individuals to do something is to show them we really care about them and want them to do this thing very much. The study done at the Western Electric Company's Hawthorne plant, mentioned earlier (Homans, 1965), demonstrated the strength of this principle. Its original purpose had been to investigate the effect of various working conditions on rate of output. Six women from a large department were chosen as subjects, and the experiment took place over a period of more than a year.

The women, whose job consisted of assembling telephone relays, worked in their regular department for the first two weeks (the first period) to provide a measure of their usual rate of output. They were average workers. After this initial period, they were removed from the department and put into a special test room identical to the main assembly room, except that it was provided with a method of measuring how much work each woman did.

For the next five weeks (the second period), no change was made in working conditions. During the third period, the method of paying the women was changed. Their salary had previously depended on the amount of work turned out by the entire department (100 workers); now it depended only on the amount of work turned out by the six women. During the fourth experimental period, five-minute rest pauses were introduced into the schedule—one in the morning and one in the afternoon. In the fifth period, the length of the rest pauses was increased to ten minutes. In the sixth period, six rest periods of five minutes each were established. In the seventh, the company provided a light lunch for the workers. During the three subsequent periods, work stopped a half-hour earlier each day. In the eleventh period, a five-day workweek was established. Finally, in the twelfth experimental period all the original conditions of work were reinstated so that the circumstances were identical to those in which the women had begun.

From the point of view of the experimenters, this seemed like a good, scientific way of testing the effect of various working conditions. Presumably the rate of work would be influenced by the conditions, so it could be determined which promoted work and which interfered with it. The results, however, were not what the company expected. Regardless of the conditions, whether there were more or fewer rest periods, longer or shorter work days, each experimental period produced a higher rate of work than the one before—the women worked harder and more efficiently.

Although this effect was probably due to several factors, the most important was that the women felt they were something special, that they were treated particularly well, that they were in an interesting experiment, and they were expected to perform exceptionally. They were happy, a lot of attention was paid to them,

and they complied with what they thought the experimenter (their boss) wanted. They knew that the main measure of their work was the rate at which they produced, and they knew that this was what was being watched. It did not matter what changes were introduced. They always assumed that the changes were for the good, and that they were supposed to increase their work. So they worked harder. Each change stimulated them to more effort.

This improvement in performance due to the greater attention associated with being part of an experiment has been called the Hawthorne effect. It probably also produces greater compliance with the experimenter's wishes in many social psychology experiments. The experimenter is sincere, presumably dedicated, and talks individually to subjects to tell them what he or she wants them to do. The subjects have put themselves in the experimenter's hands, feel that the experimenter wants them to perform the acts, are having a lot of attention paid to them, and find it hard to refuse any request that is even remotely reasonable. They feel obligated to the experimenter and therefore *want* to help.

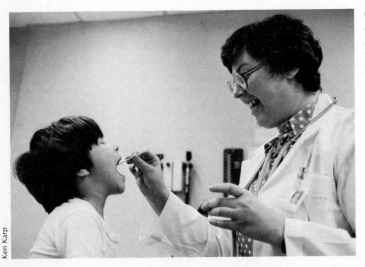

Ken Karp

Children can be induced to do quite unusual things in doctors' and dentists' offices, usually without much reward offered or punishment threatened.

Others' Expectations

To a surprising degree, people will comply with a request made by another person simply because the other person expects it. This effect is easiest to see when request is made directly. For example, having an experimenter tell subjects they should donate money, and reminding them when they do not, causes them to donate more (White, 1972).

A slightly less explicit way of communicating expectations is simply to label the person you are pressuring. If you reinforce people's images of themselves by providing a verbal name or label, it tends to make them behave according to the label you provide. In a study by Kraut (1973), people were asked to contribute to charity and were then labeled "charitable" or "uncharitable," depending on whether they had contributed. Other subjects were not actually called by the label. Later, they were asked again to contribute. The labels had the effect of making them behave the way they did the first time. Those who had given the first time and were labeled charitable gave more than those who were not labeled; and those who had not given and were labeled uncharitable gave less than if they had not been labeled.

On the other hand, labelling people in an unwanted way may make them try to compensate by behaving differently from what would be expected. Steele (1975) called people on the phone and said that it was common knowledge that they were involved in the community or said it was well known that they were not involved in the community, or said something negative that was irrelevant to the community. He then asked them to help form a food cooperative for the community. As you can see in Figure 12–3, the labels (or as he termed it, "name calling") increased compliance. But the negative labels produced even more compliance than the positive one, presumably because the subjects felt they were unfair.

In both situations, the label seems to affect the person's image. Sometimes a label can solidify that image and make the person behave consistently with it; other times, the label can make the person worry about the image and try to do something to make it better. Cognitive ele-

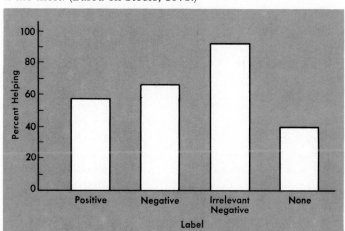

FIGURE 12–3 Any kind of label increased compliance, but a negative label, especially an irrelevant one, increased it the most. (Based on Steele, 1975.)

ments, and especially what the person thinks of herself or himself, play an important role in compliance.

Others' expectations can bring compliance even when they are only implicit. One way to maximize compliance is to place the individual in a well-controlled situation in which everything is set up to make noncompliance difficult. The individual is asked to do something and is free to refuse. However, refusal is difficult because everyone expects compliance. A familiar example can be seen in a doctor's office. Bill is sitting quietly, enjoying a magazine while waiting to see the doctor. Then the nurse asks him to come into the doctor's office. He knows the doctor is still busy with two other patients and will not be ready for another 15 minutes. He would be more comfortable where he is, and thre are no obvious threats for refusing or rewards for complying. Nevertheless, he walks into the office and waits uncomfortably, this time without his magazine and maybe without his clothes—all because the nurse asked him to do so and the situation is set up so that it is difficult for him to refuse.

The Foot-in-the-Door Technique

Sometimes the goal is to get someone to agree to a request most people ordinarily would refuse. One way of increasing compliance in such cases is to induce the person to agree first to a much smaller request. Once someone has agreed to the small action, he or she is more likely to agree to the larger one.

This is called the **foot-in-the-door technique.** It is used explicitly or implicitly by many propaganda and advertising campaigns. Advertisers often concentrate on getting consumers to do something connected with the product—even sending back a card saying they do not want it. The advertisers apparently think that any act connected with the product increases the likelihood that the consumer will buy it in the future.

A study by Freedman and Fraser (1966) demonstrated this effect. Experimenters went from door to door and told homemakers they were working for the Committee for Safe Driving. They said they wanted the women's support for this campaign and asked them to sign a petition, which was to be sent to that state's senators. The petition requested the senators to work for legislation to encourage safe driving. Almost all the women agreed to sign. Several weeks later, different experimenters contacted the same women and others who had not been approached before. At this time, all the women were asked to put in their front yards a large, unattractive sign that said "Drive Carefully."

The results were striking. Over 55 percent of the women who had previously agreed to sign the petition (a small request) also agreed to post the sign, whereas less than 17 percent of the other women agreed. Getting the women to agree to the initial small request more than tripled the amount of compliance to the large request. This effect was replicated in studies by Pliner, Heather, Kohl, and Saari (1974), and in a somewhat different setting by Snyder and Cunningham (1975). Moreover, Seligman, Bush, and Kirsch (1975) showed that the larger the first request, the greater the effect.

Why this technique works so well is not entirely clear. The most likely explanation is that people who agree to a small request get involved and committed to the issue itself, the behavior they perform, or perhaps simply the idea of taking some kind of action. Any of these factors would probably make someone more likely to comply with future requests.

Another explanation might be that in some way the individual's self-image changes. In the safe-driving experiment, for example, a woman may have thought of herself as the kind of person who does not take social action, who does not sign petitions, who does not post signs, or, perhaps, who does not even agree to things that are asked her by someone at the door. Once she had agreed to the small request, which was actually difficult to refuse, she may have changed her perception of herself slightly. Since she agreed to sign a petition, perhaps she is the kind of person who does this sort of thing. Then, when the second request was made, she was more likely to comply than she would have been otherwise.

Performing the first action changes individuals' attitudes toward themselves or the action itself. In either case, this change makes them less resistant to performing a similar act in the future, even when the second request means a much greater commitment. Some indirect support for this explanation is provided in one study (Zuckerman, Lazzaro, & Waldgeir, 1979) in which giving money for complying with the first request eliminated the effect. Supposedly the money provided an external reason for compliance and the subjects had no need to change their self-image. This is consistent with the overjustification effect described in Chapter 5 and with the self-perception explanation of the foot-in-the-door effect.

Sometimes the opposite technique from the foot-in-the-door also works. Two experiments have demonstrated that asking first for a very large request and then making a smaller one can increase compliance to the small one. In one study (Cialdini et al., 1975) subjects were asked to contribute time to a good cause. Some were asked first to give a huge amount of time. When they refused, as almost all did, the experimenter immediately said then perhaps they might agree to a much smaller commitment of time. Other subjects were asked only the smaller request, while a third group was given a choice of the two. Although 17 percent in the small-request-only condition and 25 percent in the choice condition agreed, 50 percent who first heard the large request agreed to the smaller one.

This effect is familiar to anyone who has engaged in bargaining with a used car salesman, a union, or management. The tactic is to ask for the moon and settle for less. The more you ask for at first, the more you expect to end up with eventually. The idea is that when you reduce your demands, the other person thinks you are compromising and the amount seems smaller. In a compliance situation, such as asking for charity, the same might apply—a quarter doesn't seem like much when the organization initially asked for a hundred dollars.

Clearly, both foot-in-the-door and the reverse tactic work at times, but we do not yet know when each of them will operate. One difference seems to be that the reverse effect has been shown when the smaller request follows the large one immediately and is obviously connected; the foot-in-the-door works even when the two requests are seemingly unconnected.

Limits of External Pressure

The most straightforward way to increase compliance is to exert pressure on the individual, which can be done with threats, rewards, direct requests, or social pressure. The person can also be exposed to a model who is doing what the experimenter wants. A different approach is to place the person in a controlled situation designed to put subtle pressure on him or her and to make refusal difficult. It is important in this technique to give the impression that the subject is expected to comply, that the possibility of not complying was never considered, that the experimenter is depending on the person, and that the person somehow agreed to comply by entering the situation. Another factor in this technique is the assumption of responsibility by someone other than the subject. The experimenter or someone else relieves the individual of personal responsibility, so the person feels freer to do whatever is required. The consequences are not the subject's concern or fault.

These procedures tend to increase compliance. However, they are not always easy to apply successfully in real life. Someone trying to elicit compliance often does not control large rewards, threats, or justifications; and it is rare that the person has sufficient control over the situation to produce the conditions necessary to make refusal difficult. In less ideal circumstances, people find it fairly easy to refuse even simple requests.

Sometimes the amount of external pressure that it is possible or appropriate to use produces less compliance than desired. The heroic soldier refuses to divulge the secret information even under torture; the typical nonheroic smoker refuses to give up cigarettes despite the real danger of cancer and heart disease; the letter writer refuses to use zip codes despite a variety of threats and persuasion from the Postal Service. In these cases, increasing the amount of external pressure increases compliance, but for one reason or another, it is not possible to increase the pressure beyond a certain point.

In addition, increasing the amount of external pressure sometimes actually decreases the amount of compliance. Under certain circumstances, too much pressure causes the person to do the opposite. A series of studies conducted at Duke University by Brehm (1966) explored this phenomenon, which he calls **reactance.** The basic notion behind Brehm's work is that people attempt to maintain their freedom of action. When this freedom is threatened, they do whatever they can to reinstate it. Whenever increasing the pressure on an individual is perceived as a threat to freedom of action, the person protects it by refusing to comply or by doing the opposite of what is requested. We are all familiar with the child who, when told to do something, says "I won't." But when her parents say, "All right, then, don't," the child goes ahead and does what was requested. This behavior also occurs in adults.

The clearest demonstration of reactance is an experiment (Brehm & Sensenig, 1966) in which subjects had a choice of two problems to work on. The problems were essentially identical, but the subjects were told that some people were better at one and some at the other, and the experimenter was giving them their choice. Into this simple situation was introduced external pressure in the form of a note from another subject who was supposedly making the same choice in another room. In one condition, the note read, "I choose problem A." The other

subject was expressing a preference, and this put some pressure on the subject to agree with the choice. In the other condition, the note read, "I think we should both do problem A." With this note, the other subject was not only expressing a preference, but also directly trying to influence the subject's choice.

Although the external pressure was greater in the second condition, it produced less compliance. In the low-pressure condition over 70 percent of the subjects complied by choosing the problem suggested on the note. In the high-pressure condition only 40 percent complied— 60 percent chose the other problem. This study demonstrated that even when it is possible to exert more external pressure on an individual, it may not always produce the intended effect. It may sometimes boomerang and result in less influence. This reactance effect has been shown in a variety of situations, and seems to work with both behavior and attitudes.

Another limit on external pressure is that **overjustification** undermines compliance, as noted in Chapter 5 (Deci, 1971; Lepper et al., 1973). It is not always true that the larger the reward, the more effective it will be in getting someone to do something. It is probably true that greater rewards will be more effective, as long as one is willing to continue giving them. However, we often use rewards to get someone to comply in the first place, and then withdraw the rewards and hope they will continue the behavior. For example, we might give a child an extra cookie for making her bed, or give a class a prize for finger painting. Advertisers often provide small rewards in the form of prizes or coupons for trying their products. In all these instances, those giving the rewards do not want to continue offering them.

In terms of compliance, the implication of the overjustification studies is that rewards may sometimes backfire. If the activity is basically uninteresting or even unpleasant, rewards will probably be helpful because they will increase the likelihood of compliance in the first place. And since the task is not enjoyable, there is no basic interest to undermine. But when the activity is inherently enjoyable or satisfying in any way, giving rewards may reduce future compliance. If you think that children can learn to get satisfaction from cleaning up their rooms, rewarding them too much may reduce the chance of this occurring. Similarly, if we reward people for being altruistic, for helping others, or for being responsible citizens, we may make them less good citizens in the future unless we keep supplying them with rewards. The effect of reward is sometimes limited and may depend on the initial interest in the activity and whether the amount of the reward is too great for the particular action.

CONFORMITY IN PERSPECTIVE

In general, all the techniques we have been discussing are useful for producing conformity or compliance in the short run. But they are not generally helpful if we want to produce long-term changes in people's behavior. Almost all the techniques depend in some measure on continuing monitoring or surveillance of the individual. Conformity depends on having continuing reminders of the contrary beliefs and practices of all the people around us. Obedience to an authority is most successful when the authority is physically present a great deal of the time. Rewards or threatened punishments work best when someone is there all the time to offer the reward or threaten the punishment. In most of these cases, people will just go back to their normal behavior if the influencing group or authority is no longer present. However, in many situations we are more interested in producing permanent internalized changes than we are in producing the sort of temporary behavioral changes discussed in this chapter. The processes by which those more permanent attitude changes might take place were discussed earlier in the two chapters on attitudes.

Human behavior, attitudes, thoughts, feelings, and values have almost unlimited variations. We speak in hundreds of different languages. We believe in hundreds of gods, a Trinity, one God, or no god at all. In some cultures, men have many wives; in some, they have one; and in a few, women have many husbands. In some cultures, pork is forbidden; in others, it is a delicacy. Almost every aspect of behavior—business, courtship, marriage, friendship, bargaining, communication, politics—varies from culture to culture. The diversity is so great that members of one culture often find it difficult to exist in another unless they have studied it carefully. They cannot eat the food, their sexual practices are considered unnatural, their manners rude, their every act foreign and wrong. They continually offend people and are offended themselves.

But we also have much in common. We are, after all, members of the same species; we have similar physical characteristics, needs, and abilities. Although we speak different languages, we all have language and use it quite similarly. Although we have different sexual habits, we all have family structures and prohibitions against incest. The exact forms of behavior may differ, but we do perform many of the same acts, play many of the same games, and have many of the same cares and problems. The huge differences among people must be seen against the background of the many similarities resulting from our shared humanity.

Moreover, within any culture, the similarities tend to predominate. Just as fantastic diversity exists *among* cultures, great similarity exists *within* any given culture. Almost everyone speaks the same language and has the same values and the same interests. In the United States, practically everyone likes hamburgers; in Japan, practically everyone likes sushi. The similarity of behavior and values is even greater in subcultures. The smaller the unit of society, the greater the similarity among its members. In the white, middle-class subculture in America, almost everyone has similar attitudes toward marriage and courtship, behaves the same in business, and so on. Any outsider entering a different culture is immediately struck by the fact that everyone seems to be behaving similarly. From the outsider's point of view, it looks as though the people are all conformists.

It is true that people in a culture do behave similarly. But it is important to note that this kind of comformity is an adaptive and necessary phenomenon. Members of a society must be able to assume, to some extent, that others will behave in certain ways, will have certain values, will interpret behavior in particular ways, and so on. It makes life much simpler and allows society to operate. People can interact smoothly, interpret correctly what others are doing, and communicate easily. Perhaps the most dramatic instance of this practical need is provided by language. If everyone spoke different languages or had different meanings for the same words, social interaction would be almost impossible.

Members of a society have an almost unlimited number of conventions and behaviors in common. For example, sexual relations tend to be highly ritualized and specific to a culture. How does one express affection for someone of the opposite sex without being misunderstood? How does a male communicate to a female that he wants to be friends but not lovers? The answers to these questions depend largely on the rituals and customs of the society concerned. An arm around a waist, a light kiss, and holding hands are acceptable approaches in some societies but not in others. In some societies, these gestures between a man and a woman indicate friendship; in others, they would be proposals of marriage. Not knowing these customs, or not following them, makes it difficult to make feelings and intentions known. By conforming to the norms of society, we can communicate our feelings clearly and avoid disastrous or embarrassing misunderstandings.

Similarity among the members of a culture is also due to similar backgrounds, experience, and learning. Children learn to do things in a particular way, to accept certain beliefs, and to develop certain motivations. To a great extent, all children in a society learn the same things. Then when they are adults, they behave in similar ways—not because they choose to, not because they even think about it, but because this is the way they learned to behave.

Much of the similarity of behavior and beliefs we see in a society and that we call conformity is due to necessity and learning. So although conformity usually has a negative connotation, there are often good reasons for people to be similar.

SUMMARY

1. Performing an act because everyone else performs it is called conformity. Performing an act when someone asks you to even though you would rather not perform it is called compliance.
2. Conformity is often adaptive because it is necessary to get along with others and also because other people's actions may give you information about the best way to act in a particular circumstance.
3. In controlled situations, when neither of the above considerations were relevant, there was still a great deal of conformity—about 35 percent in the Asch judgment experiments.
4. People conform because they use the information they get from others, because they trust others, because they are afraid of being deviant.
5. When the rest of the group is not unanimous, conformity drops sharply.

6. Other factors producing greater conformity are larger groups, expertise of the group, and a lack of confidence by the individual. Greater commitment to an initial position reduces conformity.

7. Compliance and obedience can be increased by the use of rewards, punishments, threats, and pressures from the situation. However, too much external pressure can backfire and produce a tendency to resist limitations on one's freedom of action that causes the individual to do the opposite of what is requested.

8. Compliance can be increased by first asking a small request and then a large one—the foot-in-the-door effect. Under some conditions, the reverse also increases compliance—a very large request followed by a small one.

SUGGESTIONS FOR ADDITIONAL READING

ASCH, S.E. (1951). Effects of group pressure upon the modification and distortion of judgments. In H. Guetzkow (ed.), *Groups, leadership, and men.* Pittsburgh: Carnegie Press. The classic study, still well worth reading.

FREEDMAN, J.L., & DOOB, A. N. (1968). *Deviancy.* New York: Academic Press. An experimental study of the effects of feeling and seeming deviant.

MILGRAM, S. (1974). *Obedience to authority: an experimental view.* New York: Harper & Row. A complete though relatively brief account of the many variations Milgram conducted of his well-known demonstration of obedience to authority.

MOSCOVICI, S. (1976). *Social influence and social change.* New York: Academic Press. A provocative discussion of how minorities can and do produce social influence, by a European Marxist social psychologist.

13

BEHAVIOR IN GROUPS

$\mathbf{W}$e are all members of groups that have enormous influence on our lives. Most of us are born into a family group and spend much of our childhood interacting with parents and siblings. As we venture into the larger social world, we encounter new groups—perhaps a neighborhood play group, a kindergarten class, Cub Scouts or Brownies, or a group at a church or synagogue. As we grow up, we begin to join clubs, sports teams, work groups, political parties, and other organizations.

In this chapter we begin by defining a group and examining some of the basic processes of group interaction including communication and competition versus cooperation. We then investigate the nature of leadership in groups, and explore group productivity and decision-making. We conclude with a brief look at some of the potentially negative aspects of group life—deindividuation and social contagion.

BASIC FEATURES OF GROUP BEHAVIOR

Defining a Group

We spend time in many different kinds of *social aggregates,* which is the general term for any collection of people (McGrath, 1984). Here are some examples of the different types:

- *A statistical aggregate:* For research purposes, it is sometimes useful to group together for analysis all members of a particular social category, such as all redheads, all women, all unemployed heads of household, or everyone over 65. Members of a statistical aggregate all have some common characteristic, although they are not likely to know each other or to interact.
- *An audience:* All the people watching the 6 o'clock news on Channel 4 in New York City are part of the same audience, even though they are not necessarily aware of one another and do not interact.
- *A crowd:* When people are in physical proximity and responding to a common situation or stimulus, we call them a crowd. Examples would be

fans gathered outside a rock star's dressing room, people lining up outside a department store waiting for a special sale to begin, or people gathering to watch a street brawl.
- *A team:* A set of people who interact regularly for some particular purpose or activity, such as a work group, sports team, or bridge club, is a team.
- *A family:* Although there are many types, families typically consist of a set of people who are related by birth or legal arrangements and who usually share a common residence.
- *Formal organization:* Larger aggregates of people often work together in some clearly structured way to accomplish a joint goal. Examples would be a school system, a church or synagogue, a national political party, the Sierra Club, or the National Rifle Association.

In everyday language we might speak of all these aggregates as "groups." But social scientists use the term *group* in a narrower, more technical way.

Groups are social aggregates in which members are *interdependent* and have at least the potential for mutual *interaction*. In most groups, members have regular face-to-face contact. This definition of a group is an extension of the basic definition of an interpersonal relationship given in Chapter 9. The definition emphasizes that the essential feature of a group is that members influence one another in some way.

Based on this definition, a statistical aggregate such as football players in general is not a group, since the people in this category do not know one another, have face-to-face contact, or influence one another. The members of the Dallas Cowboys football team are a group because they interact regularly and their actions affect one another. Similarly, all the children who watch "Sesame Street" on TV are part of a common audience, but they are not a group. However, all the children in Mrs. Garcia's second-grade class who listen to their teacher reading a story are part of a group.

Groups vary in many ways: size, duration, values and goals, and scope. One of the most important dimensions is size. The smallest group is the dyad or couple. Most research on groups has focused on small groups ranging from about 3 to 20 people. As social aggregates get much larger, they tend to become formal organizations and may no longer involve knowledge and interaction among all members. To emphasize the distinction between groups and formal organizations, some researchers prefer the term "small group" for social units in which members have face-to-face interaction.

Groups vary in duration, how long the group stays together. Families may continue to exist for many generations, with new members joining the group through birth or marriage and others leaving through death or divorce. Members of a jury might work together for a few days on a particular case, and then be disbanded at the end of the trial.

Groups also differ widely in values and goals. Consider for a moment the differences among a chess club, the local Young Republicans group, the Gay and Lesbian Student Association, and a religious education class. Which, if any, of these groups you might consider joining depends a great deal on your own personal values, interests, and goals.

The breadth or scope of activities performed by a group is another important dimension. Some groups focus on a single issue. For in-

Cheering fans at a football game are one type of social grouping.

stance, in response to a threatened tuition increase, a group of college students might form a task force to formulate alternatives and present them to the university administration. Here, a group is created for one specific purpose. In contrast, groups such as families engage in a great many different activities.

Research on small groups has sometimes studied naturally occurring groups such as families, teammates, or work groups. But there is also a long tradition of studying "concocted groups" (McGrath, 1984), groups deliberately created by a researcher. In a typical study, groups of strangers (usually college students) are brought together in a lab to spend a few hours working on a group decision-making task. We'll discuss the results of experimental studies on groups later in this chapter. For the moment, it is useful to note that whereas naturally occurring groups are often relatively enduring and broad in scope, most experimental groups are short-lived and relatively narrow in focus.

Social Roles

When a number of people are brought together in a group, they do not remain entirely undifferentiated. They develop patterns of behavior, divide tasks, adopt different roles, and so on. For example, Merei (1949) observed that after three or more meetings, groups of young children formed traditions: They decided where each child would sit in the room, who would play with which toy, what sequence of activities would be followed, and so on. In informal groups such as this one, differentiated behavior patterns emerge over time as a result of group interaction.

Often, however, the basic structure of a group is predetermined. The student entering school, the worker taking a new job, the person joining a bridge club are all confronted with a preexisting social structure. For example, in a small computer software business, there may be four distinct *positions:* the owner who created the business, the programmers who develop

new software packages, a sales representative, and a secretary. The positions in nearly any social system differ in *social status* (prestige or ranking). In the software company, the owner probably has the highest status and the largest salary; the secretary probably has the lowest status and salary.

Associated with each position is a particular **social role,** a set of rules and understandings about what the person in that position is expected to do, what the responsibilities are, and so on. Roles define the division of labor in the group. In some groups, such as the software company, positions, roles, and status are explicit and may even be described in a formal organizational chart. Individuals must adapt to the requirements of their position in the group, although they may try to redefine or renegotiate existing patterns.

Cohesiveness

In some groups, the bonds between members are strong and enduring. In other groups, members are loosely linked, lack a sense of "groupness," and tend to drift apart over time. **Cohesiveness** refers to the forces, both positive and negative, that cause members to remain in a group (Festinger, 1950). Cohesiveness is a characteristic of a group as a whole. It depends on the individual level of commitment each group member has. Our discussion of commitment in Chapter 9 is thus relevant to understanding group cohesiveness.

A key positive force is the interpersonal attraction that exists among group members (Ridgeway, 1983). When group members like each other and are connected by bonds of friendship, cohesiveness is high. Indeed, researchers have often measured cohesiveness by assessing the amount of mutual liking among group members. Second, people's motivation to remain in a group is also influenced by the instrumental goals of the group. We often participate in groups as a means to an end—a way to earn a salary, to play a sport we enjoy, to work for a worthy cause. Our attraction to a group thus depends on the match between our own needs and goals, and the activities and goals of the group. A third factor is the extent to which a group interacts effectively and harmoniously. We would undoubtedly prefer to be on a team that works efficiently, rather than on one that wastes our time and misuses our skills. More generally, anything that increases group satisfaction and morale should enhance cohesiveness.

Group cohesiveness is also affected by negative forces that discourage members from leaving, even if they are dissatisfied. Sometimes people stay in groups because the costs of leaving are high or because they have no available alternatives. We may despise our co-workers at the factory, but stay because there are no other job openings in town. We may dislike our teachers, but stay in their classes because we have no choice in the matter.

COMMUNICATION

Communication is essential to group activities, whether it be the endless talking at a committee meeting, the shared intimacies of a late-night conversation between friends, or a family conference to make plans for a weekend trip.

Who Talks

A characteristic of almost all groups is that some people talk a great deal and others say very little. The circumstances of the situation seem to have little effect on this pattern. It does not matter if the group is structured or unstructured, the problem they are discussing specific or general, the members friends or strangers. In a seminar, for example, there usually seem to be one or two people who monopolize the discussion, regardless of the topic. They do most of the talking, and the rest say only an occasional word or two.

Probably the most striking aspect of this phenomenon is that it occurs no matter what the size of the group. Regardless of how many members there are, communication follows a fairly regular pattern that can be represented by a logarithmic function. Figure 13–1 illustrates this pattern for groups of four, six, and eight. Note that in all cases one person does a great deal of talking, the next most talkative person

does considerably less, and so on. The amount of talking done by each person drops at a logarithmic rate. In an eight-member group, two people contribute 60 percent of the conversation, one other contributes 14 percent, and the other five contribute only 26 percent among them. Clearly, the exact percentage contributed by each person will vary from group to group. There are even some groups in which all members make equal contributions. But by and large, a pattern roughly similar to the one illustrated (see page 358) appears in most groups.

Talking and Leadership

There are clear links between how much group members talk and leadership in the group. If a person is designated as the group leader, say by being appointed to chair a committee, he or she is likely to participate very actively in group discussions. Even more interesting, however, is the observation that when there is no known leader, communication can influence who becomes a leader. To make someone a leader, often all that is necessary is to make the person talk more. An experiment by Bavelas, Hastorf, Gross, and Kite (1965) demonstrated this effect.

Subjects from industrial engineering classes, who did not know each other well, were re-

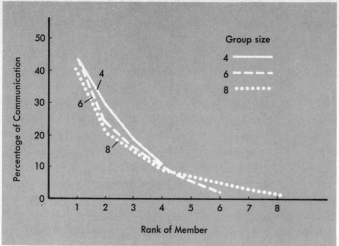

FIGURE 13-1

The amount of communication by members of a group follows a logarithmic or exponential curve. Regardless of the size of the group, the most talkative members does about 40 percent of the communicating and the amount of the other members' communication drops off sharply. (Adapted from Stephan & Mishler 1952.)

cruited to participate in group discussions. They were divided into four-man groups, given a problem to discuss for 10 minutes, and told their discussions would be observed through a one-way mirror. An observer recorded the amount of time each man talked and the number of times he talked. After the session, all participants filled out questionnaires in which they were asked to rank the other subjects on general leadership ability and a few other dimensions. Three sessions were held.

Each subject had in front of him a small box containing a red and a green light, and only he could see his own lights. Before the second discussion session, some men were told they would receive feedback on their performance. If the red light went on, it would indicate that they had been hindering or interfering with the discussion; if the green light went on, it would indicate that their contribution was helpful. In other words, they would be punished or positively reinforced for what they said.

One subject who was at or near the bottom on both verbal output and others' rankings of his leadership potential was selected from each group. During the second discussion period, he was positively reinforced (his green light was flashed) whenever he spoke. The rest of the group was punished (with red lights) for most of

their speeches. In control groups, members did not receive any feedback. When the discussion period was over, all subjects filled out the rating forms again. Finally, a third discussion session was held without reinforcement and a third rating form was filled out.

The results are shown in Table 13–1. During the second session, as one might expect, the positively reinforced subject began to talk more; conversely, the others talked less. After a while, the chosen subject was doing a much greater percentage of the talking than he had at the beginning. Moreover, this effect persisted during the third (nonreinforced) session, even though he was receiving no special encouragement.

At one level, it would be easy to say that the reinforced subject became more of a leader than before simply because he talked more. Impartial observers would see that he was taking an active, even dominant, role in the group and see him as being a leader. Another and perhaps more important test was the group's opinion. The striking result was that the group also rated him much higher on the leadership scale. In fact, he went from very low to very high.

Simple verbal activity appears to be a critical factor in determining leadership. The more active a part a person takes, the more likely he or she is to be the leader. But note that this re-

Table 13–1		
Effect of Reinforcement on Verbal Output and Ranking as Leader		
DISCUSSION PERIOD	VERBAL OUTPUT[a]	RANKING AS LEADER[b]
First (no lights)	15.7	1.77
Second (reinforcement)	37.0	3.30
Third (no lights)	26.9	2.70

[a]Figures are percentages of total group output.
[b]Figures are ranking on a scale from 1 (lowest) to 4 (highest).
Source: Adapted from Bavelas, Hastorf, Gross, and Kite (1965).

search was done in discussion groups, in which one might expect verbal activity to be particularly important. It may be that other kinds of activity are equally or more important in other kinds of groups—the strong, silent athlete may be the captain of the sports team. We do know, however, that verbal behavior is extremely important in many situations and that a person who talks a lot is for that reason alone often perceived as a leader by others.

Communication Networks

We have been discussing groups as though every member were free to communicate with every other member. Although this is true in a discussion group, there are many groups in which communications are limited. Several studies have investigated the effects of a variety of so-called **communication networks.**

The typical study in this area consists of

In this football huddle, the quarterback gives teammates instructions for the next play. This illustrates a wheel communication network in which messages are channeled through one person.

Gus Boyd, Photo Researchers, Inc.

forming a group to work on some problem and imposing limits on the communication permitted among the members. This is done by putting the subjects in separate rooms or booths and allowing them to communicate only by written messages or an intercom system. The experimenters are then able to control who can talk with whom, and a large number of different communication patterns can be imposed.

Some of these patterns are represented for groups of five people in Figure 13–2. There you can see that the structures determine freedom of communication. In the circle, all members are equal—each can talk to two neighbors and to no one else. In the chain, two of the members can each talk to only one person. Obviously, in terms of communication it is worse to be at the end of a chain. The three other members are equal in terms of the number of persons they can talk to, but the person in the middle is more central. The two intermediate people are somewhat isolated from the opposite ends. This progression is carried a step further in the Y-shaped structure. With three end members,

only one of the others is able to talk to two people, and the fifth member is able to talk to three. In the wheel, one member can talk to everyone else, but all the other members can talk only to the central one.

COMMUNICATION NETWORKS, MORALE, AND EFFICIENCY   Research shows that communication patterns such as these affect many aspects of group life (Ridgeway, 1983; Shaw, 1981). Communication networks influence group *morale*. Leavitt (1951) found that the more freedom group members had to talk, the more satisfied they were. The person who could talk to everyone was the most content, whereas those on the end of a chain, who could talk to only one other person, were the least content. Since the total morale of a group depends on the satisfaction of all group members, not just those in key positions, overall group satisfaction is highest in patterns such as the circle, where everyone has an equal opportunity to communicate.

Communication networks can also affect the *efficiency* of group problem-solving. Although

FIGURE 13–2   Examples of different types of communication networks.

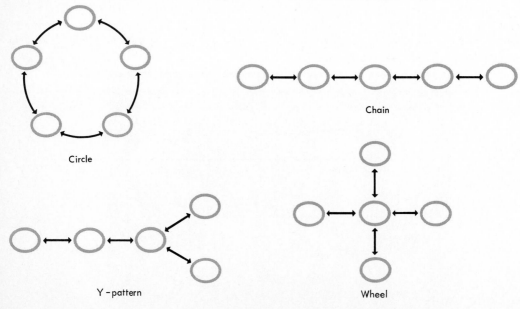

Circle

Chain

Y - pattern

Wheel

the evidence on how different kinds of networks affect group performance is not entirely consistent, most of the data suggest that centralized groups are more effective when they work on simple problems, and decentralized groups are more effective with complex problems. Imagine, for example, that each member of a group is given a card with a different symbol on it and the group task is to make a list of all the symbols. This kind of simple task is ideal for groups with highly centralized communication networks: The leader can easily collect the information from each individual and compile the final list. But complex problems are usually accomplished more effectively by groups with decentralized communication patterns, where freer interaction among members is possible.

COMPETITION VERSUS COOPERATION

In some groups, people interact cooperatively: They help each other, share information, work together for mutual benefit. In other groups, people compete: They put their own goals first and strive to outperform the rest. What determines whether group behavior is competitive or cooperative?

An important factor is the reward structure of the situation—the way in which rewards and desired outcomes are allocated. A *competitive reward structure* exists when one person's gain is another's loss. If you win a pot in poker, the other players must lose. In an Olympic swimming match, only one person can get the gold medal. If a course is graded on a curve, only a few students can get As. In these situations, the outcomes of group members are negatively linked; an individual does best when others do poorly.

In other situations, there is a *cooperative reward structure*. In order for a football team to win games, teammates must work together. People's rewards are positively linked, so that what happens to one affects all the others. The better each player does, the more likely it is that the entire team will be victorious.

An *individualistic reward structure* exists when the outcomes of individuals are independent of each other. Here, what happens to one has no impact on the others. If a teacher gives an A to everyone who gets 90 percent correct on a test, it is possible for all students to get As, or for none to get As. Each person's grade is independent of how classmates perform.

Often, the reward structure in a situation is mixed or unclear. People have choices about whether to cooperate or to compete. How do people behave when the situation permits either competition or cooperation?

Laboratory Studies

Much of the research on competition and cooperation has used laboratory games that simulate key features of everyday interaction. We will discuss research using two of the most popular games, the trucking game and the prisoner's dilemma. A common finding from these studies is that subjects (usually middle-class, white college students) tend to compete, even when cooperation would be a more rewarding strategy.

THE TRUCKING GAME   In a classic experiment on this topic, Deutsch and Krauss (1960) used a simple game called the *trucking game*. Each subject was asked to imagine that she was running a trucking company (either the Acme or the Bolt Company) and had to get a truck from one point to another as quickly as possible. The

Whether people compete or cooperate depends on the reward structure in the situation. The Olympics are fiercely competitive because only one person can get the gold medal in each event. Here Scott Hamilton receives the gold medal in figure skating. In a game of volleyball, interaction among members of each team is cooperative. A great shot by one player helps all the teammates.

two trucks were not in competition; they had different starting points and different destinations. There was, however, one hitch—the fastest route for both converged at one point to a one-lane road, and they had to go in opposite directions. This is shown in Figure 13–3. The only way both could use the road would be for one of them to wait until the other had passed through. If either truck entered the road, the other could not use it; and if they both entered the road, neither of them could move at all until

one had backed up. In addition, each player had a gate across the direct route that could be raised by pressing a button. The gate prevented the road from being used.

Each truck was provided with an alternative route that did not conflict with the other's, but was much longer. In fact, the game was set up so that taking the alternate route was guaranteed to lose points, whereas taking the direct route would gain points for both sides, even if they alternated at the one-lane section of the

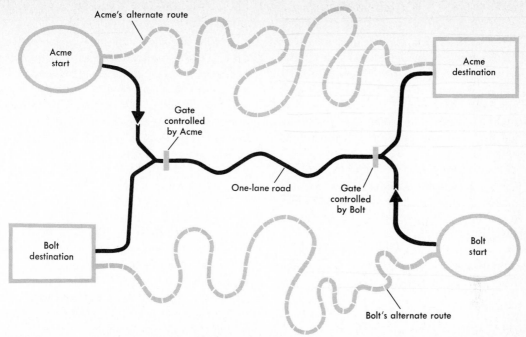

FIGURE 13–3   Road map of the trucking game. The players must get their truck to its destination as quickly as possible. Although they can do this efficiently only by cooperating and sharing the one-lane road, they often compete, particularly when gates are provided. (Adapted from Deutsch & Krauss, 1960, p. 183.)

road. The players were told that their goal was to earn as many points as possible for themselves. Nothing was said about earning more points than the other player.

The results of this experiment were striking. It was clear to the participants that the optimal strategy was to cooperate by alternating in using the one-lane road. In this way, they could both use the direct route and one would be delayed only a few seconds while the other was getting through. Despite this, there was little cooperation between the players. Instead of allowing each other to use the one-lane road, they fought for its use, raised their gates, and both of them ended up losing points.

In a typical trial, both sides would try to use the road and would meet in the middle head on. They would stubbornly stay there for a while, each refusing to retreat. The players

might laugh nervously or make nasty comments. Finally, one of them would back up, erect the barrier, and use the alternate route. On the next trial, they would do the same thing, and so it went. An occasional cooperative trial might occur, but most trials were competitive.

THE PRISONER'S DILEMMA   The tendency to compete is not due to unique characteristics of the trucking game. It also occurs in many other games, such as the *prisoner's dilemma,* so-called because it is based on a problem faced by two suspects at a police station. The district attorney thinks the suspects have committed a major crime together but has no proof against either one. The prisoners are put into separate rooms, and each is told that he has two alternatives—to confess or not to confess. If neither confesses, they cannot be convicted of a major crime. But the district attorney tells them he can get them convicted of minor crimes and that they will both receive minor punishments. If they both confess, they will be convicted of the major crime. But the district attorney says he will ask for leniency. If one of them confesses and the other does not, the confessor will be freed for helping the state, and the other suspect will get the maximum penalty. The situation is shown in Figure 13-4.

Obviously, there is a conflict. If one suspect thinks his partner is going to confess, it is essential for him to confess also; on the other hand, the best joint outcome is for neither to confess and then for both to take the minor sentences. Thus, if the suspects trust each other, they should not confess. However, if one suspect trusts his partner and is convinced he will

not confess, the first would do even better to confess and in that way be freed.

We do not know what real prisoners would do under these circumstances. In research on the problem, much of the drama is removed but the game is basically similar. Instead of playing for their freedom, subjects play for points or money. They play in pairs but usually are not allowed to talk to each other. Each player has a choice of two strategies, and each player's payoff depends both on what he does and on what his partner does.

The exact pattern of payoffs varies; a typical one is shown in Figure 13–5 for two players, Pete and Joe. If both choose option X, each gets 10 points. If Pete chooses X and Joe chooses Y, Pete loses 15 and Joe wins 15. If both choose Y, they both lose 5 points. In other words, they can cooperate (choose X) and both win, or they can compete (one or both choosing Y) and try to win a lot but risk losing.

The players are told that the goal is to score as many points as they can. It is clear to virtually all of them that the way to have the highest score is for both to select X (the cooperative choice) on every trial. But just as with the trucking game, there is a strong tendency to compete. In a typical game, only about a third of the choices are cooperative. Moreover, as the game progresses (and the players have usually won fairly few points), the number of cooperative choices actually goes down. The players choose the competitive strategy more and more, despite the fact that they know they can win more by cooperating.

One factor in this competitive behavior is that for any single play, the competitive choice has a short-run advantage. Let us analyze the game shown in Figure 13-5 more closely. If Pete selects the cooperative strategy, his payoff depends on what Joe does. If Joe chooses the cooperative strategy, Pete wins 10 points; if Joe chooses competitively, Pete loses 15 points. If Pete chooses the competitive strategy, once again his payoff depends on Joe. If Joe chooses

FIGURE 13–4 Prototype of prisoner's dilemma game. Two prisoners have the choice of confessing or not confessing. If they trust and support each other by not confessing, each receives a light sentence; if they both confess, they receive relatively heavy sentences; and if one confesses and the other does not, the former is released while the latter gets a very heavy sentence. The dilemma is that if either one has complete trust in the other, he would do best by being untrustworthy himself and confessing.

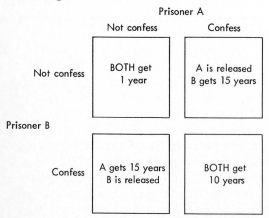

Prisoner A

	Not confess	Confess
Not confess	BOTH get 1 year	A is released B gets 15 years
Confess	A gets 15 years B is released	BOTH get 10 years

Prisoner B

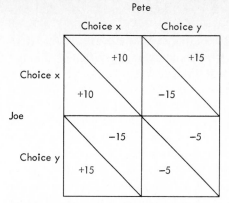

Pete

Choice x   Choice y

	Choice x	Choice y
Choice x	+10 / +10	+15 / −15
Choice y	−15 / +15	−5 / −5

Joe

FIGURE 13–5 Typical prisoner's dilemma game matrix. The top figure in each square cell indicates A's payoff; the bottom indicates B's payoff. X is a cooperative choice, because it allows both members to win. The choice of Y is competitive, because only the one who chooses it has a chance of winning and both may lose. With this matrix there is a great deal of competition.

the cooperative strategy, Pete wins 15 points; if Joe chooses competitively, Pete loses 5. In either case, Pete would do better by choosing the competitive strategy than he would by selecting the cooperative one. If Joe picks cooperatively, Pete wins 15 instead of 10; if Joe chooses competitively, Pete loses 5 instead of 15.

The dilemma is that over a long series of trials, Pete would be much better off if both he and Joe agreed to cooperate. They would both win on all trials rather than winning on some and losing on others. This would clearly maximize their individual gains, and so it would be the most rational strategy.

The only advantage of the competitive choice is that one player can score more than the other, even though he always scores less than he would have if both had picked the cooperative choice. When subjects in these studies were questioned about their reasons for behaving as they did, many of them reported that

they wanted to "beat" the other player. This occurred despite the fact that the experimenter had told them the aim of the game was to get as high a score as possible.

Determinants of Cooperation versus Competition

Many factors determine whether people interact cooperatively or competitively. Experimental game studies show that when the reward structure of a situation is mixed or ambiguous, college students often adopt a competitive strategy that prevents them from maximizing their rewards. But in situations where the reward structure is more explicit and where the rewards themselves are more important than in simulation games, rewards can enhance cooperation. The same students who strive to "beat" their partner in the trucking game may behave very cooperatively in their families or with their roommates—in settings where cooperation is expected and rewarded. Researchers have identified several other situational and personal factors that influence competition.

It has been suggested that Americans are some of the most competitive people on earth, and cross-cultural studies of children would seem to support this view (see review by Werner, 1979). A program of research by Millard Madsen (1971) and his colleagues has investigated the development of competitive behavior in children from around the world. In these studies, children are asked to play games with peers, and the extent to which they select cooperative versus competitive strategies is assessed. Children from Western technological societies are consistently more competitive than children from developing countries in Latin America, Africa, and the Middle East. In one study (Madsen, 1971), for example, 8-year-old Mexican children cooperated on about 7 of 10 trials, whereas 8-year-old Americans cooperated on less than 1 trial in 10.

Within a given society, children from urban areas are more competitive than children from rural areas. And children from middle-class homes compete more than children from lower-class homes. It appears that one of the correlates of industrialization and affluence is greater competitiveness. These differences are usually explained in terms of the rewards and values particular social environments provide for growing children.

Individual differences have also been observed. Kuhlman and Wimberley (1976) recorded people's behavior in several games, including the prisoner's dilemma. They were able to classify individuals into three types, based on how they responded in the game situations. *Cooperators* were concerned with maximizing the joint rewards received by both self and the partner. *Competitors* were oriented toward maximizing their own gains relative to those of the partner—they wanted to do better than the partner. *Individualists* were oriented toward maximizing their own gains, with no concern for the gains or losses of the partner. The researchers found that each type of person tended to assume that the partner had a similar orientation: For example, cooperators tended to expect a partner to behave cooperatively toward them. The main point is that people may vary in their predispositions to compete or cooperate.

Communication among partners is another important factor. In general, more communication leads to more cooperation. In the Deutsch and Krauss trucking game study, three different communication conditions were included. Some subjects were required to communicate; others were given the opportunity to talk if they wanted to; a third group was not allowed to communicate. Cooperation was greatest when communication was required, and least when communication was impossible.

Similar results have been found using the prisoner's dilemma game. Wichman (1970) found that competition was greatest when no communication was possible, somewhat less when partners could talk but not see each other, and least when partners could both see and talk to each other. Wichman found that when there was no communication, about 40 percent of responses were cooperative; when verbal communication was permitted, cooperation increased to more than 70 percent of trials. Communication enables partners to urge each other to cooperate, to discuss their plans, to make promises, to convince each other that they are trustworthy, to learn about each other and so on. Assuming that partners have any tendency to cooperate, knowledge about each other should facilitate it.

The size of a group also influences cooperation. In several studies, researchers have adapted the general prisoner's dilemma situation so that groups of three or more people can play. Several studies (such as Komorita & Lapworth, 1982) have found that as the size of the group increases, cooperation decreases. The specific reasons for greater competition in larger groups have not been determined. It seems likely that as groups increase in size, there will more often be at least one person who adopts an exploitative, selfish orientation. Further, larger groups may feel less pressure to cooperate because of a general diffusion of responsibility among group members.

A final factor is reciprocity. We have seen throughout this book that there is a general norm of reciprocity: People often feel obligated to return both favors and insults. There is some evidence that in the course of interaction, initial competition provokes more competition, and cooperation sometimes (but not always) encourages further cooperation. One strategy that seems especially successful in fostering cooperation is reciprocal concessions. The players take turns giving up a little. This is the traditional compromise solution to most conflicts: Each side starts with an extreme position and then retreats gradually until a common meeting ground is found.

If one player makes a small concession and then waits for the other to do the same, there is indeed greater eventual cooperation (Esser & Komorita, 1975). However, a crucial element of this strategy is timing. If one person gives in too much, he may appear weak and the other will not reciprocate. The concessions must be gradual and sequential. In fact, according to Wall (1977) the most effective technique is to make reciprocal concessions slightly larger than those made by the other person. This reinforces the other's cooperation and results in large concessions and quick agreement. Obviously this does not work unless both sides are willing to cooperate to some extent. If one is totally competitive, the one who tries cooperating will only be taken advantage of and end up with a weaker position than before.

LEADERSHIP

Some form of leadership exists in all groups. The central attribute of leadership is social influence. The leader is the person who has the most impact on group behavior and beliefs. He or she is the one who initiates action, gives orders, makes decisions, settles disputes between group members, offers encouragement, serves as a model, and is in the forefront of group activity. These examples illustrate some of the ways a leader might influence a group; any particular leader may not do all of them.

Leadership Structure

Social scientists refer to a group's unique pattern of leadership as the leadership structure of the group. In some groups, this is relatively simple. The committee responsible for planning a New Year's party at the office may consist of one enthusiastic leader and several followers. In other groups, the pattern of leadership is more complex. Who are the leaders in a professional football team? Possible leaders might include the owners, the general manager, the head coach, the captains of the various team units, the quarterback who calls the plays, or individual team members who serve as informal spokesmen for the team. In this case, various individuals are in charge of different aspects of team functioning, and each exerts influence in specific types of group activities. So whereas some groups have only one leader, other groups have two or more. In general, groups are more likely to have several leaders when they face diverse and complex tasks requiring many types of skills. Then it makes sense to have multiple leaders, each a specialist in some particular aspect of the group's activities (Ridgeway, 1983).

FORMAL AND INFORMAL LEADERS Groups differ in the extent to which their leadership structure is formal or informal. Large organizations such as a business or a school have formal organization charts indicating the official chain of command and giving guidelines about patterns of decision-making and supervision. Even in smaller groups, such as clubs and fraternities, there may be elected officers with specified responsibilities. At the other extreme, some groups have no formal leaders at all. Friendship groups are one example. Another example is the "consciousness-raising" groups designed in recent years by feminists who wanted to discuss their personal experiences and who explicitly rejected the leader-follower model of group organization. To avoid having formal leaders, consciousness-raising groups developed alternative patterns, such as having the women take turns talking and making all decisions by consensus.

What is important to recognize, however, is that groups without formal leaders still have patterns of informal leadership. One person may be more articulate and persuasive than others in group discussions, and so have more influence on decisions. Someone else may emerge as the

All groups have some form of leadership structure. When friends get together, leadership is informal—the person who is most talkative and persuasive emerges as the leader. At a business meeting, the formal leader directs group activities.

Ken Karp

3 M's Audio Visual Division

person to whom others turn to smooth over conflicts within the group. All groups, even those that say they are leaderless, have some leadership structure. And even in groups with formal leaders, there is often a pattern of informal leadership that can be very different from the official structure. The president of the student council may be the official head of the group, but unofficially it may be another officer who actually has greatest influence in decision-making.

PATHS TO LEADERSHIP   Individuals can become group leaders in several ways. One way to become a leader is to be appointed by someone

outside the group. An army lieutenant is the official leader of the company, and is appointed by people higher up in the military organization. Because of this position, the lieutenant can give orders to everyone else in the company, but none of them can give the lieutenant orders. In other situations, such as clubs or student government, a leader is elected by group members. In a third process, a group member emerges over time as a leader. When people interact repeatedly, as in a group of friends or classmates, some individuals typically emerge as informal leaders. These leaders do not have official titles, but most group members would generally agree that a particular person or set of people are the leaders. Outside observers can also spot emergent leaders by watching such things as who talks most in group discussions and whose opinions are most likely to prevail in group decision-making.

TYPES OF LEADERSHIP ACTIVITIES   In general, the leaders of any group must perform two types of activities. **Task leadership** concerns accomplishing the goals of the group—getting the work of the group done successfully. The task leader gives suggestions, offers opinions, and provides information for the group. He or she controls, shapes, directs, and organizes the group in carrying out a specific task. **Social leadership** focuses on the social and emotional aspects of group interaction. The social leader concentrates on keeping the group running smoothly and happily, is concerned about people's feelings, uses humor to relieve tension, and tries to encourage group cohesiveness.

Extensive research (see Bales, 1970; Burke, 1971) has shown that both task and social leadership are important to effective group functioning. The qualities necessary for the two types of leadership are somewhat different. A social leader must be friendly, agreeable, conciliatory, concerned about feelings, and socially oriented. A task leader must be efficient, directive, and knowledgeable about the particular task at hand. In some groups, one person will be the task leader and a different person will be the social leader. But in other situations, one person will combine the functions of both.

Who Becomes a Leader?

The search for factors that cause some people and not others to become leaders is an old one. Two contrasting views have emerged: One emphasizes the unique personal characteristics of the leader, and the other the situational forces acting on the group.

CHARACTERISTICS OF THE PERSON The "great person" theory of leadership suggests that some people, because of personality or other unique characteristics, are destined to lead. To test this idea, many empirical studies have compared the characteristics of leaders and followers (Yukl, 1981). Surprisingly few qualities have been found that consistently separate leaders from followers. In a general way, however, three factors are associated with leadership (Ridgeway, 1983).

First, leaders tend to excel in those abilities that help the group to accomplish its goals. In some situations, intelligence correlates with leadership (Mann, 1959). In other situations, leadership might be linked to political expertise, physical strength, or skills relevant to the activities and goals of the group. A great quarterback

like Roger Staubach or the star of a basketball team like Julius Erving almost automatically becomes a leader of the team. These abilities enhance a person's functioning as a task leader.

Second, leaders tend to have interpersonal skills that contribute to successful interaction. In general, being cooperative, organized, articulate, and interpersonally sensitive would be an asset. Such characteristics enhance a person's functioning as a social leader.

A third factor is motivation. Leaders usually desire recognition and prominence; they are more ambitious, achievement-oriented, and willing to assume responsibility. We emphasize, however, that although these qualities enhance a person's leadership potential, none is a sure guarantee of actually becoming a leader.

CHARACTERISTICS OF THE SITUATION Another approach to leadership emphasizes situational factors. A striking demonstration of situational forces comes from the research on communication networks described earlier in this chapter. The basic idea is that communication is essential for leadership, so the person who can communicate most freely tends to become the leader. In situations such as a wheel network, where all communications are channeled through one person, that individual should become the leader.

A study by Leavitt (1951) showed how the predetermined communication patterns in a situation affect the emergence of a leader. After working in one type of group for a while, group members were asked if there was a group leader and to name that leader. There was a clear progression from the wheel to the circle in terms of who became the leader. The number shown at each position in Figure 13-6 is the number of times the person in that position was named leader. For wheel groups, virtually everyone named the central person as the leader For the circle groups, only half the members named a leader at all, and there was little agreement about who the leader was. The other groups fell in between. It appears that simply being in a position to control communication

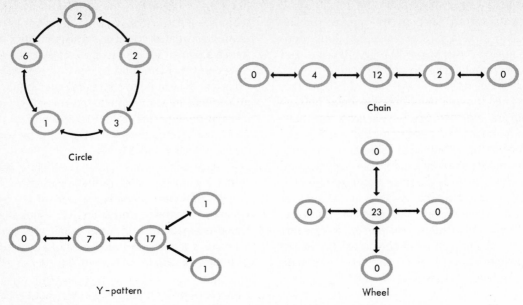

FIGURE 13–6 Communication networks and choice of leaders. The positions connected by a line can communicate directly to each other. The networks range in centrality of communication from the circle (least central, least restricted) to the wheel. The number at each position indicates the number of times the member at that position was considered the leader of the group. (Adapted from Leavitt, 1951.)

can make a person a leader, regardless of individual characteristics.

The importance of communication has not escaped the notice of the revolutionaries of the world. One of the priority targets of any takeover is a nation's radio and TV stations. We have all read that the rebel forces of some general are fighting the government's loyal troops for control of a country's radio and TV stations, or that the stations have been occupied and are broadcasting the news that the takeover is successful even though well-informed sources report that fighting continues. The aim is to take over the communication system, tell everybody the takeover has succeeded, and prevent the other side from saying it has won and from getting in touch with its troops. If one side can hold the stations long enough and assert its victory often enough, perhaps everyone will believe it and then it will become true. The side that controls communication is not only in a strong position tactically, but also has the evidence that it is

the victor: The one who can communicate is, or is seen as, the leader. This is what strategists believe, and research results indicate that, at least in small groups, it is true.

THE MATCH BETWEEN PERSON AND SITUATION Today, most researchers believe that who becomes a leader depends in large part on a match between the characteristics of the person and the needs of the particular situation confronting the group. It should be obvious that different situations require different qualities in a leader. Take the case of expertise—a clear factor in leadership. The particular types of knowledge or ability that are relevant vary dramatically from one situation to another. Being able to pitch well may be a real asset in becoming captain of the fraternity softball team, but it would not contribute much to heading the debate team. Further, expertise is a relative matter. A first-year law student might become the "legal expert" in her family, but would not necessarily become a leader among her law school class-mates or professors.

Leadership Style

Think back to your high school teachers and the different ways they led a class. One may have been a dictator who insisted on discipline and obedience. Another may have been a "nice guy" who emphasized student participation and created a relaxed classroom atmosphere. Researchers have tried to classify styles of leadership and to determine how they affect group functioning. Box 13–1 describes a classic study of "democratic" and "authoritarian" leaders. A more recent analysis of leadership style is Fiedler's contingency model.

FIEDLER'S CONTINGENCY MODEL Researchers generally agree that group performance is affected by the match between the style of the leader and the circumstances of the group. The consequences of a particular style depend on (are contingent on) various characteristics of the group itself. One prominent version of this approach is Fiedler's **contingency model of leadership effectiveness.**

Fiedler (1978, 1981) identifies two styles of leadership, corresponding roughly to the distinction between task and social leadership that we made earlier. Those leaders who give highest priority to getting the work of the group done successfully and who deemphasize relations among group members are called *task-oriented leaders*. The coach who says that "winning is the only thing" and ignores the feelings of team members is an example. In Fiedler's model, those leaders who reverse these priorities by putting group relations first and task accomplishment second are called *relationship-oriented leaders*. This sort of coach would say that it doesn't matter whether you win or lose, so long as you get along with your teammates.

Fiedler also classifies group situations along a continuum from those that are highly favorable to control by the leader to those that are unfavorable. At one extreme are high-control situations in which a leader has high legitimate power, is well liked and respected by the group, and in which the group's task is structured and clear-cut. An example would be a popular Scout leader showing a group of preteens how to set up a tent. At the other extreme are low-control situations in which the leader has little legitimate authority, has poor relations with group members, and is confronted with a task that may require creative or complex solutions. An example would be an inexperienced and unpopular student teacher who is asked to lead a group discussion with high school seniors about ways to improve school spirit.

A main goal of Fiedler's research has been to determine which types of leaders are most effective in which situations. His results, replicated in a number of different studies, are shown in Figure 13–7. Task-oriented leaders are more effective in increasing group productivity in *both* extremely high and extremely low control situations. In other words, both the Scout leader and the student teacher would be advised to give priority to the task. Relationship-oriented leaders are most effective in situations where the leader has moderate control—where the leader gets along well with group members but has a complex task, or when the leader is disliked but the task is clear.

One conclusion we can draw from Fiedler's model is that the effectiveness of either type of leader will change if there is a change in control. For example, one study of army infantry squads (Bons & Fiedler, 1976) found that a squad leader's situational control increased from moderate to high as he gained experience and on-the-job training. In accord with Fiedler's theory, task-oriented squad leaders were at first less effective than relationship-oriented leaders. But as the situation changed, task leaders increased and relationship leaders decreased in effectiveness. The key point is that no one style of leadership is effective in all situations. Ultimately, the most effective leader may be the person who can adapt his or her leadership style to match the situation.

BOX 13–1
Democratic and Authoritarian Leaders

At the end of World War II, a classic series of studies on leadership was conducted by Lewin, Lippitt, and White (1939). Kurt Lewin, a refugee from Nazi Germany, and his colleagues investigated the differences between "democratic" and "authoritarian" leaders. They formed several clubs for boys, each with an adult male leader trained to adopt a different style of leadership. In the *authoritarian style,* all decisions were made by the leader. He was very directive and controlling, gave few explanations, and remained rather aloof from the group. In the *democratic style,* boys were encouraged to discuss group policies and to make their own decisions with the assistance of the leader. Members could select their own partners and decide how to divide up the work. All clubs met for several months. To study group reactions, the researchers staged various events, such as the leader leaving the group for a while or coming late to a group meeting. The boys' behavior was observed during club meetings, and follow-up interviews were conducted outside the group.

Clear differences emerged in the behavior of members in democratic and authoritarian groups. First, the groups differed in emotional tone. The democratic groups were friendlier and more relaxed; members were more group-minded and used the word "we" (instead of "I") with greater frequency. The atmosphere in the authoritarian groups was tense. Boys showed more hostility and aggression, sometimes toward the leader and sometimes toward a group member who became the scapegoat. Boys seemed to form weaker group ties.

A second major difference was that democratic groups encouraged boys to take more initiative. If an authoritarian leader left the room, the boys stopped working on their assigned project. If a democratic leader left, the boys kept on working. Boys in authoritarian groups seemed more dependent on the leader and less capable of working on their own. Apparently, boys in democratic groups participated more, got to know other boys better, identified more with the group, and consequently were more satisfied with the group activities (Ridgeway, 1983).

It is important to note, however, that these results favoring democratic groups occurred in the context of American society. In cultures where people do not expect or value participatory democracy, results might be very different. For instance, in a society where elders are supposed to instruct the young, a democratic leader could be perceived as irresponsible, lazy, and inept, and so group morale might be lower.

Lewin, Lippitt, and White also examined the effect of democratic and authoritarian leadership styles on group productivity. They found that authoritarian groups actually spent somewhat more time working on their projects and completed slightly more projects. The researchers argued, however, that democratic groups made products of higher quality and that members took a more personal interest in their projects. Unfortunately for champions of participatory democracy, subsequent research has not supported this view (Ridgeway, 1983). Although members of democratic groups are generally happier than members of authoritarian groups, they are not necessarily any more productive.

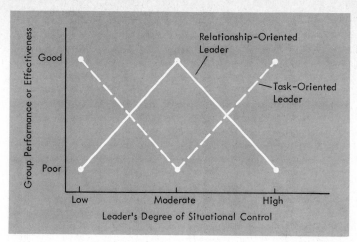

FIGURE 13–7 Fiedler's model of how group performance is determined by the leader's style and situational control. When control is either very low or very high, task-oriented leaders are more effective in encouraging productivity. When situational control is moderate, relationship-oriented leaders are more effective. (Adapted from Fiedler, 1981, p. 625.)

GROUP PERFORMANCE

Are two heads better than one? Are groups usually more successful in getting a task done than individuals alone would be? The answer to these questions depends in large part on the nature of the task involved (Hill, 1982).

Type of Task

Steiner (1972) has analyzed group productivity on several different types of tasks. An *additive task* is one in which group productivity is the sum of individual efforts. When a group of friends works together to push a pickup truck with a dead battery out of a busy intersection, the group effort is the sum of how hard each person pushes. On additive tasks, group productivity is generally superior to the efforts of any one person. (Try pushing a stalled truck by yourself if you doubt this generalization!)

A *conjunctive task* is one in which all group members must succeed for the group to succeed. For a spy team to slip successfully across enemy lines, it is essential that every member

remain undetected. A false move by any one person endangers the whole mission. For conjunctive tasks, group productivity is only as good as the least competent group member (the "weakest link"). In a *disjunctive task,* only one person needs to solve a problem for the group to succeed. If a research group is trying to solve a complex equation, any one person with the right answer can ensure the group's effectiveness. Group performance depends on the skill of the most competent member.

An even more complex situation occurs when a group has a task that can be subdivided among group members. In a football game, for example, teammates specialize in particular types of activities. Group productivity depends not only on the effort and skill of the best or worst player, but also on the group's ability to coordinate individual activities.

To investigate group performance in more detail, we'll review research findings on three topics. First, we'll consider how the performance of an individual is affected by being in a group setting versus being alone. Next, we'll

Neighbors struggle together to free a car trapped in a snowdrift. In an additive task such as this, the success group depends on the combined effort of all individuals.

look at the effectiveness of problem-solving by groups. Finally, we'll explore decision-making by groups.

Individual Performance

How does the presence of other people influence an individual's performance on a task? Consider two examples. John is an outstanding high school runner who hopes one day to try out for the Olympics. He trains very hard, and notices that he runs better with a training partner than by himself. His best performances have been during actual track meets when he was running against tough competitors. Susan is taking her first class in acting. At home in the privacy of her bedroom, she delivers her lines with accuracy and self-confidence. In front of her classmates, she stumbles over her part. As these examples suggest, the presence of others sometimes enhances and sometimes impairs an individual's performance.

FACILITATION VERSUS INHIBITION It is well known that people sometimes perform better in the presence of others than when they are alone. This is called **social facilitation,** and it has long fascinated psychologists. Indeed, experimentation in social psychology is often traced to an experiment in social facilitation conducted by Triplett in 1898. Noting that cyclists raced faster when they were in competition than when alone, Triplett devised an experiment to see whether children would work faster on a task in the presence of others. As he predicted, children worked harder pulling in a fishing reel in a group setting than alone.

Many studies have demonstrated this effect. In the 1920s, for example, Allport (1920, 1924) had subjects work on such tasks as crossing out all the vowels in a newspaper column, doing easy multiplication problems, or writing refutations of a logical argument. Even though participants always worked individually on the task, they were more productive when there were five other people in the room than when they were alone. Social facilitation has been found when the others who are present are actually performing the same task (are "co-actors"), and also when others are merely an audience.

Social facilitation is not limited to humans. It

has been found in rats, cockroaches, and parakeets. For instance, Chen (1937) found that individual ants dug three times more sand when they were in groups than when they were alone.

But sometimes the presence of others inhibits performance. In Allport's early studies (1924), people in a group setting wrote more refutations of a logical argument, but the quality of the work was lower than when they worked alone. Another study (Pessin, 1933) found that the presence of a spectator reduced individual performance on a memory task. Why does this happen?

A major answer was offered by Zajonc (1965). He suggested that being in the presence of others increases an individual's drive or motivation. Whether this increased drive facilitates or interferes with performance depends on the task. When a task requires a response that is well-learned or innate (called a "dominant response"), increased motivation is helpful. The presence of others will facilitate performance on relatively simple tasks, such as crossing out vowels or doing easy arithmetic. For a highly trained athlete, the presence of others is likely to improve performance. But when a task requires a behavior that is not well-learned, the increased motivation impairs performance. Examples would be solving difficult arithmetic problems, memorizing new material, or writing complex logical deductions. For Susan, struggling to remember her lines, an audience may simply increase stage fright and inhibit a good performance. If she were more experienced and had performed the part every night for months, the audience might help her overcome boredom and improve her performance.

Research has generally supported the basic idea that the effect of the presence of others depends on the kind of task. A recent study (Michaels, Blommel, Brocato, Linkous, & Rowe, 1982) provides an interesting illustration in a field setting. These researchers observed the behavior of people playing pool in a college student union building. They identified pairs of

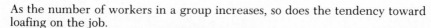

As the number of workers in a group increases, so does the tendency toward loafing on the job.

Tom McHugh, Photo Researchers, Inc.

players who were either above or below average in their play, and secretly made records of their scores. Then, teams of four confederates approached the players and watched them closely during several more rounds of play. Zajonc's theory predicts that good players will benefit from an audience, but poor players will not. The results provided clear support for this prediction. When good players were being watched by four others, their accuracy rose from 71 to 80 percent. When poor players were observed, their accuracy dropped from 36 to 25 percent.

Although there is general agreement that the presence of others increases individual drive or motivation, there is some controversy about the nature of the drive (see Geen, 1981; Guerin & Innes, 1982; Markus, 1981; Sanders, 1981). Some suggest there is an innate tendency to become aroused by the mere presence of other people. Another view is that others motivate us because we have learned to be concerned about how they may evaluate us or because we see ourselves as competing with them. A third view is that the presence of others is distracting. On easy tasks that do not require full attention, we may compensate for the distraction by trying harder and may actually perform better. But distractions created by other people work in reverse on complex tasks. These explanations are not necessarily contradictory: It is possible that all these processes can occur depending on the situation.

SOCIAL IMPACT THEORY Our discussion so far has concerned the question of when the presence of others has positive or negative effects on individual performance. Social impact theory addresses the more general issue of how strong an influence (positive or negative) these others have. As developed by Latané (1981), this theory suggests that the total impact of other people on an individual depends on their number, strength, and immediacy. This is shown schematically in Figure 13–8. The impact of other people increases as the *number* of observers in-

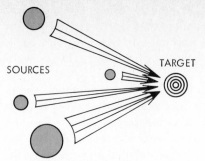

FIGURE 13–8 The impact of an audience on a target depends on the number of people present (the number of circles), the immediacy of the people (the nearness of the circles), and the strength or importance of the people (the size of the circles). (Adapted from Latané, 1981, p. 344.)

creases. Thus Susan should experience more stage fright performing in front of 50 people than 5.

Another factor is the *strength* of the social forces, the importance or power of the people present. Strength might be determined by such things as status, age, and the relationship between the individual and those others. Susan might feel significantly worse about performing in front of her teacher or a casting director than in front of her peers.

The third factor is the *immediacy* of the audience, their closeness to the individual in time or space. Susan's reactions should be stronger if she has a live audience than if she is being watched on a video monitor located in another room (Borden, 1980). Latané suggests that social impact theory can be compared to light falling on a surface: The total amount of light depends on the number of light bulbs, the wattage of the bulbs, and their closeness to the surface. The theory is still relatively new, but it does have some empirical support (Latané, 1981). For a special case of social impact theory, see Box 13–2 on social loafing.

Problem-Solving by Groups

If an advertising executive must develop catchy slogans for a campaign to encourage drivers to use seat belts, should she have her staff members work on the problem individually, or should she bring them together as a group to work jointly on the task? More generally, how do groups compare with individuals in solving problems?

BRAINSTORMING   Much of the early work on group problem-solving involved an activity called **brainstorming**. Devised by an advertising executive (Osborn, 1957), brainstorming is a technique for coming up with new or creative solutions to problems. A group is given a specific problem to discuss, such as advertising slogans for a new brand of toothpaste. Members are instructed to think of as many different suggestions as they can in a short time period.

The rules of brainstorming, as outlined by Osborn, included these:

1. Criticism is ruled out. Adverse judgment of ideas must be withheld until later.
2. Freewheeling is welcomed. The wilder an idea, the better. It is easier to tame down than to perk up.
3. Quantity is wanted. The greater the number of ideas, the more likelihood of winners.
4. Combination and improvement are sought. In addition to contributing ideas of your own, you should suggest how ideas of others can be turned into better ideas or how two or more ideas can be joined into still another one.

In a classic study on brainstorming (Taylor, Berry, & Block, 1958), subjects were assigned at random to five-person groups or to an individual condition. The people in both conditions were then given five problems and 12 minutes to work on each one. One problem was stated as follows: "Each year a great many American tourists visit Europe, but now suppose that our country wished to get many more European tourists to visit America during their vacations.

What steps can you suggest that would get more European tourists to come to this country?" The subjects were told their task was to consider the problems and to offer as many and as creative solutions as they could. There were obviously no "correct" solutions.

Subjects in the alone condition were divided at random into five-person aggregates. That is, although each worked alone, for purposes of the analysis they were considered a unit, and their total production was compared to the production of the actual groups. Taylor et al. compared 5 hours of work done by a five-person group with 5 hours done by five individuals working alone.

The results, presented in Table 13–2 (see page 380), can be considered in terms of the quantity of ideas produced and also in terms of their originality. Quantity consisted of the number of different ideas produced by the real groups and the aggregates. If two people in an aggregate produced the same idea, it was counted as only one. As the table shows, individuals working alone (the aggregates) scored higher than the actual groups. Five individuals working alone produced almost twice as many solutions and unique ideas as five people working together. Someone working alone can concentrate better and also does not worry about competing with others in order to express his or her own ideas. This and other studies have generally found that whatever stimulation a brainstorming group may produce is apparently more than offset by the interfering and distracting effects of other people (Lamm & Trommsdorf, 1973).

WHEN ARE TWO HEADS BETTER THAN ONE?   Research on brainstorming suggests that groups are not always more productive than individuals. But there are many situations in which groups are more effective. Groups have at least two important advantages: Members can check one another's work, and they provide a variety of abilities. Groups are therefore quite effective in working on tasks that involve a large number

BOX 13–2
Social Loafing

In the 1920s, a German researcher named Ringelmann conducted a study of how collective action influences individual performance (reported in Latané, 1981). Ringelmann asked German workers to pull as hard as they could on a rope, and measured their effort in kilograms of pressure using a strain gauge. Sometimes the participants worked alone and sometimes in groups of three or eight people. Common sense and research on social facilitation might predict that the men would work harder when they were part of a team than when they were alone. Just the opposite happened. When pulling alone, individuals averaged about 63 kg of pressure. In groups of three, the total group force was 160 kg, or only 53 kg per person. In groups of eight, total group pressure rose to 248 kg, but each individual's contribution fell to 31 kg—less than half the pressure exerted by individuals alone. This phenomenon—that individuals work less hard as members of a group than they would working alone—has been called **social loafing.**

More recent studies by Latané and his colleagues (Latané, Williams, & Harkins, 1979) have provided further evidence. In one study, undergraduate men were asked to make as much noise as they could by cheering or by clapping. Each person performed alone, in pairs, in groups of four, and in groups of six. The results, presented in Figure A, clearly show that the noise produced by each individual decreased as the size of the group increased. This is the same pattern Ringelmann found. The social loafing effect is similar to the bystander effect discussed in Chapter 11: As the number of witnesses to an emergency increases, the likelihood that any one person will intervene often decreases.

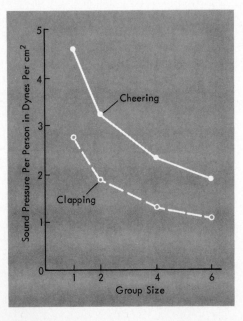

Figure A. A comparison of the intensity of noise an individual makes alone and in groups. (Adapted from Latané, Williams & Harkins, 1979, p. 825.)

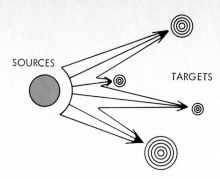

Figure B. When each individual is only one of several targets of social influence, the impact of the audience on the individual is lessened. (Adapted from Latané, 1981, p. 349.)

SOURCES

TARGETS

How can we explain the fact that the presence of others sometimes leads to social facilitation and sometimes causes social loafing? Latané proposes that these patterns occur in different situations. In facilitation situations, the individual is the sole target of influence from an audience or from co-workers (as shown in Figure 13–8). The social impact of the others is all directed at the individual; as the number of people present increases, their social impact on the individual also increases. Social loafing situations occur when group members work together on a task assigned by an outsider. As shown in Figure B, each individual is only one of several targets of the outsider's influence. When others stand with the individual as targets of forces coming from outside the group, the social impact of the outsider is divided among group members. As the size of the group increases, the pressure felt by each individual decreases.

Latané suggests that cognitive processes may contribute to social loafing. People may believe that others in the group are not working as hard as they could. Not wanting to do more than their own fair share, these people may therefore do less work. Further, individuals may feel that in a collective activity their own contribution will be less recognizable, leading to a diffusion of responsibility. As researchers learn more about the causes of social loafing, we may be able to counteract it by giving individuals a greater sense of involvement and responsibility. A recent study (Harkins & Petty, 1982) found that social loafing decreases when the task is difficult or challenging, and when individuals believe they can make a unique contribution to the group effort.

of separate operations, such as complex arithmetic problems. Situations requiring a number of different skills also tend to favor groups. If in order to solve a problem it is essential to know calculus, cellular biology, and organic chemistry, only an individual possessing all this knowledge would be able to find the answer. A group of individuals with specialized knowledge may be the most efficient way to tackle the problem. So the kind of problem often dictates whether a group or individuals will be better problem-solvers.

Group interaction can also influence productivity. We might think that highly cohesive groups would be more productive, but this is not always true. A group of friends might decide that too much studying is "bad," and so might limit the amount of studying each does. A work group might believe that an employer is treating them unfairly and agree to a slowdown. Cohe-

Table 13–2
Comparing the Brainstorming Productivity of Groups and Individuals

CONDITION	MEAN NUMBER OF DIFFERENT IDEAS	MEAN NUMBER OF UNIQUE IDEAS
Real five-person groups	37.5	10.8
Five individuals working alone (aggregates)	68.1	19.8

Source: Adapted from Taylor et al. (1958).

siveness increases productivity only when the group values high performance.

Another characteristic that can influence productivity is the fact that people of higher status in the group tend to have more influence than those of lower status. A study of Air Force crews found that the crew almost always approved solutions suggested by the high-status pilot and seldom accepted the solutions suggested by the lowest-status gunner. Unfortunately, this meant that the crews frequently rejected good ideas offered by the gunner and so were less accurate in solving problems than they would have been working alone or without regard to status differences (Torrance, 1955).

So groups may be better at solving problems when the task can be divided into separate activities that match the special skills of group members (Hill, 1982; Steiner, 1972). Groups can motivate members, can help members to catch errors, and can perform tasks beyond the abilities of any one individual. But groups can also be inefficient and distracting. It depends on the kind of problem and the kind of group.

Group Decision-Making

Do groups make better decisions than individuals? The answer, as we've repeatedly found in this book, is "it depends." Groups certainly can use members' knowledge to reach rational and thoughtful decisions. But groups are also vulnerable to some special forces. Social psychologists have examined two important ways that group processes can affect decisions—group polarization and groupthink.

POLARIZATION   Several years ago, researchers (such as Kogan & Wallach, 1967; Stoner, 1961) discovered that after taking part in a group discussion of an issue, members were willing to support riskier decisions than they had before the discussion. This finding, called the **risky shift,** sparked considerable interest, in part because it seemed to contradict the popular belief that groups are relatively conservative and stodgy about decision-making.

In a typical study, subjects read about a number of complex situations, such as the one described in Table 13–3. In each situation, several choices, ranging from very high risk to very low risk, were available. Subjects were asked to consider each situation carefully and to decide what recommendation they would make or which choice they would prefer. Subjects made their decisions individually and did not know they were going to discuss them later. Then subjects were brought into a group and asked to discuss each problem and to reach a unanimous group decision. Under these conditions, there was a strong tendency for the group decision to involve greater risk than the average of the decisions made by the individuals.

Table 13–3
An Example of the Situations Used to Study Group Polarization

Mr. E is president of a metals corporation in the United States. The corporation is quite prosperous and Mr. E has considered the possibility of expansion by building an additional plant in a new location. His choice is between building another plant in the United States, where there would be a moderate return on the initial investment, or building a plant in a foreign country, where lower labor costs and easy access to raw materials would mean a much higher return on the initial investment. However, there is a history of political instability and revolution in the foreign country under consideration. In fact, the leader of a small minority party is committed to nationalizing, that is, taking over all foreign investments.

Imagine that you are advising Mr. E. Listed below are several probabilities of continued political stability in the foreign country under consideration. Please check the lowest probability that you would consider acceptable in order for Mr. E's corporation to build in that country.

- The chances are 1 in 10 that the foreign country will remain politically stable.
- The chances are 3 in 10 that the foreign country will remain politically stable.
- The chances are 5 in 10 that the foreign country will remain politically stable.
- The chances are 7 in 10 that the foreign country will remain politically stable.
- The chances are 9 in 10 that the foreign country will remain politically stable.
- Place a check here if you think Mr. E's corporation should not build a plant in the foreign country, no matter what the probabilities.

Source: Kogan and Wallach (1967), pp. 234–5.

Many studies conducted in the United States, Canada, and Europe replicated this basic finding, but some began to find exceptions. In particular, some groups actually made more conservative decisions (see Fraser, Gouge, & Billig, 1971). Today, research has shown that when the initial opinions of group members are conservative, group discussion results in a shift toward more extreme conservatism. When the initial opinions tend toward risk, group discussion results in a shift toward greater risk. This basic finding that group discussion leads to more extreme decisions is called **group polarization** (Moscovici & Zavalloni, 1969).

Several explanations for group polarization have been offered (Myers & Lamm, 1976). The informational influence perspective emphasizes that people gain new information as a result of listening to arguments in the group discussion (Burnstein & Vinokur, 1975). Since these arguments tend to support the members' initial positions (Myers & Bishop, 1971), people will usually hear more reasons in favor of their own opinion than against it. Group discussion may also encourage members to think about various arguments and commit themselves more actively to a particular position. Discussion may convince people of the correctness of their original views, and so lead to more extreme opinions.

A second explanation concerns social comparison processes, which we discussed in Chapter 12. The idea is that group members are concerned with how their own opinions compare to those of others in the group. A desire to be liked and accepted by the group may lead individuals to conform to the general opinions of the group.

Other possible explanations have received less support. It has been suggested, for instance, that group decision rules (such as "majority rule") may contribute to polarization. It has also been suggested that people may feel freer to make risky decisions in a group because of a diffusion of responsibility for their actions.

GROUPTHINK Sometimes a seemingly reasonable and intelligent group of people comes to a decision that in retrospect is obviously a disaster. Irving Janis (1983) says this may be the result of a process he calls **groupthink.** As outlined in Figure 13–9, the process begins with the group feeling invulnerable and excessively optimistic. The group comes to a decision without allowing any member to express doubts about it. Members shield themselves from any outside

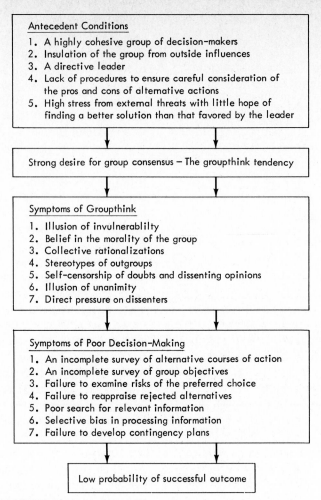

FIGURE 13–9 An analysis of groupthink. (Adapted from Janis, 1983, p. 244.)

information that might undermine this decision. Finally, the group believes its decision is unanimous, even with considerable unexpressed dissent.

Under these circumstances, the group maintains extremely high morale because of the mutual support for the decision. But since disagreements both inside and outside the group are prevented, the decisions can sometimes be disastrous.

Janis suggests that groupthink occurs most often in highly cohesive groups that are able to seal themselves off from outside opinions and that have very strong, dynamic leaders. These leaders propose a particular solution to a problem and argue strongly for it. Group members do not disagree partly because they are afraid of being rejected and partly because they do not want to lower morale. According to Janis, skeptical members do not just go along with the group; they actually convince themselves that their own doubts are trivial and not worth expressing.

Janis claims that groupthink contributed to several disastrous episodes in United States foreign policy. He cites the lack of preparation for the Japanese "surprise" attack on Pearl Harbor in 1941, the Bay of Pigs invasion in Cuba in the 1960s, the escalation of the Vietnam war during the same decade, and Nixon's attempted Watergate coverup in the early 1970s. In all these cases, a small group of powerful politicians, generally led by the president, made a decision in isolation from dissenting voices or from information that would have changed the eventual decision.

In the Bay of Pigs fiasco, President John Kennedy and his advisors hatched a plan to land anti-Castro agents, mostly Cubans living in exile in the United States, on Cuban territory. Their ultimate goal was to overthrow the Communist Castro government. The plan called for the invaders to land at the Bay of Pigs. If the initial landing was unsuccessful, the invaders were to retreat into the Escambray Mountains. The planners apparently thought this escape route was a good one, since there were anti-Castro guerrillas in these mountains. Incredibly, no one in the planning group bothered to look at a detailed map of the area. If they had, they would have realized that the mountains were separated from the landing area by 80 miles of swamps and marsh that no army could have gotten through. As it happened, the rest of the plan was also so badly conceived that the invading force was virtually wiped out before it could even consider a retreat.

Janis has offered various suggestions for combatting groupthink and enhancing the effectiveness of group decision-making. These include:

1. The leader should encourage each group member to air objections and doubts about proposed decisions. For this to be effective, the leader must be willing to accept criticism of his or her ideas.
2. The leader should initially remain impartial in discussions, stating preferences and expectations only after group members have expressed their own views.
3. The group should divide into subcommittees to discuss issues independently and then come together to hammer out differences.
4. Outside experts should be invited to participate occasionally in group discussions and should be encouraged to challenge the views of the group members.
5. At each meeting, at least one person should be assigned the role of critic or devil's advocate to challenge group ideas.

These suggestions are designed to force the group to consider many alternatives, to avoid a false illusion of consensus, and to consider all relevant information.

Empirical support for the notion of groupthink comes from two sources. First, at least some of Janis's ideas are based on and supported by basic research on group processes (Janis, 1983). Second, there have been a few direct tests of specific predictions from the model (Longley & Pruitt, 1980). In one laboratory study (Flowers, 1977), for example, teams of students met to discuss a hypothetical problem. Some group leaders were trained to use a "closed" style that should increase groupthink; others were trained to use an "open" style. As predicted, groups with open leaders made more use of the information available to them and came up with more possible solutions to the problem. Contrary to prediction, however, there was no difference in the amount of groupthink in high-cohesion groups (made up of acquaintances) and low-cohesion groups (made up of strangers).

The group processes Janis calls groupthink are apparently quite complex (see Longley & Pruitt, 1980). Many cohesive groups with strong leaders make excellent decisions. Indeed, the various groups involved in the disasters studied by Janis often made reasonable decisions on other occasions. Both the Roosevelt and Kennedy administrations are thought by many to have been extremely effective in dealing with crisis situations. More research will be needed to clarify the conditions under which decision-makers engage in groupthink.

SOCIAL CONTAGION AND DEINDIVIDUATION

Most often, behavior in groups is fairly routine: High school students go through their lessons at school, workers make decisions and perform their jobs at the factory, and so on. But occasionally, people in groups act in extreme and irrational ways.

In 1931, a young black man, accused of raping a white woman, was being held in a southern jail. There was no evidence against him except that he was in the general vicinity of the crime. A crowd gathered outside the jail, built up, and got more and more excited and enraged. Members of the crowd talked of lynching, and before long the crowd had turned into an angry mob. It rushed the jail, broke down the doors, and dragged the prisoner from his cell. He was tortured and killed in a sadistic orgy of violence.

That groups sometimes become disorganized is hardly surprising. The more interesting phenomenon is that people in groups will behave in ways they would not by themselves. In 1896 Le Bon suggested that people in a mob tend to feel and behave the same way because the emotions of one person spread through the group. When one person does something, even if it would ordinarily be unacceptable to most of the others, everyone else tends to do it also. He called this *social contagion:* Mob behavior is infectious, like a cold spreading through members of a school classroom.

As noted in our discussion of aggression (Chapter 10), Le Bon explained social contagion in terms of a breakdown of normal control mechanisms. Our actions are usually controlled by our moral sense, our value system, and the social rules we have learned. In groups, we sometimes lose a sense of responsibility for our own actions; we feel that the group is responsible. Our own control system is weakened or breaks down. Once an individual's control mechanism is weakened, primitive, aggressive, and sexual impulses are free to be expressed, and this results in violent, immoral acts.

Social psychologists (see Festinger, Pepitone, & Newcomb, 1952; Zimbardo, 1970) have translated these ideas into more modern terms. They propose that people in groups sometimes experience **deindividuation.** Personal identity is replaced by an identity with the goals and actions of the group. The individual becomes less aware of his or her own values and behavior, and instead focuses on the group and the situation (Diener, 1980). Deindividuation involves a loss of personal responsibility, as well as heightened sensitivity to what the group is doing. In a sense, each person in the group thinks of his or her own actions as being part of the *group's* behavior. This causes people to feel less responsible for their own actions and less concerned about the consequences. And it can set the stage for antisocial acts. But deindividuation can also lead an individual to act in prosocial ways —if the group favors such actions.

A key factor is anonymity. Anything that makes members of a group less personally identifiable should increase the effect. The more anonymous the group members are, the less they feel they have an identity of their own, the more irresponsibly they may behave. In a mob, most of the people do not stand out as individuals. They blend together and, in a sense, do not have an identity of their own. Conversely, to the extent that they are identifiable and feel that they are, they retain their feeling of individuality and are less likely to act irresponsibly.

In an experiment by Singer, Brush, and Lublin (1965) to test this notion, some subjects were made easily identifiable and others were made more difficult to identify. In the former condition, everyone dressed in normal clothes, which meant that each was dressed differently from the others. In addition, the subjects were called by name, and everything was done to make each one stand out as an individual. In the latter condition, all the subjects put on identical lab coats. The experimenter avoided using their names and, in general, tried to give the impression that their individual identities did not matter much. The group then discussed a variety of topics, including one that required the use of obscene language.

Groups in the low-identifiable condition showed much more freedom in all the discussions and particularly in the one involving obscene words. There were fewer pauses in the conversation, a more lively discussion, and a greater willingness to use the obscene language that was necessary for a good discussion of the topic. Subjects who were more easily identified were much more constrained and appeared quite reluctant to use the taboo words.

A more dramatic illustration of deindividuation was provided in an experiment by Zimbardo (1970). Groups of four young women were recruited to take part in a study supposedly involving empathic responses to strangers. In one condition, participants were greeted by name, wore name tags, and were easily identifiable. In another condition, subjects wore oversized white lab coats and hoods, were never called by name, and were difficult to identify. All the groups were given an opportunity to deliver electric shocks to a person not in the group. The subjects who were not identifiable gave almost twice as many shocks as the others. Apparently being less identifiable produced a marked increase in aggression, supporting the idea that loss of individuality is one cause of the violent, antisocial behavior sometimes exhibited by groups.

A clever demonstration of the deindividuation effect involved watching children who were trick-or-treating on Halloween. In this study (Diener et al., 1976), some of the children were asked their names by the adults in the homes, and others were not. Then they were given the opportunity to steal extra candy when the adult was not present. Those who had been asked their names were less likely to steal, even though the chances of getting caught were virtually zero in all cases.

Johnson and Downing (1979) have pointed out that in almost all the research, subjects have worn disguises or masks that have negative implications. Zimbardo used Ku Klux Klan outfits; most Halloween masks are of monsters or ghosts. Perhaps it is not the anonymity that in-

UPI/Bettmann Archive

When the anonymity of being in a group causes people to lose a sense of their personal identity, antisocial behavior becomes more likely. During a massive power blackout in New York City, these looters, young and old, ransacked a grocery store and carried off merchandise.

BOX 13–3
Mass Hysteria: Social Contagion and Physical Illness

One early spring, most of the 35 workers in a university computer center keypunch room were mysteriously taken ill (Stahl, 1982). They complained of a "strange and burning odor" and suffered from headaches, nausea, vomiting, hyperventilation, and tearing eyes. So serious was the problem that 10 workers were taken to the local emergency room. Many suspected that a "mystery gas" had caused the outbreak. The university called in a physician and a professor of environmental studies to investigate. The epidemic soon subsided, and the experts told workers that the problem may have been caused by an atmospheric inversion due to smoke from a local power plant. What the experts did not tell the workers was that there was absolutely no evidence from lab tests that any atmospheric inversion had actually caused the illness.

In 1983, during a time of great tension in the Israeli-occupied West Bank of the Jordan, a mass illness broke out among Arab residents. On one day alone, over 300 school girls were hospitalized, triggering violence that wounded two Israeli soldiers and a Palestinian youth. The victims, mostly teenage girls, complained of nausea, dizziness, blurred vision, and stomach aches. Many Palestinians in the area suspected that the Israelis were somehow poisoning them. Israeli officials reported that extensive investigations had found no evidence of foul play.

Both these true stories illustrate a phenomenon popularly called "mass hysteria." In a typical case, symptoms such as fainting and nausea break out among a group of people, perhaps co-workers or classmates. Victims are often young, poorly paid, and female. The symptoms spread rapidly to other group members and are blamed on some mysterious source, such as a poison gas or an insect. Experts find no physical or organic explanation for the illness, which subsides in several days. This phenomenon, technically called "mass psychogenic illness," is believed to be caused by group processes rather than physical pathogens (see the review by Colligan, Pennebaker, & Murphy, 1982).

Mass psychogenic illness generally occurs as a group reaction to severe stress. In the case of the computer center workers, the daily stress of a monotonous, low-paying job with rigid rules was compounded by heavy construction going on next door. For a two-week period, workers were exposed to frequent but unexpected dynamite blasts throughout the day. In the case of the Arab schoolgirls, stress resulted from the recent warfare and constant Arab-Israeli tensions on the West Bank.

The first victims of mass psychogenic illness are often social isolates, who may have few friends and may have had previous fainting spells. Soon, however, the illness spreads through friendship and communication networks to other group members. It is important to emphasize that the symptoms experienced in such cases are real and often quite painful and distressing. Stricken individuals are not faking illness; their suffering is genuine. What is fascinating about this fairly rare occurrence is that the cause of the illness is social-psychological rather than physiological.

Explanations for mass psychogenic illness are still preliminary. It appears that many symptoms such as hyperventilation and fainting are related to stress, and may be further heightened as rumors about "mystery gases" or other "poisons" spread. Group processes may cause the victims to define their symptoms as more serious than they might otherwise, and lead people to attribute their illness to mysterious external threats rather than to stress and anxiety.

creases the violation of norms, but the kind of disguise. To test this, anonymity was produced by having people wear Ku Klux Klan outfits or nurses' outfits consisting of white hats and coats. Those wearing outfits were compared to others wearing normal clothing. It was found that the Ku Klux Klan outfit had only a slight effect on the level of shock subjects gave (thus not replicating Zimbardo's results). Perhaps more important, the nurses' uniforms actually reduced the number of shocks given. Although anonymity sometimes produces increased aggression, these results indicate that people are influenced by social context—in this case by the uniforms they wore. If the uniform implies positive, prosocial behavior, the wearer may behave accordingly.

The critical factor in deindividuation is not membership in a group, but anonymity. Re-

search (reviewed by Diener, 1980) has shown the importance of anonymity and reduced self-awareness in creating the effect. There is no evidence that simply being in a group produces deindividuation or increases antisocial behavior. For example, Diener (1976) observed young adults in a situation in which they were free to act aggressively toward someone who would not harm them in any way. In all conditions, the subjects first observed someone else acting aggressively toward the "victim" and thus had a model to imitate. Yet subjects who were alone with the victim were actually more aggressive than those who were in a group. In this case, being in a group *decreased* aggressiveness. Being in a group leads to deindividuation only when the group provides anonymity and directs the individual's focus away from the self and toward the social setting.

SUMMARY

1. A group is a social aggregate in which people are interdependent: what happens to one person affects the outcomes for other group members. Social roles are rules and understandings about how various group members should behave; roles define the rights and responsibilities of group members. Cohesiveness refers to both the negative and positive forces that cause members to stay in a group.

2. In any group, some people usually talk more than others, and those who talk a lot tend to emerge as leaders. Limitations imposed on group communication can create various kinds of communication networks. Centralized networks (one person is allowed to talk to everyone, but the

other people can talk only to the central person) are efficient for solving simple problems. Decentralized networks produce higher morale and are probably superior for solving complex problems.

3. Much research on competition and cooperation has used laboratory games such as the trucking game and the prisoner's dilemma. In these studies, Americans often tend to compete, even when they would obtain greater external rewards for cooperation. Cross-cultural studies find more competition among children from industrialized countries, cities, and middle-class families. Situational factors affecting competition include the reward structure of the situation, the amount of communication among partners, and the size of

the group. One strategy for reducing competition is reciprocal concessions.

4. Group leaders are those who have the most impact on group behavior and beliefs. A task leader focuses on accomplishing group goals successfully. A social leader strives to maintain harmony and high morale. People who become leaders tend to excel in abilities that help the group achieve its goals, to be socially skilled, or to be highly motivated to be a leader. According to Fiedler's contingency model, the success of a leader depends on the match between the leader's style (task-oriented versus relationship-oriented) and the nature of the situation.

5. Whether people perform better alone or in a group depends on the particular activity involved. When people are performing an individual task, the presence of others usually improves performance of a well-learned behavior (social facilitation effect) but impairs performance of a novel or poorly learned behavior (social inhibition effect). When it comes to solving problems, groups can motivate, catch members' errors, and perform tasks beyond the abilities of any one person. But groups can also be inefficient and distracting.

6. There is a tendency for groups to make more extreme decisions than individuals alone. This group polarization effect sometimes leads to riskier decisions and sometimes to more conservative decisions. Highly cohesive groups with a directive leader may be vulnerable to groupthink, a decision-making process that discourages criticism and can lead to poor decisions.

7. People in groups sometimes behave in unusual or antisocial ways that individuals alone would not. This has been called social contagion. Social psychologists explain this effect in terms of deindividuation. The anonymity of groups can reduce an individual's feelings of personal responsibility, leading the individual to act more impulsively.

SUGGESTIONS FOR ADDITIONAL READING

FIEDLER, F. E. 1978. Recent developments in research on the contingency model. In L. Berkowitz (Ed.), *Group processes.* New York: Academic Press. A comprehensive review of Fiedler's theory and research.

FORSYTH, D. R. 1983. *An introduction to group dynamics.* Monterey, CA: Brooks/Cole. A readable textbook that discusses such group processes as leadership, problem-solving, and deindividuation.

JANIS, I. L. 1983. *Groupthink: Psychological studies of policy decisions and fiascoes* (2nd ed.). Boston: Houghton Mifflin. Presents Janis's theory and reviews some of the research testing hypotheses about groupthink.

PAULUS, P. B. (Ed.) 1980. *The psychology of group influence.* Hillsdale, NJ: Erlbaum. An excellent collection of articles on group behavior written by leading experts. Contains detailed discussions of such topics as social facilitation, group polarization, and deindividuation.

MCGRATH, J. E. 1984. *Groups: Interaction and performance.* Englewood Cliffs, NJ: Prentice-Hall. A comprehensive textbook covering most aspects of group functioning.

SHAW, M. E. 1981. *Group dynamics: The psychology of small group behavior* (3rd ed.). New York: McGraw-Hill. A leading textbook on the topic.

14

PREJUDICE AND POLITICS

People's prejudices concern their perceptions of other individuals and groups, and their attitudes and behavior toward them. Why does a friend's father refuse to hire Mexicans as clerks in the bank? Why do some people wind up environmentalists, or Democrats, or Moonies, or feminists? Why do we support a nuclear freeze, a balanced federal budget, or oppose prayer in the public schools? Why do some people become strongly committed to a point of view, such as supporting or not supporting an overseas war? How easy is it to change these perceptions and attitudes? How can it be done? All these questions are essentially applications of the principles discussed in earlier chapters. And they are not minor matters: Prejudice and politics are two of the most important areas of applied social psychology.

Votes determine who gets elected to public office, and therefore who runs the government.

Prejudices can determine who gets hired and who gets fired, whether it is the arbitrary judgment of a casting director in a large movie studio or the vote of a faculty meeting on a tenure decision, or the decision made by a civil service grievance panel. In court, prejudices can determine who goes to jail and who goes free. Prejudice can have a chilling effect on members of minority groups who are attempting to exercise their rights. However courageous they may be, they may sometimes want to retreat from a place where "they are not wanted." Public opinion polls increasingly play a role in government policy decisions ranging from whether or not to reinstitute capital punishment to military interventions in Lebanon or Nicaragua. In all these cases, prejudice and politics have a major impact on other lives—sometimes on thousands or millions of other lives.

PREJUDICE: WHAT IS IT?

Prejudice toward members of a social group has proved to be perhaps the most socially destructive type of attitude. Over six million European Jews were murdered by the Nazis in the 1940s, under the guise of "purifying" the European racial stock. Today only a fraction of that number of Jews remain in Europe. Over a million of Armenians living in Turkey were massacred by the Turks in the early part of this century, as were thousands of Arabs in Zanzibar following independence. The number of North American Indi-

ans dropped from an estimated 3 million in the seventeenth century to 600,000 today. The Spanish genocide of Indians in Latin America is even more appalling.

In the United States, racial prejudice against blacks by whites has been a tenacious social problem. It has resulted in an enormous catalog of social ills, ranging from the deterioration and near-bankruptcy of large cities to poverty, shorter life expectancy, high levels of crime and drug abuse, and human misery of all kinds

Public Sale of Negroes,

By RICHARD CLAGETT.

On Tuesday, March 5th, 1833 at 1:00 P. M. the following Slaves will be sold at Potters Mart, in Charleston, S. C.

Miscellaneous Lots of Negroes, mostly house servants, some for field work.

Conditions: ½ **cash, balance by bond, bearing interest from date of sale. Payable in one to two years to be secured by a mortgage of the Negroes, and appraised personal security.** *Auctioneer will pay for the papers.*

A valuable Negro woman, accustomed to all kinds of house work. Is a good plain cook, and excellent dairy maid, washes and irons. She has four children, one a girl about 13 years of age, another 7, a boy about 5, and an infant 11 months old. 2 of the children will be sold with mother, the others separately, if it best suits the purchaser.

A very valuable Blacksmith, wife and daughters; the Smith is in the prime of life, and a perfect master at his trade. His wife about 27 years old, and his daughters 12 and 10 years old have been brought up as house servants, and as such are very valuable. Also for sale 2 likely young negro wenches, one of whom is 16 the other 15, both of whom have been taught and accustomed to the duties of house servants. The 16 year old wench has one eye.

A likely yellow girl about 17 or 18 years old, has been accustomed to all kinds of house and garden work. She is sold for no fault. Sound as a dollar.

House servants: The owner of a family described herein, would sell them for a good price only, they are offered for no fault whatever, but because they can be done without, and money is needed. He has been offered $1250. They consist of a man 30 to 33 years old, who has been raised in a genteel Virginia family as house servant, Carriage driver etc., in all which he excels. His wife a likely wench of 25 to 30 raised in like manner, as chamber maid, seamstress, nurse etc., their two children, girls of 12 and 4 or 5. They are bright mulattoes, of mild tractable dispositions, unassuming manners, and of genteel appearance and well worthy the notice of a gentleman of fortune needing such.

Also 14 Negro Wenches ranging from 16 to 25 years of age, all sound and capable of doing a good days work in the house or field.

Almost all blacks in the United States are descendents of slaves forcibly imported from Africa, whereas almost all other Americans are descended from people who immigrated by choice. What kinds of behaviors might have been adaptive for people trapped in this "peculiar institution" with almost no hope for escape? What traces of those behaviors might exist today?

among blacks themselves. Racism dates back at least as far as the earliest contact between English travelers and Africans in the sixteenth century. The memoirs of the English show them to have been fascinated by the strangeness of the Africans. They were especially struck by the Africans' blackness, a color with overwhelmingly bad connotations for the Englishmen of the day. They perceived the Africans as looking like apes; as engaging in savage and uncivilized behavior; and as having "heathen" religions (Jordan, 1968). These earliest white impressions about black Africans contain most of the anti-black stereotypes still common in the twentieth century.

The importation of Africans into America as slaves codified these negative reactions. The Africans were treated as property, and often as subhuman beings. Although the slave trade was abolished in 1808, almost 90 percent of all blacks in the United States were still slaves in 1860, just before the outbreak of the Civil War. And emancipation did not noticeably improve their lot. At the beginning of World War II, the average black man in his twenties had not gone past the sixth grade in school. Most blacks lived in the South, where they were still largely segregated by law. Restaurants, movie houses, and buses had separate sections for blacks and whites. This formal, legalized segregation was not outlawed until 1964.

Prejudice and discrimination toward a wide variety of minority groups have been common throughout the history of the United States. However, the "peculiar institution" of slavery, and the legalized system of segregation that followed it, were unique to the black population. As a result, achieving equality has been much more difficult for blacks than for any other minority group. Prejudice against blacks has been difficult to eradicate. Whites today are much more accepting of formal equality than they were even twenty years ago; they strongly support black rights to equal public accommodations, public office, fair housing, and so on. But there is still strong resistance to programs that would help blacks reach full equality—for example, school integration and affirmative action (Campbell, 1971; Taylor, Sheatsley, & Greeley, 1978). This white resistance is rooted in what we call group antagonism. Because antagonism by whites toward Afro-Americans has been such a difficult and important problem in the United States, much of our discussion of prejudice will focus on it as an example.

Components of Group Antagonism

Social psychologists generally distinguish three different components of group antagonism. These roughly correspond to the three components of any attitude presented in Chapter 6: cognitive, affective, and behavioral.

THE COGNITIVE COMPONENT **Stereotypes,** the cognitive component of group antagonism, are beliefs about the personal attributes shared by people in a particular group or social category. Those applied to Jews and blacks in years gone by are shown in Table 14-1. In this study, college students were given a long list of trait adjectives, and then asked to check which ones applied to each of several groups, such as Jews, blacks (or Negroes as they were then called), and other groups. The same procedure was repeated three times—in 1933, 1951, and 1967. Note the persistence of the core themes over a long period of time: the shrewd and ambitious Jews, the ignorant and fun-loving blacks. Like any schema, stereotypes distort reality to achieve order and simplicity. In that sense, they are not necessarily bizarre, deviant, or pathological. They become destructive when they ignore the evidence of reality and are generalized to all group members.

THE AFFECTIVE COMPONENT **Prejudice** is the affective or evaluative component of group antagonism. It is an evaluation of a group or of a single individual based mainly on the person's

Table 14–1 Stereotypes in Three Generations of College Students			
TRAIT	STEREOTYPES OF JEWS (% CHECKING TRAIT)		
	1933	1951	1967
Shrewd	79%	47%	30%
Grasping	34	17	17
Sly	20	14	7
Mercenary	49	28	15
Materialistic	—	—	46
Industrious	48	29	33
Ambitious	21	28	48
Aggressive	12	—	23
Persistent	13	—	9
Talkative	13	—	3
Intelligent	29	37	37
Practical	—	—	19
Loyal to family ties	15	19	19
Very religious	12	—	7
	STEREOTYPES OF BLACKS (% CHECKING TRAIT)		
	1933	1951	1967
Superstitious	84%	41%	13%
Very religious	24	17	8
Ignorant	38	24	11
Stupid	22	10	4
Naive	14	—	4
Lazy	75	31	26
Physically dirty	17	—	3
Slovenly	13	—	5
Unreliable	12	—	6
Happy-go-lucky	38	17	27
Pleasure-loving	—	19	26
Musical	26	33	47
Ostentatious	26	11	25
Sensitive	—	—	17
Gregarious	—	—	17
Talkative	—	—	14
Imitative	—	—	13

Note: Some traits were not asked at all three time points.
Source: Adapted from Karlins et al. (1969).

group membership. It has the same like-dislike quality of the affective or evaluative dimensions discussed earlier regarding impressions (Chapter 3) and attitudes (Chapter 6). But it has the additional quality of prejudgment. The perceiver evaluates other people on the basis of their social or racial category rather than on the basis of information or facts about them as individuals. In this sense prejudice is not very reasonable, and perhaps even illogical or irrational.

THE BEHAVIORAL COMPONENT **Discrimination** is the behavioral component of group antagonism. This is the behavioral acceptance or rejection of a person based on (or at least influenced by) his or her group membership. The refusal to seat Chinese and black customers in restaurants that cater to whites is an example of discriminatory behavior. Quotas for the hiring, admission, or promotion of workers and students based on their group membership are another example. In recent years, the occasional use of quotas to aid minorities has been described as "reverse discrimination" because it favors a minority group at the expense of the majority.

The three components of group antagonism are related but are not identical. Certainly unflattering stereotypes, prejudice, and discrimination usually go together. Some people will engage in all three more often than others. And some minority groups will bear the brunt of all three more than others. But to some extent, the components are independent. Stereotypes of different groups can differ quite a bit in cognitive content, but yield equally strong negative prejudices. Historically, the majority of Americans have had quite different stereotypes about blacks and Jews, as Table 14-1 shows, but until recent years the level of prejudice against the two groups was quite similar. Nor are prejudice and discrimination always identical, as is true for any combination of attitudes and behavior. A great deal of prejudice can exist with very little discrimination, particularly if there are firm legal prohibitions against discriminatory behavior.

Origins

What are the origins of these group antagonisms? We will discuss formal theories about their origins later on in the chapter. But for now, it is important to note that the major debate has been over whether group antagonisms are based in reality or not. Most people experience their attitudes toward various social groups as simply reflecting the realities of the group's shared characteristics. We probably generally feel that we acquire these perceptions through our experience with group members, whether it is direct face-to-face experience or some other less direct kind.

For example, stereotypes may stem from the real differences among people through the categorization process we described in Chapter 4. Groupings are partly based on real differences between people—old people are plainly different from young people, and Hindus are plainly different from Irish Catholics.

Even so, most of the stereotype-generating categorization into groups is based on arbitrary social norms. We categorize on the basis of salient attributes. Salience depends to a large degree on where our attention is directed, and that usually depends on the norms we have learned. In the United States, for example, race is extremely salient. In Cuba or Brazil, it is not as salient; people's skin colors span the full range, and categorization by race is less common. In Lebanon or Northern Ireland, religious preference is the major basis for categorization; people are either Muslim or Christian, or Catholic or Protestant. Race is much less important.

A second problem with the idea of reality-based stereotypes is that the stereotype holders very often have little personal experience with the stereotyped group, and therefore cannot have acquired the stereotype by generalizing about people they have known. For example, the students who participated in the study in Table 14–1 had had very little personal contact with members of either stereotyped group. Especially in the earlier years, very few if any blacks and Jews were permitted to attend Princeton, the college these students attended.

What is most impressive therefore is that the college students surveyed shared the same standard stereotypes of these two groups, having had almost no direct contact with them. This suggests that stereotypes are largely a matter of social tradition. Gender stereotypes will be dis-

---

BOX 14–1
How Much Black Does It Take to Make a "Black"?

The arbitrariness of this categorization process is perhaps illustrated most vividly by the famous "separate-but-equal" Supreme Court decision in 1896, *Plessy* v. *Ferguson.* In the racially segregated South during the century following emancipation, the definition of who was black and who was white varied a good bit. In some states a single drop of Negro blood classified a person as a Negro. *Plessy* v. *Ferguson* defined a Louisiana pupil with one Negro great-grandparent and seven white ones as colored, and assigned the pupil to an all-Negro segregated school. The Chinese who settled in Mississippi after the Civil War were designated as colored and were subject to the same restrictions as blacks. But this categorization gradually changed, and by World War II Chinese were largely treated as if they were white. The point is that although these classifications were quite arbitrary, they had serious consequences for the people involved.

cussed in some detail in the next chapter. In that case, of course, we all have a great deal of personal experience with the group in question—but as we will see, the reigning stereotypes have much more to do with social norms than with real sex differences.

People tend to experience their own antagonisms toward other social groups as rooted in the characteristics of the groups themselves. As in other cases of the actor-observer bias in attributions discussed in Chapter 5, they attribute their own perceptions of other people to the internal dispositions of those people. These perceptions may have some "grain of truth" to them, but they are generally not fully plausible. Personal experience with the group is often quite fragmentary, and the perceptual basis for the stereotype too arbitrary, for "reality" to be an adequate explanation for the antagonisms. As we will see, learned social norms are usually the most powerful factor.

Effects on the Holder

Prejudice and stereotypes influence attitudes and behavior in almost every conceivable way. First of all, they influence *perceptions* about individual members of the target group. Sagar and Schofield (1980) presented sixth-graders with brief verbal descriptions and artist's drawings of interactions between two children, such as one asking another for cake or one bumping the other in the hallway. The races of the two children were systematically varied in the drawings. Other children were then asked to tell a story about what had happened. Both black and white children described the behavior as more mean and threatening when blacks were involved than when whites were. Presumably this is due to the stereotype that such interactions are likely to be more hostile than friendly if blacks are involved. Another example illustrates class stereotyping. Darley and Gross (1983) showed subjects a brief film of a child in a working-class urban neighborhood or a posh suburban park. Subjects were then shown a videotape of the same

child in school responding to achievement test problems. When the subjects were asked to evaluate the child's test performance, they rated it as significantly better if they had seen her in the upper-class neighborhood, presumably because the stereotype is that such upper-class children do better in school. In both cases, stereotypes colored subjects' perceptions of social interactions.

Psychological pressures toward psychological consistency (discussed in Chapter 7) frequently lead us to form attitudes that are consistent with our prejudices. The impact of racial prejudice in a mock jury situation was the focus of one study (Ugwuegbu, 1979). White college students at a Midwestern university were asked to participate as jurors in a study of jury behavior. They read a description of an alleged rape of a 19-year-old woman by a 21-year-old man on the campus. The race of both victim and defendent were varied. Then the subjects were asked how much harm the defendant intended, how responsible he was for the rape, whether or not he was guilty, and what penalty he deserved. The responses were graded to form an index of perceived culpability.

As Table 14–2 shows, a black defendant was seen as more culpable than a white, especially with a white victim. The strength of the evidence against the defendant was also varied: In a strong evidence condition, both the victim and an eyewitness could identify the assailant; in a weak evidence condition, neither was sure. A middle or "marginal" condition pitted the victim's identification against the defendant's

Table 14–2 Perceived Culpability of Male Defendant		
	MALE DEFENDANT	
FEMALE VICTIM	WHITE	BLACK
White	13.5	17.2
Black	13.6	14.2

Source: Adapted from Ugwuegbu (1979).

denials, with ambiguous reports by witnesses and police. Anti-black prejudice biased attitudes toward the black defendant, but only in the marginal evidence condition. When the evidence was clear-cut, it overrode preexisting prejudices. The need for consistency, therefore, induced people to bias their perceptions of the defendant in line with their prejudices when there was some ambiguity about the real situation.

Prejudice also influences people's political responses to minority groups. For example, in elections that pit a black candidate against a white candidate, a white voter's prejudice is often the best predictor of which candidate he or she will support. This was true in Massachusetts when a black, Edward Brooke, ran his first victorious race for the United States Senate (Becker & Heaton, 1967). And it was true in Los Angeles when a black city councilman, Tom Bradley, twice challenged the incumbent white mayor, Sam Yorty (Kinder & Sears, 1981). Bradley lost the first time and won the second. In all these

elections, the overall level of whites' prejudice was low enough that Brooke and Bradley attracted many white votes. But the best predictor of which whites voted against them was prejudice.

Prejudice is also the best predictor of how white people feel about busing schoolchildren for racial integration. The most prejudiced people are almost unanimously opposed to it, even if they are liberal in other respects. Conversely, less prejudiced whites are more favorable toward busing (Sears, Hensler, and Speer, 1979). In short, prejudice strongly influences people's political attitudes and behavior, whether it is their preferences about public policy or their voting behavior.

Prejudiced attitudes can also produce discriminatory behavior in more subtle, indirect ways. For example, parents' prejudice can affect their children's behavior. In one study, white children of prejudiced parents were less likely to engage in interracial social contact in integrated schools than were children of less

---

BOX 14–2
Anglophilia and Russophobia

Another application of the consistency idea is that "similarity breeds liking," as described in Chapter 8. We like a new person or group on the basis of the consistency of their attitudes or values with our own.

Why do we like some countries and dislike others? Nincic and Russett (1979) tested a simple theory about countries that corresponds to the reasons we like some people and dislike others: we like countries that are *similar* to ours and that share *interests* (economic or security) with us. They coded a large number of countries for similarity in terms of racial composition, language, religion, political system, and economic activity. Shared interests were indexed in terms of direct American capital investment, trade, military bases, and American military personnel stationed there.

Liking for foreign countries by American citizens was strongly affected by both factors independently. Canada was high on both and liked very much, North Vietnam low on both and much disliked. Japan was seen as dissimilar but having shared interests and was liked somewhat. The Scandinavian countries were seen as similar, but having few shared interests, and were also liked somewhat. Mexico fell about in the middle on all three dimensions.

prejudiced parents. The consequence was that the opportunity for contact with children of another race did not increase their own racial tolerance as much as it did for children of less prejudiced parents who engaged in more interaction with minority children (Stephan et al., 1978). So our prejudices can influence not only our own attitudes and behavior, but those of our children as well, and therefore can restrict their opportunities to grow up as racially tolerant persons.

Stereotypes as Self-Fulfilling Prophecies

A further effect is that our stereotypes influence not only our own behavior, but also the behavior of the *victims* of stereotyping when we interact with them. In this sense, a stereotype can be a **self-fulfilling prophecy.** This further step in the process is in some ways even more damaging. Members of the victimized group begin to live up the stereotype, to exhibit the very characteristics the stereotype says they have. If we think all Poles are bumblers, we are likely to interact with them as if we expected them to bumble at any opportunity. And, interestingly enough, this will increase the likelihood that they will behave in a stereotype-confirming way.

Much research shows that people behave in a way that confirms others' expectations. In the classroom, children conform to teachers' expectations about their competence; research subjects live up to researchers' expectations; and in therapy the client's progress may be a function of the therapist's expectations. In all these cases, one person's expectations can influence the other person's behavior, even when those expectations are based on false information about the target person. The expectation acts as a self-fulfilling prophecy, because the expectation produces the behavior in the target person (see Rosenthal & Rubin, 1978).

When applied to stereotypes, the chain of self-fulfilling prophecy involves four steps: (1) a stereotype (expectation) about how the other person will behave; (2) a change in the stereotype holder's own behavior; which (3) produces a change in the target person's behavior; and finally (4) the perception of the target person's behavior as confirming the stereotype rather than as a response to the holder's own behavior. Snyder and Swann (1978a) showed this in an ingenious way. They told each subject (the "perceiver") he was going to interact with another subject (the "target") who was described as hostile, liking contact sports, cruel, and insensitive, or as nonhostile, liking poetry and sailing, kind, and cooperative. This description set up the perceiver's stereotype of the target. Then the perceiver and target (who was also a naive subject) engaged in a series of reaction time tests that allowed both to behave in a hostile way (by administering loud, painful, distracting noises to each other).

Not surprisingly, it turned out that expecting a hostile partner led perceivers to administer more high-intensity noises. But the targets, completely ignorant of how they had been described to the other person, also administered more noise if they had been described as hostile, as shown in the top line of Table 14–3. Remember the targets had been described as hostile or nonhostile at random, so this higher level of hostile behavior had to be caused by the perceiver's expectations. And the perceivers, reasonably enough, saw the "hostile" target as more hostile than the "nonhostile" target, in view of the behavioral confirmation of their expectations. This is shown in the second line of the table.

The most interesting aspect of this experiment then followed. The target was put through the same task with a new, completely naive subject. Neither knew about the "hostile" or "nonhostile" description randomly assigned earlier to the target. Nevertheless, the target continued to live up to expectations. The third row shows he gave more noise, and the fourth row, that he was regarded as more hostile in this new interaction.

So this experiment demonstrates that expec-

Table 14–3
Effects of Perceivers' Expectations on Target Person's Behavior

	HOSTILE LABEL	NONHOSTILE LABEL
First Interaction: Informed Perceiver		
Hostile behavior	4.12[a]	3.17
Perceiver's impression of target's hostility	3.83	3.64
Second Interaction: Naive Perceiver		
Hostile behavior	4.30	2.70
Perceiver's impression of target's hostility	3.66	2.75

[a]The higher the number, the greater the hostility exhibited or perceived.
Source: Snyder and Swann (1978), p. 155.

tations affect the stereotyper's own behavior toward the person, whose behavior in return confirms the stereotype. Not only that, but the victim later behaves in a stereotype-confirming manner in other situations, even toward people who are completely ignorant of the stereotype. So even in neutral environments, with people who do not share the stereotype, the victim of prejudice still tends to exhibit stereotype-confirming behavior.

Perhaps the most destructive result is that the target person will come to believe the stereotype accurately applies to him or her. In a similar study by Fazio and his colleagues (1981), the subjects exhibited behavior in the experiment itself that confirmed the expectations of their partners. But they were then placed in a completely different social situation, where they interacted with a new confederate. The subject still lived up to the original expectations in interacting with this new person. And the subject's own self-ratings also lived up to the original partner's expectations. Through the self-perception process described earlier (Chapter 5), the subjects took their own behavior as genuinely reflecting their own personalities, even though it had been induced by the other person's expectations. In short, not only was the stereotype holder's behavior influenced by these arbitrary expectations, but the victims' behavior and self-perceptions also came to reflect the stereotype.

THEORIES OF PREJUDICE

There are four main theories of prejudice. *Realistic group conflict* theories examine when and how prejudice develops in a particular society, culture, or group. They generally focus on groups instead of individuals; they try to explain how Americans in general feel about Japan and the Japanese instead of being concerned with the attitudes of any particular individual. *Social learning* theories deal with a particular individual's prejudice, and locate the causes in the prejudiced person's learning experiences with parents, friends, teachers, and so on. *Cognitive* theories emphasize how cognitive processes such as categorization, salience, and schemas contribute to prejudice. Finally, *psychodynamic* theories look for the origins of prejudice in the prejudiced person's personality.

Group Conflict Theories

REALISTIC GROUP CONFLICT This theory argues that when two groups are in competition for scarce resources, they threaten each other. This creates hostility between them and thus produces mutually negative evaluations. So prejudice is an inevitable consequence of a reality conflict. Perhaps it can be minimized, but it cannot be eliminated altogether because it is created by unavoidable realities. This is a form of the incentive theories we presented in Chapter 1. The Palestinians and Israelis claim the same territory, so they hate each other. If blacks are hired on affirmative action programs and some whites are excluded from those jobs, whites are likely to be angry at blacks. In recent years, increasing numbers of Asian-Americans have been excelling in academic work. If they are to be admitted to prestigious universities, correspondingly fewer students from other backgrounds will be admitted. So it will not be surprising, according to realistic group conflict theory, for prejudice against Asian-Americans to rise. Some historical analyses suggest that Chinese and Japanese immigrants to the United States were well received as long as they did menial work no one else wanted to do. Only later, when they began to compete with Caucasians for jobs, did prejudice mount.

If prejudice arises because two groups really threaten each other, then the threat ought to be the strongest psychological cause of prejudice for individuals as well. In other words, the most threatened individuals ought to be the most prejudiced. The whites who most perceive their neighborhoods as being threatened with racial integration, or with crime by blacks, or with influxes of black children into the schools, ought to be the most prejudiced (Rothbart, 1976).

However, Sears and his colleagues (1979;

1980) have concluded from a number of studies that racial threats to whites' own lives have surprisingly little impact on their prejudice levels or on their preferences regarding government policies. For example, whites' opposition to busing for racial integration is generally not based on concern about their own children. Parents of white children in school districts with busing (or threatened with busing) have about the same attitudes about busing as do nonparents or those who live in areas remote from any possibility of busing (see also McConahay, 1982; Sears & Allen, 1984). In another study, whites' fears that blacks might harm them in the areas of neighborhood desegregation, economic competition, busing, and crime had no effect on their general racial attitudes. Nor did they influence whites' voting behavior in a hotly contested local (Los Angeles) mayoralty election pitting a black candidate against an incumbent white who was openly hostile toward civil rights (Kinder & Sears, 1981).

Despite the obvious appeal of realistic group conflict theories, then, considerable evidence indicates that prejudice does not necessarily have a base in such realities.

RELATIVE DEPRIVATION Another version of group conflict theories is **relative deprivation** theory. This refers to discontent that arises not simply from objective deprivation, but from the subjective feeling of being deprived relatively more than some other person or group. When people feel deprived relative to another group, they may then express their resentment in the form of group antagonism. For example, in a fast-growing economy, the economic situations of all groups may be improving quite impressively. But one group may be doing better than another, which would create feelings of relative deprivation among members of the less well-off group. This in turn might lead to antagonism against the favored group. This was one explanation for the ghetto riots of the 1960s. Although everyone was doing better, blacks felt their situations were not improving as much as those of whites, and the result was antiwhite violence. According to Bernstein and Crosby (1980), relative deprivation is most likely to produce such antagonism when people feel entitled to a particular valued object they do not have, compare themselves to some group that has it, and feel they once could have attained it but no longer can.

GROUP RATHER THAN INDIVIDUAL INTEREST These versions of realistic group conflict theory view the key mechanism as being group members' belief that their *own* lives are being or will be harmed by the target group. This is therefore an *egoistic* process of self-interest. But this assumption, that people operate out of a selfish concern for their own well-being, has been challenged in two ways.

First, Kinder & Sears (1981) found that personal racial threats had very little impact on whites' political preferences between black and white candidates. Instead, antagonism toward blacks that focused on racial symbols had a much stronger impact. These investigators (Sears & McConahay, 1973; Kinder & Sears, 1981) coined the term **symbolic racism** to describe the phenomenon.

Whites in the United States now overwhelmingly endorse the general principle of equal opportunity and oppose overt racial discrimination. But they are often quite opposed to racial progress at an abstract, symbolic level, when it violates their other values. Most do not like symbols such as "forced busing," "reverse discrimination," or "welfare." And this opposition is not based on self-interest or how these racial issues might affect them personally. It seems to be a blend of primitive antiblack feeling, anxiety, hostility, and conservative sociopolitical values.

Other research has indicated that the key fear is that one's group will be harmed, irrespective of whether or not the individual group member is personally harmed. The threat is to "us," not to "me." Even whites who live in towns with no blacks at all, or who have no children, can be upset about busing because it

signals a displacement of whites by blacks. Hence the key factor is not self-interest but group interest—the group may have a stake in a particular outcome. Therefore people may experience *fraternal* relative deprivation rather than *egoistic* relative deprivation—the feeling that the group is deprived relative to some other group, whether or not the individual is.

For example, Vanneman and Pettigrew (1972) found that working-class whites' hostility toward blacks resulted from feelings that they were not gaining as fast as blacks were; the resentment was of the gains being made by blacks as a group. Guimond and Dubé-Simard (1983) conducted a similar analysis of French-speaking residents of Quebec, a province in which English-speaking residents had for many years enjoyed many economic advantages. They found that feelings of fraternal deprivation among French-speaking residents were strongly related to their desire for political autonomy—for separation from the rest of Canada.

The egoistic versions of realistic group conflict theory usually do not have the impact on either prejudice or political preferences that group-centered versions do. Guimond and Dubé-Simard (1983) and Vanneman and Pettigrew (1972) both report that fraternal deprivation had a much stronger effect on group antagonism, nationalism, and voting behavior than did egoistic deprivation. Evidently people are much more sensitive to the symbols of how their group is doing than they are to how they themselves are doing.

Part of the reason for the small impact of egoistic discontent is that people tend to separate their attitudes about their own situations from their attitudes about society. And prejudice is first and foremost a set of attitudes about how groups should be treated in society, not about how one's own life should be going. Prejudices against particular groups focus more on how different groups should be treated and how institutions and government should be organized, and not so much on how the prejudiced person should be treated.

Tyler (1980) makes the same point in his

analysis of how people respond to crime. When people are trying to figure out whether they are personally vulnerable to crime or not, their own recent history of personal victimization plays the major role. A recent experience of having been robbed or burglarized makes people feel much more personally vulnerable to crime, and much more likely to take specific steps to protect themselves (buying a dog, putting more locks on the door). However, these personal experiences play little role in determining their estimate of the crime rate more generally. For that, people depend more on the media and on talking to acquaintances. Tyler suggests that people simply do not find their own experiences very informative about the rate of crime more generally, nor does media information tell them much about whether they themselves are at risk or not. The two arenas seem separated.

Social Learning

Social learning theory views prejudice as being learned the same way people learn other social values; it is transmitted interpersonally as part of a larger package of norms. The prejudice is a norm in the person's culture or subculture. It is acquired by the child in the process of socialization. The child acquires such prejudiced attitudes to gain acceptance by others. Finally, the continued transmission and expression of the prejudice reinforce its role as a cultural norm (Ashmore & DelBoca, 1980).

It is easy to document the existence of such social norms all over the world. For example, white North Americans' prejudice toward various national and ethnic groups was very stable through much of the twentieth century. The peoples of the British Isles have been liked much the best, and those from Asia and Africa the least. World War II hurt the Germans, Italians, and Japanese, and the Cold War hurt the Russians. Otherwise, white North Americans' prejudices have changed little. If comparable data were available from other societies, they would doubtless show the same historic enmi-

ties—for example, between Vietnamese and Cambodians, or toward untouchables in India, or tribal hatreds in Africa.

These prejudices are acquired quite early in life. The most salient ones, like racial prejudice in this country, are acquired well before adolescence. White children simply learn, by being told and by observing the society in which they live, that blacks are socially inferior in a variety of ways. To show this, Goodman (1952) observed 103 black and white children intensively for a full year. She concluded that racial awareness was already present in many children at ages 3 and 4, and that 25 percent of the 4-year-olds were already expressing strongly entrenched race-related values. No white child ever expressed a wish to be like a black child, while the black children expressed much more conflict about their color.

Certainly by the early grade school years, most American children are aware of racial differences in our society and of the prevailing norms about the races, at least in some form. As children move through grade school, they increasingly perceive differences between the races, but often do not become sensitive to differences among members of other races. The experiences children have during the grade school years are crucial, because by early adolescence racial prejudice has crystallized and is much more difficult to break down. The consequence is that prejudice is considerably stronger in some areas of the society than in others. For example, it is stronger in the South than in other regions, it is stronger in the working class than in the middle class, it is stronger among older whites (who were brought up in a more segregationist period) than among younger whites, and so on (see Maykovich, 1975; Middleton, 1976).

Parents play a particularly important role in the child's acquisition of prejudice. There are consistent correlations between parents' and children's racial and ethnic attitudes (Ashmore & DelBoca, 1976). Parents often transmit these attitudes without directly instructing their children, since attitudes can be learned by association or by imitation as well as by direct reinforcement. Children observe their parents' attitudes and behavior and pick up many nonverbal cues in their reactions to people of other races. But parents frequently are reluctant to express prejudice openly and freely. One result is that children are not perfectly accurate in the attitudes they attribute to their parents, particularly about matters not currently in the news and in the middle of controversy. As children grow older, peer groups become increasingly important. Normally peer groups mostly reinforce parents' views, because of the similarities in social background and values of people sharing a common community environment. But occasionally the parents' attitudes conflict with those in the child's environment. Children probably acquire prejudice from a broad range of cues from their parents and a broad range of other people as well.

The media represent another potential source of social learning, especially for children. Minorities have historically been given relatively little attention in the media. For example, before television, magazines such as *Life* and *The Saturday Evening Post* reached very large national audiences. As of 1949–50, blacks were in only 0.5 percent of all ads and in 2.5 percent of all nonadvertising material, despite the fact that they comprised about 10 percent of the population. Even in 1967, only 4 percent of all TV commercials included blacks (Greenberg & Mazingo, 1976). In a content analysis of Los Angeles newspapers from the late nineteenth century to the late 1960s, Johnson et al. (1971) found almost no references to blacks until the Supreme Court's school desegregation case in 1954. So far as the media were concerned, blacks were simply invisible.

And even the skimpy coverage tended to be stereotyped: 80 percent of the blacks in ads were maids, cooks, or servants for whites. The newspaper coverage that did appear was largely focused on sensational events, entertainment, and crime (Johnson et al., 1971).

All that has changed. On prime time televi-

sion, blacks appear much more often than they used to. By 1973, 14 percent of TV commercials were using blacks. Weigel, Loomis, and Soja (1980) conducted a careful content analysis of prime time television broadcasting from the 1977 and 1978 seasons. Blacks appeared in 20 percent of the product commercials, 52 percent of the situation comedies, and 59 percent of the drama shows. In situation comedies, at least one black character was visible 22 percent of the time. Moreover, the black-white interactions shown on television tend now to be egalitarian. The old days of showing blacks in subordinate roles seem to have vanished. Over 70 percent of the cross-racial interactions "occurred within institutional settings in which at least some black characters appeared to hold positions of authority or positions requiring technical sophistication" (Weigel et al., 1980, p. 889). Blacks and whites were about equally likely to have the higher-status roles in these interactions (see Table 14–4).

But—and this seems to mirror the actual state of interracial relations in the United States today—the cross-racial interactions tended to be infrequent, distant, formal, and centered on the workplace. Blacks are still given small parts; and they are still depicted quite differently from whites. Table 14–4 shows that blacks' appearances on television tended to be quite brief; some whites were almost always in view, whereas only rarely were one or more blacks in view. Further, blacks' appearances remain quite segregated. Very little of the time were blacks and whites shown as interacting with each other (less than 4 percent of the time even in comedies), and they were scarcely ever on the screen at the same time (less than 8 percent of the time even in comedies). Only 10 percent of the cross-racial interactions occurred outside the workplace, whereas 47 percent of the white-white interactions did. Black-white interactions were less intimate and involved much less shared decision-making than white-white interactions.

Cross-racial interaction is particularly distant

Table 14–4
Prime Time Commercials and Programming: Relative Frequencies of White and Black Appearances, and Cross-Racial Appearances and Interactions

TIMING CATEGORY	PERCENT OF HUMAN APPEARANCE TIME			
	DRAMA	COMEDY	TOTAL	COMMERCIALS
White appearances	99.5%	86.0%	95.8%	96.6%
Black appearances	3.3	22.0	8.3	8.5
Cross-racial appearances	2.8	7.9	4.1	5.1
Cross-racial interactions	1.5	3.6	2.0	1.7

Source: Weigel et al. (1980), p. 888.

when it is between males and females. Whereas the majority of male-female interactions involving whites had some element of flirtation or sexual involvement, 93 percent of those involving blacks and whites were rated as "ritualized greetings or situationally dictated exchanges" (p. 891). So if children were to take their cue from television today, they would assume that relations between the races were somewhat rare, distant, formal, and occur primarily at work. Cross-racial romances would be seen as quite deviant. Of course, all this is still a great improvement over the invisibility and the stereotyped behavior presented earlier in this century.

Cognitive Processes

Certain systematic cognitive biases naturally accompany impression formation. Perceivers try to develop a structured impression of another person, which necessarily breeds distortions. And they overrespond to the most salient stimuli. Such efforts can, all by themselves, produce prejudice and stereotyping.

For example, perceivers naturally categorize other people into types: tall ones, pretty ones, jocks, obnoxious ones, foreigners, or whatever. This *categorization* process helps the perceiver process information about a lot of individuals in an efficient way. But it can blur the distinctions among the members of a particular group. For example, observers of group discussions including equal numbers of blacks and whites were more likely to confuse the contributions of people within a race than to confuse their contributions across race (Taylor et al., 1978).

Categorization is often based simply on some very prominent, *salient* cues. Skin color differentiates blacks and whites; body type, hair length, clothing, and voice differentiate men and women; accent differentiates foreigners from natives, and so on. This kind of salience has a number of predictable effects. We pay more attention to salient stimuli, so these differences tend to be on our mind when we encounter members of other groups, especially when they stand out in the environment. A white researcher in a ghetto school stands out; so did Jackie Robinson when he was the first black major league baseball player.

The problem is that perceivers make more extreme evaluations of and more dispositional attributions about salient people (Taylor et al., 1977). For example, the only female in a law firm is highly salient. If she is out of work because of illness, others may say she is "sickly," self-indulgent, or maybe even malingering. If a male is out for the same reason we attribute his absence to an illness over which he has no control, perhaps extend more sympathy, and cover his workload.

Finally, if stereotypes are cognitive structures

that consist of a set of expectations regarding a social group, they can be thought of as **schemas,** with the same consequences we have already discussed in Chapter 4. New information inconsistent with schemas tends to be rejected. If someone's behavior is inconsistent with our stereotype of that person, we explain it as due to the situation, not the person. If we are forced to make an internal attribution, it probably will be to some temporary, unstable cause. A good example concerns whites' explanations for racial differences in socioeconomic status. Blacks, on the average, have always been lower in income, employment, educational level, and occupational status than whites. How do whites explain this? Years ago the main attribution for this relative lack of success was stable and internal; blacks were innately inferior in a variety of ways. Whites have gradually surrendered this notion, however. But the racial difference in status remains. So how do whites explain it now? The tendency is to invoke such unstable internal causes as lack of effort and low aspirations (Ashmore & DelBoca, 1976).

Psychodynamic Theories

Finally, some intrapersonal theories of prejudice analyze it as an outgrowth of motivational tensions within the individual. These are called *psychodynamic* theories because they emphasize the particular dynamics of the specific individual's personality, rather than factors that affect the behavior of large groups of people at the same time, such as the tensions that may arise from economic competition. One psychodynamic theory, for example, treats prejudice as displaced aggression. Displacement occurs when the source of frustration or annoyance cannot be attacked because of fear or simple unavailability. If there is a depression and a man loses his job, he feels angry and aggressive, but there is no obvious person at fault. Under these circumstances, people look for a **scapegoat** whom they can blame for their difficulties and whom they can attack.

Another psychodynamic theory treats prejudice as a personality disorder, just like a phobia about snakes or a neurotic need for approval. The best-known example of this theory is found in work on the *authoritarian personality* (Adorno et al., 1950). This impressive program of research was sponsored by the American Jewish Committee to try to understand the rise of anti-Semitism in the 1930s and the compliant behavior of Germans toward Hitler. Their conclusion was that anti-Semitism developed from a particular personality syndrome called the authoritarian personality. It is characterized by (1) rigid adherence to (and harsh punishment for deviation from) conventional values and patterns of behavior; (2) an exaggerated need to submit to, and identify with, strong authority; (3) generalized hostility; and (4) a mystical, superstitious cast of mind.

Authoritarian personalities were thought to stem from early rearing by domineering fathers and punitive mothers. As an adult, the individual repeats the experience, but now he or she is in the driver's seat. He or she bullies and punishes people who are deviant or disobedient. People of other races and religions, the handicapped or weak of all kinds, those with unconventional life styles—all fall under the authoritarian's iron boot. The authoritarian thinks his or her group is wonderful, and all other groups are disreputable and disgusting.

Research on authoritarianism quickly got caught up in disputes about data interpretation, and the psychological analysis just presented became somewhat controversial. A central problem was that researchers failed to distinguish adequately between sociocultural learning and personality factors in its explanation of ethnocentrism. For example, it was found that working-class whites were disproportionately anti-Semitic. Was this because a disproportionate number of them had authoritarian personalities? It was easy to show that working-class parents demanded more submission from their

Having a black mayor of Chicago or any other major American city would have been inconceivable as recently as the 1950s. But change does not come without conflict, as Mayor Washington and other Chicagoans could testify.

U P I/Bettmann Archive

children and dealt more harsh punishment than did middle-class parents (Lipset, 1960). Or was their anti-Semitism an historical norm that got passed down from generation to generation? Many working-class families were only a generation or two removed from areas of Europe where violent anti-Semitism had reigned for centuries. So anti-Semitism could have stemmed from learning a traditional norm, and not from a personality obsessed with authority and domination. As a result of these complexities, psychodynamic theories are not as popular in social psychology as they were some years back.

Comparison

Each of these four broad theoretical approaches points to different factors as causes of prejudice. There is some truth in all of them. For example, normal cognitive processes of categorization and of special attention to salient stimuli can increase stereotypes and discriminatory behavior. It is doubtful that such cognitive processes are sufficient to produce a consistent pattern of bias all by themselves, however. They require learning that produces prejudice against particular groups, and specific stereotypical content.

Blacks are stereotypically thought to be lazy and musical, and Chinese hard-working, though both are perceptually quite different from whites. But the perceptual distinctiveness of these minority groups may be necessary to get a pattern of group discrimination started, and it certainly helps to maintain it.

In general, social learning plays a major role in defining what is "appropriate" prejudice, what the "correct" stereotypes are, and what is acceptable behavior toward other groups and what is not. The wide variations in the treatment of any given group around the globe and across history testify to that, as do the major differences in the treatment of different groups within a society. In 1850, blacks could be bought and sold like cattle; today elaborate legal machinery protects their right to be treated like other people. Slavery hardly existed for other groups in this country, nor for blacks in most other societies. In most Muslim countries women must wear veils, may not engage in premarital or extramarital sexual relations, and do not compete with men for jobs. American women are not so restricted today, though in the nineteenth century they were much less free. Personality tensions and cognitive biases therefore operate within a cultural framework that determines how much prejudice exists, when it can be expressed, and toward whom.

Studies of conformity and obedience suggest that people's behavior can be influenced rather readily. Well-known techniques of social influence (or other forms of power) can produce behavior wholly contradictory to the person's attitudes, or even to the person's perceptions of reality. Subjects freely administer shock to inoffensive people when they are told to, or express beliefs that go against their sense perceptions.

Similarly, from the chapter on attitude change, it would appear that people's attitudes are equally susceptible to change.

But things turn out not to be so easy. As Hovland (1959) pointed out, the success of persuasion depends in part on whether it is attempted in an experimental laboratory or in the real world. In the controlled environment of a laboratory, it is generally easy to change attitudes. Even a simple written essay can produce changes in attitudes toward foreign aid, atomic submarines, tuition rates in college, brushing teeth, cancer and cigarettes, the quality of a poem, and so on. Subjects read or hear their communication, are asked to state their own beliefs, and tend to agree with the communication more after reading or hearing it than they did before (or than does a control group that did not read or hear it). Attempts to change people's attitudes in the world outside the laboratory tend to be much less successful. It is well to contrast the ease of attitude or behavior change in the laboratory with the difficulty of similar change in real life, at least of attitudes that matter, such as racial prejudices.

The Effects of Socialization

To understand why some prejudices are almost impossible to alter and others easy to change, we need to understand peoples' histories: Why are they more or less committed to their posi-

tions? As mentioned earlier, attitudes are assumed to be learned in the same way as any other disposition, through the basic processes of association, reinforcement, and imitation. Children are exposed to certain things about the world. They are also reinforced for expressing some attitudes. In addition, imitation or identification is important in the learning process. Children spend a great deal of time with their parents and after a while begin to believe as they do even when there is no deliberate attempt at influence. The same process works with peer groups, teachers, or any important figures in a child's life.

Children tend therefore to adopt the dominant attitudes of their environment. This means the parents may have a great deal of influence on some issues. For example, as shown in Table 14–5, a high percentage of high school seniors favored a given political party when both parents agreed on that party, with only about 10 percent having the opposite perference (Jennings & Niemi, 1974). The same national survey of high school seniors and their parents revealed that 83 percent agreed on a presidential candidate, and that there were similarly high levels of agreement regarding other partisan preferences.

However, parent-offspring agreement was much less in many other areas. The extent of parent influence over offspring's attitudes seems to depend most of all on the clarity and frequency of communication between them. Obviously parents are much more likely to communicate clearly and repeatedly their presidental preference in the heat of an election campaign than some subtle, relatively abstract aspect of their philosophy of life. In the same study, 92 percent of the students were able to report accurately which candidate their parent favored, but on other issues such as granting free speech to communists, they were strikingly

Table 14–5
Relationship between Party Preferences of Parents and Children

PARENT	HIGH SCHOOL SENIORS (N = 1852)			
	DEMOCRATIC	INDEPENDENT	REPUBLICAN	TOTAL
Democratic	32.6%	13.2%	3.6%	49.4%
Independent	7.0	12.8	4.1	23.9
Republican	3.4	9.7	13.6	26.7
Total	43.0	35.7	21.3	100.0

Source: Adapted from Jennings & Niemi (1974).

inaccurate—indeed, it often appeared they were simply guessing about their parents' beliefs (Niemi, 1974).

Within the family, this lack of communication leads to some predictable biases and misperceptions about one another's attitudes. One might be called a *generosity bias.* When they are ignorant of the truth children tend to attribute a socially desirable characteristic to the parent, such as having voted for the winning rather than the losing candidate. Another is the *self-directed bias,* in which a child falsely attributes the same attitude to the parent as he himself holds. On more diffuse and obscure issues, children and husbands and wives all seem to exaggerate terribly the extent to which they all agree (Niemi, 1974). These biases, and the considerable gaps in communication they attempt

to fill, limit the degree of influence parents have over children's attitudes (Tedin, 1974).

More generally, friends are the dominant influence over adolescent attitudes in a large number of areas that do not lend themselves to early, simple, repetitive, accurate communication of parental attitudes. One example is marijuana use. In the study shown in Table 14–6, adolescent use of marijuana was highly correlated with friends' use, and hardly at all with parents' drug use. The table shows, for example, that of all the students whose parent used drugs and whose best friend had used marijuana, 67 percent had themselves used marijuana. However, only 17 percent had if their best friend had not, even if a parent had.

So parents' influence tends to be more limited than many early observers originally thought

Table 14–6
Adolescent Marijuana Use Related to Best-Friend Use and Parental Drug Use

PARENT USED PSYCHOACTIVE DRUG?	BEST SCHOOL FRIEND USED MARIJUANA?	
	YES	NO
Yes	67%	17%
No	56	13

Note: Entry is percent in each category that use marijuana. Use patterns for each group are self-reported.
Source: Adapted from Kandel (1974).

(Jennings & Niemi, 1974). In general, parents have maximum influence on simple, concrete, recurrent issues like partisan choice, religious denomination, or prejudices against minority groups. They have relatively little influence on more diffuse, subjective, occasional issues, where communication is likely to be sporadic and fuzzy, such as religious philosophy, political cynicism, interpersonal trust, or civil liberties.

Nevertheless, whether the key source of influence is parents, peers, or something else, prejudice and other important attitudes tend to be acquired early. To reduce prejudice, then, one obvious solution is to change early socialization. If people are not taught prejudice to start with, perhaps it will not develop later on. This is why desegregation experts emphasize the importance of positive interracial experiences in grade school. No single socialization experience takes place in a vacuum, however, and it is hard to change a child's entire life all at once. Many of the obstacles discussed earlier exist even for young children. Prejudiced parents may sabotage anything that happens at school; and children of prejudiced parents engage in less interracial contact. Or prejudiced peers may sabotage the best efforts of parents. In addition, the larger society sets a context that always makes change more difficult. Most interracial couples have countless stories of the stares and strange looks, awkward silences, unspoken questions, innuendoes and raised eyebrows, and so on.

The Role of Higher Education

Education has always been one of the great hopes of those who wish for more interracial tolerance. If stereotypes and prejudice are based upon inaccuracy and distortion, surely being exposed to the facts should help. And education does seem to help—at least at the higher levels. People who have been to college generally are less prejudiced than those who have not. But exactly why is less clear. Their greater tolerance is related to their educational level, not some other aspect of higher status (Campbell, 1971; Stember, 1961). Future college students are generally more tolerant than those not going on to college. And the best studies show that the college experience has diverse effects that depend on many other variables (student's background, major, and type of college).

One important determinant of the effects of higher education is exposure to new peer group norms. Students who have spent most of their years living in their parents' home and surrounded by childhood friends are introduced to an environment containing many different kinds of people with many different beliefs. Not surprisingly, this exposure has a profound effect on many of them. They change many attitudes held since childhood; they reevaluate other attitudes in the light of the new information. In general, much of their belief system may undergo considerable reorganization.

A classic demonstration of such change was provided by Newcomb's (1943) study of alumnae of Bennington College. This is a small, exclusive women's college in Vermont that was started, with a very liberal faculty, in the early 1930s. Newcomb traced the changes in attitudes some students experienced during their college years. Most of the students came from affluent, conservative families, yet there were large and marked changes toward liberalism as the women progressed through the school. Newcomb's careful analysis of these attitude changes shows that they were most common among women who identified with Bennington, and who had the closest social relationships with other students and faculty. In other words, for these students, Bennington served as an important reference group, and their attitudes changed through the influence of the group.

Another interesting finding concerned the students' attitudes after they left school. Did their liberalism persist, or did they regress to their parents' conservatism? Newcomb and his associates (1967) studied the women twenty

"They sent her to Bennington to lose her Southern accent, and then she turned her back on everything."

years later and found that their political views had remained remarkably stable. Those who left college as liberals were still liberals, and the conservatives were still conservatives. More precisely, the women's senior-year attitudes were better predictors of their attitudes twenty years later than were their freshman attitudes.

Newcomb attributed this stability to the social environments the women entered after college. He found almost perfect political agreement between the graduates and their husbands; these affluent-but-liberal women had found affluent-but-liberal husbands. The occasional regressions could be attributed to the fact that some liberal women had married husbands in occupations such as banking or corporation law, and could be expected to move in a conservative world.

This study emphasized the importance of environment as a determinant of possible attitude change. However, it is a rare college that shows the political homogeneity of the small, exclu-

sive, isolated, and highly liberal Bennington campus (Newcomb's follow-up revealed that today even Bennington does not show the same degree of liberalism). The most important conclusion of the Bennington study, and indeed of this chapter, is that mere exposure to information will not be sufficient to change high-commitment attitudes. Intense, interpersonal contact such as that in the Bennington experience is necessary, and indeed may be necessary for years afterward if the change is to be maintained. Education may help reduce prejudice, but its effects are not consistent, dramatic, or swift.

Direct Contact

Another approach to prejudice reduction has been direct intergroup contact. The belief has been that contact would help break down stereotypes, and that proximity and interaction

U.S. Army Photograph

Marc Anderson

The armed services were among the
first public institutions to be racially
desegregated but for the most part
not until after World War II. The
descendents of these troops in an
all-black unit could march in racially
integrated units in the 1980s.

would increase liking as it normally does. Inter-national student exchanges, the Olympic Games, international conferences—all are pred-icated on this assumption. Does contact really work?

Since World War II, for a variety of reasons, America's major institutions have gradually be-come less segregated. The military, schools, professional sports, and most work situations are no longer fully segregated. This development has given social scientists opportunities to test the effects of contact. Racial prejudice and antagonisms decreased in World War II when black and white soldiers fought together (Stouffer et al., 1949). At the start of the war, military policy was to avoid racially mixed units. However, as time went by, white infantry replacements came to be in short supply. The Army allowed black volunteers to join previously all-white units. Surveys before this desegregation showed most white soldiers opposed it, but afterward there was much less opposition. The greatest support came from those white soldiers who were most closely associated with the blacks. No realistic conflicts arose between the groups because instead of competing, they were fighting a common enemy. Unrealistic stereotypes decreased markedly because of the greater knowledge gained by familiarity.

Some other early research also indicated that increased contact reduced antagonism, prejudice, and stereotypes. Studies on public housing have found less antagonism in both blacks and whites in integrated than in segregated areas. Deutsch and Collins (1951) compared two housing projects in which tenants were assigned to apartments without regard to race with two projects in which blacks and whites were kept in different buildings. White homemakers in the integrated projects were less prejudiced and more likely to have a black as a "best friend." Similar results have been reported in studies on integrated working conditions. When blacks were hired to work in department stores in New York City, white clerks became progressively more accepting of them. White customers had similar positive reactions. Comparable results have been found among police officers and government workers.

So most of the research indicates that greater familiarity, even under trying conditions, leads to less antagonism. The best recent reviews suggest, however, that contact, by itself, is not always beneficial. For example, school desegregation by itself has not been shown to reduce prejudice in all cases. There is relatively little research on the question, and what there is does not show a strong pattern one way or the other (see Amir, 1976; Stephan & Rosenfield, 1978).

CLOSE CONTACT Most experts have therefore concluded that the specific *type* of contact is the crucial factor. The most widely shared theory among social psychologists has been Allport's (1954) contact theory, which holds that intergroup contact decreases hostility between the races only when the contact meets three necessary conditions:

1. Close contact—it is not enough for people to co-exist in the same geographical space; they must be brought together in close interaction. Some forms of school or work desegregation do not promote very close contact, such as when white and black students are in different "tracks" in a high school and attend quite different classes, or when the executives of a firm are all white and the clerical workers are black, and they have little close interaction.
2. Cooperative interdependence—whites and blacks need to be working together for common goals and to depend upon each others' efforts, as in World War II.
3. The contact must be of equal status—resentments build up if the traditional status imbalance is maintained, and stereotypes cannot easily be broken down. Contact occurs when a black clean-up man works for a Jewish businessman, but situations of this kind simply perpetuate traditional stereotypes.

For example, Clore and co-workers (1978) ran an interracial summer camp in which campers, administrative staff, and counselors were all evenly divided between blacks and whites. The researchers tried to maximize: (1) intimate contact, by mixing the living arrangements by race; (2) cooperative interdependence, by creating primitive conditions that demanded cooperation such as fire building, cooking, and planning activities; and (3) equal status, by selecting campers from similar backgrounds. The one-week experience was successful in increasing the percentage of interracial choices campers made for partners in playing games.

Social psychologists today are quite active in trying to introduce such procedures into desegregated schools, with the idea that desegregation can reduce prejudice only if these conditions prevail. Standard educational procedures have been compared with new procedures introducing interdependent "teams" that cooperate to complete classroom assignments. For example, Eliot Aronson and his colleagues have used what they call a *jigsaw technique*. Children are placed in small learning groups, usually consisting of five or six participants. They meet in the group for about an hour a day to focus on one particular lesson. Each person is assigned one portion of the day's lesson, and is responsible for teaching that material to the rest of the group. Since no one can put together the whole picture without the information contributed by others, the students are interdependent.

Ultimately each student's learning is evaluated separately, but unless all cooperate in contributing their unique pieces of knowledge, none can do very well. Through this technique, the children get to know each other very well, and in addition they come to appreciate the abilities and contributions of all the other children. Aronson and his co-workers report good success with this technique in increasing peer liking across ethnic and racial groups, and in increasing the self-esteem of minority children (see Aronson and Osherow, 1980).

OTHER FACTORS   Close contact is not the only factor in reducing prejudice, though it may be the most important. *Successful* outcomes of cooperative efforts may be important. If people work together in wars, or games, or classroom jobs and things go badly, they may resent each other and become even more hostile. How important success is in this process is not yet clear, but it may be an important ingredient. And the norms of the surrounding community are very important. Even if the interracial experience is successful within one limited site, people will go back into their normal lives. If they are then surrounded by prejudiced people, they may quickly revert. This is one of the difficulties in trying to prevent prejudice in the children of prejudiced parents.

Using these principles of appropriate contact,

what kinds of situations would be likely to reduce prejudice, and what kinds would not? Mere desegregation would not be enough. That is, mere contact is not enough; real interaction is required. And it would have to be done in such a way as to promote equal-status relationships between the races. Being teammates on a professional football team would. Being fellow conspirators in a prison break would. Having a black janitor in an office building, or a black maid in a middle-class household, would not. Having both races in a lecture class would not. Pitting a black basketball team against a white team would not. But having interracial teams to solve homework problems in a statistics class would.

CHANCES OF SUCCESS   Are the most helpful kinds of intergroup situations common in our society? Unfortunately, through most of our history they have not been. Prior to the 1950s, American society was organized in a way that afforded almost no opportunities for equal-status, cooperative, interdependent contact between blacks and whites. Almost all American institutions were segregated. There were white colleges, and there were black colleges. Only whites were permitted to play professional sports in the major leagues. Black athletes had to play on all-black teams in black leagues. Military units were either all-black or all-white. Most blacks lived in the South, and of course in the South segregation was the law in public accommodations, schools, transportation, politics, and every other social institution. There were such gross differences between blacks and whites in income, education, and occupational status that the chance of widespread equal-status contact was minimal.

Today, contact of this type does occur in the armed forces, where blacks and whites work and fight together with more or less equal rank (at least among enlisted soldiers), and in factories and stores in which members of the two races hold comparable jobs. But in many businesses, professions, and schools, interracial contact is often between people of different status. Integration frequently occurs by bringing blacks in at the bottom of the ladder, whether as students or apprentices, or in the least desirable jobs. They then have to interact with whites who outrank them. Under these circumstances, increased contact seems less likely to have a positive effect and may even have a negative effect on relations between blacks and whites.

One of the trickiest things to ensure is continued intimate contact. There are many obstacles to it. People strongly prefer to associate with those like themselves. Every study of voluntary contacts between children in the schools has shown a strong tendency for them to associate more with their own race than any other. This is true both before and after desegregation (Schofield, 1978). It varies a great deal across settings: In some cases, there is considerable interracial mixing; in others, almost total segregation. But it shows how far we are from being a truly multiracial "melting pot." Both majority and minority have a tendency to avoid cross-racial interaction. This makes it especially difficult to get the most prejudiced people in contact with minorities. The phenomenon of "white flight," whereby white children leave desegregated schools, illustrates how hard it is to ensure any interracial contact at all, much less ensuring that the circumstances of the contact will be helpful. This is why one of the touchiest aspects of desegregation is the relative proportions of each group. If the minority proportion is too high, the majority will flee, thereby diminishing the opportunity for contact. Furthermore, desegrega-

tion requires the full support of political and judicial authorities. People have to be willing to overcome the temporary discomforts of association with unfamiliar people, and they are less likely to do so if they know they can easily escape. The practical difficulties of desegregation do not mean it should be abandoned, because there are important moral and legal reasons for it. However, it is not a magic remedy for racial prejudice.

Indeed no one approach is going to solve the problem. Intergroup antagonism seems to be a fundamental aspect of the human condition. Every society in the world takes group membership into consideration when determining how it will treat any individual. In a sense, the United States has set a higher standard for itself than most countries and has embarked on an ambitious program of group equality. The Bill of Rights and the later constitutional amendments (especially the Fourteenth) set up extremely idealistic guidelines. At the same time, the United States has tried to accommodate a bewildering variety of groups from all parts of the world, including Africans, Vietnamese, Hungarians, Hispanics, Russian Jews, and British Puritans. It is not surprising, therefore, that it should have failed to some degree. We cannot be complacent, because all too much suffering in our society is caused by racial prejudice. But it is also well to remember the very considerable harmony and group tolerance that has allowed such a Noah's Ark of humanity to coexist and cooperate for so many years.

THE MEDIA AND POLITICS

Now let us turn our attention to politics. What determines how people respond to the political world? Here we are primarily interested in how they arrive at perceptions of political leaders, and attitudes about political events and issues. To some degree such questions involve applica-

tions of principles we have discussed in earlier chapters, particularly those on social perception and attitudes. We will focus our discussion here on the role of the media in politics, because it is important and because it is a natural application of social psychology to the political world.

Three Eras

At first glance, the media seem extremely powerful in political life. Almost everyone watches television, listens to the radio, or reads a newspaper. We live in a mass media era, in which people spend more time with the media than they do with one another. But as we discovered in examining the effects of media violence on real-life behavior, the media may not dominate people's lives as much as this would imply.

THE FIRST PHASE: GREAT POWER   Research on the effects of the media in politics has gone through three phases. The first began in the 1920s and 1930s when radio became widely available throughout the Western world, and talking movies, with accompanying newsreels, became a source of mass entertainment. For the first time, political leaders could reach huge masses of people not merely through the printed word but through audio and visual channels.

Simultaneously came the rise of charismatic political leaders who were extremely effective mass communicators, such as Hitler, Mussolini, Churchill, and Franklin Roosevelt. Among the most frightening spectacles were the great public rallies held by the Nazi party, with hundreds of thousands of followers chanting and singing and marching, all seeming to be puppets in Nazi hands. Social scientists greeted such herdlike behavior with horror. Though in general they conducted little empirical analysis, they assumed that this kind of propaganda was extremely persuasive. Why? Because, they assumed, the audience was captive, attentive, and wholly gullible.

THE SECOND PHASE: MINIMAL EFFECTS   These speculations highlighted the need for more systematic test of media impact. A second phase therefore consisted of systematic empirical research on the impact of the mass media, using the new method of public opinion polling. An influential early product was *The People's Choice* (Lazarsfeld, Berelson, & Gaudet, 1948),

a careful analysis of voter decision-making during the 1940 campaign. It reported two main findings: (1) Relatively few respondents changed their preferences throughout the whole campaign, contrary to the fears of the earlier analysts. True, many voters had been undecided and subsequently made up their minds, but even these people decided according to their predispositions. (2) Those changes that did occur were not closely linked to mass media exposure. Rather, how people ultimately voted was strongly related to preexisting social background. In fact, the audiences for each candidate's campaign communications generally had been supporters even before they heard the propaganda. They chose to expose themselves to the side they already preferred. Personal contacts were more important than media propaganda. The authors concluded that the voting decision was "a social experience."

The major implication was that the media simply reinforced prior predispositions, rather than creating large numbers of converts. A good deal of such media research was done in the 1940s and 1950s, and was usually summarized with a viewpoint that might be called the **minimal effects model** (see Klapper, 1960). It asserts: Mass communication *ordinarily* does not serve as a necessary and sufficient cause of audience effects, and more often reinforces existing attitudes.

THE THIRD PHASE: RENEWED RESPECT   The last two decades have ushered in still a third era, this of renewed respect for the power of the media in politics. Partly this was due to television and the seeming devotion of the American public to it. Partly it was due to changes in the content of television: Presidents were increasingly able to reach mass audiences through "command performances" on prime time television; "media experts" became increasingly prominent in political campaigns and spent large amounts of campaign money; and the Vietnam war became "the first television war." Critiques were published of "presidential televi-

Michael Jackson is one of a series of popular musicians and entertainers that have had fabulous success in attracting large crowds. Political leaders rarely have this appeal.

sion'' decrying the president's overly easy access to a gullible public (Minow, Martin, & Mitchell, 1973); of the clever tricks used by media consultants in the ''selling of the president'' (McGinniss, 1969); and of the tendency of television news to criticize every institution in America, and create cynical and negative attitudes throughout the citizenry (Robinson, 1976).

The idea behind this ''new look'' in media research is that the media, and television in particular, do in fact have powerful persuasive effects. The pre-television ''minimal effects model'' is just outdated. Moreover, if the main obstacles to change are inadequate exposure and resistance produced by strong predispositions, as the minimal effects model suggests, the media should be especially potent in situations that overcome these obstacles (Kraus and Davis, 1976). Low media exposure should be overcome by big events, such as the political parties' nominating conventions, election-day coverage, or televised debates, or by prime time political programming that attracts the viewing public for other reasons, such as brief political commercials, television news, and information about poll results. Similarly, strong political predispositions should be neutralized under some circumstances, such as nonpartisan elections, primary elections, or voting on ballot propositions. And in general, television should be more potent now because of the long-term decline in strength of party loyalties.

Let us take a closer look at the role of the media—first assessing media impact in politics, and then looking at some areas in which the media play their most substantial role.

Limited Impact

Are the media in fact as effective as this ''new look'' suggests? In general, campaigns conducted through the mass media are not successful in producing massive changes in attitudes. There are some exceptions. In the 1960s, a clever advertising campaign built around a grammatical error (''Winston tastes good, like a cigarette should") catapulted Winston cigarettes from a small seller to the most popular cigarette in the United States. A similarly successful campaign emphasizing professional dental associations' endorsements of its role in preventing tooth decay made Crest toothpaste one of the largest sellers after its introduction. Occasionally, a person who is virtually unknown at the beginning of a political campaign can win election by virtue of intensive advertising and face-to-face contacts. "Jimmy Who?" became President-Elect Carter in 1976.

In spite of these exceptions, it is usually extremely difficult in a short period of time to produce any sizable change in people's attitudes about something they really care about and are involved in. Many apparent cases of mass persuasion turn out, on close study, to have produced remarkably little real change.

SOME MAJOR MEDIA EFFORTS Among the big media events in recent years have been televised debates between the major presidential candidates. In 1960 there were four televised debates between John F. Kennedy and Richard M. Nixon, each covered live, and whole, by all three major networks. Audience studies revealed that 55 percent of the adult population watched all four debates, and 80 percent watched at least one. Journalists widely ascribed Kennedy's narrow victory in the election to his success in these debates. Yet careful survey research revealed that there were no substantial changes in voter preference following the debates (Katz & Feldman, 1962).

Similarly, the single 1980 Carter-Reagan debate, held a week before election day and often regarded as a major influence in Reagan's last-minute victorious surge, brought only 7 percent of Carter's previous supporters to Reagan's side and cost him 1 percent of his previous supporters, according to a CBS News poll done immediately after the debate. In a close race such

changes were important, but they cannot be said to have been massive or even decisive.

Research has also examined the effects of regular media programming on political attitudes. Some television series have dealt explicitly with problems of racism and prejudice, and have been enormously popular. The television series "Roots" played to record-breaking audiences in 1976. However, exposure to the series had no significant effect on whites' perceptions of the hardships of slavery or on racial egalitarianism. Viewers' reactions to the series were most strongly determined by their preexisting racial attitudes (Hur & Robinson, 1978; Ball-Rokeach et al., 1981). Similarly, reactions to Archie Bunker, the bigoted working-class white man who was the lead character in the series "All in the Family," were strongly determined by the viewer's prior level of racial prejudice (Brigham & Giesbrecht, 1976). In both cases, reinforcement of prior predispositions, rather than attitude change, seemed to be the major effect.

Many other highly-touted media attempts at political persuasion have had similarly meager effects. People's responses to the energy crisis and to Watergate depended to a considerable extent on their prior predispositions regarding the president and his party (Sears et al., 1978). The Johnson and Nixon Administrations tried everything they could think of to rally the American public behind the Vietnam war, only to see public support ebb away steadily through the late 1960s and early 1970s. Following the energy crisis of 1973–1974, caused by the Arab oil embargo, the government tried to keep public energy consumption down. But most indices of consumption soared right back up again when the crisis was past. And let us not forget Richard Nixon's lack of success in trying to persuade the American public that he was "not a crook," despite the best of media consultants and access to prime television time to make his pitch.

EXPOSURE AND RESISTANCE

Why are the media generally so ineffective in producing major changes of political attitudes? That is, what are the major obstacles they face in political life?

Low Levels of Exposure

We will first discuss the factors that intervene between the source and the target. To paraphrase a familiar expression, "what you don't hear can't change your attitude." If a message does not reach its target, for all intents and purposes no attitudes are changed.

People in the business of affecting public attitudes know that their most critical and difficult problem is reaching the people they want to influence. Advertisers, politicians, propagandists, and teachers must devote considerable effort to making sure messages reach their intended targets. Advertising executives have to spend millions of dollars and use great ingenuity to accomplish this. They must select some medium, say, television, find a program people watch, and then try to keep them from leaving their seats or turning down the sound or switching channels during the ads. And even when all this is achieved, they reach only a small percentage of the prospective audience—perhaps 30 percent of those owning sets *if* they select the most popular program on the air.

Television news is widely thought to be enormously influential because so many people watch it. But do they? One typical study found only 23 percent of the adult (age 18 and above) population watch the nightly national news programs on CBS, NBC, or ABC on an average weeknight, and most adults (53 percent) never watched even one such program in a two-week span (J. Robinson, 1971). Even these relatively few watchers seem not to have been watching very carefully. In a telephone survey in the San

Francisco Bay Area of people who had watched one of the TV news shows earlier in the evening, Neuman (1976) found that people could recall, on the average, only 1.2 of the 19.8 stories covered in an average half-hour show. Memory improved when the interviewer ran down the list of headlines: another 4.4 stories were remembered with supporting details, and 4.3 without any details. But half the stories were completely forgotten. Similarly, the average newspaper editorial is only read by 25 percent of the newspaper's readers (Becker, McCombs, & McLeod, 1975). With so many people not in the audience, and such poor attention among those who are, massive attitude change would seem to be unlikely.

Major political events, like the presidential debates during the 1960, 1976, and 1980 presidential campaigns, would seem to have been remarkable exceptions. Eighty million people were said to have watched at least one of these debates. But more careful analysis found that only a minority watched more than one debate, and that only about a quarter of the public watched even one debate all the way through. Many would not be watching television at all, and most others would be watching other shows. Most viewers consider a football game or a good movie more interesting than a political speech.

Thus, getting through to people is difficult and chancy. Particularly in politics and public affairs, people tend to be exposed very little to persuasive messages. And regardless of the topic, the percentage of the potential audience reached by any message is quite small.

Selective Exposure

As difficult as the low level of exposure makes life for propagandists, they have other prob-

Reaching an audience is one of the problems when trying to change attitudes. Not everyone can attract this kind of a crowd just to hear a speech.

lems. When a message does get through, the person it reaches is likely already to agree with it. This is the phenomenon of **selective exposure.** People tend to be exposed relatively less to information that disagrees with what they believe. Democrats hear talks mostly by other Democrats; religious people hear talks favoring religion; and farmers tend to read articles in fa-

vor of farmers. Similar selective processes can bias processing at the perceptual, learning, or memory stages.

What evidence is there that such selective processes pose major obstacles to political communicators? There is considerable evidence that real audiences are in fact biased toward initial agreement with the propagandist. This has

---

BOX 14–3
The Ratings Game vs. Real Audiences

How can we reconcile these modest audiences with the network claims of vast audiences? The networks generally rely on Nielsen ratings, which are based mainly on whether a household's television set is on or off, though they also make some use of viewer diaries. The Nielsen ratings showed, for example, that in 1976 the average household had a TV set on 6.82 hours per day (Comstock et al., 1978, p. 89).

This figure overestimates actual viewing in several obvious ways. First of all, the Nielsen sample probably includes an excessive number of regular television viewers, since the family must contract with Nielsen to be included in the study. Second, it does not tell us if anyone is watching the set. It could be just sitting there in the living room playing to nobody. Movies taken of living rooms indicate that the TV set is on, but no human being is even in the room part of the time (19 percent in one study), and some of the time people are in the room and the set is on, but no one is watching (an additional 21 percent; see Comstock et al., 1978, p. 142). So 40 percent of the time the set is on, but no one is watching. And, finally, even when they are supposed to be watching, the viewers may be doing something else and not paying close attention. Another study videotaped people watching TV and found an amazing variety of other activities going on, including pacing, ironing, playing Monopoly, answering the phone, conversing, wrestling, dancing, and undressing (Ibid., p. 144).

---

been called **de facto selective exposure.** When the Republicans put on a television special, mostly Republicans watch. When Democrats put on a special, mostly Democrats watch (Sears & Freedman, 1967). Why does this de facto selective exposure occur?

Some assume that individuals actively seek out supportive information and avoid nonsupportive as a way of maintaining the consistency of their own attitudes. This has been called **motivated selective exposure**. This is certainly a plausible idea, but de facto selective exposure could arise for other reasons.

There has been a great deal of research on motivated selective exposure in controlled situations, but it suggests that such tendencies are rather weak. For example, during the great antiwar protests of the spring of 1968, many college students signed an antidraft petition called the "We Won't Go" pledge, and many

others gave a great deal of thought to the possibility of signing it. It was an issue of great personal importance to young men who thought they might be drafted, and possibly killed, in a war they regarded as immoral. Janis and Rausch (1970) tested for selective exposure to pro and anti communications among four different kinds of Yale students: those who immediately refused to sign the pledge, those who refused after some deliberation, those who favored the pledge and said they might sign, and those who had already signed it.

Each student was given the titles of eight articles on the war, four of which supported the pledge and four of which opposed it. Each student then rated the articles for interest in reading them. Motivated selectivity would have been reflected in a propledge student's greater interest in pro than anti messages, with the reverse holding for antipledge students. In fact, however, Janis and Rausch found motivated selectivity in only one of the four groups (those who might sign but hadn't yet), while both groups opposed to the pledge were primarily interested in counterattitudinal information. Table 14–7 shows the results. So in this study, the general trend was, if anything, for subjects to be interested in messages *opposing* their own position.

There are just about as many studies producing a preference for supportive information as there are producing a preference for nonsupportive information, and a large number show no difference at all (Sears, 1968). The most likely conclusion from the research is that motivated selectivity is not a strong force in most situations. The same tends to be true of selective learning and retention. A number of careful studies show that people do not learn supportive information more quickly than nonsupportive information, nor do they retain it longer or more completely (Smith & Jamieson, 1972; though see Frey, 1982, and Ross et al., 1981, for contrary views).

The major exception to this lack of selectivity in information acquisition is **selective attention.** A number of clever experiments have been done in which the subject is given the op-portunity to press a button to eliminate static masking a persuasive communication. Brock and Balloun (1967) found that subjects would be more likely to tune in to a supportive than to a nonsupportive message. Kleinhesselink and Edwards (1975) took it a step further, finding that people would block out nonsupportive messages as long as they were hard to refute but would happily listen to those that were easy to refute. The researchers exposed all students to a speech urging the legalization of marijuana. But the strength of arguments was varied.

In one condition, the students heard strong, difficult-to-refute arguments (prohibitions against popular drugs never work, it is better for you than alcohol, present marijuana laws encourage criminality) or weak, easy-to-refute arguments (banning marijuana would bring the American family back together and make rock musicians less paranoid). When listening to the speech, the subject could press a button to eliminate static. Buttonpressing (an index of full attention) was highest for the difficult-to-refute supportive arguments, as the selective attention hypothesis would predict. But it was also high for the easy-to-refute nonsupportive arguments. In both cases, attention was highest for the arguments that would be least threatening to the subject's

Table 14–7
Mean Scores on Interest in Being Exposed to Articles Pro and Anti the "We-Won't-Go" Pledge, Comparing Men Who Opposed and Favored the Pledge

| | OPPOSED TO PLEDGE | | IN FAVOR OF PLEDGE | |
ARTICLE	PROMPTLY REFUSED TO SIGN (n = 12)	REFUSED AFTER DELIBERATION (n = 16)	MIGHT SIGN (n = 11)	HAVE ALREADY SIGNED (n = 23)
Propledge	9.83	11.81	11.09	10.38
Antipledge	7.50	9.38	10.09	11.31
Selective exposure	−2.33	−2.43	+1.00	−0.52

Note: The ratings are of four articles, each on a 5-point scale, so the total scale is from 4 (no interest) to 20 (great interest).
Source: Janis and Rausch (1970), p. 50.

The Compliant Communicators

Another possible reason for de facto selectivity is that communicators tailor their messages to their audiences. Since similarity in attitudes increases liking (see Chapter 8), speakers should be evaluated more positively if they modified their messages to agree with their audience. This would make the audience *look* as if they were being selective, even though in reality the communicator is just trying to be ingratiating (Sears, 1968). To test this idea, Newtson and Czerlinsky (1974) had moderates on the Vietnam war communicate their positions to hawks and to doves. In every case, the speakers significantly displaced their messages toward the positions they expected the audience to hold; they communicated a more hawkish position to the hawks, and a more dovish position to the doves, than they actually held. To see if the same process works outside the laboratory, Miller and Sigelman (1978) content-analyzed Lyndon Johnson's speeches on the Vietnam war from mid-1967 to the end of his presidency in early 1969. They also coded the audiences either as hawkish (the Veterans of Foreign Wars or First Cavalry Division) or as "other" (Congress, American Milk Producers, Young Democrats). They found a substantial correlation (r = .501); more hawkish audiences attracted more hawkish speeches from President Johnson.

own position. This support for selective attention contrasts with the apparent lack of motivated selectivity in either exposure or learning.

So the work on selective exposure indicates that the communicator does not have to worry too much about the target person *deliberately* avoiding nonsupporting information. If the communicator can get the message near the targets and give them a clear choice as to whether or not to listen to it, the targets will not avoid it simply because they disagree with it.

Resistance to Persuasion

Even a communicator who has been successful in getting the message to the target is a long way from changing the target's opinion. For example, both Democrats and Republicans watched the Reagan-Carter TV debate in 1980, but they differed enormously in their evaluation of them.

The overwhelming journalistic consensus was that Reagan had "won" the debate. Yet, as you can see in Table 14–8, only 10 percent of pro-Carter viewers thought Reagan had won. New information is interpreted in terms of existing attitudes. This seems to be a typical response to most such mass communications.

New information seems to be incorporated into existing attitudes without changing them very much. Why is this so? So much resistance to attitude change suggests that the attitudes in question must reflect fairly strong commitments. In fact, this is a major problem in achieving change in real situations. The communications that attract enough attention to get past all the barriers happen also to encounter strong, highly committed attitudes in a great many people. The result is that people use modes of resolution other than attitude change to restore cognitive consistency when it is upset by a discrepant persuasive communication.

Table 14–8
Voter Judgment of Who Won the Carter-Reagan Debate, 1980

PREDEBATE PREFERENCE	CARTER	NO CHOICE	REAGAN	TOTAL (PERCENT)
Carter	69%	21%	10%	100%
Anderson	31	28	41	100
Undecided	27	43	30	100
Reagan	5	13	82	100

Note: Data from a nationwide CBS News/*New York Times* telephone survey of Americans of voting age.

Source: Adapted from CBS News release, October 29, 1980.

All the modes of resolution discussed in Chapter 7 are relevant here. For one thing, people are likely simply to reject outright arguments that are discrepant from their own previous attitude. Pressures toward cognitive consistency cause the beliefs and values that fit into the already existing structure to be more easily accepted than those that do not fit in. For example, if people consider themselves Democrats, they will be more likely to believe positive things about Democrats and negative things about Republicans. They are also more likely to favor ideas proposed by Democratic politicians than to favor those proposed by Republicans.

Source derogation also takes place. When politicians take a position on the unpopular side of a hotly contested issue, their own reputations suffer. George McGovern, in 1972, was on the "wrong" side of a whole series of issues, at least according to popular perceptions. Most people thought him too sympathetic to abortion, marijuana, reduced defense budgets, amnesty for draft resisters, busing, and campus unrest. As a consequence, voters did not change attitudes on these issues very much; rather, they derogated McGovern (Miller, Miller, Raine, & Brown, 1976). Perceptual distortions follow the same pattern. Voters distort the positions on issues taken by presidential candidates to make them more consistent with candidate preferences. The result of using all these modes of resolution is that people can expose themselves to discrepant information in the media and not show any real attitude change.

AREAS OF GREATER MEDIA IMPACT

Some Examples

Occasionally some media events, or the political events they describe, are able to produce considerable attitude change all by themselves. Following the assassination of President John F. Kennedy, at about 12:30 P.M. (CST) Friday, November 22, 1963, the three television networks covered the story virtually nonstop for four days. They covered the assassination of Lee Harvey Oswald, the alleged assassin. They also covered the religious service, the cortege to Arlington Cemetery, the burial there, several processions through the streets of Washington, and countless retrospectives and interviews with prominent people. The total coverage ranged from 60 to 71 hours across the three networks (Rubin, 1967). Public exposure was massive, with the median American adult watching almost half of this programming.

The emotional and attitudinal effects of this experience were extraordinary. According to a survey completed the following week (Sheatsley & Feldman, 1965), 53 percent said they cried, and 48 percent that they had had trouble sleeping, compared to the roughly 20 percent who did under more normal circumstances; 30 percent said they felt *more* upset than *most* people (and only 8 percent, less). Only 19 percent of the public said they had carried on "pretty much as usual." The attitudinal effects were no less impressive: Half the population called Kennedy one of the best two or three presidents in history, and only 2 percent called him "somewhat below average." Before the assassination, Kennedy had not been thought nearly so exceptional. He had run behind his party and barely won election, was rated by the public as doing no better a job than most presidents (Mueller, 1973), and indeed has as subsequently been judged by historians to be a little above average among American presidents.

It is impossible to separate the effects of the assassination itself from those of its television coverage in producing these changes. But it is widely agreed that the television coverage was instrumental in making the events among the most memorable in American history.

Another dramatic series of events was the Watergate controversy. At the height of his political fortunes, immediately after a smashing reelection victory in 1972, President Richard M. Nixon slowly but surely was revealed as having participated in covering up a burglary of Democratic party headquarters carried out by some of his campaign workers. Most of his top aides were sooner or later implicated in the scandal and forced to resign, and Nixon himself ultimately became the first American president to resign, in disgrace. The series of events lasted nearly two years, again with massive television coverage.

As a total set of events, it produced a considerable amount of attitude change, particularly toward President Nixon, of course. For example, one study showed that a crucial tape recording which became public, forcing Nixon's resignation a few days later, produced an increase of 15 percent in those desiring his forceful removal from office over a period of just three days (Lang & Stevenson, 1976; see also Chaffee, 1975; Kraus & Chaffee, 1974; Miller et al., 1975). Much of this major change must be ascribed to the media, since that was the public's primary source of information.

As we have seen, presidential debates have not themselves proved to be overwhelming persuasive instruments. But the media frequently make postdebate judgments about who "won" or "lost" the debate, and these may be quite influential. The Langs (1979) found that the immediate postviewing judgment of "who won" the first Carter-Ford debate in 1976 yielded a Carter margin of 42 to 24 percent. But media commentators quickly came to a consensus that Ford had done better than expected and concluded that he had therefore "won" the debate. The Langs found a Ford margin of 41 to 20 percent among those interviewed several days later, after all the media commentary.

A fourth exception concerns the potential influence on voting turnout of election-night broadcasts of exit polls, computer projections, concession speeches, and other premature communications about election outcomes. The concern arises because the polls are generally not yet all closed (especially on the West Coast) when results are announced. It is feared that the vote will be influenced, and especially that turnout will be reduced, if it appears that the outcome has already been settled. With the increasingly sophisticated use of exit polls, results can actually be projected long before the polls are closed in any part of the country, broadening the concern.

Recent careful studies have begun to reveal some definite dampening effects of such projections on turnout. The 1972 election featured early projections of a Nixon landslide over Mc-Govern, and a careful analysis of Census Bureau samples concluded that the network projections cut turnout in the Pacific states by about 2.7 percent (Wolfinger & Linquiti, 1981). Similarly, on election day 1980, network projections began appearing even before the polls closed in many eastern states. President Carter publicly conceded over an hour before the polls closed in California. And several prominent Democratic senators and congressmen attributed their narrow defeats to the reduced Democratic turnout caused by these media announcements.

A postelection survey found that 57 percent had heard or read some kind of election coverage, and 47 percent were aware of projections of the outcome before local poll-closing time (Jackson, 1983). Turnout was cut more than 20 percent among those who heard the projections or concession speeches and had not already voted by 6 P.M. EST. The early projections and concession speech cut turnout by an estimated overall 6 percent in the East and 11 percent in the West. Moreover, it did so much more for the losing Democrats; turnout was cut 4 percent more for Carter than for Reagan in the East, and 14 percent in the West (Jackson, 1983). Clearly, the Democratic candidates seemed to have something real to complain about. And the media, something to think about.

Overcoming Obstacles to Change

What do these positive instances of media impact on political orientations have in common? Most notably, they rank among the relatively few political events that have attracted very high levels of media exposure in the general public. The average person watched the Kennedy assassination events almost nonstop for four days. Watergate was in the headlines and dominating all news reports for about two years. Very large numbers of people prove to have learned of the media's "verdict" on presidential debates. And the election-night media projec-

tions of who has won a presidential election prove also to reach a great many people, one way or another. So part of the secret to overcoming the obstacles to change is massive exposure.

When does the wall of inadequate exposure break down? Selectivity is never perfect, whether deliberate or accidental. Throughout life and particularly as we grow older, we are exposed to information that disagrees with our attitudes. The extent to which discrepant information reaches us varies greatly and is more likely for some issues than for others. For example, most Americans develop a belief that democracy is the best political system and are rarely exposed to information inconsistent with this attitude. Similarly, devout Catholics or liberal Democrats would be more likely to be exposed to information that disagrees with their attitudes on religion or politics. Although they probably would be exposed to more supporting than nonsupporting information, they would have to face occasional disagreement.

Second, not all attitudes are emotionally laden, deeply held, and long term. The media do have a major persuasive impact when members of the audience are not especially committed to attitudes. Attitude formation toward new attitude objects, like the Ayatollah Khomeini or acid rain or the Sandinistas in Nicaragua, may depend on media coverage. And the media may be more decisive in primary and nonpartisan elections than in general elections, because these elections involve fewer standing predispositions. The nearly unknown Jimmy Carter's meteoric rise in 1976 is a good example (Patterson, 1980).

However, the evidence for substantial impact even in these cases is still not very compelling. In most of these cases, the evidence points to minimal media impact on political attitudes, or little evidence exists one way or another (Kraus and Davis, 1976). Media researchers have therefore begun to look at media effects other than persuasion. They suggest that the media play a particularly important role in providing information to the public and in focusing public attention; that is, in **agenda setting,** determining what issues are most salient to the public.

Conveying Information

Nevertheless, the media are much more successful in providing information than in changing deeply held attitudes. Presidential debates increase voters' familiarity with the candidates' positions on campaign issues (Sears & Chaffee, 1979). Children learn a great deal from television, ranging from Sesame Street to weather forecasts (Comstock et al., 1978).

One of the earliest demonstrations of this information gain from mass communication is found in the wartime research by Hovland, Lumsdaine, and Sheffield (1949). The Army commissioned them to evaluate the effectiveness of orientation films shown to draftees and volunteers. These films were intended to explain the reasons for World War II, make new soldiers more sympathetic to the war effort, and turn them into enthusiastic fighters. The researchers did find markedly increased levels of information about the war as a result of viewing the films. For example, the films clearly communicated factual details about the Battle of Britain, such as the relative sizes of the German and British air forces, the focusing of German bombings on ports and ships, and the fact that the Germans would have physically invaded England except for the resistance of the British air force. But opinions about the British and the war—such as whether the British were going all out, whether or not they would have given up with more bombing, or whether they would hold out to the end, along with attitudes toward the Germans and Japanese—were largely unaffected.

But even here it would be a mistake to expect too much from the media. Half the public heard of John Kennedy's assassination from a friend rather than from the media. In another national survey, J. Robinson (1972) found that people who watched TV news frequently were not significantly more familiar with the names of such public personalities as Ralph Nader and Bob Dylan than people who never watched TV news at all. Part of the problem is that people do not usually pay close attention to television news. And part of the problem is that TV news tends to emphasize the more entertaining features of the day's events, rather than the more serious side. For example, when it comes to elections, TV news emphasizes the "horserace" or "hoopla" aspect of the campaign, not the issues. Broadcasts focus on who is ahead, what the campaign strategies are, who made the latest mistake, and pictures of motorcades or people in funny hats, not complex policy positions (Patterson & McClure, 1976). So regular viewers hardly knew any more about candidates' policies than nonviewers.

Newspaper reading, on the other hand, does seem to contribute consistently to the public's information level. On the average, regular newspaper readers increased in their issue awareness during the 1972 campaign twice as much as did nonregular readers (Patterson & McClure, 1976, p. 52). Newspaper reading in the 1976 campaign was associated with increases in candidate and issue awareness during both the primary and general election phases of the 1976 campaign (Patterson, 1980, pp. 112, 158). National samples show newspaper reading associated with greater familiarity with news personalities, even with controls for demographic factors and other forms of media exposure (J. Robinson, 1972). The same is true for reading newsmagazines. Comparable tests show much weaker effects of television news.

Agenda Setting

Another effect is that the media can help in "setting the agenda" for people. That is, events given a great deal of media coverage tend to become foci of public attention (Comstock et al., 1978). One important study was done by Funkhouser (1973) to test whether the public's sense of priorities during the 1960s (as reflected in the

Gallup poll question asking "What is the most important problem facing the nation?") was determined by the volume of news coverage given various issues (as indexed by the number of articles in newsmagazines). He pitted media coverage against "reality," such as the number of troops actually involved in Vietnam, the crime rate, and so on. The analysis was relatively primitive, but it was clear that the public's priorities bore more relationship to media coverage than to "reality."

He suggested that the media mainly cover "newsworthy events" but soon lose interest in them, and barely cover "nonnewsworthy" events (such standing conditions as poverty or racism) at all. Thus media coverage of Watergate, especially the Senate committee hearings chaired by Senator Sam Ervin, at which John Dean made his sensational charges, helped bring that scandal to public attention. The same was true of the moonshot program, the Vietnam war, the campus unrest of the late 1960s, the ghetto riots and assassinations of the 1960s, the Iranian takeover of the American embassy in Teheran in 1979, the rising fear of war and the high unemployment rate in the early 1980s, and so on.

Several recent experiments have indicated that greater television news coverage *can* induce higher issue salience in laboratory situations (Iyengar, Peters, & Kinder, 1982; Iyengar, Peters, Kinder, & Krosnick, 1984). In one, adults viewed television newscasts in which the amount of coverage given particular issues was varied experimentally. This manipulation significantly influenced the perceived importance of these issues, even on a questionnaire given 24 hours later.

In a second, this salience manipulation influenced the basis for the respondents' evaluations of the president. They tended to base their approval of his performance on his handling of the particular issue made salient in the experiment.

The experiments, some conducted with ordinary citizens rather than college students, using real network news segments, providing a week's worth of news, and conducted under rather realistic circumstances, indicate that television news can, under the right circumstances, have an agenda-setting effect. The challenge is to determine those circumstances.

Long-Term Change

Most studies have dealt with relatively brief or short-term mass communications—single programs or short series on TV, or newspaper endorsements in a particular campaign. But many important changes of attitude may occur over extended periods of time—attitudes toward the enemy in wartime, or value changes over many years on matters such as religion or sexuality. These more gradual changes may be responsive to equally long-term patterns of media communication.

Methods of studying the long-term effects of the media are necessarily primitive. It is hard to find an adequate control group, or even a low-exposure group, when the media flood the public with a particular message for years at a time. It is difficult to isolate the unique contribution of the mass media toward attitude changes that may have been fostered by communication in schools, churches, among peer groups, at the workplace, and at many other sites throughout society. For example, American society has become dramatically more tolerant of homosexuals, divorce, women's rights, and sexual freedom since World War II. But many changes have contributed to these new attitudes. How would we isolate the contribution of, say, dramatic programs on television? The media may have helped, but so have universities, courts, legislatures, pressure groups, and protest marches.

One example is Mueller's (1973) finding that the patterns of American casualties were associated with long-term reductions in support for wars in Korea and Vietnam. The earliest casualties caused big declines in public support; later casualties made less difference, as if the public had become "hardened" to the fighting. This study provides no direct information on the media's role, but that was surely the main vehicle by which the public as a whole learned about the casualties.

A somewhat more direct test of long-term impact treats campaign expenditures as a determinant of election outcomes. Presumably the more money a candidate spends on a campaign, the more media expenditure and exposure, the more popular he or she should become. However, no simple relationship exists between voting returns and campaign expenditures. Instead, Grush et al. (1978), arguing by analogy from the "mere exposure" research in laboratory experiments (such as Zajonc, 1968), predicted that the amount of campaign expenditures ought to be most decisive when little is known about the candidates and the choice is moderately confusing. Thus campaign expenditures should most affect the vote when (1) three or more candidates are running, (2) they are all relatively unknown, and (3) only moderate levels of expenditure are involved.

These conditions held in a large number of House and Senate primaries in 1972 when no incumbent or "notorious" candidate (past incumbent, famous person, or past governor or attorney general) was running. Under these conditions, indeed, campaign expenditures were strongly related to the vote, presumably to a large degree via the media. A later study dealing with candidates in the 1976 presidential primaries (Grush, 1980) further specified this relationship. He obtained two main findings: that campaign expenditures were strongly related to voting success in the early phase of the primary season, particularly for the less successful candidates. During the later primaries, earlier successes became more important predictors than campaign expenditures. This presumably is the payoff for what Patterson called the "winner-take-all" system of news coverage of the early primaries; a few early victories are worth millions in free publicity for the later primaries.

Finally, Wattenberg (1982) has shown that media expenditures in the 1978 congressional general elections were reasonably strongly related to the intensity and salience of voters' attitudes toward candidates. This was particularly true in districts where the party organizations were not very important, and where expenditures were mainly targeted for the mass media rather than for posters, billboards, and so on. Again, the inference is that mass media exposure was responsible for the effect. One clear implication of these findings is that heavy media expenditures can have at least one reliable effect: They can boost an unknown candidate up from deep in the pack, given that there is no overwhelmingly better known candidate. But there is little evidence of that effect against a very well-known single opponent.

These studies remain rather indirect tests of media impact, however, since they do not use media content as the independent variable. Some studies do relate actual content to overall changes in public opinion. Brody and Page (1975) coded front-page news stories for their favorability to the president, and then related a summary "news discrepancy" index (favorable minus unfavorable news) to fluctuations in presidential popularity. They found a reasonably close fit for Lyndon Johnson's presidency, but not for Nixon's. A later analysis found that frequency of use of scheduled, prime time presidential broadcasts bolstered Nixon's popularity (Haight & Brody, 1977; see also Minow et al., 1973, on these broadcasts). Interestingly enough, these data also revealed that Nixon tended to schedule such broadcasts at times when his popularity was slipping.

In short, the places to look for relatively greater media impact are: agenda-setting, formation of attitudes to new attitude objects, providing information, and longer-term effects. But we should not overestimate the magnitude of effects even here. As with media violence, it is much easier to document effects in the laboratory than in real life.

SUMMARY

1. Prejudice, stereotypes, and discrimination correspond to the affective, cognitive, and behavioral components of intergroup antagonism.

2. Stereotypes and prejudice strongly influence the individual's attitudes and behavior in a variety of areas.

3. Group conflict theories view prejudice as stemming from the realities of intergroup competition; social learning theories, from the learning of conventional social norms; cognitive theories, from simple social cognition factors like categorization and salience; and psychodynamic theories, from the individual's particular personality dynamics.

4. Social learning is probably the strongest determinant of stereotypes and prejudices against minority groups.

5. Prejudices frequently develop in childhood and adolescence. Although parents have an important part in the development of commitments, they are by no means the only, or even necessarily the most important, source of prejudice acquisition.

6. Interracial contact is probably the most effective technique for reducing prejudice. But by itself, it is not extremely effective; it is more likely to be successful if it involves close contact, cooperative interdependence, and equal status.

7. Social scientists have gone through three markedly different phases in assessing the impact of the media in politics. In the 1930s it was thought to be an awesomely powerful new weapon, and in the 1940s and 1950s to have minimal effects. Today there is renewed respect for its role.

8. Far-ranging attitude changes are rarely produced by such propaganda campaigns in the real world as advertising campaigns, presidential campaigns, or presidential debates.

9. One set of obstacles to attitude change in the real world is lack of exposure to discrepant information, because of low absolute levels of exposure and selective exposure.

10. Selective exposure can occur in the absence of any general tendency for people to seek out supportive information (motivated selectivity).

11. Political propaganda also is often ineffective because it encounters highly committed attitudes, so any new information is selectively interpreted by members of the audience to reinforce their prior attitudes.

12. The media can produce massive changes in political attitudes, but usually only in those rare cases in which there is a high level of exposure.

13. The media can be effective, however, in agenda setting, providing information, or changing low-commitment attitudes, or in producing change through repeated exposure over long time periods.

SUGGESTIONS FOR ADDITIONAL READING

LANG, G., & LANG, K. (1983). *The battle for public opinion: The president, the press, and the polls during Watergate.* New York: Columbia University Press. An interesting case history of a major media event and its impact.

KINDER, D. R., & SEARS, D. O. (1985). Political behavior. In G. Lindzey and E. Aronson (Eds.), *Handbook of social psychology, 3rd ed.,* Vol. 2. New York: Random House. A most complete account of research on public opinion concerning politics in the United States. Relates that research to the social-psychological principles discussed in this chapter.

SEARS, D. O., & CITRIN, J. (1982). *Tax revolt: Something for nothing in California.* Cambridge, Mass.: Harvard University Press. An application of a social-psychological approach to the public response to problems of government taxation and spending.

15

GENDER IN SOCIAL LIFE

On a radio talk show, the host is discussing teenage sexuality with a medical expert. The second caller, Chris, asks a question about the birth control pill. The researcher begins his answer by asking Chris if she herself is considering using the pill. After a pause, Chris blurts out, "I'm a boy." Everyone seems embarrassed, the researcher apologizes, and the host rephrases the question. I, like other listeners, think about Chris's high-pitched voice and gentle manner. Would I have made the same mistake?

A noted psychologist begins a study of the behavior of young children. Concerned that knowledge of a child's gender might influence the way observers interpret the child's activities, the researcher asks parents to bring their children to the study dressed in overalls and T shirts. To the researcher's surprise, her effort to conceal the toddlers' gender backfires. Although all children arrive in denims, many of the little girls wear overalls with ruffles or bows.

You glance casually at the driver of the sports car stopped at a traffic light. Noting a gray sweatshirt and prominent chin, you assume the person is a man. But something about the face makes you look again. You quickly study the person's physique. The smooth cheeks give no hint of stubble. The shoulders are a bit broad for a woman, but perhaps she's a swimmer. The arm resting on the car door conceals the person's chest, but reveals slender, delicate fingers. Neither rings nor earrings are visible. Then the light changes and the car moves off, leaving you puzzling about the driver's gender.

As these examples indicate, gender is one of the basic categories in social life. In meeting new people, we inevitably try to identify them as male or female. There are many reasons for this tendency. One is that the English language has gender-linked pronouns such as "he" and "she," "his" and "hers."

Gender categorization usually occurs automatically, without our giving it much thought. Most of the time, cues about gender are readily available from physical characteristics such as facial hair or breasts and from style of dress. People commonly display their gender as a prominent part of their self-presentation. Instances where we cannot be certain of a person's gender call attention to the categorization process, and typically lead us to seek information to resolve the matter.

Our tendency to divide the world into masculine and feminine categories is not limited to person perception; many objects and activities are also commonly defined as masculine and feminine. At an early age, children learn that dolls and cooking utensils are for girls, and that toy trucks and guns are for boys. Most 4-year-olds believe that doctor, police officer, and construction worker are male jobs, and that secretary, teacher, and librarian are female jobs (Gettys & Cann, 1981). This process of **gender typing** continues in adulthood. In a recent study, college students identified icepicks, barbells, wrenches, and chest strengtheners as masculine objects, and eggbeaters, thimbles, rolling pins, and laundry baskets as feminine. Some objects, such as headphones, electric outlets, and corkscrews, were seen as gender-neutral (Reis & Jackson, 1981). Married couples often distinguish between "men's work," such as

BOX 15-1
The So-Called Generic Masculine
or What's All the Fuss about She/He and Chairpersons?

In English, the words "he" and "man" have had to serve two functions. They refer both to specific males and to human beings in general (Martyna, 1980). Most of us learned in high school that it is grammatically correct to say "each person took *his* turn," even when most of the people involved are female. Similarly, we were taught that "mankind" includes both sexes, just as a "chairman" can be a woman. When "he" and "man" are used to refer to both sexes, they are said to be *generic* terms. Grammarians have justified the use of the generic masculine as a convenient shorthand. Recently, however, feminists have criticized this linguistic practice, arguing that it subtly reaffirms male dominance and contributes to the "invisibility" of women in society.

Psychological research shows that the so-called generic masculine is *not* necessarily perceived as including both sexes (see review by Henley, 1979). For example, Martyna (1980) asked a large sample of students from kindergarten through college to complete sentence fragments such as "When a police officer leaves the station," "When a secretary first arrives at the office," or "When a teenager finishes high school." Martyna found that when the sentences contained a traditionally masculine role word such as "police officer," 96 percent of subjects used "he" in completing the sentence. When the sentences contained a traditionally feminine role word such as "secretary," none of the students used "he" and 87 percent used "she." In gender-neutral sentences such as that about a teenager, 65 percent of subjects used "he," 5 percent used "she," and 30 percent used alternatives such as "they." Clearly, students did not always use "he" to refer to both sexes.

Given that people do not always use the generic masculine, do they nonetheless understand it when they encounter it? MacKay and Fulkerson (1979) designed a study to find out. College students listened to a series of sentences read aloud on a tape recording. Examples included "A lawyer must frequently argue his case out of court," and "A nurse must frequently help his patients get out of bed." These sentences used the word "he" generically and so could logically refer to both males and females. Some students were asked whether each of these sentences could refer to a man, and 99 percent responded correctly that each could. In contrast, other students were asked if each sentence could refer to a woman. This time, 87 percent of responses were wrong: Students said that the sentences could not refer to a woman, when logically they could. This and other studies indicate that the use of pronouns such as "he" can bias interpretations.

We do not always use the generic masculine the way grammarians say we should. When we hear a discussion of the "best man for the job," we often conjure up a mental image of a male. When we read about the "chairman of an important committee," we assume the person is a man. If we were asked to think carefully about these terms, we would most likely acknowledge that "he" can refer to a female, but this is not our first reaction. The use of the

One consequence of these findings is that many organizations, including the American Psychological Association and most textbook publishers, have developed new guidelines for writing that explicitly discourage the use of the generic masculine. Instead, authors are urged to substitute terms that will be understood accurately, such as "chairperson" (for "chairman"), "human nature" (for "the nature of man"), or "firefighter" (for "fireman"). Alternatives to the use of the generic "he" include using the plural, alternating the use of "he" and "she" throughout the text, or using a phrase such as "he or she."

mowing the lawn, taking out the garbage, or barbecuing, and "women's work," such as housecleaning or childcare. Although a few occupations such as psychologist and personnel officer are seen by adults as gender-neutral, most jobs are perceived as gender-typed (Shinar, 1975). You should have no trouble guessing how most people categorize the following jobs: secretary, brain surgeon, truck driver, elementary school teacher, nurse, and judge.

This distinction between male and female is a universal organizing principle in all human societies. As children, boys and girls are expected to learn different skills and to develop different personalities. As adults, men and women typically assume distinctive gender-linked roles as husband or wife, mother or father. Cultures vary in exactly what is defined as masculine or feminine and in the degree to which they accentuate gender differences or similarities. But the use of gender to structure at least some elements of social life has been basic.

Hella Hammid, Photo Researchers, Inc.

Irene Springer

The tendency to categorize things as masculine versus feminine extends to colors, toys, occupations and fashions. In recent years, however, gender distinctions have become somewhat less rigid. One sign of change is hair styles.

GENDER IN THE EYE OF THE BEHOLDER

We begin with a seemingly simple question: How does the gender of other people influence our perception and evaluation of them and their behavior? The emphasis here is on gender as a characteristic of the *target* of impression formation. Research shows that our beliefs about what typical men and women are like can color our perceptions of individuals and bias our evaluations of their performance.

Gender Stereotypes

How do you think men and women differ? Do you believe that one sex is usually more aggressive or more nurturant than the other? How do the sexes typically compare on such qualities as being courageous, neat, logical, gentle, squeamish, dominant, or gullible? Beliefs about the personal attributes of women and men are **gender stereotypes.** All stereotypes, whether based on gender, race, ethnicity, or other groupings, refer to an image of what the typical member of a particular social category is like. But a useful distinction can be made between cultural and personal stereotypes (Ashmore, 1981).

CULTURAL STEREOTYPES We are all exposed to images of the sexes presented by our culture. Movies, pop music, television, and other mass media convey messages about the nature of masculinity and femininity. So do religious teachings, educational materials, art, and literature. The societal-level images of the sexes conveyed in these places are **cultural stereotypes.** You probably know these stereotypes quite well, although you may not have thought about them very much.

On TV, for example, we can see anxious housewives desperately trying to avoid tell-tale spots on the family's clothes or pondering the best food for a finicky cat. Young women ap-

pear obsessed with staying thin or competing for men's attention by wearing the right pantyhose or jeans. Off camera, the voices of male experts solemnly offer advice. On screen, men in impressive offices extol the virtues of razor blades or copying machines. Systematic research has found that the most common TV commercial depicts a male expert instructing a female consumer about a particular product. In a typical study (McArthur & Resko, 1975), 70 percent of men were shown as experts, whereas 86 percent of women were product users. Female experts and male consumers were the exception.

A trip to an art museum would also find men and women portrayed in traditional gender-typed activities. A study of highly acclaimed paintings and sculptures found that men were often shown in professional work or warfare, whereas women usually did housework or childcare (O'Kelly, 1980). Significantly more women than men were portrayed as passively "doing nothing." Nearly a quarter of women but only 2 percent of men were depicted as "objects" who were not engaged in any identifiable activity.

These studies and other analyses of newspaper articles, award-winning children's books, university textbooks, and other diverse elements of culture have found several general themes in the portrayal of the sexes. Whereas men are shown in a wide variety of social roles and activities, women are more often restricted to domestic and family roles. Men are commonly portrayed as experts and leaders, women as subordinates. Men are usually depicted as more active, assertive, and influential than women. And although females are slightly more than half the population, they are often under represented in the media. In recent years there have been efforts to change these media images so they portray men and women in less rigidly gender-typed ways. We are slowly beginning to see a few women in the business world and a few men in the kitchen.

Do these cultural portraits of the sexes actually have an effect on people's daily lives? Evidence suggests that they can. An example is provided by research on TV commercials. Television now reaches 95 percent of American homes, and some social critics claim that Americans may have a TV set on as many as four or five hours a day. An experimental study of women college students demonstrated the potential influence of TV (Jennings, Geis, & Brown, 1980). Participants were randomly assigned to one of two conditions. Half the participants saw four commercials depicting the sexes in traditional roles. Men were portrayed as the authorities and were the center of attention; women were shown as sex objects or in domestic roles. The experimental commercials were closely modeled after real ones. In one, for example, a tiny woman serves her large, hungry husband a packaged dinner. The implicit message is that the wife's role is to cater to and please her husband. In another, an attractive man authoritatively extols the virtues of an alcoholic beverage. At the close of the commercial, a seductive woman slithers up and coyly says that she would also choose the same drink. Here the woman is presented as a sex object who follows the man's advice. In the second experimental condition, women participants saw reversed-role versions of the same commercials in which the females were the central figures and the males were shown in the homemaking and seductive roles.

Results indicated that exposure to TV commercials had a significant effect on subsequent behavior. After watching the films, participants engaged in one of two tasks. Some performed a test designed to measure their conformity, while others were rated on self-confidence as they gave a short, extemporaneous speech. Women who watched traditional commercials conformed more and showed less self-confidence than women who watched the nontraditional commercials. The researchers concluded that

regardless of whether people buy the product advertised in commercials, they may buy the implicit images of femininity and masculinity conveyed.

PERSONAL STEREOTYPES   As individuals, we may or may not agree with cultural depictions of the sexes. **Personal stereotypes** are our own unique beliefs about the attributes of groups of people such as women and men. Individuals construct personal stereotypes in at least two different ways.

One way individuals think about gender is in terms of general personality traits that characterize each sex. Most of us have beliefs about the global features that distinguish males and females. To get some idea of your own views on this matter, read the list of adjectives in Table 15–1. Decide whether you personally think each trait is more characteristic of men or of women, or equally true of both sexes. You probably found this a fairly easy task. People usually develop broad generalizations about the traits shared by men and women and about the traits that distinguish the sexes. As Table 15–1 shows, most respondents in one study (Rosenkrantz et al., 1968) rated men higher on traits associated with competence, such as leadership, objectivity, and independence. In contrast, most people rated women higher on traits associated with warmth and expressiveness, such as gentleness and awareness of the feelings of others. How do your own personal gender stereotypes compare with these findings?

A second way in which people think about gender is to develop images of different types of males and females (Brewer, Dull, & Lui, 1981; Clifton, McGrath, & Wick, 1976; Taylor, 1981). Instead of thinking about females "in general," we may think of more specific categories of women, such as mothers, career women, beauty queens, tomboys, or spinsters. Similarly, instead of having a single, uniform image of males, our beliefs about men may distinguish such types as fathers, businessmen, hardhats, sissies, jocks, chauvinists, or nerds. These more specific *social types* describe different kinds of

Table 15–1
Common Gender Stereotypes

MORE CHARACTERISTIC OF MEN	MORE CHARACTERISTIC OF WOMEN
Aggressive	Gentle
Independent	Tactful
Unemotional	Talkative
Objective	Religious
Dominant	Aware of feelings of others
Like math and science	Neat in habits
Active	Interested in own appearance
Competitive	Quiet
Logical	Express tender feelings
Worldly	Enjoy art and literature
Self-confident	Cry easily
Act as leader	Dependent
Adventurous	Do not use harsh language
Ambitious	Strong need for security

College students rated the "typical man" and the "typical woman" on a long list of adjectives. Traits that 75 percent of students thought were more characteristic of men are shown in the left column. Traits that 75 percent of students thought were more characteristic of women are shown in the right column.

Source: Adapted from Rosenkrantz, Vogel, Bee, Broverman, & Broverman (1968), p. 291.

males and females who embody distinctive clusters of traits. Thus one person might believe that mothers are nurturant and self-sacrificing, that beauty queens are gorgeous but empty-headed, or that tomboys are youthful, athletic, and adventurous. An important point is that social types often incorporate some attributes typically associated with the other sex: A career woman may be seen as assertive and independent (masculine traits) as well as attractive and tactful (feminine traits).

Activating Stereotypes

What determines whether we relate to another person largely on the basis of stereotypes or as a unique individual? In other words, what situations increase or decrease the influence of stereotypes? Social psychologists are just beginning to answer this question. Two important factors are the amount of information we have about the person and the salience of the person's group membership.

AMOUNT OF INFORMATION The less information available about a person, the more likely we are to perceive and react to him or her on the basis of stereotypes. For example, when adults know nothing about a baby except its gender, they tend to react to the child in stereotyped ways. In one study (Condry & Condry, 1976), adults watched a videotape of a baby. Although everyone watched the same videotape, half were told they were watching a boy and half were told they were watching a girl. People who thought the child was a boy rated the child as significantly more active and forceful than people who thought the child was a girl. The child's response to a jack-in-the-box toy was rated as showing more "fear" if the child was a girl, and more "anger" if the child was a boy.

In another study (Sidorowicz & Lunney, 1980), college students actually interacted with a baby described either as a boy or a girl. Both boy and girl babies were used. Half the time the gender label was correct; half the time it was not. The dependent variable of interest was

When we have little information about a person, we tend to rely on gender stereotypes. If you saw this attractive woman in a supermarket, you might assume that to be a suburban homemaker. In reality, Geraldine Ferraro is the first woman nominated for Vice President by a major U.S. political party.

which of three toys the adult selected to use in playing with the child. Among those who thought they were playing with a boy, 65 percent selected the football, 20 percent selected the doll, and 15 percent selected the gender-neutral teething ring. In contrast, among adults who thought the child was a girl, 80 percent selected the doll, 15 percent the football, and 5 percent the teething ring. In this situation, since the adults knew nothing about the preferences of the individual child, they apparently made guesses based on gender stereotypes.

When we have more information about the unique attributes of a particular person, we rely less on stereotypes. For instance, we may believe that most males are highly assertive, and so assume when we meet a new man that he too will be assertive. But we may also have learned from past experience that our friend Leon is a shy and unassuming male.

A study by Locksley and her colleagues (1980) demonstrated this idea and showed that providing relevant information about the assertiveness of a specific person eliminated the effects of stereotypes. In this study, Locksley first determined that undergraduates held the stereotype that males are more assertive than females. Then she asked participants to rate particular men and women on assertiveness, based on case histories about them. Some of the case histories contained information directly relevant to the person's assertiveness. For example, one story depicted Nancy as quite assertive:

> The other day Nancy was in a class in which she wanted to make several points about the readings being discussed. But another student was dominating the class discussion so thoroughly that Nancy had to abruptly interrupt this student in order to break into the discussion and express her own views. (p. 827)

Other case histories contained information irrelevant to assertiveness. Results clearly showed the effect of information.

When students had no relevant information, they rated male targets as more assertive than female targets. But when participants had specific knowledge about the person's past actions, their judgments of male and female targets were virtually identical. In other words, the effect of the gender stereotype was eliminated when people had relevant information about the individual.

SALIENCE OF GROUP MEMBERSHIP   A second factor that can activate the use of stereotypes is the salience of the person's group membership, in this case gender (Taylor, 1981). For example, a person's gender is more salient when he or she is in a numerical minority, such as being the only woman in an all-male work group. "Token integration" often creates groups with just one minority person. Token or "solo" status calls attention to the person's distinctive social category and makes solos especially vulnerable to stereotyping. A study by Taylor (1981) illustrates this point. Students evaluated the members of a six-person tape-recorded discussion group.

BOX 15–2
Making Stereotypes Come True

A young man goes on a blind date with a woman he has never met before. Based on hearsay, he believes her to be a rather traditional "Southern belle" type. Accordingly, he dresses rather formally, puts on his most gentlemanly manners, and treats her in a somewhat old-fashioned way. Just as he expected, she defers to his suggestions, waits for him to open doors, and acts in what he considers a very "ladylike" way. Only later does he learn that his advance information was wrong; she is, in fact, usually a fairly assertive nonconformist. This story shows how expectations can become self-fulfilling prophecies. The man's beliefs about his date shaped his own behavior toward her. The woman, wanting to spend a pleasant evening, responded by acting in a conventionally "ladylike" way herself. The result was that the man's expectations set in motion an interpersonal process that appeared to confirm his prior beliefs.

Gender stereotypes often become self-fulfilling prophecies. This point was cleverly demonstrated in a study by Berna J. Skrypnek and Mark Snyder (1982). A male college student is led to believe that his partner for an experiment is either a stereotypic man (independent, assertive, ambitious, and masculine), or a stereotypic woman (shy, gullible, soft-spoken, and feminine). In reality, the partner is always a woman, a naive subject who has been randomly assigned the label of "man" or "woman." Since the two partners communicate from separate rooms by a system of lights, the partner's real gender is never revealed. The woman is told nothing about her partner, how she has been described to him, or the goals of the study. In this way the researchers systematically manipulate the gender expectations of the male subject.

In the first phase of the study, the partners must negotiate how to divide work on 12 hypothetical tasks. Some tasks are traditionally masculine (fixing a light switch or baiting a fish hook), some are feminine (icing a birthday cake or ironing a shirt), and some are neutral (coding test results, washing windows). The rules set by the experimenter give the man greater initiative in the bargaining process. As predicted, the man's expectations about his partner shape his own actions significantly. If he thinks his partner is a conventional woman, the male subject is more likely to select masculine tasks for himself and to refuse to switch tasks than if he thinks his partner is a man. As a result, the female subject winds up being assigned more of the feminine tasks if she is arbitrarily labeled a "female" than if she is believed to be a "male."

In the second phase, the researchers investigate whether this initial behavior pattern would continue over time. Accordingly, they change the rules of the interaction so that the woman now has greater control over the bargaining. Nonetheless, a woman who is labeled as "female" continues to select more feminine tasks than does a woman labeled as a "male." The woman actually comes to initiate behavior consistent with the gender to which she has been randomly assigned!

This study provides a powerful demonstration that in dyadic interactions, one person's beliefs and stereotypes about another can channel their interaction so that the other person engages in stereotype-confirming

> behavior. Our actions are shaped not only by our own interests and preferences, but also by the expectations of those with whom we interact. When others expect us to act in gender-typed ways and communicate these expectations through their behaviors, we may put aside personal preferences and instead act out the others' stereotypes.

Some groups had just a "solo" man or just a "solo" woman; others were evenly divided between men and women.

After listening to the tape, subjects rated the group's members. In actuality, the solo's contribution to the discussion was identical to that of one of the members of the gender-balanced group. But Taylor found that the solos were perceived as talking more and making a stronger impression than members of the more gender-balanced groups. In addition, solos tended to be perceived as playing gender-stereotyped roles. Solo women were seen as "motherly, nurturant types, bitches, or as the group secretary." Solo men were perceived as "father figures, leaders, or macho types." Group composition accentuated the solo's gender and fostered stereotyped perceptions of the solo's behavior.

The Dangers of Stereotypes

As Chapter 4 on social cognition indicated, it is quite natural for us to try to simplify complex life experiences by categorizing and generalizing. Personal stereotypes, like other social schemas, are one way in which we try to make sense of life. But like other mental crutches, stereotypes have certain inherent problems. One is that stereotypes always oversimplify and sometimes are dead wrong, as we'll see later in the chapter. For example, the belief that men are more intelligent than women has been disproved by scientific research. Unfortunately, people seldom examine the accuracy of their stereotypes. If we encounter someone who does not fit a stereotype, we often simply decide the person is "the exception that proves

the rule." We do nothing to change our stereotype. Further, as Box 15–2 indicates, we sometimes act in ways that turn stereotypes into self-fulfilling prophecies.

A second problem is that stereotypes exaggerate differences *between* groups and minimize differences *within* groups. Gender stereotypes can make it seem that all men are alike, when in fact there are enormous individual differences among men. The same is true about differences among women. And gender stereotypes can also make it seem that men and women are utterly different, when in fact similarities are usually much greater than differences. For example, there is great variation among men in aggressiveness: individuals range from nonassertive males who wouldn't hurt a fly to mass murderers. In contrast, the average difference between males and females in aggressiveness, while real, is much smaller in magnitude. Gender stereotypes can create a very distorted view of human nature.

A final danger of stereotypes is that they are often used to justify prejudice and discrimination against members of certain groups. Historically, the false belief that women were not as smart as men and that women lacked ambition was used to deny women an education and to keep them at home.

Stereotypes that have a basis in fact can also be misused in a discriminating way. There are, for example, small but consistent sex differences in math ability (favoring men) and in verbal ability (favoring women). Yet if we were recruiting applicants for a job such as newspaper writer that requires verbal skills, it would be foolish to exclude all male candidates, since some men are likely to be verbally gifted and some women may not be. Recruitment and hiring practices that categorically reject one sex are not only discriminatory but unwise. A sounder policy is to use a task-relevant selection procedure, such as giving all applicants a skill test and then selecting the high performers.

Evaluating Performance

Do we typically give women and men equal credit for equal work? Or do gender stereotypes distort judgments of performance? In the world of work, stereotypes often depict men as more competent than women. In one national survey (Rosen & Jerdee, 1978), for example, male managers generally perceived women workers as lower than men in skill, motivation, and work habits. Women were believed to be less employable and promotable, and to have less ability to make decisions and to cope with stress. Research shows that general stereotypes such as these can bias evaluations of the performance of individuals (see review by Nieva & Gutek, 1981). This evaluation bias can cut both ways, however; sometimes it favors men, and occasionally it favors women.

One of the first demonstrations of gender bias in evaluation was provided by Philip Goldberg in 1968. He investigated whether women were biased in evaluations of other women. Goldberg selected six professional articles from such fields as law, elementary education, and art history. The articles were edited to about 1,500 words each and combined in test booklets. The experimental manipulation concerned the gender of the authors. The same article bore a male name (such as John T. McKay) in one booklet and a female name (such as Joan T. McKay) in another. Each booklet contained three articles by "men" and three by "women." College women read the six articles and then rated each on persuasiveness, style, and competence.

Results indicated that the same article was judged more favorably when it had a male author than when it had a female author. Goldberg's results appeared to show that women are

indeed prejudiced against women. But before leaping to a hasty conclusion, it is important to know that Goldberg's findings sparked a rash of research. The results of over a hundred studies indicate that a pro-male bias is common, but by no means universal. The challenge today is to understand when and how gender bias occurs.

One important factor influencing evaluation is the gender typing of the task or job. In general, men have an advantage in masculine jobs and women have an advantage in feminine jobs. In one study (Cash, Gillen, & Burns, 1977), professional personnel consultants rated applicants' résumés for masculine jobs (automobile salesperson), feminine jobs (office receptionist), and gender-neutral jobs (motel desk clerk). For masculine jobs, men were perceived as better qualified, were expected to be more successful, and were given stronger recommendations. For feminine jobs, women were rated more favorably. For gender-neutral jobs, men and women were given similar ratings.

In another study (Levinson, 1975), students responded by phone to job ads that had appeared in the newspaper. Some of the jobs were traditionally masculine (bus driver, management trainee, security guard) and some were feminine (receptionist, housekeeper, dental assistant). None required advanced training. A male and female applicant with identical qualifications called about each job.

Gender bias was said to occur when the "sex-appropriate" caller was encouraged to apply, but the "sex-inappropriate" caller was not. In one case, for example, a female caller for a restaurant management training program was told that her having only two years of college and no prior management experience disqualified her. A male with the identical background was scheduled for an interview. In all, 28 percent of the women asking about masculine jobs and 44 percent of the men asking about feminine jobs were discouraged. This suggests considerable gender bias linked to the gender typing of occupations.

A second factor influencing evaluation bias is the amount of relevant information available about the person. Gender bias in evaluations is most common when little information is provided about the individual's ability. One study (Frank & Drucker, 1977) gave extensive information about a male or female manager, including copies of letters, memos, and other materials allegedly written by the person. Subjects used this material as a basis for evaluating the manager's sensitivity, organizing and decision-making ability, and communication effectiveness. The experimental manipulation was whether the materials were written by "John Griffin" or "Joan Griffin." Given all this information about the specific individuals, no evaluation bias occurred; John and Joan were rated identically.

Finally, there is some evidence that stereotype-breaking behavior can occasionally win a person "extra" credit. In particular, when a woman excels in a traditionally masculine job, she may be perceived more favorably than an equally successful man. Abramson et al. (1977) found that a highly successful female attorney was rated more vocationally competent than an identically successful male attorney. Similarly, Taynor and Deaux (1973) presented students with descriptions of a person whose quick thinking in an armed robbery helped the police capture a criminal. When the person was a woman, she received more positive evaluations than a man in the identical situation. The unusualness of a woman's successful performance in masculine situations appears to win her a more favorable evaluation than her male counterpart. Whether something comparable occurs for men who excel in traditionally feminine activities is an interesting but unanswered question.

So far, we have considered evaluations of the quality of women's and men's performance. Another way in which gender bias can occur is in the attributions people make to explain success or failure. Research has found that men's success is more often seen as resulting from ability. In contrast, women's success is more often attributed to the ease of the task (Feather & Simon, 1975), to extreme effort (Taynor & Deaux, 1975), or to luck (Deaux & Emswiller, 1974). Ability attributions usually produce more favorable evaluations of successful performance. Differences in attributions for men's and women's performance may create a subtle bias that diminishes recognition of women's skills and instead explains female success as due to situational or chance factors.

In summary, a person's gender can influence the way we evaluate the person and explain his or her performance. Evaluation bias often favors men, especially in masculine situations. However, women may have an advantage in feminine situations and when they excel in masculine activities. When substantial information is available about the stimulus person, evaluation bias often disappears. Finally, it appears that female and male evaluators are equally prone to en-

Sally Ride is the first woman to become a U.S. astronaut. As a woman in a largely male profession, Dr. Ride's solo status makes her gender especially salient.

NASA

gage in evaluative bias based on the performer's gender.

Having seen how the perceptions of other people are affected by whether they are female or male, we turn now to the question of how gender influences our self-perception.

GENDER AND THE SELF

Gender is a basic element in self-concept. Knowing that "I am a woman" or "I am a man" is a core part of our personal identity. Further, many people perceive themselves as having gender-typed interests and personalities.

Gender Identity

Knowledge that we are a male or female, our sense of **gender identity,** is acquired early in life. By age 2 or 3, children are aware of their own gender and can tell us whether they are a girl or a boy. By age 4 or 5, children can correctly label others by gender. However, this understanding of gender differs from that of adults. Research by Kohlberg (1966) and other developmental psychologists has documented the surprising fact that young children think they can change gender if they want to.

In one study, Kohlberg showed children a picture of a girl and asked whether she could be a boy if she wanted to or if she played boys' games or if she wore a boy's haircut and clothes. Most of the 4-year-olds said that she *could.* By age 6 or 7, however, children insisted that such a gender transformation would be impossible. Kohlberg believes this shift in children's conception of gender is part of a more general pattern of cognitive development. The same 4-year-old who says she could change gender might also say the family cat could become a dog by cutting off its whiskers. Adults know that if you pour a pint of water from a tall skinny glass into a short fat one, the volume of water stays the same. But the 4-year-old would probably disagree, perhaps arguing that the short glass had less.

Young children do not see the physical world as constant. As children get older, a combination of experience and maturation enables them to reach a more advanced stage of mental development in which they understand that gender, water volume, and other physical properties remain the same despite changes in external appearance. An important developmental milestone occurs when children understand that gender is fixed and unchanging: Once a boy (or a girl), always a boy (or girl).

Knowing that we are male or female does not mean we think about our gender identity all the time. In one study (McGuire & Padawer-Singer, 1976), for example, only about 20 percent of sixth-graders spontaneously mentioned their gender when asked to "tell us about yourself" and to "describe what you look like." For many children, other characteristics were more salient, as for a girl who answered: "I am twelve years old. I was born in South Carolina. I have two sisters and a dog. I have a babysitting job every day after school. . . . I hate arithmetic but I like our teacher" (pp. 746–747). The salience of gender identity depends on many factors, including the proportion of males and females in our environment. The study described above found that boys and girls were twice as likely to mention their own gender if their classroom at school had an excess of children of the other sex. We are apparently more aware of our own gender when we are in a numerical minority. This is like the token or solo effect discussed earlier for gender stereotypes, where the gender of a lone man or woman in a group is more salient to observers than it would be in a gender-balanced group.

For most of us, the acquisition of gender identity is a smooth and trouble-free process. We are classified as male or female at birth, treated as a boy or girl by our parents, and easily learn our own gender as we grow up. For a few people, however, developing gender identity is a problem. Transsexuals are a case in point. Such individuals are biologically members of one gender, but develop the belief that they are really members of the other. In the most common case, a person is to all outward appearances a male, but that person's psychological reality is being a woman trapped in a male body.

The causes of transsexualism are still a mystery. Most often, transsexuals show no signs of biological abnormality. Genetically, hormonally, and physiologically, they are "normal" members of their gender. Yet at a very early age they develop a self-concept at odds with their physical characteristics. This puzzling situation is profoundly disturbing to the individuals involved. Efforts to help transsexuals by psychotherapy have had very little success; it is not easy to change a deeply rooted sense of gender identity. As a result, some have advocated sex-change surgery as one way to reconcile this mind-body problem.

Psychological Masculinity, Femininity, and Androgyny

Gender identity is an either-or matter; people believe they are either a male or a female. However, individuals differ markedly in the degree to which they perceive themselves as having all the different masculine or feminine characteristics that make up conventional gender stereotypes. In terms of their **gender self-concept,** a highly "masculine" person would be one who believes he possesses the attributes, interests, preferences, and skills society typically associates with maleness. A highly "feminine" person would believe she possesses the attributes, interests, preferences, and skills associated with femaleness. Psychologists have long been interested in measuring individual differences in self-perceptions of psychological masculinity and femininity.

A typical masculinity-femininity test might ask such questions as whether a person prefers showers (masculine) or tub baths (feminine), whether the person would rather work as a building contractor (masculine) or librarian (feminine), whether the person is active (masculine) or passive (feminine). An important feature of these tests is that they view masculinity and femininity as mutually exclusive polar opposites. People get a single score on the test: High scores indicate masculinity (many masculine choices) and low scores indicate femininity (few masculine choices).

In more recent times, some psychologists have challenged this one-dimensional view of psychological masculinity and femininity (see Spence & Helmreich, 1978, 1980). Sandra Bem (1974, 1981), for example, proposed that some people might see themselves as having both masculine and feminine characteristics. Such a person might enjoy both carpentry and cooking, might be very assertive (a masculine trait) at work but very nurturant (a feminine trait) at home, and so on. Bem called these people psychologically **androgynous,** borrowing from the Greek terms for male (andro) and female (gyne). Bem emphasized that the androgynous person is not a moderate who falls halfway between extreme masculinity and femininity. Rather, the androgynous person views himself or herself as combining strong masculine and strong feminine attributes.

To investigate this idea, Bem constructed a new test with separate dimensions for masculinity and for femininity, making it possible for a person to score high on both. In the Bem Sex Role Inventory, people rate their personal qualities using 60 adjectives: 20 masculine (assertive, independent), 20 feminine (affectionate, understanding), and 20 gender-neutral (sincere, friendly). When Bem administered her test to samples of college students, she found some traditionally gender-typed individuals, both masculine men (who scored high on M and low on F) and feminine women (who scored high on F and low on M). More interesting, however, was the fact that some people rated themselves high on both masculine and feminine characteristics, showing the androgynous pattern Bem predicted.

The exact percentages of gender-typed and androgynous people vary somewhat from study to study. Typical are results from a recent study of California college students (Bernard, 1980). Roughly 40 percent of students perceived themselves as traditionally gender-typed, and 25 percent were androgynous. An "undifferentiated" subgroup included 29 percent of men and 21 percent of women who scored low on both masculine and feminine traits. Finally, a few people showed a pattern of reverse gender typing—specifically feminine men (5 percent) and masculine women (12 percent). The important point is that although traditional gender typing is the most common pattern, a sizable minority of people perceive themselves as combining both masculine and feminine qualities.

Research on androgyny has raised basic questions about how psychological masculinity and femininity affect well-being. One long-standing view has been that to ensure mental health, boys and men should be masculine in their interests and attributes, whereas girls and women should be feminine. This *congruence model* (Whitley, 1983) proposes that adjustment is enhanced when there is an "appropriate" match between gender and self-concept. In contrast, the newer *androgyny model* of well-being argues that it is better for people to have both masculine and feminine traits. In particular, it has been proposed that androgynous individuals surpass traditionally sex-typed individuals in having greater behavioral flexibility and higher self-esteem.

BEHAVIORAL FLEXIBILITY   Bem hypothesized that masculine people will perform well in situations

calling for task competence or assertiveness; feminine people will do well in situations requiring nurturance or emotional expressivity; and androgynous people will do well in both types of situations. Some empirical support for this prediction has been found. In one study (Bem, 1975), masculine and androgynous individuals did better than feminine individuals on a test of ability to resist group pressure for conformity. In another study (Bem, Martyna, & Watson, 1976), feminine and androgynous individuals did better on tasks requiring nurturance, including playing with a baby and responding to a transfer student who was having problems adjusting to a new college.

At this point, research on the behavior of androgynous people is still relatively new, and definitive conclusions must await further evidence. It seems safe to say, however, that existing findings challenge the congruence model and suggest that androgynous people may be at least as effective as gender-typed people in social interactions (Pleck, 1981).

SELF-ESTEEM   Feeling good about oneself is a key ingredient in mental health. The congruence model predicts that self-esteem should be highest for masculine men and feminine women—people with "appropriate" gender self-concepts. In contrast, the adrogyny model asserts that androgynous individuals who perceive themselves as having both positive masculine and positive feminine attributes should have higher self-esteem than gender-typed individuals. A large number of studies have investigated this topic (Whitley, 1983), and they suggest an unexpected conclusion.

Basically, research once again provides no support for the congruence model. And results offer only weak support for the androgyny model. Instead, the biggest factor influencing self-esteem seems to be how a person scores on psychological masculinity. Both masculine and androgynous individuals usually have high self-esteem. The added benefit for androgynous people of being feminine as well as masculine is statistically significant, but very small in size.

Researchers are still puzzling about why masculinity appears to be so central to self-esteem. One possibility is that in this culture, self-esteem is closely linked to the kinds of traits traditionally labeled as masculine, such as independence, assertiveness, and competence. Another possibility is that self-esteem scales are biased and do not adequately assess elements of self-esteem that are associated with femininity; in other words, the pattern of results is due to a methodological weakness in the tests being used.

SOME CAUTIONS   Research on the behavioral flexibility and self-esteem of gender-typed and androgynous individuals challenges the model that "appropriate" gender typing is essential to mental health. Masculine men and feminine women do not seem to have an advantage over androgynous individuals. But although the concept of androgyny has provided a useful correction to earlier work on masculinity and femininity, we should be cautious about accepting it uncritically.

First, androgyny measures are very limited in scope; they focus on self-perceptions of task competence and emotional expressiveness. In actuality, most people probably view masculinity and femininity much more broadly as including appearance, sexual behavior, and social roles as well as personality (Myers & Gonda, 1982). Further, these different components of masculinity and femininity are probably not part of a single, consistent dimension (Spence & Helmreich, 1980). One woman might, for instance, think of herself as masculine in personality (assertive, ambitious, and independent), feminine in appearance (short and voluptuous), and androgynous in social roles (both a wife-mother and a career woman). Existing androgyny instruments do not capture this complexity.

Second, androgyny is possible only in areas such as personality; a person could perceive himself or herself as warmly nurturant in some situations and coldly competitive in others. But in different domains, masculinity and femininity actually are mutually exclusive. In reproduction, for example, insemination and childbearing are each exclusive to one sex.

Third, current work on androgyny tells us little about how salient masculinity and femininity actually are in people's thinking about themselves. The Bem Sex Role Inventory and other tests ask people to rate themselves on traits society labels as masculine or feminine (Spence & Helmreich, 1980). But responses to these tests do not tell us whether people spontaneously label their own actions this way. If gender typing is really important, a person might think: "Gee, it makes me feel feminine to have prepared such a fine meal for my family," or "I feel more masculine for having stood up to my boss today." But if gender typing is not so vital, people might recognize their own nurturance or assertiveness, but identify these as human traits unrelated to gender. We just do not know how prominent masculine and feminine labels actually are in people's self-concepts.

Finally, discussions of masculinity and femininity often touch on personal values and ideals. For those who endorse more traditional views about the sexes, the preservation of clear-cut distinctions between masculinity and femininity is an important goal. For those who want to expand the options available to both sexes, the blurring of distinctions is seen as desirable. Indeed, some feminists have rejected androgyny as an ideal because it preserves the notion that there are distinct masculine and feminine qualities even as it gives permission to people to have both types of attributes. Instead, some (such as Garnets & Pleck, 1979) have argued that we should move toward "sex-role transcendence." Personal attributes and preferences should no longer be associated with gender. Psychological research can clarify how gender affects our self-concept and can identify the consequences of various patterns, but it cannot tell people what ideals to adopt for their own lives.

So far, our discussion of gender has focused on perception—impressions of others and of ourselves. Now we turn to the topic of actual differences in the behavior of women and men.

GENDER DIFFERENCES IN BEHAVIOR:
THEORETICAL APPROACHES

People debated about sex differences long before the invention of social psychology. For centuries, personal experience and intuition were the basis for such discussions. Today, scientific theories and research are providing a more balanced and comprehensive understanding of gender differences in behavior.

Early discussions often asked whether gender differences were caused by "nature or nurture," by biology or learning. We now know that such simple dichotomies are misleading. A full explanation of gender differences must consider both the biological capacities of the sexes and the social environment in which males and females live. It has also become clear that there is no single, general explanation for *all* differences between males and females. Rather, the causes of gender differences in math ability may be quite distinct from the causes of gender differences in self-disclosure, and so on. Three broad perspectives on the causes of gender differences emphasize the influence of biology, of learning, and of social situations.

The Influence of Biology

Gender differences are undoubtedly affected by biology. Physical differences in height, in the ability to bear children and to breastfeed them, and so on, are obvious. The impact of sex hormones, both on the unborn fetus and on adults, is a lively topic of investigation, as are possible sex differences in the brain. Some sociobiologists are even suggesting that genetic evolution contributes to gender differences in human behavior (see Box 15–3).

The point social psychologists emphasize is that basic biological differences can be greatly increased or reduced by social forces. For example, sex differences in physical size and strength may once have given males a clear-cut advantage over females in warfare. But with modern aircraft and push-button weapons, brute force is less important for soldiers of either gender. Childbirth provides another illustration of the interplay of biology and society. Women are physically capable of having a dozen or more babies during a lifetime, but because of contemporary social attitudes and contraceptive technology, the typical American woman has only two or three children. Today, American wives typically outlive their husbands by several years. But in colonial days, when women had many children and childbirth was hazardous, the situation was reversed—men usually lived longer than women. The impact of biological gender differences can vary dramatically depending on the social environment.

The Influence of Learning

This perspective begins with the idea that society has different expectations and standards for the behavior of males and females. Imagine a father whose young daughter enters the living room dressed in Mommy's earrings, silk robe, and high heels, and climbs on Daddy's knee. The father is likely to smile at his daughter, give her a big hug, and compliment her on being such a pretty little girl. Now imagine that a 4-year-old boy were to do exactly the same thing. Although a modern Daddy might not punish his son, it is likely he would communicate firmly that feminine clothes are not appropriate for boys.

The term **social role** refers to cultural rules about how a particular type of person should behave. Roles define ideal or at least acceptable

BOX 15-3
The Evolution of Gender Differences

In his book, *The Evolution of Human Sexuality* (1979), Donald Symons outlines a sociobiological analysis of gender differences. Like other sociobiologists, he looks to genetic inheritance and the process of evolution for the causes of many gender differences.

Symons argues that humans have evolved in ways that maximize the likelihood of their individual genes being passed on to offspring and thus "surviving" in future generations. Whereas men produce many sperm, women typically produce only one egg per month and then must invest time and energy in pregnancy and nursing a baby. As a result, the most effective reproductive strategies for the two sexes differ. For men, the survival of one's own genes ("reproductive success") is enhanced by impregnating as many women as possible and investing little time and energy in the rearing of any one child. Hence men are biologically disposed to have many sexual partners and limited contact with infants. In contrast, for women reproductive success depends on maximizing the chances that the few children a woman can produce will survive to maturity. Women are disposed to be involved in the care of infants and to seek a long-term relationship with a man who can also contribute to the development of their children.

Symons and other sociobiologists believe that males and females have distinctive genetically based dispositions. They recognize, however, that whether such dispositions are translated into gender differences in actual behavior depends a good deal on the environment. The sociobiological perspective is still quite controversial, but it provides a good example of how biological factors might influence gender differences in attitudes and behavior.

conduct. And many of the most important roles are linked to gender: There are different behavior codes for sons and daughters, husbands and wives, boyfriends and girlfriends, and so on. As children grow up, they learn these social roles through processes such as reinforcement and modeling (see Chapter 1). Children learn about roles from many sources, including parents, friends, teachers, and the popular media.

The result is that males and females acquire different attitudes, interests, skills, and personality traits based on the gender-linked roles in their society. The fact that women differ significantly from each other, just as men are a varied group, is also explained by differences in the learning experiences of each person.

The Influence of Social Situations

Behavior is not solely determined by biological dispositions or learned personality traits. A third major influence is the social setting. A man might talk about football and cars with his male buddies, peppering his speech with four-letter words, but "clean up his act" and change the topic of conversation with a new girlfriend.

BOX 15–4
Too Many Women: Sex Ratios and Social Life

In a recent book, *Too Many Women: The Sex Ratio Question* (1982), Marcia Guttentag and Paul Secord investigate the social effects of the ratio of males to females in society. Although approximately equal numbers of males and females are born each year, the ratio of male-to-female adults of marriageable age is quite variable cross-culturally. It is affected by wars, the hazards of childbearing, migration, infanticide of girl children, and so on. On the American frontier, for example, men outnumbered women, often by substantial proportions. By contrast, in 1980, for every 100 women aged 33 to 37 in the United States, there were only 84 men. What are the consequences of extreme variations in sex ratios between the sexes?

Guttentag and Secord begin by arguing that in all societies, men have relatively greater structural power than women: Men control the economy, religion, government, and so on. However, sex ratios influence patterns of dominance in the personal relations of men and women in courtship and marriage. When there is an undersupply of women, as in America before World War II, young women are highly valued and protected. Men are eager to form a committed relationship through marriage. Women gain status through marriage, and are able to achieve economic mobility by "marrying up." Husband and wife roles are highly differentiated and complementary. Both sexes stress sexual monogamy, although a double standard may permit greater sexual freedom for men.

In contrast, Guttentag and Secord propose that when women are in oversupply, as in the 1970s and 1980s in America, women often feel personally devalued and powerless. Marriage and commitment are deemphasized in the relations between the sexes. The divorce rate is high, and the rate of remarriage is high only for men. A high proportion of women are never married or divorced, and single-parent families headed by women increase. Sexual permissiveness is the prevailing value system, although options are greater for men than for women. Under such conditions, feminist movements are likely to arise.

The basic argument of Guttentag and Secord—that sex ratios in society have a profound impact on heterosexual relationships—is provocative. The researchers support their argument with examples of societies ranging from ancient Greece to medieval Europe to contemporary Africa. Their views will undoubtedly spark a lively scientific debate, and their work provides a fascinating illustration of a way in which societal-level factors may influence the daily lives of women and men.

The gender of the person we are with is one powerful situational determinant of behavior. Empirical support for this idea comes from a study of who interrupts whom in casual conversations. The researchers (Zimmerman & West, 1975) unobtrusively tape-recorded the conversations of male-male, female-female, and male-female pairs as they chatted spontaneously in coffee shops, drugstores, and other public places. Interruptions were ten times more frequent in the male-female conversations than in the same-sex ones. More striking, in same-sex pairs, men and women were equally likely to initiate an interruption; but in mixed sex dyads, men initiated 96 percent of all interruptions. A laboratory study of conversations in mixed-sex groups (McMillan, Clifton, McGrath, & Gale, 1977) found similar but less extreme results. As shown in Table 15–2, men and women were equally likely to interrupt another person of the same sex. But when cross-sex interruptions occurred, it was five times more likely for a man to interrupt a woman as vice versa. For another illustration of the impact of group gender composition, this time in the society as a whole, see Box 15–4.

Our desire to be liked by other people often leads us to conform to their expectations about how males and females should behave, regardless of personal beliefs. In a recent experiment (von Baeyer, Sherk, & Zanna, 1981), college women participated in a simulated job interview. By random assignment, half the women were led to believe that the male interviewer had quite traditional attitudes about women's roles, and half believed that he rejected traditional roles. As predicted, the women applicants tried to impress the interviewer. Women who thought the interviewer preferred traditional women dressed in a more "feminine" way (wore more makeup and jewelry), talked less during the interview, described themselves in a more stereotypically feminine way, and were evaluated as more "attractive" by male raters than women who thought the interviewer preferred nontraditional women. The desire to be

	Table 15–2 Mean Number of Interruptions per Half-Hour in Mixed-Gender Discussion Groups

GENDER OF PERSON WHO IS INTERRUPTED	GENDER OF INTERRUPTER	
	MALE	FEMALE
Male	2.36	0.93
Female	5.24	2.50

Source: Adapted from McMillan, Clifton, McGrath, & Gale (1977).

liked and accepted by others can lead us to act in more or less gender-typed ways, depending on the situation.

Situational constraints can prevent people from acting in accord with their own preferences and beliefs about gender. For example, many parents believe mothers should have greater responsibility for child care than fathers, and mothers usually do spend more time with children, even when the mother has a full-time job. However, an exception occurs when a wife's work schedule literally prevents her from doing all the childcare. One study (Berk & Berk, 1979) found that when wives worked an evening shift so that they had to leave home before dinner, fathers wound up, of necessity, giving the kids dinner and putting them to bed. The more general point is that a variety of situational factors, such as the gender composition of a group, the expectations of other people, or the constraints of a work schedule, can have great impact on how men and women behave.

THE SOCIAL BEHAVIOR OF MEN AND WOMEN

In recent years, a great deal of research has compared the behavior of males and females, especially that of American children and college students. But the results of these studies are often contradictory and sometimes downright confusing. It turns out to be considerably more difficult to pin down gender differences in behavior than might be imagined.

In 1974, Eleanor Maccoby and Carol Jacklin published a landmark book called *The Psychology of Sex Differences.* They reviewed hundreds of studies of sex differences in many psychological characteristics, such as verbal ability and aggressiveness. Maccoby and Jacklin attempted to evaluate this research carefully, excluding studies with methodological weaknesses and accepting as true only those findings replicated in several studies by different investigators. They concluded that sex differences had been established in only four areas:

1. Females score higher than males in verbal ability, such as reading and vocabulary.
2. Males score higher than females in mathematical ability.
3. Males score higher than females on visual-spatial ability.
4. Males are more aggressive than females.

Equally important, Maccoby and Jacklin concluded that some stereotypes about sex differences were clearly wrong. The sexes do not differ in overall intelligence, nor in general level of achievement motivation or striving for excellence. The authors also debunked the idea that girls are better at rote learning and simple repetitive tasks, whereas boys are better at tasks requiring higher-level cognitive processing.

Maccoby and Jacklin emphasized individual intellectual abilities in their review. As social psychologists, we are more concerned with social skills and behaviors. We have described such sex differences throughout this book. In Chapter 9, for example, we considered gender differences in self-disclosure, power, and love. Here we will take a closer look at male-female differences in aggression, conformity, and nonverbal communication.

Aggression

One of the most consistent gender differences is the greater frequency of aggressive behavior by males (Maccoby & Jacklin, 1974). Around the world, it is men who are the warriors. Violent crime is also largely a male domain. Whether it be the activities of teenage gangs, underworld crime figures, or a lone assassin, it is usually men who use physical force in illegal pursuits. According to FBI statistics, 87 percent of those arrested for murder in 1981 were men (see Table 15–3 for other statistics). During childhood, boys are usually rated as more aggressive than girls by teachers, parents, and peers. So whether it be socially approved aggression in wartime, illegal violence, or children's play, males take the lead in aggressive behavior.

In Chapter 10, a basic distinction was made

Table 15–3
FBI Statistics Comparing Arrests for Violent Crimes by Men and Women

TYPE OF OFFENSE	1972			1981		
	TOTAL NUMBER	MEN (%)	WOMEN (%)	TOTAL NUMBER	MEN (%)	WOMEN (%)
Murder and nonnegligent manslaughter	12,312	84%	16%	16,082	87%	13%
Forcible rape	15,455	100	0	24,713	99	1
Robbery	90,245	94	6	124,737	93	7
Aggravated assault	125,798	87	13	220,194	87	13
All violent crime	243,810	90	10	385,726	90	10

Source: Adapted from *Uniform Crime Reports: Crime in the United States, 1981.* Federal Bureau of Investigation, U.S. Department of Justice, August 26, 1982.

between aggressive behavior and aggressive impulses or feelings. On a behavioral level, males are clearly more aggressive than females, but is this also true for aggressive impulses? The evidence here is mixed. The appearance of gender differences among young children can be taken as evidence of a greater male disposition to aggressiveness, perhaps based partly on biology. But other evidence suggests that situational pressures may inhibit aggressive tendencies in females more than for males (Frodi, Macaulay, & Thome, 1977).

Our society is more tolerant of aggression in males than in females. As children, for instance, boys are much more likely to be given toy guns and missile launchers. As a result of social pressures, females may feel more guilt, anxiety, and fear about aggressive acts, and so inhibit their aggressive impulses. When situational constraints are removed, however, female inhibitions about aggression are reduced. Consider, for example, the studies of children's aggression toward a plastic Bobo doll described in Chapter 10. In a free-choice situation, where the appropriateness of aggression was unclear, girls were significantly less aggressive than boys. But when children were offered a reward for aggressive behavior, boys and girls were equally aggressive (Bandura, Ross, & Ross, 1961).

In real life, men are much more likely than women to behave aggressively. In the lab, most studies find males to be more aggressive, although a significant minority of studies finds no gender differences at all. These findings may reflect male-female differences in aggressive impulses, in learned behaviors based on the rewards males and females experience for aggression, in situational pressures encouraging greater male aggression, or in some combination of factors.

Conformity

Stereotypes portray women as more yielding, gullible, and conformist than men. For many years, psychological research appeared to support this idea. An earlier edition of this book reported a gender difference in conformity, and explained it as resulting from socialization processes that teach men to be independent and women to be submissive. Recently, however, new evidence has seriously challenged the view that women are generally more easily influenced than men.

Careful reviews of the empirical research on social influence (such as Eagly, 1978, 1983) indicate that significant sex differences actually occur in only a minority of studies. Eagly found 62 studies that had investigated sex differences in persuasion—that is, the extent to which a person is influenced by hearing arguments in favor of or against an issue. Only 16 percent of these studies found that women were significantly more easily persuaded; the vast majority found no differences. Similarly, Eagly found 61 studies of responses to group pressures for conformity, as in the Asch experiment described in Chapter 12. Here again, only 34 percent found that women conformed significantly more; in most cases, the sexes did not differ significantly. Further, in those cases where sex differences did occur, they were usually small in magnitude (Eagly & Carli, 1981). In short, the most common finding is that the sexes respond similarly to attempts at influence.

Other data suggest that when sex differences do occur, they may have more to do with the gender typing of the task than with a general disposition for women to conform. People are generally more likely to conform if they lack information about a topic or consider it unimportant. Thus women are more likely to conform on tasks traditionally viewed as masculine, and men are more likely to conform when confronted with feminine tasks. This point was demonstrated by Sistrunk and McDavid (1971). They asked college women and men to answer a questionnaire about matters of fact and opinion, some concerning masculine topics such as sports cars, politics, and mathematics, and others concerning feminine areas such as cosmetics, sewing, or cooking.

To introduce conformity pressure, the questionnaire indicated next to each question how a majority of college students had supposedly responded. Results clearly showed the effect of gender typing. Men conformed more than women on feminine items; women conformed more than men on masculine items. Overall, there were no significant differences between the level of conformity of men and of women. In addition to the gender typing of the test materials, it also appears that the gender of the researcher can affect the chances of finding sex differences. Studies by male researchers have found sex differences more often than studies by female researchers (Eagly & Carli, 1981). Unfortunately, the explanation for this pattern is still not known.

If empirical studies find little evidence that women are generally more easily influenced than men, why does the stereotype persist that women are much more yielding? Eagly and Wood (1982) suggest that the answer lies in the roles men and women typically play in society. In real life, an important determinant of social influence is a person's prestige or power relative to others in a group. In a business, for example, subordinates are expected to go along with the boss; a nurse usually follows a physician's orders. Since men typically have higher occupational status than women, it is more common to observe a woman yielding to a man than vice versa.

Although this behavior pattern is actually based on status, people may mistakenly infer that women have a general tendency to go along with others. To test this idea, Eagly and Wood (1982) had students read a description of a man influencing a female co-worker or a woman influencing a male co-worker. Subjects then answered questions about the people described. When subjects had no information about the job titles of these persons, they assumed that women held lower-status jobs and that women were more likely to comply behaviorally with men than vice versa. When explicit job titles were provided, subjects believed that compliance would be based on status rather than gender. Such results support the idea that stereotypes about women's greater influenceability are based in part on knowledge that men often have more prestigious and powerful positions in society.

Nonverbal Communication

Stereotypes about female "intuition" suggest that women may be better than men at decoding or "reading" nonverbal behavior. Thus it might be speculated that mothers are more expert than fathers at telling whether a crying baby is hungry, wet, or suffering gas pains. Similarly, the stereotype would suggest that women may be better able to sense whether another person is feeling depressed or embarrassed or tired. Many studies have addressed this question by comparing men's and women's accuracy at decoding another person's emotions from facial cues, body language, or tone of voice.

In a typical study, subjects watch a videotape of a person expressing a series of emotions, such as happiness, disgust, or fear. After viewing each segment of the film, subjects indicate which of several emotions they think is being expressed. In other studies, subjects listen to voices that have been "content filtered"—altered so that the words are garbled and only the tone is distinct. Judith Hall (1978) reviewed 75 such studies that permitted gender comparisons. In 68 percent, women were better decoders than men; in 13 percent, men were better than women; and in 19 percent no gender differences occurred.

This gender difference has been found in schoolchildren, teenagers, and adults. Several possible explanations have been offered. One is that females have a genetically "programmed" sensitivity to nonverbal cues because of their role in caring for preverbal infants. Another suggestion is that women are trained to be experts in emotional matters, and so learn to be more skillful in nonverbal communication.

How would you react if asked to imagine finding a dead animal that had been lying in the sun for several days or to imagine that a friend has come to visit? Research shows that the facial expressions of this New Guinea tribesman are remarkably similar to those of American college students given the same instructions. Can you tell which photos show anger, happiness, sadness, or disgust.

From P. Ekman and W. V. Friesen. *Unmasking the face.* Englewood Cliffs, N.J.: Prentice-Hall, 1975, p. 27. (Answers in numerical order are happiness, sadness, anger and disgust.)

GENDER DIFFERENCES IN PERSPECTIVE: CHANGING ROLES

Aside from the biological facts of life, just how different are males and females? Psychological research offers no simple conclusion. At the level of basic abilities and personal dispositions, gender differences are often small in magnitude, no more than a few points on a standardized test. For example, Eagly (1983) estimated that gender explains only about 1 percent of all the variability between people in conformity and persuasibility. Similarly, Hall (1978) estimated that gender accounts for only 4 percent of variation in decoding nonverbal messages. Hyde (1981) reported that gender explains only 1 percent of individual differences in verbal ability, 1 percent in math ability, and 4.5 percent in visual-spatial ability. For these types of behaviors,

the range of human variation is great and the average differences between the sexes are small. Such gender differences may be "statistically significant," yet essentially trivial. Other alleged gender differences, such as in general intelligence or achievement motivation, have been disproved.

At the same time, our everyday experiences repeatedly show that men and women often use their basic talents and drives in different ways. A man with high achievement strivings may channel his energies into starting his own business; a traditional woman with equally great desire for achievement may take up gourmet cooking or become a "super mom." Clear-cut differences do exist between the activities that

Suzanne Szasz, Photo Researchers, Inc.

Tim Davis, Photo Researchers, Inc.

Traditional rules about what males and females should and shouldn't do are breaking down. More women hold paid jobs than ever before, and men are showing increased interest in homemaking and childcare. Here, a twelve-year-old girl earns money delivering newspapers and a first grade boy gets a sewing lesson at school.

are usually "men's work" and those that are "women's work."

But newspapers today are filled with stories about the changing roles of men and women. Whether a writer heralds these changes as a "stride toward equality" or laments the collapse of "traditional values," few would deny that the lives of men and women are not what they used to be. One way to assess these changes is to compare contemporary gender roles with the older, traditional patterns. Traditional gender roles were organized around two basic principles. The first idea was that men and women should perform distinctive activities, that there should be a division of labor by gender. The second idea was that men should be the dominant sex, both at home and in society at large.

Let us look now at these social roles and how they are changing.

Division of Labor

There is much evidence that rigid distinctions between what men should do and what women should do are breaking down. During this century, women have increasingly come to do things formerly considered "for men only." In particular, women's participation in paid work has increased dramatically, decreasing men's exclusive role as the family breadwinner. In 1940, only 15 percent of married women worked for pay, but by 1975 the figure had risen to 44 percent (Bane, 1976). Today, more than half of all married women have paying jobs, including many mothers of small children. Women have begun to enter occupations such as law, medicine, and engineering that were once the near exclusive domain of men. Women have also made gains in higher education; in 1978, more women than men entered college for the first time in United States history. These are changes of great personal and social significance.

Yet women are far from equal partners in the world of work. Women continue to be concentrated in lower-status "female jobs" such as secretary, nurse, and teacher. Partly as a result, the average woman worker earns only about 57 cents for every dollar earned by a man. Even when women make it into high-status jobs, they often experience bias not encountered by their male peers.

Are men today doing more things formerly considered "for women only"? Everyday examples of such changes are easy to find. It is not unusual these days to see a father in the delivery room assisting in the birth of his child or taking his toddler to the supermarket. In public schools, many home economics classes have gone "coed"; more boys are learning to cook and to babysit. However, men's participation in housework and childcare—*family work* as some call it—is still relatively small. One study (Robinson et al., 1977) found that husbands' total family work averaged only 11.2 hours per week.

A surprising finding from research by Robinson and others is that the amount of time a husband spends on housework and childcare is *not* related to whether or not his wife has a paid job. A husband whose wife has a 40-hour a week job spends no more time on household chores than a husband whose wife is home full time. Women perform most homemaking and childcare activities, regardless of whether they have a paid job or not. The only difference is that employed wives spend less time on family work (about 28 hours per week) than do full-time homemakers (about 53 hours per week). Recent studies (Pleck, 1981) show some signs

that men in dual-worker marriages may be beginning to do a little more at home, but the change is very small. Homemaking and childcare continue to be largely "women's work."

Male Dominance

The second basic idea in traditional gender roles is that males should be the leaders both at home and in society at large. Changes are clearly occurring in both arenas. In the public section, laws denying women the vote, forbidding women to own property, and in general defining women as second-class citizens are largely a thing of the past. In recent years we've seen the first woman elected governor and the first woman appointed to the U.S. Supreme Court. Nonetheless, the numbers of women in the power circles of society are still small. In 1980, women were only 2 percent of U.S. senators and 4 percent of members of the House of Representatives. For an example closer to home, consider the college you attend. Chances are that there are many women secretaries and a few women professors, but that the chairperson of your department, most of the deans and top-level administrators, and the president are male. Women are still very far from being equal partners in public affairs.

In the family, the extent of male dominance is harder to assess. As we discussed in Chapter 9, marriages in which the husband is the all-powerful patriarch are uncommon today. Nonetheless, proponents of the traditional pattern of greater male power are easy to find. A striking example is the bestseller *Fascinating Womanhood,* by Helen Andelin (1963). She advocates a benevolent form of male dominance, arguing that women should defer to their husbands and take pleasure in being cared for. The man, she writes, should be the "undisputed head of the family." The wife "must accept him as her leader, support and obey him" (pp. 134–135). But although male dominance has vocal supporters, many people today reject this view.

In 1981, when Lady Diana married Prince Charles, the future king of England, she broke with tradition in her wedding vows: She did not promise to obey her husband. A Westminster Abbey clergyman explained: "Marriage is the kind of relationship where there should be two equal partners, and if there is to be a dominant partner it won't be settled by this oath" (*Los Angeles Times,* July 2, 1981, 18). Many other young couples seem to share this view (Peplau, 1979), and it seems likely that male dominance is less pronounced than it used to be (Scanzoni & Scanzoni, 1976).

In contemporary society, multiple definitions of gender roles co-exist. The options available to people today, both at work and in personal relationships, are much less limited by gender than in the past.

SUMMARY

1. Gender is one of the most basic categories in social life. The process of labeling people, things, and activities as "masculine" and "feminine" is called gender typing.
2. Gender stereotypes are beliefs about the typical personal attributes of males and females. Cultural stereotypes are societal-level images of the sexes found in the media, art, and literature. Personal stereotypes are the unique beliefs held by an individual about the typical attributes of men and women.
3. Stereotypes are most likely to influence our perception of other people when we have little information available and when a person's gender is especially salient. One problem with gender stereotypes is that they can bias evaluations of the performance of individual men and women.
4. Gender identity, knowledge that we are female or male, is acquired early in childhood. An important developmental milestone occurs when children come to understand that gender is constant and unchanging. Transsexuals have a severe gender identity problem: They believe their true psychological gender is different from their biological gender.
5. Beliefs about masculinity and femininity are important elements in our self-concept. Males who rate themselves high on masculine traits and low on feminine traits and females who rate themselves high in femininity and low in masculinity are traditionally gender-typed. Androgynous people rate themselves high in both masculine and feminine qualities. Recent research has challenged the congruence model assertion that psychological well-being is greatest for people who are traditionally gender-typed in their self-concept.
6. There are three major theoretical perspectives on gender differences in behavior. A biological approach emphasizes the impact of physical differences, sex hormones, and genetics. A learning approach emphasizes ways in which society shapes behavior; through such processes as reinforcement and modeling, people acquire stable characteristics linked to gender. Social psychologists have been most interested in a third approach, the influence of social situations. People's behavior varies from situation to situation, depending on such factors as the gender composition of the group, social roles and expectations, and the nature of the task or activity.
7. In daily life, women and men often use their basic talents and drives in gender-linked ways. Traditional gender roles prescribed a division of labor by sex and conferred greater power on men. Although both patterns are still evident, the options available to people today are less constrained by gender than in the past.

SUGGESTIONS FOR ADDITIONAL READING

ALLGEIER, E. R., & McCORMICK, N. B. (Eds.) 1983.   *Changing boundaries: Gender roles and sexual behavior.* Palo Alto, CA: Mayfield. Experts in the field discuss the many ways that gender affects sexuality and close relationships.

EAGLY, A. H. 1983.   Gender and social influence: A social psychological analysis. *American Psychologist,* 971–981. A thorough review of research on gender differences in conformity.

HENLEY, N. M. 1977.   *Body politics: Power, sex, and nonverbal communication.* Englewood Cliffs, NJ: Prentice Hall. A very readable analysis of gender differences in the use of touch, space, time, and other aspects of nonverbal communication.

HYDE, J. S., & ROSENBERG, B. G. 1984.   *Half the human experience: The psychology of women* (3rd ed.). Lexington, MA: D.C. Heath. An up-to-date and comprehensive text on the psychology of gender.

PLECK, J. H. 1981.   *The myth of masculinity.* Cambridge, MA: MIT Press. A detailed analysis of research and theories on masculinity; somewhat technical, but well worth the effort.

SPENCE, J. T., & HELMREICH, R. 1978.   *Masculinity and femininity: Their psychological dimensions, correlates, and antecedents.* Austin, TX: University of Texas Press. Presents a program of research on masculinity, femininity, and androgyny.

TAVRIS, C., & WADE, C. 1984.   *The longest war: Sex differences in perspective* (2nd ed.). New York: Harcourt Brace Jovanovich. A basic introduction to research and theories about gender differences, written in a very readable style.

16

ENVIRONMENTAL PSYCHOLOGY

Over the past ten or fifteen years, people have become more and more concerned about the environment. The environmental movement has focused attention on the quality of the air we breathe and the water we drink, on how new dam construction harms wildlife, and how strip mining devastates the landscape and causes floods. We are beginning to realize that virtually all aspects of the world around us can have profound and potentially negative effects on our health and well-being.

Social scientists, including psychologists, have also become concerned about how the environment affects us. Just as toxic chemicals in the air and the ground can damage physical health, so other characteristics of the environment can damage mental and social health. Noise, crowding, building design, and community structure all determine the quality of our lives and our day-to-day functioning. **Environmental psychology** is a relatively new branch of psychology that focuses on the relationships between the physical environment and human behavior and well-being. We will consider some of the main findings of environmental psychologists. We begin with how humans use space.

HUMAN SPATIAL BEHAVIOR

How do people use the space around them to regulate their social interactions? This is one of the questions asked by environmental researchers, who use the term **proxemics** to refer to the study of human spatial behavior (Hall, 1959). We will consider two aspects of how humans use space: personal space and territoriality.

Personal Space

Suppose you are standing by yourself in a physician's waiting room, and the nurse walks up to you. How close does she actually come? Three inches? Ten inches? Two feet? Suppose you are sitting on a park bench and a well-dressed man sits down immediately next to you. How does that make you feel? Would you feel differently if he sat down five feet away? How close to other people do you usually stand? Does it make any difference if they are friends, strangers, or members of your family? Does it make any difference if you are standing at a cocktail party, on a bus, or on line at the Post Office?

As these examples suggest, people have preferred distances for social interaction, depending on who they are with and the activity. People treat the physical space immediately around them as though it were a part of themselves; this zone has been called their **personal space.** According to Sommer (1969):

Personal space refers to an area with an invisible boundary surrounding the person's body into which intruders may not come. Like [porcupines], people like to be close enough to obtain warmth and comradeship but far enough away to avoid pricking one another. (p. 26)

In social interactions, people try to maintain an acceptable balance between being too close for comfort or awkwardly distant.

Personal space is often measured by the physical distance a person maintains from others. But personal space involves much more than physical distance. At very close distances, we can touch and smell another person, talk in hushed whispers, and see their features very clearly. At far distances, we may need to talk loudly and have quite different possibilities for social contact.

Edward Hall (1959), an anthropologist, suggested four basic zones for interpersonal interaction. *Intimate distance,* from 0 to 18 inches, is illustrated by a couple making love, by a mother nursing an infant, by wrestlers locked in a tight hold. *Personal distance,* from 18 inches to 4 feet, is the distance for friendly conversation. *Social distance,* from 4 to 7 feet, is the distance for a formal business meeting. *Public distance,* from 12 to 25 feet, requires a loud voice and is illustrated by someone giving a lecture. According to Hall, the social situation deter-

mines which of these zones people prefer to use. Intimate and personal distance are typically used for informal interactions with friends, family, or close associates. Social and public distances are used for more formal interactions among casual acquaintances or strangers.

Research has generally supported Hall's basic idea (Stokols, 1978). For instance, friends prefer to stand closer together than do strangers (Ashton, Shaw & Worsham, 1980), and people who want to seem friendly choose smaller distances (Lott & Sommer, 1967; Patterson & Sechrest, 1970). People who are sexually attracted to each other also stand close (Allgeier & Byrne, 1973). Although most people do not think much about personal space, we are nonetheless aware of the unwritten rules about space use in our culture. For example, we know that standing close together is usually a sign of friendship or interest. It may be one of the most important and easiest ways of telling someone you have just met that you like him or her. The other person is immediately aware of your interest, and if the person is not interested, he or she will generally move away to make that clear.

Group Differences in Spatial Behavior

Many factors affect our use of space. As an anthropologist, Hall was especially interested in cross-cultural differences in spatial behavior. If you have traveled much outside the United States, you have no doubt noticed that people in other countries differ in how close they stand while talking. People in some cultures stand closer together than you are accustomed to, whereas people in other cultures maintain a greater distance. Research in this area has found that cultural norms determine typical personal space preferences. White North Americans, the English, and the Swedes stand the farthest apart; Southern Europeans stand closer; and Latin Americans and Arabs stand the closest (Watson & Graves, 1966; Little, 1968; Sommer, 1969). Although much observation remains to be done in Africa, Eastern Europe, and Asia, it is clear that consistent differences exist all over the world.

Personal space refers to a zone surrounding a person's body that is treated as an extension of the self. In this uncrowded library, each student has a comfortable island of personal space.

These cultural differences might be considered a piece of interesting but trivial information if it were not for the fact that preferences in personal distance can sometimes have important consequences. People from cultures with different preferences may misinterpret one another's actions. For example, an American and a Pakistani have a problem when they stand next to each other to talk. The American likes to stand about three or four feet away, whereas the Pakistani would ordinarily stand much closer. Obviously, they cannot both have their way. If they are unaware of the cultural difference, they may execute a little dance around the room. The Pakistani feels uncomfortably far away and moves closer. The American feels uncomfortable and retreats, which in turn causes the Pakistani to move closer again. Moreover, as this is going on, the Pakistani may feel that the American is being cold and unfriendly, while the American thinks the other is being overly intimate and pushy.

In addition to cross-cultural variations, personal space may also vary within a culture. As you may have guessed, men and women tend to use personal space somewhat differently. Pairs of women stand closer together than do pairs of men (Horowitz et al., 1970), and women often tend to stand closer to whomever they are with (Hartnett et al., 1970; Leibman, 1970). Violent prisoners prefer greater distances than do nonviolent prisoners (see Gilmour & Walkey, 1981).

Territorial Behavior

You arrive at the library to study for your final exam in social psychology. To your distress, every seat is taken. Most seats are physically occupied by someone, and the rest are "staked out" with coats, books, briefcases, and other markers. You consider whether or not to move someone's belongings and take the chair, but think better of it, not wanting to face an argument.

People often lay claim to a particular place as "theirs." A **territory** is an area controlled by a specific individual or group. Territorial behavior includes actions designed to stake out or mark a territory and to claim ownership. Whereas personal space is physically connected to a person—a distance from the person's body to that of other people—territories do not necessarily require physical presence. As the library example suggests, people often try to guard their territory from intrusion while they are absent.

Territorial behavior is a way that people regulate social interaction, and it can serve many specific functions. Territorial rules can simplify and bring order to daily interactions. For instance, when family members share bedrooms, they usually designate some areas for personal use. Each person has his or her own part of the closet, dresser, or side of the bed (Altman, Nelson, & Lett, 1972). Family members tend to have fixed places at the dinner table, places that are changed only when people are eating alone or when guests are present. Territoriality also contributes to the maintenance of privacy—control over the information others have about us and the extent to which social contact occurs. The goal of territorial behavior is not necessarily to be alone, but rather to control access to oneself and one's property. Finally, territorial behavior provides a way to communicate information about our self and our interests. The rose-covered white picket fence surrounding a suburban house marks the property line, but it also conveys an image of the owners.

TYPES OF TERRITORIES   Altman (1975) has distinguished three main types of human territories. A *primary territory* is owned and used exclusively by an individual or group. A house or apartment, for example, is clearly owned by a person or family, controlled on a relatively permanent basis, and important in their daily lives. Unwelcome intrusions into a primary territory are a serious matter.

A *secondary territory* is a space that is used regularly, but shared with others. You may always take the same seat in your chemistry lab and get annoyed if someone else sits in it before you arrive, but you know that the space is not exclusively yours. Secondary territories are semi-public, and so there is more ambiguity of ownership and control. *Public territories* are places like a park or airport waiting lounge where everyone presumably has an equal right of access. We may stake out a spot on the beach with a beach chair and blanket, but we

BOX 16–1
The Home Team Advantage in Sports

In competitive sports, teams usually do better when playing at home than "on the road." A study of professional basketball, baseball, and football teams found that all teams won a greater percentage of their home games than games played elsewhere (Hirt & Kimble, 1981). The home field advantage was most striking for basketball, where professional teams won about 65 percent of home games but only 35 percent of away games. An analysis of the 1976–77 National Basketball Association season found that even teams who finished last in their division won nearly 60 percent of their home games (Watkins, 1978). And even the most powerful division champions performed relatively poorly on the road. Schwartz and Barsky (1977) have concluded that playing at home is as strong a factor in a team's performance as the quality of the players.

Why is it better to play on your home territory? Greater familiarity with the home field and the fatigue of travel may contribute, but they are not the whole answer (Schwartz & Barsky, 1977). Psychological factors are also important. Territorial dominance may be one explanation. Home teams may do better because they are on their own turf. Visitors may feel wary and inhibited because they are not on their home ground. An even more important factor may be the behavior of the spectators. A team usually has more fans on hand for home games. According to Schwartz and Barsky, the social support provided by the home audience is a crucial factor. They also suggested that encouragement from an audience is most effective when it is sustained for some time and when the audience is most compact (high in social density). This may explain why the home team advantage is most pronounced for indoor sports such as basketball, where spectators are in a small enclosed space, rather than for outdoor games such as football, which are played in large arenas.

Audience encouragement may influence sports performance through the process of social facilitation, discussed in Chapter 13. In this view, supportive audiences increase an athlete's arousal or motivation. When someone performs a well-learned task, increased arousal usually improves performance. Thus highly skilled athletes should benefit from heightened arousal.

In a recent extension of this work, Greer (1983) looked at negative behavior by fans, such as booing and hissing. Researchers observed the behavior of home and visiting men's college basketball teams over a two-year period. The researchers noted every instance of sustained crowd protest that lasted for at least 15 seconds, and then recorded the behavior of both teams during the next five minutes. Performance measures included scoring, violations, and turnovers.

Greer found that very short crowd protests occurred in virtually every game, but sustained outbursts happened only about half the time, for a total of 15 games. Ten of these booing incidents were directed at the referees for calls made against the home team. In four cases, the protest expressed displeasure with referees who failed to call violations on visiting players. One protest was directed at the players on the visiting team. All protests were in support of the home team. Following these episodes, there was a consistent know that our claim is temporary; getting a choice spot depends on getting there ahead of the other beachgoers.

TERRITORIAL MARKERS   One interesting research focus has been the way people mark and personalize their territories. **Territorial markers** often serve a preventive function. They let others know that a particular area is claimed. In a study of behavior in the library, Becker (1973) found that people were least likely to select a table that was physically occupied by another person. Not surprisingly, physical presence is a strong marker. But people were also discouraged by the presence of books and personal belongings on a table; the more markers present, the greater the avoidance. Quite subtle gestures can also serve as territorial markers.

A study in a game arcade (Werner, Brown, & Damron, 1981) found that body gestures were territorial markers. A confederate stood by an electronic game called Space Invaders. The researchers varied how far the confederate stood from the machine, and whether or not the confederate placed a hand on the edge of the machine. The confederate never touched the actual controls. New players were significantly less likely to approach the machine when the confederate stood close and when he touched the machine. In public settings where it is not possible to use permanent markers, touch and physical proximity may be subtle signs of temporary "ownership."

Territorial markers also serve to display aspects of an individual's personality or interests. In one study (Vinsel, Brown, Altman, & Foss, 1980), photographs were taken of the wall decorations in dorm rooms of newly entering first-

We use territorial markers to claim a particular space and prevent unwanted intrusions. This woman has used her shoes, bookbag, and newspaper to indicate her control of the area.

year university students. Virtually all students hung at least one object, such as a poster or photograph, on the wall by the bed. Women were more likely than men to use relationship items, such as personal photos; men were more likely to use impersonal items such as a sports poster. Differences were also found between the markers of students who later dropped out of the university and those who remained in school. The decorations of continuing students showed more identification with the new school and community, such as school posters and maps of the local area. The displays of dropouts suggested a greater commitment to past life and families.

Defending and Sharing Space

Personal space and territorial behavior are used to control social interaction. On the one hand, we want to defend ourselves and our territory from unwanted "invasions." But equally important, we often want to share ourselves and our space with friends and loved ones. Thus, our reaction to someone who enters our space can vary greatly, depending on the way we define the situation.

Our attributions about the other person's motives—whether we interpret the actions as friendly, rude, or possibly even dangerous—are important. A study by Koneci and his associates (1975) involved having a confederate stand very close to a person who was waiting on a corner to cross the street. In this situation, people apparently interpreted the stranger's behavior as an unwelcome invasion, and crossed the street much faster than usual to escape from the stranger's presence.

Another experiment (Sundstrom & Sundstrom, 1977) investigated the effect of having a stranger ask permission to sit next to a person. Confederates approached a same-sex stranger sitting on a public bench. Before sitting down, half the confederates asked permission—they asked whether it was OK if they sat down on the bench. The other half of the time, the confederates sat down without asking permission. It appears that women and men interpreted this situation quite differently.

Women seem to have interpreted the request for permission as the beginning of an unwanted social contact. They left sooner when the confederate asked permission than when the confederate did not. In contrast, men seemed to have interpreted the request for permission as a sign of politeness. Men who were asked permission stayed on the bench longer than men who were not asked. The point is that our reactions to others who enter our space depend on how we interpret the situation and the person's motives.

When physical space is limited and we are forced to share it with others, we may feel crowded. The misery of squeezing into a packed bus on a hot summer day is one example. The experience of crowding has been an important research topic in environmental psychology.

CROWDING

One hundred million people every year, one billion people every ten years—that is the rate at which the population of the world is increasing. As you can see in Figure 16–1, it took tens of thousands of years for the world population to reach half a billion. Two hundred years passed before the population doubled and reached 1 billion. But the next doubling to 2 billion took only eighty years, and the doubling to 4 billion only forty-five years. At the present rate of growth, the number of people on earth will double again and reach 8 billion in only thirty-five years.

Fortunately, we are beginning to see the first signs that the population explosion may be slowing down. The government of China, which has almost a quarter of the population of the world, is making a determined effort to reduce

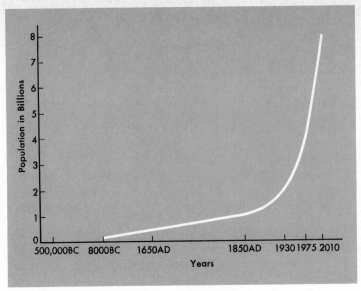

FIGURE 16–1 Growth of world population.

the birth rate. Other governments, including some in South America and Africa, which have traditionally had extremely high birth rates, are also beginning to encourage people to limit family size. Probably the most promising sign is that people all over the world now seem to desire smaller families more than they did in the past. Families in which women typically would have had seven or eight children twenty years ago now have only four or five. Nonetheless, there is no question that, barring some catastrophe, the population of the world will continue to increase well into the twenty-first century and perhaps beyond that.

This population explosion has serious consequences for practically every aspect of our lives. It strains the economic resources of the world, exhausts natural resources, pushes up the cost of fuel, food, and every other necessary item, and leads to pollution. As populations increase, resources must be shared by more and more people. There is just so much good land, so much oil, so much wood for houses, and so on. In the United States, for example, the national parks are so crowded that it is practically "standing room only" in the more popular ones. They are still beautiful, but they are no longer a place to enjoy in solitude.

One of the consequences of the population explosion is that the concentration of people in and around cities is increasing steadily. Most of the populations of the United States, Canada, and the other industrialized countries have become increasingly concentrated in and around urban centers. Even though the central cities have actually lost population over the past 20 or 30 years, the larger metropolitan areas have grown enormously because suburbs have become so large. Therefore, the question of how crowding affects us is of more and more concern.

Definitions

Researchers who study the effects of crowding find it essential to distinguish between objective measures of population density and subjective feelings of being crowded (Stokols, 1972). **Social density** refers to the objective number of people in a given space. Density might be measured in terms of the number of people per square foot. **Crowding** refers to the subjective experience of feeling cramped and not having enough space. Density may or may not be unpleasant, but crowding is always unpleasant and

BOX 16–2
Crowding in Animals

Biologists and ethologists have done a great deal of research on how nonhuman animals react to high-density experiences. Although animals do not complain of subjective feelings of crowding, they do sometimes display signs of distress when population density is high.

In many studies, small groups of animals, usually rats or mice, have been put in an enclosed space, provided with food, water, and other necessities, and otherwise left alone (Snyder, 1968; Southwick, 1955; Terman, 1974). Under these circumstances, a dramatic phenomenon occurs. The group behaves normally for a while, and the population grows. Then, at some point, the population peaks and either stops growing or declines sharply. Instead of continuing to produce more offspring that survive, the animals sometimes cease reproducing or produce offspring that die very soon. In other words, normal reproductive functions are severely disrupted merely because the animals are enclosed in a limited area.

In addition, there is substantial evidence that animals living under conditions of high density, or simply being enclosed, suffer physiological damage. Their adrenal glands become enlarged (Christian, 1975; To & Tamarin, 1977). Their reproductive organs decrease in size or in activity (Davis & Meyer, 1973; Snyder, 1968).

Finally, there is some evidence that social behavior is also affected. In a famous series of studies, Calhoun (1962) placed rats in cages specifically designed to produce very high densities in certain areas. The animals in these cages exhibited a wide range of abnormal behavior. They fought violently, mated indiscriminately, trampled nests and the young who were in them, and failed to build adequate nests in the first place. Calhoun called this phenomenon of antisocial and disruptive behavior a **behavioral sink**. Although other work (Terman, 1974) has failed to find these effects on aggressiveness, there is little doubt that under some circumstances high density does cause a breakdown in normal social behavior.

The rats in Calhoun's behavioral sink were simultaneously exposed to very small physical spaces and to many other animals. Subsequent research has tried to examine separately the effects of these two factors. Results suggest that the sheer amount of space available is not the crucial element. Animals alone in small cages do not show these effects. Rather, the harmful effects are linked to being enclosed *in groups*. Animals in groups suffer negative effects, regardless of the physical size of their cages (Terman, 1974). In many situations, social density seems to be more important than physical space (Freedman, 1979).

In any case, humans are not rats. We have much more complex social systems, higher levels of cognitive functioning, all sorts of rules and laws and customs with which to deal with the environment, and a flexible system of communication with other people. Generalizing from work on other animals to humans is always both difficult and questionable. This is particularly true when complicated social factors and interpersonal relations are involved. Thus, although this work on other animals is suggestive, we must look at research on humans to discover how they respond to crowding.

negative, by definition. When we say we feel "crowded," we are usually complaining.

Moreover, this feeling of being crowded can occur regardless of the amount of space we actually have available. It is more likely to be aroused when we are cramped, but we sometimes feel crowded even when we have plenty of space around us. There are times when three is a crowd no matter how much space is available. If you like to swim at deserted beaches, the presence of a few other people may make you feel that the beach is overcrowded, whereas you might not feel crowded at a party even if there were fifty other people in a fairly small room. Crowding refers to the psychological state of discomfort and stress associated with wanting more space than is available.

Theories of Human Crowding

When do people experience the presence of others as crowding? A number of explanations have been given that emphasize cognitive processes—the way people perceive, interpret, and react to their social environment.

SENSORY OVERLOAD   Stanley Milgram (1970) proposed that whenever people are exposed to too much stimulation, they experience sensory overload and can no longer deal with all the stimulation. Social density is one source of stimulation that can sometimes produce overstimulation and feelings of being crowded. Milgram believes that sensory overload is always unpleasant and interferes with a person's ability to function properly. People deal with overload by screening out some of the stimulation and attending only to what is most important.

Individual differences in reactions to social density may reflect differences in preferred level of stimulation. Some people may like high levels of stimulation—they like the radio blaring all the time, study in busy rooms, and watch television while carrying on a conversation or doing a crossword puzzle. Others like low levels of stimulation. When they work, it has to be quiet; if they watch television, they do not want any distractions. For high-stimulation people, high social density may be the right level of stimulation and so be perceived as pleasant and excit-

ing. In contrast, for low-stimulation people, high social density may be disruptive and so be perceived as crowding.

DENSITY-INTENSITY   A different explanation (Freedman, 1975) is that high density intensifies usual reactions to a social situation. Just as turning up the volume on a stereo magnifies our reaction to music, so increasing density magnifies our reaction to other people. If we dislike the music, we will dislike it more when it is loud than when it is soft; if we like it, we will like it more when it is loud. Similarly, whatever our response to other people who are near us, increasing density intensifies that response. If we like them, we will like them more; if we dislike them, we will dislike them more. If we are afraid, nervous, angry, aggressive, friendly, or anything else in low-density situations, we will feel more of it in high-density situations.

Some direct support for this view is provided by a series of studies by Freedman and his colleagues (Freedman, 1975). In this research, situations were deliberately made pleasant or unpleasant. Increasing density should intensify responses, making the pleasant situation more pleasant and the unpleasant more unpleasant. That is what these studies show.

This explanation of crowding seems to fit quite nicely into many of our everyday experiences. Sometimes the presence of many people is unpleasant and sometimes it is pleasant, but generally it does appear to intensify the social situation. Riding a bus is not always pleasant. If the bus is crowded, it can become really unpleasant. Or consider a party. If there are only 20 people in a huge room, the party tends to be flat, unexciting, dull. In fact, under these circumstances people will usually collect in the kitchen or at one end of the room. The same 20 people in a small room will make a much better party, assuming of course that they are pleasant people. If they are unpleasant, the small room will produce a less pleasant experience than the large room. In other words, basically positive situations usually become more positive when density is increased; negative ones become more negative.

LOSS OF CONTROL   High density can make people feel they have less control over their actions, and so create feelings of being crowded (Baron & Rodin, 1978). The idea is that with so many people in a small space, each individual is less able to control the situation, to move around freely, to avoid undesired contact.

This loss of control can have several negative features. Since people usually want as much control as possible over their lives, simply feeling powerless or helpless is, in itself, negative. Further, high density may prevent people from maintaining a desired degree of privacy (Altman, 1975). High density may also lead to problems in the coordination of activities. When three people share a small dorm room, they may literally bump into each other, make it difficult for individuals to study or sleep when they want, and so on. Under high-density conditions, people are more likely to interfere with each other's activities, leading to feelings of frustration and anger (Schopler & Stockdale, 1977).

Research has begun to provide evidence that a lack of perceived control produces the feeling of being crowded. For example, Sherrod (1974) had students work under high-density conditions and provided some with a button that, if pushed, would signal the experimenter to remove them from the situation. Although no one actually used the button, students who were given this sense of control over their environment were less negatively affected by the high density.

Closely related to control may be the ability to predict what a situation will be like. Kline and Harris (1979) told subjects to anticipate a high- or low-density room, and then confirmed or did not confirm their expectation. The results were that the objective number of people in the room by itself had no effect. Instead, subjects did better when their expectations were confirmed than when their expectations were not confirmed. In other words, there were no negative effects of being in a high-density room so long as it was anticipated.

It is likely that sensory overload, density intensification, and loss of control can all play a part in producing the experience of crowding. With these general principles in mind, we now turn to empirical studies of crowding.

Researchers have used many approaches to study the effects of human crowding. We will consider three types of research. One approach examines the impact of population density in cities on such social ills as crime and suicide. Another investigates the effects of crowded living conditions in families, schools, and prisons. A third approach has used laboratory studies to conduct controlled experiments on exposure to high-density situations.

Population Density in Cities

Several studies have concentrated on the effects of population density in the largest metropolitan areas of the United States. The measure of density is the number of people per square mile. In other words, this type of study is concerned simply with how many people live within the boundaries of the city relative to the size of the city. How does this measure of density affect the quality of life? For example, does density correlate with the amount of crime in the cities? It has been found (Freedman, Heshka, & Levy, 1973) that there is a small but significant correlation between density and crime when only those two factors are considered (r = about .35).

Of course, density tends to be highly correlated with other factors such as income, and income in turn is also highly correlated with crime rate. It is therefore impossible to tell from the simple correlation whether density causes crime or whether some other factor, such as income, leads to both higher density and higher crime rates. This is the "third-variable" problem discussed in Chapter 2. When researchers have used statistical procedures to control for the effect of income and other social factors, the relationship between population density and crime disappears. Across the major U.S. metropolitan areas, once income is controlled, there seems to be little relationship between density and crime rates. For example, Los Angeles has one of the lowest densities but one of the highest crime rates in the United States. So density is not responsible for crime.

This result may seem surprising, given our stereotype of urban life as crowded and crime-ridden. Yet studies show that most people in major cities function well psychologically (Fischer, 1976). The incidence of mental disturbance is

Population density refers to the number of people concentrated in a particular area. Major cities such as Hong Kong have very high population densities.

no higher in large cities than in smaller communities (Srole, 1972). People in cities are no more likely to commit suicide than people in smaller communities (Gibbs, 1971). In fact, urban dwellers say they are just as happy as people who live in suburbs, small towns, or rural areas (Shaver & Freedman, 1976). In a book on the urban experience, Fischer writes that he found "little evidence that urbanites are more stressed, disordered, alienated, or unhappy than ruralites" (1976, p. 177). Population density in cities is not the generally harmful factor it is often thought to be.

Residential Density

Several studies have examined the effects of social density in households on well-being. Probably the most impressive research of this type was conducted by Mitchell (1971), who went into a vast number of homes in Hong Kong, one of the most crowded cities in the world. He measured the exact size of each family's living space, computed the density of people in the home, and took measures of anxiety, nervousness, and other symptoms of mental strain. In this study, a typical person shared a space of about 400 square feet with ten or more people. Yet despite these cramped conditions, Mitchell found no appreciable relationship between density and pathology. Similar results were found in a study in Toronto (Booth, 1976).

Another opportunity to study residential crowding is provided by young adults living in dormitory settings. Studies at Rutgers University (Karlin, Epstein, & Aiello, 1978) compared students living two to a room versus three to a room, all in rooms designed to hold two students. Tripled students reported significantly more stress and disappointment than doubled students. These effects were more severe for women students, who attempted to make their cramped quarters into a homelike enivronment, than for men, who spent more time away from their rooms. Tripled students of both sexes got significantly lower grades. However, in later years, when students were no longer living in high-density environments, their grades improved. In another study, students in triple rooms reported feeling less control over their environments (Baron, Mandel, Adams & Griffen, 1976), suggesting that this may be one reason for the negative effects of tripled dorms.

The effects of limited living quarters can be quite variable, however. One dramatic demonstration comes from a case study of Peace Corps volunteers (MacDonald & Oden, 1973). In this study, five married couples agreed voluntarily to share an unpartitioned 30- by 30-foot room during the twelve-week training program. The volunteers agreed to this experience in order to gain some insight into the hardships they might encounter once overseas. They were compared to other Peace Corps couples living in more spacious hotel rooms.

Despite their very dense living conditions, the couples living communally showed no adverse effects and saw their experience as a positive challenge. They apparently developed high morale and a spirit of cooperation. Clearly, those who volunteered for the communal living arrangement may have had different personalities than the nonvolunteers, and they knew that the situation was only temporary. The point of the example, however, is that very high density living can be a positive experience under certain circumstances.

Studies of prison inmates also provide evidence about the effects of residential density. Prisoners housed in single cells have been found to have lower blood pressure than inmates living in dormitory-type cells (D'Atri, 1975; McCain, Cox, & Paulus, 1976). Research based on archival data has also linked high-density living quarters in prison to higher death rates and to psychiatric problems (McCain et al., 1976).

In reviewing these mixed findings, Epstein (1981) proposed that the negative effects of residential density are least likely when residents have a cooperative attitude and some degree of perceived control. Families seem to suffer least from crowded homes, presumably because they have control over their homes and have established patterns of interacting that minimize the problems of high-density living. At the other extreme, prisoners, who have little control over their environment and may have little motivation to cooperate, show negative effects from high density living.

Laboratory Studies

To further clarify the complex effects of density, researchers have turned to carefully controlled laboratory experiments. Participants in these studies are typically exposed to very high density conditions for a short period of time. In some ways, this is quite like many real-world encounters with crowding that are also fairly short in duration. For example, a New Yorker may find herself in a crowded elevator or subway for a few minutes, on a crowded sidewalk while going to work, or in a packed department store. Experiments dealing with short-term crowding may be helpful in telling us how such crowding in the real world affects us.

The standard procedure for most of this experimental work is to put some people in a small room, the same number of people in a large room, and look for any differences on a wide variety of measures. The general pattern of results is clear: High density is not generally harmful to people. As we will see, this does not mean that high density is good for people, nor that it never has bad effects. What it means is that the effects are complicated. We will consider laboratory studies of the impact of density on task performance and social behavior, and then consider gender differences in reactions to crowding.

TASK PERFORMANCE Quite a few studies have investigated task performance under crowded and uncrowded conditions. There are two reasons why this is an important issue. The first is a practical one: People often work under high-density conditions, and we would like to know

These workers are exposed to very high density conditions on the job. Yet research shows that so long as space is adequate for the physical demands of the job, performance does not necessarily suffer.

how this affects performance. If it turned out that high density interfered with their work, presumably managers in factories, offices, and other workplaces would try to reduce density. The second reason for studying this is theoretical: It is well established that when people are under stress or are aroused for any reason, they tend to do less well on difficult and complex tasks, though they often perform better on easy, familiar tasks. If people perform less well on complex tasks when they are crowded, this would indicate that high density is stressful or arousing. Most of the research indicates that high density has little or no effect on task performance.

Freedman, Klevansky, and Ehrlich (1971) had hundreds of subjects of various ages and backgrounds work on many different tasks. Some subjects worked under very cramped conditions (as little as 3 to 4 square feet per person), whereas others had lots of space. There were no consistent differences of any kind. This finding has been repeated in many other experiments (Griffitt & Veitch, 1971; Stokols et al., 1973; Nogami, 1976). Further evidence that density does not necessarily impair task performance comes from studies of people working and living in such cramped environments as submarines, space ships, or air raid shelters. Not

everyone who participates in such experiences enjoys them, but most people do just fine and perform quite competently (Smith & Haythorn, 1972).

Although research on task performance generally shows little negative impact from high density, there are some exceptions to this general pattern. A few studies (Paulus, 1980b) have found that density impairs task performance. Sometimes both sexes are negatively affected by high density (Evans, 1979), but sometimes only men perform less well under high density, whereas women perform slightly better (Paulus et al., 1976). The results of these studies are at odds with the majority of other research. Nevertheless, they suggest that for some people high density may impair performance. In addition, these studies raise the possibility that there may be important sex differences in response to density.

Finally, whenever a particular job requires a lot of room or moving around, and whenever the presence of other individuals in a small space directly interferes with the performance of the task, performance will be hurt. Heller, Groff, and Solomon (1977) demonstrated this; and McCallum and associates (1979) showed that when the resources available were inadequate for the number of people, performance suffered. Obviously, other people can get in the way if there is not enough space. You cannot play a good game of tennis if there are 40 people on the court; 9 people cannot play the same piano simultaneously (or at least they will not play it very well); and even reading a newspaper on a bus is difficult if you are so cramped that you cannot turn the pages. This is not a psychological effect in the usual sense of the word. Rather, it is a purely physical consequence of not having adequate space to perform a particular task.

SOCIAL BEHAVIOR   It seems that crowding might be more likely to affect social behavior than task performance. After all, when people are in close proximity, their social relationships may change in response to the situation. Actually, research on this issue has found no consistent overall effects of density on social behavior. People in crowded conditions are not in general more aggressive, more friendly, more nervous, or less happy than people under less crowded conditions. Studies of adults (Freedman, 1975; Nogami, 1976) have found no consistent differences between high- and low-density conditions.

The findings regarding children's reactions to variations in density are somewhat less consistent. Several studies have observed children in playgrounds or school playrooms. Ginsberg and associates (1977) found that boys engaged in more fighting in smaller playgrounds, although the fights did not last as long as they did in larger areas. In contrast, a series of careful observations by Smith and Connelly (1972) indicated no effect of density on the amount of fighting. Rohe and Patterson (1974) suggest that as long as there are adequate facilities and toys, the amount of space makes little difference. This seems to have been supported by two studies (Loo & Smetana, 1978) that found little overall effect of density on aggressiveness, anger, happiness, or positive group interactions among preschoolers and 10-year-old boys.

Thus, with a few exceptions, this work generally indicates few overall effects of variations in density on social behavior or mood. But when less space is combined with reduced facilities, the effect may be negative. And we should remember that this often occurs in the real world. People who have less space in their homes, for example, typically have fewer facilities as well. Children who are provided a tiny playroom in a poorly equipped school are probably also given relatively few toys to play with. But the negative consequences then are due mainly to the poor facilities, not to the lack of space. On the other hand, to return to a point made earlier, some games cannot be played in too small a space. Basketball and running games require a large play area. In these instances, high density will interfere with the games and may accordingly reduce the fun.

SEX DIFFERENCES   Several studies suggest that men may be more adversely affected by high density than women. In two experiments (Freedman et al., 1972), all-male or all-female groups were put in high- or low-density conditions and various measures were taken of their competitiveness and the severity of sentencing they gave in a mock jury situation. It was found that men tended to respond more competitively and to give more severe sentences in the high-density condition than they did in the low-density condition. Women were actually less competitive and gave milder sentences under conditions of high density. Figure 16–2 shows the results of the jury study. In addition, the men in the group liked each other less under conditions of high density. In mixed-sex groups, there were no effects of density.

Other research has also found sex differences in response to crowding, but the effects are not entirely consistent. Most of the studies find that males are more sensitive to density than females, and that males tend to respond more negatively (Ross et al., 1973; Stokols et al., 1973; Paulus, 1980b). This is consistent with the finding described earlier in this chapter that men seem to prefer greater interpersonal distance in their interactions.

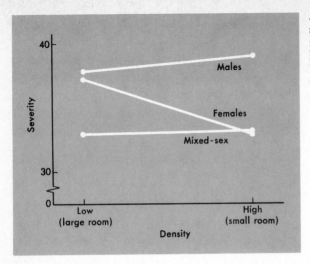

FIGURE 16–2 The effect of density on severity of sentences given by all male, all-female, and mixed-sex groups. Females give less severe sentences, males more severe in high-density situations. The effect in this study is much stronger for females than for males. (Based on Freedman et al., 1972.)

ENVIRONMENTAL STRESS: NOISE

It's Monday morning and Charlie begins his day driving to work. As he pulls onto the already congested freeway, he closes the car windows to keep out the noise and pollution of the city. Later, driving through a particularly narrow and dangerous stretch of highway, he feels his muscles tensing and notices that he is gripping the steering wheel. The summer day has begun to heat up, and Charlie feels a trickle of perspiration forming on his back. The urban landscape of highways, factories, and dreary tenements does little to improve his mood. Charlie fondly remembers the weekend he just spent in the mountains, where the air was crisp and clean. The country sounds of birds and crickets were a welcome relief from the din of the city. The lovely mountains and woods had created an atmosphere of calm and relaxation.

The physical environment has strong effects on our feelings and social interactions. One important factor is the extent to which the physical environment is stressful. Some environmental stressors, such as earthquakes or floods, are sudden and powerful; they dramatically alter people's lives. Also important, however, are the daily hassles created by environments that expose us to noise, heat, air pollution, and other irritants (Evans, 1982). Much research on stress in the physical environment has studied the effects of noise, and we will focus our discussion on that topic.

Unless you are in a specially constructed soundproof chamber, you are always exposed to noise. For those with normal hearing, sound is one of the most important means of knowing about and experiencing the world. A silent world is virtually impossible to imagine. However, psychologists are especially concerned about the effects of noise because so much of modern industrial life involves the production of noise, and because the amount of noise to which people are exposed in cities is often extremely high.

Not only do traffic, construction, machinery of all kinds, and powerful stereo equipment produce noise of great intensity, but millions of people in a relatively small area create high noise levels. In fact, one of the most striking as-

Laimute E. Druskis

The quiet serenity of the country is becoming a rare experience. In industrialized societies, most people live and work in cities where they are exposed to high levels of noise.

pects of cities is their constant high noise levels, as compared to suburbs and rural areas. According to the U.S. Bureau of the Census (1973), excessive noise is the most common neighborhood complaint of community residents. Just what effect does noise have on us?

Short-Term Noise

Sometimes we are exposed to short bursts of very loud noise—sounds of a dynamite blast from the construction site next door or the shrill barking of a neighbor's dog. Our initial reaction to a burst of very loud noise is strong. Everyone is familiar with one typical response—the so-called startle reflex. An unexpected loud noise causes us to jump, flex our stomach muscles, blink, and generally react physically. Even if we are expecting the noise, we respond physiologically with increased blood pressure, sweating, and other signs of arousal. In addition, loud noise interferes with our ability to perform tasks. We do less well on both simple and complex tasks. Clearly, loud noise is upsetting, causes

physiological arousal, and prevents us from functioning at our usual level.

ADAPTATION   However, these disruptive effects generally last only a short while. The most important finding from studies of short-term noise is that people adapt very quickly. It takes only a few minutes for physiological reactions to disappear and for performance to return to normal. After 10 minutes or less, people who are subjected to short bursts of extremely loud noise behave very much like people who hear moderate or low noise. This is true even for noise levels over 100 decibels, which is roughly equivalent to a big jet coming in low over your head or a huge truck rumbling by right next to you. As long as the noise is not so loud that it actually produces pain or physical damage, people adapt to it very quickly (Glass & Singer, 1972).

You can see this effect in a study by Glass and Singer in which people were exposed to background noise (no noise condition) or to a meaningless jumble of noise at 108 decibels in short burst for 23 minutes. As shown in Figure 16–3, the loud noise did cause physiological arousal, but the arousal lasted only a few min-

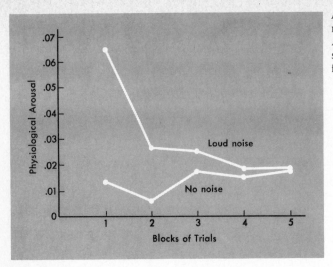

FIGURE 16–3 Physiological response (GSR) to loud noise. After a strong initial response, subjects adapt quickly. (Adapted from Glass & Singer, 1972.)

utes. Moreover, after 4 minutes, all subjects did equally well on a variety of tasks, including simple arithmetic, matching sets of numbers (deciding whether 68134 and 68243 are identical), scrambled words, and higher-level mathematics. Once they have gotten used to the noise, people perform almost any task as well with loud noise as they do in quieter environments.

There are a few important exceptions to this finding, however. In particular, noise does seem to affect performance on some kinds of tasks, expecially complex ones. Donald Broadbent (1957) and others have shown that certain kinds of monitoring tasks are more difficult to do with loud noise. For example, if someone is required to watch three dials to be sure none of them goes over a certain point, high levels of noise interfere with performance. Similarly, it is apparently harder to do two tasks at the same time in a noisy environment. In one study (Finkelman & Glass, 1970), subjects had to repeat digits they heard over headphones while at the same time turning a steering wheel to track a moving line. Noise level did not affect the primary task, which was the tracking, but it made the subjects less accurate at repeating the digits. Presumably, noise is distracting and interferes with the performance of complex tasks that already strain our capacity to concentrate.

Most of the time we are only doing one thing at a time, so the effects of noise are probably quite limited. On the other hand, it is well to remember that some sensitive jobs do involve exactly the kinds of complex monitoring tasks that seem to be affected by loud noise. The pilot of a plane must watch many different dials while operating a variety of instruments; flight controllers have similar problems; and even the typical driver of a car has many things to attend to at once. (It is a little frightening to realize that these critical jobs, especially those of pilot and flight controller, are performed under conditions of considerable noise.) With this potentially important exception, short-term exposure to loud noise appears to have little detrimental effect.

THE IMPORTANCE OF PREDICTABILITY AND CONTROL However, this is not the whole story about short-term noise. We have seen throughout this book that our reactions to situations are influenced by our ability to predict what will happen and to control it. A series of experiments by Glass and Singer (1972) demonstrated that loud noise may have negative aftereffects if the noise is not under the control of the individual. In particular, if the noise is predictable (occurring every 60 seconds or only when there is a warning) or if the person can turn off the noise, no bad effects occur. But if the noise seems to be totally out of the control of the person, certain kinds of performance may suffer once the noise ceases.

The experiments were straightforward but ingenious. Subjects heard bursts of noise for a set period of time while they performed tasks. Then they performed other tasks with no noise. The crucial variation was that the circumstances under which the noise occurred gave the person a sense of control or did not. In one study, people heard short bursts of loud or soft noise. The major variation was that the noise bursts came either exactly 1 minute apart (and were therefore predictable) or at random intervals. Even though subjects heard just as much noise in the two conditions, the effects were entirely different.

During the noise section of the study, all groups performed equally well regardless of how loud the noise was or whether it was predictable. But afterward, as shown in Table 16–1, those who had heard the predictable noise performed better than those who had heard random noise. In fact, unpredictable soft noise caused more errors than predictable loud noise. This was true despite the fact that subjects reported finding the predictable and unpredictable noise equally annoying.

In other studies, subjects were given a feeling of control by telling them they could stop the noise whenever they wanted to by pressing a button or by signaling their partner, who would then stop it. Even though subjects never did actually stop the noise, this feeling of control was apparently enough to eliminate the negative effects. There was no decline in performance either during or after the noise.

A later study (Sherrod, Hage, Halpern & Moore, 1977) replicated and extended these results. Subjects were allowed to start the noise, stop it, both start or stop it, or allowed no control whatever. As in the earlier work, control reduced the negative effects of the noise. Moreover, the more control they had, the better the people performed. In this study, unlike any previous work, the presence of uncontrollable noise actually caused subjects to do less well on a proofreading task while the noise was present. In line with the earlier work, the main result was that those exposed to controllable noise performed better on problems after the noise ended.

The importance of control may help us understand the effects of noise in the real world. Most of the noise in a city is fairly constant or predictable. There is the continuous noise of cars and trucks on the streets, periodic noise of trains in some communities, and the general din caused by many people. On the other hand, some noise is both unpredictable and uncontrollable. Jackhammers, firecrackers, backfiring cars, planes, and sudden loud music from radios fill the air with noise at random intervals and are therefore probably much more annoying than the usual background noise. It seems likely that the absolute level of the noise is less important than this unpredictability. Indeed, it is unpredictable kinds of noises that most people complain about.

Long-Term Exposure to Noise

Some research suggests that long-term exposure to noise can have detrimental effects. A large apartment house in New York City is built over a highway, and because of the design of the building, the noise levels inside are quite high. Lower floors are almost always noisier than higher ones, and this situation provides an ideal setting for a natural experiment on the effects of

Table 16–1
Aftereffects of Predictable and
Unpredictable Noise on Proofreading

CONDITION	NUMBER OF ERRORS
No noise	26.4
Soft predictable	27.4
Soft unpredictable	36.7
Loud predictable	31.8
Loud unpredictable	40.1

Source: Adapted from Glass and Singer (1972).

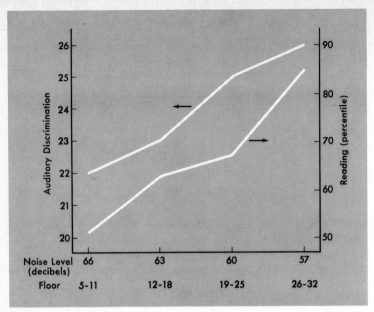

FIGURE 16-4 Noise level in apartment and children's reading and auditory skills. The lower the noise level, the better the children performed. (Adapted from Cohen, Glass, & Singer, 1973.)

long-term noise. Cohen, Glass, and Singer (1973) measured reading achievement and ability to make auditory discriminations of children who had lived in the building for at least four years.

As you can see in Figure 16-4, those who lived on lower floors did worse on both measures. The louder the noise on their floor, the less well they read and the poorer their auditory discriminations. More recent studies (such as Heff, 1979; Cohen, Evans, Krantz, Stokols & Kelly, 1981) have also found that noisy environments can impair children's intellectual performance. Studies further suggest that although people are able to adapt to short-term noise, they may not adapt to long-term noise, such as that experienced by those who live near a busy airport (Cohen & Weinstein, 1981).

How Noise Affects Social Behavior

In recent years, researchers have begun to investigate the impact of noise on social behaviors (Cohen & Weinstein, 1981). One finding is

that noise appears to reduce attention to social cues. In one study (Cohen & Lezak, 1977), students watched slides while learning lists of nonsense syllables in a noisy or a quiet room. The slides showed people in common daily activities and in dangerous situations. For example, one slide showed two men shaking hands in front of a house; another showed one man threatening another with a knife in front of a house. After seeing the slides, students were unexpectedly asked questions about them. Those exposed to noise remembered significantly fewer of the social situations than did those in the quiet condition.

Similarly, in a field study (Korte & Grant, 1980) pedestrians on noisy streets were less likely to notice unusual objects on the sidewalk (such as a woman holding a large teddy bear) than were pedestrians on a quiet street. In other words, loud noise may cause people to narrow the focus of their attention and so miss social cues in the environment.

In the chapter on prosocial behavior, we reviewed several studies showing that people are less helpful in noisy situations than in quiet ones. There is also some evidence that noise can increase aggressiveness (Geen & O'Neal, 1969). In one study (Donnerstein & Wilson, 1976), students were either angered or treated in a neutral manner, and then were given an opportunity to give electric "shocks" to another person as part of a learning experiment. Angered students in a noisy room gave significantly more shocks than did nonangered students or angered students in a quiet room.

A second experiment (Donnerstein & Wilson, 1976) demonstrated that perceived control can alter the noise-aggression link. In this study, students first worked on math problems in a high-noise or no-noise condition. Later, students were able to give electric "shocks" to another person as part of a learning experiment. Some students had been angered by a confederate of the researcher; some had not. Students who had been exposed to loud noise and angered gave more shocks than those who had not been angered or who had not been exposed to the noise. However, angered students who had been able to control the loud noise (to turn it off if they wanted to) were no more aggressive than those not exposed to the noise, even when they did not actually use their control.

These and other studies suggest that noise can sometimes increase aggressive behavior, but that this may only occur when people perceive no control over the noise and when they have an independent reason to be angry. In other words, noise may not be a direct cause of aggression, but rather may intensify preexisting aggressive tendencies.

ARCHITECTURAL DESIGN

One of the most fascinating questions facing environmental psychologists is how the design of buildings, roads, and shopping centers affects us. Certainly the structures we produce, the so-called **built environment,** are an extremely important part of our world. And some of them seem to "work" better than others. Some houses are pleasant to be in and function smoothly, others are not. Some stores minimize congestion and generally make the shopping experience relatively pleasant; others have the reverse effect. And the same is true about virtually every other structure we build.

Architects are deeply concerned with making their designs work well, but by and large they have to rely entirely on their own intuition and experience. Until very recently there was no systematic research on how design affects people, and even now psychologists and sociologists are only beginning to study the problem seriously. But at least they are beginning to understand some of the ways in which design influences people, and perhaps soon they will be able to give some guidance to architects based on solid research. For the moment, most of the research done by psychologists has been on the structure of dormitories (obviously of interest to many people at universities) and high-rise versus low-rise housing.

Dormitory Design

College dormitories are generally built according to two different designs. One type has single or double rooms located along a long corridor, with social areas and bathrooms shared by all corridor residents. A second type has suites of rooms consisting of several bedrooms located around a common living room, usually with the residents of just these bedrooms sharing bathroom facilities. The amount of space available to each resident is approximately the same for both designs. Yet the two designs seem to have different effects on the residents.

A series of studies (Baum & Valins, 1977; Baum et al., 1978) compared corridor and suite arrangements. The research indicates that students who live in suite-type dormitories are more sociable and friendlier. At first glance, this seems obvious. Clearly, if you share a living room with, say, nine other people (five bedrooms with two people each), you will get to know these nine other students. In a sense, you have a "family" living situation. If you share a room with only one person, it takes greater effort to get to know other people on the floor.

As we noted in Chapter 8, proximity is one of the major factors in liking and friendship. The suite arrangement puts more people in close proximity and therefore should lead to more friendships. Thus far, this follows directly from our knowledge of the effects of proximity and certainly would be expected. The striking aspect of Baum's and Valins's work is that these sociability differences seem to carry over into the world outside the dormitory. When the students are observed in the psychology laboratory, the suite residents are friendlier than the corridor residents. For example, in one study a student arrived at the laboratory and was shown into a room in which another student (actually a confederate) was sitting. There were several chairs in the room, and the question was how close to the other student the subject would sit. Suite residents tended to sit closer than corridor residents, and to initiate more conversations.

One problem with this research is that students are not always randomly assigned to rooms. Perhaps more sociable people request assignment to suites. Another problem is that suites are sometimes newer than corridor dorms, and the two types of housing are sometimes located on different parts of the campus. To overcome these problems, Baum and Davis (1980) conducted an intervention experiment. They obtained permission to assign first-year women students randomly to living conditions. To further control the environment, the researchers devised the architectural intervention shown in Figure 16–5.

Baum and Davis selected two identical long-corridor floors in the same building, each housing about 40 students. On the intervention floors, they converted several bedrooms in the middle of the corridor into lounges and installed doors to divide the corridor into two smaller units, each housing about 20 students. As a further comparison, they studied a "short" corridor in another building that also housed about 20 students. In all settings, students had about the same amount of physical space, and the density was relatively high. The researchers gave questionnaires to dorm residents at the beginning of the school year and at several times during the year. They made systematic observations of social interactions in the dorm and of behavior in a laboratory situation.

The results of this experiment were very consistent with earlier findings. After living in the dorm for several weeks, residents on the short corridors reported feeling less crowded, having fewer problems regulating social contacts in the dorm, and having a greater sense of control over life in the dorm than did students on the long corridor. Short-corridor residents also reported that they were more successful in forming friends in the dorm, and they were observed to have more social interactions in lounges and corridors. In the laboratory, students who had been randomly assigned to short corridors showed greater friendliness toward a research confederate and expected to have more control over the experiment than did long-corridor residents. These results provide strong evidence that an architectural design feature—in this case the size of the residential living group—can significantly affect feelings and social interactions.

Two main factors appear to be at work in these dormitory settings. First, smaller residential units (suites and short corridors) are more conducive to group formation and friendship than are larger units. Since it is usually more pleasant to interact with friends than with strangers, dorm designs that encourage friendships are experienced as more positive. Second, smaller residential units increase students' sense of personal control over the environment. In long-corridor dorms, students are constantly being required to meet and interact with many

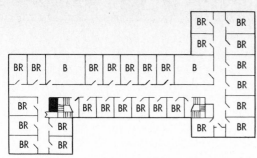

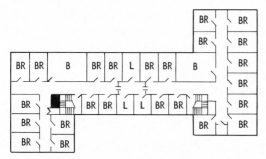

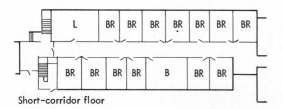

Long-corridor floor

Intervention floor

Short-corridor floor

BR = Bedroom
B = Bathroom
L = Lounge

FIGURE 16–5

Floor plans of the dormitory floors. The intervention floor was originally identical to the long-corridor floor but was remodeled to form two short corridors separated by doors and lounges. The short-corridor floor was in another building. (Adapted from Baum & Davis, 1980, p. 475.)

others on the floor. When they walk to the bathroom or common lounge areas, they necessarily share the corridor and facilities with many others, most of whom are not friends and with whom they might prefer not to interact.

Thus, they are overloaded with social contacts and have difficulty avoiding them. In contrast, those who live in suites or short corridors have a self-contained living unit they share only with people they get to know quite well. They therefore have much more control over their social interactions, which presumably increases satisfaction with their residence and their general sense of control over their lives.

High-Rise and Low-Rise Housing

Although students are naturally quite concerned about dormitory design, a much more serious problem for our society is how high-rise housing affects people. Since the 1950s, vast numbers of high-rise buildings have been constructed for our rapidly expanding population. Some of these buildings are huge—thirty or forty stories, with hundreds or even thousands of individual apartments. Others are smaller. But all contrast sharply with the private homes or four- or five-story apartment houses characteristic of previ-

BOX 16–3
Building Better Classrooms

College classrooms are often drab and dreary places. Walls are painted a variation of "institutional gray"; furniture is easy to clean, but uncomfortable and unattractive. Chairs are lined up in straight rows facing the teacher's desk or lectern. In one study (Farrenkopf, 1974), over 80 percent of students at one university rated their classrooms negatively, describing them as ugly, cramped, stuffy, uncomfortable, and so on. Research by environmental psychologists is beginning to show that unattractive classrooms are not only unappealing, they may also affect academic performance.

In a demonstration study by Sommer and Olsen (1980), a typical small classroom was converted into what the researchers called a "soft classroom." Rows of chairs were replaced with cushioned benches around the walls, carpets were added, lighting was made softer, and colorful mobiles were hung. Students reacted enthusiastically with such comments as "It's dynamite," or "I'm really impressed!" Comparisons of student behavior in the soft classroom and other classrooms on campus suggested that student participation in class discussion was two or three times greater in the more attractive room.

A more carefully controlled study of classroom environments was conducted by Wollin and Montage (1981). They selected two identical classrooms located side by side in the psychology building. The control classroom, which they called the "sterile classroom," had white walls, a gray carpet, and rows of plastic desks. The experimental classroom, which they called the "friendly classroom," was redecorated with the help of a design consultant. Several walls were painted bright colors, art posters were hung

on the walls, large plants were added to the room, and brightly colored Chinese kites were hung from the ceiling. In addition to traditional desks, a part of the room was outfitted with area rugs, color-coordinated cushions, and wooden cubes to provide nontraditional seating.

The researchers investigated how these two different environments affected performance in actual college classes. Two professors teaching introductory psychology agreed to participate in the study, although they were not informed of the purpose of the research. When school began, each class was randomly assigned to one of the two rooms. Halfway through the term, the classes switched rooms, so that students in both classes spent half the term in the control room and half in the "friendly" room. Students were not told they were being studied; the switch in rooms was explained as occurring because the original room was needed for videotaping.

The most striking finding from this study is that students performed significantly better on regular course exams when they were in the friendly rather than the sterile classroom. It thus appears that the physical environment can affect the amount of learning that occurs, at least as measured by scores on tests. In addition, students were asked to evaluate their instructor halfway through the term and again at the end of the term. The instructors were rated significantly more positively during the time the class met in the attractive classroom. In the experimental room instructors were evaluated as more knowledgeable, more interesting, and better organized than they were in the control room. So our evaluations of other people are at least partly influenced by the physical setting in which we interact with them.

---

ous housing. It has become a matter of great social importance to determine whether high-rise housing of this sort is a good environment in which to live.

THE FAILURES: PRUITT IGOE Some high-rise buildings have been failures. They have gotten run down, the halls have been defaced, the apartments have been allowed to deteriorate, crime and vandalism have made the buildings unsafe, and people have moved out whenever they were able. The most dramatic example of this kind of failure is the Pruitt Igoe project built in the 1950s in St. Louis. Designed by a leading architect, the complex had 33 high-rise buildings with 2,800 modern apartments. Built with public funds for low- and middle-income families, this "showcase" project became a disaster.

Located in the midst of an urban slum, the project never attracted middle-income families who could afford to live in better neighborhoods, and so rental revenues were less than anticipated. Teenage gangs invaded the halls and elevators to rob and terrorize residents. Walls were covered with graffitti, and physical conditions deteriorated as needed maintenance and repairs were not made. Tenants who could find other housing moved out. Ultimately, conditions deteriorated to such a point that the buildings were condemned and torn down. This multimillion-dollar housing project was a total loss.

PSYCHOLOGICAL EFFECTS: SOME IMPORTANT FACTORS On the one hand, we know that most high-rise buildings, both public and private, have been successful at least to the extent that people continue to live in them and function reasonably well. In cities such as Toronto, San

Francisco, and Boston, high-rise apartments and condominiums in fashionable neighborhoods are considered very desirable. The central question addressed by environmental psychologists is whether high-rise and low-rise buildings have different psychological effects on residents, and in particular, whether high-rise housing is typically harmful.

In general, research does not find major differences between the health or general well-being of those who live in high-rise versus low-rise housing. A few studies (Holahan & Wilcox, 1978; McCarthy & Saegert, 1978) have found that high-rise residents are less happy with their social relations, more concerned about safety, and feel more crowded. But other studies (Michelson, 1977; Friedman, 1979) have found the opposite: High-rise residents reported feeling more content with their buildings and more satisfied with their social relations. Overall, few consistent differences have been found.

In understanding these results, it is important to keep in mind that the experience of high-rise living can vary considerably: Living in the penthouse of a beautiful high-security apartment building is quite different from living at the top of a poorly maintained public housing project in a rundown area. Further, it is likely that high-rise housing (or for that matter any kind of housing) may not be suitable for everyone. Although none of the research produced consistent differences between high- and low-rise housing, there is no question that some people prefer one or the other.

Parents with young children often complain that high-rise housing presents great difficulties in supervising the children (Michelson, 1970). Someone who lives on the twentieth floor cannot watch a child in the playground on the street floor. Many parents are reluctant to let their young children ride elevators alone, so that even if they can play on the street, it is inconvenient to get them there. Perhaps because of this, residents of high-rise housing are often less satisfied with their housing than are people who live in their own homes. Moreover, high-rise residents do not value the friendliness of their neighborhood as much (Wellman & Whitaker, 1974). None of these differences is large or related to any noticeable differences in health or general satisfaction, but the differences do exist. In other words, people complain more about high-rise housing, even though research has not shown any actual negative effects.

As with the dormitory design studies, research on high-rise housing faces enormous difficulty in equating the residents of the various kinds of buildings. People are not randomly assigned to housing in our society, so that residents of different buildings almost always differ in potentially important ways. In cities like New York, which has many high-rise apartments, upper-, middle-, and working-class families all live in high-rise buildings. Many people who can afford to live anywhere choose to live in a high-rise building in the middle of New York City. In other words, high-rise buildings are not only for low-income families. But middle- and upper-class families do generally have a choice, whereas poorer families often are forced to live in a high-rise because it is the only housing available.

This lack of choice may itself cause problems, and it should therefore probably be a matter of public policy to provide choice for all people. That is, if we continue to build high-rise apartments for low-income people, we should also provide the alternative of low-rise buildings for these same people. Although high-rise buildings may not have any negative effects, being forced to live in one (or to live anywhere with no choice) may be psychologically harmful.

LIFE IN THE CITY

The United States and Canada are largely urban societies, with more than 70 percent of the population living in or around cities. So it becomes important to ask how living in cities differs from living elsewhere. This question is especially relevant today. In addition to financial problems, our cities are beset by high crime rates, run-down schools, heavy welfare rolls, and high unemployment. In recent years, public opinion about cities has become increasingly negative. In a 1978 Gallup poll asking Americans whether they would prefer to live in a city, a suburb, a small town or on a farm, only 13 percent chose the city. Of those who actually lived in cities, only 21 percent said they preferred city living.

City dwellers are more likely than others to criticize their community, and to complain about schools, housing, taxes, and lack of safety (Fischer, 1976). On the other hand, people continue to move to metropolitan areas, suggesting that cities must also hold positive attractions. In fact, as we will see, research indicates that city life does not have negative psychological effects on people. The city may not be to everyone's liking, but it is not inherently harmful to mental health or personal relationships.

PHYSICAL AND SOCIAL ENVIRONMENT   The experience of living in cities is affected by both the physical and the social environment (Fischer, 1976). Physically, big cities are typically noisier, dirtier, and more polluted than small towns. Urban population density often necessitates high-rise apartments rather than single-family homes. In the city, trees and grass give way to concrete and asphalt. But although such factors as noise and high-rise buildings may be unpleasant, they do not necessarily have negative consequences. Further, cities offer many advantages that may compensate for the difficulties of urban life. It is in cities that we find major art museums, theaters, and concert halls; the latest medical tech-

City dwellers are routinely exposed to crowds and to people from many different social backgrounds. Whether the experience of city life is perceived as exciting and stimulating, or as cramped and unpleasant, is largely a matter of personal taste.

Rhoda Galyn, Photo Researchers, Inc.

nology; financial and political centers; specialized stores and services.

The social context of city living also differs from that of towns and rural areas. High social density is the hallmark of the city, and urbanites are more often exposed to crowds. Cities also have people from many ethnic, racial, and religious backgrounds. The social composition of cities differs from that of small towns. Cities tend to attract people who are younger, less likely to be married, have fewer children, and are higher in socioeconomic status. New immigrants are also likely to gravitate to urban centers. Do these differences in the physical and social environment of cities harm city dwellers?

PHYSICAL AND MENTAL HEALTH   In terms of physical and mental health, living in town versus city is not an important factor (Fischer, 1976). Whatever advantages people in small communities may have in terms of lower stress and a more healthful environment are apparently offset by the urbanite's greater access to health care services. Rates of mental disturbance and psychosis are about the same for those who live in cities, small towns, and even rural communities (Srole, 1972). Nor do city people feel any more anxious or unhappy than other people.

In a survey of a large number of Americans (Shaver & Freedman, 1976), those who lived in cities said that they were just as happy and calm as those who lived in small towns or rural areas. These findings are all the more striking since city dwellers do report less satisfaction with their living environment than those who live outside of cities. Apparently dissatisfaction with facets of city living does not affect people's personal feelings of happiness and overall life satisfaction.

A study (Franck, 1980) of people who had recently moved to New York City or to a small town in upstate New York sheds light on this finding. The newcomers in this research were all beginning graduate students who were interviewed during the first year in their new environment. Newcomers to New York City were more likely than those in the small town to re-

port that the move increased their fears about crime and safety, and made them more distrustful of other people. City residents were more likely to report being stressed by exposure to panhandlers, drunks, addicts, and "crazies."

However, the big city people also reported many compensating positive features of the urban experience. They came to enjoy the variety of people they saw in the city and felt that they had become more broadminded. In other words, city life has not only unique problems, but unique pleasures as well.

SOCIAL RELATIONS   It has been suggested that one of the most pernicious effects of urban life may be to weaken social relationships. Sociologist George Simmel (1903) thought that city residents would be so overloaded by superficial contacts that they would have fewer intimate friends than those who live in smaller communities. However, despite the common belief that life in the big city leads to alienation and social isolation, empirical research seriously challenges this view.

In a recent survey study, Claude Fischer (1982) obtained detailed information about the social relations of more than 1,000 people living in large cities, suburbs, small towns, and semirural areas in northern California. Overall, no differences were found between city dwellers and others in the number of their social ties or the quality of their social relations. For example, city dwellers were as likely as townspeople to report having someone they could talk to about personal matters; the overall level of social support available to an individual was not related to community size.

Fischer did find, however, that people in cities differed somewhat in the types of relationships they had. Urbanites reported fewer ties to relatives, neighbors, or church groups, and more ties to friends, co-workers, and others with similar interests or hobbies. Fischer explains this pattern largely in terms of self-selection. For instance, city dwellers are more likely to be young, unmarried, or foreign-born—all factors that would reduce relations with relatives, and increase ties to friends and associates. The important point is that those who live in big cities report just as much "social connectedness" as those who live in smaller communities.

The newcomer study adds further to this portrait of city life. Franck (1980) found that newcomers to New York City and to a smaller town were equally successful in making friends, but it took the city dwellers somewhat longer to do so. Shortly after arriving, city dwellers reported having fewer friends than those in the small town, but several months later this difference had disappeared. City dwellers said they found it harder to make friends, but ultimately they had just as many friends as people in the smaller community.

The one aspect of social relations that is affected by community size is interaction with strangers (Korte, 1980). We have already seen that city dwellers are more fearful of crime, more concerned about their personal safety, and more distrustful of others. Perhaps not surprisingly, people in cities are less likely to help a stranger in distress than are people in smaller communities (see Chapter 11). Research (Korte, 1980) has found that in urban environments people are usually less likely to help someone who dials a wrong telephone number, to return a "lost" letter, to do small favors, to help a lost child, or to let a stranger use a phone.

DIVERSITY OF LIFE STYLE   Although city dwellers are less helpful to strangers, they are also more accepting of others whose life styles differ from their own. The populations of small towns tend to be more homogeneous than those of cities with respect to race, religion, ethnic background, sexual orientation, political views, and just about anything else you can think of. People who do not fit comfortably in a small town often seek like-minded companions in the big city. Cities tend to attract people who are "different" from the average, and to treat these groups better. It is not surprising, for example, that the largest and most visible homosexual communities are found in major metropolitan areas. It is not that cities produce alternate life styles, but rather that city dwellers are more accepting of individual differences.

In fact, one study (Hansson & Slade, 1977) found that city people were actually more helpful toward an extremist group, in this case the Communist Party, than were people in small towns. In this study, the experimenters dropped letters that were addressed to an individual, to someone who was apparently performing at the "Pink Panther Lounge," or to the Communist Party headquarters. The researchers counted how many of each "lost" letter were returned. The townspeople returned somewhat more letters to the individual and the Pink Panther Lounge, but many fewer to the Communist Party. The authors concluded that people in small towns may be somewhat more helpful as long as the person in need belongs to an acceptable category; the city people were much more helpful toward nonconformists.

By this point, it should be clear that reactions to the city depend on the particular individual. Just as some people like high levels of stimulation and others do not, so some people are city lovers and some are not. Individuals have optimal levels of stimulation, which may actually change as they live in one type of environment or another (Geller, 1980). If you like a high level of stimulation, you may enjoy cities, find them exciting and invigorating, and dislike small towns as dull and uninteresting. The key issue is the match between the person's characteristics and the community. Indeed, research (Shaver & Freedman, 1976) indicates that people who do not like their community (whatever it is) tend to be less happy and healthy. Although the size of the community does not affect happiness, an individual's satisfaction with the community does.

SUMMARY

1. Environmental psychology considers how the physical environment affects people's behavior and well-being. The field has concentrated on such topics as how humans use space, crowding, noise, the design of buildings, and life in the city.

2. Proxemics is a general term for the study of how people use space. Personal space refers to the physical space immediately around a person that the person treats as an extension of the self. The distance we prefer to stand from other people depends on our ethnic background, our gender, and our relation to the people. Hall has distinguished four basic zones for interpersonal interaction: intimate, personal, social, and public distance.

3. A territory is an area controlled by a person or group. Altman has distinguished primary, secondary, and public territories. People use various markers to identify and lay claim to their territory. Our reaction to someone who enters our territory depends on how we interpret the act—as friendly, rude, hostile, and so on.

4. Crowding is the subjective experience of feeling cramped and not having enough space. In contrast, social density refers to the objective number of people in a given area. According to the sensory overload theory of crowding, high social density creates an unpleasantly high level of stimulation. According to the density-intensity theory, high social density intensifies usual reactions to a social situation, making bad situations worse and good ones better. A third theory emphasizes that high density may cause people to experience a distressing loss of personal control.

5. Research shows that crowding does not necessarily have harmful consequences. High population density in cities is not a cause of crime or mental illness. In laboratory studies, even very high density conditions do not usually impair task performance or lead to antisocial behavior. In some situations, however, high density can be harmful. For example, students living in tripled dorm rooms and prisoners sharing cramped cells may show signs of distress. Men seem to be more sensitive to social density than women. High density is probably most harmful when it interferes with accomplishing specific goals and when it is associated with a perceived loss of control.

6. Noise affects us less than we might think. As long as noise is not so loud that it causes physical damage, people adapt to short exposure to loud noise and perform most tasks at their normal level. Only complex tasks seem to be impaired by short-term loud noise. Prolonged exposure to loud noise can have negative effects on hearing and intellectual performance.

7. Architectural design can influence people's behavior. College students who live in suite-type dormitories and in small living units are more sociable and friendlier than those who live on long corridors. Smaller residential units may make it easier to form friendships and may increase a sense of personal control. However, high-rise housing is not necessarily worse than low-rise housing.

8. Urban living is not generally less healthy than living in other kinds of communities. People often find that the difficulties of city life are offset by the advantages of being in a cultural and business center. The effect of community size depends on the preferences and characteristics of the individual.

SUGGESTIONS FOR ADDITIONAL READING

BAUM, A., & SINGER, J. E. (Eds). 1982. *Advances in environmental psychology. Vol 4. Environment and health.* Hillsdale, NJ: Erlbaum. The latest volume in this continuing series presents research on how health is affected by such environmental factors as crowding, noise, and air quality.

EVANS, G. W. (Ed.). 1981. Environmental stress. *Journal of Social Issues, 37.* The entire issue of this journal is devoted to studies of the effects of environmental factors as crowding, noise, and air quality.

FISCHER, C. S. 1984. *The urban experience,* 2nd ed. New York: Harcourt Brace Jovanovich. A readable review of research and theories about life in cities.

FISHER, J. D., BELL, P. A. & BAUM, A. (1984). *Environmental psychology* (2nd ed.). New York: Holt, Rinehart, and Winston. An up-to-date survey of the field of environmental psychology.

FREEDMAN, J. L. 1975. *Crowding and behavior.* San Francisco: Freeman. Presents all research on crowding up to that date, as well as the author's theory.

SOMMER, R. 1969. *Personal space: The behavioral basis for design.* Englewood Cliffs, NJ: Prentice-Hall. A classic discussion of the topic.

GLOSSARY

Actor-Observer Bias The tendency for observers to overestimate the importance of the actor's dispositions, and for the actor to overestimate the importance of the situation, in explaining the actor's behavior.

Affective Component Emotional feelings associated with beliefs about an attitude object; consists mainly of the evaluation of the object (like-dislike, pro-con).

Agenda-Setting Mass communications that focus the public's attention on certain issues, and therefore determine what issues the public is concerned about. If the media focus intensively on inflation, the public becomes concerned with inflation; if they focus on Central America, so will the public.

Aggression Any action intended to hurt others; may also refer to internal state of wanting to hurt others (aggressive feelings).

Aggression Anxiety Anxiety about expressing overt aggression, usually with respect to a particular target.

Altruism An act performed voluntarily to help others when there is no expectation of receiving a reward in any form.

Androgynous In psychology, the term used to refer to people who believe they possess both traditionally feminine and traditionally masculine characteristics. An androgynous person's self-concept includes both masculine and feminine qualities—for instance, seeing oneself as both independent and nurturant, strong and emotionally expressive.

Antisocial Aggression Aggressive acts such as murder that violate commonly accepted social norms.

Applied Research Research designed to answer questions about specific, real-world issues, usually without concern for any general theoretical or scientific issues.

Archival Research Techniques based on the analysis of data already available in published records.

Assimilation The tendency to perceive a communication of low discrepancy as being even less discrepant than it is in fact. That is, the target overestimates agreement with a communicator who disagrees only moderately with him or her.

Association Linking different stimuli that occur together in place and time. Through pairing, evaluations of one stimulus become associated with those of the other; one of the basic processes by which learning occurs.

Attitude Enduring response disposition with a cognitive component, an affective component, and a behavioral component. We develop and hold attitudes toward persons, objects, and ideas.

Attitude-Discrepant Behavior Acts inconsistent with a person's attitudes. When an individual behaves in a way inconsistent with a belief, dissonance is produced and there is a tendency for the attitude to change.

Attribution Process by which people make inferences about the causes of attitudes or behavior. *Attribution theory* describes the principles by which these attributions are determined, and the effect they have.

Averaging Principle The theory that various informational inputs about a person or other attitude object are processed solely in terms of their evaluation of the object, then averaged together to form an overall attitude.

Balance Model or Theory Heider's theoretical model, in which unbalanced relationships (those with an odd number of negative relationships) between two persons and an object tend to change toward balanced ones.

Basic Research Research designed to examine general relationships among phenomena rather than specific questions about particular issues.

Behavioral Component That part of an attitude consisting of the person's tendencies to act toward the attitude object. A child's attitude toward her pet cat may include the tendencies to pet it and cuddle it.

Behavioral Intention The person's intention to behave, which is a crucial determinant of actual behavior according to the "theory of reasoned action." How much you intend to study for an exam is a major determinant of how much you actually will study for it.

Behavioral Sink The term used by Calhoun to describe the finding that rats placed in very high-density cages showed antisocial and disruptive behavior.

Behaviorism The learning theory popular for many years, and associated with Watson, Pavlov, and Skinner. It investigated only overt behavior, not subjective states such as thoughts, feelings, or attitudes. It placed primary emphasis on learning and reinforcement as the determinants of behavior.

Body Language Information transmitted about attitudes, emotions, and so on by nonverbal bodily movements and gestures, such as posture, stance, touch, and so on.

Brainstorming A technique for coming up with new and creative solutions for problems. Members of a group discuss a problem and generate as many different solutions as they can, withholding criticism until all possibilities have been presented.

Breakpoints The perceived starting or ending points of a behavioral act, as perceived by an observer.

Built Environment Buildings, roads, shopping centers, and other structures built by humans.

Bystander Effect The more people present, the less likely it is that any one person will offer help to a person in distress. The diffusion of responsibility created by the presence of other people is one explanation of the bystander effect.

Categorization The process by which we perceive stimuli in groups or categories rather than perceiving each individual stimulus in isolation from the others.

Catharsis Freud's idea that the aggressive drive can be reduced by expressing and thus releasing aggression.

Central Traits Extent to which a trait is central to an impression through being associated with the stimulus person's other characteristics. Traits such as warm or cold are considered central because they are important in determining impressions.

Cognitive Component That part of an attitude consisting of the person's beliefs, knowledge, and facts about the attitude object.

Cognitive Consistency Tendency for people to seek consistency among their attitudes; regarded as a major determinant of attitude formation and change.

Cognitive Dissonance Theory developed by Festinger according to which inconsistency (dissonance) between two cognitive elements produces pressure to make these elements consonant. It has been applied to a wide range of phenomena, including decisions and attitude-discrepant behavior.

Cognitive Miser Description of people as having limited information-processing capabilities, and therefore adopting various cognitive shortcuts. For example, we cannot perceive all stimuli in our perceptual field at once, so we focus on the most salient ones.

Cognitive Response Theory The theory that attitude change following receipt of communication depends on the cognitive responses it evokes. If it produces negative thoughts, it will be rejected; if it evokes positive thoughts, it will be accepted. Counterarguing is a crucial mechanism for resisting persuasion, according to this theory.

Cohesiveness The forces, both positive and negative, that cause members to remain in a group. Cohesiveness is a characteristic of a group as a whole, and results from the degree of *commitment* of each individual group member to the group.

Commitment to an Attitude The extent to which a person is tied to, involved in, or for any reason finds it difficult to give up an attitude, judgment, or other kind of position. Higher commitment reduces conformity and attitude change.

Commitment to a Relationship All the forces that act to keep a person in a relationship or group. Positive forces include interpersonal attraction and satisfaction with a relationship; negative forces include such barriers to ending a relationship as the lack of alternatives or having made large investments in the relationship.

Companionate Love A somewhat practical type of love that emphasizes trust, caring, and tolerance of the partner's flaws. Companionate love may develop slowly in a relationship as partners become more interdependent. *See also* passionate love.

Comparison Level One standard we use to evaluate the quality of our social relationships. Our comparison level refers to the level of benefits we believe we deserve based on our past experience in relationships.

Comparison Level for Alternatives A second standard we use to evaluate the quality of our social relationships. Our comparison level for alternatives refers to evaluating one particular relationship against other relationships that are currently available to us.

Compliance Performance of an act at another's request.

Conformity Voluntary performance of an act because others also do it.

Contagious Violence Spreading of the aggressive feelings or behavior of a small number of people throughout the entire group, as described by Le-Bon and others. Most frequently used to describe mob violence.

Contingency Model of Leadership Effectiveness Fiedler's model distinguishing between task-oriented and relationship-oriented leaders. When the group situation is either highly favorable or highly unfavorable to control by the leader, task-oriented leaders are more effective. In intermediate situations where the leader has moderate control, relationship-oriented leaders are more successful.

Contrast Tendency to perceive a communicator's position as being farther away from the individual's own position than it actually is.

Correlational Research Design Passively measuring two variables and determining whether or not they are associated with each other. Studies relating smoking to lung cancer are correlational: They measure the amount of smoking each person has done and whether or not he or she gets lung cancer, and determine whether the two are related. The major problem with correlational designs is determining whether or not the correlation, if it exists, reflects a cause-and-effect relationship.

Covariation Attributing a particular event to a particular cause when the two always occur together and never occur separately. The *covariation model* describes the particular kinds of information we use in arriving at causal attributions for social events.

Credibility How expert a communicator is perceived to be about the topic of communication and how much he or she is trusted by the individual receiving the communication.

Crowding The subjective experience of feeling cramped and not having enough space.

Cultural Stereotypes Societal-level images of members of a social group such as those found in art, literature, religious teachings, and the mass media.

Deindividuation Loss of a sense of personal identity and responsibility in a group, which can lead people to do things they would normally not do when alone. Anonymity is a key factor in deindividuation.

Dependent Variable The responses to the independent variable being manipulated or measured in a study.

Deviant Being seen as or actually being different from others.

Discounting Cue A cue associated with a communication that reduces its persuasive influence, such as a low-prestige source. If, over time, the association between communication and the cue erodes, the influence of the communication may increase.

Discounting Principle The tendency in making attributions to reduce reliance upon one particular cause to the extent that other plausible causes exist. If, for example, a judge gives the death penalty to a criminal, we might conclude that she was generally a tough judge, but we would be less likely to do so if we also discovered that the law demanded the death penalty for the crime that was committed.

Discrepancy The distance between the communicator's and the target's position on the issue discussed in the communication. A communicator may argue that tuition should be doubled; that position will be highly discrepant to a student who believes it should not change, but only moderately discrepant to a student who thinks a modest increase is reasonable.

Discrimination The behavioral component of group antagonism. People discriminate against the disliked group by refusing its members access to desired jobs or educational opportunities, or to country clubs, restaurants, places of entertainment, and so on.

Disinhibition General loosening of the tight control over anger when it has once been released under socially approved conditions; that is, once a person has committed a socially approved aggressive act, he or she has fewer inhibitions about aggressing under other conditions.

Displacement Expression of aggression toward a target other than the source of frustration or annoyance. Typically, it occurs because the original source is not available or because the reasons for restraining aggression against this other target are weaker.

Distraction Stimulus that draws attention away from a persuasive message. It sometimes increases attitude change by making it harder for people to defend a position against the arguments in the message.

Emotional Loneliness A type of loneliness that results from the absence of an intimate attachment relationship, such as might be provided for children by their parents or for adults by a spouse or close friend. *See also* loneliness; social loneliness.

Empathic Concern Feelings of sympathy and caring for others—in particular, sharing vicariously or indirectly in the suffering of other people. Strong feelings of empathic concern would motivate a person to help someone in need.

Environmental Psychology A relatively new branch of psychology that studies the relationships between the physical environment and human behavior and well-being.

Equity Theory An offshoot of social *exchange theory* that focuses on fairness in relationships. A relationship is said to be equitable when the ratio of a person's profits to contributions is the same for everyone. The theory postulates that when individuals perceive inequity in a relationship, they feel distress and take steps to restore equity.

Evaluation Most important basic dimension underlying impression formation and attitudes; the goodness or badness of another person, object, or concept.

Exchange Theory An analysis of interpersonal interaction in terms of the costs and benefits each person gives and receives. Because people in a relationship or group are interdependent (that is, the outcomes one person receives depend on what others do and vice versa), individuals must coordinate their behavior to maximize their joint benefits. This is one of the incentive or rational choice theories of social interaction.

Expectancy-Value Theory A theory of decision

making that predicts the person will choose whatever is highest in goal desirability and probability of goal attainment.

Experimental Research Design Type of research in which the researcher randomly assigns people to two or more conditions, varies in a controlled manner the treatment each condition is given, and then measures the effects on the subjects' responses. Though experiments are often difficult to arrange, they have the advantage of yielding clear information about cause and effect, because any differences between groups in the outcome of the experiment must of necessity be due to the variables that were experimentally manipulated.

External Validity Extent to which the results of a study are generalizable to other populations and settings.

Fantasy Aggression An imagined act of aggression. It may tend to reduce direct aggression.

Field Experiment Study in which variables are systematically manipulated and measured in real-life, nonlaboratory settings.

Figure-Ground Principle The principle that people's attention is drawn to stimuli that stand out against a background. Figural stimuli are those that stand out; the background is called the ground. This basic perceptual principle has generated much of the research on salience in the area of social perception.

Foot-in-the-Door Technique Method of increasing compliance with a large request by first getting the person to comply with a smaller request.

Frustration The blocking or thwarting of goal-directed behavior. A child is frustrated when a parent refuses to let her color the bathroom wallpaper with crayons or smear her ice cream on the dining room table.

Fundamental Attribution Error The tendency for observers to overestimate the causal importance of a person's dispositions and underestimate the importance of the situation when they explain the person's actions.

Gender Identity The knowledge that we are male or female. Our gender identity is acquired early in life.

Gender Self-Concept The degree to which a person perceives that he or she possesses traditionally masculine or feminine characteristics.

Gender Stereotypes Beliefs about the typical personal attributes of women and men. According to traditional gender stereotypes, for example, women are believed to be nurturant and passive, and men are seen as independent and aggressive.

Gender Typing The process of labeling things and activities as "masculine" and "feminine." For ex-

ample, many people consider dolls, ruffles, and housecleaning to be feminine.

Gestalt The view that people form coherent and meaningful perceptions based on the entire perceptual field, so that the whole is different from the sum of its parts.

Group A social aggregate in which members are interdependent (have mutual influence on one another) and have at least the potential for mutual interaction.

Groupthink Term coined by Janis to describe an impairment in decision-making and sound judgment that can occur in highly cohesive groups with a strong, dynamic leader. Group members isolate themselves from outside information, try to please the group leader, and agree on a decision even if it is irrational.

Group Polarization When a group discusses an issue, people often come to support more extreme positions than they did initially. This sometimes leads to a *risky shift* and sometimes to a cautious shift, depending on the initial views of group members.

Halo Effect A liked person being perceived as having good qualities of all kinds, even in things the perceiver is ignorant of.

Hawthorne Effect The fact that when workers are involved in an experiment, performance tends to improve, because they receive more attention, get more involved in their work, and feel more important. Named after a famous experiment done at the Hawthorne plant of the Western Electric Company.

Illusion of Control A bias in causal attribution whereby we perceive ourselves as being able to control our lives and events around us more than is probably the case in fact.

Imitation Learning by watching what others do and doing the same; also applies to forming attitudes by modeling those of others, such as parents or teachers.

Implicit Personality Theory The ordinary person's theory about which personality traits go with other traits, such as that "weak" goes with "cowardly," or "calm" goes with "decisive."

Independent Variable The variable in a study that is interpreted as the cause of changes in the dependent variable. The independent variable may be systematically manipulated by the experimenter in an experiment, or passively measured in a correlational study.

Informed Consent The requirement that research subjects must freely choose to participate, after being informed of what the study is about, the procedures that will be used, and the costs and benefits of the study.

Inoculation McGuire's notion that people are more resistant to the effects of persuasive communications when they are exposed to weak counter-arguments.

Instrumental Aggression Aggression committed not with the intent of hurting another person for the sake of hurting, but to use hurting as a means to some other end. Usually wars are intended not to hurt ordinary soldiers, who in fact do get hurt in great numbers, but to gain land, wealth, prestige, or resources.

Interdependence The condition in which two or more people have some degree of mutual influence on each other's feelings, beliefs, or behavior.

Just World The belief that people get what they deserve. If good things happen to people, it is because they have worked hard, been honest, or been foresighted; if bad things happen to them, it is because they were lazy, careless, dumb, or dishonest. One consequence is that victims are blamed for their misfortunes, even if in reality they are not to blame.

Learned Helplessness The feeling of helplessness and possible depression when people discover they have no control over their outcomes.

Loneliness The psychological discomfort we feel when our social relations lack some essential feature. This deficit may be quantitative (too few relationships), or qualitative (unsatisfying relationships).

Matching Principle In dating and marriage, people tend to select partners who are similar to themselves in attitudes, values, ethnic background, religion, social class, education, and many other personal characteristics.

Mere Exposure Effect Simply being exposed frequently to a person or object tends to increase our liking for that person or object. Repeated exposure is most likely to enhance liking when our initial reaction to the person is neutral or positive, when no conflict of interests exists, and when the repetition is not so great that it causes satiation.

Middle-Range Theories Theories that attempt to account for major categories of behavior, but do not attempt to cover human behavior in general. They might attempt to account for most kinds of attitude change, *or* attribution, *or* aggression, but not all three.

Minimal Effects Model The description of mass communications as mainly reinforcing the recipient's prior attitudes, rather than as creating widespread attitude change.

Minimal Risk The idea that the risk anticipated in any research project must be no greater than the risk encountered in daily life.

Misattribution Assigning the cause of a particular behavior or emotional state to a stimulus other than the actual cause, such as thinking a lecture is exciting when actually you are excited by having drunk ten cups of coffee.

Motivated Selectivity The idea that people deliberately seek supportive information and avoid nonsupportive information as a way of maintaining the consistency of their own attitudes. The evidence indicates that this generally does not occur.

Naive Psychology The ordinary person's informal theories about what determines human behavior.

Negativity Effect Tendency for impressions to be more influenced by negative traits than by positive traits. Hence positive impressions are more vulnerable to change than negative impressions.

Nonverbal Leakage The communication of true emotions through nonverbal channels even when the person's verbal communication tries to cover them up.

Norm *See* social norms.

Norm of Reciprocity The norm that we are expected to reward those who reward us. For example, if people help us, we feel obligated to help them in return.

Norms of Social Justice Norms about fairness and the just distribution of resources developed by human groups. Norms of social justice may contribute to prosocial behavior.

Norm of Social Responsibility A social norm dictating that we should help others who depend on us. This may be one cause of prosocial behavior.

Obedience Performing an action because of an order or request.

Overjustification Giving people high rewards for performing a task undermines their intrinsic interest in the task, presumably because they attribute their liking for the task to the reward rather than to their own intrinsic interest in the task.

Paralanguage Information conveyed by variations in speech other than actual words and syntax, such as pitch, loudness, hesitations, and so on.

Passionate Love The emotionally charged type of love that sometimes characterizes the early stages of romantic relationships.

Person Perception Process of forming impressions of others, making judgments about their personalities, and adopting hypotheses about the kind of persons they are.

Personal Distress Our own personal reactions to the suffering of others may include horror, shock, helplessness, or concern. Since personal distress focuses on the self, it can motivate people to ignore or avoid the suffering of others, rather than to offer assistance.

Personal Space The physical space immediately around their bodies that people treat as though it were a part of themselves. Hall has suggested four basic zones for interpersonal interaction: intimate, personal, social, and public distance.

Personal Stereotypes An individual's own beliefs about the attributes of members of particular groups. Personal stereotypes may be similar to or different from cultural stereotypes.

Positivity Bias General tendency to express positive evaluations of people more often than negative evaluations. Also called the *leniency effect.*

Prejudice The affective component of group antagonisms; disliking a group, or members of a group.

Prosocial Aggression Aggressive acts that support commonly accepted social norms, such as a boxer hitting an opponent.

Prosocial Behavior Any act that helps or is designed to help others, regardless of the helper's motives. Prosocial behavior is a broader category than *altruism.*

Proxemics The term used by Hall to describe the study of how people use space.

Psychoanalytic Theory Theory of human behavior based originally on Freud's work. It emphasizes instincts, unconscious motivation, and the ego defenses people construct to protect themselves against their own irrational drives. More generally, this is called psychodynamic theory.

Random Assignment Placement of subjects into experimental conditions in a manner which guarantees that the choice is made entirely by chance, such as by using a random number table; essential characteristic of an experiment.

Random Sample A group of people participating in a study who are selected from the broad population by a random process, and therefore who are representative of that broad population.

Reactance Brehm's concept that people attempt to maintain their freedom of action. When this freedom is threatened, they do whatever they can to restore it: Reactance is aroused, and compliance decreases.

Realistic Group Conflict The theory that antagonism between groups arises from real conflicts of interest and the frustrations those conflicts produce. Two groups in conflict over the fishing rights in a certain segment of the ocean may start to hold prejudices and act aggressively toward each other as a result of the reality-based intergroup conflict.

Reference Group The group's norm can act as a persuasive force leading to attitude change, or pre-

vent change by supporting the individual's position when it is attacked.

Reinforcement The process by which a person or animal learns to perform a particular response by being rewarded when it is performed.

Relative Deprivation The theory that the amount of social discontent depends upon the level of deprivation relative to what other people or groups have, or what the deprived person or group had in the past, rather than upon the absolute amount of deprivation. Hunger should therefore produce the most discontent when the hungry people previously had more to eat, or when others around them have more, regardless of how much or how little food they have in absolute terms.

Reverse-Causality Problem The problem that arises in correlational research when the presumed cause might in fact be the actual effect. Children who watch a lot of television do most poorly in school. But is their television viewing causing poor grades? Or does their poor school performance cause them to escape from schoolwork and watch TV instead?

Risky Shift The phenomenon that after taking part in a group discussion of an issue, people are sometimes willing to support riskier decisions than they were before the group discussion. This is part of a more general process of *group polarization,* which can lead either to riskier or more cautious decisions, depending on the initial views of group members.

Salience The quality that makes a particular stimulus stand out and be noticed. Bright, noisy, colorful, unusual, and novel stimuli are usually the most salient.

Sanctioned Aggression Aggression that is permissible (though not necessarily encouraged) according to the norms of the individual's social groups.

Scapegoat A person who, because he or she is weak, different, and easily distinguishable, tends to be selected as a target of displaced aggression.

Schema An organized system or structure of cognitions about some stimulus or type of stimulus, such as a person, personality type, group, role, or event.

Selective Attention Tendency for people to pay more attention to a supportive message than to a non-supportive message.

Selective Exposure Tendency for persuasive communications not to reach the intended audience because audience members tend to be exposed mostly to sources they agree with. Should be distinguished from *motivated selectivity,* a presumed psychological tendency to avoid nonsupportive information.

Self-Fulfilling Prophecy The tendency for an individual's expectations about the future to influence that future. Prejudice can serve as a self-fulfilling prophecy by determining how the prejudiced person acts toward the victim, which may in turn influence the victim to act in a way that confirms the first person's prejudices.

Self-Serving Bias Attributional bias that is motivated by a need to raise or protect the perceiver's self-esteem. People explain their successes as internally caused thus boosting their self-esteem, while they deny blame for their failures, thus losing no self-esteem.

Shift of Meaning Tendency for the connotations of a trait to change when placed in a different context. This is the explanation for context effects given by cognitive theories of impression formation.

Social Density The objective number of people in a given space, such as the number of people living per square mile in a major city.

Social Exchange Theory *See* Exchange Theory

Social Facilitation The tendency for people (and some kinds of animals) to perform better on simple, well-learned tasks when others are present than when they are alone.

Social Leadership Activities designed to promote group harmony and *cohesiveness*. The social leader focuses on the social and emotional aspects of interaction in order to keep the group running smoothly and happily. *See also* Task Leadership.

Social Learning Theory A modern derivative of behavioral theory that places primary emphasis on how people learn from one another, especially through social reinforcement and imitation.

Social Loafing The phenomenon that individuals sometimes work less hard as members of a group than they would if they worked alone. Individuals may feel that their own efforts will be less recognizable in a group, which leads to a diffusion of responsibility.

Social Loneliness Type of loneliness that results when a person lacks a sense of social integration or community that might be provided by a network of friends, co-workers, or neighbors.

Social Norms The standards of behavior that determine whether specific actions, attitudes, or beliefs are approved or disapproved by the individual's social group. Hurting an innocent person violates the norms of most social groups and would be disapproved; believing in God is consistent with the norms of most social groups and would be approved by members of those groups.

Social Penetration Altman and Taylor's theory about the process by which people gradually attain closeness and intimacy in a relationship. The theory emphasizes that as relationships develop, self-disclosure increases in both breadth (range of topics) and depth (intimacy).

Social Power A person's ability deliberately to influence the behavior, thoughts, or feelings of another person. Raven and his colleagues have identified six major bases of social power: reward, coercion, legitimate authority, expertise, information, and referent power.

Social Role A set of *social norms* (rules and understandings) about how a person in a particular social position is expected to behave. Roles define the rights and responsibilities of members of couples, groups, and other social units.

Sociobiology A relatively new field in biology that uses evolutionary theory to explain social behavior in humans and other animals.

Stereotype Beliefs about the characteristics of members of a group or social category. This is the cognitive component of group antagonism.

Symbolic Racism Opposition to the progress of blacks, or to policies promoting that progress, that is based both in antagonism toward blacks and in support for traditional values.

Task Leadership Activities designed to accomplish the goals of a group and to get the work of the group done successfully. The task leader directs and organizes the group in carrying out a specific task.

Territorial Markers Objects and nonverbal gestures that people use to mark and personalize their territories. For example, a person may stake out a seat in the library using a bookbag, sunglasses, and notebook.

Territory An area controlled by a specific individual or group. Altman has distinguished primary, secondary, and public territories.

Theoretical Question Research question stemming from a theory.

Third-Variable Problem A problem with interpreting correlational research. When two variables are correlated with each other, is one the cause of the other? Or is some third variable the cause of both? Couples' satisfaction with their sex life is correlated with how long they remain a couple. But is sexual compatibility the cause of long-lasting relationships? Or are both caused by a more general level of trust and understanding?

Transfer of Affect The theory that attitude change takes place by transferring the affect associated with one attitude object to another. Watching a beautiful model use a particular brand of soap in the shower transfers the positive affect associated with her to the brand of soap, supposedly compelling the viewer to buy that brand.

REFERENCES

ABELSON, R. P. (1976). Script processing in attitude formation and decision making. In J. S. Carroll and J. W. Payne (Eds.), *Cognition and social behavior.* Hillsdale, NJ: Erlbaum.

ABRAMSON, L. Y., SELIGMAN, M. E. P., & TEASDALE, J. D. (1978). Learned helplessness in humans: Critique and reformulation. *Journal of Abnormal Psychology, 87,* 49–74.

ABRAMSON, P. E., GOLDBERG, P. A., GREENBERG, J. H., & ABRAMSON, U. M. (1977). The talking platypus phenomenon: Competency ratings as a function of sex and professional status. *Psychology of Women Quarterly, 2,* 114–124.

ADORNO, T. W., FRENKEL-BRUNSWIK, E., LEVINSON, D. J., & SANFORD, R. N. (1950). *The authoritarian personality.* New York: Harper & Row.

AHAMMER, I. M., & MURRAY, J. P. (1979). Kindness in the kindergarten: The relative influence of role playing and prosocial television in facilitating altruism. *International Journal of Behavioral Development, 2,* 133–157.

AHMED, S. M. S. (1979). Helping behavior as predicted by diffusion of responsibility, exchange theory, and traditional sex norms. *Journal of Social Psychology, 109,* 153–154.

AIELLO, J. R., & AIELLO, T. (1974). The development of personal space: Proxemic behavior of children 6 through 16. *Human Ecology, 2,* 177–189.

AIELLO, J. R., & COOPER, R. E. (1972). The use of personal space as a function of social affect. *Proceedings of the 80th Annual Convention of the American Psychology Association, 7,* 207–208.

AINSWORTH, M. D. S. (1973). The development of infant-mother attachment. In B. M. Caldwell & H. N. Ricciuti (Eds.), *Review of child development research* (Vol. 3). Chicago: University of Chicago Press.

AJZEN, I., & FISHBEIN, M. (1980). *Understanding attitudes and predicting social behavior.* Englewood Cliffs, NJ: Prentice-Hall.

ALLEN, V. L., & LEVIN, J. M. (1971). Social support and conformity: The role of independent assessment of reality. *Journal of Experimental Social Psychology, 7,* 48–58.

ALLGEIER, E. R., & BYRNE, D. (1973). Attraction toward the opposite sex as a determinant of physical proximity. *Journal of Social Psychology, 90,* 213–219.

ALLGEIER, E. R., & McCORMICK, N. B. (Eds.). (1983). *Changing boundaries: Gender roles and sexual behavior.* Palo Alto, CA: Mayfield.

ALLOY, L. B., ABRAMSON, L. Y., & VISCUSI, D. (1981). Induced mood and the illusion of control. *Journal of Personality and Social Psychology, 41,* 1129–1140.

ALLPORT, F. H. (1920). The influence of the group upon association and thought. *Journal of Experimental Psychology, 3,* 159–182.

ALLPORT, F. H. (1924). *Social psychology,* Boston: Riverside Editions, Houghton Mifflin.

ALLPORT, G. W. (1935). Attitudes. In C. Murchison, (Ed.), *A handbook of social psychology.* Clark University Press.

ALLPORT, G. W. (1954). *The nature of prejudice.* Garden City, NY: Doubleday Anchor.

ALTMAN, I. (1975). *The environment and social behavior.* Monterey, CA: Brooks/Cole.

ALTMAN, I., & HAYTHORN, W. W. (1965). Interpersonal exchange in isolation. *Sociometry, 23,* 411–426.

ALTMAN, I., NELSON, P. A., & LETT, E. E. (1972). The ecology of home environments. *Catalog of Selected Documents in Psychology.* Washington, DC: American Psychological Association.

ALTMAN, I., & TAYLOR, D. A. (1973). *Social penetration: The development of interpersonal relationships.* New York: Holt, Rinehart & Winston.

AMATO, P. R. (1983). Helping behavior in urban and rural environments: Field studies based on a taxonomic organization of helping episodes. *Journal of Personality and Social Psychology, 45*(3), 571–586.

AMIR, Y. (1976). The role of intergroup contact in change of prejudice and ethnic relations. In P. A. Katz (Ed.), *Towards the elimination of racism* (pp. 245–308). Elmsford, NY: Pergamon Press.

ANDELIN, H. B. (1963). *Fascinating Womanhood.* New York: Bantam.

ANDERSON, N. H. (1959). Test of a model for opinion change. *Journal of Abnormal and Social Psychology, 59,* 371–381.

ANDERSON, N. H. (1965). Averaging vs. adding as a stimulus-combination rule in impression formation. *Journal of Experimental Psychology, 70,* 394–400.

ANDERSON, N. H. (1966). Component ratings in impression formation. *Psychonomic Science, 6,* 279–280.

ANDERSON, N. H. (1968a). A simple model for information integration. In R. P. Abelson et al. (Eds.), *Theories of cognitive consistency: A sourcebook.* Chicago: Rand McNally.

ANDERSON, N. H. (1968b). Likableness ratings of 555 personality-trait words. *Journal of Personality and Social Psychology, 9,* 272–279.

ANDERSON, N. H., & HUBERT, S. (1963). Effects of concomitant verbal call on order effects in personality impression formation. *Journal of Verbal Learning and Verbal Behavior, 2,* 379–391.

ANDREWS, K. H., & KANDEL, D. B. (1979). Attitude and behavior. *American Sociological Review, 44,* 298–310.

APPLE, W., & HECHT, K. (1982). Speaking emotionally: The relation between verbal and vocal communication of affect. *Journal of Personality and Social Psychology, 42,* 864–875.

APPLE, W., STREETER, L. A., & KRAUSS, R. M. (1979). Effects of pitch and speech rate on personal attributions. *Journal of Personality and Social Psychology, 37,* 715–727.

APSLER, R., & SEARS, D. O. (1968). Warning, personal involvement, and attitude change. *Journal of Personality and Social Psychology, 9,* 162–166.

ARCHER, R. L. & BERG, J. H. (1978). Disclosure reciprocity and its limits: A reactance model. *Journal of Experimental Social Psychology, 14,* 527–540.

ARMS, R. L., RUSSELL, G. W., & SANDILANDS, M. L. (1979). Effects on the hostility of spectators of viewing aggressive sports. *Sociometry, 42,* 275–79.

ARMSTRONG, E. A. (1965). *Bird display and behavior: An introduction to the study of bird psychology* (2nd ed.). New York: Dover.

ARONSON, E., & CARLSMITH, J. M. (1963). The effect of the severity of threat on the devaluation of forbidden behavior. *Journal of Abnormal and Social Psychology, 66,* 584–588.

ARONSON, E., & LINDER, D. (1965). Gain and loss of esteem as determinants of interpersonal attractiveness. *Journal of Experimental Social Psychology, 1,* 156–171.

ARONSON, E., & OSHEROW, N. (1980). Cooperation, social behavior, and academic performance: Experiments in the desegregated classroom. In L. Bickman (Ed.), *Applied social psychology annual* (Vol. 1). Beverly Hills, CA: Sage Publications.

ARONSON, E., TURNER, J. A. & CARLSMITH, J. M. (1963). Communicator credibility and communication discrepancy as determinants of opinion change. *Journal of Abnormal and Social Psychology, 67,* 31–36.

ARONSON, E., WILLERMAN, B., & FLOYD, J. (1966). The effect of a pratfall on increasing interpersonal attractiveness. *Psychonomic Science, 4,* 227–228.

ASCH, S. E. (1946). Forming impressions of personality. *Journal of Abnormal and Social Psychology, 41,* 258–290.

ASCH, S. E. (1951). Effects of group pressure upon the modification and distortion of judgments. In H. Guetzkow (Ed.), *Groups, leadership and men.* Pittsburgh, PA: Carnegie Press.

ASHMORE, R. D. (1970). The problem of intergroup prejudice. In B. E. Collins, *Social psychology: Social influence, attitude change, group processes, and prejudice.* Reading, MA: Addison-Wesley.

ASHMORE, R. D. (1981). Sex stereotypes and implicit personality theory. In D. L. Hamilton (Ed.), *Cognitive processes in stereotyping and intergroup behavior* (pp. 37–82). Hillsdale, NJ: Erlbaum.

ASHMORE, R. D., & DEL BOCA, F. K. (1976). Psychological approaches to understanding intergroup conflict. In P. A. Katz (Ed.), *Towards the elimination of racism* (pp. 73–124). Elmsford, NY: Pergamon Press.

ASHMORE, R. D., & DEL BOCA, F. K. (1981). Conceptual approaches to stereotypes and stereotyping. In D. L. Hamilton (Ed.), *Cognitive processes in stereotyping and intergroup behavior.* Hillsdale, NJ: Erlbaum.

ASHTON, N. L., SHAW, M. E., & WORSHAM, A. P. (1980). Affective reactions to interpersonal distances by friends and strangers. *Bulletin of the Psychonomic Society, 15,* 306–308.

AUSTIN, W. (1980). Friendship and fairness: Effects of type of relationship and task performance on choice distribution rules. *Personality and Social Psychology Bulletin, 6,* 402–408.

AVERILL, J. R. (1983). Studies on anger and aggression: Implications for theories of emotion. *American Psychologist, 38,* 1145–1160.

AVERILL, J. R., & BOOTHROYD, P. (1977). On falling in love in conformance with the romantic ideal. *Motivation and Emotion, 1*(3), 235–247.

BALES, R. F. (1970). *Personality and interpersonal behavior.* New York: Holt, Rinehart & Winston.

BALL-ROKEACH, S. J., GRUBE, J. W., & ROKEACH, M. (1981). Roots: The next generation—Who watched and with what effect? *Public Opinion Quarterly, 45,* 58–68.

BANDURA, A., ROSS, D., & ROSS, S. A. (1961). Transmission of aggression through imitation of aggressive models. *Journal of Abnormal and Social Psychology, 63*(3), 575–582.

BANE, M. J. (1976). *Here to stay: American families in the twentieth century.* New York: Basic Books.

BARKER, R. G., DEMBO, T., & LEWIS, D. (1941). Frustration and regression: An experiment with young children. *University of Iowa Studies in Child Welfare, 18* (1).

BARON, R. A. (1971a). Magnitude of victim's pain cues and level of prior anger arousal as determinants of adult aggressive behavior. *Journal of Personality and Social Psychology, 17,* 236–243.

BARON, R. A. (1971b). Aggression as a function of magnitude of victim's pain cues, level of prior anger arousal, and aggressor-victim similarity. *Journal of Personality and Social Psychology, 18,* 48–54.

BARON, R. A. (1974). Aggression as a function of victim's pain cues, level of prior anger arousal, and exposure to an aggressive model. *Journal of Personality and Social Psychology, 29,* 117–124.

BARON, R. A. (1977). *Human aggression.* New York: Plenum Press.

BARON, R. A., & BALL, R. L. (1974). The aggression-inhibiting influence of nonhostile humor. *Journal of Experimental Social Psychology, 10,* 23–33.

BARON, R. A., & BELL, P. A. (1975). Aggression and heat: Mediating effects of prior provocation and exposure to an aggressive model. *Journal of Personality and Social Psychology, 31,* 825–832.

BARON, R. A., & BELL, P. A. (1976). Aggression and heat: The influence of ambient temperature, negative affect, and a cooling drink on physical aggression. *Journal of Personality and Social Psychology, 33,* 245–255.

BARON, R. A., & BELL, P. A. (1977). Sexual arousal and aggression by males: Effects of type of erotic stimuli and prior provocation. *Journal of Personality and Social Psychology, 35,* 79–87.

BARON, R. M., MANDEL, D. G., ADAMS, C. A., & GRIFFEN, L. M. (1976). Effects of social density in university residential environments. *Journal of Personality and Social Psychology, 34,* 434–446.

BARON, R. M., & RODIN, J. (1978). Perceived control and crowding stress: Processes mediating the impact of spatial and social density. In A. Baum & Y. Epstein (Eds.), *Human response to crowding.* Hillsdale, NJ: Erlbaum.

BAR-TAL, D., BAR-ZOHAR, Y., GREENBERG, M. S., & HERMON, M. (1977). Reciprocity behavior in the relationship between donor and recipient and between harm-doer and victim. *Sociometry, 40*(3), 293–298.

BATSON, C. D., COCHRAN, P. J., BIEDERMAN, M. F., BLOSSER, J. L., RYAN, M. J., & VOGT, B. (1978). Failure to help when in a hurry: Callousness or conflict? *Personality and Social Psychology Bulletin, 4,*(1), 97–101.

BAUM, A., AIELLO, J. R., & CALESNICK, L. E. (1978). Crowding and personal control: Social density and the development of learned helplessness. *Journal of Personality and Social Psychology, 36,* 1000–1011.

BAUM, A., & DAVIS, G. E. (1980). Reducing the stress of high-density living: An architectural intervention. *Journal of Personality and Social Psychology, 38*(3), 471–481.

BAUM, A., & SINGER, J. E. (Eds.). (1982). *Advances in environmental psychology: Vol 4. Environment and health.* Hillsdale, NJ: Erlbaum.

BAUM, A., & VALINS, S. (1977). *Architecture and social behavior: Psychological studies of social density.* Hillsdale, NJ: Erlbaum.

BAUMEISTER, R. F. (1982). A self-presentational view of social phenomena. *Psychological Bulletin, 91,* 3–26.

BAVELAS, A., HASTORF, A. H., GROSS, A. E., & KITE, W. R. (1965). Experiments on the alteration of group structures. *Journal of Experimental Social Psychology, 1,* 55–70.

BECKER, F. D. Study of spatial markers. (1973). *Journal of Personality and Social Psychology, 26*(3), 439–445.

BECKER, J. F., & HEATON, E. E., Jr. (1967). The election of Senator Edward W. Brooke. *Public Opinion Quarterly, 31,* 346–358.

BECKER, L. B., McCOMBS, M. E., & McLEOD, M. M. (1975). The development of political cognitions. In Steven H. Chaffee (Ed.), *Political communication: Issues and strategies for research* (pp. 21–63). Beverly Hills, CA: Sage Publications.

BELL, R. (1968). A reinterpretation of the direction of effects in studies of socialization. *Psychological Review, 75,* 81–85.

BEM, D. J. (1965). An experimental analysis of self-persuasion. *Journal of Experimental Social Psychology, 1,* 199–218.

BEM, D. J. (1967). Self-perception: An alternative interpretation of cognitive dissonance phenomena. *Psychological Review, 74,* 183–200.

BEM, S. L. (1974). The measurement of psychological androgyny. *Journal of Consulting and Clinical Psychology, 42,* 155–162.

BEM, S. L. (1975). Sex role adaptability: One consequence of psychological androgyny. *Journal of Personality and Social Psychology, 31,* 634–643.

BEM, S. L. (1981). Gender schema theory: A cognitive account of sex typing. *Psychological Review, 88,* 354–364.

BEM, S. L., MARTYNA, W., & WATSON, C. (1976). Sex typing and androgyny: Further explorations of the expressive domain. *Journal of Personality and Social Psychology, 43,* 1016–1023.

BENSON, P. L., KARABENICK, S. A., & LERNER, R. M. (1976). Pretty pleases: The effects of physical attractiveness, race, and sex on receiving help. *Journal of Experimental Social Psychology, 12,* 409–415.

BENTLER, P. M., & SPECKART, G. (1981). Attitudes "cause" behaviors: A structural equation analysis. *Journal of Personality and Social Psychology, 40,* 226–238.

BERK, R. A., & BERK, S. F. (1979). *Labor and leisure at home: Content and organization of the household day.* Beverly Hills, CA: Sage Publications.

BERKOWITZ, L. (1965). Some aspects of observed aggression. *Journal of Personality and Social Psychology, 2,* 359–369.

BERKOWITZ, L. (1968). Responsibility, reciprocity, and social distance in help-giving: An experimental investigation of English social class differences. *Journal of Experimental Social Psychology, 4,* 46–63.

BERKOWITZ, L. (1970). The contagion of violence. In W. J. Arnold and M. M. Page (Eds.), *Nebraska Symposium on Motivation.* Lincoln: University of Nebraska Press.

BERKOWITZ, L. (1972). Social norms, feelings, and other factors affecting helping and altruism. In L. Berkowitz (Ed.), *Advances in experimental social psychology* (Vol. 6). New York: Academic Press.

BERKOWITZ, L. (1983). Aversively stimulated aggression: Some parallels and differences in research with animals and humans. *American Psychologist, 38,* 1135–1144.

BERKOWITZ, L., & FRODI, A. (1979). Reactions to a child's mistakes as affected by her/his looks and speech. *Social Psychology Quarterly, 42,* 420–425.

BERKOWITZ, L., & GEEN, R. G. (1966). Film violence and the cue properties of available targets. *Journal of Personality and Social Psychology, 3,* 525–530.

BERKOWITZ, L., & GEEN, R. G. (1967). Stimulus qualities of the target of aggression: A further study. *Journal of Personality and Social Psychology, 5,* 364–368.

BERKOWITZ, L., & RAWLINGS, E. (1963). Effects of film violence on inhibitions against subsequent aggression. *Journal of Abnormal and Social Psychology, 66,* 405–412.

BERNARD, J. (1972). *The future of marriage.* New York: Bantam.

BERNARD, L. C. (1980). Multivariate analysis of new sex role formulations and personality. *Journal of Personality and Social Psychology, 38,* 323–336.

BERNSTEIN, M., & CROSBY, F. (1980). An empirical examination of relative deprivation theory. *Journal of Experimental Social Psychology, 16,* 442–456.

BERNSTEIN, W. M., & STEPHAN, W. G., & DAVIS, M. H. (1979). Explaining attributions for achievement: A path analytic approach. *Journal of Personality and Social Psychology, 37,* 1810–1821.

BERSCHEID, E. (1983). Emotion. In H. H. Kelley et al., *Close relationships* (pp. 110–168). New York: Freeman.

BERSCHEID, E., GRAZIANO, W., MONSON, T., & DERMER, M. (1976). Outcome dependency: Attention, attribution, and attraction. *Journal of Personality and Social Psychology, 34,* 978–989.

BERSCHEID, E., & WALSTER, E. (1967). When does a harmdoer compensate a victim? *Journal of Personality and Social Psychology, 6,* 435–441.

BERSCHEID, E., & WALSTER, E. H. (1978). *Interpersonal attraction* (2nd ed.), Reading, MA: Addison-Wesley.

BICKMAN, L. (1971). The effect of another bystander's ability to help on bystander intervention in an emergency. *Journal of Experimental Social Psychology, 7,* 367–379.

BICKMAN, L., & KAMZAN, M. (1973). The effect of race and need on helping. *Journal of Social Psychology, 89,* 73–77.

BIRDWHISTELL, R. I. (1970). *Kinesics and context: Essays on body motion communication.* Philadelphia: University of Pennsylvania Press.

BLAU, P. M. (1964). *Exchange and power in social life.* New York: Wiley.

BLUMENTHAL, M. D., KAHN, R. L., ANDREWS, F. M., & HEAD,

K. B. (1972). *Justifying violence: Attitudes of American men.* Ann Arbor, MI: Institute for Social Research.

BOCHNER, S., & INSKO, C. A. (1966). Communicator discrepancy, source credibility, and opinion change. *Journal of Personality and Social Psychology, 4,* 614–621.

BOND, M. H., & DUTTON, D. G. (1975). The effect of interaction anticipation and experience as a victim on aggressive behavior. *Journal of Personality, 43*(3), 515–527.

BONS, P. M., & FIEDLER, F. E. (1976). Changes in organizational leadership and the behavior of relationship- and task-motivated leaders. *Administrative Science Quarterly, 21,* 433–472.

BOOTH, A. (1976). *Urban crowding and its consequences.* New York: Praeger.

BORDEN, R. J. (1980). Audience influence. In P. B. Paulus (Ed.), *Psychology of group influence* (pp. 99–132). Hillsdale, NJ: Erlbaum.

BORGIDA, E., & CAMPBELL, B. (1982). Belief relevance and attitude-behavior consistency: The moderating role of personal experience. *Journal of Personality and Social Psychology, 42,* 239–247.

BORGIDA, E., & HOWARD-PITNEY, B. (1983). Personal involvement and the robustness of perceptual salience effects. *Journal of Personality and Social Psychology, 45,* 560–570.

BOWLBY, J. (1969). *Attachment and loss: Vol. 1. Attachment.* New York: Basic Books.

BRADBURN, N. (1969). *The structure of psychological well-being.* Chicago: Aldine.

BRADLEY, G. W. (1978). Self-serving biases in the attribution process: A reexamination of the fact or fiction question. *Journal of Personality and Social Psychology, 36,* 56–71.

BRAIKER, H. B., & KELLEY, H. H. (1979). Conflict in the development of close relationships. In R. L. Burgess & T. L. Huston (Eds.), *Social exchange in developing relationships.* New York: Academic Press.

BRAMEL, D., TAUB, B., & BLUM, B. (1968). An observer's reaction to the suffering of his enemy. *Journal of Personality and Social Psychology, 8,* 384–392.

BREHM, J. W. (1956). Post-decision changes in desirability of alternatives. *Journal of Abnormal and Social Psychology, 52,* 384–389.

BREHM, J. W. (1966). *A theory of psychological reactance.* New York: Academic Press.

BREHM, J. W., & SENSENIG, J. (1966). Social influence as a function of attempted and implied usurpation of a choice. *Journal of Personality and Social Psychology, 4,* 703–707.

BREHM, S. S., & BREHM, J. W. (1981). *Psychological reactance: A theory of freedom and control.* New York: Academic Press.

BREWER, M. B., DULL, V., & LUI, L. (1981). Perceptions of the elderly: Stereotypes as prototypes. *Journal of Personality and Social Psychology, 41*(4), 656–670.

BRIAR, S. (1966). Welfare from below: Recipients' view of the public welfare system. In J. Brock (Ed.), *The law of the poor.* San Francisco: Chandler.

BRIGHAM, J. C., & GIESBRECHT, L. W. (1976). All in the family: Racial attitudes. *Journal of Communication, 26,* 75–84.

BROADBENT, D. E. (1957). Effects of noise on behavior. In C. M. Harris (Ed.), *Handbook of noise control.* New York: McGraw-Hill.

BROCK, T. C. (1965). Communicator-recipient similarity and decision change. *Journal of Personality and Social Psychology, 1,* 650–654.

BROCK, T. C., & BALLOUN, J. L. (1967). Behavioral receptivity to dissonant information. *Journal of Personality and Social Psychology, 6,* 413–428.

BRODY, R. A., & PAGE, B. I. (1975). The impact of events on presidential popularity: The Johnson and Nixon administrations. In A. Wildavsky (Ed.), *Perspectives on the presidency* (pp. 136–148). Boston: Little, Brown.

BRUNER, J. S., & TAGIURI, R. (1954). The perception of people. In G. Lindzey (Ed.), *Handbook of social psychology* (Vol. 2, pp. 634–654). Reading, MA: Addison-Wesley.

BRYAN, J. H., & TEST, N. A. (1967). Models and helping: Naturalistic studies in aiding behavior. *Journal of Personality and Social Psychology, 6,* 400–407.

BULMAN, R. J., & WORTMAN, C. B. (1977). Attributions of blame and coping in the "real world": Severe accident victims react to their lot. *Journal of Personality and Social Psychology, 35,* 351–363.

BURGESS, E. W., & WALLIN, P. (1953). *Engagement and marriage.* Philadelphia: Lippincott.

BURGESS, R. L., & HUSTON, T. L. (Eds.). (1979). *Social exchange in developing relationships.* New York: Academic Press.

BURKE, P. J. (1971). Task and social-emotional leadership role performance. *Sociometry, 34,* 22–40.

BURNSTEIN, E., & VINOKUR, A. (1975). What a person thinks upon learning he has chosen differently from others: Nice evidence for the persuasive-arguments explanation of choice shifts. *Journal of Experimental Social Psychology, 11,* 412–426.

BUSS, A. H. (1961). *The psychology of aggression.* New York: Wiley.

BUUNK, B. (1982). Anticipated sexual jealousy: Its relationship to self-esteem, dependency, and reciprocity. *Personality and Social Psychology Bulletin, 8,* 310–316.

BYRNE, D. (1971). *The attraction paradigm.* New York: Academic Press.

BYRNE, D., & WONG, T. J. (1962). Racial prejudice, interpersonal attraction and assumed dissimilarity of attitudes. *Journal of Abnormal and Social Psychology, 65,* 246–253.

CACIOPPO, J. T., & PETTY, R. E. (1979). Effects of message repetition and position on cognitive response, recall, and persuasion. *Journal of Personality and Social Psychology, 37,* 97–109.

CALDWELL, M. A., & PEPLAU, L. A. (1982). Sex differences in same-sex friendship. *Sex Roles, 8,*(7), 721–732.

CALHOUN, J. B. (1962). Population density and social pathology. *Scientific American, 206,* 139–148.

CAMPBELL, A. (1971). *White attitudes toward black people.* Ann Arbor, MI: Institute for Social Research.

CAMPBELL, D. T. (1975). On the conflicts between biological and social evolution and between psychology and moral tradition. *American Psychologist, 30* (12), 1103–1126.

CAMPBELL, D. T., & STANLEY, J. C. (1963). *Experimental and quasiexperimental designs for research.* Chicago: Rand McNally.

CANTOR, J. R., ZILLMANN, D., & BRYANT, J. (1975). Enhancement of experiences of sexual arousal in response to erotic stimuli through misattribution of unrelated residual excitation. *Journal of Personality and Social Psychology, 32,* 69–75.

CANTOR, N., & MISCHEL, W. (1977). Traits as prototypes: Effects on recognition memory. *Journal of Personality and Social Psychology, 35,* 38–48.

CANTOR, N., MISCHEL, W., & SCHWARTZ, J. (1982). Social knowledge: Structure, content, use, and abuse. In A. H. Hastorf, & A. M. Isen (Eds.), *Cognitive social psychology.* New York: Elsevier.

CANTRIL, H. (1940). *The invasion from Mars.* Princeton, NJ: Princeton University Press.

CARLSMITH, J. M., & ANDERSON, C. A. (1979). Ambient temperature and the occurrence of collective violence: A new analysis. *Journal of Personality and Social Psychology, 37,* 337–344.

CARLSMITH, J. M., ELLSWORTH, P., & WHITESIDE, J. (1968). *Guilt, confession and compliance.* Unpublished manuscript, Stanford University.

CARLSTON, D. E., & SHOVAR, N. (1983). Effects of performance attributions on others' perceptions of the attributor. *Journal of Personality and Social Psychology, 44*(3), 515–525.

CASH, T. F., GILLEN, B., & BURNS, D. S. (1977). Sexism and "beautyism" in personnel consultant decision making. *Journal of Applied Psychology, 62,* 301–310.

CATER, D., & STRICKLAND, D. (1975). *TV violence and the child.* New York: Russell Sage.

CHAFFEE, S. H. (Ed.). (1975, October). *American Politics Quarterly, 3.*

CHAIKEN, S. (1979). Communicator physical attractiveness and persuasion. *Journal of Personality and Social Psychology, 37,* 1387–1397.

CHAIKEN, S., & BALDWIN, M. W. (1981). Affective-cognitive consistency and the effect of salient behavioral information on the self-perception of attitudes. *Journal of Personality and Social Psychology, 41,* 1–12.

CHAIKEN, S., & EAGLY, A. H. (1976). Communication modality as a determinant of message persuasiveness and message comprehensibility. *Journal of Personality and Social Psychology, 34,* 605–614.

CHAIKEN, S., & EAGLY, A. H. (1983). Communication modality as a determinant of persuasion: The role of communicator salience. *Journal of Personality and Social Psychology, 45,* 241–256.

CHAIKIN, A. L., & DERLEGA, V. J. (1974). Liking for the norm-breaker in self-disclosure. *Journal of Personality, 42,* 117–129.

CHEN, S. C. (1937). Social modification of the activity of ants in nest-building. *Physiological Zoology, 10,* 420–436.

CHRISTIAN, J. J. (1975). Hormonal control of population growth. In B. E. Elefheriou & R. L. Sprott (Eds.), *Hormonal correlates of behavior* (Vol. 1). New York: Plenum Press.

CIALDINI, R. B., BAUMANN, D. J. & KENRICK, D. T. (1981). Insights from sadness: A three-step model of the development of altruism as hedonism. *Developmental Review, 1,* 207–223.

CIALDINI, R. B., VINCENT, J. E., LEWIS, S. K., CATALAN, J., WHEELER, D., & DARBY, B. L. (1975). Reciprocal consessions procedure for inducing compliance: The door-in-the-face technique. *Journal of Personality and Social Psychology, 31,* 206–215.

CLARK, R. D., & WORD, L. E. (1972). Why don't bystanders help? Because of ambiguity? *Journal of Personality and Social Psychology, 24,* 392–400.

CLARK, R. D., & WORD, L. E. (1974). Where is the apathetic bystander? Situational characteristics of the emergency. *Journal of Personality and Social Psychology, 29,* 279–287.

CLIFTON, A. K., MCGRATH, D., & WICK, B. (1976). Stereotypes of woman: A single category? *Sex Roles, 2,* 135–148.

CLINE, V. H., CROFT, R. G., & COURRIER, S. (1973). Desensitization of children to television violence. *Journal of Personality and Social Psychology, 27,* 360–365.

CLORE, G. L., BRAY, R. B., ITKIN, S. M., & MURPHY, P. (1978). Interracial attitudes and behavior at a summer camp. *Journal of Personality and Social Psychology, 36,* 107–116.

CLORE, G. L., & BYRNE, D. (1974). A reinforcement-affect model of attraction. In T. L. Huston (Ed.), *Foundations of interpersonal attraction* (pp. 143–165). New York: Academic Press.

COHEN, C. E. (1981). Person categories and social perception: Testing some boundaries of the processing effects of prior knowledge. *Journal of Personality and Social Psychology, 40,* 441–452.

COHEN, S., EVANS, G. W., KRANTZ, D. S., STOKOLS, D., & KELLY, S. (1981). Aircraft noise and children: Longitudinal and cross-sectional evidence on adaptation to noise and the effectiveness of noise abatement. *Journal of Personality and Social Psychology, 40,* 331–345.

COHEN, S., GLASS, D. C. & SINGER, J. E. (1973). Apartment noise, auditory discrimination, and reading ability in children. *Journal of Experimental Social Psychology 9,* 407–422.

COHEN, S., & LEZAK, A. (1977). Noise and attentiveness to social cues. *Environment and Behavior, 9,* 559–572.

COHEN, S., & WEINSTEIN, N. (1981). Nonauditory effects of noise on behavior and health. *Journal of Social Issues, 37*(1), 36–70.

COLEMAN, J. F., BLAKE, R. R. & MOUTON, J. S. (1958). Task difficulty and conformity pressures. *Journal of Abnormal and Social Psychology, 57,* 120–122.

COLLIGAN, M. J., PENNEBAKER, J. W., & MURPHY, L. R. (1982). *Mass psychogenic illness: A social psychological analysis.* Hillsdale, NJ: Erlbaum.

COMMISSION ON OBSCENITY AND PORNOGRAPHY. (1970). *The Report of the Commission on Obscenity and Pornography.* New York: Bantam.

COMSTOCK, G. (1975). *Television and human behavior: The key studies.* Santa Monica, CA: The Rand Corporation.

COMSTOCK, G. (1982). Violence in television content: An overview. In D. Pearl, L. Bouthilet, & J. Lazar (Eds.), *Television and behavior: Ten years of scientific progress and implications for the eighties: Vol. II: Technical reviews.* Rockville, MD: National Institute of Mental Health.

COMSTOCK, G., CHAFFEE, S., KATZMAN, N., MCCOMBS, M., & ROBERTS, D. (1978). *Television and human behavior.* New York: Columbia University Press.

CONDRY, J., & CONDRY, S. (1976). Sex differences: A study

in the eye of the beholder. *Child Development, 47,* 812–819.

COOK, T. D., & FLAY, B. R. (1978). The persistence of experimentally induced attitude change. In L. Berkowitz (Ed.), *Advances in experimental social psychology* (Vol. 11, pp. 2–59). New York: Academic Press.

COOPER, J., & JONES, R. A. (1970). Self-esteem and consistency as determinants of anticipatory opinion change. *Journal of Personality and Social Psychology, 14,* 312–320.

COZBY, P. C. (1973). Self-disclosure: A literature review. *Psychological Bulletin, 79,* 73–91.

CROCKER, J., HANNAH, D. B., & WEBER, R. (1983). Person memory and causal attributions. *Journal of Personality and Social Psychology, 44*(1), 55–66.

CUNNINGHAM, M. R. (1979). Weather, mood, and helping behavior: Quasi-experiments with the sunshine Samaritan. *Journal of Personality and Social Psychology, 37*(11), 1947–1956.

CUNNINGHAM, M. R., STEINBERG, J. & GREV, R. (1980). Wanting to and having to help: Separate motivations for positive mood and guilt-induced helping. *Journal of Personality and Social Psychology, 38*(2), 181–192.

CUTRONA, C. E. (1982). Transition to college: Loneliness and the process of social adjustment. In L. A. Peplau & D. Perlman (Eds.), *Loneliness: A sourcebook of current theory, research and therapy* (pp. 291–309). New York: Wiley-Interscience.

DABBS, J. M., JR., & LEVENTHAL, H. (1966). Effects of varying the recommendations in a fear-arousing communication. *Journal of Personality and Social Psychology, 4,* 525–531.

DARLEY, J. M., & BATSON, C. D. (1973). "From Jerusalem to Jericho": A study of situational and dispositional variables in helping behavior. *Journal of Personality and Social Psychology, 27,* 100–108.

DARLEY, J. M., & GROSS, P. H. (1983). A hypothesis-confirming bias in labeling effects. *Journal of Personality and Social Psychology, 44*(1), 20–33.

DARLEY, J. M., & LATANÉ, B. (1968). Bystander intervention in emergencies: Diffusion of responsibility. *Journal of Personality and Social Psychology, 8,* 377–383.

DARWIN, C. (1871). *The descent of man.* London: Murray.

DARWIN, C. (1872). *The expression of the emotions in man and animals.* London: Murray.

D'ATRI, D. A. (1975). Psychophysiological responses to crowding. *Environment and Behavior, 7,* 237–250.

DAVIDSON, A. R., & JACCARD, J. J. (1979). Variables that moderate the attitude-behavior relation: Results of a longitudinal survey. *Journal of Personality and Social Psychology, 37,* 1364–1376.

DAVIS, G. J., & MEYER, R. K. (1973). FSH and LH in the snowshoe hare during the increasing phase of the 10-year cycle. *General Comparative Endocrinology, 20,* 53–60.

DAVIS, J. D. (1976). Self-disclosure in an acquaintance exercise: Responsibility for level of intimacy. *Journal of Personality and Social Psychology, 33,* 787–792.

DAVIS, J. D. (1977). Effects of communication about interpersonal process on the evolution of self-disclosure in dyads. *Journal of Personality and Social Psychology, 35,* 31–37.

DEAUX, K., & EMSWILLER, T. (1974). Explanations of successful performance on sex-linked tasks: What is skill for the male is luck for the female. *Journal of Personality and Social Psychology, 29,* 80–85.

DECI, E. (1971). Effects of externally mediated rewards on intrinsic motivation. *Journal of Personality and Social Psychology, 18,* 105–111.

DENGERINK, H. A., SCHNEDLER, R. W., & COVEY, M. K. (1978). Role of avoidance in aggressive responses to attack and no attack. *Journal of Personality and Social Psychology, 36,* 1044–1053.

DEPAULO, B. M., ROSENTHAL, R., EISENSTAT, R. A., ROGERS, P. L., & FINKELSTEIN, S. (1978). Decoding discrepant nonverbal cues. *Journal of Personality and Social Psychology, 36,* 313–323.

DEPAULO, B. M., ROSENTHAL, R., GREEN, C. R., & ROSENKRANTZ, J. (1982). Diagnosing deceptive and mixed messages from verbal and nonverbal cues. *Journal of Personality and Social Psychology, 18,* 433–446.

DERLEGA, V. J., & CHAIKIN, A. L. (1975). *Sharing intimacy: What we reveal to others and why.* Englewood Cliffs, NJ: Prentice-Hall.

DERLEGA, V. J., DURHAM, B., GOCKEL, B., & SHOLIS, D. (1981). Sex differences in self-disclosure: Effects of topic content, friendship, and partner's sex. *Sex Roles, 7*(4), 433–447.

DERLEGA, V. J., & GRZELAK, A. L. (1979). Appropriate self-disclosure. In G. J. Chelune (Ed.), *Self-disclosure: Origins, patterns, and implications of openness in interpersonal relationships.* San Francisco: Jossey-Bass.

DEUTSCH, M., & COLLINS, M. E. (1951). *Interracial housing: A psychological evaluation of a social experiment.* Minneapolis: University of Minnesota Press.

DEUTSCH, M., & GERARD, H. B. (1955). A study of normative and informational social influences upon individual judgment. *Journal of Abnormal and Social Psychology, 51,* 629–636.

DEUTSCH, M., & KRAUSS, R. M. (1960). The effect of threat on interpersonal bargaining. *Journal of Abnormal and Social Psychology, 61,* 181–189.

DIAMOND, I. (1980). Pornography and repression: A reconsideration. *Signs: Journal of Women in Culture and Society, 5,* 686–701.

DIENER, E., & DEFOUR, D. (1978). Does television violence enhance program popularity? *Journal of Personality and Social Psychology, 36,* 333–341.

DIENER, F. (1976). Effects of prior destructive behavior, anonymity, and group presence on deindividuation and aggression. *Journal of Personality and Social Psychology, 33,* 497–507.

DIENER, F. (1980). Deindividuation: The absence of self-awareness and self-regulation in group members. In P. B. Paulus (Ed.), *Psychology of group influence.* Hillsdale, NJ: Erlbaum.

DIENER, F., FRASER, S. C., BEAMAN, A. L., & KELEM, Z. R. T. (1976). Effects of deindividuation variables on stealing among Halloween trick-or-treaters. *Journal of Personality and Social Psychology, 33,* 178–183.

DION, K. K. (1972). Physical attractiveness and evaluations of children's transgressions. *Journal of Personality and Social Psychology, 24,* 285–290.

DION, K. K., BERSCHEID, E., & WALSTER, E. (1972). What is

beautiful is good. *Journal of Personality and Social Psychology, 24,* 285–290.

DION, K. L., & DION, K. K. (1973). Correlates of romantic love. *Journal of Consulting and Clinical Psychology, 41,* 51–56.

DOLLARD, J., DOOB, J., MILLER, N., MOWRER, O., & SEARS, R. (1939). *Frustration and aggression.* New Haven, CT: Yale University Press.

DONNERSTEIN, E. (1980). Aggressive erotica and violence against women. *Journal of Personality and Social Psychology, 39,* 269–277.

DONNERSTEIN, E. (1983). Erotica and human aggression. In R. Geen & E. Donnerstein (Eds.), *Aggression: Theoretical and empirical reviews.* New York: Academic Press.

DONNERSTEIN, E., & BARRETT, G. (1978). Effects of erotic stimuli on male aggression toward females. *Journal of Personality and Social Psychology, 36,* 180–188.

DONNERSTEIN, E., & BERKOWITZ, L. (1981). Victim reactions in aggressive erotic films as a factor in violence against women. *Journal of Personality and Social Psychology, 41,* 710–724.

DONNERSTEIN, E., & DONNERSTEIN, M. (1972). White rewarding behavior as a function of potential for black retaliation. *Journal of Personality and Social Psychology, 24,* 327–333.

DONNERSTEIN, E., & DONNERSTEIN, M. (1975). The effects of attitudinal similarity on interracial aggression. *Journal of Personality, 43,* 485–502.

DONNERSTEIN, E., & DONNERSTEIN, M., & EVANS, R. (1975). Erotic stimuli and aggression: Facilitation or inhibition. *Journal of Personality and Social Psychology, 32,* 237–244.

DONNERSTEIN, E., DONNERSTEIN, M., SIMON, S., & DITTRICHS, R. (1972). Variables in interracial aggression: Anonymity, expected retaliation, and a riot. *Journal of Personality and Social Psychology, 22,* 236–245.

DONNERSTEIN, E., & HALLAM, J. (1978). Facilitating effects of erotica on aggression against women. *Journal of Personality and Social Psychology, 36,* 1270–1277.

DONNERSTEIN, E., & WILSON, D. W. (1976). Effects of noise and perceived control on ongoing and subsequent aggressive behavior. *Journal of Personality and Social Psychology, 34,* 774–781.

DOOB, A. N., & WOOD, L. (1972). Catharsis and aggression: The effects of annoyance and retaliation on aggressive behavior. *Journal of Personality and Social Psychology, 22,* 156–162.

DUCK, S., & GILMOUR, R. (Eds.). (1981). *Personal relationships* (Vol. 1). New York: Academic Press.

DWECK, C. S. (1975). The role of expectations and attributions in the alleviation of learned helplessness. *Journal of Personality and Social Psychology, 31,* 674–685.

DYCK, R. J., & RULE, B. G. (1978). Effect on retaliation of causal attributions concerning attack. *Journal of Personality and Social Psychology, 36,* 521–529.

EAGLY, A. H. (1978). Sex differences in influenceability. *Psychological Bulletin, 85,* 86–116.

EAGLY, A. H. (1983). Gender and social influence: A social psychological analysis. *American Psychologist, 38*(9), 971–981.

EAGLY, A. H., & CARLI, L. L. (1981). Sex of researchers and sex-typed communications as determinants of sex differences in influenceability: A meta-analysis of social influence studies. *Psychological Bulletin, 90*(1), 1–20.

EAGLY, A. H., & TELAAK, K. (1972). Width of the latitude of acceptance as a determinant of attitude change. *Journal of Personality and Social Psychology, 23,* 388–397.

EAGLY, A. H., & WARREN, R. (1976). Intelligence, comprehension, and opinion change. *Journal of Personality, 44,* 226–242.

EAGLY, A. H., & WOOD, W. (1982). Inferred sex differences in status as a determinant of gender stereotypes and social influence. *Journal of Personality and Social Psychology, 43,* 915–928.

EAGLY, A. H., WOOD, W., & CHAIKEN, S. (1978). Causal inferences about communicators and their effect on opinion change. *Journal of Personality and Social Psychology, 36,* 424–435.

EDWARDS, W. (1954). The theory of decision-making. *Psychological Bulletin, 51,* 380–417.

EISENBERG, N. (Ed.). (1982). *The development of prosocial behavior.* New York: Academic Press.

EKMAN, P. (1982). *Emotion in the human face* (2nd ed.). Cambridge, Eng.: Cambridge University Press.

EKMAN, P., & FRIESEN, W. V. (1971). Constants across cultures in the face and emotion. *Journal of Personality and Social Psychology, 17,* 124–129.

EKMAN, P., & FRIESEN, W. V. (1974). Detecting deception from the body or face. *Journal of Personality and Social Psychology, 29,* 288–298.

EKMAN, P., FRIESEN, W. V., & SCHERER, K. (1976). Body movements and voice pitch in deceptive interaction. *Semiotica, 16,* 23–27.

ELLSWORTH, P. C., & CARLSMITH, J. M. (1973). Eye contact and gaze aversion in an aggressive encounter. *Journal of Personality and Social Psychology, 28,* 280–292.

ELLSWORTH, P. C., FRIEDMAN, H. S., PERLICK, D., & HOYT, M. E. (1978). Some effects of gaze on subjects motivated to seek or to avoid social comparison. *Journal of Personality and Social Psychology, 14,* 69–87.

EMSWILLER, T., DEAUX, K., & WILLITS, J. E. (1971). Similarity, sex, and requests for small favors. *Journal of Applied Social Psychology, 1*(3), 284–291.

EPSTEIN, Y. M. (1981). Crowding stress and human behavior. *Journal of Social Issues, 37*(1), 126–144.

ERON, L. D., HUESMANN, L. R., LEFKOWITZ, M. M. & WALDER, L. O. (1972). Does television violence cause aggression? *American Psychologist, 27,* 253–263.

ESSER, J. K., & KOMORITA, S. S. (1975). Reciprocity and concession making in bargaining. *Journal of Personality and Social Psychology, 31,* 864–872.

EVANS, G. (1979). Behavioral and physiological consequences of crowding in humans. *Journal of Applied Social Psychology, 9,* 27–46.

EVANS, G. (Ed.). (1982). *Environmental stress.* New York: Cambridge University Press.

FARRENKOPF, T. (1974). *Man-environment interaction: An academic department moves into a new building.* PhD dissertation, University of Massachusetts.

FAZIO, R. H. (1981). On the self-perception explanation of the overjustification effect: The role of the salience of initial attitude. *Journal of Experimental Social Psychology, 17,* 417–426.

Fazio, R. H., Chen, J., McDonel, E. C., & Sherman, S. J. (1982). Attitude accessibility, attitude-behavior consistency, and the strength of the object-evaluation association. *Journal of Experimental Social Psychology, 18,* 339–357.

Fazio, R. H., Effrein, E. A., & Falender, V. J. (1981). Self-perceptions following social interaction. *Journal of Personality and Social Psychology, 41,* 232–242.

Fazio, R. H., & Zanna, M. P. (1981). Direct experience and attitude-behavior consistency. In L. Berkowitz (Ed.), *Advances in experimental social psychology* (Vol. 14). New York: Academic Press.

Feather, N. T., & Simon, J. G. (1975). Reactions to male and female success and failure in sex-linked occupations: Impressions of personality, causal attributions, and perceived likelihood of different consequences. *Journal of Personality and Social Psychology, 31*(1), 20–31.

Feldman, N. S., Higgins, E. T., Karlovac, M., & Ruble, D. N. (1976). Use of consensus information in causal attributions as a function of temporal presentation and availability of direct information. *Journal of Personality and Social Psychology, 34,* 694–698.

Feldman, R. E. (1968). Response to compatriot and foreigner who seek assistance. *Journal of Personality and Social Psychology, 10*(3), 202–214.

Feldman, S. (1983). Economic individualism and American public opinion. *American Politics Quarterly, 11,* 3–30.

Fenigstein, A. (1979). Does aggression cause a preference for viewing media violence? *Journal of Personality and Social Psychology, 37,* 2307–2317.

Feshbach, S. (1955). The drive-reducing function of fantasy behavior. *Journal of Abnormal and Social Psychology, 50,* 3–12.

Feshbach, S. (1961). The stimulating versus cathartic effects of a vicarious aggressive activity. *Journal of Abnormal and Social Psychology, 63,* 381–385.

Feshbach, S. (1970). Aggression. In P. Mussen (Ed.), *Carmichael's Manual of Child Psychology* (Vol. 2). New York: Wiley.

Feshbach, S., & Singer, R. D. (1971). *Television and aggression.* San Francisco: Jossey-Bass.

Festinger, L. (1950). Informal social communication. *Psychological Review, 57,* 271–282.

Festinger, L. (1954). A theory of social comparison processes. *Human Relations, 7,* 117–140.

Festinger, L. (1957). *A theory of cognitive dissonance.* Evanston, IL: Row, Peterson.

Festinger, L., & Carlsmith, J. M. (1959). Cognitive consequences of forced compliance. *Journal of Abnormal and Social Psychology, 58,* 203–210.

Festinger, L., & Maccoby, N. (1964). On resistance to persuasive communications. *Journal of Abnormal and Social Psychology, 68,* 359–366.

Festinger, L., Pepitone, A., & Newcomb, T. (1952). Some consequences of deindividuation in a group. *Journal of Abnormal and Social Psychology, 47,* 383–389.

Festinger, L., Riecken, H. W., & Schachter, S. (1956). *When prophecy fails.* Minneapolis: University of Minnesota Press.

Festinger, L., Schachter, S., & Back, K. (1950). *Social pressures in informal groups: A study of human factors in housing.* New York: Harper & Row.

Fiedler, F. E. (1978). Recent developments in research on the contingency model. In L. Berkowitz (Ed.), *Group processes* (pp. 209–225). New York: Academic Press.

Fiedler, F. E. (1981). Leadership effectiveness. *American Behavioral Scientist, 24*(5), 619–632.

Finkelman, J. M., & Glass, D. C. (1970). Reappraisal of the relationship between noise and human performance by means of a subsidiary task measure. *Journal of Applied Psychology, 54,* 211–213.

Fischer, C. S. (1976). *The urban experience.* New York: Harcourt Brace Jovanovich.

Fischer, C. S. (1982). *To dwell among friends: Personal networks in town and city.* Chicago: University of Chicago Press.

Fischer, W. F. (1963). Sharing in pre-school children as a function of amount and type of reinforcement. *Genetic Psychology Monographs, 68,* 215–245.

Fishbein, M., & Ajzen, I. (1975). *Belief, attitude, intention and behavior: An introduction to theory and research.* Reading, MA: Addison-Wesley.

Fisher, J. D., Bell, P. A., & Baum, A. (1984). *Environmental psychology* (2nd ed.) New York: Holt, Rinehart & Winston.

Fisher, J. D., Nadler, A., & Whitcher-Alagna, S. (1982). Recipient reactions to aid. *Psychological Bulletin, 91,* 33–54.

Fiske, S. T. (1980). Attention and weight in person perception: The impact of negative and extreme behavior. *Journal of Personality and Social Psychology, 38,* 889–906.

Fiske, S. T., & Taylor, S. (1984). *Social cognition.* Reading, MA: Addison-Wesley.

Flowers, M. L. (1977). A laboratory test of some implications of Janis's groupthink hypothesis. *Journal of Personality and Social Psychology, 35,* 888–896.

Foa, U. G. (1971). Interpersonal and economic resources. *Science, 71,* 345–351.

Foa, U. G., & Foa, E. B. (1974). *Societal structures of the mind.* Springfield, IL: Charles C Thomas.

Folkes, V. S. (1982). Forming relationships and the matching hypothesis. *Personality and Social Psychological Bulletin, 8*(4), 631–636.

Folkes, V. S., & Sears, D. O. (1977). Does everybody like a liker? *Journal of Experimental Social Psychology, 13*(6), 505–519.

Forsyth, D. R. (1983). *An introduction to group dynamics.* Monterey, CA: Brooks/Cole.

Franck, K. A. (1980). Friends and strangers: The experience of living in urban and nonurban settings. *Journal of Social Issues, 36,*(3), 52–71.

Frank, F. D., & Drucker, J. (1977). The influence of evaluatee's sex on evaluation of a response on a managerial selection instrument. *Sex Roles, 3,* 59–64.

Fraser, C., Gouge, C., & Billig, M. (1971). Risky shifts, cautious shifts, and group polarization. *European Journal of Social Psychology, 1,* 7–30.

Freedman, J. L. (1963). Attitudinal effects of inadequate justification. *Journal of Personality, 31,* 371–385.

Freedman, J. L. (1964). Involvement, discrepancy, and change. *Journal of Abnormal and Social Psychology, 69,* 290–295.

Freedman, J. L. (1965). Long-term behavioral effects of cognitive dissonance. *Journal of Experimental Social Psychology, 1,* 145–155.

FREEDMAN, J. L. (1975). *Crowding and behavior.* New York: Viking Press.

FREEDMAN, J. L. (1979). Reconciling apparent differences between the responses of humans and other animals to crowding. *Psychological Review, 86,* 80–85.

FREEDMAN, J. L., & DOOB, A. N. (1968). *Deviancy.* New York: Academic Press.

FREEDMAN, J. L., & FRASER, S. C. (1966). Compliance without pressure: The foot-in-the-door technique. *Journal of Personality and Social Psychology, 4,* 195–202.

FREEDMAN, J. L., HESHKA, S., & LEVY, A. (1973). Population density and pathology: Is there a relationship? *Journal of Experimental Social Psychology, 11,* 539–52.

FREEDMAN, J. L., KLEVANSKY, S., & EHRLICH, P. (1971). The effect of crowding on human task performance. *Journal of Applied Social Psychology, 1,* 7–25.

FREEDMAN, J. L., LEVY, A. S., BUCHANAN, R. W., & PRICE, J. (1972). Crowding and human aggressiveness. *Journal of Experimental Social Psychology, 8,* 528–548.

FREEDMAN, J. L., & SEARS, D. O. (1965). Warning, distraction, and resistance to influence. *Journal of Personality and Social Psychology, 1,* 262–266.

FREEDMAN, J. L., & STEINBRUNER, J. D. (1964). Perceived choice and resistance to persuasion. *Journal of Abnormal and Social Psychology, 68,* 678–681.

FREEDMAN, J. L., WALLINGTON, S., & BLESS, E., (1967). Compliance without pressure: The effect of guilt. *Journal of Personality and Social Psychology, 7,* 117–124.

FRENCH, J. (1944). Organized and unorganized groups under fear and frustration. *University of Iowa studies: Studies in child welfare.* Iowa City: University of Iowa.

FRENCH, J. & RAVEN, B. (1959). The bases of social power. In D. Cartwright (Ed.), *Studies in social power* (pp. 150–167). Ann Arbor, MI: Institute for Social Research.

FREY, D. (1982). Different levels of cognitive dissonance, information seeking, and information avoidance. *Journal of Personality and Social Psychology, 43,* 1175–1183.

FRIED, R., & BERKOWITZ, L. (1979). Music hath charms . . . and can influence helpfulness. *Journal of Applied Social Psychology, 9,* 199–208.

FRIEDMAN, L. (1979). *The relationship of some architectural variables to the social behavior of building residents.* Unpublished doctoral dissertation, Columbia University.

FRIEDRICH, L. K., & STEIN, A. H. (1973). Aggressive and prosocial television programs and the natural behavior of preschool children. *Monographs of the Society for Research in Child Development, 38* (4, Serial No. 151).

FRODI, A., MACAULAY, J., & THOME, P. R. (1977). Are women always less aggressive than men? A review of the experimental literature. *Psychological Bulletin, 84*(4), 634–660.

FUNKHOUSER, G. R. (1973). The issues of the sixties: An exploratory study in the dynamics of public opinion. *Public Opinion Quarterly, 37,* 62–75.

GARNETS, L., & PLECK, J. (1979). Sex role identity, androgyny, and sex role transcendence: A sex role strain analysis. *Psychology of Women Quarterly, 3,* 270–283.

GEEN, R. G. (1981). Evaluation apprehension and social facilitation: A reply to Sanders. *Journal of Experimental Social Psychology, 17,* 252–256.

GEEN, R. G., & O'NEAL, E. C. (1969). Activation of cue-eliciting aggression by general arousal. *Journal of Personality and Social Psychology, 11,* 289–292.

GEEN, R. G., & PIGG, R. (1970). Acquisition of an aggressive response and its generalization to verbal behavior. *Journal of Personality and Social Psychology, 15,* 165–170.

GEEN, R. G., & QUANTY, M. B. (1977). The catharsis of aggression: An evaluation of a hypothesis. In L. Berkowitz (Ed.), *Advances in experimental social psychology* (Vol. 10, pp. 2–39). New York: Academic Press.

GELLER, D. M. (1980). Responses to urban stimuli: A balanced approach. *Journal of Social Issues, 36*(3), 86–100.

GERGEN, K. J., ELLSWORTH, P., MASLACH, C., & SEIPEL, M. (1975). Obligation, donor resources, and reactions to aid in three cultures. *Journal of Personality and Social Psychology, 31,* 390–400.

GERGEN, K. J., GERGEN, M. M., & METER, K. (1972). Individual orientations to prosocial behavior. *Journal of Social Issues, 8,* 105–130.

GETTYS, L. D., & CANN, A. (1981). Children's perceptions of occupational sex stereotypes. *Sex Roles, 7*(3), 301–308.

GIBBS, J. P. (1971). Suicide. In R. K. Merton & R. A. Nisbet (Eds.), *Contemporary social problems* (3rd ed., pp. 271–312). New York: Harcourt Brace Jovanovich.

GILMOUR, D. R., & WALKEY, F. H. (1981). Identifying violent offenders using a video measure of interpersonal distance. *Journal of Consulting and Clinical Psychology, 49,* 287–291.

GILOVICH, T. (1981). Seeing the past in the present: The effect of associations to familiar events on judgments and decisions. *Journal of Personality and Social Psychology, 40,* 797–808.

GILOVICH, T., JENNINGS, D. L., & JENNINGS, S. (1983). Causal focus and estimates of consensus: An examination of the false-consensus effect. *Journal of Personality and Social Psychology, 45,* 550–559.

GINSBURG, H. J., POLMAN, V. A., YANSON, M. S., & HOPE, M. L. (1977). Variation of aggressive interaction among male elementary school children as a function of changes in spatial density. *Environmental Psychology and Nonverbal Behavior, 2,* 67–75.

GLASS, D. C., & SINGER, J. E. (1972). *Urban stress.* New York: Academic Press.

GOETHALS, G. R., COOPER, J., & NAFICY, A. (1979). Role of foreseen, foreseeable, and unforeseeable behavioral consequences in the arousal of cognitive dissonance. *Journal of Personality and Social Psychology, 37,* 1179–1185.

GOETHALS, G., & KLOS, D. S. (Eds.). (1970). *Experiencing youth: First-person accounts.* Boston: Little, Brown.

GOFFMAN, E. (1952). On cooling the mark out: Some aspects of adaptation to failure. *Psychiatry, 15,* 451–463.

GOLDBERG, P. (1968). Are women prejudiced against women? *TransAction, 5*(5), 28–30.

GOLDSTEIN, J. H., & ARMS, R. L. (1971). Effects of observing athletic contests on hostility. *Sociometry, 34,* 83–90.

GOLDSTEIN, J. H., DAVIS, R. W., & HERMAN, D. (1975). Escalation of aggression: Experimental studies. *Journal of Personality and Social Psychology, 31,* 162–170.

GOODMAN, M. E. (1952). *Race awareness in young children.* Reading, MA: Addison-Wesley.

GORANSON, R. E., & BERKOWITZ, L. (1966). Reciprocity

and responsibility reactions to prior help. *Journal of Personality and Social Psychology, 3,* 227–232.

GOTTMAN, J. M. (1979). *Marital interaction: Experimental investigations.* New York: Academic Press.

GOULD, R., & SIGALL, H. (1977). The effects of empathy and outcome on attribution: An examination of the divergent-perspectives hypothesis. *Journal of Experimental Social Psychology, 13,* 480–491.

GOULDNER, A. W. (1960). The norm of reciprocity: A preliminary statement. *American Sociological Review, 25,* 161–179.

GRAMZA, A. F. (1967). Responses of brooding nighthawks to disturbance stimulus. *Auk, 84*(1), 72–86.

GREENBERG, B. S., & MAZINGO, S. L. (1976). Racial issues in mass media institutions. In P. A. Katz, (Ed.), *Towards the elimination of racism* (pp. 309–340). Elmsford, NY: Pergamon Press.

GREENBERG, J., & COHEN, R. L. (Eds.), (1982). *Equity and justice in social behavior.* New York: Academic Press.

GREENBERG, J., PYSZCZYNSKI, T., & SOLOMON, S. (1982). The self-serving attributional bias: Beyond self-presentation. *Journal of Experimental Social Psychology, 18,* 56–67.

GREENBERG, M. S., & FRISCH, D. M. (1972). Effects of intentionality on willingness to reciprocate a favor. *Journal of Experimental Social Psychology, 8,* 99–111.

GREENWALD, A. G. (1968). Cognitive learning, cognitive response to persuasion, and attitude change. In A. G. Greenwald, T. C. Brock, and T. M. Ostrom, (Eds.), *Psychological foundations of attitudes* (pp. 147–170). New York: Academic Press.

GREENWELL, J., & DENGERINK, H. A. (1973). The role of perceived versus actual attack in human physical aggression. *Journal of Personality and Social Psychology, 26,* 66–71.

GREER, D. L. (1983). Spectator booing and the home advantage: A study of social influence in the basketball arena. *Social Psychology Quarterly, 46*(3), 252–261.

GRIFFIT, W., & VEITCH, R. (1971). Hot and crowded: Influences of population density and temperature on interpersonal affective behavior. *Journal of Personality and Social Psychology, 17,* 92–98.

GROSS, A. E., & LATANÉ, J. G. (1974). Receiving help, reciprocation, and interpersonal attraction. *Journal of Applied Social Psychology, 4*(3), 210–223.

GROSS, A. E., WALLSTON, B. S., & PILIAVIN, I. M. (1979). Reactance, attribution, equity, and the help recipient. *Journal of Applied Social Psychology, 9*(4), 297–313.

GRUDER, C. L., ROMER, D., & KORTH, B. (1978). Dependency and fault as determinants of helping. *Journal of Experimental Social Psychology, 14,* 227–235.

GRUSH, J. E. (1980). Impact of candidate expenditures, regionality, and prior outcomes on the 1976 Democratic presidential primaries. *Journal of Personality and Social Psychology, 38,* 337–347.

GRUSH, J. E., MCKEOGH, K. L., & AHLERING, R. G. (1978). Extrapolating laboratory exposure research to actual political elections. *Journal of Personality and Social Psychology, 36,* 257–70.

GUERIN, B., & INNES, J. M. (1982). Social facilitation and social monitoring: A new look at Zajonc's mere presence hypothesis. *British Journal of Social Psychology, 21,* 7–18.

GUIMOND, S., & DUBE-SIMARD, L. (1983). Relative deprivation theory and the Quebec nationalist movement: The cognition-emotion distinction and the personal-group deprivation issue. *Journal of Personality and Social Psychology, 44,* 526–535.

GURIN, G., VEROFF, J., & FELD, S. (1960). *Americans view their mental health: A nationwide survey.* New York: Basic Books.

GUTTENTAG, M., & SECORD, P. F. (1982). *Too many women: The sex ratio question.* Beverly Hills, CA: Sage Publications.

HACKER, H. M. (1981). Blabbermouths and clams: Sex differences in self-disclosure in same-sex and cross-sex friendship dyads. *Psychology of Women Quarterly, 5*(3), 385–401.

HAIGHT, T. R., & BRODY, R. A. (1977). The mass media and presidential popularity: Presidential broadcasting and news in the Nixon administration. *Communication Research, 4,* 41–60.

HALL, E. T. (1959). *The silent language.* Garden City, NY: Doubleday.

HALL, J. A. (1978). Gender effects in decoding nonverbal cues. *Psychological Bulletin, 85*(4), 845–857.

HALL, K. R. L. (1960). Social vigilance behavior of the chacuma baboon (Papio ursinus). *Behaviour, 16* (3,4), 261–294.

HAMILTON, D. L. (1981). Cognitive representations of persons. In E. T. Higgins, C. P. Herman, & M. P. Zanna (Eds.), *Social cognition: The Ontario symposium* (Vol. 1). Hillsdale, NJ: Erlbaum.

HAMILTON, D. L., & ZANNA, M. P. (1972). Differential weighting of favorable and unfavorable attributions in impressions of personality. *Journal of Experimental Research in Personality, 6,* 204–212.

HAMILTON, D. L., & ZANNA, M. P. (1974). Context effects in impression formation: Changes in connotative meaning. *Journal of Personality and Social Psychology, 29,* 649–654.

HANSSON, R. O., & SLADE, K. M. (1977). Altruism toward a deviant in city and small town. *Journal of Applied Social Psychology, 7,* 272–279.

HARKINS, S. G., & PETTY, R. E. (1982). Effects of task difficulty and task uniqueness on social loafing. *Journal of Personality and Social Psychology, 43*(6), 1214–1229.

HARTMANN, D. P. (1969). Influence of symbolically modeled instrumental aggression and pain cues on aggressive behavior. *Journal of Personality and Social Psychology, 11,* 280–288.

HARTNETT, J. J., BAILEY, K. G., & GIBSON, F. W., JR. (1970). Personal space as influenced by sex and type of movement. *Journal of Psychology, 76,* 139–144.

HARVEY, J. H., WEARY, G., & HARRIS, B. (1981). *Perspectives on attributional processes.* Dubuque, IA: Wm. C. Brown.

HASS, R. G., & GRADY, K. (1975). Temporal delay, type of forewarning and resistance to influence. *Journal of Experimental Social Psychology, 11,* 459–469.

HATKOFF, S., & LASSWELL, T. E. (1979). Male-female similarities and differences in conceptualizing love. In M. Cook & G. Wilson (Eds.), *Love and attraction.* Oxford, Eng.: Pergamon Press.

HEFF, H. (1979). Background and focal environmental

conditions of the home and attention in young children. *Journal of Applied Social Psychology, 9,* 47–69.

HEIDER, F. (1958). *The psychology of interpersonal relations.* New York: Wiley.

HELLER, J. F., GROFF, B. D., & SOLOMON, S. H. (1977). Toward an understanding of crowding: The role of physical interaction. *Journal of Personality and Social Psychology, 35,* 183–190.

HENDRICK, C., & HENDRICK, S. (1983). *Liking, loving, and relating.* Monterey, CA: Brooks/Cole.

HENDRICK, C., HENDRICK, S., FOOTE, F. H., & SLAPION-FOOTE, M. J. (in press). Do men and women love differently? *Journal of Social and Personal Relationships.*

HENLEY, N. M. (1977). *Body politics: Power, sex, and nonverbal communication.* Englewood Cliffs, NJ: Prentice-Hall.

HENLEY, N. M. (1979, May). *This new species that seeks a new language: On sexism in language and language change.* Paper presented at Conference on Language and Gender, Santa Cruz, CA.

HENNIGAN, K. M., HEATH, L., WHARTON, J. D., DEL ROSARIO, M. L., COOK, T. D., & CALDER, B. J. (1982). Impact of the introduction of television on crime in the United States: Empirical findings and theoretical implications. *Journal of Personality and Social Psychology, 42,* 461–477.

HIGBEE, K. L. (1969). Fifteen years of fear arousal: Research on threat appeals, 1953–1968. *Psychological Bulletin, 72,* 426–444.

HIGGINS, E. T., & BRYANT, S. L. (1982). Consensus information and the fundamental attribution error: The role of development and in-group versus out-group knowledge. *Journal of Personality and Social Psychology, 43,* 889–900.

HIGGINS, E. T., RHODEWALT, F., & ZANNA, M. P. (1979). Dissonance motivation: Its nature, persistence, and reinstatement. *Journal of Experimental Social Psychology, 15,* 16–34.

HILL, C. T., RUBIN, Z., & PEPLAU, L. A. (1976). Breakups before marriage: The end of 103 affairs. *Journal of Social Issues, 32*(1), 147–168.

HILL, G. W. (1982). Group versus individual performance: Are N + 1 heads better than one? *Psychological Bulletin, 91,* 517–539.

HIRT, E., & KIMBLE, C. E. (1981, May). *The home-field advantage in sports: Differences and correlates.* Paper presented at the Midwestern Psychological Assoc., Detroit.

HODGES, B. H. (1974). Effect of valence on relative weighting in impression formation. *Journal of Personality and Social Psychology, 30,* 378–381.

HOFFMAN, C., MISCHEL, W., & MAZZE, K. (1981). The role of purpose in the organization of information about behavior: Trait-based versus goal-based categories in person cognition. *Journal of Personality and Social Psychology, 40,* 211–225.

HOFFMAN, M. L. (1981). Is altruism part of human nature? *Journal of Personality and Social Psychology, 40*(1), 121–137.

HOKANSON, J. E. (1961). Vascular and psychogalvanic effects of experimentally aroused anger. *Journal of Personality, 29,* 30–39.

HOKANSON, J. E., & BURGESS, M. (1962). The effects of

three types of aggression on vascular processes. *Journal of Abnormal and Social Psychology, 64,* 446–449.

HOLAHAN, C. J., & WILCOX, B. L. (1978). Residential satisfaction and friendship formation in high- and low-rise student housing: An interactional analysis. *Journal of Educational Psychology, 70*(2), 237–241.

HOMANS, G. C. (1965). Group factors in worker productivity. In H. Proshansky and L. Seidenberg (Eds.), *Basic studies in social psychology.* New York: Holt, Rinehart & Winston.

HOOK, J. G., & COOK, T. D. (1979). Equity theory and the cognitive ability of children. *Psychological Bulletin, 86,* 429–445.

HOROWITZ, M. J., DUFF, D. F., & STRATTON, L. O. (1970). Personal space and the body buffer zone. In H. Proshansky, W. Ittelson, & L. Rivlin (Eds.), *Environmental psychology: Man and his physical setting.* New York: Holt, Rinehart & Winston.

HOUSE, J. S. (1981). *Work stress and social support.* Reading, MA: Addison-Wesley.

HOUSE, J. S., & WOLF, S. (1978). Effects of urban residence on interpersonal trust and helping behavior. *Journal of Personality and Social Psychology, 36,* 1029–1043.

HOVLAND, C. I. (1959). Reconciling conflicting results derived from experimental and survey studies of attitude change. *American Psychologist, 14,* 8–17.

HOVLAND, C. I., HARVEY, O. J., & SHERIF, M. (1957). Assimilation and contrast effects in reactions to communication and attitude change. *Journal of Abnormal and Social Psychology, 55,* 244–252.

HOVLAND, C. I., & JANIS, I. L. (1959). Summary and implications for further research. In C. I. Hovland and I. L. Janis (Eds.), *Personality and persuasibility.* New Haven, CT: Yale University Press.

HOVLAND, C. I., & JANIS, I. L., & KELLEY, H. H. (1953). *Communication and persuasion.* New Haven: Yale University Press.

HOVLAND, C. I., LUMSDAINE, A. A., & SHEFFIELD, F.D. (1949). *Experiments on mass communication.* Princeton, NJ: Princeton University Press.

HOVLAND, C. I., & PRITZKER, H. A. (1957). Extent of opinion change as a function of amount of change advocated. *Journal of Abnormal and Social Psychology, 54,* 257–261.

HOVLAND, C. I., & SEARS, R. R. (1940). Minor studies of aggression: Correlation of lynchings with economic indices. *Journal of Psychology, 9,* 301–310.

HOVLAND, C. I., & WEISS, W. (1952). The influence of source credibility on communication effectiveness. *Public Opinion Quarterly, 15,* 635–650.

HUESMANN, L. R. (1982). Television violence and aggressive behavior. In D. Pearl, L. Bouthilet, & J. Lazar (Eds.), *Television and behavior: Ten years of scientific progress and implications for the eighties: Vol. II. Technical reviews.* Rockville, MD: Nat'l. Inst. of Mental Health.

HUNT, M. M. (1959). *The natural history of love.* New York: Knopf.

HUR, K. K., & ROBINSON, J. P. (1978). The social impact of "Roots." *Journalism Quarterly, 55,* 19–24.

HUSTON, T. L. (1983). Power. In H. H. Kelley et al., *Close relationships* (pp. 169–219). New York: Freeman.

HUSTON, T. L., RUGGIERO, M., CONNER, R., & GEIS, G. (1981). Bystander intervention into crime: A study based on naturally-occurring episodes. *Social Psychology Quarterly, 44*(1), 14–23.

HYDE, J. S. (1981). How large are cognitive gender differences? A meta-analysis using w² and d. *American Psychologist, 36,* 892–901.

HYDE, J. S., & ROSENBERG, B. G. (1984). *Half the human experience: The psychology of women* (3rd ed.). Lexington, MA: Heath.

INKELES, A. (1983). *The third century.* Stanford, CA: Hoover Institution Press.

ISEN, A. M. (1970). Success, failure, attention, and reaction to others: The warm glow of success. *Journal of Personality and Social Psychology, 15,* 294–301.

ISEN, A. M., CLARK, M., & SCHWARTZ, M. F. (1976). Duration of the effect of good mood on helping: Footprints on the sands of time. *Journal of Personality and Social Psychology, 34,* 385–393.

ISEN, A. M., & LEVIN, P. F. (1972). Effects of feeling good on helping: Cookies and kindness. *Journal of Personality and Social Psychology, 21,* 384–388.

ISEN, A. M., & SIMMONDS, S. F. (1978). The effect of feeling good on a helping task that is incompatible with good mood. *Social Psychology Quarterly, 41,* 346–349.

IYENGAR, S., KINDER, D. R., PETERS, M. D., & KROSNICK, J. A. (1984). The evening news and presidential evaluations. *Journal of Personality and Social Psychology, 46,* 778–787.

IYENGAR, S., PETERS, M. D., & KINDER, D. R. (1982). Experimental demonstrations of the "not-so-minimal" consequences of TV news programs. *The American Political Science Review, 76*(4), 848–858.

JACKSON, J. E. (1983). Election night reporting and voter turnout. *American Journal of Political Science, 27,* 615–635.

JAFFE, Y., MALAMUTH, N., FEINGOLD, J., & FESHBACH, S. (1974). Sexual arousal and behavioral aggression. *Journal of Personality and Social Psychology, 30,* 759–764.

JANIS, I. L. (1967). Effects of fear arousal on attitude change: Recent developments in theory and experimental research. In L. Berkowitz (Ed.), *Advances in Experimental Social Psychology* (Vol. 3, pp. 166–224). New York: Academic Press.

JANIS, I. L. (1983). *Groupthink: Psychological studies of policy decisions and fiascoes* (2nd ed., rev.). Boston: Houghton Mifflin.

JANIS, I. L., & FESHBACH, S. (1953). Effects of fear-arousing communications. *Journal of Abnormal and Social Psychology, 48,* 78–92.

JANIS, I. L., & GILMORE, J. B. (1965). The influence of incentive conditions on the success of role playing in modifying attitudes. *Journal of Personality and Social Psychology, 1,* 17–27.

JANIS, I. L., & MANN, L. (1965). Effectiveness of emotional role-playing in modifying smoking habits and attitudes. *Journal of Experimental Research in Personality, 1,* 84–90.

JANIS, I. L., & RAUSCH, C. N. (1970). Selective interest in communications that could arouse decisional conflict: A field study of participants in the draft-resistance movement. *Journal of Personality and Social Psychology, 14,* 46–54.

JANOFF-BULMAN, R. (1979). Characterological versus behavioral self-blame: Inquiries into depression and rape. *Journal of Personality and Social Psychology, 37,* 1798–1809.

JELLISON, J. M., & GREEN, J. (1981). A self-presentation approach to the fundamental attribution error: The norm of internality. *Journal of Personality and Social Psychology, 40,* 643–649.

JENNINGS, J., GEIS, F. L., & BROWN, V. (1980). Influence of television commercials on women's self-confidence and independent judgment. *Journal of Personality and Social Psychology, 38*(2), 203–210.

JENNINGS, M. K., & NIEMI, R. G. (1974). *The political character of adolescence.* Princeton, NJ: Princeton University Press.

JERVIS, R. (1976). *Perception and misperception in international politics.* Princeton, NJ: Princeton University Press.

JOHNSON, P. B., SEARS, D. O., & McCONAHAY, J. B. (1971). Black invisibility, the press, and the Los Angeles riot. *American Journal of Sociology, 76*(4), 698–721.

JOHNSON, R. D., & DOWNING, L. L. (1979). Deindividuation and valence of cues: Effects of prosocial and antisocial behavior. *Journal of Personality and Social Psychology, 37,* 1532–1538.

JONES, E. E. (1979). The rocky road from acts to dispositions. *American Psychologist, 34,* 107–117.

JONES, E. E., & HARRIS, V. A. (1967). The attribution of attitudes. *Journal of Experimental Social Psychology, 3,* 1–24.

JONES, E. E., & NISBETT, R. E. (1972). The actor and the observer: Divergent perceptions of the causes of behavior. In E. E. Jones et al., *Attribution: Perceiving the causes of behavior.* Morristown, NJ: General Learning Press.

JONES, E. E., & SIGALL, H. (1971). The bogus pipeline: A new paradigm for measuring affect and attitude. *Psychological Bulletin, 76,* 349–364.

JONES, E. E., WORCHEL, S., COETHALS, G. R., & GRUMET, J. F. (1971). Prior expectancy and behavioral extremity as determinants of attitude attribution. *Journal of Experimental Social Psychology, 7,* 59–80.

JONES, W. H. (1982). Loneliness and social behavior. In L. A. Peplau & D. Perlman (Eds.), *Loneliness: A sourcebook of current theory, research and therapy* (pp. 238–254). New York: Wiley-Interscience.

JORDAN, W. D. (1968). *White over black: American attitudes toward the Negro, 1550–1812.* Chapel Hill: University of North Carolina Press.

KANDEL, D. (1974). Inter- and intragenerational influences on adolescent marijuana use. *Journal of Social Issues, 30,* 107–135.

KANDEL, D. (1978). Similarity in real-life adolescent friendship pairs. *Journal of Personality and Social Psychology, 36,* 306–312.

KANIN, E. J., DAVIDSON, K. R., & SCHECK, S. R. (1970). A research note on male-female differentials in the experience of heterosexual love. *Journal of Sex Research, 6*(1), 64–72.

KANOUSE, D. E., & HANSON, L. R., JR. (1972). Negativity in evaluations. In E. E. Jones et al., *Attribution: Perceiving and causes of behavior* (pp. 47–62). Morristown, NJ: General Learning Press.

KAPLAN, K. J., FIRESTONE, I. J., DEGNORE, R., & MORRE, M. (1974). Gradients of attraction as a function of disclosure probe intimacy and setting formality: On distinguishing attitude oscillation from attitude change—Study one. *Journal of Personality and Social Psychology, 30,* 638–646.

KAPLAN, R. M., & SINGER, R. D. (1976). Television violence and viewer aggression: A reexamination of the evidence. *Journal of Social Issues, 32,* 35–70.

KARLIN, R. A., EPSTEIN, Y. M., & AIELLO, J. R. (1978). Strategies for the investigation of crowding. In A. Esser & B. Greenbie (Eds.), *Design for community and privacy.* New York: Plenum Press.

KARLINS, M., COFFMAN, T. L., & WALTERS, G. (1969). On the fading of social stereotypes: Studies in three generations of college students. *Journal of Personality and Social Psychology, 13,* 1–16.

KATZ, D., & BRALY, K. W. (1933). Racial stereotypes of 100 college students. *Journal of Abnormal Social Psychology, 28,* 280–290.

KATZ, E., & FELDMAN, J. J. (1962). The debates in the light of research: A survey of surveys. In S. Kraus (Ed.), *The great debates* (pp. 173–223). Bloomington: Indiana University Press.

KEATING, C. F., MAZUR, A., SEGALL, M. H., CYSNEIROS, P. G., DIVALE, W. T., KILBRIDE, J. E., KOMIN, S., LEAHY, P., THURMAN, B., & WIRSING, R. (1981). Culture and the perception of social dominance from facial expression. *Journal of Personality and Social Psychology, 40,* 601–614.

KEATING, C. H., JR. (1970). Report of Commissioner Charles H. Keating, Jr. In *The Report of the Commission on Obscenity and Pornography.* New York: Random House.

KELLEY, H. H. (1950). The warm-cold variable in first impressions of persons. *Journal of Personality, 18,* 431–439.

KELLEY, H. H. (1967). Attribution theory in social psychology. In D. Levine (Ed.), *Nebraska Symposium on Motivation.* Lincoln: University of Nebraska Press.

KELLEY, H. H. (1952). Attribution in social interaction. In E. E. Jones et al., *Attribution: Perceiving the causes of behavior.* Morristown, NJ: General Learning Press.

KELLEY, H. H. (1979). *Personal relationships: Their structures and processes.* Hillsdale, NJ: Erlbaum.

KELLEY, H. H. (1983). Love and commitment. In H. H. Kelley et al., *Close relationships* (pp. 265–314). New York: Freeman.

KELLEY, H. H., BERSCHEID, E., CHRISTENSEN, A., HARVEY, J. H., HUSTON, T. L., LEVINGER, G., McCLINTOCK, E., PEPLAU, L. A., & PETERSON, D. R. (1983). *Close relationships.* New York: Freeman.

KELLEY, H. H., & THIBAUT, J. W. (1978). *Interpersonal relations: A theory of interdependence.* New York: Wiley-Interscience.

KELLEY, H. H., & VOLKART, E. H. (1952). The resistance to change of group-anchored attitudes. *American Sociological Review, 17,* 453–465.

KELLEY, H. H., & WOODRUFF, L. (1956). Members' reactions to apparent group approval of a counternorm communication. *Journal of Abnormal and Social Psychology, 52,* 67–74.

KELLEY, S., JR., & MIRER, T. W. (1974). The simple act of voting. *American Political Science Review, 68,* 572–591.

KELMAN, H. C., & HOVLAND, C. I. (1953). "Reinstatement" of the communicator in delayed measurement of opinion change. *Journal of Abnormal and Social Psychology, 48,* 327–335.

KENRICK, D. T., & GUTIERRES, S. E. (1980). Contrast effects and judgments of physical attractiveness: When beauty becomes a social problem. *Journal of Personality and Social Psychology, 38,* 131–140.

KENRICK, D. T., & JOHNSON, G. A. (1979). Interpersonal attraction in aversive environments: A problem for the classical conditioning paradigm? *Journal of Personality and Social Psychology, 37,* 572–579.

KERNIS, M. H. & WHEELER, L. (1981). Beautiful friends and ugly strangers: Radiation and contrast effects in perception of same-sex pairs. *Personality and Social Psychology Bulletin, 7,* 617–620.

KIDDER, L. H., FAGAN, M. A., & COHN, E. S. (1981). Giving and receiving: Social justice in close relationships. In M. J. Lerner & S. C. Lerner (Eds.), *The justice motive in social behavior: Adapting to times of scarcity and change* (pp. 235–259). New York: Plenum Press.

KINDER, D. R., & ABELSON, R. P. (1981). *Appraising presidential candidates: Personality and affect in the 1980 campaign.* Paper presented at the annual meeting of the American Political Science Association, New York.

KINDER, D. R., & SEARS, D. O. (1981). Prejudice and politics: Symbolic racism versus racial threats to the good life. *Journal of Personality and Social Psychology, 40,* 414–431.

KINDER, D. R., & SEARS, D. O. (1985). Public opinion and political action. In G. Lindzey & E. Aronson (Eds.), *Handbook of social psychology* (3rd ed.). Reading, MA: Addison-Wesley.

KING, C. E., & CHRISTENSEN, A. (1983). The relationship events scale: A Guttman scale of progress in courtship. *Journal of Marriage and the Family, 45,* 671–678.

KINGDON, J. W. (1967). Politicians' beliefs about voters. *The American Political Science Review, 61,* 137–145.

KLAPPER, J. T. (1960). *The effects of mass communications.* Glencoe, IL: Free Press.

KLEIN, K., & HARRIS, B. (1979). Disruptive effects of disconfirmed expectancies about crowding. *Journal of Personality and Social Psychology, 37,* 769–777.

KLEINHESSELINK, R. R., & EDWARDS, R. W. (1975). Seeking and avoiding belief-discrepant information as a function of its perceived refutability. *Journal of Personality and Social Psychology, 31,* 787–790.

KLINNERT, M. D. (1981, April). *Infants' use of mothers' facial expressions for regulating their own behavior.* Paper presented at the meeting of the Society for Research in Child Development, Boston.

KNOX, R. E., & INKSTER, J. A. (1968). Postdecision dissonance at post time. *Journal of Personality and Social Psychology, 8,* 319–323.

KOGAN, N., & WALLACH, M. A. (1967). Risk taking as a function of the situation, the person, and the group. In G. Mandler (Ed.), *New directions in psychology* (Vol. III). New York: Holt, Rinehart & Winston.

KOHLBERG, L. (1966). A cognitive-developmental analysis of children's sex-role concepts and attitudes. In E. E.

Maccoby (Ed.), *The development of sex differences.* Stanford, CA: Stanford University Press.

KOMAROVSKY, M. (1967). *Blue-collar marriage.* New York: Vintage.

KOMORITA, S. S., & LAPWORTH, C. W. (1982). Cooperative choice among individuals versus groups in *N*-person dilemma situation. *Journal of Personality and Social Psychology, 42,* 487–496.

KONECNI, V. J. (1975). Annoyance, type and duration of post-annoyance activity, and aggression: The "cathartic" effect. *Journal of Experimental Psychology: General, 104,* 76–102.

KONECNI, V. J., & DOOB, A. N. (1972). Catharsis through displacement of aggression. *Journal of Personality and Social Psychology, 23,* 379–387.

KONECNI, V. J., & EBBESEN, E. B. (1976). Disinhibition versus the cathartic effect: Artifact and substance. *Journal of Personality and Social Psychology, 34,* 352–365.

KONECNI, V. J., LIBUSER, L., MORTON, H., & EBBESEN, E. B. (1975). Effects of a violation of personal space on escape and helping responses. *Journal of Experimental Social Psychology, 11,* 288–299.

KORTE, C. (1971). Effects of individual responsibility and group communication on help-giving in an emergency. *Human Relations, 24,* 149–159.

KORTE, C. (1980). Urban-nonurban differences in social behavior and social psychological models of urban impact. *Journal of Social Issues, 36*(3), 29–51.

KORTE, C. (1981). Constraints on helping in an urban environment. In J. P. Rushton & R. M. Sorrentino (Eds.), *Altruism and helping behavior.* Hillsdale, NJ: Erlbaum.

KORTE, C., & GRANT, R. (1980). Traffic noise, environmental awareness, and pedestrian behavior. *Environment and Behavior, 12,* 996–1003.

KRAUS, S., & CHAFFEE, S. H. (Eds.). (1974). *Communication research.* Beverly Hills, CA: Sage Publications.

KRAUS, S., & DAVIS, D. (1976). *The effects of mass communication on political behavior.* University Park, PA: Pennsylvania State University Press.

KRAUSS, R. M., APPLE, W., MORENCY, N., WENZEL, C., & WINTON, W. (1981). Verbal, vocal, and visible factors in judgments of another's affect. *Journal of Personality and Social Psychology, 40,* 312–320.

KRAUSS, R. M., GELLER, V., & OLSON, C. (1976, September). *Modalities and cues in the detection of deception.* Paper presented at the American Psychological Association meeting.

KRAUT, R. E. (1973). Effects of social labelling on giving to charity. *Journal of Experimental Social Psychology, 9,* 551–562.

KRAUT, R. E. (1978). Verbal and nonverbal cues in the perception of lying. *Journal of Personality and Social Psychology, 36,* 380–391.

KRAUT, R. E., & POE, D. (1980). Behavioral roots of person perception: The deception judgments of customs inspectors and laymen. *Journal of Personality and Social Psychology, 39,* 784–798.

KRECH, D., & CRUTCHFIELD, R. A. (1948). *Theory and problems of social psychology.* New York: McGraw-Hill.

KUHLMAN, D. M., & MARSHELLO, A. F. J. (1975). Individual differences in game motivation as moderators of pre-programmed strategy effects in Prisoner's Dilemma. *Journal of Personality and Social Psychology, 32,* 922–931.

KUHLMAN, D. M., & WIMBERLEY, D. L. (1976). Expectations of choice behavior held by cooperators, competitors, and individualists across four classes of experimental game. *Journal of Personality and Social Psychology, 34,* 69–81.

KULIK, J. A. (1983). Confirmatory attribution and the perpetuation of social beliefs. *Journal of Personality and Social Psychology, 44*(6), 1171–1181.

KUNDA, Z. & SCHWARTZ, S. H. (1983). Undermining intrinsic moral motivation: External reward and self-presentation. *Journal of Personality and Social Psychology, 44,* 763–771.

KUTNER, B., WILKINS, C., YARROW, P. R. (1952). Verbal attitudes and overt behavior involving racial prejudice. *Journal of Abnormal Social Psychology, 47,* 649–652.

LAMM, H., & TROMMSDORF, G. (1973). Group versus individual performance on tasks requiring ideational proficiency (brainstorming): A review. *European Journal of Social Psychology, 3,* 361–388.

LANDY, D., & ARONSON, E. (1969). The influence of the character of the criminal and his victim on the decisions of simulated jurors. *Journal of Experimental Social Psychology, 5,* 141–152.

LANDY, D., & SIGALL, H. (1974). Beauty is talent: Task evaluation as a function of the performer's physical attractiveness. *Journal of Personality and Social Psychology, 29,* 299–304.

LANG, G. E., & LANG, K. (1979). Immediate and mediated responses: First debate. In S. Kraus (Ed.), *The great debates: Carter vs. Ford 1976* (pp. 298–313). Bloomington: Indiana University Press.

LANGER, E. J. (1975). The illusion of control. *Journal of Personality and Social Psychology, 32,* 311–328.

LAPIERE, R. T. (1934). Attitudes vs. actions. *Social Forces, 13,* 230–237.

LARSON, R., CSIKSZENTMIHALYI, M., & GRAEF, R. (1982). Time alone in daily experience: Loneliness or renewal? In L. A. Peplau & D. Perlman (Eds.), *Loneliness: A sourcebook of current theory, research and therapy* (pp. 40–53). New York: Wiley-Interscience.

LASSWELL, M., & LOBSENZ, N. M. (1980). *Styles of loving.* New York: Ballantine Books.

LASSWELL, T. E., & LASSWELL, M. (1976). I love you but I'm not in love with you. *Journal of Marriage and Family Counseling, 2*(3), 211–224.

LATANÉ, B. (1981). The psychology of social impact. *American Psychologist, 36,* 343–356.

LATANÉ, B., & DARLEY, J. M. (1968). Group inhibition of bystander intervention in emergencies. *Journal of Personality and Social Psychology, 10,* 215–221.

LATANÉ, B., & DARLEY, J. M. (1970). *The unresponsive bystander: Why doesn't he help?* New York: Appleton-Century-Crofts.

LATANÉ, B., & NIDA, S. (1981). Ten years of research on group size and helping. *Psychological Bulletin, 89*(2), 308–324.

LATANÉ, B., WILLIAMS, K., & HARKINS, S. (1979). Many hands make light the work: The causes and consequences of social loafing. *Journal of Personality and Social Psychology, 37,* 822–832.

LAU, R. R. (1979). *Negativity in person perception with applications to political behavior*. Unpublished doctoral dissertation, University of California, Los Angeles.

LAU, R. R., & RUSSELL, D. (1980). Attributions in the sports pages. *Journal of Personality and Social Psychology, 39*, 29–38.

LAZARSFELD, P. F., BERELSON, B., & GAUDET, H. (1948). *The people's choice* (2nd ed.). New York: Columbia University Press.

LEAVITT, H. J. (1951). Some effects of certain communication patterns on group performance. *Journal of Abnormal and Social Psychology, 46*, 38–50.

LEBON, G. (1896). *The crowd: A study of the popular mind*. London: Ernest Benn.

LEDERER, L. (Ed.). (1980). *Take back the night: Women on pornography*. New York: Morrow, 1980.

LEE, J. A. (1973). *The colors of love*. New York: Bantam Books.

LEE, J. A. (1977). A typology of styles of loving. *Personality and Social Psychology Bulletin, 3*, 173–182.

LEIBMAN, M. (1970). The effects of sex and race norms on personal space. *Dissertation Abstracts International, 31*, 3038–3039.

LEPPER, M., GREENE, D., & NISBETT, R. (1973). Undermining children's interest with extrinsic rewards: A test of the "overjustification hypothesis." *Journal of Personality and Social Psychology, 28*, 129–137.

LERNER, M. J. (1965). The effect of responsibility and choice on a partner's attractiveness following failure. *Journal of Personality, 33*, 178–187.

LERNER, M. J. (1970). The desire for justice and reactions to victims. In J. McCauley and L. Berkowitz (Eds.), *Altruism and helping behavior*. New York: Academic Press.

LERNER, M. J. (1980). *The belief in a just world: A fundamental delusion*. New York: Plenum Books.

LEVENTHAL, H. (1970). Findings and theory in the study of fear communications. In L. Berkowitz, (Ed.), *Advances in experimental social psychology* (Vol. 5), pp. 120–186). New York: Academic Press.

LEVINE, R. A., & CAMPBELL, D. T. (1972). *Ethnocentrism: Theories of conflict, ethnic attitudes, and group behavior*. New York: Wiley.

LEVINGER, G. (1979). A social psychological perspective on marital dissolution. In G. Levinger & O. C. Moles (Eds.), *Divorce and separation: Context, causes, and consequences*. New York: Basic Books.

LEVINGER, G., & SNOEK, J. G. (1972). *Attraction in relationship: A new look at interpersonal attraction*. Morristown, NJ: General Learning Press.

LEVINSON, R. M. (1975). Sex discrimination and employment practices: An experiment with unconventional job inquiries. *Social Problems, 22*, 533–543.

LEWIN, K., LIPPITT, R., & WHITE, R. K. (1939). Patterns of aggressive behavior in experimentally created social climates. *Journal of Social Psychology, 10*, 271–299.

LEYENS, J. P., CAMINO, L., PARKE, R. D., & BERKOWITZ, L. (1975). Effects of movie violence on aggression in a field setting as a function of group dominance and cohesion. *Journal of Personality and Social Psychology, 32*, 346–360.

LINDER, D. E., COOPER, J., & JONES, E. E. (1967). Decision freedom as a determinant of the role of incentive magnitude in attitude change. *Journal of Personality and Social Psychology, 6*, 245–254.

LIPSET, S. M. (1960). *Political man*. Garden City, NY: Doubleday.

LITTLE, K. B. (1968). Cultural variations in social schemata. *Journal of Personality and Social Psychology, 10*, 1–7.

LOCKSLEY, A., BORGIDA, E., BREKKE, N., & HEPBURN, C. (1980). Sex stereotypes and social judgment. *Journal of Personality and Social Psychology, 39*(5), 821–831.

LOCKSLEY, A., ORTIZ, V., & HEPBURN, C. (1980). Social categorization and discriminatory behavior: Extinguishing the minimal intergroup discrimination effect. *Journal of Personality and Social Psychology, 39*, 773–783.

LONDON, P. (1970). The rescuers: Motivational hypotheses about Christians who saved Jews from the Nazis. In J. Macaulay & L. Berkowitz (Eds.), *Altruism and helping behavior* (pp. 241–250). New York: Academic Press.

LONG, G. T., & LERNER, M. J. (1974). Deserving, the 'personal contract', and altruistic behavior in children. *Journal of Personality and Social Psychology, 29*, 551–556.

LONGFELLOW, C. (1979). Divorce in context: Its impact on children. In G. Levinger & O. C. Moles (Eds.), *Divorce and separation: Context, causes and consequences*. New York: Basic Books.

LONGLEY, J., & PRUITT, D. G. (1980). Groupthink: A critique of Janis's theory. In L. Wheeler (Ed.), *Review of personality and social psychology* (Vol. 1). Beverly Hills, CA: Sage Publications.

LOO, C., & SMETANA, J. (1978). The effects of crowding on the behavior and perception of 10-year-old boys. *Environmental Psychology and Nonverbal Behavior, 2*, 226–249.

LORGE, I. (1936). Prestige, suggestion, and attitudes. *Journal of Social Psychology, 7*, 386–402.

LOTT, D. F., & SOMMER, R. (1967). Seating arrangements and status. *Journal of Personality and Social Psychology, 7*, 90–95.

LYNCH, J. G., JR., & COHEN, J. L. (1978). The use of subjective expected utility theory as an aid to understanding variables that influence helping behavior. *Journal of Personality and Social Psychology, 36*, 1138–1151.

MACCOBY, E. E., & JACKLIN, C. N. (1974). *The psychology of sex differences*. Stanford, CA: Stanford University Press.

MACDONALD, W. S., & ODEN, C. W. (1973). Effects of extreme crowding on the performance of five married couples during twelve weeks of intensive training. *Proceedings of 81st Annual Convention of the American Psychological Association, 8*, 209–210.

MACKAY, D. G., & FULKERSON, D. G. (1979). On the comprehension and production of pronouns. *Journal of Verbal Learning and Verbal Behavior, 18*, 661–673.

MADSEN, M. C. (1971). Developmental and cross-cultural differences in the cooperative and competitive behavior of young children. *Journal of Cross-Cultural Psychology, 2*, 365–371.

MALAMUTH, N. (1981). Rape fantasies as a function of exposure to violent sexual stimuli. *Archives of Sexual Behavior, 10*, 33–47.

MALAMUTH, N., & CHECK, J. V. P. (1981). The effects of mass media exposure on acceptance of violence against women: A field experiment. *Journal of Research in Personality, 15,* 436–446.

MALAMUTH, N. & DONNERSTEIN, E. (1982). The effects of aggressive-pornographic mass media stimuli. In Leonard Berkowitz (Ed.), *Advances in experimental social psychology* (Vol. 15). New York: Academic Press.

MALOF, M., & LOTT, A. J. (1962). Ethnocentrism and the acceptance of Negro support in a group pressure situation. *Journal of Personality and Social Psychology, 65,* 254–258.

MANN, L. (1977). The effect of stimulus queues on queue-joining behavior. *Journal of Personality and Social Psychology, 35,* 437–442.

MANN, L. (1981). The baiting crowd in episodes of threatened suicide. *Journal of Personality and Social Psychology, 41,* 703–709.

MANN, L., & JANIS, I. L. (1968). A follow-up study on the long-term effects of emotional role playing. *Journal of Personality and Social Psychology, 8,* 339–342.

MANN, R. D. (1959). A review of the relationship between personality and performance in small groups. *Psychological Bulletin, 56,* 241–270.

MANSTEAD, A. S. R., PROFFITT, C., & SMART, J. L. (1983). Predicting and understanding mothers' infant-feeding intentions and behavior: Testing the theory of reasoned action. *Journal of Personality and Social Psychology, 44,* 657–671.

MARKUS, H. (1977). Self-schemata and processing information about the self. *Journal of Personality and Social Psychology, 35,* 63–78.

MARKUS, H. (1981). The drive for integration: Some comments. *Journal of Experimental Social Psychology, 17,* 257–261.

MARTYNA, W. (1980). The psychology of the generic masculine. In S. McConnell-Ginet, R. Borker, & N. Furman (Eds.), *Women and language in literature and society* (pp. 69–78). New York: Praeger.

MARUYAMA, G., FRASER, S. C., & MILLER, N. (1982). Personal responsibility and altruism in children. *Journal of Personality and Social Psychology, 42*(4), 658–664.

MATHEWS, K. E., & CANON, L. K. (1975). Environmental noise level as a determinant of helping behavior. *Journal of Personality and Social Psychology, 32*(4), 571–577.

MATLIN, M., & STANG, D. (1978). *The Pollyanna principle: Selectivity in language, memory, and thought.* Cambridge, MA: Schenkman.

MAUSNER, B. (1954). The effect of one partner's success in a relevant task on the interaction of observer pairs. *Journal of Abnormal and Social Psychology, 49,* 557–560.

MAY, J. L., & HAMILTON, P. A. (1980). Effects of musically evoked affect on women's interpersonal attraction toward and perceptual judgements of physical attractiveness of men. *Motivation and Emotion, 4,* 217–228.

MAYKOVICH, M. K. (1975). Correlates of racial prejudice. *Journal of Personality and Social Psychology, 32,* 1014–1020.

MCARTHUR, L. A. (1972). The how and what of why: Some determinants and consequences of causal attribution. *Journal of Personality and Social Psychology, 22,* 171–193.

MCARTHUR, L. Z. (1981). What grabs you? The role of attention in impression formation and causal attribution. In E. T. Higgins, C. P. Herman, & M. P. Zanna (Eds.), *Social cognition: The Ontario symposium* (Vol. 1). Hillsdale, NJ: Erlbaum.

MCARTHUR, L. Z., & POST, D. L. (1977). Figural emphasis and person perception. *Journal of Experimental Social Psychology, 13,* 520–535.

MCARTHUR, L. Z., & RESKO, B. G. (1975). The portrayal of men and women in American TV commercials. *Journal of Social Psychology, 97,* 209–220.

MCCAIN, G., COX, V. C., & PAULUS, P. B. (1976). The relationship between illness, complaints and degree of crowding in a prison environment. *Environment and Behavior, 8,* 283–290.

MCCALLUM, P., RUSBULT, C. E., HONG, C. K., WALDEN, T. A., & SCHOPLER, J. (1979). Effects of resource availability and importance of behavior on the experience of crowding. *Journal of Personality and Social Psychology, 37,* 1304–1313.

MCCARTHY, D., & SAEGERT, S. (1978). Residential density, social overload, and social withdrawal. *Human Ecology, 6,* 253–272.

MCCLELLAND, D. C. (1976). *The achieving society: With a new introduction.* New York: Irvington.

MCCONAHAY, J. B. (1982). Self-interest versus racial attitudes as correlates of anti-busing attitudes in Louisville: Is it the buses or the blacks? *Journal of Politics, 44,* 692–720.

MCCORMICK, N. B. (1979). Come-ons and put-offs: Unmarried students strategies for having and avoiding sexual intercourse. *Psychology of Women Quarterly, 4,* 194–211.

MCCORMICK, N. B., & JESSER, C. J. (1983). The courtship game: Power in the sexual encounter. In E. R. Allgeier & N. B. McCormick (Eds.), *Changing boundaries: Gender roles and sexual behavior* (pp. 64–86). Palo Alto, CA: Mayfield.

MCFARLAND, C., & ROSS, M. (1982). Impact of causal attributions on affective reactions to success and failure. *Journal of Personality and Social Psychology, 43,* 937–946.

MCGINNISS, J. (1969). *The selling of the president, 1968.* New York: Trident Press.

MCGRATH, J. E. (1984). *Groups: Interaction and performance.* Englewood Cliffs, NJ: Prentice-Hall.

MCGUIRE, W. J. (1960). A syllogistic analysis of cognitive relationships. In M. J. Rosenberg et al. (Eds.), *Attitude organization and change.* New Haven, CT: Yale University Press.

MCGUIRE, W. J. (1969). The nature of attitudes and attitude change. In G. Lindzey and E. Aronson (Eds.), *The handbook of social psychology* (Vol. 3, 2nd ed., pp. 136–314). Reading, MA: Addison-Wesley.

MCGUIRE, W. J. (1981). The probabilogical model of cognitive structure and attitude change. In R. E. Petty, T. M. Ostrom, & T. C. Brock (Eds.), *Cognitive responses in persuasion.* Hillsdale, NJ: Erlbaum.

MCGUIRE, W. J., & PADAWER-SINGER, A. (1976). Trait salience in the spontaneous self-concept. *Journal of Personality and Social Psychology, 33*(6), 743–754.

MCGUIRE, W. J., & PAPAGEORGIS, D. (1961). The relative efficacy of various types of prior belief defense in producing immunity against persuasion. *Journal of Abnormal and Social Psychology, 62,* 327–337.

MCMILLAN, J. R., CLIFTON, A. K., MCGRATH, D., & GALE, W. S. (1977). Women's language: Uncertainty or interpersonal sensitivity and emotionality? *Sex Roles, 3*(6), 545–559.

MEHRABIAN, A. (1972). *Nonverbal communication.* Chicago: Aldine-Atherton.

MEREI, F. (1949). Group leadership and institutionalization. *Human Relations, 2,* 23–29.

METALSKY, G. I., ABRAMSON, L. Y., SELIGMAN, M. E. P., SEMMEL, A., & PETERSON, C. (1982). Attributional styles and life events in the classroom: Vulnerability and invulnerability to depressive mood reactions. *Journal of Personality and Social Psychology, 43,* 612–617.

MEYER, J. P. (1980). Causal attribution for success and failure: A multivariate investigation of dimensionality, formation, and consequences. *Journal of Personality and Social Psychology, 38,* 704–718.

MEYER, J. P., & KOELBL, S. L. M. (1982). Students' test performances: Dimensionality of causal attributions. *Personality and Social Psychology Bulletin, 8*(1), 31–36.

MEYER, J. P., & MULHERIN, A. (1980). From attribution to helping: An analysis of the mediating effects of affect and expectancy. *Journal of Personality and Social Psychology, 39*(2), 201–210.

MICHAELS, J. W., BLOMMEL, J. M., BROCATO, R. M., LINKOUS, R. A., & ROWE, J. S. (1982). Social facilitation and inhibition in a natural setting. *Replications in Social Psychology, 2,* 21–24.

MICHELSON, W. (1970). *Man and his urban environment: A sociological approach.* Reading, MA: Addison-Wesley.

MICHELSON, W. (1977). *Environmental choice, human behavior, and residential satisfaction.* New York: Oxford University Press.

MIDDLETON, R. (1976). Regional differences in prejudice. *American Sociological Review, 41,* 94–117.

MIDLARSKY, E., BRYAN, J. H., & BRICKMAN, P. (1973). Aversive approval: Interactive effects of modeling and reinforcement on altruistic behavior. *Child Development, 44,* 321–328.

MILAVSKY, J. R., KESSLER, R., STIPP, H., & RUBENS, W. S. (1982). Television and aggression: Results of a panel study. In D. Pearl, L. Bouthilet, & J. Lazar (Eds.), *Television and behavior: Ten years of scientific progress and implications for the eighties: Vol. II. Technical reviews.* Rockville, MD: National Institute of Mental Health.

MILGRAM, S. (1961). Nationality and conformity. *Scientific American, 205,* 45–51.

MILGRAM, S. (1963). Behavioral study of obedience. *Journal of Abnormal and Social Psychology, 67,* 371–378.

MILGRAM, S. (1965). Some conditions of obedience and disobedience to authority. *Human Relations, 18,* 57–75.

MILGRAM, S. (1970). The experience of living in cities. *Science, 167,* 1461–1468.

MILGRAM, S., BICKMAN, L., & BERKOWITZ, L. (1969). Note on the drawing power of crowds of different size. *Journal of Personality and Social Psychology, 13,* 79–82.

MILGRAM, S., & SHOTLAND, R. L. (1973). *Television and antisocial behavior: Field experiments.* New York: Academic Press.

MILLER, A. G. (1975). Actor and observer perceptions of the learning of a task. *Journal of Experimental Social Psychology, 11,* 95–111.

MILLER, A. G. (1976). Constraint and target effects in the attribution of attitudes. *Journal of Experimental Social Psychology, 12,* 325–339.

MILLER, A. G., JONES, E. E., & HINKLE, S. (1981). A robust attribution error in the personality domain. *Journal of Experimental Social Psychology, 17,* 587–600.

MILLER, A. H., BRUDNEY, J., & JOFTIS, P. (1975). *Presidential crises and political support: The impact of Watergate on attitudes toward institutions.* Paper presented at the annual meeting of the Midwest Political Science Association, Chicago.

MILLER, A. H., MILLER, W. E., RAINE, A. S., & BROWN, T. A. (1976). A majority party in disarray: Policy polarization in the 1972 election. *American Political Science Review, 70,* 753–778.

MILLER, D. T., & ROSS, M. (1975). Self-serving biases in the attribution of causality: Fact or fiction? *Psychological Bulletin, 82,* 213–225.

MILLER, L. W., & SIGELMAN, L. (1978). Is the audience the message? A note on LBJ's Vietnam statements. *Public Opinion Quarterly, 42,* 71–80.

MILLER, S. (1981). *Contemporary racial conflict: The nature of white opposition to mandatory busing.* Unpublished doctoral dissertation, University of California, Los Angeles.

MINOW, N. N., MARTIN, J. B., & MITCHELL, L. M. (1973). *Presidential television.* New York: Basic Books.

MINTZ, A. (1946). A reexamination of correlations between lynchings and economic indices. *Journal of Abnormal and Social Psychology, 41,* 154–160.

MISCHEL, W. (1979). On the interface of cognition and personality: Beyond the person-situation debate. *American Psychologist, 34,* 740–754.

MITA, T. H., DERMER, M., & KNIGHT, J. (1977). Reversed facial images and the mere-exposure hypothesis. *Journal of Personality and Social Psychology, 35,* 597–601.

MITCHELL, R. E. (1971). Some social implications of high-density housing. *American Sociological Review, 36,* 18–29.

MONSON, T. C., & SNYDER, M. (1977). Actors, observers, and the attribution process: Toward a reconceptualization. *Journal of Experimental Social Psychology, 13,* 89–111.

MORELAND, R. L., & ZAJONC, R. B. (1982). Exposure effects in person perception: Familiarity, similarity and attraction. *Journal of Experimental Social Psychology, 18,* 395–415.

MORGAN, C. J. (1978). Bystander intervention: Experimental test of a formal model. *Journal of Personality and Social Psychology, 36,* 43–55.

MORGAN, C. J., & LEIK, R. K. (1979). Simulation theory development: The bystander intervention case. In R. B. Smith & B. Anderson (Eds.), *Social science methods: Vol. 3: Theory construction.* Halstead Press.

MORIARTY, T. (1975). Crime, commitment, and the responsive bystander. Two field experiments. *Journal of Personality and Social Psychology, 31,* 370–376.

MORRIS, W. N., & MILLER, R. S. (1975). The effects of consensus-breaking and consensus-preempting partners on reduction in conformity. *Journal of Experimental Social Psychology, 11,* 215–223.

MORTON, T. L. (1978). Intimacy and reciprocity of exchange: A comparison of spouses and strangers. *Journal of Personality and Social Psychology, 36,* 72–81.

MOSCOVICI, S., & ZAVALLONI, M. (1969). The group as a

polarizer of attitudes. *Journal of Personality and Social Psychology, 12,* 125–135.

Moss, M. K., & Page, R. A. (1972). Reinforcement and helping behavior. *Journal of Applied Social Psychology, 2,* 360–371.

Mueller, C., & Donnerstein, E. (1977). The effects of humor-induced arousal upon aggressive behavior. *Journal of Research in Personality, 11,* 73–82.

Mueller, J. E. (1973). *War, presidents, and public opinion.* New York: Wiley.

Murphy, G., Murphy, L. B., & Newcomb, T. N. (1937). *Experimental social psychology* (rev. ed.). New York: Harper.

Murstein, B. I. (1972). Physical attractiveness and marital choice. *Journal of Personality and Social Psychology, 22,* 8–12.

Myers, A. M., & Gonda, G. (1982). Utility of the masculinity-femininity construct: Comparison of traditional and androgyny approaches. *Journal of Personality and Social Psychology, 43*(3), 514–523.

Myers, D. G., & Bishop, G. D. (1971). Enhancement of dominant attitudes in group discussion. *Journal of Personality and Social Psychology, 20,* 386–391.

Myers, D. G., & Lamm, H. (1976). The group polarization phenomenon. *Psychological Bulletin, 83,* 602–627.

National Institute of Mental Health (1982). *Television and behavior: Ten years of scientific progress and implications for the eighties: Vol. I: Summary report.* Rockville, MD: National Institute of Mental Health.

Neuman, W. R. (1976). Patterns of recall among television news viewers. *Public Opinion Quarterly,* 115–123.

Newcomb, T. M. (1943). *Personality and social change.* New York: Dryden Press.

Newcomb, T. M. (1961). *The acquaintance process.* New York: Holt.

Newcomb, T. M. (1963). Persistance and regression of changed attitudes: Long-range studies. *Journal of Social Issues, 19,* 3–14.

Newcomb, T. M. (1968). Interpersonal balance. In R. P. Abelson et al., *Theories of cognitive consistency: A sourcebook.* New York: Rand-McNally.

Newcomb, T. M., Koenig, K. E., Flacks, R., & Warwick, D. P. (1967). *Persistence and change: Bennington College and its students after 25 years.* New York: Wiley.

Newtson, D. (1976). Foundations of attribution: The perception of ongoing behavior. In J. H. Harvey, W. J. Ickes, & R. F. Kidd (Eds.), *New directions in attribution research* (Vol. 1). Hillsdale, NJ: Erlbaum.

Newtson, D., & Czerlinsky, T. (1974). Adjustment of attitude communications for contrasts by extreme audiences. *Journal of Personality and Social Psychology, 30,* 829–837.

Newtson, D., Engquist, G., & Bois, J. (1977). The objective basis of behavior units. *Journal of Personality and Social Psychology, 35,* 847–862.

Niemi, R. G. (1974). *How family members perceive each other.* New Haven, CT: Yale University Press.

Nieva, V., & Gutek, B. (1981). *Women and work: A psychological perspective.* New York: Praeger.

Nincic, M., & Russett, B. (1979). The effect of similarity and interest on attitudes toward foreign countries. *Public Opinion Quarterly, 43,* 68–78.

Nisbett, R. E., & Borgida, E. (1975). Attribution and the psychology of prediction. *Journal of Personality and Social Psychology, 32,* 932–943.

Nisbett, R. E., Caputo, C., Legant, P., & Marecek, J. (1973). Behavior as seen by the actor and as seen by the observer. *Journal of Personality and Social Psychology, 27,* 154–164.

Nisbett, R. E., & Ross, L. (1980). *Human inference: Strategies and shortcomings of social judgment.* Englewood Cliffs, NJ: Prentice-Hall.

Nisbett, R. E., & Schachter, S. (1966). Cognitive manipulation of pain. *Journal of Experimental Social Psychology, 2,* 227–236.

Nogami, G. Y. (1976). Crowding: Effects of group size, room size, or density? *Journal of Applied Social Psychology, 6,* 105–125.

Norman, R. (1975). Affective-cognitive consistency, attitudes, conformity, and behavior. *Journal of Personality and Social Psychology, 32,* 83–91.

Norman, R. (1976). When what is said is important: A comparison of expert and attractive sources. *Journal of Experimental Social Psychology, 12,* 294–300.

Novak, D. W., & Lerner, M. J. (1968). Rejection as a consequence of perceived similarity. *Journal of Personality and Social Psychology, 9,* 147–152.

O'Kelly, C. (1980). Sex-role imagery in modern art: An empirical examination. *Sex Roles, 6*(1), 99–112.

Orvis, B. R. (1977). *The bases, nature, and affective significance of attributional conflict in young couples.* Unpublished doctoral dissertation, University of California, Los Angeles.

Orvis, B. R., Kelley, H. H., & Butler, D. (1976). Attributional conflict in young couples. In J. H. Harvey, W. Ickes, & R. F. Kidd (Eds.), *New directions in attribution research* (Vol. 1, pp. 353–386). Hillsdale, NJ: Erlbaum.

Osborn, A. F. (1957). *Applied imagination.* New York: Scribners.

Osgood, C. E., Suci, G. J., & Tannenbaum, P. H. (1957). *The measurement of meaning.* Urbana: University of Illinois Press.

Pallak, M. S., Sogin, S. R., & Van Zante, A. (1974). Bad decisions: Effect of volition, locus of causality, and negative consequences on attitude change. *Journal of Personality and Social Psychology, 30,* 217–227.

Pancer, S. M., McMullen, L. M., Kabatoff, R. A., Johnson, K. G., & Pond, C. A. (1979). Conflict and avoidance in the helping situation. *Journal of Personality and Social Psychology, 37,* 1406–1411.

Park, R. D., Berkowitz, L., Leyens, J. P., West, S. G., & Sebastian, R. J. (1977). Some effects of violent and nonviolent movies on the behavior of juvenile delinquents. In L. Berkowitz (Ed.), *Advances in experimental social psychology* (Vol. 10, pp 136–173). New York: Academic Press.

Parlee, M. B. (1979, October). The friendship bond. *Psychology Today,* pp. 43–54, 113.

Patterson, M. L., & Sechrest, L. B. (1970). Interpersonal distance and impression formation. *Journal of Personality, 38,* 161–166.

Patterson, T. E. (1980). *The mass media election: How Americans choose their president.* New York: Praeger.

PATTERSON, T. E., & MCCLURE, R. D. (1976). *The unseeing eye*. New York: Putnam.

PAULUS, P. B. (Ed.). (1980a). *The psychology of group influence*. Hillsdale, NJ: Erlbaum.

PAULUS, P. B. (1980b). Crowding. In P. B. Paulus (Ed.), *The psychology of group influence*. Hillsdale, NJ: Erlbaum.

PAULUS, P. B., ANNIS, A. B., SETA, J. J., SCHKADE, J. K., & MATTHEWS, R. W. (1976). Density does affect task performance. *Journal of Personality and Social Psychology, 34,* 248–253.

PEPLAU, L. A. (1979). Power in dating relationships. In J. Freeman (Ed.), *Women: A feminist perspective* (2nd ed.). Palo Alto, CA: Mayfield.

PEPLAU, L. A., & GORDON, S. L. (in press). Women and men in love: Gender differences in close heterosexual relationships. In V. E. O'Leary, R. K. Unger, & B. S. Wallston (Eds.), *Women, gender and social psychology*. Hillsdale, NJ: Erlbaum.

PEPLAU, L. A., & PERLMAN, D. (1982). *Loneliness: A sourcebook of current theory, research and therapy*. New York: Wiley-Interscience.

PERLMAN, D., & OSKAMP, S. (1971). The effects of picture content and exposure frequency on evaluations of Negroes and whites. *Journal of Experimental Social Psychology, 7,* 503–514.

PERLMAN, D., & PEPLAU, L. A. (in press). Loneliness research: Implications for interventions. In L. A. Peplau & S. Goldston (Eds.), *Preventing the harmful consequences of severe and persistent loneliness*. Washington, DC: U.S. Government Printing Office.

PESSIN, J. (1933). The comparative effects of social and mechanical stimulation on memorizing. *American Journal of Psychology, 45,* 263–270.

PETERSON, C., SCHWARTZ, S. M., & SELIGMAN, M. E. P. (1981). Self-blame and depressive symptoms. *Journal of Personality and Social Psychology, 41,* 253–259.

PETERSON, D. R. (1983). Conflict. In H. H. Kelley et al., *Close relationships*. New York: Freeman.

PETTY, R. E., & BROCK, T. C. (1981). Thought disruption and persuasion: Assessing the validity of attitude change experiments. In R. E. Petty, T. M. Ostrom, and T. C. Brock (Eds.), *Cognitive responses in persuasion*. Hillsdale, NJ: Erlbaum.

PETTY, R. E., & CACIOPPO, J. T. (1977). Forewarning, cognitive responding, and resistance to persuasion. *Journal of Personality and Social Psychology, 35,* 645–656.

PETTY, R. E., & CACIOPPO, J. T. (1979). Issue involvement can increase or decrease persuasion by enhancing message-relevant cognitive responses. *Journal of Personality and Social Psychology, 37,* 1915–1926.

PETTY, R. E., & CACIOPPO, J. T. (1981). *Attitudes and persuasion: Classic and contemporary approaches*. Dubuque, IA: Wm. C. Brown.

PETTY, R. E., OSTROM, T. M., & BROCK, T. C. (1981). Historical foundation of the cognitive response approach to attitudes and persuasion. In R. E. Petty, T. M. Ostrom, & T. C. Brock (Eds.), *Cognitive responses in persuasion*. Hillsdale, NJ: Erlbaum.

PETTY, R. E., WELLS, G. L., & BROCK, T. C. (1976). Distraction can enhance or reduce yielding to propaganda: Thought disruption versus effort justification. *Journal of Personality and Social Psychology, 34,* 874–884.

PHILLIPS, D. P. (1983). The impact of mass media violence on U.S. homicides. *American Sociological Review, 48,* 560–568.

PILIAVIN, I. M., PILIAVIN, J. A., & RODIN, J. (1975). Costs, diffusion, and the stigmatized victim. *Journal of Personality and Social Psychology, 32*(3), 429–438.

PILIAVIN, I. M., RODIN, J., & PILIAVIN, J. A. (1969). Good Samaritanism: An underground phenomenon? *Journal of Personality and Social Psychology, 13*(4), 289–299.

PILIAVIN, J. A., DOVIDIO, J. F., GAERTNER, S. L., & CLARK, R. D. (1981). *Emergency intervention*. New York: Academic Press.

PINES, A., & ARONSON, E. (1983). Antecedents, correlates, and consequences of sexual jealousy. *Journal of Personality, 51* (1), 108–136.

PLECK, J. H. (1981). *The myth of masculinity*. Cambridge, MA: The MIT Press.

PLINER, P., HEATHER, H., KOHL, J. & SAARI, D. (1974). Compliance without pressure: Some further data on the foot-in-the-door technique. *Journal of Experimental Social Psychology, 10,* 17–22.

PRENTICE-DUNN, S., & ROGERS, R. W. (1980). Effects of deindividuating situational cues and aggressive models on subjective deindividuation and aggression. *Journal of Personality and Social Psychology, 39,* 104–113.

PRICE, G. H., & DABBS, J. M. (1974). Sex, setting and personal space: Changes as children grow older. *Personality and Social Psychology Bulletin, 1,* 362–363.

RANDS, M., & LEVINGER, G. (1979). Implicit theories of relationship: An intergenerational study. *Journal of Personality and Social Psychology, 37,* 649–661.

RAVEN, B. H., & RUBIN, J. Z. (1983). *Social psychology* (2nd ed.). New York: Wiley.

REGAN, D. T. (1968). *The effects of a favor and liking on compliance*. Unpublished doctoral dissertation, Stanford University.

REGAN, D. T., & FAZIO R. (1977). On the consistency between attitudes and behavior: Look to the method of attitude formation. *Journal of Experimental Social Psychology, 13,* 28–45.

REGAN, D. T., & TOTTEN, J. (1975). Empathy and attribution: Turning observers into actors. *Journal of Personality and Social Psychology, 32,* 850–856.

REIS, H. T., & JACKSON, L. A. (1981). Sex differences in reward allocation: Subjects, partners and tasks. *Journal of Personality and Social Psychology, 40*(3), 465–478.

RHINE, R. J., & SEVERANCE, L. J. (1970). Ego-involvement, discrepancy, source credibility, and attitude change. *Journal of Personality and Social Psychology, 16,* 175–190.

RIDGEWAY, C. L. (1983). *The dynamics of small groups*. New York: St. Martin's Press.

RIESS, M., ROSENFELD, P., MELBURG, V., & TEDESCHI, J. T. (1981). Self-serving attributions: Biased private perceptions and distorted public descriptions. *Journal of Personality and Social Psychology, 41,* 224–231.

ROBINSON, J. P. (1970). Public reaction to political protest: Chicago, 1968. *Public Opinion Quarterly, 34,* 1–9.

ROBINSON, J. P. (1971). The audience for national TV news programs. *Public Opinion Quarterly, 35,* 403–405.

ROBINSON, J. P. (1972). Mass communication and information diffusion. In F. G. Kline and P. J. Tichenor (Eds.), *Current perspectives in mass communication research* (pp. 71–93). Beverly Hills, CA: Sage Publications.

ROBINSON, J., & MCARTHUR, L. Z. (1982). Impact of salient vocal qualities on causal attribution for a speaker's behavior. *Journal of Personality and Social Psychology, 43,* 236–247.

ROBINSON, J. P., YERBY, J., FIEWEGER, M., & SOMERICK, N. (1977). Sex-role differences in time use. *Sex Roles, 3,* 443–458.

ROBINSON, M. J., (1976). Public affairs television and the growth of political malaise: The case of "the selling of the Pentagon." *American Political Science Review, 70,* 409–432.

ROCHA, R. F., & ROGERS, R. W. (1976). Ares and Babbitt in the classroom: Effects of competition and reward on children's aggression. *Journal of Personality and Social Psychology, 33,* 588–593.

ROGERS, R. W., & MEWBORN, C. R. (1976). Fear appeals and attitude change: Effects of a threat's noxiousness, probability of occurrence, and the efficacy of coping responses. *Journal of Personality and Social Psychology, 34,* 54–61.

ROGERS, R. W., & PRENTICE-DUNN, S. (1981). Deindividuation and anger-mediated interracial aggression: Unmasking regressive racism. *Journal of Personality and Social Psychology, 41,* 63–73.

ROHE, W., & PATTERSON, A. (1974). The effects of varied levels of resources and density on behavior in a day care center. In D. Carson (Ed.), *EDRA V,* pp. 161–171.

ROKEACH, M., & MEZEI, L. (1966). Race and shared belief as factors in social choice. *Science, 151,* 167–172.

ROLLINS, B. C., & BAHR, S. (1976). A theory of power relationships in marriage. *Journal of Marriage and the Family, 38,* 619–627.

ROSEN, B., & JERDEE, T. H. (1978). Perceived sex differences in managerially relevant characteristics. *Sex Roles, 4,* 837–843.

ROSENBERG, M. J. (1960). An analysis of affective-cognitive consistency. In C. I. Hovland and M. J. Rosenberg (Eds.), *Attitude organization and change.* New Haven, CT: Yale University Press.

ROSENBERG, S., NELSON, C., & VIVEKANANTHAN, P. S. (1968). A multidimensional approach to the structure of personality impressions. *Journal of Personality and Social Psychology, 9,* 283–294.

ROSENFELD, L. B. (1979). Self-disclosure avoidance: Why I am afraid to tell you who I am. *Communication Monographs, 46,* 63–74.

ROSENKRANTZ, P., VOGEL, S., BEE, H., BROVERMAN, I., & BROVERMAN, D. M. (1968). Sex-role stereotypes and self-concepts in college students. *Journal of Consulting and Clinical Psychology, 32,* 287–295.

ROSENTHAL, R., & RUBIN, D. B. (1978). Interpersonal expectancy effects: The first 345 studies. *The Behavioral and Brain Sciences, 3,* 377–415.

ROSS, A. S. (1971). Effect of increased responsibility on bystander intervention: The presence of children. *Journal of Personality and Social Psychology, 19*(3), 306–310.

ROSS, L. (1977). The intuitive psychologist and his shortcomings: Distortions in the attribution process. In L. Berkowitz (Ed.), *Advances in experimental social psychology* (Vol. 10). New York: Academic Press.

ROSS, L., AMABILE, T. M., & STEINMETZ, J. L. (1977). Social roles, social control, and biases in social-perception processes. *Journal of Personality and Social Psychology, 35,* 485–494.

ROSS, L., GREENE, D., & HOUSE, P. (1977). The "false consensus effect": An egocentric bias in social perception and attribution processes. *Journal of Experimental Social Psychology, 13,* 279–301.

ROSS, M. (1975). Salience of reward and intrinsic motivation. *Journal of Personality and Social Psychology, 32,* 245–254.

ROSS, M. LAYTON, B., ERICKSON, B., & SCHOPLER, J. (1973). Affect, facial regard, and reactions to crowding. *Journal of Personality and Social Psychology, 28,* 69–76.

ROSS, M., MCFARLAND, C., & FLETCHER, G. J. O. (1981). The effect of attitude on the recall of personal histories. *Journal of Personality and Social Psychology, 40,* 627–634.

ROSS, M., & SICOLY, F. (1979). Egocentric biases in availability and attribution. *Journal of Personality and Social Psychology, 37,* 322–336.

ROTHBART, M. (1976). Achieving racial equality: An analysis of resistance to social reform. In P. A. Katz (Ed.), *Towards the elimination of racism.* New York: Pergamon Press.

RUBENSTEIN, C. M., & SHAVER, P. (1982). The experience of loneliness. In L. A. Peplau & D. Perlman (Eds.), *Loneliness: A sourcebook of current theory, research and therapy* (pp. 206–223). New York: Wiley-Interscience.

RUBIN, B. (1967). *Political television.* Belmont, CA: Wadsworth.

RUBIN, L. (1976). *Worlds of pain.* New York: Basic Books.

RUBIN, Z. (1970). Measurement of romantic love. *Journal of Personality and Social Psychology, 16,* 265–273.

RUBIN, Z. (1973). *Liking and loving: An invitation to social psychology.* New York: Holt, Rinehart & Winston.

RUBIN, Z. (1975). Disclosing oneself to a stranger: Reciprocity and its limits. *Journal of Experimental Social Psychology, 11,* 233–260.

RUBIN, Z. (1980). *Children's friendships.* Cambridge, MA: Harvard University Press.

RUBIN, Z., HILL, C. T., PEPLAU, L. A., & DUNKEL-SCHETTER, C. (1980). Self-disclosure in dating couples: Sex roles and the ethic of openness. *Journal of Marriage and the Family, 42,* 305–317.

RUBIN, Z., PEPLAU, L. A., & HILL, C. T. (1981). Loving and leaving: Sex differences in romantic attachments. *Sex Roles, 7*(9), 821–835.

RUBLE, D. N., & FELDMAN, N. S. (1976). Order of consensus, distinctiveness, and consistency information and causal attributions. *Journal of Personality and Social Psychology, 34,* 930–937.

RUSBULT, C. E. (1980). Commitment and satisfaction in romantic associations: A test of the investment model. *Journal of Experimental Social Psychology, 16,* 172–186.

RUSBULT, C. E. (1983). A longitudinal test of the investment model: The development (and deterioration) of satisfaction and commitment in heterosexual involvements. *Journal of Personality and Social Psychology, 45,* 101–117.

RUSBULT, C. E., & ZEMBRODT, I. M. (1983). Responses to dissatisfaction in romantic involvements: A multidimensional scaling analysis. *Journal of Experimental Social Psychology, 19,* 274–293.

RUSBULT, C. E. ZEMBRODT, I. M., & GUNN, L. K. (1982). Exit, voice, loyalty, and neglect: Responses to dissatisfaction in romantic involvements. *Journal of Personality and Social Psychology, 43,* 1230–1242.

RUSHTON, J. P. (1980). *Altruism, socialization and society.* Englewood Cliffs, NJ: Prentice-Hall.

RUSHTON, J. P., & CAMPBELL, A. C. (1977). Modeling, vicarious reinforcement and extraversion on blood donating in adults: Immediate and long-term effects. *European Journal of Social Psychology, 7,* 297–306.

RUSHTON, J. P., & TEACHMAN, G. (1978). The effects of positive reinforcement, attributions, and punishment on model-induced altruism in children. *Personality and Social Psychology Bulletin, 4*(2), 322–325.

RYAN, W. (1971). *Blaming the victim.* New York: Vintage.

SAEGERT, S., SWAP, W., & ZAJONC, R. B. (1973). Exposure, context, and interpersonal attraction. *Journal of Personality and Social Psychology, 25,* 234–242.

SAGAR, H., & SCHOFIELD, J. W. (1980). Racial and behavioral cues in black and white children's perceptions of ambiguously aggressive acts. *Journal of Personality and Social Psychology, 39,* 590–598.

SALANCIK, G. R., & CONWAY, M. (1975). Attitude inferences from salient and relevant cognitive content about behavior. *Journal of Personality and Social Psychology, 32,* 829–840.

SAMPSON, E. E. (1977). Psychology and the American ideal. *Journal of Personality and Social Psychology, 35,* 767–782.

SANDERS, G. S. (1981). Driven by distraction: An integrative review of social facilitation theory and research. *Journal of Experimental Social Psychology, 17,* 227–251.

SARNOFF, I., & ZIMBARDO, P. G. (1961). Anxiety, fear, and social affiliation. *Journal of Abnormal and Social Psychology, 62,* 356–363.

SATOW, K. L. (1975). Social approval and helping. *Journal of Experimental Social Psychology, 11,* 501–509.

SCANZONI, L. D., & SCANZONI, J. (1976). *Men, women, and change.* New York: McGraw-Hill.

SCHACHTER, S. (1951). Deviation, rejection, and communication. *Journal of Abnormal and Social Psychology, 46,* 190–207.

SCHACHTER, S. (1959). *The psychology of affiliation.* Stanford, CA: Stanford University Press.

SCHACHTER, S., & SINGER, J. E. (1962). Cognitive, social and physiological determinants of emotional state. *Psychological Review, 69,* 379–399.

SCHLEGEL, R. P., CRAWFORD, C. A., & SANBORN, M. D. (1977). Correspondence and mediational properties of the Fishbein model: An application to adolescent alcohol use. *Journal of Experimental Social Psychology, 13,* 421–430.

SCHLENKER, B. R., HALLAM, J. R, & McCOWN, N. E. (1983). Motives and social evaluation: Actor-observer differences in the delineation of motives for a beneficial act. *Journal of Experimental Social Psychology, 19,* 254–273.

SCHMITT, D. R., & MARWELL, G. (1972). Withdrawal and regard reallocation as responses to inequity. *Journal of Experimental Social Psychology, 8,* 207–221.

SCHNEIDER, D. J., & MILLER, R. S. (1975). The effects of enthusiasm and quality of arguments on attitude attribution. *Journal of Personality, 43,* 693–708.

SCHOFIELD, J. (1978). School desegregation and intergroup relations. In D. Bar-Tal and L. Saxe (Eds.), *Social psychology of education: Theory and research.* New York: Wiley.

SCHOPLER, J., & STOCKDALE, J. E. (1977). An interference analysis of crowding. *Journal of Environmental Psychology and Nonverbal Behavior, 1,* 81–88.

SCHRAMM, W., & CARTER, R. F. (1959). Effectiveness of a political telethon. *Public Opinion Quarterly, 23,* 121–127.

SCHUMAN, H., & JOHNSON, M. P. (1976). Attitudes and behavior, *Annual Review of Sociology, 2,* 161–207.

SCHWARTZ, B., & BARSKY, S. (1977). The home advantage. *Social Forces, 55,* 641–661.

SCHWARTZ, S. H. (1977). Normative influences on altruism. In L. Berkowitz (Ed.), *Advances in experimental social psychology* (vol. 10). New York: Academic Press.

SCHWARTZ, S. H. (1978). Temporal instability as a moderator of the attitude-behavior relationship. *Journal of Personality and Social Psychology, 36,* 715–724.

SCHWARTZ, S. H., & GOTTLIEB, A. (1980). Bystander anonymity and reactions to emergencies. *Journal of Personality and Social Psychology, 39*(3), 418–430.

SCHWARZ, N., & CLORE, G. L. (1983). Mood, misattribution, and judgments of well-being: Informative and directive functions of affective states. *Journal of Personality and Social Psychology, 45*(3), 513–523.

SEARS, D. O. (1968). The paradox of de facto selective exposure without preferences for supportive information. In R. P. Abelson, E. Aronson, W. J. McGuire, T. M. Newcomb, M. J. Rosenberg, & P. H. Tannenbaum (Eds.), *Theories of cognitive consistency: A sourcebook* (pp. 777–787). Chicago: Rand-McNally.

SEARS, D. O. (1982). *Positivity bias in evaluation of public figures.* Paper presented at the annual meeting of the American Political Science Association, Denver.

SEARS, D. O. (1983). The person-positivity bias. *Journal of Personality and Social Psychology, 44,* 233–250.

SEARS, D. O., ALLEN, H. M., JR. (1984). The trajectory of local desegregation controversies and whites' opposition to busing. In N. Miller and M. Brewer (Eds.), *Groups in contact: The psychology of desegregation.* New York: Academic Press.

SEARS, D. O., & CHAFFEE, S. H. (1979). Uses and effects of the 1976 debates: An overview of empirical studies. In S. Kraus (Ed.), *The great debates, 1976: Ford vs. Carter* (pp. 223–261). Bloomington: Indiana University Press.

SEARS, D. O., & FREEDMAN, J. L. (1967). Selective exposure to information: A critical review. *Public Opinion Quarterly, 31,* 194–213.

SEARS, D. O., FREEDMAN, J. L., & O'CONNOR, E. F., JR. (1964). The effects of anticipated debate and commitment on the polarization of audience opinion. *Public Opinion Quarterly, 28,* 615–627.

SEARS, D. O., HENSLER, C. P., & SPEER, L. K. (1979). Whites' opposition to "busing": Self-interest or symbolic politics? *American Political Science Review, 73,* 369–384.

SEARS, D. O., LAU, R. R., TYLER, T. R., & ALLEN, H. M., JR. (1980). Self-interest vs. symbolic politics in policy attitudes and presidential voting. *American Political Science Review, 74,* 670–684.

SEARS, D. O., & MCCONAHAY, J. B. (1973). *The politics of violence: The new urban blacks and the Watts riot.* Boston: Houghton Mifflin. Reprinted by University Press of America, 1981.

SEARS, D. O., & WHITNEY, R. E. (1973). Political persuasion. In I. deS. Pool, W. Schramm, F. W. Frey, N. Maccoby, and E. B. Parker (Eds.), *Handbook of communication* (pp. 253–289). Chicago: Rand-McNally.

SEARS, R. R., WHITING, J. W. M., NOWLIS, V., & SEARS, P. S. (1953). Some child-rearing antecedents of aggression and dependency in young children. *Genetic Psychological Monographs, 47,* 135–236.

SEGAL, M. W. (1974). Alphabet and attraction: An unobtrusive measure of the effect of propinquity in a field setting. *Journal of Personality and Social Psychology, 30* (5), 654–657.

SELIGMAN, C., BUSH, M., & KIRSCH, K. (1975). Relationship between compliance in the foot-in-the-door paradigm and size of first request. *Journal of Personality and Social Psychology, 33,* 517–520.

SELIGMAN, M. E. P. (1975). *Helplessness: On depression, development, and death.* San Francisco: Freeman.

SHANTEAU, J., & NAGY, G. F. (1979). Probability of acceptance in dating choice. *Journal of Personality and Social Psychology, 37,* 522–533.

SHAVER, P., & FREEDMAN, J. L. (1976, August). Happiness. *Psychology Today.*

SHAVER, P., & KLINNERT, M. D. (1982). Schachter's theories of affiliation and emotion: Implications of developmental research. In L. Wheeler (Ed.), *Review of personality and social psychology* (Vol. 3). Beverly Hills, CA: Sage Publications.

SHAVER, P., & RUBENSTEIN, C. (1980). Childhood attachment experience and adult loneliness. In L. Wheeler (Ed.), *Review of personality and social psychology* (Vol. 1, pp. 42–73). Beverly Hills, CA: Sage Publications.

SHAW, M. E. (1981). *Group dynamics: The psychology of small group behavior* (3rd ed.). New York: McGraw-Hill.

SHEA, J. D. C. (1981). Changes in interpersonal distances and categories of play behavior in the early weeks of preschool. *Developmental Psychology, 17,* 417–425.

SHEATSLEY, P. B., & FELDMAN, J. J. (1965). A national survey of public reactions and behavior. In B. S. Greenberg and E. B. Parker (Eds.), *The Kennedy assassination and the American public* (pp. 149–177). Stanford, CA: Stanford University Press.

SHEPOSH, J. P., DEMING, M., & YOUNG, L. E. (1977, April). *The radiating effects of status and attractiveness of a male upon evaluating his female partner.* Paper presented at the annual meeting of the Western Psychological Association, Seattle, Washington.

SHERIF, M. (1935). An experimental study of stereotypes. *Journal of Abnormal and Social Psychology, 29,* 371–375.

SHERROD, D. R. (1974). Crowding, perceived control and behavioral aftereffects. *Journal of Applied Social Psychology, 4,* 171–186.

SHERROD, D. R., & DOWNS, R. (1974). Environmental determinants of altruism: The effects of stimulus overload and perceived control on helping. *Journal of Experimental Social Psychology, 10,* 468–479.

SHERROD, D. R., HAGE, J. N., HALPERN, P. L., & MOORE, B. S. (1977). Effects of personal causation and perceived control on responses to an aversive environment: The more control, the better. *Journal of Experimental Social Psychology, 13,* 14–27.

SHINAR, E. H. (1975). Sexual stereotypes of occupations. *Journal of Vocational Behavior, 7,* 99–110.

SHOTLAND, R. L., & HUSTON, T. L. (1979). Emergencies: What are they and do they influence bystanders to intervene? *Journal of Personality and Social Psychology, 37* (10), 1822–1834.

SHOTLAND, R. L., & STRAW, M. K. (1976). Bystander response to an assault: When a man attacks a woman. *Journal of Personality and Social Psychology, 34,* 990–999.

SIDOROWICZ, L. S., & LUNNEY, G. S. (1980). Baby X revisited. *Sex Roles, 6* (1), 67–74.

SIEBENALER, J. B., & CALDWELL, D. K. (1956). Cooperation among adult dolphins. *Journal of Mammology, 37,* 126–128.

SIGALL, H., & LANDY, D. (1973). Radiating beauty: The effects of having a physically attractive partner on person perception. *Journal of Personality and Social Psychology, 28,* 218–224.

SIGALL, H., & OSTROVE, N. (1975). Beautiful but dangerous: Effects of offender attractiveness and nature of the crime on juridic judgment. *Journal of Personality and Social Psychology, 31,* 410–414.

SIMMEL, G. (1903). *Sociology of Georg Simmel.* New York: MacMillan, 1950. Translation of German edition.

SINGER, J. E., BRUSH, C., & LUBLIN, S. D. (1965). Some aspects of deindividuation: Identification and conformity. *Journal of Experimental Social Psychology, 1,* 356–378.

SISTRUNK, F., & MCDAVID, J. W. (1971). Sex variable in conforming behavior. *Journal of Personality and Social Psychology, 17* (2), 200–207.

SIVACEK, J., & CRANO, W. D. (1982). Vested interest as a moderator of attitude-behavior consistency. *Journal of Personality and Social Psychology, 43,* 210–221.

SKOLNICK, P. (1977). Helping as a function of time of day, location, and sex of victim. *Journal of Social Psychology, 102,* 61–62.

SKRYPNEK, B. J., & SNYDER, M. (1982). On the self-perpetuating nature of stereotypes about women and men. *Journal of Experimental Social Psychology, 18,* 277–291.

SLOCHOWER, J., WEIN, L., WHITE, J., FIRSTENBERG, S., & DIGUILIO, J. (1980). Severe physical handicaps and helping behavior. *Journal of Social Psychology, 112,* 313–314.

SMITH, P. K., & CONNELLY, K. (1972). Patterns of play and social interaction in preschool children. In N. B. Jones (Ed.), *Ethological studies of child behavior.* Cambridge, Eng.: Cambridge University Press.

SMITH, S., & HAYTHORN, W. H. (1972). Effects of compatibility, crowding, group size, and leadership seniority on stress, anxiety, hostility and annoyance in isolated groups. *Journal of Personality and Social Psychology, 22,* 67–79.

SMITH, S., & JAMIESON, B. D. (1972). Effects of attitude and ego involvement on the learning and retention of controversial material. *Journal of Personality and Social Psychology, 22,* 303–310.

SNIDERMAN, P. M., & BRODY, R. A. (1977). Coping: The

ethic of self-reliance. *American Journal of Political Science, 21,* 501–522.

SNYDER, A., MISCHEL, W., & LOTT, B. (1960). Value, information, and conformity behavior. *Journal of Personality, 28,* 333–342.

SNYDER, M., & CUNNINGHAM, M. R. (1975). To comply or not comply: Testing the self-perception explanation of the "foot in the door" phenomenon. *Journal of Personality and Social Psychology, 31,* 64–67.

SNYDER, M., & SWANN, W. B. JR. (1976). When actions reflect attitudes: The politics of impression management. *Journal of Personality and Social Psychology, 34,* 1034–1042.

SNYDER, M., & SWANN, W. B. JR. (1978). Hypothesis-testing processes in social interaction. *Journal of Personality and Social Psychology, 36,* 1202–1212.

SNYDER, M. L., & JONES, E. E. (1974). Attitude attribution when behavior is constrained. *Journal of Experimental Social Psychology, 10,* 585–600.

SNYDER, M. L., STEPHAN, W. G., & ROSENFIELD, D. (1976). Egotism and attribution. *Journal of Personality and Social Psychology, 33,* 435–441.

SNYDER, R. L. (1968). Reproduction and population pressures. In E. Steller and J. M. Sprague (Eds.), *Progress in physiological psychology.* New York: Academic Press.

SOGIN, S. R., & PALLAK, M. S. (1976). Bad decisions, responsibility, and attitude change: Effects of volition, foreseeability, and locus of causality of negative consequences. *Journal of Personality and Social Psychology, 33,* 300–306.

SOLANO, C. H., BATTEN, P. G., & PARISH, E. A. (1982). Loneliness and patterns of self-disclosure. *Journal of Personality and Social Psychology, 43,* 524–531.

SOLOMON, L. Z., SOLOMON, H., & STONE, R. (1978). Helping as a function of number of bystanders and ambiguity of emergency. *Personality and Social Psychology Bulletin, 4* (2), 318–321.

SOMMER, R. (1969). *Personal space: The behavioral basis of design.* Englewood Cliffs, NJ: Prentice-Hall.

SOMMER, R., & OLSEN, H. (1980). The soft classroom. *Environment and Behavior, 12* (1), 3–16.

SOUTHWICK, C. H. (1955). The population dynamics of confined house mice supplied with unlimited food. *Ecology, 36,* 212–215.

SPENCE, J. T., & HELMREICH, R. (1978). *Masculinity and femininity: The psychological dimensions, correlates, and antecedents.* Austin: University of Texas Press.

SPENCE, J. T., & HELMREICH, R. L. (1980). Masculine instrumentality and feminine expressiveness: Their relationships with sex role attitudes and behaviors. *Psychology of Women Quarterly, 5* (2), 147–163.

SPRAFKIN, J. N., LIEBERT, R. M., & POULOS, R. W. (1975). Effects of a prosocial televised example on children's helping. *Journal of Experimental Child Psychology, 20,* 119–126.

SROLE, L. (1972). Urbanization and mental health: Some reformulations. *American Scientist, 60,* 576–583.

STAHL, S. M. (1982). Illness as an emergent norm or doing what comes naturally. In M. J. Colligan, J. W. Pennebaker, & L. R. Murphy (Eds.), *Mass psychogenic illness: A social psychological analysis* (pp. 183–198). Hillsdale, NJ: Erlbaum.

STECK, L., LEVITAN, D., MCLANE, D., & KELLEY, H. H. (1982).

Care, need, and conceptions of love. *Journal of Personality and Social Psychology, 43,* 481–491.

STEELE, C. M. (1975). Name-calling and compliance. *Journal of Personality and Social Psychology, 31,* 361–369.

STEIN, A. H., & FRIEDRICH, L. K. (1972). Television content and young children's behavior. In J. P. Murray, E. A. Rubinstein, & G. A. Comstock (Eds.), *Television and social behavior: Vol. 2. Television and social learning.* Washington, DC: U.S. Government Printing Office.

STEIN, D. D., HARDYCK, J. A., & SMITH, M. B. (1965). Race and belief: An open and shut case. *Journal of Personality and Social Psychology, 1,* 281–289.

STEINEM, G. (1980). Erotica and pornography: A clear and present difference. In L. Lederer (Ed.), *Take back the night: Women on pornography.* New York: Morrow.

STEINER, I. D. (1972). *Group process and productivity.* New York: Academic Press.

STEMBER, C. H. (1961). *Education and attitude change.* New York: Institute of Human Relations Press.

STEPHAN, F. F., & MISHLER, E. G. (1952). The distribution of participation in small groups: An exponential approximation. *American Sociological Review, 17,* 598–608.

STEPHAN, W. G., & ROSENFIELD, D. (1978). Effects of desegregation on racial attitudes. *Journal of Personality and Social Psychology, 36,* 795–804.

STERNBERG, R. J., CONWAY, B. E., KETRON, J. L., & BERNSTEIN, M. (1981). People's conceptions of intelligence. *Journal of Personality and Social Psychology, 41,* 37–55.

STOKOLS, D. (1972). On the distinction between density and crowding: Some implications for future research. *Psychological Review, 79,* 275–277.

STOKOLS, D. (1978). Environmental psychology. *Annual Review of Psychology, 29,* 253–295.

STOKOLS, D., RALL, M., PINNER, B., & SCHOPLER, J. (1973). Physical, social, and personal determinants of the perception of crowding. *Environment and Behavior, 5,* 87–115.

STONER, J. A. F. (1961). *A comparison of individual and group decisions involving risk.* Unpublished master's thesis. School of Industrial Management, MIT.

STORMS, M. D. (1973). Videotape and the attribution process: Reversing actors' and observers' points of view. *Journal of Personality and Social Psychology, 27,* 165–175.

STORMS, M. D. & NISBETT, R. E. (1970). Insomnia and the attribution process. *Journal of Personality and Social Psychology, 16,* 319–328.

STOUFFER, S. A., SUCHMAN, E. A., DEVINNEY, L. C., STAR, S. A., & WILLIAMS, R. M., JR. (1949). *The American soldier: Adjustment during army life.* New York: Wiley.

STRAUS, M. A. GELLES, R. J. & STEINMETZ, S. K. (1981). *Behind closed doors: Violence in the American family.* Garden City, NY: Doubleday Anchor Books.

STRAYER, F. F., WAREING, S., & RUSHTON, J. P. (1979). Social constraints on naturally occurring preschool altruism. *Ethology and Sociobiology, 1,* 3–11.

SUEDFELD, P. (1982). Aloneness as a healing experience. In L. A. Peplau & D. Perlman (Eds.), *Loneliness: A sourcebook of current theory, research and therapy* (pp. 54–69). New York: Wiley-Interscience.

SUNDSTROM, E., & SUNDSTROM, M. G. (1977). Personal space invasions: What happens when the invader asks permission? *Environmental Psychology and Nonverbal Behavior, 2,* 76–82.

SURGEON GENERAL'S SCIENTIFIC ADVISORY COMMITTEE. (1972) *Television and growing up: The impact of televised violence: Report to the Surgeon General.* U.S. Public Health Service, Dept. of Health, Education, and Welfare Publication N. HSM 72-9090. Rockville, MD: National Institute of Mental Health.

SWANN, W. B., JR., & STEPHENSON, B. (1981). Curiosity and control: On the determinants of the search for social knowledge. *Journal of Personality and Social Psychology, 40,* 635–642.

SWENSEN, C. H. (1972). The behavior of love. In H. A. Otto (Ed.), *Love today* (pp. 86–101). New York: Dell.

SYMONS, D. (1979). *The evolution of human sexuality.* New York: Oxford University Press.

TAJFEL, H., BILLIG, M. G., BUNDY, R. P., & FLAMENT, C. (1971). Social categorization and intergroup behavior. *European Journal of Social Psychology, 1,* 149–178.

TARDE, G. (1903). *The laws of imitation.* New York: Holt, Rinehart & Winston.

TAVRIS, C., & WADE, C. (1984). *The longest war: Sex differences in perspective* (2nd ed.). New York: Harcourt Brace Jovanovich.

TAYLOR, D. G., SHEATSLEY, P. B. & GREELEY, A. M. (1978). Attitudes toward racial integration. *Scientific American, 238,* 42–49.

TAYLOR, D. W., BERRY, P. C. & BLOCK, C. H. (1958). Does group participation when using brainstorming facilitate or inhibit creative thinking? *Administrative Science Quarterly, 2,* 23–47.

TAYLOR, S. E. (1975). On inferring one's attitudes from one's behavior: Some delimiting conditions. *Journal of Personality and Social Psychology, 31,* 126–131.

TAYLOR, S. E. (1981a). The interface of cognitive and social psychology. In J. H. Harvey (Ed.), *Cognition, social behavior, and the environment.* Hillsdale, NJ: Erlbaum.

TAYLOR, S. E. (1981b). A categorization approach to stereotyping. In D. L. Hamilton (Ed.), *Cognitive processes in stereotyping and intergroup behavior* (pp. 83–114). Hillsdale, NJ: Erlbaum.

TAYLOR, S. E. (1982). Social cognition and health. *Personality and Social Psychology Bulletin, 8* (3), 549–562.

TAYLOR, S. E. (1983). Adjustment to threatening events: A theory of cognitive adaptation. *American Psychologist, 38,* 1161–1173.

TAYLOR, S. E., & CROCKER, J. (1981). Schematic bases of social information processing. In E. T. Higgins, C. P. Herman, & M. P. Zanna (Eds.), *Social cognition: The Ontario symposium,* (Vol. 1). Hillsdale, NJ: Erlbaum.

TAYLOR, S. E., CROCKER, J., FISKE, S. T., SPRINZEN, M., & WINKLER, J. D. (1979). The generalizability of salience effects. *Journal of Personality and Social Psychology, 37,* 357–368.

TAYLOR, S. E., & FISKE, S. T. (1975). Point of view and perceptions of causality. *Journal of Personality and Social Psychology, 32,* 439–445.

TAYLOR, S. E., & FISKE, S. T. (1978). Salience, attention, and attribution: Top of the head phenomena. In L. Berkowitz, (Ed.), *Advances in experimental social psychology* (Vol. 11, pp. 249–288). New York: Academic Press.

TAYLOR, S. E., FISKE, S. T., CLOSE, M., ANDERSON, C., & RUDERMAN, A. (1977). *Solo status as a psychological variable: The power of being distinctive.* Unpublished manuscript, Harvard University.

TAYLOR, S. E., FISKE, S. T., ETCOFF, N. L., & RUDERMAN, A. J. (1978). Categorical and contextual bases of person memory and stereotyping. *Journal of Personality and Social Psychology, 36,* 778–793.

TAYLOR, S. E., & THOMPSON, S. C. (1982). Stalking the elusive "vividness" effect. *Psychological Review, 89,* 155–181.

TAYNOR, J., & DEAUX, K. (1973). When women are more deserving than men: Equity, attribution and perceived sex difference. *Journal of Personality and Social Psychology, 28,* 360–367.

TAYNOR, J., & DEAUX, K. (1975). Equity and perceived sex differences: Role of behavior as defined by the task, the mode and the action. *Journal of Personality and Social Psychology, 32,* 381–390.

TEDIN, K. L. (1974). The influence of parents on the political attitudes of adolescents. *American Political Science Review, 68,* 1579–1592.

TERMAN, C. R. (1974). Behavioral factors associated with cessation of growth of laboratory populations of prairie deermice. *Research in Population Ecology, 15,* 138–147.

TESSLER, R. C., & SCHWARTZ, S. H. (1972). Help-seeking, self-esteem, and achievement motivation: An attributional analysis. *Journal of Personality and Social Psychology, 27,* 318–326.

TESSOR, A. (1978). Self-generated attitude change. In L. Berkowitz (Ed.), *Advances in experimental social psychology* (Vol. 11). New York: Academic Press.

THIBAUT, J. W., & KELLEY, H. H. (1959). *The social psychology of groups.* New York: Wiley.

THOMAS, M. H., HORTON, R. W., LIPPINCOTT, E. C., & DRABMAN, R. S. (1977). Desensitization of portrayals of real-life aggression as a function of exposure to television violence. *Journal of Personality and Social Psychology, 35,* 450–458.

THOMPSON, S. C., & KELLEY, H. H. (1981). Judgments of responsibility for activities in close relationships. *Journal of Personality and Social Psychology, 41,* 469–477.

THOMPSON, W. C., COWAN, C. L., & ROSENHAN, D. L. (1980). Focus of attention mediates the impact of negative affect on altruism. *Journal of Personality and Social Psychology, 38,* 291–300.

TILKER, H. A. (1970). Socially responsible behavior as a function of observer responsibility and victim feedback. *Journal of Personality and Social Psychology, 14,* 95–100.

TO, L. P. & TAMARIN, R. H. (1977). The relation of population density and adrenal gland weight in cycling and noncycling voles (Microtus). *Ecology, 58,* 928–934.

TOI, M., & BATSON, C. D. (1982). More evidence that empathy is a source of altruistic motivation. *Journal of Personality and Social Psychology, 43,* 281–292.

TORRANCE, E. P. (1955). Some consequences of power difference on decision making in permanent and temporary three-man groups. In A. P. Hare, E. F. Bogatta, & R. F. Bales (Eds.), *Small groups: Studies in social interaction.* New York: Knopf.

TRIPLETT, N. (1898). The dynamogenic factors in pacemaking and competition. *American Journal of Psychology, 9,* 507–533.

TRIVERS, R. L. (1971). The evolution of reciprocal altruism. *Quarterly Review of Biology, 46,* 35–57.

TUCKER, L., HORNSTEIN, H. A., HOLLOWAY, S., & SOLE, K. (1977). The effects of temptation and information about a stranger on helping. *Personality and Social Psychology Bulletin, 3* (3), 416–421.

TURNER, R. H. (1962). Role-taking: Process versus conformity. In A. H. Rose (Ed.), *Human behavior and social processes: An interactionist approach.* Boston: Houghton Mifflin.

TYBOUT, A. M. & SCOTT, C. A. (1983). Availability of well-defined internal knowledge and the attitude formation process: Information aggregation versus self-perception. *Journal of Personality and Social Psychology, 44* (3), 474–91.

TYLER, T. R. (1978). *Drawing inferences from experiences. The effect of crime victimization experiences upon crime-related attitudes and behaviors.* Unpublished doctoral dissertation, University of California, Los Angeles.

TYLER, T. R., & DEVINITZ, V. (1981). Self-serving bias in the attribution of responsibility: Cognitive versus motivational explanations. *Journal of Experimental Social Psychology, 17,* 408–416.

TYLER, T. R., & SEARS, D. O. (1977). Coming to like obnoxious people when we must live with them. *Journal of Personality and Social Psychology, 35,* 200–211.

UGWUEGBU, D. C. E. (1979). Racial and evidential factors in juror attribution of legal responsibility. *Journal of Experimental Social Psychology, 15,* 133–146.

U.S. BUREAU OF THE CENSUS. (1973). *Annual housing survey: 1973 U.S. and regions: Part B, Indicators of housing and neighborhood quality.* Current Housing Report Series H-150-73-B. Washington DC: U.S. Government Printing Office.

VALINS, S. (1966). Cognitive effects of false heart-rate feedback. *Journal of Personality and Social Psychology, 4,* 400–408.

VALINS, S., & RAY, A. A. (1967). Effects of cognitive desensitization on avoidance behavior. *Journal of Personality and Social Psychology, 7,* 345–350.

VANNEMAN, R. D., & PETTIGREW, T. F. (1972). Race and relative deprivation in the urban United States. *Race, 13,* 461–486.

VINSEL, A., BROWN, B. B., ALTMAN, I., & FOSS, C. (1980). Privacy regulation, territorial displays, and effective individual functioning. *Journal of Personality and Social Psychology, 39* (6), 1104–1115.

VON BAEYER, C. L., SHERK, D. L., & ZANNA, M. P. (1981). Impression management in the job interview: When the female applicant meets the male (chauvinist) interviewer. *Personality and Social Psychology Bulletin, 7* (1), 45–52.

WALL, J. A., JR. (1977). Operantly conditioning a negotiator's concession making. *Journal of Experimental Social Psychology, 13,* 431–440.

WALLER, W. (1938). *The family: A dynamic interpretation.* New York: Dryden Press.

WALLERSTEIN, J. S., & KELLY, J. B. (1975). The effects of pa-rental divorce: Experiences of the preschool child. *Journal of the America. Academy of Child Psychiatry, 14,* 600–616.

WALSH, J. (1983). ABC objections to linkage of aggression to TV violence in NIMH report brings social scientists into contention in novel public skirmish. *Science, 220,* 804–805.

WALSTER, E., ARONSON, E., & ABRAHAMS, D. (1966). On increasing the persuasiveness of a low-prestige communicator. *Journal of Experimental Social Psychology, 2,* 325–342.

WALSTER, E., ARONSON, E., ABRAHAMS, D., & ROTTMAN, L. (1966). Importance of physical attractiveness in dating behavior. *Journal of Personality and Social Psychology, 4,* 508–516.

WALSTER, E., & WALSTER, G. W. (1963). Effects of expecting to be liked on choice of associates. *Journal of Abnormal and Social Psychology, 67,* 402–404.

WALSTER, E., & WALSTER, G. W. (1978). *A new look at love.* Reading, MA: Addison-Wesley.

WALSTER, E., & WALSTER, G. W., & BERSCHEID, E. (1978). *Equity: Theory and research.* Boston: Allyn & Bacon.

WALSTER, E., & WALSTER, G. W., & TRAUPMANN, J. (1978). Equity and premarital sex. *Journal of Personality and Social Psychology, 36,* 82–92.

WATSON, R. I., JR. (1973). Investigation into deindividuation using a cross-cultural survey technique. *Journal of Personality and Social Psychology, 25,* 342–345.

WATKINS, M. (1978, January 9). Why N.B.A. teams succeed at home. *The New York Times,* p. C23.

WATSON, O. M., & GRAVES, T. (1966). Quantitative research in proxemic behavior. *American Anthropologist, 68,* 971–985.

WATTENBERG, M. P. (1982). From parties to candidates: Examining the role of the media. *Public Opinion Quarterly, 46,* 216–227.

WATTS, W. A., & HOLT, L. E. (1979). Persistence of opinion change induced under conditions of forewarning and distraction. *Journal of Personality and Social Psychology, 37,* 778–789.

WEIGEL, R. H., LOOMIS, J. W., & SOJA, M. J. (1980). Race relations on prime time television. *Journal of Personality and Social Psychology, 39,* 884–893.

WEIGEL, R. H., VERNON, D. T. A., & TOGNACCI, L. N. (1974). Specificity of the attitude as a determinant of attitude-behavior congruence. *Journal of Personality and Social Psychology, 30,* 724–728.

WEINER, B. (1974). *Achievement motivation and attribution theory.* Morristown, NJ: General Learning Press.

WEINER, B. (1979). A theory of motivation for some classroom experiences. *Journal of Educational Psychology, 71,* 3–25.

WEINER, B. (1980). A cognitive (attribution)-emotion-action model of motivated behavior: An analysis of judgments of help-giving. *Journal of Personality and Social Psychology, 39* (2), 196–200.

WEINER, B. (1982). The emotional consequences of causal attributions. In M. S. Clark & S. T. Fiske (Eds.), *Affect and cognition: The seventeenth annual Carnegie symposium on cognition.* Hillsdale, NJ: Erlbaum.

WEISS, R. S. (1973). *Loneliness: The experience of emotional and social isolation.* Cambridge, MA: MIT Press.

WEISS, R. S. (1974). The provisions of social relationships.

In Z. Rubin (Ed.), *Doing unto others.* Englewood Cliffs, NJ: Prentice-Hall.

WEISS, W., & FINE, B. J. (1956). The effect of induced aggressiveness on opinion change. *Journal of Abnormal and Social Psychology, 52,* 109–114.

WELLMAN, B., & WHITAKER, M. (1974). *High-rise, low-rise: The effects of high-density living.* Toronto: Ministry of State, Urban Affairs, Canada, B.74.29.

WELLS, G. L., & HARVEY, J. H. (1977). Do people use consensus information in making causal attributions? *Journal of Personality and Social Psychology, 35,* 279–293.

WELLS, W. D. (1973). *Television and aggression: Replication of an experimental field study.* Unpublished manuscript, Graduate School of Business, University of Chicago.

WERNER, C. M., BROWN, B. B., & DAMRON, G. (1981). Territorial marking in a game arcade. *Journal of Personality and Social Psychology, 41* (6), 1094–1104.

WERNER, E. E. (1979). *Cross-cultural child development.* Monterey, CA: Brooks/Cole.

WHITE, G. L. (1976). *The social psychology of romantic jealousy.* Doctoral dissertation, University of California, Los Angeles, University Microfilms No. 77-7700.

WHITE, G. L. (1980). Physical attractiveness and courtship progress. *Journal of Personality and Social Psychology, 39,* 660–668.

WHITE, G. L. (1981). Jealousy and partner's perceived motive for attraction to a rival. *Social Psychology Quarterly, 44* (1), 24–30.

WHITE, G. M. (1972). Immediate and deferred effects of model observation and guided and unguided rehearsal on donating and stealing. *Journal of Personality and Social Psychology, 21,* 139–148.

WHITE, L. A. (1979). Erotica and aggression: The influence of sexual arousal, positive affect, and negative affect on aggression behavior. *Journal of Personality and Social Psychology, 37,* 591–601.

WHITLEY, B. E. (1973). Sex role orientation and self-esteem: A critical meta-analytic review. *Journal of Personality and Social Psychology, 44,* 765–778.

WHYTE, W. H. JR. (1956). *The organization man.* New York: Simon and Schuster.

WICHMAN, H. (1970). Effects of isolation and communication on cooperation in a two-person game. *Journal of Personality and Social Psychology, 16,* 114–120.

WICKER, A. W. (1969). Attitudes versus action: The relationship of verbal and overt behavior responses to attitude objects. *Journal of Social Issues, 25* (4), 41–78.

WICKER, A. W. (1971). An examination of the "other variables" explanation of attitude-behavior inconsistency. *Journal of Personality and Social Psychology, 19,* 18–30.

WIESENTHAL, D. L., ENDLER, N. S., COWARD, T. R., & EDWARDS, J. (1976). Reversibility of relative competence as a determinant of conformity across different perceptual tasks. *Representative Research in Social Psychology, 7,* 319–342.

WILDER, D. A. (1977). Perception of groups, size of opposition, and social influence. *Journal of Experimental Social Psychology, 13,* 253–258.

WILKE, H., & LANZETTA, J. T. (1970). The obligation to help: The effects of amount of prior help on subsequent helping behavior. *Journal of Experimental Social Psychology, 6,* 488–493.

WILLIAMSON, J. B. (1974). The stigma of public dependency: A comparison of alternative forms of public aid to the poor. *Social Problems, 22,* 213–238.

WILSON, E. O. (1971). *The insect societies.* Cambridge, MA: Belknap Press of Harvard University Press.

WILSON, E. O. (1975). *Sociobiology, the new synthesis.* Cambridge, MA: Harvard University Press.

WILSON, L., & ROGERS, R. W. (1975). The fire this time: Effects of race of target, insult, and potential retaliation on black aggression. *Journal of Personality and Social Psychology, 32,* 857–864.

WILSON, T. D., & LASSITER, G. D. (1982). Increasing intrinsic interest with superfluous extrinsic constraints. *Journal of Personality and Social Psychology, 42,* 811–819.

WOLFINGER, R., & LINQUITI, P. (1981). Tuning in and turning out. *Public Opinion, 4,* 56–60.

WOLFSON, M. R., & SALANCIK, G. R. (1977). Observer orientation and actor-observer differences in attributions for failure. *Journal of Experimental Social Psychology, 13,* 441–451.

WOLLIN, D. D., & MONTAGNE, M. (1981). College classroom environment. *Environment and Behavior, 13* (6), 707–716.

WONG, P. T. P., & WEINER, B. (1981). When people ask "why" questions, and the heuristics of attributional search. *Journal of Personality and Social Psychology, 40,* 650–663.

WOOD, W. (1982). Retrieval of attitude-relevant information from memory: Effects on susceptibility to persuasion and on intrinsic motivation. *Journal of Personality and Social Psychology, 42,* 798–810.

WOOD, W., & EAGLY, W. H. (1981). Stages in the analysis of persuasive messages: The role of causal attributions and message comprehension. *Journal of Personality and Social Psychology, 40,* 246–259.

WOODWORTH, R. D. (1938). *Experimental psychology.* New York: Holt.

WORCHEL, S. The darker side of helping: The social dynamics of helping and cooperation. (in press). In D. Bar-Tal et al., *The development and maintenance of prosocial behavior.* New York: Plenum Press.

WORTMAN, C. B. (1975). Some determinants of perceived control. *Journal of Personality and Social Psychology, 31,* 282–294.

WORTMAN, C. B. (1976). Causal attributions and personal control. In J. H. Harvey, W. Ickes, and R. F. Kidd (Eds.), *New directions in attribution research* (Vol. 1, pp. 23–52). Hillsdale, NJ: Erlbaum.

WYER, R. S., JR. (1974). Changes in meaning and halo effects in personality impression formation. *Journal of Personality and Social Psychology, 29,* 829–835.

YUKL, G. A. (1981). *Leadership in organizations.* Englewood Cliffs, NJ: Prentice-Hall.

ZAJONC, R. B. (1965). Social facilitation. *Science, 149,* 269–274.

ZAJONC, R. B. (1968). Attitudinal effects of mere exposure. *Journal of Personality and Social Psychology,* (Monograph Suppl., Pt. 2), 1–29.

ZANNA, M. P., & COOPER, J. (1974). Dissonance and the pill: An attribution approach to studying the arousal properties of dissonance. *Journal of Personality and Social Psychology, 29,* 703–709.

ZANNA, M. P., & HAMILTON, D. L. (1977). Further evidence for meaning change in impression formation. *Journal of Experimental Social Psychology, 13,* 224–238.

ZILLMANN, D., & BRYANT, J. (1974). Effect of residual excitation on the emotional response to provocation and delayed aggressive behavior. *Journal of Personality and Social Psychology, 30,* 782–791.

ZILLMANN, D., & SAPOLSKY, B. S. (1977). What mediates the effect of mild erotica on annoyance and hostile behavior in males? *Journal of Personality and Social Psychology, 35,* 587–596.

ZIMBARDO, P. G. (1970). The human choice: Individuation, reason and order versus deindividuation, impulse and chaos. In N. J. Arnold and D. Levine (Eds.), *Nebraska symposium on motivation, 1969.* Lincoln: University of Nebraska Press.

ZIMBARDO, P. G., WEISENBERG, M., FIRESTONE, I., & LEVY, B. (1965). Communicator effectiveness in producing public conformity and private attitude change. *Journal of Personality, 33,* 233–256.

ZIMMERMAN, D. H., & WEST, C. (1975). Sex roles, interruptions and silences in conversation. In B. Thorne & N. Henley (Eds.), *Language and sex: Difference and dominance* (pp. 105–129). Rowley, MA: Newbury House.

ZUCKERMAN, M. (1979). Attribution of success and failure revisited, or: The motivational bias is alive and well in attribution theory. *Journal of Personality, 47,* 245–287.

ZUCKERMAN, M., AMIDON, M. D., BISHOP, S. E., & POMERANTZ, S. D. (1982). Face and tone of voice in the communication of deception. *Journal of Personality and Social Psychology, 43,* 347–357.

ZUCKERMAN, M., DEPAULO, B. M., & ROSENTHAL, R. (1981). Verbal and nonverbal communication of deception. In L. Berkowitz (Ed.), *Advances in experimental social psychology* (Vol. 14). New York: Academic Press.

ZUCKERMAN, M., LARRANCE, D. T., SPIEGEL, N. H. & KLORMAN, R. (1981). Controlling nonverbal displays: Facial expressions and tone of voice. *Journal of Experimental Social Psychology, 17,* 506–524.

ZUCKERMAN, M., LAZZANO, M. M., & WALDGEIR, D. (1979). Undermining effects of the foot-in-the-door technique with extrinsic rewards. *Journal of Applied Social Psychology, 9,* 292–296.

INDEX

NAME INDEX

SUBJECT INDEX